DATE DUE AUG − − 2006

DEMCO 38-296

Key Readings in Crisis Management

What is Crisis Management and why is it so important?

Key Readings in Crisis Management brings together an international collection of some of the most important work in the field of crisis management over the past thirty years.

The book is divided into four main sections, each containing a variety of readings:

- Understanding crisis management
- Modelling the crisis management process
- The crisis of management: cultural and psychological dynamics of risk and crisis management
- Crisis management in practice

Each section is accompanied by an editorial commentary written by a leading name in the field of crisis management.

This reader is an essential text for courses on crisis and risk management across a variety of subject areas.

Denis Smith is Professor of Management at the University of Glasgow.

Dominic Elliott is Paul Roy Professor of Business Continuity and Strategic Management at the University of Liverpool Management School.

Key Readings in Crisis Management

Systems and structures for prevention and recovery

Edited by

Denis Smith and Dominic Elliott

Routledge
Taylor & Francis Group

LONDON AND NEW YORK

First published 2006
by Routledge
2 Park Square, Milton Park, Abingdon, Oxon OX14 4RN

Simultaneously published in the USA and Canada
by Routledge
270 Madison Ave, New York, NY 10016

Routledge is an imprint of the Taylor & Francis Group, an informa business

Typeset in Perpetua and Bell Gothic by
RefineCatch Limited, Bungay, Suffolk
Printed and bound in Great Britain by
TJ International Ltd, Padstow, Cornwall

British Library Cataloguing in Publication Data
A catalogue record for this book is available from the British Library

Library of Congress Cataloging in Publication Data
Smith, Denis, 1956–
Key readings in crisis management: systems and structures for prevention and recovery / Denis Smith and Dominic Elliott.
p. cm.
Includes bibliographical references and index.
ISBN 0–415–31520–4 (hard cover) – ISBN 0–415–31521–2 (soft cover)
1. Crisis Management. I. Elliott, Dominic, 1963– II. Title.
HD49.S645 2006
658.4'056–dc22
2005015497

ISBN10: 0–415–31520–4 (hbk)
ISBN10: 0–415–31521–2 (pbk)
ISBN10: 0–203–56328–X (ebk)

ISBN13: 978–0–415–31520–3 (hbk)
ISBN13: 978–0–415–31521–0 (pbk)
ISBN13: 978–0–203–56328–1 (ebk)

Contents

SECTION THREE
The crisis of management: cultural and psychological dynamics of risk and crisis management

SECTION FOUR
Crisis management in practice

Conclusions

Dedication

A book of this nature is clearly the result of the work of many others and thanks need to be given at the outset to the large number of people who made this possible.

In the first instance, thanks are due to the authors and publishers of the original works for allowing them to be reprinted here. It is our view, that these papers provide the reader with a solid introduction to the nature of crisis management as it is currently understood and the advances in our understanding of the processes of crisis are, in no small measure, due to many of the authors whose work is included here. There are also papers that deal with events that are deemed to be of some significance as they changed the way in which the sector understood how crises could occur.

Thanks are also due to those who agreed to provide a commentary on the various sections of readings. This was a potentially difficult process and we would like to thank our commentators, Arjen Boin and Larry Barton, for providing discussion pieces that also extend our current understanding of the nature of crisis as well as highlighting areas of significance around the papers within the section. Each of them took time from their own busy schedules to deliver commentaries that make important contributions to the literature in their own right.

At Liverpool, Jean Burnett and Viv Moss played a major role behind the scenes and we owe them a significant vote of thanks. At Routledge, Emma Joyes, Rachel Crookes and Jacqueline Curthoys managed to ensure that we delivered the manuscript despite some delays. Emma dealt with our inevitable excuses with good humour but was sufficiently stern to force us back on track. Thank you all.

Finally, both editors would like to thank their respective families for putting up with the long absences from family life that are inevitably associated with a project of this nature. Although we might not often show it, we do appreciate the support.

The original genesis of this book took place several years ago following a series of conversations between Denis Smith and Bill Richardson. The initial aim was to produce an authored text that dealt with the broad range of issues facing managers from the impacts associated with crises. At the time, the body of literature was felt to be in too much of a state of flux to produce a book that would do justice to the complex nature of crisis. Whilst the project was on hold, Bill sadly, and prematurely died. This reader was inspired by the initial discussions with Bill and the book is dedicated to his memory.

Denis Smith and Dominic Elliott
Liverpool 2005

Acknowledgements

This book brings together many of the leading researchers in this field and provides a unique resource collection of seminal papers, commentaries and new work. Of course we may be accused of being eclectic in our choice, although that some of these papers are truly seminal would not be challenged by many. The book begins by examining the issues from a broad systems perspective and this provides a firm foundation for subsequent sections, which deal with modelling and conceptual issues in crisis; sectoral aspects of disasters and the psychological and cultural dynamics of disasters and crisis. Each section has a commentary and analysis, which is written by a leading scholar in the field.

We would like to express our thanks to a number of colleagues including Jean Burnett and Viv Moss at the University of Liverpool; Emma Joyes and Rachel Crookes at Routledge, for their ongoing patience and the authors and publishers who have agreed to us reprinting their work.

The authors and publisher of this book gratefully acknowledge the following for permission to use the material in this book:

Chapter 2, originally published as 'The limits of safety: The enhancement of a theory of accidents', (1994) *Journal of Contingencies and Crisis Management*, 2 (4): pp. 212–220. Reprinted by permission of Blackwell Publishing.

Chapter 3, originally published as 'Understanding industrial crises', (1988) *Journal of Management Studies*, 25 (2): pp. 283–303. Reprinted by permission of Blackwell Publishing.

Chapter 4, originally published as 'The structure of man-made organizational crisis', *Technological Forecasting and Social Change*, (1988) 33: pp. 83–107. Reprinted by permission of Elsevier Publications.

Chapter 5, originally published as 'Organisational pathology and industrial crisis', (1988) *Industrial Crisis Quarterly* 2 (1): pp. 65–74. Reprinted by permission of SAGE Publications Inc.

Chapter 8, originally published as 'The organizational and inter-organizational development of disasters', (1976) *Administrative Science Quarterly*, 21: pp. 378–397. Reprinted by permission of Cornell University.

Chapter 9, originally published as 'Crisis prone versus crisis avoiding organisations', (1988) *Industrial Crisis Quarterly*, 2: pp. 53–63. Reprinted by permission of SAGE Publications Inc.

Chapter 10, originally published as 'Beyond contingency planning – Towards a model of crisis management' (1990) *Industrial Crisis Quarterly*. 4 (4): pp. 263–275. Reprinted by permission of SAGE Publications Inc.

Chapter 11, originally published as 'Some characteristics of one type of High Reliability Organization' (1990) *Organization Science*, 1 (2): pp. 160–177. Reprinted by permission of Institute for Operations Research and the Management Sciences.

Chapter 12, originally published as 'Systems analysis of failures as a quality management tool' (1994) *British Journal of Management*, 5: pp. 205–213. Reprinted by permission of Blackwell Publishing.

Chapter 13, originally published as 'Organizational learning from disasters' (1988) in *Emergency Planning for Industrial Hazards*, London: Elsevier Applied Science, pp. 297–313. Reprinted by permission of Elsevier Publications.

Chapter 14, originally published as 'Enacted sensemaking in crisis situations' (1988) *Journal of Management Studies*, 25: pp. 305–317. Reprinted by permission of Blackwell Publishing.

Chapter 16, originally published as 'Human errors: A taxonomy for describing human malfunction in industrial installations' (1982) *Journal of Occupational Accidents*, 4: pp. 311–335. Reprinted by permission of Elsevier Publications.

Chapter 17, originally published as 'The contribution of latent human failures to the breakdown of complex systems' (1990) *Philosophical Transactions of the Royal Society of London*, B, 37: pp. 475–484. Reprinted by permission of The Royal Society.

Chapter 18, originally published as 'The collapse of sensemaking in organizations: The Mann Gulch Disaster' (1993) *Administrative Science Quarterly*, 38: pp. 628–652. Reprinted by permission of Cornell University.

Chapter 19, originally published as 'Storming and catastrophic systems failure' (1992) *Industrial Crisis Quarterly*, 6: pp. 295–312. Reprinted by permission of SAGE Publications Inc.

Chapter 21, originally published as 'Designs for crisis decision units', (1977) *Administrative Science Quarterly*, 22: pp. 640–657. Reprinted by permission of Cornell University.

Chapter 22, originally published as 'Collective minds in organizations: Heedful interrelating on flight decks' (1993) *Administrative Science Quarterly*, 38: pp. 357–381. Reprinted by permission of Cornell University.

Chapter 23, originally published as 'Football stadia disasters in the United Kingdom: Learning from tragedy', (1993) *Industrial and Environmental Crisis Quarterly*, 7 (3): pp.205–229. Reprinted by permission of SAGE Publications Inc.

Chapter 1

Denis Smith

CRISIS MANAGEMENT – PRACTICE IN SEARCH OF A PARADIGM

Introduction

THERE IS LITTLE DOUBT that the notion of crisis has now become an important construct within 'management' – as both an academic discipline and also as a community of practice. However, despite an increased awareness of the notion of crisis, there is still considerable ambiguity about what the term means. In some respects 'crisis' is, perhaps, one of the most misused words within modern society and there is considerable ambiguity around many of the core processes that underpin the construct. The term 'crisis' is often used to describe events and situations that are difficult to deal with, but not necessarily potentially damaging or destructive. There is also considerable overlap, at least in common usage, between the related terms of 'disaster', 'business continuity' and, to an extent, 'risk'. There has been discussion within the literature around new ways of conceptualising the relationship between 'risk' and 'crisis' management (Barton and Hardigree, 1995; Shaluf, Ahmadun and Said, 2003), particularly in the aftermath of the terrorist attacks of 11 September 2001 (Moore, 2004). Some have pointed out that, in practice, the distinction often made between the two functions was that risk management was seen to have a focus on the identification of potential problems, whereas crisis management was concerned with the management of the crisis event itself (Barton and Hardigree 1995). Although that distinction has become increasingly blurred over time, there is still a perceived distinction between the two approaches (Moore, 2004) that might not be helpful in terms of preventing such events from occurring. The view adopted here is that failure to manage risks within an organization or society will generate the potential for a wider crisis and, as such, risk is seen as being a sub-set of the much wider crisis process – a point that will be returned to later.

The rationale for this collection of essays lies in an attempt to address the broad range of processes that are dealt with under this generic heading of 'crisis management' and to provide the reader with an entrée into the academic literature that has attempted to develop our understanding of the processes, procedures and problems that are embedded in the broad crisis process. The papers provide the reader with an overview of some of the key debates that have taken place within the crisis management literature. These include the various ways of conceptualizing the crisis process, the ways in which failure potential becomes embedded within organizational systems and processes, the manner in which we make sense of crisis events and issues around problems associated with managing the 'acute' phase of a crisis, as well as dealing with its aftermath. Invariably, this collection is not inclusive and gaps within this sample of the literature will be all too evident to those familiar with that wide body of research. However, this collection can be seen as an entry point into the diverse bodies of research that characterize the emerging field of crisis management.

The aim of this opening chapter is to outline some key issues that the reader may wish to reflect upon as they work through the remaining papers. We provide a working definition of crisis and explore some, but invariably not all, of the theoretical dimensions of the process. In order to provide a basis for that discussion, we should first outline the nature of crisis 'in practice'. An understanding of both the nature and processes that underpin a crisis are clearly important if organizations are to have any prospect of dealing with them once they occur or, more significantly, trying to prevent them from occurring in the first place.

The nature of crisis 'in practice'

The nature of 'crisis' can be illustrated by reference to some of the more celebrated, or infamous, events that have become symbolic of the term. There have, of course, been many reminders of the pervasive and interconnected nature of crises within modern society during the last thirty years and any examples of such 'events' will be far from inclusive or, indeed, conclusive. The examples given here have been chosen to illustrate the interconnected and spatial dynamics of a crisis but they are not meant to be seen as all-encompassing – such a list would be problematic in itself and would require many more pages than are available to us here. The events discussed below show how crises can be constructed within a spatial setting (and often bring with them a sense of place and time), display emergent properties, and are represented as complex, non-linear events (Smith, 2005a) that generate problems for those who are responsible for attempting to manage them. It is against this background that managers within organizations have often developed their own situation-specific definitions of crisis, and developed their planning and response strategies accordingly.

The practical nature of a crisis is an important consideration. If an organization or its main stakeholders perceive that it is in a state of almost perpetual crisis, then it could be argued that this might indicate a deep-seated malaise within the organization. This set of 'cultural' problems will become exposed when an incident escalates into a 'crisis'. Invariably, some triggering event is seen as the catalyst that exposes any internal weaknesses in the organization. The notion of 'trigger events' as a means of exposing such deep-seated problems has developed with the literature as an important concept in explaining the manner in which such events emerge and, to an extent, escalate (Smith, 1990, 1995; Turner, 1976, 1978). However, the trigger event is not usually the root cause of the crisis but rather the mechanism through which vulnerabilities within the organization are exposed. Many of these vulnerabilities are not recognized by managers within the organization due to a set of processes which generate a form of institutional blindness. One might argue that the notion of crisis (and the associated concept of disaster) as seen 'through the eyes of the beholder' (or more accurately 'beholders') (Smith, 2005b) is an important first step in the 'practice' of crisis management. By recognizing that an organization is in a state of crisis, managers can take action to try to alleviate the problem and may, as a consequence, prevent matters from getting worse. All too often, however, organizations only recognize a crisis when it has reached what can be termed as 'the operational phase' (Smith, 1990). At this point damage has already taken place and the role of managers is largely that of attempting to stop the crisis escalating further. Effective crisis management, it can be argued, takes place before the operational phase and requires organizations to develop capabilities aimed at recognizing and acting upon early warnings and weak signals around potential problems (Reason, 1990, 1997; Turner, 1976, 1978). However, the sheer diversity of potential examples of crisis is such that it makes all-encompassing procedures for identifying and acting upon such warnings difficult. The complexity surrounding such processes can be illustrated by examining a selection of significant crisis events.

The accidents at Bhopal and Chernobyl both illustrated the devastating potential for harm that exists within modern industrial processes (Hazarika, 1987; Lapierre and Moro, 2002; Mould, 2000; Shrivastava, 1987). These were both catastrophic events that killed large numbers of people. In both cases, the final death toll may not be known with any accuracy due to a range of problems related to latent versus immediate deaths, difficulties in information gathering, and issues concerning the hazard range of the substances released from both sites. Whilst both events were catastrophic they also triggered a wider problem for their respective industries that went beyond the immediate companies and countries involved in the accidents. Following the Chernobyl accident, the nuclear industry could no longer deny that significant accidents could occur in reactors (even though many Western operators argued that the 'event' was a result of Soviet 'management' and systems) and public concern around potential risks was heightened. The effects of the fallout were far reaching (Davies, 1986) and even caused problems as far removed from the site of the accident as Cumbria in the UK, where concerns were expressed over the safety of sheep farming and its food products (Michael, 1992).

After Bhopal, the chemical industry was also faced with a heightened level of public concern, especially in many Western countries, over the risks of potential releases from neighbouring plants. In the UK, the Chemical Industries

Association embarked upon a major public relations programme in an attempt to try and reassure local publics about the safety of chemical plant operations in their locality. Despite such effects, there was some evidence of growing public concern over risks from such plants (Irwin, Dale, and Smith, 1996) and this prompted considerable efforts to be made (much of which was enforced by legislation) aimed at informing the public about the potential hazards and what actions they should take in an emergency. The sector was also faced with criticism surrounding what was seen as the exporting of hazardous processes and waste materials to those countries that were perceived as having a weaker regulatory framework or lower levels of public concern over risk. Whilst debates around hazardous waste disposal began in the 1970s and continued through the 1980s, they were given fresh impetus by the accident at Bhopal due to the perceived exploitation by multinationals of countries with weaker regulatory systems than those in the West. These waste debates illustrated once again the spatial dynamics of risk but also highlighted the temporal aspects of the problem (Clark, Smith and Blowers, 1992; Sheldon and Smith, 1992; Smith, 1991; Smith and Blowers, 1991, 1992). In many cases, the wastes concerned had been buried decades before and it had been a case of 'out of sight and out of mind' (Smith, 1991; Smith and Blowers, 1991, 1992). It was public concerns about waste materials buried at the Love Canal site in the USA that raised the issue of waste and its transfers high into the public consciousness (Smith and Blowers, 1991, 1992). The resultant policy debates saw many states within the USA ban the importation of waste for disposal and this, in turn, led to an increase in the international transfers of waste. The most controversial of these involved the transfers of waste from Western countries (including a number of European states) to West Africa, culminating in the attempt to return the waste on board the infamous Karin B waste ship (Smith, 1991). What is apparent from this set of examples is that crises can be interconnected in their nature and that it is possible for a particular 'event' in one organization to impact upon the sector as a whole and possibly trigger other problems elsewhere.

A range of high profile transport accidents also highlighted the problems that can occur when socio-technical systems fail. The collision of aircraft on the ground at Tenerife (Weick, 1990) and the mid-air collision over Ueberlingen in Germany, but close to the Swiss border, (Anon, 2005), illustrate the range of problems that can exist around the complex interaction between air traffic control, airline operators and the various associated technologies within aviation. In these cases, it was not a single organization that was responsible for the accidents but rather an interaction between various 'actors' within the wider system of production. Despite our increased reliance on advanced technologies, both accidents involved a complex chain of events that generated conditions in which human factors combined with the technology in place and the prevailing environmental conditions at the time. The Tenerife collision occurred in Spanish territory, under the control of Tenerife air traffic control and involved a Dutch KLM and a US Pan American Boeing 747 (Weick, 1990). A collision between two such planes was often held to be the worst case accident scenario and was deemed to be of such low probability as to be almost impossible. There is little doubt that much of the reasoning behind this view was that the technical systems in place would prevent any such collision from occurring – a view that was still prevalent at the time of the Ueberlingen crash. The Ueberlingen crash also illustrated the trans-boundary nature of crises. The planes involved were a Russian Tupolev 154 and a DHL Boeing 757 cargo aircraft, who were both being controlled by Swiss air traffic control, and the resultant debris was found on both sides of the Swiss-German border (Anon, 2005). Aviation has a long history of the use of advanced technologies in accident prevention and it had been suggested that collision-avoidance systems would have prevented such a mid-air collision from taking place. However, a complex chain of interactions between human factors and systems elements that conspired to create the conditions for such a catastrophic failure.

Advanced high-technology commercial systems were not the only ones found to be vulnerable to such a potential for failure. The loss of the Russian submarine, the Kursk, in 2000 marked the worst peacetime disaster ever to face the Russian navy (Truscott, 2002) and pointed to the vulnerability of military systems at a time when the USA was on the verge of reprioritizing its 'defence' programmes under the Bush administration. The vulnerability of such systems of mass destruction was not a new phenomenon (Sagan, 1993). Indeed, much of the early theoretical developments of risk analysis took place around the Minuteman programme as military planners wanted to try to make certain that they dealt with the hazards of an unprogrammed (and therefore illegal or accidental) launch (Irwin, Smith and Griffiths, 1982). Of course, the reliability of military and associated intelligence decision-making processes and practices has more recently been called into question following the war(s) in Iraq and other, more localized, conflicts and operations. What these examples make clear is that the nature of crisis is not limited to a particular ideological setting or restricted to commercial activities. Form of technology crisis is rather a pervasive process that transcends political, ideological, social and technological boundaries.

Some crises also point to the problems that exist around our knowledge of the processes that typify modern organizational practices, or the impacts that industrial production can have upon society or the environment. There are several examples that illustrate the nature of this problem. The BSE, or 'mad cow', crisis in the UK and its subsequent 'export' to other countries, serves as a good example of how an emergent problem can create a significant issue for both policy- and decision-makers. This is especially apparent when the evidence upon which to make judgments is weak, or where there is a lack of proof that clearly (and unambiguously) points to an existing problem. What the BSE crisis also illustrated was the difficult trade-offs that can exist in taking a precautionary approach to 'risk' policy when there is little proof of harm (but also little proof of safety) (Calman and Smith, 2001; Dormont, 2002; Flynn and Marsden, 1992; Klein, 2000; Little, 2001; Pennington, 2003). The costs associated with such an action would have had a major impact upon the UK's farming industry and, with little *unequivocal* proof at the point at which the decisions were taken, the government was unwilling to take radical (and preventative) action. These actions were subsequently criticized within the public inquiry into the BSE crisis and the eventual discovery of the potential for BSE to 'jump the species barrier' created major difficulties for both the government of the day and the food industry.

Other problems of this nature can also be seen around global warming, food additives, genetic modification (Irwin, 2001; Strand, 2001) and a range of problems within health care (Redfern, Keeling and Powell, 2000; Rosenthal, 1987, 1995; Sitford, 2000; Smith, 2002). In part, many of these 'crises' can be seen to emerge from the potentially incompatible requirements for safe processes at lowest possible cost or maximum short-term benefit! These types of events sit at the heart of modern society and also illustrate the importance of reputation within the crisis management process.

Crises can also be created by deliberate acts. The terrorist attacks on the USA on September 11th 2001 (Chomsky, 2001; Conover *et al.*, 2002; Evans, 2001; Greenberg, 2002), along with subsequent other terrorist atrocities, have changed forever some of our notions of risk within an urban setting and have shown the powerful influence of networks, space and place as elements in the construction of hazard. It was not just the nature of these attacks, their ferocity and callousness, but the fact that they illustrated, all too dramatically, the point that risk transcends boundaries in ways that had never been adequately considered by policy makers and managers.

The examples given above, also demonstrate the point that the analysis of crises does not fall neatly within any particular analytical or theoretical paradigm in the literature. Indeed, it could be argued that the practice of crisis management is beginning to challenge many of the core assumptions that are held within some disciplines. 'Management' would be a good example of this shift in approach, as many crises illustrate the failures that have taken place within management processes and practices. The examples used above can, however, be used to illustrate the importance of several generic factors within crisis events (see Smith, 2005a; Smith, 2005b; Smith, 2005c).

The first of these is the notion of *place*. Many of these crises are associated with a particular location and setting. Whilst it is possible for crises to be widespread, they are often clearly linked to a specific context, setting, or 'organization'. Place is also important from the perspective of the victims of crisis events. In many cases, the victims are brought together within a particular setting rather than being randomly distributed (the attacks on September 11th demonstrate the importance of place in this regard).

In addition, *time* is also clearly of importance in influencing both the nature of the crisis and its consequences. All of the examples of crisis discussed above point to the importance of time in helping to shape the configuration of the event as it unfolds. With modern organizational systems that are geared towards efficiency, such 'tight-coupling' (Perrow, 1984) is a key factor in shaping the manner in which the crisis emerges and evolves and also in affecting the abilities of the organization to respond to the task demands that the crisis generates.

A third aspect of crisis would seem to involve the processes of *emergence* and *scale* and the manner in which complex, non-linear problems are faced by managers (Smith, 2005b; Smith, 2005c). Such events also illustrate the inherent *vulnerability* that can exist within organizations (Smith, 2005c), an issue that has not had the attention that it deserves outside of research on natural hazards and those communities that are affected by such 'events'. All too often, the initial trigger escalates an incident into a serious accident because the organization does not have an effective contingency plan to cope with the *scale* of the event, or because the incident emerges in ways that were not foreseen prior to the actual accident. The accident then has the potential to escalate still further and move the organization into a crisis.

Finally, the examples given earlier also point to the difficulties associated with a 'contingency approach' to dealing with crises. In each of the cases highlighted, it is likely that few, if any, contingency plans would have allowed those charged with managing the events to ensure that effective mitigation took place, and this illustrates a common problem within much of crisis practice as well as theory. Too great a focus on the contingency approaches to dealing with the demands of the 'operational crisis' (Smith, 1990) will always leave organizations having to cope with significant levels of damage and harm, as well as the risk of reputation-related problems.

Against this background we can now briefly consider the frameworks for analyzing crises that have been used as a guiding principle for this collection.

The nature of crisis in theory

At this point in our deliberations, it is important to try and attempt a definition of crisis and to try to suggest ways in which it is possible for management to intervene effectively in both the prevention and mitigation of crises. It is our contention here that a focus on any one phase of a crisis will create significant problems for management and, as a consequence, a more holistic approach needs to be taken. This does, however, create significant problems for 'management' – both in terms of its theoretical underpinnings and its practice. As a first stage in this discussion, it is first necessary to attempt a definition of 'crisis' that is used within this collection of essays.

Crises are, by definition, complex events that confound the abilities of those who try to manage them. They also present significant challenges around managerial attempts at bringing the events back under control. One might argue, therefore, that a crisis can be defined as:

> 'a damaging event, or series of events, that display emergent properties which exceed an organisation's abilities to cope with the task demands that it generates and has implications that can effect a considerable proportion of the organisation as well as other bodies. The damage that can be caused can be physical, financial, or reputational in its scope. In addition, crises will have both a spatial and temporal dimension and will invariably occur within a sense of "place". Crises will normally be "triggered" by an incident or another set of circumstances (these can be internal or external to the organisation), that exposes the inherent vulnerability that has been embedded within the "system" over time.'
>
> (Smith, 2005a)

Whilst many definitions of crisis have been put forward within the literature, this particular collection has been put together using this definition as a guiding framework. Obviously there remain some inherent ambiguities within any attempt at defining a 'crisis'. In many respects these can be seen to relate to the nature of a crisis compared to other damaging events covered by the terms 'risk' and 'disaster'. It is the overlap between these three terms, and the context in which they are often used (sometimes almost interchangeably), that creates difficulties of interpretation. At this point, it is worth trying to differentiate the meaning of these terms within the context of our present discussions.

There is little doubt that recent events have conspired to make the issues of 'risk' and 'disaster' amongst the most powerful defining constructs of the current century. It has been suggested that we now live within a 'risk society' (Beck, 1986, 1992; Giddens, 1990) in which uncertainty and the consequences of core activities have conspired to generate a level of fear amongst large sections of society (Glassner, 1999). The notion of risk has also been widely dealt with within the literature, although it too has proved to be a difficult construct, both within policy making and within the social sciences. For example, there were two major attempts to deal with issues around risk that were undertaken on behalf of the Royal Society (Royal Society, 1983, 1992), and the academic literature is replete within debates around the nature of risk and its social construction (Irwin Smith and Griffiths, 1982; Smith and Tombs, 2000). For our present purposes, 'risk' is seen as a function of the probability of an event occurring and the consequences of that event – in other words, it is a function of probability times consequence. In the wider organizational settings covered by this collection of essays, it is possible to see risk management as representing an attempt to deal with issues at the operational level of activities. Most risk management is concerned with the ways in which small-scale failures of components can aggregate upwards to generate 'higher level events'. At this point, the failure to manage risks may ultimately result in a scale of event that generates a crisis for the organization. However, by separating the two terms out from each other in practice, we may well be contributing to the generation of the potential for failures and the lack of an organizational capability to deal with them once they occur. Risk and crisis should be seen as part of the same continuum and organizations need to develop their management strategies accordingly.

In a similar way, the study of disasters is also faced with debates about the nature of the core construct of the term and its 'realization' in practice, and there has been considerable debate surrounding what a 'disaster' means (Perry and Quarantelli, 2005; Quarantelli, 1978a, 1978b, 1998a, 1998b; Steinberg, 2000, 2001, 2002). Whilst there is a body of research that states that disasters must have a natural trigger (Stallings, 1998, 2005), there is also a view that suggests that the outcomes are as important as the underlying processes that generate the harm (Steinberg, 2000, 2001, 2002). To the victims of these 'events' it doesn't matter whether the trigger is natural or socio-technical, it is the damage and trauma caused that becomes the focus of their attention. The terms crisis and disaster have, over time, been used to describe the same class of events. What is clear, however, is that a disaster is generally seen as a much narrower phenomenon than a crisis and, for our present purposes, a disaster will be defined as a naturally occurring event that is triggered by geo-physical processes. Whilst the scale of the damage associated with such a disaster might well generate a subsequent crisis, we will not be considering 'natural' hazards within this collection in any systematic way. There is a wide body of literature that deals with such naturally occurring phenomena and there is also a body of literature that has attempted to address the nature of a 'disaster' and the responses that can be made to such events (Alexander, 1993; Bianco *et al.*, 1999; Chester, 1993; Menoni, 2001; Pelling, 2001, 2002; Perry and Quarantelli 2005; Quarantelli, 1978a, 1978b, 1998a, 1998b; Raphael, 1986)

Conclusions

The aim of this collection is to provide a set of readings that provide an introduction to a range of issues around the processes of crisis management. Invariably, this is not a definitive collection. These papers represent insights into some of what we believe to be important issues facing organizations and the collection provides a resource to address some of the key issues around several major themes including: the definition of crisis; the processes that shape the nature and scope of crisis events; the manner in which people and the organizations in which they work 'make sense' of these processes; the role of human agency (including latent and active error) in the creation of those conditions that allow crises to incubate; and the processes through which organizations may begin to learn effective lessons from crises and change their ways of working as a consequence. Each of the various sections of the book represents an attempt to bring together papers in a way that is logical within the section theme. There is also considerable value to be gained from looking at the papers in a cross-theme manner, and the various theoretical relationships between the sections are also important. The collection provides an initial map into a complex but important literature. If it causes managers to think more carefully about the processes that underpin crises then it will have served its purpose.

References

Alexander, D. (1993) *Natural Disasters*, Routledge: London.

Anon (2004) Indian Ocean earthquake; http://en.wikipedia.org/wiki/2004_Indian _Ocean_earthquake 7th April 2005 11:00 hours.

Anon (2005) Mid-air collision inquiry begins; http://archives.cnn.com/2002/ WORLD/europe/07/02/midair.crash/ 27th March 2005 21:48 hours.

Barton, L. and Hardigree, D. (1995) Risk and crisis management in facilities: emerging paradigms in assessing critical incidents, *Facilities,* 13 (9/10): 11–14.

Beck, U. (1986) *Risikogesellschaft: Auf dem Weg in eine andere Moderne*, Suhrkamp Verlag: Frankfurt.

Beck, U. (1992) *Risk Society: Towards a new modernity*, M. Ritter, trans., SAGE: London.

Bianco, F., Castellano, M., Milano, G., Vilardo, G., Ferrucci, F., and Gresta, S. (1999) 'The seismic crises at Mt. Vesuvius during 1995 and 1996', *Physics and Chemistry of the Earth, Part A: Solid Earth and Geodesy*, 24 (11–12): 977–983.

Calman, K. and Smith, D. (2001) 'Works in theory but not in practice? Some notes on the precautionary principle', *Public Administration*, 79 (1): 185–204.

Chester, D. (1993) *Volcanoes and society*, Edward Arnold: London.

Chomsky, N. (2001) *9–11*, New York, NY: Seven Stories Press.

Clark, M., Smith, D., and Blowers, A. (eds) (1992) *Waste Location: Spatial aspects of waste management, hazards and disposal*, Routledge: London.

Conover, S., Stein, Z., Susser, E., and Susser, M. (2002) 'New York besieged: 11 September and after' *J Epidemiol Community Health,* 56 (1): 2–3.

Davies, R. (1986) 'Commentary: the effect of the accident at Chernobyl upon the nuclear community', *Science, Technology and Human Values,* 11 (4): 59–63.

Dormont, D. (2002) 'Prions, BSE and food', *International Journal of Food Microbiology*, 78: 181–189.

Evans, S. (2001) 'Ground Zero' in J. Baxter and M. Downing (eds), *The day that shook the world: Understanding September 11th*, 21–34, BBC Worldwide Ltd: London.

Flynn, A. and Marsden, T. (1992) 'Food regulation in a period of agricultural retreat: the British experience', *Geoforum*, 23 (1): 85–93.

Giddens, A. (1990) *The Consequences of Modernity*, Polity Press: Cambridge.

Glassner, B. (1999) *The Culture of Fear: Why Americans are afraid of the wrong things*, Basic Books: New York, NY.

Greenberg, J. W. (2002) 'September 11, 2001: A CEO's story', *Harvard Business Review*, 80 (10): 58–64.

Hazarika, S. (1987) *Bhopal: The lessons of a tragedy*, Penguin Books: New Delhi.

Irwin, A. (2001) '*Sociology and the Environment: a critical introduction to society, nature and knowledge*', Polity: Cambridge.

Irwin, A., Smith, D., and Griffiths, R. F. (1982) 'Risk analysis and public policy for major hazards', *Physics in Technology*, 13 (6): 258–265.

Irwin, A., Dale, A., and Smith, D. (1996) 'Science and Hell's Kitchen – The local understanding of hazard issues', in A. Irwin and B. Wynne (eds), *Misunderstanding Science? The public reconstruction of science and technology*, 47–64, Cambridge University Press: Cambridge.

Klein, R. (2000) 'The politics of risk: the case of BSE', *British Medical Journal*, 321: 1091–1092.

Lapierre, D. and Moro, J. (2002) *Five Past Midnight in Bhopal*, Warner Books: New York .

Little, G. (2001) 'BSE and the regulation of risk', *Modern Law Review*, 64 (5): 730–756.

Menoni, S. (2001) 'Chains of damages and failures in a metropolitan environment: some observations on the Kobe earthquake in 1995', *Journal of Hazardous Materials*, 86 (1–3): 101–119.

Michael, M. (1992) 'Lay discourses of science: science-in-general, science-in-particular, and self', *Science, Technology and Human Values,* 17 (3): 313–333.

Moore, D. A. (2004) 'The new risk paradigm for chemical process security and safety', *Journal of Hazardous Materials*, 115: 175–180.

Mould, R. F. (2000) *Chernobyl Record: The definitive history of the Chernobyl catastrophe*, Institute of Physics Publishing: Bristol.

Pelling, M. (2001) 'Natural disaster', in N. Castree and B. Braun (eds), *Social nature. Theory, practice, and politics*, 170–188, Blackwell Publishers: Oxford.

Pelling, M. (2002) 'Assessing urban vulnerability and social adaptation to risk', *IDPR*, 24 (1): 59–76.

Pennington, H. (2003) *When Food Kills: BSE, E.coli and disaster science*, Oxford University Press: Oxford.

Perrow, C. (1984) *Normal Accidents*, Basic Books: New York.

Perry, R. W. and Quarantelli, E. L. (eds) (2005) *What is a disaster? New answers to old questions*, Xlibris: Philadelphia.

Quarantelli, E. L. (1978a) 'Some basic themes in sociological studies of disaster', in E. L. Quarantelli (ed.), *Disasters – theory and research:* 1–14, SAGE: Beverly Hills, CA.

Quarantelli, E. L. (ed.) (1978b) Disasters – theory and research, SAGE: Beverly Hills, CA.

Quarantelli, E. L. (1998a) 'Introduction. The basic question, its importance, and how it is addressed in this volume', in E. L. Quarantelli (ed.) *What is a disaster? Perspectives on the question*, 1–7, Routledge: London.

Quarantelli, E. L. (ed.) (1998b) '*What is a Disaster? Perspectives on the question*', London: Routledge.

Raphael, B. (1986) '*When Disaster strikes: A handbook for the caring professions*, Unwin Hyman: London.

Reason, J. T. (1990) *Human Error*, Oxford University Press: Oxford.

Reason, J. T. (1997) *Managing the Risks of Organizational Accidents*, Ashgate: Aldershot.

Redfern, M., Keeling, J., and Powell, E. (2000) *The Royal Liverpool Children's Inquiry Report*, The Stationary Office: London.

Rosenthal, M. M. (1987) *Dealing with Medical Malpractice: The British and Swedish experience*, Tavistock: London.

Rosenthal, M. M. (1995) *The Incompetent Doctor*, Open University Press: Milton Keynes.

Royal Society (1983) *Risk Assessment: A Study Group Report*, Royal Society: London.

Royal Society (1992) *Risk: Analysis, perception and management*, Royal Society: London.

Sagan, S. D. (1993) *The Limits of Safety: Organizations, accidents, and nuclear weapons*, Princeton University Press: Princeton, NJ.

Shaluf, I. M., Ahmadun, F., and Said, A. M. (2003) 'A review of disaster and crisis', *Disaster Prevention and Management*, 12 (1): 24–32.

Sheldon, T. A. and Smith, D. (1992) Assessing the health effects of waste disposal sites: Issues in risk analysis and some Bayesian conclusions, in M. Clarke, D. Smith and A. Blowers (eds), *Waste Location: Spatial aspects of waste management, hazards and disposal*, 158–186, Routledge: London.

Shrivastava, P. (1987) Bhopal. Anatomy of a crisis, Ballinger Publishing Company: Cambridge, Mass.

Sitford, M. (2000) *Addicted to murder – the true story of Dr Harold Shipman*, London: Virgin Publishing.

Smith, D. (1990) 'Beyond contingency planning – Towards a model of crisis management', *Industrial Crisis Quarterly*, 4 (4): 263–275.

Smith, D. (1991) 'The Kraken wakes – the political dynamics of the hazardous waste issue', *Industrial Crisis Quarterly*, 5 (3): 189–207.

Smith, D. (1995) 'The Dark Side of Excellence: Managing Strategic Failures', in J. Thompson (ed.), *Handbook of Strategic Management*, 161–191, Butterworth-Heinemann: London.

Smith, D. (2002) 'Not by error, but by design – Harold Shipman and the regulatory crisis for health care', *Public Policy and Administration,* 17 (4): 55–74.

Smith, D. (2005a) 'What's in a name? The nature of crisis and disaster – a search for signature qualities, Working Paper, University of Liverpool Science Enterprise Centre: Liverpool.

Smith, D. (2005b) 'In the eyes of the beholder? Making sense of the system(s) of disaster(s)', in R. W. Perry and E. L. Quarantelli (eds), *What is a disaster? New answers to old questions*, Xlbris: Philadelphia.

Smith, D. (2005c) 'Business (not) as usual – crisis management, service interruption and the vulnerability of organisations', *Journal of Services Marketing*, 19 (5): pp. 309–320.

Smith, D. and Blowers, A. (1991) 'Passing the buck – Hazardous waste disposal as an international problem', *Talking Politics*, 4 (1): 44–49.

Smith, D. and Blowers, A. (1992) 'Here today there tomorrow: the politics of transboundary hazardous waste transfers', in M. Clark, D. Smith and A. Blowers (eds), *Waste location: Spatial aspects of waste management, hazards and disposal*, 208–226, Routledge: London.

Smith, D. and Tombs, S. (2000) 'Of course it's safe, trust me! Conceptualising issues of risk management within the risk society', in E. Coles, D. Smith and S. Tombs (eds), *Risk Management and Society*, 1–30, Kluwer: Dordrecht.

Stallings, R. (1998) 'Disaster and the theory of social order', in E. L. Quarantelli (ed), *What is a Disaster? Perspectives on the question*, 127–145, Routledge: London.

Stallings, R. (2005) 'Disaster, crisis, collective stress, and mass deprivation', in R. W. Perry and E. L. Quarantelli (eds), *What is a disaster? New perspectives on old questions*, Xlbris: Philadelphia.

Steinberg, T. (2000) *Acts of God: The Unnatural History of Natural Disasters in America*, Oxford University Press: New York.

Steinberg, T. (2001) 'The secret history of natural disaster', *Environmental Hazards*, 3: 31–35.

Steinberg, T. (2002) 'Down to earth: Nature, agency, and power in history', *The American Historical Review*, vol. 107: 58 paragraphs, accessed 2nd January 2004 online: http://www.historycooperative.org/journals/ahr/107.3/ah0302000798.html

Strand, R. (2001) 'The role of risk assessments in the governance of genetically modified organisms in agriculture', *Journal of Hazardous Materials*, 86 (1–3): 187–204.

Truscott, P. (2002) *Kursk: Russia's lost pride*, Simon and Schuster: London.

Turner, B. A. (1976) 'The organizational and interorganizational development of disasters', *Administrative Science Quarterly*, 21: 378–397.

Turner, B. A. (1978) *Man-made disasters*, Wykeham: London.

Weick, K. E. (1990) 'The vulnerable system: An analysis of the Tenerife air disaster', *Journal of Management*, 16: 571–593.

Understanding crisis management

Chapter 2

Charles Perrow

THE LIMITS OF SAFETY: THE ENHANCEMENT OF A THEORY OF ACCIDENTS

Introduction

SCOTT SAGAN HAS WRITTEN an extraordinary book which, among other things, draws a sharp contrast between two theories of accidents in large scale systems with catastrophic potential. High Reliability Theory (HRT) believes we can do such things as learn from our operating and regulatory mistakes, put safety first and empower lower levels, thereby making risky systems quite safe. Sagan contrasts this with Normal Accident Theory (NAT) which says, among other things, that no matter how hard we try there will be serious accidents because of the interactive complexity (which allows the inevitable errors to interact in unexpected ways and defeat safety systems) and tight coupling (in which small errors propagate into major ones) of most risky systems. Catastrophic accidents are 'normal' (though rare) because they are inherent in the system. Sagan checks out the two theories with an amazing and frightening account of accidents and close calls in the US nuclear weapons system during the Cold War. He finds much more support for NAT than for HRT.

Todd La Porte, arguably a founder of the most important branch of HRT, disputes Sagan's interpretation of the two theories. He embraces NAT, denies that it is all that different from HRT and especially denies that HRT is at all optimistic. La Porte has written a spirited rebuttal to the theory part of Sagan's book (he praises the empirical accounts).

In contrast to La Porte, I think Sagan's theoretical work is very valuable, and as important as his empirical materials. We should draw the sharp distinction that he does between the two theories. It is not all that common in the study of organizations that theories are as explicitly contrasted and subject to systematic evaluation; Sagan has performed a signal service here. And it is even less common that theorists such as La Porte and myself, are called upon to comment on the theoretical review. If this exchange between Sagan, La Porte and myself does nothing to advance theory in this area I will be both surprised and very disappointed.

I will outline the two theories, briefly, then indicate the improvements that I think Sagan has made in Normal Accident Theory, and suggest how this reformulation and some others that I will make would considerably reduce the difference between La Porte and Sagan while preserving enough distinctiveness to provide us with two sharp tools rather than one.

High reliability theory

HRT is a growing enterprise, not limited to the work of La Porte and his associates. While I will focus upon the latter, it is necessary to emphasize that the perspective is shared with at least two other important works that emphasize much the same things. The first of this is Morone and Woodhouse's (1986) *Averting Catastrophe: Strategies for Regulating Risky Technologies*. They look at the record in the US for the management of toxic chemicals, nuclear power, recombinant DNA research, ozone layer depletion and global warming problems. Despite dire warnings about all, they point out that no catastrophes have occurred in the US in these areas and they say this is because of a deliberate process by which risks are monitored, evaluated and reduced. They provide a list of organizational processes and strategies that reduce the risk. Although noting that these processes and strategies are not always fully developed or perfectly implemented, they optimistically believe that 'taken together, the strategies we found in use suggest the elements of a complete system for averting catastrophes' (Morone and Woodhouse, 1986: 8). NAT would scoff at these rosy prospects and argue that the new risky systems have not had time to disclose their danger and some are getting riskier.

Wildavsky's (1988) *Searching for Safety* points to the considerable degree of safety achieved in contemporary society and argues that it is due to 'entrepreneurial activity' (as opposed to regulatory activity) in a variety of complex systems. He gives two 'universal strategies' for achieving safety: anticipation, which involves efforts to predict and prevent potential dangers from arising before they have ever occurred; and resilience, efforts to cope with dangers once they become manifest. He examines nuclear power plants, the human body's immune system, and the Food and Drug Administration's drug approval process. Arguing from a markedly neo-conservativist stance, he is generally critical of governmental regulations and of 'interveners' who would increase those regulations or restrict activities seen as highly risky. Normal accident theorists have not paid much attention to Wildavsky's call for more errors in risky systems so that we can learn more, or his view of a benighted, fearful public hampering free enterprise that would pursue the risks that supposedly made the US great. I would argue that political risks such as universal suffrage make a great nation, not the industrial risks that killed employees.

The main example of HRT, in the sense that it is the most developed, empirical, sophisticated and expansive, is the wonderfully inter-disciplinarian Berkeley group of Todd La Porte (political science), Karlene Roberts (business school, psychology) and Gene Rochlin (engineering), with some help from Michigan social psychologist Karl Weick. Their publications are many (Roberts, 1990, 1993; La Porte and Consolini, 1991; see Clarke, 1993 for an extensive review). This is the branch that Sagan properly chooses to contrast with NAT.

They initially looked at three 'nearly error free operations', the Federal Aviation Administration's air traffic control system, the Pacific Gas and Electric's electric power system, including the Diablo Canyon nuclear power plant, and the peacetime flight operations of three United States Navy aircraft carriers. These have achieved high levels of reliable and safe operations through the design and management of organizations. While they say more needs to be done, nevertheless they maintain that 'we have begun to discover the degree and character of effort necessary to overcome the inherent limitations to securing consistent, failure-free operations in complex social organizations' (La Porte quoted in Sagan, 1993: 15). This is a strong and unequivocal statement, repeated in La Porte's comment in this issue of the *Journal of Contingencies and Crisis Management*: we will get failure-free operations through more effort. Other quotes from their work could be provided demonstrating a decidedly optimistic view of the possibilities of failure-free operations (Clarke, 1993; Sagan, 1993).

All three HRT branches are aware of the vast cognitive limitations of human beings; they do not expect increased safety to come from improvements in individual rationality. There is a strain of 'voluntarism' in the La Porte branch; a belief that making a greater effort will overcome difficulties. But primarily the three branches believe that organizations can compensate for human limitations and, therefore, can be significantly more rational and effective than individuals − if individuals try. Furthermore, these organizational compensations are unproblematic; they do not involve more complexity or new irrationalities but are solely positive.

I am not very clear about the role of 'individual effort' in their scheme; it is clearly hortatory, and perhaps that is all that is intended. NAT, however, is bleakly explicit on this account: while it is better to try hard than not, because of system characteristics trying hard will not be enough.

Regardless of the individual effort theme, the crux of the difference between the two theories lies in one's faith in organizations. Sagan (1993) notes HRT uses a closed, rational system view of organizations; the La Porte branch is explicit regarding this (La Porte and Consolini, 1991: 23–24).

Organizations are rational in that they have highly formalized structures and are oriented towards the achievement of clear and consistent goals; in this case safe operations. They are relatively closed systems in that they go to great effort to minimize the effect that people or events outside of the organization might have on the organization. The main effect of the opening to the environment in HRT is that it demands safety, but otherwise no great effort is made to theorize environmental effects upon the operating system (for example, the shoddy construction of nuclear plants is not noted as a particular risk since it is not a part of the operating system; the isolation of the aircraft carrier is not contrasted to the political pressures upon the air traffic control system).

Achieving high reliability

The research of the different high reliability groups has produced similar explanations for positive safety records within a wide variety of systems. Sagan (1993) identifies four critical causal factors (and La Porte agrees):

- Political elites and organizational leaders put safety and reliability first as a goal;
- high levels of redundancy in personnel and technical safety measures;
- the development of a 'high reliability culture' in decentralized and continually practiced operations; and
- sophisticated forms of trial and error organizational learning.

Regarding goals, leaders must place a high priority on safety because safety costs money; 'richer is safer' as Wildavsky (1988) nicely puts it. Also, since HR organizations require clear operational goals, safety must have a high priority in order to communicate this objective clearly and consistently. Redundancy is obvious; the only way one can build 'reliable systems from unreliable parts' (Von Neuman, quoted in Sagan, 1993: 19) is to have multiple and independent channels of communication, decision making, and implementation. Duplication is a substitute for perfect parts (and carries no costs in increased complexity and opportunities for failure).

Next, it is important to decentralize decision-making authority. Operators in a nuclear power plant need discretion; aboard aircraft carriers anyone can halt a landing or takeoff, no matter what their rank; at air traffic control centres supervisors and controllers may switch responsibilities when necessary and informal teams are often formed to trade advice and manage dangerous operations; and airline captains can delegate the task of piloting to subordinates during crises. This helps create a 'culture of reliability' within the organization. This culture is also achieved through recruiting, socialization and training.

One of the differences between NAT and this aspect of HRT is that NAT asserts that systems that are both complexly interactive and tightly coupled require decentralization to cope with the unexpected interactions, but centralization to cope with the tight coupling, and they can't do both (Perrow, 1984: 332). The NAT claim of incompatible demands in most risky systems, rejected by HRT, is also an example of the incompatibility of the two theories, despite La Porte's suggestion that they are compatible.

There must be continuous operations and training. Most organizations emphasize stability and routinization in operations and deliberately reduce the amount of challenge and variety. HR organizations, however, should maximize challenge and variety in their continuous operations. This is difficult, they might have noted; one can't keep shutting down a nuclear power plant for training purposes since it provides a base load of electricity; one cannot keep firing off armed nuclear missiles to gain experience; and we have no record of carrier safety in times of actual combat – they are nearly error free only in training.

The final element that they mention is the strong capability to learn. Again, repeated trials and errors are important, though sometimes they refer to trials without errors because of the catastrophic consequence of mistakes. Wildavsky (1988: 25), for example, argues that there are too many government regulations on potentially hazardous technologies, because 'without trials there can be no new errors; but without these errors there is also less new learning'.

One might note one infrequent, but perverse, barrier to learning at this point, originally identified, I believe, by Turner (1978; 224) in *Man-made Disasters*, where accident investigations convert ill structured problems into well structured ones (see also Vaughan, 1994). Accident investigations are 'left censored' in that they examine only systems that failed, not the ones with the same characteristics that have not failed. Finding failures A and B in the system that had the accident, they assume these caused the accident. They do not look at similar systems that have not had accidents that might also have failures A and B, but not failure C in a somewhat remote part. The failure of C is not noted in the system with the accident and correcting for A and B may not do the trick, if C, perhaps in conjunction with A and B, or even with X and Y, caused the accident.

But the reverse problem should be noted. If we only examine systems without failures, as the HRT are prone to do, we are 'selecting on the dependent variable', that is, examining favourable outcomes only and then predicting what brought them about. The striking case of this problem is the US Occupational and Safety and Health Agency (OSHA) which examined Union Carbides' Institute, West Virginia plant shortly after Union Carbide's Bhopal disaster. The Institute plant also produced the deadly MIC gas. They gave the plant a clean bill of health, a 'it could never happen here' rating. Some 18 months after Bhopal, the Institute plant had a similar accident. OSHA went in again and found the plant full of violations and said that it was 'an accident waiting to happen' and levied a hefty fine (greatly reduced later) (Perrow, 1986). It is the familiar case of 'I will see it when I believe it'. HRT is perhaps not sufficiently alert to these problems of analysis.

Sagan examines dozens of often incredible accidents and near misses in the US nuclear defence system and repeatedly finds that safety was not the prime goal; learning did not take place; decentralization did not help or was revoked and there was little chance for realistic trials. For example, during the Cuban Missile Crisis, an Air Force sentry in Minnesota shot at a fence-climbing intruder and sounded the sabotage alarm. But at the Air Defence Command Base airfield in nearby Wisconsin the wrong alarm sounded, indicating a nuclear attack. The pilots of nuclear armed interceptors prepared for take off, but were stopped at the last minute by an officer flashing his car lights on the runway. It was a bear that tried to climb the fence in Minnesota.

Also during the Missile Crisis, a U-2 spy plane got lost when the *Aurora Borealis* obscured the stars and Soviet interceptors tried to shoot it down. The Alaskan command post ordered it home, but it ran out of fuel over Siberia. American interceptors, armed with air-to-air nuclear missiles, which they had full capability to launch on their own, went to protect the U-2 from Soviet fighters. Also during the Cuban Missile Crisis, a test tape of a missile launch from Cuba appeared on the radar operator's screens just as a satellite appeared over the horizon. After checking the data twice, the operators notified everyone of a real attack and the missile was projected to impact near Tampa.

My own favourite example is the incredible chapter on the 1968 Thule bomber accident (Sagan, 1993, Chapter 4) and how little was learned from it. Strategic Air Command (SAC) used a B-52 bomber as a redundant warning device. It flew above a critical warning radar, had thermonuclear weapons on board and crashed. SAC did not think through the implications of what would happen if the plane crashed, thus producing a warning of nuclear attack – in this case a false one. But the case is more than a compelling example of how adding redundancy can inadvertently cause an accident. It also shows how SAC's purpose, to do more flying, make things more exciting, expand its operational scope and so on – the role of 'interests' or operational, rather than official, goals – created a blind spot: airborne alert forces could occasionally crash and the crash might involve some common mode failures such as setting off a realistic threat of an enemy nuclear attack. Once the crash occurred, flights were cancelled but learning did not seem to take place. The SAC actively avoided an interpretation of the event that said that things were not perfect and that some redundancies had new risks. Instead, they provided strategic rationales to avoid a review of the incident and said that the flights were no longer necessary because other means were reliable.

The dangers of going native

There is something faintly 'B school' about the High Reliability Theory list; no one can be against clear safety goals, learning, experience and so on. Would that the world of organizations were receptive to such 'family values' credos as are offered by leadership theory and human resource management tracts. NAT has a healthy scepticism about goals, training and the absence of group interests.

It is also easy to be awed by these behemoths and the intense level of activity in some of them, such as flight exercises at night on the rolling deck of an aircraft carrier. I cannot even walk through a nuclear power plant without being awed by the immensity of controlled power and danger. The reflection that the plant that I am in has been safe for 15 years and might be for ten more, erodes the critical scrutiny I should maintain. I remember being very impressed by one such visit and chastened to later read that it was closed down for gross violations after a series of near misses.

The landing and takeoff carrier experiences of the Berkeley team are impressive and the system is awesome. But is the carrier so distinctive? Is it even complexly interactive and tightly coupled? When I think of the rolling mill operation in steel plants I studied in the 1960s, they seemed to be every bit as dangerous, as decentralized and as imbued with a safety culture as the prime exemplar of HR organizations; the aircraft carrier deck with its intense activity. Yet there were failures and deaths, probably at a rate not significantly different from that of the naval carriers. Like the deck of the carrier, with jets sometimes coming in or leaving every 50 seconds, action in the rolling mill was repetitive (though complicated skills were involved), permitting continuous learning, open observation of everyone's behaviour and the possibility of stopping an essentially loosely coupled process in emergencies. In this sense, the sobriquet 'High Reliability Organizations' probably applies to more organizations than HRT would expect. Some industrial units are run at these intense rates.

We can be optimistic about these types of operations, as High Reliability theorists are. But are carriers typical of risky systems, the kind characterized by (using Sagan's label) Normal Accident Theory? I think not, with one exception; but first let us look at NAT.

Normal accident theory

NAT predicts 'systems accidents' rather than the more ubiquitous commonplace failures of operators, equipment, procedures, environment and so on (called 'component failure accidents', where there is no significant unexpected inter-action of failures). It focuses on something quite different than the elements of HRT (safety goals, redundancies and learning which all organizations attempt). It argues that major accidents are inevitable in some systems. Since nothing is perfect, if the organization is 'complexly interactive' rather than linear, and 'tightly coupled' rather than loosely coupled, small errors can interact in unexpected ways and the tight coupling will mean a cascade of increasingly large failures. A failure in a linear system (assembly line) is anticipated, comprehensible and generally visible. It can be fixed and probably won't happen again. Complexly interactive systems can have independent failures, each insignificant in itself, that interact in unexpected and even incomprehensible ways such as to evade or defeat the safety devices set up to respond to the individual failures. If the system is also 'tightly coupled', the initial failures cannot be contained or isolated and the system stopped; failures will cascade until a major part of the system or all of it will fail. Loosely coupled systems have the slack to absorb disturbances; defective units can be segregated, production can be stopped or follow alternative paths and substitutions of personnel or materials are possible. Tightly coupled systems do not have these options. Tight coupling is sometimes designed in as an economy measure, but often there is no other known way to produce the output without tight coupling. If the system has catastrophic potential – has toxic or explosive parts, or if it functions in a hostile environment such as in space, the air, or on or under water – we may have scores of deaths and/or the pollution of a significant part of the environment.

This is the theory that Sagan so effectively contrasts to HRT. The essence is that no matter how hard we might try, the characteristics of complexly interactive and tightly coupled systems will cause a major failure, eventually.

Of the major systems studied by HRT, only the Diablo Canyon nuclear power plant is tightly coupled and complexly interactive with catastrophic potential. It has not yet had a serious accident and this is cited as evidence of a High Reliability operation. The operation may be highly reliable, but an open systems view would point out that it is not encouraging that initially the contractors installed a major safety system upside down and backwards without realizing it and that the plant is on an earthquake fault line. Air traffic control has been able to reduce tight coupling and is basically a linear system rather than a complexly interactive one. It is not all that clear to me how coupled and complexly interactive power grids are. I judged them as quite tightly coupled but moderately linear (Perrow, 1984: 97); they have little catastrophic potential so I did not carefully analyze their operations and failures. Flight operations on the aircraft carriers are basically linear and since landings and takeoffs can be easily stopped or delayed, the system may be seen as loosely coupled. Even so it has not been tested in actual combat. The friendly fire that kills one's own troops in combat situations suggests that there are some things for which there is no adequate training, even in linear and loosely coupled systems. The evidence assembled by this branch of HRT, then, is hardly conclusive with regard to the risky systems NAT worries about: nuclear power; nuclear weapons; marine transport; aircraft (as distinct from the airways); chemical plants; genetic engineering and space missions (see for example Perrow, 1984: 97; others have extended this list).

Sagan's two major contributions

As noted at the outset, Sagan (1993) allows us to theorize about accidents in risky systems in a far more explicit way than has been the case. Too much has been implicit in all the work cited so far; it has been guided by theories, certainly, but different ones and the difference has been unacknowledged. Thus the work of accident theorists has been under-theorized.

The first advantage of Sagan's theoretical work is that it calls attention to the different theoretical models of organizations involved and the consequences of this. For an organizational theorist this is an exciting achievement (and it is embarrassing to find that I had to be told that I was, as with the Moliere character, 'speaking prose'). He allows me to more sharply conceptualize NAT than I did in my book. I noted in passing that I was using a Garbage Can Theory (Cohen, March and Olsen, 1988) with power (Perrow, 1984: 10, 261, 330–339), but not anticipating the emergence of a set of High Reliability Theorists with a contrasting model, I did not reflect upon the consequences of model choice. Sagan dramatically draws our attention to it and for this alone his work is significant.

I also failed to stress that risky systems are likely to have high degrees of uncertainty associated with them and thus one can expect (assuming bounded rationality) 'Garbage Can' processes; that is, unstable and unclear goals misunderstanding and mis-learning, happenstance, confusion as to means and so on (March and Olsen, 1979; Perrow, 1986: 131–154; Cohen, March and Olsen, 1988). A Garbage Can approach, appropriate where there is high uncertainty about means or techniques, appropriate structures and even goals, invites a pessimistic view of such things as efficiency or safety. A more rational, B-school model invites optimism. I think this is the basis of the contradictory claims wherein Sagan insists that HRT is optimistic and La Porte insists that it is not.

Since the risky systems being observed have not been around very long, settling the issue on the basis of outcomes – how many serious accidents – is impossible; the controversy is properly over processes and this means the models of organizations used.

The second advantage of Sagan's theoretical work is the awareness of the need to emphasize the role of group interests in producing accident-prone systems. Group interests and power pervaded my (1984) book, but I did not note that many organizational theories were inattentive to not only bounded rationality, but to interests and power. The issue, I argued, was not risk, but power; the power of elites to impose risk on the many for the benefit of the few. Sagan makes this a researchable question, rather than an assumption and the analysis of the rôle of group interests in the systems he studies is vital to his story and to our understanding of catastrophes. An interest theory says that a variety of groups within and without the organization will attempt to use it for their own ends and these may not be consistent with the official goals or the public interest. Indeed, Sagan argues that even if elites do place safety first and try hard to enforce this goal, clashes of power and interest at lower levels may defeat it. HRT, by assuming that safety can be put first, assumes that elites or others who use the organization will have safety goals foremost and those subordinate to them will share them; NAT is profoundly sceptical on this score. Sagan's data clearly supports NAT and the value of an interest view of organizations.

But why would system elites not put safety first? Here an expanded version of NAT is vital. The harm, the consequences, are not evenly distributed; the latency period may be longer than any decision maker's career; few managers are punished for not putting safety first even after an accident, but will quickly be punished for not putting profits, market share or prestige first. Managers come to believe their own rhetoric about safety first because information indicating otherwise is suppressed for reasons of organizational politics. Above all, it is hard to have a catastrophe, so the risk to any one set of managers or elites is small; while it is substantial for society as a whole.

The difficulty of having a catastrophe

The last point deserves emphasis; it was forced upon me by the Bhopal accident. It is rarely the case that we cannot say of any disaster 'it could have been worse', but we cannot say this in the case of the accident at Union Carbide's Bhopal plant in India. Chemical plants with catastrophic potential have been around for nearly 100 years, but there have been few catastrophes. Plants capable of killing thousands with one blow have been around for about 30 or 40 years, but there has only been one Bhopal. The US Environmental Protection Agency estimated in 1989 that in the previous 25 years there were 17 releases of toxic chemicals in volumes and levels of toxicity exceeding those that killed at least 3,000 in Bhopal. But mostly because of sheer luck only five people were killed in these accidents (Shabecoff, 1989).

The reason is the 'flip' side of Normal Accident Theory: just as it takes just the right combination of failures to defeat all the safety devices, so does it take just the right combination of circumstances to produce a catastrophe. With Bhopal these included sufficient quantities of toxic materials released; no warning of the release; no awareness of the toxicity; a concentrated population; weather conditions that brought the cloud over the population; people in their houses and asleep; permeable houses; and denial by the plant officials for some hours of a release and then of the toxicity of the release. Remove any one or two variables (except for the last, which merely made the disaster worse) and it would have been a close call or a small event.

We have had explosive clouds drift over sleeping suburbs in the US but not find an ignition source; the Union Carbide plant in Institute West Virginia had an accident that was similar to the Union Carbide plant in Bhopal some 18 months later, but the gas was less toxic, there was less of it and the wind took it away from concentrated settlements. Warnings are crucial: the Grand Teton dam failure in the US had a couple of hours and very few deaths; the Vaiont dam failure in Italy had none and 3,000 perished.

We may have been lucky that the space shuttle *Challenger* blew up; the next shuttle flight, with the same multiple problems and high risks of the *Challenger*, was to take up 47 pounds of highly toxic plutonium which could have drifted as a powder over the Florida coast after an explosion. We were very lucky with Chernobyl, for if the toxic cloud had not gone straight up several thousand feet before lazily dispersing, but had been carried by winds directly over nearby Kiev with its two million inhabitants, the disaster would have been immediate and unimaginable.

Incidentally, I do not find that Bhopal, the *Challenger*, Chernobyl or the *Exxon Valdez* accidents are normal accidents, though NAT helps us understand them and the aftermaths. They are alarmingly banal examples of organizational elites not trying very hard at all and are what I call 'component failure accidents'. Bhopal made me realize how hard it is to have a catastrophe where hundreds or thousands perish with one blow; everything must be just right. Elites must be aware of this when they increasingly populate the earth with risky systems, and when the number of male-made industrial disasters is rising sharply.

Error-avoiding and error-inducing systems

Sagan, then, has highlighted the importance of two things more or less missing from HRT; limited rationality models and group interests. There is another important factor that bears upon the second criticism La Porte makes of Sagan. I have argued that even if we try hard there will be accidents in certain types of systems, but we don't even try hard, because of bounded rationality and group interests. But will we, La Porte in effect asks, try harder in some cases than others and can we learn from this? Or, to take it out of the motivational tense, are some systems more error-inducing than others, and why, and what could we do about it?

I made a first attempt at this question in 1984 with *Normal Accidents*, extended it in an article finished in 1992 (Perrow, 1994) and, since then, have been elaborating it to include the failure of non-risky systems. I will confine myself to the 1992 formulation on risky systems here. An organization, such as a chemical plant, exists in a system which includes technological advances, regulatory agencies, vendors, unions, communities, competitors and a market for its goods. There are important system characteristics which determine the number of inevitable (though often small) failures which might interact unexpectedly and the degree of coupling which determines the spread and management of the failures. Some of these are:

- Experience with operating scale – did it grow slowly, accumulating experience, or rapidly with no experience with the new configurations or volumes?
- Experience with the critical phases – if starting and stopping are the risky phases, does this happen frequently (takeoffs and landings) or infrequently (nuclear plant outages)?
- Information on errors – is this shared within and between the organizations? (Yes in the Japanese nuclear power industry; barely in the US). Can it be obtained, as in air transport, or does it go to the bottom with the ship?
- Close proximity of elites to the operating system – they fly on airplanes but don't ship on rusty vessels or live only a few blocks from chemical plants.
- Organizational control over members – solid with the naval carriers, partial with nuclear defence, mixed with marine transport (new crews each time), absent with chemical and nuclear plants (and we are hopefully reluctant to militarize all risky systems).
- Organizational density of the system's environment (vendors, subcontractors, owners/operators trade associations and unions, regulators, environmental groups, and competitive systems) – if rich, there will be persistent investigations and less likelihood of blaming God or the operators and more attempts to increase safety features.

I found naval carriers and air transport to be error-avoiding systems; nuclear plants, nuclear defence and nuclear waste and marine transport to be error-inducing systems; and space programs and chemical plants to be error-neutral.

These are system characteristics that can make things safer or less safe: Some are generic and can hardly be changed – nuclear defences can't really be tested nor can nuclear plants induce utility executives to be in attendance continually, or start up and shut down as frequently as airplanes. Others could be altered; nuclear plants and crude oil tankers could have grown in size slowly; the Coast Guard need not have been captured by the industry or de-funded by President Reagan. The system characteristics profoundly affect the degree to which the safety-inducing factors that HRT emphasizes, such as safety goals, learning, training and empowerment could be established. In this way we can use the four features mentioned earlier that HRT has identified.

But a contrast of error-avoiding and error-inducing systems also permits an 'optimistic' element in what Sagan describes as a basically pessimistic theory. It shows that inevitable as normal accidents may be, their frequency can be significantly affected by the configuration of the system, because that configuration can encourage, in an error-inducing system, the small errors that make the unanticipated interaction of errors possible.

The most important thing about the systems view of accidents is that it allows work to go forward by both HRT and NAT. La Porte is correct to note that Sagan did not significantly advance the search for operational and procedural changes that can improve the reliability of organizations that manage hazardous technologies. That was not his objective even though it is La Porte's agenda. I think Sagan had other important things to do; clarifying and adding to our theories of organizational safety which were necessary before one could proceed with La Porte's agenda. Sagan is far from indifferent to this agenda, however. For example, he points to a basic structural change that is required to make the nuclear system safer – taking nuclear warheads off alert and placing them in storage far away from the missiles and aircraft that make the system so tightly coupled today. I also advocated such things as the decoupling of spent storage pools from nuclear reactor buildings.

Summary and a final word on optimism

In summary, we are in a position to argue that complexly interactive and tightly coupled systems will inevitably experience the unexpected interaction of (quite possibly small, and normally insignificant) errors that will defeat safety devices (both theories seem to agree with this). Secondly, systems with catastrophic potential are particularly vulnerable to the problems of bounded rationality and 'Garbage Can' processes which will encourage multiple errors and de-emphasize safety goals. HRT would say, I presume, that this limitation can be overcome. Thirdly, in addition to a bounded rationality and open systems view of these organizations, we must include the matter of 'interests' (group interests or interest aggregation), a matter which Sagan rightly stresses in his account. Production pressures, profit pressures, growth, prestige, departmental power struggles and so on will supplant safety concerns. The HRT and NAT theories diverge here. Fourthly, some risky systems are, in addition, error-prone because of both internal processes and the environment they continually interact with, further restricting and even defeating safety attempts.

The first and second – inevitable accidents and quite imperfect organizations – affect all risky systems. Some systems, in addition, have strong interest components that compromise safety, but not all of them (for example, marine transport is profit-oriented, nuclear power utilities in the US are not particularly so). And finally some systems conspire to avoid errors (air transport, aircraft carriers) because of their characteristics and others are error-inducing (marine transport, nuclear weapons, US nuclear power). Changing the latter will be extremely difficult and requires changing many other contiguous systems.

We return to the optimistic/pessimistic issue one last time. First, there is the question of whether, as Sagan puts it, the glass is 99 per cent full or 1 per cent empty. High reliability theorists speak of 'nearly error-free operations', and the normal accident theorist would say that she is not impressed with those criteria. The issue is only in part the frequency of errors, because there are always errors in risky systems. But most of them are caught by safety devices, redundancies and so on and are insignificant. For NAT we would need a metric which would measure the frequency at which errors, even though they may be small and insignificant by themselves, interact in unexpected ways that can defeat or bypass safety systems. On the other hand, take the notion that organizations are after all pretty sloppy, are chaotic garbage cans and riddled with interests; the observation that so alarms normal accident theorists. It does not take into account the presence of many almost self-correcting features of some risky systems, the error-avoiding ones such as air transport. Bounded rationality is not appreciably more evident in marine transport than in air transport, but there is much less scope for it in the latter and this should prevent any sweeping generalizations about risky systems by those enchanted by NAT and disenchanted by our survival prospects. In short, one should be careful with the metrics when being pessimistic or optimistic; it is not just error rates but interaction possibilities and the chances for learning, trials, investigations and so on; and these reside in the larger system characteristics.

I, for one, found the confrontation of Sagan and La Porte and his colleagues to be very productive. I cannot speak for the many others who have contributed to the further development of NAT, but I think we need both formulations and research from both perspectives. NAT and HRT took the theory of accidents out of the hands of economists and engineers and put it into the hands of organizational theorists; Sagan has brought that theory of accidents much closer to maturity.

References

Clarke, L. (1993) 'Drs. Pangloss and Strangelove Meet Organizational Theory: High Reliability Organizations and Nuclear Weapons Accidents', *Sociological Forum*, Volume 8, Number 4, pp. 675–689.

Cohen, M. D., March, J. G. and Olsen, J. P. (1988) 'A Garbage Can Model of Organizational Choice', in March, J. G. (ed.), *Decisions and Organizations*, Basil Blackwell: London, pp. 294–334.

La Porte, T. R. and Consolini, P. M. (1991) 'Working in Practice but Not in Theory', *Journal of Public Administration Research and Theory*, Volume 1, Number 1, Winter, pp. 19–47.

March, J. G. and Olsen, J. P. (1979) *Ambiguity and Choice in Organizations*, Universitetsforleget: Bergen.

Morone, J. and Woodhouse, E. J. (1986) *Averting Catastrophe: Strategies for Regulating Risky Technologies*, University of California Press: Berkeley.

Perrow, C. (1984) *Normal Accidents: Living with High Risk Systems*, Basic Books: New York.

Perrow, C. (1986) *Complex Organizations* (third edition), Random House, New York.

Perrow, C. (1994) 'Accidents in High Risk Systems', *Technology Studies*, Volume 1, Number 1.

Roberts, K. (1990) 'Some Characteristics of One Type of High Reliability Organizations', *Organization Science*, Volume 1, Number 2, pp. 160–176.

Roberts, K. (ed.) (1993) *New Challenges to Understanding Organizations*, Macmillan: New York.

Sagan, S. D. (1993) *The Limits of Safety: Organizations, Accidents and Nuclear Weapons*, Princeton University Press: New Jersey.

Shabecoff, P. (1989) 'Bhopal Disaster Rivals 17 in US', *New York Times*, 30 April.

Turner, B. (1978) *Man-made Disasters*, Wykeham: London.

Vaughan, D. (1994) 'Risk, Work Group Culture, and the Normalization of Deviants' (unpublished paper), pp. 1–30.

Wildavsky, A. (1988) *Searching for Safety*, Transaction Books: New Brunswick.

Chapter 3

Paul Shrivastava, Ian I. Mitroff, Danny Miller and Anil Miglani

UNDERSTANDING INDUSTRIAL CRISES[1]

PRIVATE CORPORATIONS AND PUBLIC organizations are facing a new class of strategic problems caused by the harmful effects of their own activities or the effects of environmental forces on their activities. Some of these problems are serious enough to assume crisis proportions for society, and threaten the very survival of implicated organizations. Understanding and coping with such industrial crises is a challenge facing organizational researchers and practitioners alike.

A key objective of organizational theory and management sciences has been to understand the behaviour of organizations and to discover technically efficient ways of organizing. Some researchers have also focused on management of organization-environment relationships for achieving organizations' long-term objectives (Pfeffer, 1982; Schendel and Hofer, 1979). This research predominantly focuses on improving financial performance, productivity and technological efficiency. Unfortunately, it ignores the *harmful* effects of organizational activities (Keeley, 1984).

Organizational activities have a variety of potentially damaging side-effects on their stakeholders and on the natural environment. For example, industrial accidents, environmental pollution, product injuries, and occupational diseases can cause severe harm to consumers, workers, the public and the environment. Usually the damage is small, is widely dispersed over time and across multiple subjects, and does not cause public alarm or major risk. Organizations deal with such side-effects in an *ad hoc* and piecemeal way (Kinghorn, 1985). Occasionally however, damage can be major and sudden, or it can accumulate to a crisis that seriously threatens corporations, government agencies and the public (Gephart, 1984; Masuch, 1985).

Industrial crises are becoming important because of their increased frequency the extensive damage they cause, and their cost to organizations and society. More importantly, there seems to be an inexhorable systemic logic in industrial societies that makes these crises almost inevitable. Industrial technologies are becoming progressively more complex and potentially harmful (Perrow, 1984). Organizations are becoming larger in size and scope. As the Chernobyl nuclear disaster illustrates, the impacts of industrial crises sometimes transcend organizational and national boundaries to create harm on a global scale.

This article conceptualizes industrial crises and defines the domain for studying them by describing their key characteristics and the logic of their occurrence. These are illustrated using three recent crises – the Bhopal accident, the Tylenol poisonings, the space shuttle Challenger explosion. A typology of crisis-triggering events is also presented.

The societal context of industrial crises

Industrial crises can be understood only within the context of the evolution of industrial societies. Following Habermas (1975), we view this evolution as proceeding on two distinct but connected fronts: the development of forces of production, and the development of normative order in society. Mismatches between these forces create 'steering problems' for society by disrupting the principles of social organization. Steering problems lead to crises if they extend beyond the organizational principles of any given society.

Modern industrial societies and those attempting to industrialize rapidly are characterized by monopolistic or oligopolistic economies, large multinational corporations, and expanding state interventionism. The normative order in these societies is becoming increasingly secularized. Older forms of legitimacy based on religion and custom are being supplanted by technical administrative rationality. The state's administrative capability to control the economic system and to moderate its fluctuations is in large measure the source of its legitimacy. But the state is only partially able to stabilize the economy and its institutions. Periodic economic crises are inevitable (Offe, 1984; O'Connor, 1987).

Economic steering problems are treated largely as issues of rational administration by the state. Failure to deal with these or to manage economic growth generates what Habermas calls a 'rationality crisis' – the inability of the state and its agencies to manage economic growth successfully. Prolonged rationality crisis causes the state to lose legitimacy, resulting in a 'legitimacy crisis', or the mass withdrawal of support and loyalty. It forces changes in existing social structures and institutions. A legitimation crisis can then devolve into a 'motivational crisis' – a decline in moral commitment to the normative order. In the absence of traditional moral values, the commitment of the masses to the normative order in modern societies is at best fragile. Technocratic/administrative legitimation can only provide temporary and provisional acceptance of a materially successful economic system. Thus, the potential for these crises is endemic in modern industrial societies (Giddens, 1983; Habermas, 1975).

Economic crises are endemic to industrial and industrializing societies.

Economic conditions in those societies promote rapid and rapacious industrial development without commensurate investments into the development of infrastructure for enhancing safety. The gap between needed and available safety infrastructure to support hazardous technological systems continues to increase as industrial development progresses. This increases the probability of crisis occurring in the industrial system. This is reflected in countries like Mexico, India, Nigeria, Malaysia, etc. Industrial output of these countries accounts for 30–35 per cent of their respective GNPs (like many of the industrialized countries). However, their investments in the areas of industrial safety and environmental and health protection is much smaller than in the industrialized nations.

Industrial crises are situations in which organized industrial activities are the source of major damage to human life, and natural and social environments. They often occur in an environment of economic crisis characterized by insufficient growth, unemployment, fiscal deficits, budgetary and competitive pressures on individual organization, and an inadequate industrial infrastructure. Crises invariably extend beyond the organization of origin to encompass a broad range of economic, social and political agents and forces. They may also possess elements of rationality and legitimacy crises, and eventually threaten social structures and institutions.

Characteristics of industrial crises

Although industrial crises have destructive effects similar to natural disasters (earthquakes, floods, hurricanes, etc.), the two are very different. Industrial crises are disasters caused by human agencies and the social order; natural disasters are acts of nature (Fritz, 1961; Quarantelli, 1978). The impacts of natural disasters are localized to a geographic region and specific time periods. The impacts of industrial crises sometimes transcend geographic boundaries and can even have trans-generational effects. For example, the impact of the radiation from the Chernobyl Nuclear Power Plant accident was felt in a dozen countries outside the Soviet Union, and is expected to cause an unknown number of increased cancer deaths for the next 30 years (Hohenemser et al., 1986).

Industrial crises and natural disasters follow different paths of evolution. The worst consequences of the latter are felt at the place and time of occurrence, after which the effects are progressively reduced (Kreps, 1984). In contrast, industrial crises do not always have their worst consequences at the point of occurrence. They unfold in complex ways and sometimes, as in the toxic waste poisoning in Japan's Minamata Bay or Love Canal, New York, the worst effects occur long after the triggering event and its causes have been identified.

Industrial crises are both organizational and inter-organizational phenomena. They are caused by human, communication, and technological failures within and among organizations. Organizations also become involved in mitigating the effects of crises (Turner, 1978). Thus industrial crises cannot be dealt with at the level of single organizations.

Industrial crises have a number of key defining characteristics, which are discussed below.

1   *Triggering event.* Industrial crises are triggered by specific events identifiable according to place, time, and agents. They represent sudden destructive events or new information about destructive aspects of existing products, processes and practices. Triggering events have a very low probability of occurrence, but there are often warnings of their occurrence (Kates, 1977). Given their low probability assessments, these warnings are often not taken seriously.

Triggering events take many forms. They may conveniently be divided into production and consumption related harm. On the production side, crises can be triggered in the production system, the production environment, and *via* post-production effects. Production system related harm can occur through personal accidents, transportation accidents, and systems accidents which cause major damage to workers and surrounding communities. Harm in the production environment occurs in the form of occupational diseases and workplace hazards. Post-production harm takes the form of environmental pollution and toxic waste disposal problems, both of which have triggered crises in the past.

On the consumption side, misuse of safe products, product sabotage and the use of defective products are the most common sources of harm. Certain side-effects of consumption also create crises, both for individual organizations and for whole industries (for example, links between smoking and cancer caused decline in demand in the tobacco industry). Figure 1 presents types and examples of harm and crises caused by these industrial activities.

This typology covers a wide range of potential crisis-triggering events arising from industrial activities. While it may not comprehensively represent all possible types of crises, it can serve as a useful starting point. Triggering events initiate crisis processes in several domains such as product markets, financial markets, national and regional economies, the physical environment, medical and public health areas, legal and governmental actions, and social relations. These events become the reference points for identifying crises.

2   *Large-scale damage to human life and environment.* The triggering event and the subsequent crisis cause much perceived or real damage to human life and/or the natural environment. The former include death, injuries, delayed health effects, and health effects on future generations. Environmental damages include destruction of vegetation, pollution of air, water, and soil, changes in weather patterns, mutation of natural life species, etc. Lack of information, uncertainty about consequences, and highly subjective perceptions of risks, further enhance perceptions of damage (Renn, 1986; Turner, 1978).

3   *Large economic costs.* Industrial crises involve high costs, often running into hundreds of millions of dollars (Smets, 1985). Organizations in which crises originate are held legally liable for compensating victims for damages. There are additional costs associated with technical damage control, rescue and relief, cleaning up contamination, rebuilding production facilities, recalling defective products, redesigning defective products/processes, and

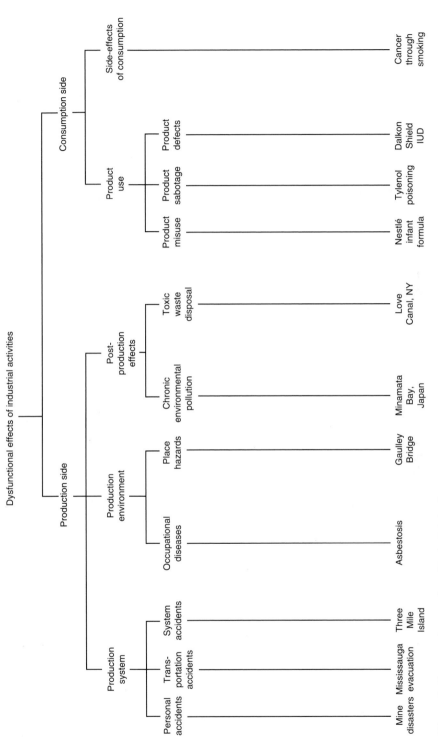

Figure 1 Types and examples of industrial crises

health care for affected persons. Often crises create open-ended liabilities for some organizations, thereby making their costs impossible to estimate. For example, government agencies and voluntary social work organizations involved in mitigating the effects of crises incur large costs in rescue, relief and rehabilitation tasks. Some of these tasks last for many years beyond initial estimates because of delayed effects or discovery of new information about effects on health.

4   *Large social costs.* The social costs of crises are high because they involve disruptions in social, political, and cultural arrangements. Crises are associated with large scale evacuation of people, rehabilitation of affected persons, reorganization, of family interdependencies and changes in the social order (Fritz, 1961; Kreps, 1984). Conflicts over causes and consequences of crises create political disruptions. Public leaders, ruling political parties, and government agencies associated with the causes of, and recovery from crises are subjected to immense social and political pressures (Erickson, 1976).

5   *Causes of crises.* Crises are caused by two interacting sets of failures. Inside organizations, a complex set of Human, Organizational, and Technological (HOT) factors, lead to the triggering event. These in turn, interact with Regulatory, Infrastructural and Preparedness (RIP) failures in the organizations' environments. Human factors include operator and managerial errors, purposive acts such as sabotage and terrorist attacks or acts of war. Organizational factors include policy failures, inadequate resource allocations for safety, strategic pressures which allow managers to overlook hazardous practices and conditions, communication failures, misperceptions of the extent and nature of hazards, inadequate emergency plans, and cost pressures which curtail safety (Miller and Freisen, 1980; Miller and Freisen, 1984; Turner, 1978). Technological systemic factors include faulty design, defective equipment, contaminated or defective materials and supplies, and faulty technical procedures (Perrow, 1984). Crises may also be triggered by acts of nature such as floods, earthquakes, lightning, tornadoes, etc.

The organizational environment plays an important role in causing crises. More specifically, it causes triggering events to escalate into full-blown crises. Regulatory failures allow hazardous technologies to enter communities ill-prepared to handle them. The physical and social infrastructure supporting industrial activities and specific industrial units also determines a community's capacity to prevent and cope with industrial crises. Weak infrastructure characterized by a lack of monitoring and surveillance capacity, and by inadequate essential services (water, electricity, transportation, communication, etc.) allows hazardous conditions to exist within communities, and fails to anticipate and prevent triggering events from occurring. Preparedness failures in the form of inadequate on- and off-site emergency plans, lack of emergency medical capacity, and ill-prepared civil defence authorities, leads to proliferation of harm from the triggering events. In the absence of emergency preparation, even small incidents have grave effects, and major accidents become catastrophic (Shrivastava, 1987).

Developing countries usually have an acute shortage of infrastructural facilities. Many have industrialized very rapidly in the past 25 years, without evolving a commensurate infrastructure. For example, in Brazil, India, Malaysia, Mexico, Nigeria, Singapore, and Venezuela the percentage of Gross Domestic Product from industrial activities is increasing rapidly and is as high as that of industrialized countries – between 30 and 40 per cent (World Bank, 1985). However, these developing countries do not have the resources to build an infrastructure that makes industries safe. The consequence is that major industrial accidents in developing countries lead to far more deaths and injuries than in industrialized countries (Shrivastava, 1987; Smets, 1985). In the last ten years the accidents with the most fatalities have all occurred in the factories of developing countries.

6   *Multiple stakeholder involvement and conflict.* Multiple stakeholders are inevitably involved in causing, communicating, and mitigating the effects of industrial crises. Involvement of multiple agencies creates numerous, long-drawn conflicts over responsibility, liability and recovery costs. Key stakeholders are corporations, both private and public, which own or manage the facilities in which the crises are triggered. They are legally liable for damages. In some countries, such as the USA, liability can extend beyond the corporation to equipment manufacturers, design and engineering consultants, raw material suppliers, and state agencies. Insurance companies, and industry/trade associations are also affected.

The media play a key role in communicating crisis events to the public. They shape public perceptions and responses to crises. Despite the deployment of enormous media resources, coverage of crisis events is fragmented, lacks objective data, and is equivocal. This is caused by a tendency of stakeholders to control information, and by a genuine lack of information about causes. Such coverage extends the crisis by giving rise to myths, false alarms and heightened perceptions of harm (Gephart, 1984; Molotch and Lester, 1975; Shrivastava, 1985).

State or government agencies in charge of industrial, social, regulatory, and public health infrastructure are stakeholders in two ways. They help in mitigating the effects of the crises, and they provide regulatory and monitoring services to prevent similar crises from recurring. State agencies also bear the political burden of these crises (Lagadec, 1982). However, voluntary organizations represent a diverse set of public interest stakes in crises. They provide relief services and create public pressure on other organizations to aid victims in recovering from damages (Kreps, 1984).

The most profoundly affected stakeholders are, of course, the victims who suffer damage to life and property. These include workers in production facilities, consumers, and communities in which hazardous facilities are located. Even unborn children become victims because of genetic effects or delayed medical effects. Sometimes even remote observers of crisis events suffer deeply. For example, children who watched the space shuttle Challenger blow up on the TV were found to have suffered psychological trauma (Goleman, 1986).

7   *Responses to crises.* Crises elicit *responses* from stakeholders that attempt to

mitigate destruction and social disruption and prevent future crises of a similar kind from occurring. Immediate responses aim at technical damage control, and rescue and relief of injured persons. These responses have to be made under severe time pressures, inadequate and conflicting information, breakdown of normal social and organizational systems, intense media scrutiny and an emotionally charged environment (Bouillette and Quarantelli, 1971). Long-term organizational responses focus on inquiries into causes and consequences of crises, conflict resolution, compensation and rehabilitation of victims, and technological and organizational improvements. Other responses focus on changing environmental conditions, enhancing infrastructural services, and changing regulations governing industries.

Crises are composed of many loosely coupled *interdependent events* often taking place in geographically dispersed locations and at different times. Each event sets the stage for others to occur in a chain reaction that proliferates the crisis. Within a chain, events are causally linked, but parallel chains of events may be loosely coupled. Events in a chain are sometimes difficult to anticipate and prevent, and only indirectly affect other chains. For example, event chains in the technological domain are only loosely coupled with event chains in the legal domain, or with event chains in relief and rehabilitation domains. Part of the reason for loose coupling is that different actors and agencies are in charge of each event chain, and there is poor co-ordination and information exchange between them (Turner, 1976).

In addition to the primary effects described earlier, crises have indirect impacts on stakeholders. These impacts represent intermediate outcomes from the chain of events that constitute the crisis. Some of these outcomes change important contextual factors. They may lead to corporate bankruptcies, regulatory changes, or changes in insurance rates. These effects are delayed and represent lessons learned by remote observers and stakeholders.

8   *Crisis resolution and crises extension.* Decision-makers attempt to resolve a crisis by mitigating its effects. Technical recovery is sought through organizational and technological process improvements. Economic recovery is sought through compensation to victims. Business recovery is pursued through financial and product market changes, and settlement of damage claims. Social recovery requires the reintegration of victims into social systems and normalization of social relations (Quarantelli, 1978).

Often recovery from damages is viewed as the resolution of the crisis. However, few efforts are made to eliminate the original causes, perhaps because these cannot be identified with certainty. The focus on symptoms rather than causes leaves organizations vulnerable to similar crises that can deepen and extend the original problem (Shrivastava, 1987).

A model of industrial crises

The relationships between these characteristics of industrial crises are schematically drawn in figure 2. Preconditions for crisis triggering events are created by

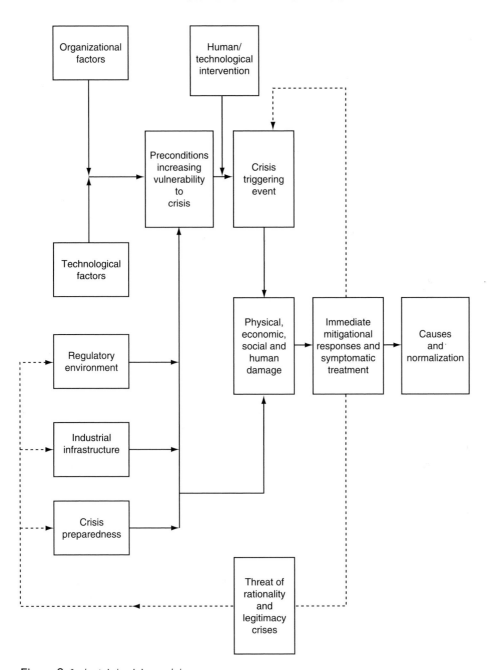

Figure 2 Industrial crisis model

organizational and environmental conditions. These include strategic, operating and technological characteristics of production facilities and products, and the quality of regulatory, infrastructural and crisis preparedness systems that support industrial activities. Under certain conditions, human and technological failures trigger crises. Triggering events cause damage to life, environment and property. The extent of damage is greater in situations where the infrastructure is weak and crisis preparedness systems are inadequate. Damages elicit responses and corrective actions in the form of technological damage control, rescue and relief, compensation to victims, organizational improvements and regulatory changes. Affected stakeholders recover from symptoms without necessarily eliminating the causes of the crisis. Post-crisis normalization can take a long time, and involves the reassessment of and changes in social institutions and structures. However, since the fundamental causes of crisis are not addressed, even minor follow-up incidents extend and deepen the crisis for involved organizations.

The above characteristics of crises are illustrated in the next section by using data from three disparate events – the Bhopal crisis, the Tylenol poisonings and the space shuttle Challenger explosion. These events involve both public and private sector organizations, operate in both domestic and multinational environments, and deal with a broad range of product and process technologies. The events were partly chosen for their differences, to emphasize the diverse scope and nature of the industrial crisis phenomenon. Before comparing them each event is briefly introduced.

Industrial crisis illustrations and comparisons

The Bhopal crisis. The accident that triggered the Bhopal crisis occurred at the Union Carbide (I) Ltd pesticide plant, located in the densely populated centre of the city of Bhopal, less than two miles from the Bhopal Railway Station which served as the hub of commerce and transportation. The plant manufactured and stored large quantities of a highly poisonous chemical called Methyl Isocyanate (MIC) used for manufacturing the pesticide SEVIN. People living around the plant, local authorities, medical personnel, and even Union Carbide workers, were not aware of the extreme toxicity of MIC, nor did they have any contingency plans to follow in case of a large-scale accidental release of the chemical.

The MIC manufacturing plant was commissioned in 1981, but had received inadequate maintenance and was in a rundown condition. From the time of its establishment, it had operated at less than 50 per cent of capacity because of declining demand for pesticides. Severe cost pressures had prompted management to curtail expenditures on safety practices, maintenance, and personnel (International Confederation of Free Trade Unions, 1985).

On 2 December, 1984, around 11 pm, due to a faulty pipe washing operation a large quantity of water entered the storage tank 610. Water reacted violently with MIC in a runaway trimerization chain reaction. Before any remedial actions could be taken, large quantities of MIC were released into the atmosphere until the reaction ended without intervention at about 2 am (Union Carbide Corporation, 1985; Varadarajan *et al.*, 1985).

Outside the plant, the city of Bhopal was thrown into complete chaos and panic. No one knew the appropriate emergency procedures to deal with the accident. Residents from nearby neighbourhoods fled haphazardly breathing more poisonous gases as they escaped. The medical system with its 1800 hospital beds (already occupied) and 300 doctors, was overwhelmed by the emergency.

Before the week ended over 2500 people were reported dead, and over 200,000 were injured. Incalculable damage was done to the natural environment. Over 2000 animals died and another 7000 were injured. Standing crops and vegetation in affected areas were destroyed. The social and economic life of the city was disrupted by two large scale evacuations involving 200,000 and 400,000 people respectively (Morehouse and Subramaniam, 1986).

Union Carbide was sued for damages by injured victims and by the Government of India. Its stock price plummeted and remained undervalued for several months, during which equity arbitragers acquired a large stake in the company. Eight months after the Bhopal accident, there was a series of similar accidents at the company's Institute, West Virginia, plant. This further eroded the company's credibility and the public's faith in its ability to run operations safely. At that time, a takeover attack was made by GAF corporation. Management successfully defended the company against the takeover attempt, but at the cost of having to divest 20 per cent of its most profitable assets (Shrivastava, 1987).

The Tylenol poisonings. On 29 September, 1982, three people died in a Chicago suburb from consuming extra-strength Tylenol capsules. A day later another two people died of the same cause in another Chicago suburb. Somebody had contaminated these capsules with cyanide, a highly poisonous substance. The poisonous capsules were traced back to multiple lots. This created a public impression that large numbers of poisoned capsules were on drug store shelves, exposing vast numbers of innocent consumers to grave risk. It prompted the manufacturer McNeil Labs, a subsidiary of Johnson & Johnson, Inc. to telex its 15,000 retailers to remove 11 million bottles of regular and extra strength Tylenol from their shelves.

The Federal Drug Administration immediately initiated nationwide testing of Tylenol and discovered strychnine-laced capsules in Oroville, California. This spread of poisoning created an even larger public scare and forced the company again to recall its product. Eventually the company had to recall 31 million bottles of its products at a cost of over $100 million. Soon, affected consumers filed multi-million dollar law suits against Johnson & Johnson, Inc.

The mystery of these poisonings was never resolved. While product sabotage was suspected, the Chicago Police Department investigating the incident was unable to identify suspects or establish motives. It was not known whether the saboteur was an insider or an outsider. Tylenol was brought back into the market with triple tamper-resistant packaging. Over time it re-established itself as the leading pain killing drug. The company's market share which had dropped from 35 per cent to 8 per cent recovered from this costly market decline within eight months. With this recovery, the management and the public considered the crisis to be over (Mitroff and Kilmann, 1984). This was considered a remarkably successful case of corporate crisis management.

Then in February 1986, cyanide laced Tylenol caused the death of a woman in Bronxville, New York. Several bottles of poisoned capsules were discovered in stores around the area. The incident made national media headlines and alarmed the public around the country about the risks of taking Tylenol and other over-the-counter capsule medications. The poisoned capsules were traced back to two production facilities in Puerto Rico and Pennsylvania. The company initiated another national recall of the capsules. It announced plans to abandon altogether the manufacture of Tylenol in 'capsule' form. It substituted capsules with a caplet form of medication, and redesigned its production facilities. Recalls and production retooling were estimated to cost the company over $150 million.

The shuttle Challenger disaster. On 28 January, 1986, at 11.39 am the worst space disaster in history occurred at the Cape Canaveral space centre of the National Aeronautics and Space Administration (NASA). The space shuttle Challenger exploded 74 seconds after take-off, killing all 6 crew members and one civilian passenger – the first teacher in space. This was one of the most highly publicized 'show-case flights' of the shuttle, which gave its failure even more impact.

The explosion was caused by the failure of the right side solid rocket booster that powered the shuttle. The launch took place at very low temperature, which caused the seals of the solid rocket booster to malfunction. The President's Commission of Inquiry uncovered a number of other factors that contributed to the disaster. Investigations revealed management system failures such as ignoring warnings from subcontractors, budget pressures to adopt less expensive methods of risk management, blocking of information at middle levels of management, communication distortions, faulty design of booster seals, and strategic pressures to maintain flight schedules in the face of obviously hazardous conditions (Boffey, 1986; Diamond, 1986; Rogers *et al.*, 1986).

The impact of the disaster was wide-ranging. It resulted in the deaths of seven people. The entire nation was stunned while witnessing the event on television. School children who eagerly watched this flight because it carried the first school teacher into space were especially traumatized (Goleman, 1986). The economic cost of replacing the shuttle was estimated at $2 billion. Primary subcontractors to NASA suffered a significant decline in their stock prices. The delay of subsequent shuttle launchings jeopardized nearly 20,000 jobs and was said to pose some security risk to the country. The political impact of the disaster extended well beyond NASA, to the Reagan Administration. NASA management came under severe critical scrutiny, as did the Administration's role in pressuring the Agency to launch the shuttle under hazardous conditions (Harris and Beazley, 1986; Noble, 1986).

Even as investigations into the accident continued, a series of smaller accidents with other rocket launches deepened the crisis. On 18 April, 1986, a Titan rocket carrying a sensitive military payload exploded at lift-off. In early May, a Delta rocket, deemed one of the most reliable, failed in flight and had to be destroyed. These follow-up accidents eroded the public's faith in NASA's technological capabilities and brought the agency under further critical scrutiny.

Characteristics of industrial crises as manifested in these events are compared in table 1. While the events are very different on the surface, they exhibit striking similarities on most attributes, suggesting that these attributes have broad explanatory value. One of the more interesting features of this comparison is the variety of manifestations that each attribute can take. For example, damage to human life ranged from 6 deaths in the case of Tylenol to 3000 deaths and 300,000 injuries in the case of Bhopal. Social costs included traumatization of

Table 1 Industrial crisis characteristics

Characteristics	Challenger	Tylenol	Bhopal
Triggering event (Low probability event but there are warnings of its occurrence)	Shuttle Challenger explosion Thiokol and Rockwell engineers warned NASA of the hazard of launching at low temperature	Poisoning deaths caused by the ingestion of cyanide laced Tylenol capsules	Uncontrolled emision of 42 tons of MIC from a storage tank A 1982 safety survey identified problems that caused the accident. News reports warned community of hazard
Extent of damage and perception of damage to life and environment	7 crew members dead	5 deaths in 1982 plus 1 death in 1986 Threat of poisoning nation-wide	3000 dead 300,000 injured 2000 animals dead and 7000 injured Plants and crops destroyed
Economic costs	$2 billion shuttle replacement costs Six primary contractors' stock prices and revenues decline 20,000 jobs jeopardized Critical delays in launching military payload	$100 million in recalls and costs in 1982 and drop in market share from 35 to 8% Product liability claims $150 million in recalls and production retooling in 1986	Government spent over $30 million in relief Damage compensation estimated to cost UCC $350 million to $4 billion Takeover attempt by GAF forced UCC to divest 20% of its assets
Social costs	Nation's technological prestige damaged Political liabilities created for the Reagan administration Children traumatized	Nation-wide public health scare	2 major evacuations of 200 and 400 thousand people respectively Legitimacy of goverment threatened *continued*

Table 1 *Continued*

Characteristics	*Challenger*	*Tylenol*	*Bhopal*
Causes	Communicative distortions (a) Inter-organizational-McDonald's strenuous objections about O-rings not conveyed to NASA top management	Poisoning was a deliberate human act	Low morale, poor safety training and practices Manning down of operators from 12 to 6, supervisors from 2 to 1
Human	Rockwell's ice 'objections' interpreted as 'concern' by NASA managers (b) Within NASA disagreements at technical level not conveyed to strategic decision-makers by Reinartz		Institute, W. Va plant warning of runaway reaction not relayed to UCIL
Organizational	Flight too strategic to NASA to be delayed Long-term budgetary pressures forced design modifications	Capsule form too strategic to be dropped after 1st incident. It accounted for 7% of world wide sales and 15–20% of profits	Facility was strategically unimportant to make needed safety investments
Strategic	Lack of direction		
Operational	Seriousness of Thiokol's concerns about cold temperature O-ring performance not appreciated by NASA for 7 months creating *preconditions* for disaster NASA pressured Thiokol engineers to reverse decisions and OK the launch Cost pressures made NASA use cheaper risk analysis method FM and EA instead of FTA	Investigation dropped without finding source of poisoning creating *precondition* for another poisoning	Nitrogen pressure system faulty for 6 weeks creating *preconditions* for runaway reaction Implementation of operational safety survey not monitored Cost cutting pressures lead to poor maintenance and reduced safety
Technological Design	O-rings were defective, 40 redesign options were being evaluated	Original packaging not tamper-proof Redesigned triple tamper-proof package not foolproof	Plant *design* allowed for large scale storage of MIC RVVH-PVH jumper line connection was a *design* modification that allowed water to enter storage tank

Procedure	Thiokol engineers' warnings about O-ring erosion were ignored		Tank 610 abandoned after Nitrogen pressurization failure without remedying causes Worker did not insert slip blind during pipe washing 3 safety devices non-operational Contaminated MIC was used
Supplies			
Multiple stakeholders	20 Corporations (sub contractors to NASA) Federal Government and NASA US and world public, the media Crew members and their families	J and J, McNeil Labs FBI, NY and Chicago police Victims, entire nation at risk, US media	UCC, UCIL, Chemical industry in US and India Lawyers Government of MP and India Affected community and remote communities at risk, world media
Crisis responses	National mourning led by President Reagan Presidential Inquiry	Product recalls and packaging changes Police inquiry	Rescue and neutralization of remaining 22 tons of MIC Judicial and technical inquiry
Long-term	Re-evaluating manned flights Rescheduling flights and search for options to launch military pay loads	Product redesign and production retooling Abandoning of capsule form	Medical treatment and rehabilitation Law suits and conflict resolution
Parallel chain of events	Financial markets reacted by devaluating contractors' stocks Presidential Commission of Inquiry	Market recalls and consumer reactions FBI and police inquiry	Relief and rehabilitations of victims Legal proceedings in US and India Financial markets reaction and takeover bid for UCC
Crisis resolution and extension	Crisis displaced by other international events Crisis extended by the explosion of the Titan rocket in April, 1986	Crisis considered resolved by the recovery of market share Crisis extended by the second round of poisoning	Crisis considered resolved with mitigational responses and stock price recovery Crisis for UCC extended by accidents in W. Va.

children and damage to technological prestige of the US in the case of Challenger and two major evacuations involving several hundred thousand people in Bhopal. Similarly, economic costs to involved organizations ranged from about a quarter billion dollars for Johnson & Johnson to over 2 billion dollars for NASA.

The causes of crises are highly varied, however. Each crisis involves simultaneous interactions among variables inside organizations with those in their environment. The role of environmental agents is de-emphasized in most explanations of technological accidents. This analysis shows that environmental variables set up the preconditions for accidents, cause triggering events, and also exacerbate the effects of accidents after they occur. A common form of interaction in which failures occur is communication between organizational decision-makers and outsiders. At NASA, and to a lesser extent at Union Carbide, communication failures played a primary role in causing the crises.

Another interesting feature of these crises is that responses to them often do not eliminate their causes. The Tylenol saboteurs remain unapprehended even now. Similarly, causes of the Bhopal accident remain under dispute, and unresolved three years after the accident. The causes of the Challenger explosion included wide-scale failures in management and decision-making systems, and failures in technical design and operating procedures. The far-reaching and radical organizational and technical changes needed for eliminating these causes have not yet been implemented.

Concluding remarks

This article has attempted to provide a framework for understanding industrial crises. Several important implications emerge from this analysis. The first concerns our view of organizations. Strategic management researchers have traditionally viewed organizations as neutral, rational, technical systems of *production*. The three cases discussed here challenge this view. They illustrate that organizations are simultaneously systems of *production and of destruction*. Sometimes they even destroy more value than they produce. Often what is productive for one stakeholder is destructive for another. Hence organizations must be designed and operated not only to maximize their productivity, but also to minimize their destructive potential.

The second issue concerns our view of organization-environment relationships. Organizational researchers typically consider only the market and economic aspects of environments to be important. However, as has been argued earlier, several parts of the environment – the regulatory system and the physical infrastructure, as well as the community's crisis preparedness – also need to keep pace with the increasing complexity in organizations and their technologies. Therefore, organizational activities may be constrained equally by the physical environment in which they are situated and by the social and economic environment.

A third issue concerns the study of organizations in crises and of crisis management. If our explanations of crises are correct, they cannot be understood simply as organizational phenomena. Crises have fundamental trans-organizational causes, involving social, political, and cultural variables. Therefore, their prevention and management cannot be achieved at the organizational level alone. Changes must occur in social and cultural institutions, and strategies must be developed to promote more effective social control of technologies.

Note

1   This research was supported in part with funds from the Tenneco Foundation

References

Boffey, P. (1986) 'Rocket engineer tells of pressures for a launching', *New York Times*, 26 February.

Bouillette, J. R. and Quarantelli, E. R. (1971) Types of patterned variation in bureaucratic adaptations to organizational stress: After variation, *Social Inquiry*, 41: 39–45.

Diamond, S. (1986) 'NASA wasted billions, federal audits disclose', *New York Times*, 23 April.

Erikson, K. T. (1976) *Everything in its Path*, New York: Simon and Schuster.

Fritz, C. E. (1961) 'Disasters', in Merton, R. and Nisbet, R. (eds), *Social Problem*, New York: Harcourt Brace and World, pp. 651–94.

Gephart, R. P. (1984) 'Making sense of organizationally based environment disasters' *Journal of Management*, 10(2): 205–25.

Giddens, A. (1983) *Profiles and Critiques in Social Theory*, Berkeley, CA: University of California Press.

Goleman, D. (1986) 'Openness is key in solacing young' *New York Times*, 30 January.

Habermas, J. (1975) *Legitimation Crisis*, Boston: Beacon Press.

Harris, R. J. and Beazley, J. E. (1986) 'Aerospace firms brace for costly impact of space-program delay after explosion', *Wall Street Journal*, 29 January.

Hohenemser, C. *et al.* (1986) 'An early report on the Chernobyl disaster', *Environment*, 16 June.

International Confederation of Free Trade Unions (1985) *The Trade Union Report on Bhopal*, Geneva: International Confederation of Free Trade Unions.

Kates, R. W. (ed) (1977) *Managing Technological Hazard: Research Needs and Opportunities*, Boulder, CO: Institute of Behavioral Science, University of Colorado, Monograph no. 25.

Keeley, M. (1984) 'Impartiality and participant interest theories of organizational effectiveness', *Administrative Science Quarterly*, 29(1): 1–25.

Kinghorn, S. (1985) 'Corporate harm: an analysis of structure and process', paper presented at the conference on Critical Perspectives in Organizational Analysis, 5–7 September, Baruch College, CUNY, New York.

Kreps, G. A. (1984) 'Sociological inquiry and disaster research', *Annual Review of Sociology*, 10: 309–30.

Lagadec, P. (1982) *Major Technological Risk*, New York: Pergamon.

Masuch, M. (1985) 'On harmful organizations', paper presented at the conference on Critical Perspectives in Organizational Analysis, Baruch College, CUNY, 5–7 September.

Miller, D. and Freisen, P. H. (1980) 'Momentum and revolution in organizational adaptation', *Academy of Management Journal*, 25: 589–613.

Miller, D. and Freisen, P. H. (1984) *Organizations: A Quantum View*, Englewood Cliffs, NJ: Prentice-Hall.

Mitroff, I. I. and Kilmann, R. H. (1984) *Corporate Tragedies: Product Tampering, Sabotage and Other Disasters*, New York: Praeger.

Molotch, H. and Lester, M. (1975) 'Accidental news: the great oil spill', *American Journal of Sociology*, 81: 235–60.

Morehouse, W. and Subramaniam, A. (1986) *The Bhopal Tragedy: What Really Happened and What it Means for American Workers and Communities at Risk*, New York: Council on International Public Affairs.

Noble, J. W. (1986) 'Shuttle crash: where clues have led so far', *New York Times*, 25 February.

O'Connor, J. (1987) *The Meaning of Crisis*, Berkeley, CA: University of California Press.

Offe, C. (1984) *Contradictions of the Welfare State*, Cambridge, MA: MIT Press.

Perrow, C. (1984) *Normal Accidents: Living with High Risk Technologies*, New York: Basic Books.

Pfeffer, J. (1982) *Organizations and Organization Theory*, New York: Pitman.

Quarantelli, E. L. (ed.) (1978) *Disasters: Theory and Research*, Beverly Hills, CA: Sage.

Renn, O. (1986) 'Risk perception: a systematic review of concepts and research results', in *Avoiding and Managing Environmental Damage from Major Industrial Accidents*, proceedings of an international conference, Air Pollution Control Association, Pittsburgh.

Rogers, W. *et al.* (1986) *Report of the Presidential Commission on the Space Shuttle Challenger Accident*, Washington, D.C.

Schendel, D. and Hofer, C. W. (1979) *Strategic Management*, Boston: Little, Brown.

Shrivastava, P. (1985) 'Organizational myths in industrial crises', working paper, Industrial Crisis Institute, New York, NY.

Shrivastava, P. (1987) *Bhopal: Anatomy of a Crisis*, Cambridge, MA: Ballinger.

Smets, H. (1985) 'Compensation for exceptional environmental damage caused by industrial activities', paper presented at the conference on Transportation, Storage and Disposal of Hazardous Materials, IIASA, Laxenburg, Austria, 1–5 July.

Turner, B. A. (1976) 'The organizational and interorganizational development of disasters', *Administrative Science Quarterly*, 21: 378–97.

Turner, B. A. (1978) *Man Made Disasters*, London: Wykeham.

Union Carbide Corporation (1985) *Bhopal Methyl Isocyanate Incident Investigation Team Report*, Danbury, CT: Union Carbide Corporation, March.

Varadarajan, S. *et al.* (1985) *Report on Scientific Studies on Factors Related to Bhopal Toxic Gas Leakage*, New Delhi: Council on Scientific and Industrial Research.

World Bank (1985) *World Development Report*, New York: Oxford University Press.

Chapter 4

Ian I. Mitroff, Terry C. Pauchant and Paul Shrivastava

THE STRUCTURE OF MAN-MADE ORGANIZATIONAL CRISES: CONCEPTUAL AND EMPIRICAL ISSUES IN THE DEVELOPMENT OF A GENERAL THEORY OF CRISIS MANAGEMENT

Introduction

The rise of corporate disasters

IN 1979, THE THREE MILE ISLAND Nuclear Power Plant had an accident leading to the near meltdown of its reactor core. The accident not only cost billions of dollars for Metropolitan Edison, the company that owned the plant, but it also altered the very fate of the nuclear power industry in the United States [20]. The plant owners and operators paid 26 million dollars for evacuation, financial losses, and medical surveillance; 4 billion dollars was the estimated cost of repairs and the production of electricity via other means. (The most recent case, that of Chernobyl, is even worse, for its repercussions for the nuclear industry are worldwide.)

In 1982 an unknown person or persons (possible psychopathic) contaminated dozens of Tylenol capsules with cyanide, which caused the deaths of eight people and 100 million dollars loss in recalled packages for Johnson and Johnson (J&J); in 1986, a second poisoning incident forced J&J to reluctantly withdraw all its Tylenol capsules from the market at a loss of 150 million dollars. The company abandoned capsule form of medication and had to redesign its production facility. The full costs of withdrawing products from the shelves and of switching from the production of capsules to other forms of medication has cost significantly more – in the range of 500 million dollars.

In December 1984, the worse industrial accident in history occurred; Poisonous methyl isocyanate gas leaked from a storage tank at a Union Carbide plant in Bhopal, India, killing approximately 3,000 people and injuring another 300,000, in addition to causing unknown damage to flora and fauna in the area. Union Carbide was sued by victims for billions of dollars. The compensation settlement in this case is likely to be between 500 million dollars and 1 billion dollars. In addition, the company was forced to sell off 20% of its most profitable assets to prevent a takeover attack mounted by the GAF Corporation, which had acquired Carbide's undervalued stocks after the accident [26].

In May/June 1985, deadly bacteria in Jalisco cheese caused the deaths of 84 people in California and the financial bankruptcy of the company that produced the product.

The list of recent corporate crises is virtually unending. It includes executive kidnappings, hijackings both in the air and at sea, hostile takeovers, and acts of terrorism such as the bombing of factories and warehouses; most recently, slivers of glass were found in Gerber's baby food, and other major products (Contact) have been the object of still more incidents of product tampering. What was unthinkable and sporadic now happens on an ever-increasing and daily basis; furthermore, the time between major incidents is shrinking precipitously [25, 31].

Corporate crises are characterized by low-probability, high-consequence organizational events that threaten the most fundamental goals of an organization [25]. Such crises are triggered by major industrial accidents, environmental jolts, product defects, occupational hazards, and pollution incidents that arise from within corporations. These triggering events cause extensive damage (and its perception) to human life and the environment. Corporations are usually held liable for these damages caused by crises, and they thereby suffer severe financial and reputational setbacks [9, 25].

An indication of the rising frequency of corporate crises is provided by the number of product-injury lawsuits terminating in million-dollar awards. This number has increased dramatically in the past decade. In 1974 there were less than 2,000 product-injury suits filed in U.S. courts. By 1984, the number had jumped to 10,000. In 1975, juries had awarded less than 50 compensation awards of greater than 1 million dollars each. In 1985, there were more than 400 such awards [25]. The costs of product- and production-related harm has been one factor in the recent crisis in the liability insurance industry. Many forms of liability insurance have simply vanished, and all forms of insurance have become prohibitively expensive and are available only for small coverages.

The basic purpose of this paper is to contribute to the development of a general theory of crisis management. One of the most critical issues attendant to the development of such a theory is, 'How general can a general theory of crisis management be?' Even though crises differ widely in their underlying causes, treatment, and prevention, are there nonetheless some general patterns or structures that underlie the crises? If so, what are they? How generally applicable are such structures and patterns to the prediction, treatment, and prevention (i.e. to the general management) of all crises?

The paper proceeds in three main parts. The first consists of a conceptual overview at the macro level of crisis management. The second part consists of a presentation of the empirical findings from a nationwide questionnaire designed to check on the conceptual models. The third part ends with a discussion of the implications of both the conceptual and empirical findings plus suggestions for further research.

The paper utilizes a distinctive blend and contrast between theoretical/ conceptual models and empirical findings. While the empirical findings are used in a critical sense to test the adequacy of the prior theoretical conceptions, neither final nor complete epistemic weight is accorded to them. The reason is that, especially in recent years, the modern philosophy of science has recognized that the interplay between theory and data is much more complex than had been acknowledged previously [3, 6, 7, 14, 17, 32]. To be sure, data do indeed test theories, but only if certain complexities are taken into account, complexities that are usually not even acknowledged in the standard accounts of scientific methodology [see 13, 14] for in-depth discussions of the 'standard accounts' and their limitations).

Modern philosophers of science have recognized that *data are neither completely independent of theories nor neutral with respect to them* [3, 6, 7, 32]. The crucial point is that *if data are used to test theories, which they usually are, then it is also the case that theories are used to direct our attention to the data that are appropriate to test the theories under scrutiny*. In a word, all data are theory-dependent or theory-laden with concepts drawn from the very theory that they are presumed to test. The danger is that instead of data providing a test that is supposedly completely independent of the theory, the data are so coupled with the theory being tested that they will provide instead unintended verification of the theory. The fear, in other words, is that the relationship between theory and data is a highly incestuous one instead of being an independent one (various proposals to counteract this are complex and extend far beyond the scope of this paper [see 3, 13, 14, 17]).

In this paper, we proceed by first taking the prior conceptual and theoretical models (frameworks) as 'provisionally true.' We first consider the prior theoretical models or frameworks as 'what if' statements. Given their 'what if' epistemic status, we then interpret the empirical data *as if* the frameworks *were true*, and, hence we deduce what can be concluded *from* the data *given* this assumption. Under this way of proceeding, the data are *not* used to test the prior theoretical conceptions, but rather, *the prior theoretical conceptualizations are used to give order and meaning to the data*. After this, we then analyze the data not only to see what patterns emerge from them, but also to see if they are consistent with the prior theoretical patterns. In this part of the paper, the data are then used to give a quasi-independent interpretation and 'test' of the prior theoretical models. However, once again it is important to emphasize that there is a constant and repeated interplay between theory and data.

Typologies of crises

Figure 1 presents an expanded list of crises classified according to two primary dimensions: 1) the originating source of a crisis, and 2) whether it is due

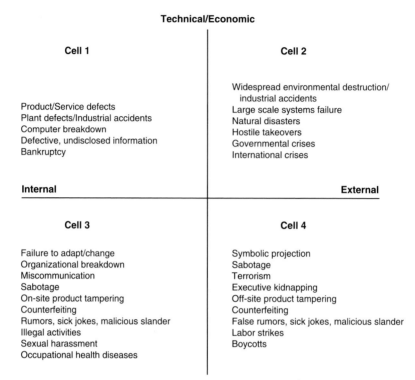

Figure 1 Different types of corporate crises

primarily to technical or human/organizational factors. The dimensions arise from an application of the Jungian typology that has been shown previously to be applicable to a wide range of organizational phenomena [12].

Figure 1 differentiates between those crises that arise from *within*, or *internal* to, an organization and those that arise *external* to it. This dimension corresponds to a combination of Jung's introvert/extrovert and sensing/intuition distinctions. The difference is between those factors that are looked at in the *short run* and/or as *internal* to the environment and those that are looked at in a *longer time span* and/or as *external* to the organization. This distinction is critical because, as we argue later, the management of crises is not the same for all of them.

Figure 1 also differentiates between those crises that are caused primarily by *technical/economic* breakdowns or factors and those that are caused by *people/organizational/social* breakdowns. This distinction thus corresponds to Jung's thinking/feeling dimension [12]. The difference is between those crises that are primarily or immediately traceable to human actions (e.g. rumors, terrorism) and those that are primarily or more immediately traceable to technical or economic factors (e.g. hostile takeovers, plant defects).

Figure 1 lists a broader array of crises than that used to introduce this paper because the initial set is unfortunately only a small subset of those crises that are possible. At the same time, Figure 1 does not pretend to be complete, because completeness is impossible in the field of crisis management. Essentially, we are dealing with an open-ended, emergent, or ill-structured phenomenon, not a well structured one. Completeness is not one of the principal defining characteristics of ill-structured phenomena [3, 13, 14]. The figure only attempts to provide some conceptual boundary to the phenomena by indicating the different kinds of crises that fit in the various cells.

By the same token, Figure 2 attempts to show various kinds of underlying causes that can be identified with the various types of crises shown in Figure 1. And, finally, Figure 3 shows the wide variety of actions that are potentially open to organizations in blunting, preparing for, coping with, and recovering from the various kinds of crises that we can identify. Figures 2 and 3 are also organized around the Jungian framework.

Figure 3 shows that in contrast to the general impression held by many managers that there is too little or nothing that organizations can do to blunt potential crises, there is in fact an exactly opposite problem. Organizations are faced with the problem of choosing between too many options, none of which include perfect prevention or complete containment.

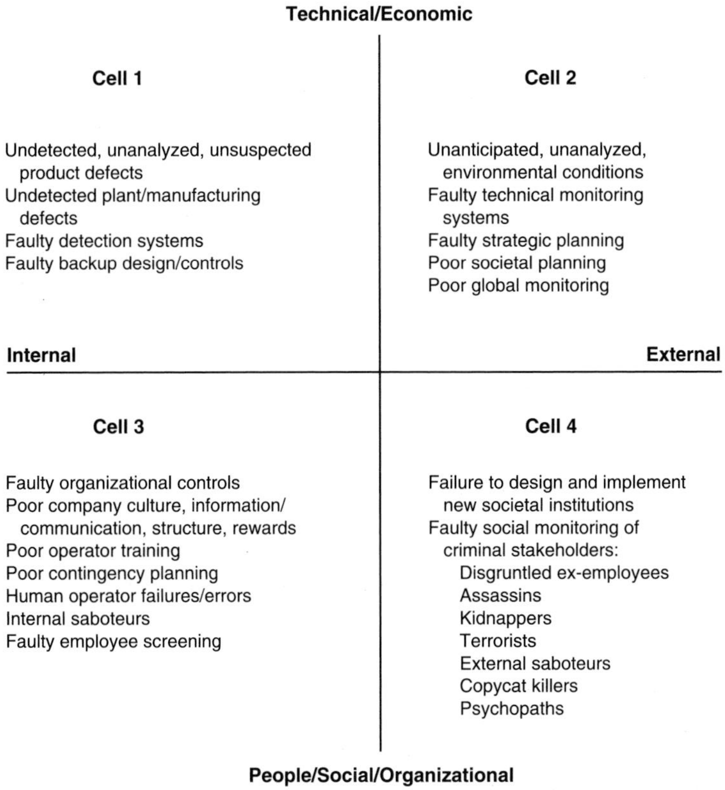

Technical/Economic

Cell 1	**Cell 2**
Undetected, unanalyzed, unsuspected product defects	Unanticipated, unanalyzed, environmental conditions
Undetected plant/manufacturing defects	Faulty technical monitoring systems
Faulty detection systems	Faulty strategic planning
Faulty backup design/controls	Poor societal planning
	Poor global monitoring

Internal ———————————————— **External**

Cell 3	**Cell 4**
Faulty organizational controls	Failure to design and implement new societal institutions
Poor company culture, information/ communication, structure, rewards	Faulty social monitoring of criminal stakeholders:
Poor operator training	Disgruntled ex-employees
Poor contingency planning	Assassins
Human operator failures/errors	Kidnappers
Internal saboteurs	Terrorists
Faulty employee screening	External saboteurs
	Copycat killers
	Psychopaths

People/Social/Organizational

Figure 2 Causes and sources of corporate crises

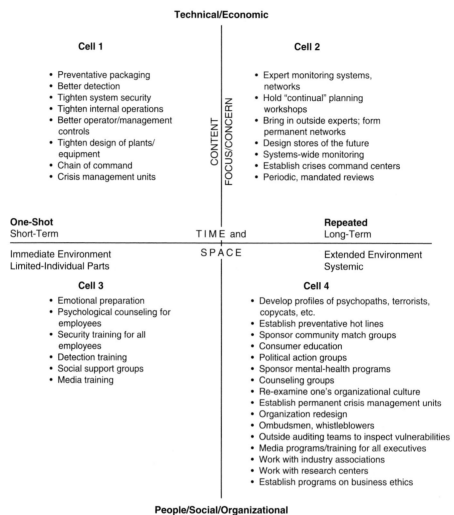

Figure 3 Preventative organizational actions

Based on the Jungian schema, it is possible to state two basic hypotheses, the first of which follows:

Hypothesis 1 – Organizational crises will be distributed evenly over the Jungian typology.

This hypothesis follows from the premise that organizations do not control or have only partial control over the crises they experience. *If* this is indeed the case, and if as Jungian theory postulates, each of the types is equally functional or has a fundamental contribution to make within any given organizational setting [12], then one should expect to find no preference for the occurrence or distribution of crises across the typology.

The second hypothesis follows from the fact that although each of Jung's personality or behavioral types is equally possible from a *theoretical* standpoint, they are not evenly distributed in any particular person, social setting, or institutional setting. In Western societies in particular, one finds a marked and general preference for 'extroverted thinking.' Thus, one would expect to find:

> *Hypothesis 2* – The actions that organizations undertake to attempt to thwart or to prevent crises will be significantly skewed towards technical actions.

Notice that in principle, each hypothesis is capable of influencing the other strongly. Thus, if organizations only engage selectively in certain preventative actions, then this may in fact raise their potential for certain kinds of crises. In this sense, organizations may in fact partially 'control' or 'design' the types of crises they face – consciously as well as unconsciously.

Other factors must also be noted that markedly affect the interpretation and subsequent testing of the hypotheses. In the vast majority of cases, it is possible to classify a particular crisis as either primarily or even solely fitting in a particular cell of Figure 1. The same is also true of Figures 2 and 3. In other cases, a particular crisis or preventative action may be classified as fitting in more than one cell simultaneously. This arises because of the differing conceptual interpretation that can be placed on a particular crisis or action. For instance, some crises such as terrorism that are obviously a human-induced social act are relatively easy to classify. Others, however, such as defective products, are much more difficult to classify. The primary classification fits in the internal/technical cell, in that a product defect is exactly what its name implies, a technological defect that is internal to a product, i.e. latent within the property structure of the product. However, a moment's reflection shows that there is a basic difficulty that underlies all crises and perhaps even the actions and policies of all organizations.

The primary cause of the Challenger failure was a defective O-ring, i.e. a defective technical part [23]. But the underlying cause of failure was a faulty, defective organization that seriously compromised its safety and quality standards and indeed can be said to have actively intervened to inhibit and block organizational communication. Hence, a more accurate proposition is that underlying every major crisis, technical and human errors or factors are equally involved. In some cases, these factors will be relatively easy to classify in one cell or another as the primary cause of a particular disaster. For some, equal weight will have to be given to both factors. In reality, there may be no clean way of ever separating the two, especially if one takes a systemic view or a systems approach to crisis management [3, 12, 13].

The difficulty in classification may also be a matter of one's basic philosophical outlook – for instance, whether one is a technological determinist or a social determinist or both or neither [3]. In order to prompt the discussion, we have classified the factors according to what the authors took to be the primary meaning that is given to each through a review of the literature in crisis management. In those few cases where a crisis or action could not be assigned primarily to one cell or quadrant, it was assigned to those cells where it could fit under reasonable multiple interpretations. If one regards the Jungian typology as a theoretical or conceptual 'factor structure,' then this is equivalent to implying that certain items load equally on more than one factor.

The importance of grouping crises, while it is perhaps obvious, should be stressed. If there is some order underlying various crises, then does this order help organizations prepare for a block or family of crises rather than merely treat each separately and even in a fragmented manner? If such an order exists, does it, in other words, help organizations to give coherence to their crisis management efforts? Instead of having to monitor each crisis separately, can they be monitored in groups or families so that, for instance, a certain group might be signaled by the same kinds of warnings?

Method

In late November and early December 1986, questionnaires were mailed to the public affairs officers of the *Fortune* 1,000 corporations. The questionnaire was designed by the authors and mailed under the auspices of the public affairs office of the National Association of Manufacturers (NAM). In this way, it was hoped that public affairs officers would be induced to fill out a questionnaire on a topic that is highly sensitive. The topic of the crisis potential of leading American corporations was also of vital interest to NAM. While the questionnaire did not call for the respondents to disclose any detailed plans or preparations for crises, it did ask them to indicate the number of incidents that had affected their organizations over the past three years. (Because of space limitations and the desire to insure that the respondents would fill out the questionnaire, subsets of the items from Figure 1 were used for evaluation.) It also asked them to indicate whether their current vulnerability was greater or less than it was three years ago. In addition, the questionnaire asked respondents to indicate the range and extent of various preventative measures that they were undertaking in an attempt to lessen the crisis potential of their organizations (subsets of the items from Figure 3 were used for this purpose). The questionnaire also listed various attitudinal items to gauge general attitudes towards crisis management (see Table 4 for a listing of attitudinal items). It also surveyed whether they had a crisis management team and who was on it.

Of the 1,000 questionnaire that were mailed, 114 were returned. Given the length of the questionnaire plus its sensitivity, a response rate of 11.4% is acceptable. Further, because of the extreme sensitivity of the topic, the questionnaires were not coded in any way that would reveal the identity of the responding organizations. However, the respondents could write in the name of their organization if they so wished; 47 respondents did so. Included among them are the names of America's largest and most visible corporations. Furthermore, in every case, respondents were asked to indicate their industry or primary business. The businesses and industries identified comprise a complete spectrum that includes banking, chemicals, food, health, heavy manufacturing, high technology, pharmaceuticals, power utilities, etc. Thus, there are reasons to believe that the sample and its results represent the state of crisis management. This is not to say that the population of respondents is not biased to begin with, since public affairs officers are more likely to be sensitive to the topic of crisis management than are other executives. If a crisis occurs, the public affairs officers are the executives most likely to have to communicate with the outside world as well as internally, within their corporations.

As we indicate in the beginning of this paper, the results will be analyzed not only in number of steps but also with regard to a variety of perspectives. The first perspective essentially takes the Jungian framework as conceptually or theoretically validated and asks, 'given' the framework, how do the responses of the questionnaire fit on it? To examine this, we performed basic statistical analyses (frequencies, t-tests) on the responses to selected items from Figures 1 and 3. More sophisticated factor analyses were also performed to see how the structure that emerged from the data fit with the a priori structures derived from the Jungian framework. Later analyses ask how the empirical results modify the theoretical grouping of items to suggest a potential order that may be different from that suggested by the Jungian framework – particularly since considerable judgment is involved in sorting items onto the initial framework.

Results

Jungian factors

To the right of each item on Figures 4 and 5 is *the mean* of the responses to the item. Each item is positioned within the set of items that compose a theoretical factor based on the Jungian framework (e.g. see Figure 1). Thus, for instance, on Figure 4 under factor 1, the mean of the responses to how many incidents of plant/equipment defects were experienced in the last three years was 1.97. Given the scale score, this is equivalent to the statement, 'The average number of experienced incidents of plant/equipment defects was between 1 and 5.' The average for each cell or factor is also given in Figures 4 and 5. In addition, the $\propto$ coefficient or the measure of the internal reliability for each factor is known as well.

Appropriate paired t-tests were performed between the factor scores for each cell (each factor consists of an equal weighting of all the items in a cell). Except for factors 2 and 3 in Figure 4, there is a significant difference between all of the factors taken two at a time at the 0.001 level or better (0.0001). Thus, if we regard the Jungian schema as 'given,' then Hypothesis 1 is rejected; in other words, organizational crises are *not* distributed evenly over the Jungian typology. In fact, inspection of Figure 4 reveals that the incidents experienced most frequently are product defects, environmental accidents, and plant/equipment defects in that order, and in fact, factor 1 has the highest cell mean ($\bar{X} = 1.78$).

Figure 5 shows that Hypothesis 2 is confirmed; i.e. organizational actions are significantly skewed towards the adoption/utilization of some behaviors more than others in an attempt by organizations to lessen their crisis potential. For instance, Figure 5 reveals that limited, short-term, technical actions predominate.

As helpful and revealing as the quantitative results are, they become even more powerful when they are coupled with qualitative data. The item on

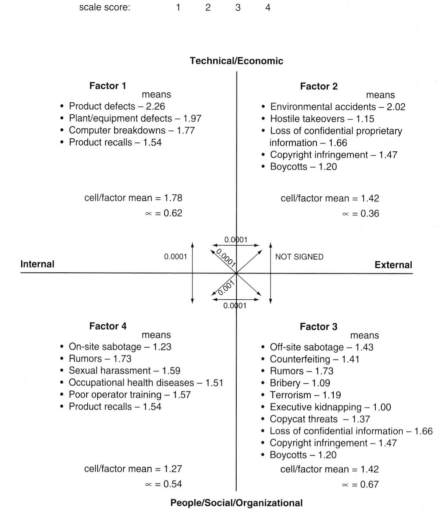

Figure 4 Different types of corporate crises grouped according to Jungian theoretical factors

Figure 5 that received the lowest rating ($\bar{X} = 1.35$) that organizations were engaging in was 'emotional preparation for crises by bringing in psychological consultants.' From direct personal interviews conducted by the first author with the executives of organizations that have been struck by major product-tampering incidents, it is clear that major crises not only cause significant financial impacts, but they also cause significant lasting emotional impacts. The conversations and reports by such executives reveal that nightmares are frequently reported on the anniversary of major product-tampering incidents – that executives, when they are summoned out of their sleep at night by telephone calls, experience relief when the call only reports the breakdown of a car by one of their children or relatives.

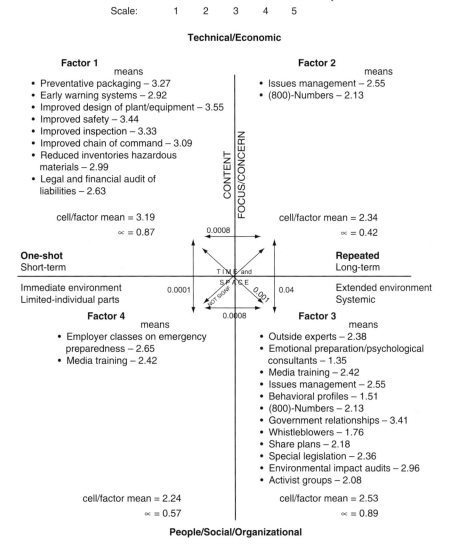

Figure 5 Preventative organizational actions

The first author also talked with NASA officials who reported that soon after the space shuttle Challenger exploded, NASA had to set up an emergency medical hot line. Not only were the employees experiencing normal grief to begin with, but they were also plagued by guilt concerning whether they had done enough to prevent the accident. This guilt and stress was intensified further, sometimes beyond the breaking point, when the employees returned home to be confronted by their children, who asked, 'Mommy, Daddy, were you responsible for killing the astronauts?' As a result their inability to cope with the stress caused by the accident plus feelings of guilt induced by such questions, a number of employees experienced severe stress and had to be counseled.

The point is again that major crises and disasters not only wreak extreme financial havoc on organizations, but also extreme emotional and personal havoc as well [22]. Hence, it is all the more significant to find that of all the items in Figure 5, the item having to do with emotional preparation for crises by calling in outside psychological consultants received the lowest score of the preparatory actions in which organizations can engage. This may be explained by two factors: First, organizations are reluctant to call in outsiders on so sensitive an issue in general; and second, organizations may be generally insensitive to the emotional needs of their employees, particularly when they are under stress in a major crisis. Indeed, there is further evidence from the questionnaire to support this when one looks at the members who are on a crisis management team. From Table 4, it can be seen that outsiders are virtually unrepresented at all on crisis management teams. This may appear to conflict with the fact that the item 'outside expert' ('brought in outside experts to review plants and operations') has a mean of 2.38. However, the main point still stands, in that outside experts are mainly brought in only to advise on technical matters, not on emotional issues.

Finally, the $\propto$ coefficients lend some empirical support to the Jungian factors themselves. With the exception of factors 2 in both Figures 4 and 5, the $\propto$ coefficient or the internal reliability of the scales range from good (0.52) to excellent (0.89).

Empirically derived factors

Orthogonal factor analyses using varimax rotation to exclude the least consistent structural dimensions were performed. For an item to be included in a factor, a loading close to 0.6 was used as the criterion for inclusion. Through the use of an eigenvalue of one as a cutoff, six factors emerged from the empirical data on the frequency of occurrence (Figure 4) of various crisis incidents over the last three years; five factors emerged from the empirical data describing the frequency of actions (Figure 5) that organizations were undertaking to lessen their crisis potential. In both cases, the factors were reduced to four through the employment of two additional, more stringent criteria. First, the $\propto$ or reliabilities of the factors were examined. Second, metric multidimensional scaling (MDS) analyses were performed on the data. In both cases, factor solutions were selected that met four stringent criteria: 1) more than 10% of the variance had to be explained by each factor, 2) each item had to load close to 0.60 on each factor in order to be included, 3) a factor had to have a reliability coefficient or $\propto$ of 0.70 or better (only one factor, factor 4 in Table 1, did not meet this criterion although its $\propto$ was still of a reasonable magnitude), 4) the clustering patterns from MDS were similar to the factor uncovered through factor analysis. In effect, this procedure amounts to the derivation or extraction of factors through triangularization, i.e. the imposition of a more severe selection process. The results of the analyses for both sets of data are shown in Table 1 and Figure 6 for the frequencies of various crises and Table 2 and Figure 7 for the frequencies of various actions that organizations are undertaking in order to lower their crisis potential.

Table 1 VARIMAX rotated factor loadings of type of crises[a]

	Factor 1	Factor 2	Factor 3	Factor 4
α (reliability)	.69	.71	.85	.57
Eigenvalues	3.26	2.78	2.65	1.91
% Variance explained	17.2	14.6	14.0	10.0
Cumulative variance	17.2	31.8	45.8	55.8
Factor loadings				
Counterfeiting of products	.62[b]			
Sexual harassment	.67	.29		
Occupational health diseases	.67			
Loss of confidential information	.74	.31		.27
Copyright infringement	.63		.22	.22
Boycotts	.58		.22	
Product defects		.62		.25
Defects in plants or equipment		.81		
Poor operator training/screening	.33	.66		
Computer breakdowns	.34	.60		
Off-site product tampering	.22		.85	
Terrorism			.74	
Copycat threats			.89	
Bribery				.71
Product recalls	.23			.80
Rumors, malicious slander	.50	.39		
Industrial/environmental accidents	.31	.55	.32	
On-site product tampering		.41	.31	.46
Hostile takeover		−.24	−.26	.51

[a] N = 83.
[b] Underlined items represent those that are included in a factor.

As indicated by the variations, eigenvalues, percentages of variance explained, and the MDS Mappings, the factor solutions are good in both cases. Comparisons with Figures 4 and 5 reveal some interesting findings. Factor 2 in Figure 6 is almost identical with that of factor 1 of Figure 4. This implies that the cluster-labeled internal-technical crises make sense from both prior theoretical considerations and *a posteriori* or empirical considerations.

Factor 3 of Figure 6 also makes sense. It represents a subset of factor 3 of Figure 4. Indeed, this is one of the more interesting factors to emerge from the analyses. Empirically, it says that the items representing the most extreme forms of human behavior (i.e. psychopathic and sociopathic) all cluster together. Thus, the 'people/social/organizational' factors of Figure 4 are split apart into two factors in Figure 6. Factor 3 contains the more extreme forms, while factor 1 contains the less extreme.

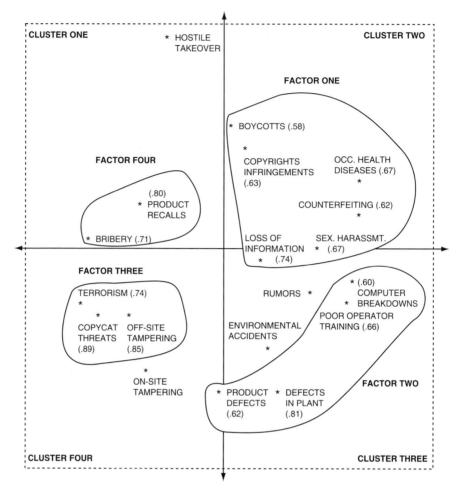

TWO-DIMENSIONAL, MDS TYPE OF CRISES. KRUSKAL STRESS = .274; RSQ = .586.

Figure 6 Frequency of incidents factors

Figure 7, which shows the actions that organizations are undertaking to blunt potential crises, permits an even easier interpretation of all four factors. Factor 1 is a 'media/information' factor. As such, it is primarily a subset of factor 3 of Figure 5. Factor 2 of Figure 7 is a combination of 'internal-technical improvements' or 'inspection/control activities.' As such, it is a subset of factor 1 of Figure 5. Factor 3 of Figure 7 is a 'behavioral' factor. It is another subset of factor 3 of Figure 5. And, finally, factor 4 of Figure 7 is best described as a 'monitoring' factor. It is a combination of items from factors 1 and 3 of Figure 5.

The conclusion from both sides of empirical factors is that, while there are obvious points of departure from the Jungian factors, the departures are neither extreme nor serious. The empirically derived factors not only make sense in themselves, but they also relate well to the initial theoretically derived factors based on the Jungian framework.

Table 2 VARIMAX rotated factor loadings of undertakings[a]

	Factor 1	Factor 2	Factor 3	Factor 4
α (reliability)	.83	.78	.72	.76
Eigenvalues	3.83	3.12	2.76	2.70
% Variance explained	18.2	14.9	13.1	12.9
Cumulative variance	18.2	33.1	46.2	59.1
Factor loadings				
Early warning systems	.66[b]	.22	.31	.33
Media training	.68		.28	.24
Special 800 number	.66		.34	
Relationships with government	.62	.32		
Sharing of crisis plan within industry	.74			.38
Improved security and safety	.27	.75		
Improved design plants/equipment	.20	.79		
Improved inspection/maintenance		.81		.32
Emotional preparation for crises			.73	
Behavioral profiles of terrorists	.26		.78	
Whistleblower programs			.64	
Relationships with activist groups	.41	.23	.56	
Reduction of hazardous inventories				.72
Development of special legislation			.42	.56
Legal and financial audit of liabilities	.33		.20	.69
Preventive product packaging	.57	.63	.39	
Employee classes	.48	.37	.20	
Improved chain of command		.53		.46
Environmental impact audit	.51			.47
Issues management program	.41		.30	.49
Use of outside experts	.29	.32		.31

[a] $N = 45$.
[b] Underlined items represent those that are included in a factor.

The use of factor scores

We can summarize thus far: Two sets of four principal factors arise from 1) the frequencies of different types of experienced crises (incidents) and 2) the different types of actions that organizations can and are undertaking to meet such crises. The four principal factors from the analysis of crises are:

1   A combination of a) *external threats* to the corporation as a whole and its products based on *faulty* or deliberately falsified information and/or products (boycotts, copyright infringements, counterfeiting, loss of confidential/proprietary information); and b) *internal threats* to persons (occupational health diseases and sexual harassment)

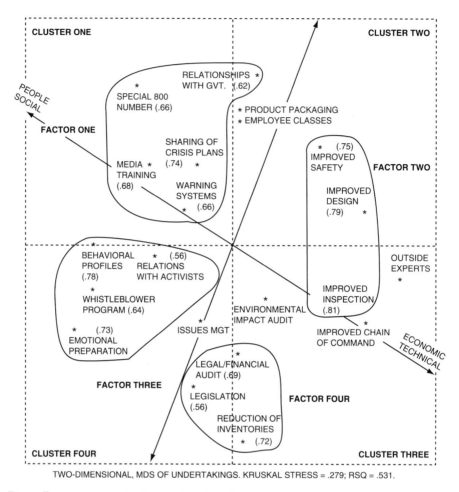

TWO-DIMENSIONAL, MDS OF UNDERTAKINGS. KRUSKAL STRESS = .279; RSQ = .531.

Figure 7 Actions organizations undertaking factors

2   *Breaks*/defects in operators, equipment, and facilities (computer break-downs, poor operator training, plant defects, product defects)
3   Extreme or *psychopathic threats* (terrorism, copycat threats, off-site tampering)
4   *External actions/threats* (product recalls, bribery)

The four principal factors from the analysis of undertakings are:

1   *Environmental information*/monitoring (relationships with governments, special 800 numbers, sharing of crisis plans, media training, warning systems)
2   *Improved design/control* (improved safety, improved design, improved inspections)
3   *Behavioral* (behavioral profiles, relations with activists, whistle-blower programs, emotional preparation)
4   *Auditing* (legal/financial audits, legislation, reduction of inventories)

For greater ease of discussion, understanding, and interpretation, we will refer to these factors simply as follows:

1   Crisis factors
    a.   E/I Threats
    b.   Breaks
    c.   Psycho
    d.   E Threats
2   Undertaking factors
    a.   E Inf
    b.   Design/Control
    c.   Behave
    d.   Audit

Given these factors, the following questions naturally arise: 1) What, if any, are the relationships between the two sets of factors? 2) What are the relationships between the factors and the attitudinal items that were part of the extended questionnaire? These questions were explored through the use of factor scores based on the items entering into the constitution of the factors and their factor loadings.

Table 3 shows the correlations between the factor scores. The most highly significant correlations permit some interesting interpretations. First, consider the highest and most significant of the correlations, 0.58. Not only is it *not* surprising that extreme or psychopathic threats should be coupled with greater information monitoring of the external environment, but it is conceptually comforting that they are coupled, since they are among the most extreme threats that the external environment can throw at the modern corporation. In other words, the rather high p value between E Inf and Psycho not only lends welcome conceptual and face validity to the factors, but it also supports the proposition that the modern corporation faces a whole new series of stakeholder threats

Table 3 Correlation coefficients between factor scores

| | Accidents/crises | | | |
Undertakings	E/I Threats	Breaks	Psycho	E Threats
E Inf	NS	NS	0.58[c]	NS
Design/control	0.34[a]	NS	NS	0.27[d]
Behave	0.27[b]	NS	0.34[a]	0.21[b]
Audit	0.42[a]	NS	NS	NS

NS, not significant.
[a]$p < 0.01$.
[b]$p < 0.10$.
[c]$p < 0.001$.
[d]$p < 0.05$.

that are more extreme in severity than those that have emerged from the (in comparison) much more 'relatively benign' stakeholders of the past, i.e. competition, government agencies, activist groups, unions, etc. Copycat killers, terrorists, and off-site tamperers represent degrees of threat and terror that depart much more from normalcy than either corporations or executives have faced or have been educated to deal with in the past [16].

Second, by the same token, it is comforting to find also that greater E/I Threats are related to greater Design/Control and Auditing activities. And finally, it is also not surprising but comforting to find that greater Psychopathic threats are related to enhanced Behavioral activities.

What is surprising is that there are not significant p values between E Inf and E/I Threats, Breaks, and any of the undertakings, to mention only two sets of relationships. The topic is certainly deserving of further study. Are the lack of relationships an artifact of the data, sample, study, design, etc.?

Attitudinal questions

Table 4 shows the means and percentages of the responses to a variety of attitudinal and factual questions that were addressed to the respondents. In addition to being interesting and providing valuable information on their own, the questions provide even deeper insights when they are coupled with the factor scores. Table 5 shows the correlations between the frequency of Crisis Management Unit meetings (item no. 7, Table 4), the amount of claims paid in dollars over the last three years (item no. 8, Table 4) and the crisis factor scores. What is interesting is the emergence of the extremely high p of 0.84 and its high of significance *when* bribery, which is one of the items composing the factor E Threats, has the *lowest* frequency of occurrence of all of the crises. Also, the other item, recalls, which also enters in the composition of E Threats, is ranked eighth out of 19 (executive kidnappings received no occurrences from the respondents and was dropped from the original list of 20 crises; therefore, it did not enter into the factor analyses). Even though correlation does not necessarily imply direction of causality (unless we possess other information that we currently do not have), this nonetheless raises the following important question for future inquiries: If the amount of claims paid in dollars is significantly correlated with bribery and recalls, and if the current level of bribery especially is low in frequency, but if acts of bribery increase in the future, can we expect the amount of claims to increase even more? Or, is the high p value an artifact of the data or the fact that it is based on a small percentage of the sample (20%) reporting usable data?

Finally, while the frequency of CMU meetings are correlated significantly with the factor Psycho, an extreme *behavioral* factor, how does this square with the fact the greatest undertakings lie with a combination of internal and external *technical* actions or undertakings? In other words, is the match between reality (the incidence of various crises) and actions (undertakings) appropriate? Are we bumping up against the fact that ours is a society that believes in its general as well as corporate culture in the efficacy of technological solutions to all

Table 4 Attitudinal and factual responses

No	Item	Mean
1.	Every organization should have a permanent crisis management unit or team?	2.49[a]
2.	Most organizations, unless they first experience a major crisis, will not engage in a serious program of crisis management. Why, why not? (Briefly describe_____)	2.73[a]
3.	A company should withdraw its products from the market or shut down its facilities at the first signs that they might cause harm to the public.	3.45[a]
4.	A company should withdraw its products or shut down its facilities only after ordered to by federal and state agencies.	5.97[a]
5.	What, if any, are the most important lessons your company has learned regarding crisis management? (Briefly describe _____)	

No	Item	Response No. (%)
6.	Does your organization have a formal crisis management unit or team?	Yes 42 (38) No 68 (62)
	Are you a member of it?	Yes 32 (42) No 45 (58)
	If your organization has a crisis management unit or team, are the following individuals members of it?	
	Chief Executive Officer	Yes 25 (68) No 12 (32)
	Chief Financial Officer	Yes 21 (60) No 14 (40)
	Chief Operating Officer	Yes 27 (82) No 6 (18)
	Chairman of the Board	Yes 12 (46) No 14 (54)
	Director of Engineering	Yes 25 (78) No 7 (22)
	Director of Marketing	Yes 15 (50) No 15 (50)
	Outsiders	Yes 1 (5) No 21 (96)
	Director of Research	Yes 11 (42) No 15 (57)
	Chief Legal Counsel	Yes 34 (90) No 4 (10)
	Director of Environmental Affairs	Yes 24 (80) No 6 (20)
	Director of Security	Yes 25 (83) No 5 (17)
	Director of Personnel	Yes 23 (68) No 11 (32)
	Director of Safety	Yes 20 (67) No 10 (33)
	Director of Public Affairs	Yes 32 (87) No 5 (13)

No	Item	Mean
7.	How often does your CMU team meet?	3.61[b]
8.	What is the approximate amount of liability claims in $ your company settled in the past three years?	

[a] 7-point scale: '1' = agree strongly; '7' = disagree strongly.
[b] Scale: weekly = 1; once a month = 2; quarterly = 3; annually = 4; only when a crisis occurs = 5; doesn't apply = 6; don't know = 7.

problems, even if, like the Challenger, they demand solutions that are based on integrated programs of *behavioral, technical, organizational, and social* factors?

Table 4 shows that 38% ($N = 42$) out of those organizations responding to item no. 6 ($N = 110$) had a CMU. Since it is known from previous surveys [8] that approximately only 50% of U.S. corporations have contingency plans to cope with crisis, and more importantly since we don't know the *quality* of those plans, the 38% survey response may be either high or low depending upon the quality of those CMUs, which is also unknown. What we can do, however, is examine the differences in factor scores between those organizations reporting the existence of a CMU and those reporting that they do not have one.

Table 6 shows that there are significant differences between those organizations having a CMU and those not having one, both in the frequency of crises they experience and the actions they undertake to lower their crisis potential. Do those organizations that experience greater EI Threats for example, thereby set up a CMU, or does the setting up of a CMU thereby allow an organization to be more cognizant of the frequency of experienced crises? The question is not an idle one, since we know from other sectors of society (e.g. police reports) that

Table 5 Correlations between claims paid, frequency of CMU meetings, and factors

	E/I Threats	Breaks	Psycho	E Threats
Frequency of CMU Meetings (item no. 7)	NS	NS	0.40[a]	NS
Claims paid in dollars (item no. 8)	0.46[b]	NS	NS	0.84[c]

NS, not significant.
[a] $p < 0.10$.
[b] $p < 0.05$.
[c] $p < 0.001$.

Table 6 Differences in factor scores between organizations having a CMU versus those not having a CMU

Factors	N	X̄CMU	X̄NO-CMU	T Diff	Sig Diff
Crises					
E/I Threats	41	1.49	1.30	1.78	0.08
Breaks	40	1.83	1.79	0.20	NS
Psycho	25	1.63	1.16	2.21	0.04
E Threats	30	1.27	1.30	−0.34	NS
Actions					
E Inf	43	3.27	2.06	6.10	0.001
Design/control	53	3.72	3.16	2.95	0.004
Behav	23	2.02	1.35	3.93	0.0003
Audit	48	3.07	2.32	3.47	0.0009

NS, not significant.

the setting up of institutionalized mechanisms to detect severe events affects the reporting of them, since it affects the basic observation of them to begin with. Also, does engaging in more preventative actions follow from or precede the setting up of a CMU, or do these occur simultaneously?

Qualitative responses

Table 4 shows that the questionnaire asked the participants to respond to a couple of open-ended items. Fifty-eight, or 51%, of the respondents gave written answers in addition to their numerical responses to item no. 2. The overwhelming response was the mistaken belief by organizations that 'it can't happen to me.' In other words, both the verbal answers and numerical scores to item no. 2 support the interpretation that organizations remain primarily in the denial stage of crisis management. This stands in sharp contrast to the major lessons that organizations report they have learned. Sixty-nine respondents (60% of the sample) wrote responses to item no. 5 (Table 4). The chief answer was that the most important lesson they learned was 'to plan as far ahead as possible in advance of what can happen.' In general, the qualitative responses confirm the importance of the phases of crisis management outlined in Figures 9 and 10 of the section that follows immediately.

Discussion

The preceding results and analyses take on added significance when they are seen in the broader perspective of a systems approach to crisis management (CM). A systems approach to CM can be captured in two models. Figures 8 and 9 present the most basic *process* models of CM that the authors have been able to formulate based on a review of the literature. Both models attempt to identify as many of the phases that are necessary for the effective management of crises from a process standpoint. It is important to stress that neither model appears explicitly in the literature. Both were formulated by the present authors through reviews of the current literature on crisis management and by using prior theoretical conceptions and models developed by the first author [see 15].

The models in Figures 8 and 9 can be entered and exited from any point, and any direction can be proceeded in, which reflects both the systemic nature as well as the wide variety of epistemic and organizational patterns that are possible in CM. We shall discuss Figure 8 mainly by proceeding clockwise and starting with the entry point labeled 'detection.' The circle labeled 'detection' is meant to stand for all those systems that an organization has in place for the primary purpose of scanning both the external and internal environments for signals of impending crises. We have placed this function *prior to* the sloping line labeled 'prevention/preparation' in order to make the point that it is difficult, but not necessarily impossible, to engage systematically and comprehensively in acts of prevention or preparation for undetected crises. A review of the literature of crisis management reveals that most experts in the field of CM agree that

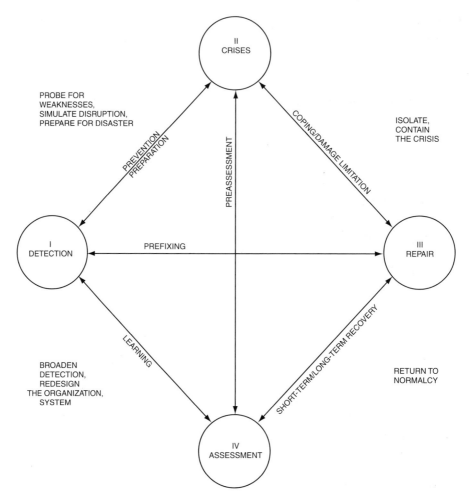

Figure 8 A preventative model of crises management

detection is logically and organizationally prior to prevention [2, 8, 28, 29]. One may in fact be able to prevent what one has not detected through normal, everyday, unintended managerial programs. But the point is that the prevention achieved in such instances will be based more on luck and happenstance rather than on deliberate organizational intention and intervention.

Point two of Figure 8 indicates that no organization will ever be perfect in the complete prevention of or preparation for all crises. Indeed, complete prevention is not one of the basic aims of either crisis planning or of CM. The *process* of constantly testing and revising one's crisis plans is hypothesized to allow an organization to cope more effectively with those crises that do occur because its prior planning activities have enabled the organization to 'learn how to roll with the punches more effectively' [8]. In other words, the fundamental purpose of crisis planning is not seen as the production of formal plans that sit on a shelf or that will perfectly prevent all crises. The fundamental point of crisis planning is to allow an organization to engage in both the necessary intellectual and

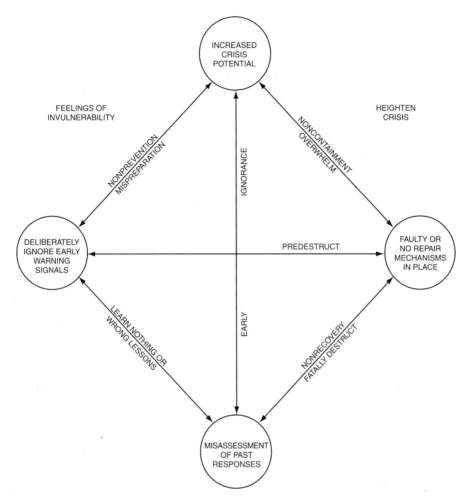

Figure 9 A crisis creation model or 'Design for Disaster'

emotional learning that will allow it to cope more effectively with those crises that do occur. Most organizations will not have the luxury of learning during a crisis, when one's responses will be stressed to the point of breaking and when rigidity and defensiveness most likely guide organizational responses [30].

Point three is meant to represent the major *tested* and *in-place* structures and mechanisms that an organization has for guiding both its short-term and long-term recovery efforts. Point four is meant to raise the important points of what an organization has learned from its past crises and, hence, what efforts it means to take to revise both its detection, preparation, and recovery mechanisms.

It can be hypothesized that the more an organization denies its vulnerability, the more its activities will be directed to the right-hand side of Figure 8. That is, the more it will respond *re*actively to crises, the more it will be engaged in cleanup efforts 'after the fact.' Conversely, it is also hypothesized that the more crises an organization anticipates, the more it will engage in *pro*active behavior directed toward activities on the left-hand side of the model. Table 6 shows that this may be one of the crucial differences between those organizations with a CMU and those without one.

The model embodies some lessons that are vital to CM. The first and perhaps single most important one is that prior to its actual occurrence, nearly every potential crisis is thought to leave a repeated trail of early warning signals [8]. Thus, if organizations could only learn to read these warning signals and to attend to them more effectively, then there is much they could do to prevent many crises from ever occurring (that is, they could engage in programs of prevention based on information in Table 2 and Figure 7). For example Shrivastava [26] has shown that for a year and a half prior to the tragic explosion in Bhopal, India, at Union Carbide's Indian subsidiary, messages repeatedly passed from the parent office in Danbury, Connecticut, to the Indian plant warning it to fix potential problems that could cause a catastrophic explosion. Thus, the signals were sent, but the system either chose to ignore and not to act on the warnings (see Figure 9).

Given today's extremely litigious environment and a news media that is more vigilant than ever, it is the height of folly and delusion for any organization to believe that it will not be judged by how well it does on *every* phase of Figure 8. In fact, one can regard it as almost a virtual certainty that one's prior plans and performance on every phase of the model *will* become available to an ever-vigilant press.

Because the field of crisis management is still in its infancy, the primary data are available mainly through the reports of experts in the field in quasi-professional magazines and journals [e.g. 3, 5, 10, 18, 19, 21, 24]. Most experts believe that the more potential crises an organization can think of and prepare for, the more quickly and successfully it will recover from any crises that strike it [8, 27]. This is not, as we have stressed earlier, because planning is always perfect, but rather because going through the *process* of planning teaches an organization how to cope more effectively with whatever does occur. In fact, a cardinal rule of crisis management appears to be: *No crisis ever happens exactly as it was planned for.*

The tragic explosion of the space shuttle reinforces and illustrates virtually every point in Figures 8 and 9. The Presidential Commission Report [23] on the cause of the space shuttle disaster painstakingly examined the contending, probable causes of the disaster. The report suggested that the explosion was caused by the failure of two large, critical O-rings that were supposed to keep the highly flammable rocket fuel from spilling from its casing and igniting the shuttle's main engines. The real importance of the Presidential Commission Report consists in showing the major role that organizational factors play in both the prevention and cause of major disasters. The underlying, precipitating causes of the shuttle failure had little to do with technology per se. The Presidential Commission Reports, after locating the technical cause of the disaster, spends the overwhelming majority of its pages establishing the accompanying human and organizational causes. These pages include reproduction of a long series of memos that flowed between NASA and one of its prime subcontractors, Morton Thiokol. The memos are, in effect, an audit trail of early-warning signals. If NASA had attended to them then, it is very likely that the disaster could have been prevented. One of the most painful memos starts with the anguished cry, 'Help!' It goes on to say if the shuttle continues to fly with the current O-ring design, then NASA is almost guaranteed to incur a disaster. The memos that follow reveal an organization that is impervious to hearing bad news, so that instead of deliberately designing monitoring systems to consciously pick up danger signals, in effect it designed a management system to intentionally block them out or downgrade their seriousness.

For this very reason, the authors have presented both Figures 8 and 9. Figure 8 represents a normative statement of what organizations *should do ideally* in order to 'lessen' their disaster potential. If anything, the situation is asymmetrical. Figure 9 shows the factors that are almost 'guaranteed' to cause a major disaster from which an organization will not recover, i.e. if 1) it deliberately blocks important warning signals; if 2) it does not put in place prevention and preparatory mechanisms; and if 3) it has no tested in-place damage limitation and recovery mechanisms, then it seems almost designed to have a disaster that it will not be able to prevent, contain, or recover from. To see this, it is enough to consider just the damage limitation phase of Figures 8 and 9. The prime purpose of such mechanisms is to limit the spreading of a disaster once it has occurred, so that it will not engulf other parts of the organization.

Figures 8 and 9 show that there are a wide variety of mixed options that are open to every organization. These mixed options result from an interweaving of the models in Figures 8 and 9. That is, it is possible to regard both Figures 8 and 9 as providing pure components that can be weaved together in a wide variety of patterns, so that parts of Figure 8 can be meshed with parts of Figure 9 to constitute models that are admixtures of the two. Thus, e.g. if just one part of Figure 8 is substituted with its corresponding part from Figure 9, then the disaster potential of an organization is raised accordingly. The point is that in each and every case, we are dealing with the performance of a system that is measured *multiplicatively* [1, 3], not additively. That is, the performance of the resulting system is not merely the sum of the performances of the separate parts, but instead of their multiplication. In symbols, Perf. TOTAL SYSTEM $= \pi$ Perf. PART, where π stands for multiplication, so that the total system performance is reduced by the performance of its weakest part no matter how high the performance is of the stronger parts.

Concluding remarks

The relationship between the empirical results, analyses, and the process models of CM (Figures 8 and 9) is highly important. If different types of crises leave different kinds of early-warning signals; calls for different kinds of preparatory and prevention mechanisms; necessitate different damage limitation, recovery, and learning mechanisms; then does the fact that certain crises cluster or factor together help organizations in giving coherence to their CM efforts? If, as the current research has demonstrated, crises group together in certain clusters, then are there certain kinds of 'action portfolios' that organizations can engage in or undertake to lower their potential susceptibility to blocks of crises? For instance, instead of preparing for each and every kind of crisis or disaster, which may be an organizational impossibility because of the sheer overload such a task would necessitate, one can obtain greater across-the-board coverage by preparing for certain limited groups or types that span the spectrum of crises? Is it enough, in other words, for organizations to form a *crisis portfolio* based on the probable occurrence of *at least one* type of crisis from each of the factors in Table 1 and Figure 6? Conversely, is it also enough to form a crisis portfolio of available blocking actions based on the consideration of *at least one* preventative action from each of the factors in Table 2 and Figure 7? Are these actions sufficient to give both minimum coherence and minimum protection (robustness) to organizations?

The field of crisis management is still in its infancy. Much additional work, both of a conceptual/theoretical and an empirical nature remains to be done. Nevertheless, the present study has been successful in shedding important light on the essential phases of crisis management (Figures 8 and 9) and the structure (i.e. organization) of crises and preventative actions.

Future research is needed to check on the validity of the models and the structures identified as well as proposed here. How many more major crises will we have to experience before these issues raised will get the attention they so strongly deserve?

References

1. Ackoff, R. (1981) *Creating the Corporate Future*, Wiley: New York.
2. Andriole, S. (1985) (ed.) *Corporate Crisis Management*, Petrocelli Books: Princeton, N.J.
3. Churchman, C. West (1971) *The Design of Inquiring Systems*, Basic Books: New York.
4. Draper, N. (1986) Training Managers To Meet The Press, *Training* 23 (8) 30–38.
5. Feinberg, M. (1987) Crash Course in Crisis Management, *Working Woman* 12 (1), 24–28.
6. Feyerabend, Paul, 'Against Method: Outline Of An Anarchistic Theory of Knowledge.' Minnesota Studies In The Philosophy of Science, Volume 4: 17–130. Minneapolis: University of Minnesota Press.
7. Feyerabend, Paul (1965) Problems of Empiricism, in *Beyond the Edge of Certainty*, Robert Colodny (ed.) Prentice Hall: Englewood Cliffs, N.J., pp. 145–260.
8. Fink, Stephen (1986) *Crisis Management*, AMACOM: New York.
9. Gephart, R. P. (1984) Making Sense of Organizationally Based Environmental Disasters, *Journal of Management* 10 (2): 205–225.
10. Kahn, R. (1985) Information Processing Technology For Emergency Management, Information Society 3 (4): 303–311.
11. Milburn, T. W., Schuler, R. S., and Watman, K. H. (1984) Organizational Crisis. Part I: Definition and Conceptualization, *Human Relations* 36 (12): 1141–1160.

12. Mitroff, Ian I. (1983) *Stakeholders of the Organizational Mind: Toward a New View of Organizational Policy Making*, Jossey-Bass: San Francisco.

13. Mitroff, Ian I. (1974) *The Subjective Side Of Science: A Philosophical Enquiry Into The Psychology Of The Apollo Moon Scientists*, Elsevier: Amsterdam, Holland.

14. Mitroff, I. I., (1973) Systems Inquiry, and the Meaning of Falsification, Philosophy of Science 40 (2): 255–276.

15. Mitroff, I. I., Betz, F., Pondy, L. R., and Sagasti, F. On Managing Science In The Systems Age: Two Schemas For The Study Of Science As A Whole Systems Phenomenon, *Interfaces* 4 (93): 46–58.

16. Mitroff, Ian I., and Kilmann, Ralph H. (1978) *Methodological Approaches to Social Science*, Jossey-Bass: San Francisco.

17. Mitroff, Ian I., and Kilmann, Ralph H. (1984) *Corporate Tragedies: Product Tampering, Sabotage, and Other Catastrophes*, Praeger: New York.

18. Nudell, M. (1986) Contingency Planning For Terrorism, Part I, *Risk Management* 33 (7): 20–24.

19. Nudell, M. (1986) Contingency Planning For Terrorism, Part II, *Risk Management* 33 (8): 30–36.

20. Perrow, Charles (1984) *Normal Accidents*, Basic Books: New York.

21. Phelps, N. (1986) Setting Up A Crisis Recovery Plan, *Journal of Business Strategy* 6 (4): 5–10.

22. Raphael, Beverly (1986) *When Disaster Strikes, How Individuals and Communities Cope with Catastrophe*, Basic Books: New York.

23. Report of the President's Commission on the Space Shuttle Challenger Accident (1986) Order No. 04000000496–3. Government Printing Office, GPO Superintendent of Documents: Washington, D.C.

24. Rich, L. A. (1986) Just In Case The Worst Case Happens, *Chemical Week* 139 (21): 43–45.

25. Shrivastava, P. A Cultural Analysis of Conflicts in Industrial Crises, *International Journal of Mass Emergencies and Disasters* in press.

26. Shrivastava, Paul (1987) *Bhopal. Anatomy of a Crisis*, Ballinger Publishing Comp: Cambridge, Ma.

27. Shrivastava, P., and Mitroff, I. (1987) Strategic Planning for Corporate Crises, *Columbia Journal of World Business*, Summer.

28. Smart, C. F., and Stanbury, W. T. (eds) (1978) *Studies in Crisis Management*, Butterworth: Toronto.

29. Starbuck, W. H., Greve, A., and Hedberg, B. L. T. (1978) Responding to Crisis, *Journal of Business Administration* 9: 111–137.

30. Staw, B., Sandelands, L. E., and Dutton, J. E. (1981) Threat Rigidity Effects in Organizational Behavior: A Multi-level Analysis. *Administrative Science Quarterly* 26: 501–524.

31. Turner, B. A. (1978) Man Made Disaster, Wykeham Publications: London.

32. Wedeking, G., Duhem, Quinn, and Grunbaum (1969) On Falsification, *Philosophy of Science* 36: 375–380.

Bettelheim, B. (1943) Individual and Mass Behavior in Extreme Situations, *Journal of Abnormal and Social Psychology*, 38: 417–452.

Billings, R. S., Milburn, T. W., and Schaalman, M. L. (1980) A Model of Crisis

Perception: A Theoretical and Empirical Analysis, Administrative Science Quarterly, 25: 300–316.

Brown, L., Chandler, W. U., Flavin, C., Pollock, C., Postel, S., Starke, L., Wolf, E. C. (eds) (1985, 1986) *State of the World*, W. W. Norton and Co.: New York.

Chase, W. H. (1984) *Origins of the Future*, Issue Action Publications, Inc.: Stamford, CT.

Dutton, J. E. (1986) The Processing of Crisis and Non-Crisis Strategic Issues, *Journal of Management Studies*, 23 (5): 501–517.

Erman, D. M., and Lundman, R. (eds) (1978) *Corporate and Governmental Deviance*, Oxford University Press, New York.

Hohenemser, C., *et al.* (1986) An Early Report on the Chernobyl Disaster, *Environment*, June 16.

Littlejohn, R. F. (1986) When The Crisis Is Terrorism, *Security Management* 30 (8): 38–41.

Meyer, A. D. (1982) Adapting to Environmental Jolts, *Administrative Science Quarterly* 27: 515–537.

Milburn, T. W., Schuler, R. S., and Watman, K. H. (1984) Organizational Crisis. Part II: Strategies and Responses, *Human Relations*.

Mitroff, I. I., and Shrivastava, P. Effective Crisis Management, *Columbia Journal of Business*, in press.

Nelkin, D. (1977) Technological Decisions and Democracy. Sage Publications, Beverly Hills: Calif.

Sills, D. L., Wolf, C. P., and Shelanski, V. B. (eds.) (1982) *Accident at Three Mile Island: The Human Dimension*, Westview Press: Boulder, Colo.

Slovic, P., Fischoff, B., and Lichtenstein, S. (1979) Rating the Risks, *Environment* 21 (3): 14–39 (1979).

Tolba, M. K. (1982) Development Without Destruction: Evolving Environmental Perceptions, Tycooly International Publishing: Dublin.

Chapter 5

Danny Miller

ORGANIZATIONAL PATHOLOGY AND INDUSTRIAL CRISIS

THE FIELD OF INDUSTRIAL crisis management is still very new. It is not surprising then that it stands to benefit from better and more encompassing definitions of crisis as well as from a more precise grasp of the contingencies that give rise to crises. This paper attempts to make some progress in this area. First, it derives a classification of industrial crises outcomes based on their effects on the different stakeholders of the corporation. Next, it uses a taxonomy of pathological organizations to show how each common type can give rise to outcomes in each of the crisis categories. Some examples are given of firms that faced crises. But these examples are used only to make *conjectures* about some relationships between organizational functioning and negative results rather than to ascribe blame or responsibility to any group of managers for any particular crisis.

Typically, industrial crises have been considered to be accidents or disasters caused by business and public organizations. These include severe cataclysms in the workplace that damage the environment or injure workers and citizens. They also include damage done to consumers by poorly designed or unsafe products (Shrivastava, Mitroff, Miller and Miglani, 1998). But crises can be defined more broadly – as serious financial setbacks, psychological suffering, and environmental damage that can occur as a result of corporate activities.

We shall look at crisis outcomes as they influence the various constituencies or stakeholders of the organization: these include managers, workers, shareholders, and the general society. Each of these constituencies are placed in jeopardy by very different types of organizational crisis outcomes. Shareholders and sometimes managers are hurt by severe deterioration in financial performance: their returns on investment, salaries and job security are influenced by poor organizational performance. But managers are also hurt by political factors

– by a poor working environment that is torn with conflict, stultified by bureaucracy, or rife with suspicion. Finally, society as a whole is hurt by still another set of organizational outcomes – for example the pollution of the environment by irresponsible firms, the consumption of hazardous products, and the misallocation of resources brought about by illegal corporate activities such as bribes, kickbacks, and restrictive trade practices.

In fact, several earlier typologies attempted to classify industrial crises. Mitroff, Pauchant and Shrivastava (1988) have focussed on problems with psychological roots. Lagadec (1982), Perrow (1984), Shrivastava (1987) have concentrated on the various types of technological crises that result in harm to the environment. Meyers (1986) has looked primarily at financial and business crises. Our approach was to unify these perspectives. It seemed useful to distinguish between at least three types of crises and their outcomes. The first are *financial* and jeopardize the survival of the organization – and thus the returns to shareholders and the job security of its managers and line workers. Bankruptcy is the most extreme example, but we include hostile takeovers, liquidity crises, and depleted capital reserves. The second class of outcomes are *pyschological or interpersonal* and have to do with the social and working climate of the organization – with its corporate culture. These can endanger the mental and physical health of managers and line workers by creating stress, conflict, extreme apathy, disenchantment, alienation, and even depression in the work environment. These outcomes are crises in themselves as they can engender illness and much suffering. But they can also lead to carelessness, even sabotage, which results in accidents at the workplace and inferior products. Finally, there are the *societal/environmental* crisis outcomes such as pollution, industrial accidents (the Bhopal toxic leak, for example), bribes and corruption of government officials, price gouging, and dangerous faulty products (Dalkon shield), etc.

Having derived this rough and tentative classification of crises it is useful to explore the kinds of organizations that could give rise to them. In order to do this, we have used a by now rather established taxonomy of pathological organizations. This classification of failing types of firms derives from the empirical work done by Miller (1976), and the subsequent development of the types by Miller and Friesen (1978, 1984) and Kets de Vries and Miller (1984, 1988).

Essentially, these authors have discovered five types of sick organizations: the suspicious, the compulsive, the dramatic, the depressive, and the detached or fragmented. It is interesting that these organizational types are really gestalts among a large number of attributes of strategy, structure, corporate culture, environment, and chief executive personality.

Perhaps some definitions are in order. The strategy of an organization is the product-market scope it defines for itself and the competitive distinctive competences that it develops (Hofer and Schendel, 1978). Its structure is the set of administrative procedures – the hierarchy, the allocation of responsibility and authority, the nature and membership of committees (integrative devices) – that are used to develop and implement the strategy (Jackson and Morgan, 1982; Lawrence and Lorsch, 1967; March and Simon, 1958). The corporate culture includes the goals, interpersonal styles, and overriding beliefs and ideologies of the dominant group of managers (Deal and Kennedy, 1982). Environment is the nature of the firm's markets – its customers, competitors, and the legal and social infrastructure (Lawrence and Lorsch, 1967; Thompson, 1967). Finally, personality encompasses the enduring, entrenched needs, goals, basic assumptions and beliefs of top managers (Kets de Vries and Miller, 1984).

It has been shown that the elements of strategy, structure, corporate culture and executive personality seem to combine in a mutually reinforcing way to form extremely durable and change-resistant configurations (Miller, 1987; Miller and Friesen, 1984; Kets de Vries and Miller, 1984, 1988). We will discuss five such configurations very briefly as they have already been described elsewhere (Kets de Vries and Miller, 1984, 1988). Our primary task will be to show how each of the organizational types can engender the three types of crisis outcomes that we have discussed above. It is important to note that these pathological types of organizations do not inevitably cause industrial crises. All we wish to argue in this paper is that such firms have a greater susceptibility to, or proclivity towards, the various crises we shall be discussing. It should be noted too that there are many extra-organizational causes, beyond the scope of our discussion here, that can also engender crises and aggravate their severity. These include the nature of the technologies used (Lagadec, 1982; Perrow, 1984), the political and physical infrastructure of society (Shrivastava, 1987; Thompson and Hawkes, 1962), and the parameters of prevailing economic and social systems (Arnold, 1981; Zimmerman, 1987).

The compulsive organization

The compulsive firm is wed to ritual. Every detail is planned in advance and carried out in a routinized, preprogrammed fashion. Thoroughness and conformity with established procedures are emphasized.

Such firms are exceedingly hierarchical, and they generally develop an elaborate set of formal policies, rules and procedures. These extend beyond production and marketing decisions to dress codes, corporate credos and suggested employee beliefs and attitudes.

The strategy making style of the compulsive firm shows the same preoccupation with detail and established procedures. Firms have a very narrow and well defined distinctive competence which entirely determines the organization's strategy. The marketplace, too often, is almost totally ignored.

The kinds of financial crisis outcomes of this organizational type stem from a failure to adapt to the wants and needs of customers and the inroads of more flexible and innovative competitors. Market share is lost because merchandise is outdated, or inappropriate. Prices and profit margins fall for the same reason. Ultimately, some of these organizations become buggy whip manufacturers and perish. The rigid, hidebound bureaucracy run by the first Henry Ford produced, for many years, a Model T that became so antiquated and undesirable to potential customers as to bring Ford to the brink of bankruptcy and allow the ascendance of General Motors as a major competitor (Kets de Vries and Miller, 1988). The Facit company of Sweden produced outmoded manual office equipment long after electrification by competitors had rendered Facit's products obsolete.

Interpersonal crises in these firms may be even more serious. There is little scope among managers for creative interaction or initiative. Power is too centralized, and rules are too confining to allow room for personal growth. Managers become depressed and apathetic. The best people leave, creating a brain drain and a competence crisis. Also, some of these organizations routinize their processes so much that line workers suffer even more intensely than middle managers from monotonous, stultifying jobs. Alienation and boredom increase the propensity for accidents and lengthy strikes. All of these things happened at Ford during the last years of the founder's tenure.

Firms are so narrowly focussed that they fail to adapt to the needs of their own customers, let alone broader society. They make almost no significant innovations and contribute very little to overall economic growth. Environmental crises are produced because compulsive firms simply do not consider social goals to be important. The lack of concern for responsible social behavior creates irresponsible behavior – such as pollution, chemical spills, accidents, etc. Ford's anti-union and anti-semetic activities, as well as his administrative follies, were both the results of an apparently compulsive personality (Kets de Vries and Miller, 1988).

The dramatic organization

The dramatic organization is hyperactive, impulsive, dramatically venturesome, and dangerously uninhibited. Its top executives live in a world of hunches and first impressions rather than facts, and they take on extraordinarily ambitious and widely disparate projects in desultory fashion. Power is extremely centralized in the hands of the entrepreneurial chief executive who has a flair for the dramatic and reserves only to himself the prerogative to initiate bold ventures. The power of the second tier executives is severely limited, and the CEO becomes terribly overloaded with administrative responsibilities. The increasing complexity of operations, and the limited administrative apparatus cause the firm to get out of control.

The financial crisis outcome here generally stems from overexpansion and the poor husbanding of resources. Firms diversify into projects and businesses in which they have little expertise. This, coupled with the administrative bottleneck that shunts all problems to the top of the organization, allows problems lower down to go unattended for too long. Resources are squandered and profits plummet. A prime example of this was Automatic Sprinkler Corp. of the 1960s run by the energetic Harry Figgie. The firm expanded boldly and rapidly, aquiring a host of diverse subsidiaries that were in a poor state of repair. The firm doubled, even tripled its size every two or three years. Unfortunately, power was centralized in the hands of the increasingly overburdened CEO who was too busy to become aware of the many operating problems in the divisions. These problems were never recognized by the top managers who, in any event, had too few controls in place and too little expertise to be able to do much about them. Ultimately, the financial results were disastrous and much divestment was necessary (Miller, 1976).

Interpersonal problems are caused by a corporate culture that centers around the charismatic and often overbearing personality of the leader. Middle level managers must tow the line and pay hommage to the boss at regular intervals or they risk losing their jobs. Also, their talents are underutilized as they have too little power to make decisions. Many dramatic organizations are highly acquisitive, moving from one takeover to another, and divesting businesses that fail to quickly become profitable. The result is that many managerial and line operating jobs are in great peril at all times. There is virtually no employment security. Layoffs on a massive scale are common. This was the case at some of the major conglomerates of the 1960's such as Litton, LTV, Boise Cascade and Textron – where major and very painful consolidations, resulting in the loss of many jobs, followed periods of unbridled expansion.

The emphasis on short-run returns can also create environmental and social problems. Cost cutting drives can reduce safety in the workplace and result in inferior products. Plant closures can devastate small communities.

The depressive organization

The depressive organization is characterized by inactivity, lack of confidence, extreme conservatism, insularity, and entrenched bureaucracy. Only those things that have been pre-programmed and routinized and require absolutely no special initiative ever get done. Everything else is ignored.

These firms are usually quite old and well-established, generally serving a single mature market that has had the same technology, customer buying patterns, and competitors for a very long time. Depressive organizations are found most often in protected environments where trade agreements, collusions, restrictive trade practices, and substantial tariffs that limit competition are the rule. The high level of stability – indeed stagnation – and the absence of serious competition, lull the firm to sleep.

The major financial threat is that these firms become so stagnant that they lose their viability, even in their protected markets. The inroads made by foreign competition can be devastating (recall the steel, textile and automobile industries of the U.S.). Market shares shrink, margins erode, profits plummet, and capital equipment becomes antiquated, rendering firms less and less competitive.

The corporate climate or culture of these firms is stultifying and depressing. There is no room for initiative, creativity, or autonomous decision making. The most talented managers leave or become extremely disenchanted and lethargic. The general workforce has much difficulty maintaining competitive wages, and layoffs are common. A&P, Eastern Airlines, and Allis Chalmers went through periods in which their resources were badly depleted because they failed to update their management resources, products and services (Kets de Vries and Miller, 1988; Miller, 1976). Many of the most talented managers left the firms for more rewarding, less oppressive careers elsewhere.

The environmental and social cost is that the nation loses its international competitiveness in an industry. Also, industries with a high percentage of such depressive organizations are most likely to have too few slack resources to adopt environmental protection measures or to keep their capital base productive. The textile, steel and automotive industries in the United States have lagged far behind their international competitors, failing to update products and production equipment. Many of the firms in these industries are, or were, stagnant bureaucracies (Kets de Vries and Miller, 1988).

The detached (fragmented) organization

The detached organization is characterized by a leadership vacuum. Its top executive discourages interaction, believing that most relationships will end painfully for him. In some organizations, the second tier of executives compensates for the leader's lack of involvement. Frequently however, the detached organization is a political battlefield in which second-tier managers battle one another to fill the leadership vacuum. The initiatives of one group of managers are often neutralized or defeated by those of an opposing group.

Strategy in such organizations has more to do with individual goals and internal politics than any threats or opportunities in the external environment.

The financial costs these organizations have to pay are largely due to an inability to formulate an internally consistent strategy. Resources are squandered as the firms move simultaneously in conflicting directions. Subunits and departments work at cross purposes so that cooperative collaboration is impossible. Projects are bungled, and product lines suffer because functional areas such as marketing, R&D, and production cannot work together. Customers are lost.

The interpersonal and psychological costs of working in the detached organization are in many ways the greatest. The animosity between departments creates great tensions and a highly unpleasant working environment. Power struggles and vocational stress abound. Often, it is those with the greatest political acumen who are promoted rather than those who have the most appropriate skills for the job. This was a complaint at the sprawling Societé Génèrale of Belgium in the late 1960's. The powerful divisional managers created their own strategies and ran their own fiefdoms, oblivious to what was good for the organization. They almost never cooperated with one another and conflict was the rule (Kets de Vries and Miller, 1988).

The poor coordination among functional areas can create poorly designed and hazardous products that inflict costs at the environmental level. Political compromises can result in sloppy designs and unduly risky technologies.

Union Carbide may have been something of a detached organization at the time of the Bhopal tragedy during which toxic gas was released into the environment. This leak resulted in tremendous loss of life in the general community. Carbide's Indian subsidiary was only very loosely controlled by the head office. The local managers were very independent. Also, political conflicts may have been signalled by the fact that there were 8 different plant managers at Bhopal in 13 years. Loose controls and inexperience may have been the causes of poor safety monitoring. Indeed the operational safety survey had not been carried out for over two years (Shrivastava, 1987).

The suspicious organization

This paranoid organization, suspicious of people and events both inside and outside the firm, places strong emphasis on intelligence and controls. Such organizations tend to develop sophisticated methods of gathering information in order to identify threats and challenges from the government, from competitors, and from customers. Suspicious organizations also strive to maintain strict control over internal matters by monitoring all aspects of the firm's operations.

Suspicious firms tend to be reactive, which can interfere with the development of a consistent strategy. External forces, rather than overall goals or organizational needs, determine the firm's direction.

One strategy that is used quite frequently by suspicious firms is diversification. To reduce the risk of relying on any one market, suspicious firms often enter into a number of unrelated businesses. Although these are run by different divisional managers, the managers are kept in line by sophisticated information systems and narrowly defined goals.

Financially, the risks are much the same as those for the dramatic organization. Overcentralization and too much diversity result in unprofitable divisions. The organization spreads itself too thin strategically to develop any real distinctive competences. Market power is eroded.

The interpersonal climate is pervaded by suspicion and hostility – directed toward the environment, which is always perceived as dangerous and threatening. Managers spy upon each other and try to question one another's motives and loyalties. The stresses created are enormous.

Managers try to reduce the environmental threats by lobbying, industrial spying, restrictive trade practices, payoffs to officials, and other forms of graft. The firm has no social conscience and immorality prevails.

There is evidence that ITT under Harold Geneen was a suspicious organization (Kets de Vries and Miller, 1988). Replete with sophisticated, computerized controls and scrutinizing head office planning committees, ITT tried to ensure that it would meet with few suprises. But its desire for control – for ensuring a 'safe' environment for itself – seemed to extend to underwriting efforts, and lobbying illegally, to topple the Allende regime in Chile. Suspicion, it seems, bred pernicious interference. The firm was also held to be a fiercely unpleasant place to work by many of the managers who had endured the Geneen regime.

Conclusion

Prescriptions are very difficult to arrive at when dealing with these pathological types of organizations. All that we can say is that classification must precede any remedial efforts within the organization. It is necessary to determine the nature of the organization's pathologies before attempting to deduce its proclivities to the three categories of industrial crises that we have discussed. This can best be done by objective third parties who have much experience in organizational diagnosis and intervention. Kets de Vries and Miller (1984, 1988) present instruments for organizational diagnosis that can help managers identify whether their firms are dangerously similar to any of the five pathological types we have discussed here.

Having identified the dominant syndrome and the underlying dynamics of an organization's problem, it is necessary to obtain the commitment to change from the very highest and most powerful levels of the organization. And since these individuals are themselves so often responsible for the problems, it can be very difficult to obtain their cooperation. One way would be to illustrate the dangers (and the potential crisis outcomes) of the pathological type or types that most closely resemble the organization. This can be done by using regular strategic audits and discussing the results broadly – among top and middle managers and across all functional areas. Boards of directors should participate whenever possible. External consultants, as well as staff experts and middle level managers should contribute to the audit to ensure that it circumvents the tunnel vision of the top executives. Every attempt must be made to avoid scapegoating and the politicization of the diagnosis and change processes. The admission of error often erodes an executive's credibility and power base. This is one of the greatest obstacles to change.

As we have seen, the pathologies of the five common types are very deeply ingrained and their component problems are highly interdependent and mutually supportive. They form unified gestalts that resist alteration to the point of bouncing back to their original configuration whenever a small change is made (Miller and Friesen, 1984). Thus, as a rule, only revolutionary or 'quantum' change, rather than incremental and piecemeal adjustments, can move the organization to a healthier configuration (Miller and Friesen, 1984). Since counteracting the pathological styles requires such major changes it will entail significant resource expenditures and will usually have to involve the strategies, decision making styles, power distribution, structure, and especially the top management of the firm. Kets de Vries and Miller (1984, 1988) deal with some of the political and psychological avenues for amassing the leverage required to change such unhealthy organizations.

References

Arnold, W.B. (1981) 'The economics of risk to life', *American Economic Review*, 71: 54–64.

Deal, T. and Kennedy, A. (1982) *Corporate cultures*, Addison-Wesley: New York.

Hofer, C. and Schendel, D. (1978) *Strategy formulation*, West, St. Paul: MN.

Jackson, J. and Morgan, C. (1982) *Organization theory*, Prentice Hall, Englewood Cliffs: NJ.

Kets de Vries, M. and Miller, D. (1984) *The neurotic organization: Diagnosing and changing counterproductive styles of management*, Jossey Bass, San Francisco: CA.

Kets de Vries, M. and Miller, D. (1988) *Unstable at the top: Inside the troubled organization*, New American Library: New York.

Lagadec, P. (1982) *Major technological risk: An assessment of industrial disasters*: Pergamon Press: Oxford.

Lawrence, P. and Lorsch, J. (1967) *Organization and environment*, Harvard, Boston: MA.

March, J.G. and Simon, H.A. (1958) *Organizations*, Wiley: New York.

Meyers, G.C. (1986) *When it hits the fan: Managing the nine crises of business*, Houghton Mifflin, Boston: MA.

Miller, D. (1987) *Strategy making in context: Ten empirical archetypes*, Doctoral dissertation, McGill University: Montreal.

Miller, D. and Friesen, P.H. (1978) 'Archetypes of strategy formulation', *Management Science*, 24: 921–933.

Miller, D. and Friesen, P.H. (1984) *Organizations: A quantum view*, Prentice Hall, Englewood Cliffs: NJ.

Mitroff, I., Pauchant, T. and Shrivastava, P. (1988) 'The structure of man-made organizational crises: Conceptual and empirical issues in the development of a general theory of crisis management', *Technological Forecasting and Social Change*, forthcoming.

Perrow, C. (1984) *Normal accidents*, Basic Books: New York.

Shrivastava, P. (1987) *Bhopal: Anatomy of a crisis*, Ballinger, Cambridge: MA.

Shrivastava, P., Mitroff, I., Miller, D. and Miglani, A. (1988) 'The anatomy of organizational crisis', *Journal of Management Studies*, forthcoming.

Thompson, J.D. (1967) Organizations in action, McGraw-Hill: New York.

Thompson, J.D. and Hawkes, R.W. (1962) *Disaster, community organization, and administrative process*, in G.W. Baker and D.W. Chapman, (eds.), *Man and society in disaster*, Basic Books: New York.

Zimmerman, R. (1987) 'The government's role as stakeholder in industrial crises', *Industrial Crisis Quarterly*, 1 (3): 34–45.

Chapter 6

Arjen Boin

ORGANIZATIONS AND CRISIS: THE EMERGENCE OF A RESEARCH PARADIGM

Four classic readings

THE FIELD OF ORGANIZATIONAL crisis management got a jump-start in the 1980s.[1] It was an era of new and frightening technological crises: the near-catastrophe of the Three Miles Island (TMI) nuclear reactor (1979) and the Chernobyl disaster (1986); the Bhopal tragedy (1984) and the *Challenger* disaster (1986) – these became paradigmatic cases for organization theorists interested in crisis and the management of adversity. Most of the readings selected for this book were written in that era of 'industrial crises.'

The articles under review in this section share this common backdrop. They are marked by a sense of urgency to understand the nature and dynamics of 'industrial crises.' The authors – all seasoned organization theorists – wrestle with the finding that organizational success factors may become the causes of untold horror; Shrivastava and his colleagues (1988: 297) ominously observe that 'organizations are simultaneously systems of production and of destruction.' They all work toward a comprehensive theory of crisis management, even though their understanding of crisis is limited by the newness of the subject.

The selected articles also differ in what they offer. Danny Miller tries to identify the causes of crisis by looking at causes of organizational failure: he assumes – quite mistakenly as we will see – that the various types of organiza-tional pathologies identified in earlier work will help to understand crises caused by organizations. Ian Mitroff and colleagues introduce a very useful typology of corporate crises and toy with a 'systems approach' to understand how these crises arise. Paul Shrivastava (together with Miller and Mitroff) put together a list of factors that are said to cause these crises, but they fail to explain just how that may happen. These three papers – all published in 1988 – give us a sense of the frantic and joint effort to understand what are commonly referred to as 'industrial crises.' Several authors continued these efforts well into the 1990s.

The fourth article under discussion differs from the rest as it flows from an alternative research strand.[2] In the wake of the TMI near-miss, a selected group of American scholars sought to understand what happened (Sills, Wolf and Shelanski, 1981). They were especially interested to learn how complex organizations worked with high-risk technologies. Three classic bodies of work emerged: Charles Perrow's *Normal Accidents* (1984), Aaron Wildavsky's *Searching for Safety* (1988) and the Berkeley formulation of High Reliability Theory. Perrow's article reflects the deep controversy that has since separated High Reliability and Normal Accident theorists. Incidentally, it also suggests just how productive such discord can be for the sake of theoretical development.

This chapter offers a commentary on these articles. This commentary aims to do four things. First, it will clarify the concept of crisis. The authors employ the term in various ways, which precludes a comparative discussion of their articles. Second, it will summarize and discuss what these articles tell us about the causes of crises. Third, it will map the implications for crisis management: can practitioners use these insights to prevent crises in their organization? The chapter concludes with the formulation of future research challenges: what is it that we simply do not know and where should we go to find answers? Throughout this commentary, we ask whether a paradigm of organizational crisis research is emerging within these articles.

The industrial crisis

For a paradigm to emerge, some sort of agreement on core definitions, key questions and common approaches must exist.[3] The four articles suggest that – at the time of their writing – no such paradigm existed. The authors do not work with a clear definition of crisis, they ask different questions, and toy with various approaches. At the same time, the articles provide tantalizing clues for conceptual and theoretical convergence.

The absence of a shared label for crisis is striking: the authors write about industrial crises, organizational crises, corporate crises and risky systems. The term 'industrial crisis' is an obvious product of its time: it became briefly popular in the 1980s when organization theorists (they were not alone here) worried about the harm large-scale organizations did to the environment (Bhopal and Chernobyl being the defining cases).[4] The terms 'organizational' and 'corporate' crises reflect a broader take on adverse effects produced by organizations (Tylenol and *Challenger* come into play). The discussion about 'risky systems' supersedes the organizational level all together: Perrow examines how society deals with dangerous technologies through the use of complex organizations.

It is clear that the authors did not share a definition of the phenomenon under study (from here on we will talk about the 'organizational crisis'). More specifically, the authors seem unsure how to define both the 'organizational' and the 'crisis' part of the phrase.

The term crisis is used in an oddly offhanded manner (Perrow does not use the term at all), as if everybody understands the word in the same way. Academics rarely agree on key terms, however, 'crisis' being no exception. The term crisis is most commonly used in reference to a period of discontinuity, during which the core values of a system (a small group, organization, town, society or the world) have come under threat. It is often assumed that such a threat requires the urgent reaction of leaders, who must make critical decisions under conditions of uncertainty (cf. Rosenthal, Charles and 't Hart, 1989; Rosenthal, Boin and Comfort, 2001). By using rather generic definitions, crisis researchers can study and compare such different phenomena as nuclear disasters, acts of terrorism, product recalls, mayhem on financial markets and devastating tsunamis.

Note that crisis is not defined in terms of outcomes: it is the destabilizing threat that is at the heart of the definition, not the damage that it caused. Moreover, crisis is defined in a subjectivist sense, as academics tend to speak of a crisis only when people (who exactly remains a matter of discussion) perceive an urgent threat. After all, it would be strange (but not impossible) to analyze a crisis nobody actually experienced.

All this saves the term for academic use. It is impractical at best to define crisis in terms of negative outcomes, if only because it is impossible to agree on the amount of damage (number of deaths; financial losses) 'required' to qualify some form of adversity as a crisis. If one wants to talk about outcomes, the much better defined concept of 'disaster' seems more appropriate.[5] Whether some form of adversity may be termed disastrous or not is, as disaster sociologists have come to agree, a matter of social construction (Bovens and 't Hart, 1996; Quarantelli, 1998; Quarantelli and Perry, 2005). Crisis is thus better not defined in terms of outcome.

The authors of the articles under review here do, of course, exactly that. Miller (1988: 65) offers a 'classification of industrial crises outcomes based on their effects' while Shrivastava et al. (1988: 285) discuss the '*harmful* effects of organizational activities.' What these authors are really talking about is organizational *failure*. Crisis is used as a synonym for *really bad* performance; it has very little to do with the crisis-as-challenge concept introduced above.

The authors also wrestle with the 'organizational' dimension of crisis. If one defines crisis in terms of threat to a system, an organizational crisis would be interpreted to revolve around some threat to the organization. The authors do this: they analyze the impact of faulty products (Tylenol and *Challenger*) on the organization, noting, for instance, the stress that crisis can cause within an organization. However, they seem even more concerned with the threat caused *by* organizations, a concern Perrow shares.

All this makes for confused reading. Three Mile Island is treated as a paradigmatic case, even though it hardly qualifies as an industrial crisis for it did not cause much 'damage to human life and/or the natural environment' (Shrivastava et al., 1988: 288). The Enron case would have a hard time qualifying as an industrial crisis, but 'cancer through smoking' apparently is (Shrivastava et al., 1988: 289). Mitroff, Pauchant and Shrivastava (1988) offer a very nice typology of corporate crises (based on causal dimensions), but it remains unclear to which organizational misadventures exactly the typology can be applied.

The confusion thickens as the authors ask (if only implicitly) different questions. Judging by the answers they seek to provide, we may surmise that the authors are interested in the *causes* of organizational crises, the *dynamics* of the crisis process, the *effects* of crisis (both inside and outside the organization), and the means of effectively *managing* the crisis. To be sure, these are all important questions. But they are best treated separately, as answers to each question typically require different theoretical approaches.

The absence of a uniform approach in these four articles is therefore not surprising. Without a clear definition of key variables and without a shared sense of what are the most relevant questions, the authors understandably engage in a largely a-theoretical, inductive search for a 'general theory of crisis management' (Mitroff, Pauchant and Shrivastava, 1988: 84). To accomplish just that, it will be necessary to book progress on these issues.

Fortunately, Perrow's article – bound to become a true classic – contains solutions to most if not all of these problems. These solutions are not explicitly formulated, for the article serves an altogether different purpose.[6] It is, however, possible to distill from Perrow's article a clear definition of the phenomenon to be explained, the questions to be asked, and the approach to be used. This will be done in the following sections. The resulting perspective, it is argued, provides an effective framework for understanding organizational crises.

Towards a systems approach of crisis dynamics

In his work on 'risky systems,' Perrow (1984) explores why and how organizational control of dangerous technologies breaks down occasionally. The crisis is the critical phase during which the operators of the technology begin to lose control, which typically evokes a frantic search for solutions. Three Mile Island is, once again, the illustration of choice: Perrow describes how Three Mile Island operators ran a race against the clock to save the power plant from nuclear meltdown (it is worth remembering here that they ultimately won that race. We will return to this point in the next Section).

Based on Perrow, we could define crisis as a breakdown of the organization's core technology, which requires an urgent response under conditions of deep uncertainty with regard to the causes and possible solutions of the problem at hand. Perrow is really only interested in organizations that deal with dangerous technology, but breakdown of core technology is a crisis for every organization (Thompson, 1967). Note that crisis is *not* defined in terms of consequences (be it for the environment or the organization itself). It is, of course, possible to do that: the Three Mile Island breakdown caused a crisis among frightened citizens and politicians; it caused a crisis for the nuclear industry (Baumgartner and Jones, 1993); and it damaged the reputation of Three Mile Island – but these are different types of crisis that should be distinguished from the organizational crisis under discussion here.[7]

Before we further explore Perrow's thoughts on the causes of organizational breakdown, we should see what the other articles bring to bear on the subject. It is true that the authors worked with different definitions and asked different questions, but they have intimate knowledge about organizational processes. They are students of organizational failure, so we can legitimately ask what they have to say on this topic.

The first thing we learn from these articles is that theories of organizational malperformance do not explain breakdowns of core technology. Miller's (1988) effort is illustrative in this regard. Drawing from his earlier work on organizational pathologies, Miller asserts that 'five types of sick organizations' are more prone to produce adverse outcomes (which he calls crises). There is a distinct tautological flavor to this argument, as he defines the various pathologies largely in terms of the organization's inability to create meaningful relations with its environment: organizations are 'sick' because they cannot adapt, a condition that lies at the heart of Miller's crisis. Moreover, it remains unclear how organizations develop these pathologies in the first place.

But Miller does have a point when he argues that, for a variety of reasons, some organizations cannot adapt to a changing environment. The underlying pathology is the continuous reliance on core technologies that were once the key to success; but it is this 'leaning' on proven formulas that sets the organization up for breakdown (we will return to this point).

Mitroff et al. (1988: 86) offer a nice figure that helps us to make an analytical distinction between causes of breakdown. A breakdown can be caused by internal or external factors, which may be classified in terms of technical-economic or social-organizational factors. Much of the article deals with two hypotheses that are not very relevant for our concern. Toward the end of the article, however, the authors produce – more or less out of nowhere – a 'preventative model of crises management' (ibid., p. 102). This model is really a model of crisis causation, as it displays the underlying thesis of their work: crises are the product of failed crisis management. In other words: crises occur – in fact, they are 'almost guaranteed' (Mitroff et al., 1988:105) – within an organization because the organization did not prevent them and suffered from 'failures of foresight.'

This latter phrase refers to Barry Turner's (1978) seminal work on organizations and crisis.[8] This work is often used to support the common misconception that 'nearly every potential crisis is thought to leave a repeated trail of early warning signals' (Mitroff et al., 1988: 104). The crisis is presented in this line of thinking as an ontological entity, something 'out there.' It is envisioned to produce barely audible signals that announce its impending arrival. If only organizations would pay attention! It is easy in hindsight, as both Perrow and Turner note, to reinterpret the ill-structured mess of crisis and depict it as a highway to failure. The real question, however, is not whether an organization can 'hear' a crisis coming, but whether it is possible to recognize a crisis once it has 'arrived.'

The article by Shrivastava et al. (1988) also refers to Turner's treatise. They repeat Turner's characterization of crisis as a process of escalation. Turner's thesis, which informed Perrow's theory on normal accidents, holds that crisis is the product of rather common errors or glitches that propagate through the organization. The errors cause other errors, which tap into yet other vulnerabilities. As the dominoes fall, it is a question of time before the critical technology of an organization begins to fail. One can see the complimentarity of Turner's arguments: the failure to detect and the escalatory nature of the process together explain how crises can consume an organization within a seemingly short period of time.

Unfortunately, both articles give short shrift to the underlying causes of organizational breakdown. Apparently under the assumption that big failures must have big causes, the authors collect and present a seemingly exhaustive shopping list of potential 'triggers' that can set the escalatory chain in motion.[9] Looking back at a crisis, these triggers usually can be found. The problem is, as Perrow (1994) points out, that the authors fail to check whether these triggers are present in organizations that did not suffer from similar breakdowns under similar circumstances.

Such a comparative exercise would show that the identified 'triggers' of crisis are ubiquitous in the great majority of organizations. Operator and managerial errors, policy failures, cost pressures, environmental shocks, faulty design, defective equipment – what organization is safe from these 'normal' factors? If crises, as Shrivastava *et al.* (1988: 287) claim, are 'almost inevitable' – which is a logical inference from the ubiquity argument – why do so few organizations suffer from catastrophic breakdown?

The answer is simple if somewhat mystifying: it takes 'just the right combination of circumstances to produce a catastrophe' (Perrow, 1994: 217). To understand why this is the case, we must return to Turner's theory of organizational breakdown and consider Perrow's elaboration of it.

Crisis as a 'normal' outcome of modern organization

Turner (1978) argues that the causes of organizational breakdown are found in the 'search for rationality' that is characteristic of modern organizations. As he tries to harness the dangerous potential of increasingly powerful technologies, Organization Man must build increasingly rational structures and processes. His capacity for rational design is limited, however. His rational structures will therefore produce unintended consequences, which are bound to go unnoticed because of the inherent impossibilities of information. The unintended consequences make use of the rational organization to propagate; the rational organization magnifies the errors into disaster.

Turner's theory presents us with a paradox: the causes of organizational breakdown lie in the efforts to build perfect organizations. Viewed from this perspective, it is not the 'sick' organization described by Miller that is most likely to produce a disaster, it is the modern and efficient organization that demands our attention. Disastrous breakdowns, Turner tells us, require organizing ability (Turner and Pidgeon, 1997: 151):

> Accidents are produced, then, by failures of intent, by errors [. . .]
> Errors are only likely to develop into large-scale accidents or disasters
> if they occur in an organizational decision hierarchy or power hier-
> archy at a point at which they are likely to be magnified, and possibly
> to be compounded with other smaller errors, by the operation of the

normal administrative processes. They are most likely to produce large-scale accidents, that is to say, if they are linked with the negentropic tendencies of an organization or of a cluster of organizations, so as to become major 'anti-tasks' which the organization then inadvertently executes.

In his classic *Normal Accidents*, Perrow (1984) illuminates the argument by introducing the concepts of complexity and tight coupling. The more complex an organization, its core technology and their interactions become, the harder it is for operators (who are the most knowledgeable with regard to the technology) to understand the system. Operators are bound to misinterpret small 'glitches' and may initiate remedial actions that fuel rather than dampen the emerging crisis. If an organization is also tightly coupled, the misunderstood errors travel rapidly throughout the organizational system. Together, Perrow argues, complexity and tight coupling make for 'normal accidents' (cf. Turner, 1978).

This line of thinking suggests an 'inexorable systemic logic in industrial societies that makes crises almost inevitable' (Shrivastava *et al.*, 1988: 286). As Western societies are becoming ever more complex and tightly coupled (think of globalization or the use of new technologies), we would expect more breakdowns to occur. There is precious little evidence to support this expectation, however.[10] If anything, modern technology seems to become *safer*. So why do some organizations suffer 'normal' breakdowns whereas many others do not?

Richer is safer, explains Wildavsky (1988). Wealthy organizations and societies can afford slack in their systems; moreover, they can afford to experiment and learn from mistakes. Rich organizations and societies have become more resilient over time, which compensates for the unintended consequences of complexity and tight coupling. Perrow (1994: 213) scoffs at this notion, but does not refute it.

This brings us to the question of crisis management: could it be that organizations learn to deal with complexity and tight coupling? Have they found ways to discover emerging crises in time? Have they perhaps learned to 'de-couple' organizational systems (cf. Nutt, 2004)? Have organizations learned to become reliable?

Implications for crisis management

Mitroff, Pauchant and Shrivastava (1988: 105) think there might be 'certain kinds of "action portfolios" that organizations can engage in or undertake to lower their potential susceptibility to [. . .] crises'.[11] This makes sense. If an organization is confronted with multiple occurrences of similar crisis types, one may expect that organization to develop an 'action portfolio.' In fact, an organization must learn if it is to survive (an organization can only handle so many crises). At the same time, we know that organizations are 'bad learners' – the barriers against learning are tremendous (Argyris and Schön, 1978).

Perrow does not believe organizations can do anything to prevent breakdowns or control their consequences. His theory is predicated on precisely this assumption: modern technology cannot be understood and to think we can is what makes it all the more dangerous. NAT, Perrow (1994: 213) repeats, is 'bleakly explicit on this account: while it is better to try hard than not, because of system characteristics *trying hard will not be enough*' (emphasis added).

How about all those organizations that have dealt with dangerous technology for years without any major accidents? Take, for instance, the U.S. nuclear defense system (studied by Sagan (1993) and the subject of Perrow's review (1994)). Despite all the blunders, near-misses, and the described lack of intention to learn, this system has not produced the disaster that NAT predicts it should have experienced. To this example we can add the collection of shoddy nuclear power plants in eastern Europe, the ever-expanding air traffic, transportation of dangerous goods through mega-cities – the list can be long.

Perrow (1994) offers three answers: coincidence, time and academic incompetence. In discussing the US nuclear defense system, Perrow gives us several incredible examples of accidents – the bear and the test tape stand out – that we are led to believe *nearly* caused a nuclear war. But as was the case with Three Mile Island, these accidents did not blow up the world. This is pure coincidence, Perrow wants us to believe. Luck may have saved the day, but it cannot save a theory.

His second argument addresses long records of safety that at least some organizations can defend. Just wait, says Perrow (1994: 32), 'we simply have not given [these systems] a reasonable amount of time to disclose [their] potential.' Something bad will happen in due course. But how long should we wait? Any prediction is good without a time limit, so how do we test this theory?

His third argument takes the form of an attack on 'B-school' academics who study reliable organizations with long track records of safety. Perrow (1994: 215) wonders whether these organizations are 'distinctive' or 'even complexly interactive and tightly coupled.' In other words, HRT scholars have not done their homework. He may be right that some of these HROs are not complex and tightly coupled (Marais, Dulac and Leveson, 2004). That leaves us wondering, however, about the general applicability of NAT: which organizations, then, *are* complex and tightly coupled (apart from nuclear power plants)?

This 'B-school' – made up of the scholars who have parented High Reliability Theory (HRT) – attracts Perrow's scorn and drives his line of argumentation. The HRT scholars observed a small set of organizations with excellent safety records, trying to find out what is different about these organizations. They found that these reliable organizations are set apart from other organizations by a pervasive safety culture, which nurtures a common awareness of potential vulnerabilities ('it can happen to us') and a particular organizational mode.[12]

What makes HRT scholars 'optimists' is their – implicitly formulated – belief that this safety culture is amenable to design efforts. A well-entrenched organizational culture is indeed, at least partly, the outcome of consistent management efforts – this is a well-documented finding in the institutional strand of organization research (see for instance Perrow, 1986). Organization leaders can make their organization more reliable, HRT scholars argue, by importing the elements of a safety culture and by bringing the organizational structure in line with such a culture (Weick and Sutcliffe, 2002).

Perrow will have none of this, dismissing both the importance of culture and the potential role of leaders (and, we might add, his own earlier work). He is especially critical of the organizational solutions proposed by the high reliable school. In order to cope with complexity and tight coupling, organizations must centralize (to de-couple) and decentralize (to understand what's going on) – 'they can't do both' (Perrow, 1994: 214). But they can according to Weick (1987). Organizations centralize by instilling core values (safety for instance) in their employees, which allows for a substantial degree of lower-level discretion. This is, of course, precisely what HROs do. The most impressive characteristic of the HRO is its dominant safety culture, which guides the employees in the use of their decisional freedom (a result of decentralization).

Perrow (1994: 215) also dismisses the notion that redundancy may limit the vulnerability of complex and tightly coupled systems: 'adding redundancy can inadvertently cause an accident.' That may be true (Rijpma, 1997). But redundancy also makes a system more loosely coupled. Perrow cannot have his cake and eat it too: tight coupling is either important or not. If tightly coupled and loosely coupled systems are both vulnerable to breakdown, the coupling factor does not explain anything. The strength of NAT would be severely undermined.

Perrow (1994: 212) sees no constructive role for organizational leaders, in which he has absolutely no confidence. These 'elites increasingly populate the earth with risky systems' and cause a 'sharply rising number of male-made disasters.' Here we arrive at the base line of Perrow's vision: modern, large-scale organizations and the elites that run them are bad. If nothing bad happened yet, don't hold your breath – it will. If nothing happens when it should have – Perrow (1999) forecasted the breakdown of the US electrical grid system as a result of Y2k problems – it is coincidence.

Aspiring optimists should thus look somewhere else to understand the relation between organizational characteristics and performance. Interestingly, Perrow does offer a way forward by introducing a set of error-inducing factors that increase the vulnerability of organizations. This suggests some sort of contingency model, which juxtaposes the organizational culture of an organization with the environment of that organization. An organization that is set in an error-inducing environment and combines dangerous technology with a 'culture of sloppy management' (Turner, 1978) is, we could then hypothesize, much more likely to experience devastating breakdowns than its well-managed counterpart that happens to exist in a safety-inducing environment. This line of thinking could perhaps restart the stalled debate between NAT and HRT scholars.

It is on this optimist–pessimist dimension that the papers under review diverge rather widely. All authors seem propelled by a desire to understand the causes and dynamics of organizational crises. Most authors seem to share the idea that 'complete prevention is impossible' (Mitroff, Pauchant and Shrivastava 1988: 102). They believe that whatever organizations do, something unforeseen will happen that causes a dangerous breakdown. They have a point, if only because Mother Nature can undo whatever safety devices managers have designed. What sets Perrow apart from the rest, however, is his resistance against any efforts to improve organizational safety. If a paradigm of organizational crisis is to emerge, this sense of unwarranted pessimism should make no part of it.

All articles under review here provide building blocks – some bigger than others – for the construction of such a paradigm. The discussion of these articles makes clear, however, that more building blocks are needed. The concluding section will point toward promising research strands that may help to produce additional insights.

Prospects for future research

To judge an emerging field of inquiry by discussing four articles (selected by others than yourself) is a risky affair in itself. To provide some added value for the reader, the reviewer must juggle definitions and concepts, highlight findings that the authors may never have intended as such, and create a debate that never existed between the original authors. At the same time, we may argue that this discovery of common ground is what characterizes an emerging paradigm. In this review, we have explored the common ground with regard to organizational crisis – arbitrarily defined here as a breakdown of core technology.

Two questions have clearly inspired the authors of all four articles. First, they seek to find out the causes and dynamics of organizational crisis. Second, they explore what organizations can do to cope with these crises. The authors give us different answers, as we have seen above. Let us now see what type of research may help to expand the common ground these authors and others share.

Charles Perrow's normal accident theory captures how most organization theorists picture breakdowns. In all articles, one can find the references to vulnerable systems in which an escalatory process of breakdown is triggered. In fact, these dynamics can be found in other systems as well. Financial crises are described in terms of vulnerabilities, triggers, complexity and tight coupling (see for instance Eichengreen, 2002). Prison riots have similar dynamics (Boin and Rattray, 2004). So there appears to be agreement that organizational crises occur after vulnerable systems are triggered into some spiral of adverse dynamics.

The problem appears to be that anything can serve as a trigger: human error, faulty equipment, a faulty payment or, in the case of prison riots, a small fight between two inmates. The triggers that are often identified after a crisis are so ubiquitous in most organizations that do not suffer from crises that they cannot really explain anything. In fact, it appears that analysts are prone to 'discover' these triggers in hindsight as they try to construct a convincing narrative of the crisis (Baumgartner and Jones, 1993).

Vulnerability does not explain much either. Many complex and tightly coupled systems do not suffer breakdowns and 'survive' environments that seem decidedly 'error inducing.' In fact, simple and loosely coupled systems in friendly environments have also been known to suffer breakdowns. The crucial issue, I suspect, is rapid migration: organizations break down after a rapid increase in vulnerability which they are unprepared to handle. We must find out what drives this migration process. Answers are most likely to be found in the interaction between error-inducing factors and the coping strategies of organization.

Complexity theory may well provide the framework for such a type of analysis.[13] This rapidly growing body of theoretical work investigates why complex systems develop toward what is called 'the edge of chaos,' a vulnerable state that may easily and rapidly escalate into decline. Part of the answer, as we may also surmise from the work under review, is that the most vulnerable states tend to be the most productive states for complex systems. Systems may have an inbuilt tendency to develop an optimal balance between their internal configurations and their environment; in order to maintain that balance, systems must continuously correct small deviations in that balance. A powerful source of disintegration, as Miller (1988) points out, may then be the unfounded reliance of proven success formulas. The same mechanisms that feed cycles of success may come to fuel spirals of decline.

A second question that guided this review asks what organizations can do to prepare for inevitable breakdown. The debate between NAT and HRT writers has been spirited (to say the least) and informative. However, we should be careful not to limit future research to the parameters set forth in this debate. The crucial question is not whether organizations can prevent crises or at least nip them in the bud. Surely, we must explore whether the precepts of reliable management can explain why some organizations perform better in this regard than others. Empirical research is scant on both accounts, a situation that favors style over substance.

The question that has gained relevance in recent times pertains to organizational resilience: why do some organizations 'bounce back' in the face of a crisis, whereas others succumb to the forces of adversity? The little empirical and theoretical research that is available (Freeman, Hirschhorn and Maltz, 2004) suggests that the same factors that explain the institutional strength of an organization also explain its capacity to survive crises. To complicate matters, these same 'success' factors appear to make organizations vulnerable to crisis. Much work, in short, remains to be done.

This volume of articles provides a welcome source of inspiration for academics who wish to pursue this research agenda. Additional perspectives are needed, however. Moreover, the theories forwarded in these articles must be tested in empirical research that compares both failed and failure-free organizations (in both the public and private sectors). The combination between multidisciplinary and empirical research holds the biggest promise for a paradigm of organizational crisis studies.

Notes

1   At the time, the field of organizational crisis management was 'still in its infancy' (Mitroff, Pauchant and Shrivastava 1988: 106). Elsewhere I have argued that the field of crisis management (still) does not exist, even though recent developments certainly seem to move in that direction (Boin, 2004).

2   In this chapter, we will continue to distinguish between the three articles on industrial crisis and Perrow's discussion piece.

3   Compare with similar discussions in the field of disaster studies (Quarantelli, 1998; Quarantelli and Perry, 2005).

4   The popularity of the term is illustrated by the fate of the journal *Industrial Crisis Quarterly*, which Shrivastava launched in the mid-1980s. It has been renamed several times since and is now published as *Organization and Environment*.

5   Note that in the abstract of their article, Shrivastava *et al.* define crises as 'organizationally-based *disasters* which cause extensive damage and social disruption' (emphasis added).

6   Perrow's article is part of a symposium on Scott Sagan's (1993) *The Limits of Safety*, in which Sagan contrasts Perrow's (1984) normal accident theory with high reliability theory. Other contributors to the symposium were Todd LaPorte, Gene Rochlin and Scott Sagan. The articles by these other authors are recommended reading.

7   We could label the other crises as 'societal', 'institutional' (Boin and 't Hart, 2000) and 'reputational' (Booth, 2000).

8   See also the symposium on the occasion of the publication of the second and revised edition (Turner and Pidgeon, 1997), which appeared in the *Journal of Contingencies and Crisis Management* (1997).

9   Mitroff, Pauchant and Shrivastava (1988: 89) provide a clear example of big crisis-big cause thinking: 'The primary cause of the Challenger failure was a defective O-ring, i.e. a defective technical part. But the underlying cause of failure was a faulty, defective organization.' This is a gross simplification, which is not supported by careful analysis (Vaughan, 1996).

10   Perrow (1994) discusses this issue in the afterword and postscript to the second edition of *Normal Accidents*.

11   Mitroff's subsequent work has been devoted to helping organizations develop these 'action portfolios' (see f.i. Mitroff, 2003).

12   For an excellent summary of this work, see Weick and Sutcliffe (2002).

13   For an introduction to complexity theory, see Axelrod and Cohen (2000).

References

Argyris, C. and Schön, D. (1978) *Organizational Learning: A theory of action perspective*, Addison Wesley: Reading.

Axelrod, R. and Cohen, M. D. (2000) *Harnessing Complexity: Organizational Implications of a Scientific Frontier*, Basic Books: New York.

Baumgartner, F. R. and Jones, B. D. (1993) *Agendas and Instability in American Politics*, University of Chicago Press: Chicago.

Boin, R. A. (2004) 'Lessons from Crisis Research', *International Studies Review*, Vol. 6, pp. 165–174.

Boin, R. A. and 't Hart, P. (2000) 'Institutional Crises and Reforms in Policy Sectors', in H. Wagenaar (ed.) *Government Institutions: Effects, Changes and Normative Foundations*, Kluwer Academic Publishers: Boston, pp. 9–31.

Boin, R. A. and Lagadec, P. (2000) 'Preparing for the Future: Critical Challenges in Crisis Management', *Journal of Contingencies and Crisis Management*, Vol. 8, No. 4, pp. 185–191.

Boin, R. A. and Rattray, W. A. R. (2004) 'Understanding Prison Riots: Towards a threshold theory', *Punishment & Society*, Vol. 6, No. 1, January, pp. 47–65.

Booth, S. (2000) 'How Can Organizations Prepare for Reputational Crises?', *Journal of Contingencies and Crisis Management*, Vol. 8, No. 4, pp. 197–207.

Bovens, M. and 't Hart, P. (1996) *Understanding Policy Fiascoes*, Transaction: London.

Eichengreen, B. (2002) *Financial Crises and What to do about Them*, Oxford University Press: Oxford.

Freeman, S. F., L. Hirschhorn and M. Maltz (2004) *Organizational resilience and moral purpose*, Sandler O'Neill & Partners, L. P. in the aftermath of September 11, 2001 (working paper).

Marais, K., Dulac, N. and Leveson, N. (2004) 'Beyond Normal Accidents and High Reliability Organizations: The Need for an Alternative Approach to Safety in

Complex Systems', paper presented at the Engineering Systems Division Symposium, MIT, Cambridge, March 29–31.

Miller, D. (1988) 'Organizational Pathology and Industrial Crisis', *Industrial Crisis Quarterly*, Vol. 2, pp. 65–74.

Mitroff, I. (2003) *Crisis Leadership: Planning for the Unthinkable*, John Wiley: Hoboken, NJ.

Mitroff, I., Pauchant, T. and Shrivastava, P. (1988) 'The Social Structure of Man-made organizational crises: Conceptual and Empirical Issues in the Development of a General Theory of Crisis Management', *Technological Forecasting and Social Change*, Vol. 33, pp. 83–107.

Nutt, P. C. (2004) 'Organizational De-development', *Journal of Management Studies*, Vol. 41, No. 7, pp. 1083–1103.

Perrow, C. (1984) *Normal Accidents: Living with High-risk Systems*, Basic Books: New York.

Perrow, C. (1986) *Complex Organizations* (third edition), Random House: New York.

Perrow, C. (1994) 'The Limits of Safety: The Enhancement of a Theory of Accidents', *Journal of Contingencies and Crisis Management*, Vol. 2, No. 4, pp. 212–220.

Quarantelli, E. L. (ed.) (1998) *What is a Disaster? Perspectives on the Question*, London: Routledge.

Quarantelli, E. L. and Perry, R. W. (eds) (2005) *What is a Disaster? New Answers to Old Questions*, Xlibris Press: Philadelphia.

Rijpma, J. A. (1997) 'Complexity, Tight-coupling and Reliability: Connecting Normal Accidents Theory and High Reliability Theory', *Journal of Contingencies and Crisis Management*, Vol. 5, No. 1, pp. 15–23.

Rosenthal, U., Boin, R. A. and Comfort, L. (eds) (2001) *Managing Crises: Threats, Dilemmas, Opportunities*, Charles C. Thomas: Springfield, IL.

Rosenthal, U., Charles, M. T. and 't Hart, P. (eds) (1989) *Coping with Crises: The Management of Disasters, Riots and Terrorism*, Charles C. Thomas: Springfield, IL.

Sagan, S. D. (1993) *The Limits of Safety: Organizations, Accidents and Nuclear Weapons*, Princeton University Press: Princeton.

Shrivastava, P., Mitroff, I., Miller, D. and Miglani, A. (1988) 'Understanding Industrial Crises', *Journal of Management Studies*, Vol. 25, No. 4, pp. 285–303.

Sills, D., Wolf, C. and Shelanski, V. (eds) (1981) *The Accident at Three Mile Island: The Human Dimension*, Westview Press: Boulder.

Thompson, J. D. (1967) *Organizations in Action: Social Science Bases of Administrative Theory*, McGraw-Hill: New York.

Turner, B. A. (1978) *Man-made Disasters*, Wykeham: London.

Turner, B. A. and Pidgeon, N. F. (1997) *Man-made Disasters* (second edition), Butterworth-Heinemann: London.

Vaughan, D. (1996) *The Challenger Launch Decision*, The Chicago University Press: Chicago.

Weick, K. E. (1987) 'Organizational Culture as a Source of High Reliability', *California Management Review*, Vol. 29, No. 2, pp. 112–127.

Weick, K. E. and Sutcliffe, K. M. (2002) *Managing the Unexpected: Assuring High Performance in an Age of Complexity*, Jossey Bass: San Francisco.

Wildavsky, A. (1988) *Searching for Safety*, Transaction Books: New Brunswick.

Modelling the crisis management process

Chapter 7

Denis Smith

MODELLING THE CRISIS MANAGEMENT PROCESS: APPROACHES AND LIMITATIONS

Introduction

THERE ARE A NUMBER of 'frameworks' that can be used to analyze the various stages of a crisis and some of the more relevant ones are included within this section. Whilst each framework has considerable merits, it is the potential overlap between them that surfaces important issues for research and practice. Invariably, the manner in which we conceptualize the various processes that underpin crises will be important in helping to shape our understanding of the ways in which crises emerge and evolve. Each of the various frameworks offered within the wider literature approach the processes by which crises are generated in different ways. Some simply focus on the 'operational' phase of the crisis and neglect causal processes, whilst others take a more holistic approach. However, it is our view that it is important to ensure that the various phases of a crisis are considered in a more 'holistic manner'; as a failure to take account of the range of causal, operational and crisis recovery issues will severely curtail the overall effectives of the process. A narrow focus on the development of contingency plans within the operational phase of a crisis, for example, may inhibit wider attempts at crisis prevention and restrict crisis management to a narrow 'business recovery' approach. Such a restricted view of crisis is inherently problematic, both practically and theoretically (Smith, 1990, 1995). One outcome of an operational focus is that managers often fail to see how their actions can generate the conditions in which contingency plans can be bypassed. The development of such plans and their associated structural responses, without reference to the broader set of psycho-social, cultural and systems-based issues within the organization, will fail to address the core problem of crisis incubation.

Within such a reactive approach to dealing with crisis, managers can easily become the 'authors of their own misfortune' and create the conditions in which crises (often at lower, more operational, levels) can develop. It will be these crises that 'management' will subsequently have to manage.

The question remains as to why organizations have shown such an unwillingness, or inability, to address such latent problems (Reason, 1997). It is our view that there are several barriers within organizations that conspire to create problems associated with a wider recognition of such latent errors, and each of the papers included in this section address different elements of this process. These barriers can be considered to exist at several levels and we need to consider them in more detail.

Barriers and constraints in crisis management

The first set of barriers, those dealing with problems around the individual, can be classified as a set of psycho-social issues relating to perception, assumptions, core beliefs and a range of psychological processes that shape behaviour (Ackroyd and Thompson, 1999; Dixon, 1976; Rasmussen, 1982, 1983; Reason, 1990c; Vaughan, 1999). In addition, the difficulties that people have in perceiving the nature of the problems that they face can severely inhibit their abilities to 'make sense' of the situation (Weick, 1988, 1993, 1995), thus increasing the risk of error.

The second set of barriers operate at the cultural and group level of the organization. They reflect the wider set of issues around the ways that the organization works, the behaviour of groups within a specific organizational setting and the role that management style can play in the creation of cultural norms and behaviours (Esser and Lindoerfer, 1989; Janis, 1982, 1989; Smith, 2000b; Vaughan, 1997).

The final set of barriers exist at the systems level and include a range of structural and environmental pressures and constraints that impact upon the organization at various points in space and time (Fortune and Peters, 1994, 1995, 2005; Gladwell, 2000; Mintzberg, 1983; Perrow, 1984; Turner, 1976, 1978). The systems level barriers also include issues around complexity and its impact upon management (Murray, 1998; Ortegon-Monroy, 2003) and technology (Chiles, 2002; Smith, 2000a; Tenner, 1996).

Taken together, these issues can form powerful barriers to the early recognition of crisis potential within an organization, but they also provide points at which change can be made to deal with the strategic implications of crises. The various papers included in this section of the book offer different perspectives on these elements and each paper presents a broad framework within which to consider many of the core processes around crisis generation and management. However, several caveats need to be made at this point around our abilities to set crisis processes within a conceptual 'framework'.

The choice of the term framework here is an attempt to highlight the difficulties that exist in modelling crisis. A 'model' should have a degree of predictive validity built into it and should also provide a guiding framework for management that allows them to deal with future threats at certain points in time. It is difficult to ague that there are sufficiently robust 'models' available to us within the field of crisis management at the present time. At best, it could be argued that we have frameworks within which to consider the processes that are at work. There are several reasons for this which need to be examined in more detail.

Theoretical limitations around crisis frameworks

First, most research in this area has been undertaken by post-hoc crisis evaluation. Many of the 'events' studied have largely been of such a scale as to attract a considerable amount of external attention. This has been largely a result of the difficulties that exist in gaining access to information from organizations, mainly due to the inherent sensitivity surrounding crises. Crises that result in public inquiries or accident investigations have generated a considerable amount of published information that can be analyzed by researchers. Examples of such crises include: the loss of the space shuttles Challenger and Columbia (Esser and Lindoerfer, 1989; Heimann, 1993; Moorhead, Ference and Neck, 1991; Nelson, 2001; Vaughan, 1997, 1999), problems around BSE ('mad cow' disease) (Atkins and Bowler, 2001; Collee and Bradley, 1997; Dormont, 2002; Little, 2001; Pennington, 2003), the accident at Bhopal (Hazarika, 1987; Lapierre and Moro, 2002; Shrivastava, 1987), and the terrorist attacks of September 11th 2001 (Chomsky, 2001, 2003; Greenberg, 2002; Halliday, 2002; Holtz *et al.*, 2003; Kendra and Wachtendorf, 2003; Posner, 2003). Unfortunately, this means that much of the theoretical development has been based upon the processes that surround severe cases or extreme events rather than more 'normal' forms of adverse events that can result in crises for organizations.

This takes us into our second major constraint. Given the fact that much of the research to date has been based upon such 'extreme' events, some questions remain as to how much predictive validity these frameworks might have. Of particular importance here are the processes through which 'events' and incidents escalate – an issue identified by Handy (Handy, 1994, 1995) as the 'point(s) of inflection' (see also, Smith, 2006, this volume). This process of 'managing ahead of the curve' (Smith, 2006) remains a significant challenge to management theory, practice and research. It also raises a significant problem in trying to observe the behaviour of organizations prior to the onset of a crisis. It can be argued, for example, that organizational behaviours can change during a crisis. This may be a result of the changing task demands of the event, but also as a consequence of a range of potential culpability issues that might cause people to hide their actions as an incident escalates into a crisis. Because of the obvious difficulties associated with identifying potential organizations for research and getting access prior to a crisis, much of our current theoretical understandings are based upon retrospective analysis. There are some exceptions to this, with the work of Mitroff and Pauchant (Mitroff *et al.*, 1989; Pauchant and Mitroff, 1992) serving as a good example.

Third, the literature has, in some cases been developed within 'disciplinary' or even 'national silos'. Several important strands of research have been developed within the disciplines of sociology, psychology (including human factors and ergonomics), engineering and management. Given the diverse nature of this work (which could all be covered by the label 'crisis management') it is important to recognize that some theoretical frameworks proposed within the literature may not draw upon the wider pool of findings that is available across the various disciplines. A related issue also concerns that body of research which is undertaken within the various 'sectoral' contexts and also across the public-private sector divide. Again, there are potential problems around the validity of findings in one situational context (including the various spatial and temporal settings of the research) and another. There are some situational contexts, for example, in which the findings of research, or the elements of good practice, may not be perceived as being relevant to others, even though there are valid reasons for the comparison (one example might be taking lessons from health care and applying them to practices in the nuclear industry). However, we would argue that there is considerable learning potential that exists across the various disciplinary, cultural, and sector boundaries.

Finally, a barrier can be seen to exist around some of the core assumptions that are built into the various disciplinary perspectives and theories. For example, management theory has, until recently, struggled to take account of the incubation of crises and has simply seen such events as failures in performance (largely at the level of the individual), rather than as a failure of the main theories used to describe organizational activities and processes. An example of this is the notion of 'organizational misbehaviour', where some authors have noted that misbehaviours are normal facets of organizational life and should not be seen simply as deviant activities (Ackroyd and Thompson, 1999). However, there is a growing awareness that management – as both a theoretical perspective and a form of praxis – can create a set of conditions in which the potential for failure can become embedded in procedures and protocols. Put another way, managers can become the authors of their own misfortune.

These issues create a context in which it has proved difficult for organizations and managers therein, to conceptualize and act upon the various precursors to crisis. As a consequence, attention has been focused on the task demands that are generated by crises as they 'emerge' and this has been represented in terms of the structural and contingency responses required by organizations. The papers presented here represent a different perspective on this 'contingency' approach as they seek to move beyond contingency planning and formulate a more strategic perspective on crisis management. It is against this background that we need to consider the papers included in this section.

Crisis 'models' as frameworks for analysis

This particular section of the book brings together several research contributions to our understanding of the nature of the crisis process. Each of the papers presented here represent a different perspective on the problems around crises and, taken as a whole, offer considerable opportunities for making connections across the frameworks that are proposed by the various authors. The rationale for bringing these papers together in this volume was that, taken as a whole, they offer important insights into the strategic nature of the crisis management process and, more importantly, on the ways in which strategic processes can 'incubate' crisis potential. The papers recognize the importance of both the creation of crisis potential and the subsequent development of response strategies as important and interlinked strategic processes. In addition, much of the work reproduced here also recognizes the significance of organizational learning as a means of both feeding information back into the strategy process around crisis prevention and response, and also challenging the core assumptions and beliefs of senior managers.

One of the early seminal papers in this area was the work undertaken by Turner (Turner, 1976, 1978) who argued that organizations can 'incubate' the potential for crisis as a function of relatively routine management processes. Turner argued that a series of factors would shape the precautionary norms that an organization seeks to put into place to control its activities. These norms and assumptions may well lead to a gap between the task demands generated by a 'crisis' (Turner used the phrase 'man-made disaster') and the controls that were in place. It was this gap between assumptions and controls and, what can be described as 'emergent' properties within a crisis, that generated the incubation potential for crisis. What Turner also identified was the central role of 'management' (in its various guises) as a key factor in shaping the conditions within which existing defenses can also be eroded. He highlighted the strategic nature of 'crisis' and pointed to the manner in which decisions taken elsewhere within the organization can help to shape the emergence of a crisis. Turner was also amongst the first to recognize the importance of organizational learning (which he termed 'full cultural readjustment') within crisis management. He saw learning as a means of helping to prevent future problems by challenging and changing core assumptions, beliefs and values, and helping to improve early warning detection. Turner and Toft's paper (this volume) moves Turner's early thinking forward and develops this discussion around organizational learning. Both papers need to be linked together in order to see Turner's arguments in a more holistic way. There is little doubt that the relationship between learning and incubation is a key area for both theory and precipice and managers need to pay close attention to the range of potential barriers that exist in many organizations (see Smith, 2001; Smith and Elliott, 2005). Turner's contribution to the crisis literature should not be underestimated (Pidgeon, 1998; Weick, 1998) and his initial work can be seen to have influenced a significant amount of subsequent research in the field.

The strategic dimension of crisis is also highlighted in the work of Mitroff and Pauchant (Mitroff *et al.*, 1989; Pauchant and Mitroff 1992). Their research has been important in terms of our conceptualization of the crisis-prone and crisis-prepared organization and the multi-layered processes around which crises become generated. Their work builds upon the work of Turner by maintaining the strategic focus of the crisis management process and by extending the incubation metaphor into the notion of a crisis-prone organization.

They argued that it is possible to look at an organization by using the metaphor of an onion, with the various layers offering new insights into the way in which the entity is constructed. Because the outer layers of the onion are the most visible, we would tend to focus more of our attention on this layer but we also need to recognize the important contribution that the inner layers make. In organizational terms, we all too often focus attention on the easily observed and measure facets of the organization and may fail to take account of the more subtle and deep-seated processes that give shape to these outer layers. In proposing their 'onion model', they argue that the outer layer could be considered as an organization's strategy and planning processes, as these would be clearly visible though published plans and procedures. These plans are normally accessible to those outside of the organization and are often used in the aftermath of a crisis event to judge performance against 'intention'. An organization that has developed a strategy for dealing with the potential for crisis, will have formalized its procedures and protocols in such a way that they should be accessible by those staff who need to work within the organization's strategic frameworks. Any external assessment of an organization's capabilities would invariably focus attention on these plans. The next level of activity within the 'onion' would be expressed in terms of the structural approaches that the organization has taken to ensure that its strategy can be implemented. These structural procedures include the nature and role of crisis management teams along with a range of specialist units. The creation of such teams will be dependent upon the nature of the organization's core activities and processes. For example, the oil, gas and chemical industries might require specialist oil spill response teams or chemical spill teams and these would be built into the emergency plans for the organization. Other elements of structure would reflect the different task demands faced by each organization and would include strategic business units, subsidiary companies and the like (Mintzberg, 1983; Perrow, 1961, 1967). The structure that an organization has will also determine the ways in which information flows are dealt with and may impact upon the effectiveness of communication and decision-making (Fortune and Peters, 1994, 1995, 2005). In terms of their crisis response teams, many organizations work on a three-tier system (based upon the Bronze-Silver-Gold command structure used within the emergency services). This is represented as the various incident management teams, the 'liaison' group and the crisis team, with the latter being the team that considers the strategic-level issues facing the organization as a result of the crisis (Smith, 2000b, 2004).

Taken together these outer two layers of the 'onion' represent the most common organizational approaches to dealing with the management of crises – namely, structural and contingency responses. Too many organizations, however, believe that by dealing with these outer layers they would be satisfying the main requirements of crisis management. Mitroff and Pauchant argue that the innermost layers of the 'onion' represent extremely powerful and yet often-neglected elements of organizations – namely, assumptions and the core beliefs and values of senior managers. These two inner layers also reflect the earlier work of Turner, especially around the importance of assumptions in creating gaps in controls (strategy and structure). The issue of core beliefs and values also raises issues around the relationship between the 'ethical' approach of the organization and its crisis prone nature – an area that has not been widely researched within the literature (Smith and Tombs, 1995; Tombs and Smith, 1995).

It is the interaction between the various levels of an onion that will determine the organization's crisis prone or crisis prepared nature. By focusing on the outer layers without considering the impact of the central core, organizations risk generating a dislocated strategy for managing crises and one that may lead to the failure of their contingency plans when implemented. In addition, the focus on the outer core of the onion may also allow for the incubation of a crisis, especially given the important role that assumptions play in the findings of Turner's work.

In order to address some of these issues, Mitroff and Pauchant have attempted to develop instruments that can be used to categorize an organization within a crisis prone/prepared continuum. Whilst such instruments invariably bring problems of interpretation with them, the potential that such an approach offers for an audit framework remains an interesting area for further investigation.

The paper by Smith (Smith, 1990) sets out a framework for conceptualizing the process of crisis management. Crisis management can be seen here as an interrelated process of prevention, response and recovery that can extend over considerable periods of time (see Figure 1). In order to shift the focus away from the contingency approaches to crisis, this paper argues that there are two other important phases that need to be considered along with the 'operational crisis'. These are the 'crisis of management' and the 'crisis of legitimation'. Each of these phases is interconnected and the notion of crisis incubation is seen as a long standing and continuous process. The core of this paper centres on the manner in which a crisis can escalate, an issue that has been developed further in subsequent work (Smith, 2005) and the early notion of the interconnected nature of crises (Sipika and Smith, 1993; Smith, 1995; Smith and Sipika, 1993). The links between the various phases of a crisis and the evolution of crises across the timeline has been likened to 'pathways of vulnerability' (Smith, 2000a; Smith, 2005).

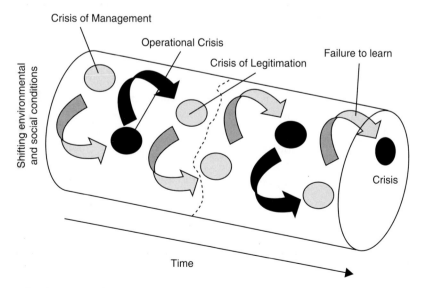

Figure 1 The notion of a crisis timeline involving the three phases of crisis management

The first phase of this framework, the crisis of management, represents that period in which the potential for a crisis becomes 'incubated'. This phase addresses the strategic and systems-level issues that can generate problems for organizations at the more functional and operational levels of activity. The important elements here can be seen to be around communication, culture and decision-making processes and the ways in which these factors generate vulnerability. It is in this phase that the potential is developed that would allow an incident or an accident to escalate into a more serious event. This process has been termed 'tight coupling' and 'interactive complexity' by Perrow and reflects the speed of interaction between elements and the complex emergence of failure (Perrow, 1984). Perrow argues that such failures are designed into the system and often represent the 'normal' way of working. Much of this potential for failure is created as a function of attempts at making the organization more efficient (through 'just in time' processes, for example) or by the extended nature of its supply chains. Similarly, the failure of management to respond to incidents in an effective manner could allow an initial event to develop quickly into a crisis. The processes through which this escalation can occur are dealt with at several points in this collection. The main issues for consideration within this initial phase of the process include: the role of management in the generation of errors lower down the organization, weaknesses in the management structure, constrained decision-making and communication, and the problems that arise as a result of the interaction between the organization and its environment. These issues will ultimately be reflected in the failures of contingency planning to address the scope and scale of the problems that face the organization in the operational phase of the crisis.

The second phase of the framework – the operational crisis – takes place when the event escalates to such a point that damage is caused or the reputation of the organization becomes threatened. In some larger organizations, this phase is often formally triggered when a senior manager determines that the event has the potential to damage the reputation of the group or the main parent company of the various business units (Smith, 2000b, 2004). This phase of a crisis is also inevitably the most visible, due to the damage that is being caused. By and large, this damage requires that an additional level of resource is brought to bear in order to contain the demands of the events, and, eventually, to return them to 'normal'. This phase is also characterized by the role of external agencies – often acting in the role of 'rescuers' – who will often assume (short-term) control of the damaging event until such time as the demands return to a level that can be handled by more routine management processes. However, where there is loss of life associated with the crisis then there will also be a requirement for the collection of evidence. This requirement may remain with external agencies for a considerable period of time after the 'operational' phase. There is considerable potential for this process to escalate the crisis still further as media coverage of any investigation will have an impact upon reputation, share price and, to an extent, legal status. Thus, a crisis does not end at the point at which the 'acute problem' is brought under control, but may escalate still further as the crisis moves to more of a reputational problem in the 'legitimation' phase.

The final phase of this framework raises the issues of turnaround management, reputation recovery, and a range of processes aimed at securing the organization's legitimacy with its external and internal stakeholders. These are all issues that need to be considered by managers in the 'crisis of management' phase rather than in the operational and 'legitimation' phases. This final phase also includes the processes of organizational learning, which is as generating many of the conditions necessary to deal with future problems of crisis incubation within the crisis of management (Elliott, Smith and McGuinness, 2000; Smith, 2001).

The development of a 'learning organization' can also be seen to sit at the core of research into, what have become known as, 'high reliability organizations' (HROs) (Clarke, 1993; LaPorte and Consolini, 1991; Roberts, 1989; Sagan, 1993; Weick, 1987). The paper by Roberts (Roberts, 1990) deals with some of the main characteristics of HROs and this concept represents an area of considerable research opportunity for improving the ways in which an organization deals with many of the contributory factors that generate crises. This is especially the case around the nature and role of human errors and violations in exposing the vulnerability that is inherent within safety-critical systems (Reason, 1990b; Reason, 1997, 2001).

There is little doubt that the core principles of HROs are seductive. If we can design and maintain organizations that are close to being error free, especially in high risk environments (Roberts and Rousseau, 1989), then we will be close to dealing with many of the core problems around crisis incubation. Whilst the nature and validity of HRO theory (termed HRT by Sagan, 1993) has been called into question (Perrow, 1994; Sagan, 1993) and has been the subject of vigorous debate (LaPorte, 1994; LaPorte and Rochlin, 1994; Perrow, 1994), it does present some important and interesting challenges for management theory and practice. Reason (2000) observes that for high reliability organizations:

> '. . . the pursuit of safety is not so much about preventing isolated failures, either human or technical, as about making the system as robust as is practicable in the face of its human and operational hazards. High reliability organisations are not immune to adverse events, but they have learnt the knack of converting these occasional setbacks into enhanced resilience of the system'.
>
> (p. 770)

This generation of organizational resilience is clearly an important challenge for future crisis research.

The early work on HROs has been focused on those organizations that are high in 'failure potential' (or more accurately, 'consequence potential') such as air traffic control, military systems (aircraft carrier operations) and the management of nuclear power plants. The opportunities to migrate the concepts developed in these industries to other high-risk activities, such as health care, is considerable and may generate greater insights into the processes by which organizations 'incubate' crisis potential. What this work has suggested is that HROs have developed systems and processes which ensure that knowledge is made explicit, communicated and acted upon by all people within the organization (Roberts, 1989). They have also developed a culture of training and continuous improvement that allows organizational members to become, and remain, motivated and willing to learn. It also provides them with the skills (and confidence) needed to deal with the complex set of task demands generated by the system in which they work (Roberts, 1989). As Reason (2000) points out, these practices do not prevent failures or errors from occurring but they do seem to contribute to the organization's reliance and capabilities to prevent these incidents from escalating into catastrophic accidents.

Another area in which HRO research offers some interesting opportunities for further consideration is around the relationships that exist between 'managers' and other organizational members. This seems to be especially important in the way that this relationship impacts upon decision-making and communication within HROs (Rousseau, 1989; Turner, 1994; Weick, 1987). Processes to deal with the problems of upward communication and the potential for distortion that can exist in that process, also assume a high priority within a HRO's activities (Rousseau, 1989). Similarly, a key element in the HRO's ability to process large amounts of information, in a time-dependent environment, is seen as being a function of the slack in human capital that is available to the organization (Roberts, 1989). This 'redundancy' also allows for a process of continuous training and development that is also seen to underpin the performance of the HRO (Roberts, 1989). There are clearly some interesting and important research developments that emerge out of this body of work that are worthy of wider consideration. If for no other reason, the findings of this research are important as they may well cause managers to reflect upon the ways in which they work. Added to that, the potential benefits that will accrue from further research into the concept of a HRO makes this body of work important to the crisis literature.

The paper by Fortune and Peters (Fortune and Peters, 1994) also takes a 'systems perspective' in dealing with failure, and recognizes the importance of the interaction between various strategic elements of an organizational system – environment, decision-making, resource allocation, communication – as a means of creating the conditions of crisis (Fortune and Peters, 1995, 2005). Much of the work within human error and organizational failure adopts a systems perspective as a means of exploring the wider context of failure. Moving beyond the errors of the individual to a consideration of the wider set of influencing factors has proved to be an important contribution of the systems approach. Whilst a considerable amount of literature adopts a systems perspective on failure, few contributions to that debate have elaborated on what that means from a theoretical and a practical viewpoint.

The paper by Fortune and Peters sets out a useful framework for looking at an organization's processes and procedures as a means of assessing the potential vulnerability that exists within the system. What this framework offers, in common with many systems approaches, is a means of trying to capture and evaluate the various interactions between elements that can contribute to a failure within the system 'as a whole'. The main contribution of this paper is that it allows for the other work within this section to be contextualized within a framework of a wider systems approach. The purposes of much of the systems literature lies in setting out a complex set of issues and processes in a manner that can be understood by a range of people from different backgrounds and perspectives. It can also serve as a means of surfacing core beliefs and assumptions – a key factor in crisis prevention. Indeed, in setting out that systems framework, the aim is invariably to capture the richness associated with such differing views as a means of portraying the individual's understanding of the problems. Fortune and Peters help to frame that wider sensemaking process – an issue that is a central theme of the final paper in this section.

One of the problems that impacts upon all of the frameworks discussed so far, relates to the manner in which we interpret, or make sense of, the complex set of factors, processes and procedures that take place within an organization. The paper by Weick (Weick, 1988) deals with the set of processes around 'sense-making'. This process represents one of the most important 'psycho-social' activities that take place within an organization. Put simply, if we cannot make sense of the events that we are trying to manage then clearly it will generate difficulties for our decision-making and strategies for intervention. If the organization is to develop an ability to move beyond its fixed set of contingency plans and processes when dealing with 'emergence' within crises, then it will clearly need to develop its sensemaking capabilities. When a set of events moves outside of the limits covered by the contingency plans, then the difficulties around sensemaking will generate problems associated with responding to the emergent nature of these events. If there is no plan to guide the behaviour of people in such circumstances then they will need to develop a greater understanding of the event that they are dealing with and develop control strategies in a 'real time' setting. Problems occur when the processes of sense-making breakdown and organizational members take decisions in a pressured, highly volatile environment (Weick, 1988, 1990, 1993). The inability to make sense of what is going on around them will clearly inhibit the ability of both individuals and an organization's crisis teams to deal with the demands of the event (Smith, 2000b, 2004). Sensemaking within organizations remains at the heart of the crisis management process. It represents an opportunity to develop effective ways of interpreting and acting upon the 'events' that managers and 'operators' have to deal with. It also presents us with considerable challenges, which require changes to the ways in which organizational members think and interrelate with each other.

Conclusions

The papers in this section have been brought together to illustrate the various perspectives that can be taken on the 'modelling' of crises. Taken as a whole, the papers highlight some important focal points within the literature and it is possible to identify a number of key themes that emerge from this body of work.

The first is that crises have a psycho-social dynamic. This dynamic takes place across the three main phases of a crisis as identified by Smith (Smith, 1990, 1995) and plays an important role in determining the effectiveness of management intervention in 'containing' *and* 'preventing' crisis escalation. There are clearly important *psycho-social* issues around the incubation of crisis potential within an organization, and especially around the relationship between latent and active errors (Rasmussen, 1982, 1983; Reason, 1990a, 1990b, 1990c, 1997, 2004). Other elements of the psycho-social include the processes of sensemaking and perception as well as the abilities of people within the organization to communicate effectively both before, during and following a crisis (Fortune and Peters, 1994, 1995; Weick, 1990, 1993). There are also significant psycho-social factors at work in the prevention of organizational learning around a range of crisis issues.

The various frameworks also point to the importance of a range of *cultural issues* that impact upon the generation of crises and, in particular, on the relationship that exists between the strategies, plans and structures developed by the organization and the core beliefs, values and assumptions held by organizational members. Attempts at designing and managing organizational cultures to deal with the demands of high-risk organizations have attracted considerable discussion within the research literature on crises.

Finally, a series of *systems-level issues* are also highlighted that point to the importance of organizational strategy and the shaping effects of wider environmental factors in generating the conditions for crisis. In addition, these systems issues also provide us with some insights into the important role played by emergence, escalation and complexity in the bypassing of organizational controls and the complex processes that surround the interactions between elements of the organization and its networks/supply chains, stakeholders and operating environments. These issues remain important areas for research and practice.

The papers included within this section provide a foundation for much of what follows in this collection of essays. The processes surrounding our understanding of crises will impact upon our abilities to identify and manage such events. By failing to recognize the complex and evolving nature of this process, we risk condemning our organizations to crises in the future.

References

Ackroyd, S. and Thompson, P. (1999) *Organizational Misbehaviour*, SAGE: London.

Atkins, P. and Bowler, I. (2001) *Food in society: Economy, culture, geography*, Arnold: London.

Chiles, J. R. (2002) *Inviting disaster: Lessons from the edge of technology*, Harper Business: New York.

Chomsky, N. (2001) *9–11*, Seven Stories Press: New York, NY.

Chomsky, N. (2003) *Power and terror: Post-9/11 talks and interviews*, Seven Stories Press: New York.

Clarke, L. (1993) 'Drs. Pangloss and Strangelove Meet Organizational Theory: High Reliability Organizations and Nuclear Weapons Accidents', *Sociological Forum*, 8 (4): 675–689.

Collee, J. G. and Bradley, R. (1997) 'BSE: a decade on – part 2', *The Lancet*, 349: 715–721.

Dixon, N. (1976) *On the psychology of military incompetence*, Basic Books: New York.

Dormont, D. (2002) 'Prions, BSE and food', *International Journal of Food Microbiology*, 78: 181–189.

Elliott, D., Smith, D. and McGuinness, M. (2000) 'Exploring the failure to learn: Crises and the barriers to learning', *Review of Business*, 21 (3): 17–24.

Esser, J. K. and Lindoerfer, J. S. (1989) 'Groupthink and the Space Shuttle Challenger accident: Toward a quantitative case analysis', *Journal of Behavioral Decision Making*, 2: 167–177.

Fortune, J. and Peters, G. (1994) 'Systems analysis of failures as a quality management tool', *British Journal of Management*, 5: 205–213.

Fortune, J. and Peters, G. (1995) *Learning from failure – The systems approach*, John Wiley and Sons: Chichester.

Fortune, J. and Peters, G. (2005) *Information systems: Achieving success by avoiding failure*, Wiley: Chichester.

Gladwell, M. (2000) *The Tipping Point: How little things can make a big difference*, Abacus: London.

Greenberg, J. W. (2002) 'September 11, 2001: A CEO's story' *Harvard Business Review*, 80 (10): 58–64.

Halliday, F. (2002) *Two hours that shook the world. September 11, 2001: Causes and consequences*, Saqi Books: London.

Handy, C. (1994) *The empty raincoat: Making sense of the future*, Hutchinson: London.

Handy, C. (1995) *The age of unreason: New thinking for a new world*, Random House: London.

Hazarika, S. (1987) *Bhopal: The lessons of a tragedy*, Penguin Books: New Delhi.

Heimann, C. F. L. (1993) 'Understanding the Challenger Disaster: Organizational Structure and the Design of Reliable Systems', *American Political Science Review*, 87 (2): 421–435.

Holtz, T. H., Leighton, J., Balter, S., Weiss, D., Blank, S., and Weisfuse, I. (2003) 'The public health response to the World Trade Center disaster', in B. S. Levy and V. W. Sidel (eds), *Terrorism and public health. A balanced approach to strengthening systems and protecting people*, 19–48. Oxford University Press: New York.

Janis, I. L. (1982) *Groupthink: Psychological studies of policy decisions and fiascos* (2nd ed.), Houghton Mifflin: Boston.

Janis, I. L. (1989) *Crucial decisions: Leadership in policymaking and crisis management*, Free Press: New York, NY.

Kendra, J. M. and Wachtendorf, T. (2003) 'Elements of resilience after the World Trade Center disaster: reconstituting New York City's emergency operations centre', *Disasters*, 27 (1): 37–53.

Lapierre, D. and Moro, J. (2002) *Five past midnight in Bhopal*, Warner Books: New York.

LaPorte, T. (1994) 'A strawman speaks up: Comments on "The Limits to Safety"', *Journal of Contingencies and Crisis Management*, 2 (4): 207–211.

LaPorte, T. and Consolini, P. M. (1991) 'Working in practice but not in theory: Theoretical challenge of high reliability', *Journal of Public Administration Research and Theory*, 1: 19–47.

LaPorte, T. and Rochlin, G. (1994) 'A rejoiner to Perrow', *Journal of Contingencies and Crisis Management*, 2 (4): 221–227.

Little, G. (2001) 'BSE and the regulation of risk', *Modern Law Review*, 64 (5): 730–756.

Mintzberg, H. (1983) *Structure in fives: Designing effective organizations*, Prentice-Hall International: London.

Mitroff, I. I., Pauchant, T. C., Finney, M., and Pearson, C. (1989) 'Do (some) organizations cause their own crises? Culture profiles of crisis prone versus crisis prepared organizations', *Industrial Crisis Quarterly*, 3: 269–283.

Moorhead, G., Ference, R., and Neck, C. P. (1991) 'Group decision fiascoes continue: Space Shuttle Challenger and a revised groupthink framework', *Human Relations*, 44 (6): 539–550.

Murray, P. J. (1998) 'Complexity theory and the Fifth Discipline', *Systemic Practice and Action Research*, 11 (3): 275–293.

Nelson, D. A. (2001) *NASA new millennium problems and solutions*, Xlibris: Philadelphia, PA.

Ortegon-Monroy, M. C. (2003) 'Chaos and complexity theory in management: an exploration from a critical systems thinking perspective', *Systems Research and Behavioral Science*, 20: 387–400.

Pauchant, T. C. and Mitroff, I. I. (1992) *Transforming the crisis-prone organization. Preventing individual organizational and environmental tragedies*, Jossey-Bass Publishers: San Fransisco.

Pennington, H. (2003) *When food kills. BSE, E.coli and disaster science*, Oxford University Press: Oxford.

Perrow, C. (1961) 'The Analysis of Goals in Complex Organizations', *American Sociological Review*, 26 (6): 854–66.

Perrow, C. (1967) 'A Framework for the Comparative Analysis of Organizations', *American Sociological Review*, 32 (2): 194–208.

Perrow, C. (1984) *Normal Accidents*, Basic Books: New York.

Perrow, C. (1994) 'The limits of safety: The enhancement of a theory of accidents', *Journal of Contingencies and Crisis Management*, 2 (4): 212–220.

Pidgeon, N. F. (1998) 'Shaking the kaleidoscope of disasters research – a reply', *Journal of Contingencies and Crisis Management*, 6 (2): 97–101.

Posner, G. (2003) *Why America slept: The failure to prevent 9/11*, Random House: New York, NY.

Rasmussen, J. (1982) 'Human errors. A taxonomy for describing human malfunction in industrial installations', *Journal of Occupational Accidents*, 4: 311–333.

Rasmussen, J. (1983) 'Skills, rules, knowledge: signals, signs and symbols and other distinctions in human performance models', *IEEE Transactions on Systems, Man and Cybernetics*, 13: 257–267.

Reason, J. (1990a) 'The contribution of latent human failures to the breakdown of complex systems', *Philosophical Transactions of the Royal Society of London B: Biological Sciences*, 327: 475–484.

Reason, J. (2000) 'Human error: models and management', *British Medical Journal*, 320 (7237): 768–770.

Reason, J. (2004) 'Beyond the organisational accident: the need for "error wisdom" on the frontline', *Quality and Safety in Health Care*, 13 (suppl 2): ii28–33.

Reason, J. T. (1990b) 'The contribution of latent human failures to the breakdown of complex systems', *Philosophical Transactions of the Royal Society of London B*, 37: 475–484.

Reason, J. T. (1990c) *Human error*, Oxford University Press: Oxford.

Reason, J. T. (1997) *Managing the risks of organizational accidents*, Ashgate: Aldershot.

Reason, J. T. (2001) 'Understanding adverse events: the human factor', in C. Vincent (ed.), *Clinical risk management: Enhancing patient safety*, 2nd ed., 9–30, BMJ Books: London.

Roberts, K. H. (1989) 'New challenges in organizational research: high reliability organizations', *Industrial Crisis Quarterly*, 3: 111–125.

Roberts, K. H. (1990) 'Some characteristics of one type of High Reliability Organizations', *Organization Science*, 1 (2): 160–176.

Roberts, K. H. and Rousseau, D. M. (1989) 'Research in nearly error free, high reliability organizations: having the bubble', *IEEE Transactions*, 36 (2): 132–139.

Rousseau, D. M. (1989) 'The price of success? Security-oriented cultures and high reliability organizations', *Industrial Crisis Quarterly*, 3: 285–302.

Sagan, S. D. (1993) *The limits of safety: Organizations, accidents, and nuclear weapons*, Princeton University Press: Princeton, NJ.

Shrivastava, P. (1987) *Bhopal: Anatomy of a crisis*, Ballinger Publishing Company: Cambridge, Mass.

Sipika, C. and Smith, D. (1993) 'From disaster to crisis: the failed turnaround of Pan American Airlines', *Journal of Contingencies and Crisis Management*, 1 (3): 138–151.

Smith, D. (1990) 'Beyond contingency planning: Towards a model of crisis management', *Industrial Crisis Quarterly*, 4 (4): 263–275.

Smith, D. (1995) 'The Dark Side of Excellence: Managing Strategic Failures', in J. Thompson (ed.), *Handbook of Strategic Management*, 161–191, Butterworth-Heinemann: London.

Smith, D. (2000a) 'On a wing and a prayer? Exploring the human components of technological failure', *Systems Research and Behavioral Science*, 17: 543–559.

Smith, D. (2000b) 'Crisis Management Teams: Issues in the management of operational crises', *Risk Management: An International Journal*, 2 (3): 61–78.

Smith, D. (2001) 'Crisis as a catalyst for change: Issues in the management of uncertainty and organizational vulnerability', *E-risk: Business as usual?* 81–88, British Bankers Association/Deloitte and Touche: London.

Smith, D. (2004) 'For whom the bell tolls: Imagining accidents and the development of crisis simulation in organisations', *Simulation and Gaming*, 35 (3): 347–362.

Smith, D. (2005) 'Business (not) as usual – crisis management, service interruption and the vulnerability of organisations', *Journal of Services Marketing*, 19 (5): 309–320.

Smith, D. (2006) 'The crisis of management – managing ahead of the curve', in D. Smith and D. Elliott (eds), *Key readings in crisis management: Systems and structures for prevention and recovery*, Routledge: London.

Smith, D. and Elliot, D. (2005) 'Moving Beyond Denial: Exploring the Barriers to Learning from Crisis', Working Paper, Centre for Risk and Crisis Management, University of Liverpool.

Smith, D. and Sipika, C. (1993) 'Back from the brink – post crisis management', *Long Range Planning*, 26 (1): 28–38.

Smith, D. and Tombs, S. (1995). 'Self regulation as a control strategy for Major Hazards', *Journal of Management Studies*, 32 (5): 619–636.

Tenner, E. (1996) *Why things bite back: Technology and the revenge effect*, Fourth Estate: London.

Toft, B. and Reynolds, S. (1994) *Learning from disasters*, Butterworth: London.

Tombs, S. and Smith, D. (1995) 'Corporate responsibility and crisis management: Some insights from political and social theory', *Journal of Contingencies and Crisis Management*, 3 (3): 135–148.

Turner, B. A. (1976) 'The organizational and interorganizational development of disasters', *Administrative Science Quarterly*, 21: 378–397.

Turner, B. A. (1978) *Man-made disasters*, Wykeham: London.

Turner, B. A. (1994) 'Causes of disaster: Sloppy management', *British Journal of Management*, 5: 215–219.

Vaughan, D. (1997) 'The trickle down effect: policy decisions, risky work, and the Challenger tragedy', *California Management Review*, 39 (2): 80–102.

Vaughan, D. (1999) 'The Dark Side of Organizations: Mistake, Misconduct, and Disaster', *Annual Review of Sociology*, 25: 271–305.

Weick, K. E. (1987) 'Organizational culture as a source of high reliability', *California Management Review*, 29: 112–127.

Weick, K. E. (1988) 'Enacted sensemaking in crisis situations', *Journal of Management Studies*, 25: 305–317.

Weick, K. E. (1990) 'The vulnerable system: An analysis of the Tenerife air disaster', *Journal of Management*, 16: 571–593.

Weick, K. E. (1993) 'The collapse of sensemaking in organizations: The Mann Gulch Disaster', *Administrative Science Quarterly*, 38: 628–652.

Weick, K. E. (1995) *Sensemaking in organizations*, SAGE: Thousand Oaks.

Weick, K. E. (1998) 'Foresights of failure: An appreciation of Barry Turner', *Journal of Contingencies and Crisis Management*, 6 (2): 72–75.

Chapter 8

Barry A. Turner

THE ORGANIZATIONAL AND INTERORGANIZATIONAL DEVELOPMENT OF DISASTERS

ADMINISTRATIVE ORGANIZATIONS MAY BE thought of as cultural mechanisms developed to set collective goals and make arrangements to deploy available resources to attain those goals. Given this concern with future objectives, analysts have paid considerable attention to the manner in which organizational structures are patterned to cope with unknown events – or uncertainty – in the future facing the organization and its environment (Crozier, 1964; Thompson, 1967; Lawrence and Lorsch, 1967).

Uncertainty creates problems for action. Actors' organizations resolve these problems by following rules of thumb, using rituals, relying on habitual patterns, or, more self-consciously, by setting goals and making plans to reach them. These devices provide the determinateness and certainty needed to embark upon organizational action in the present. But since organizations are indeterminate open systems, particularly in their orientation to future events (Thompson, 1967: 10), members of organizations can never be sure that their present actions will be adequate for the attainment of their desired goals.

Prediction is made more difficult by the complex and extensive nature of the tasks that must be carried out to fulfill organizational goals of any significance. Many tasks, particularly the more important ones, are loosely formulated, directed to ill-defined or possibly conflicting ends, and lacking unequivocal criteria for deciding when the goals have been attained. This situation is resolved sometimes by creating small areas of certainty which can be handled. At other times the problem is redrawn in a more precise form which ignores features that are difficult to specify or are nonquantifiable. Action is made possible in organizations by the collective adoption of simplifying assumptions about the environment, producing what Simon (1957) called a framework of 'bounded rationality.'

When a task which was formerly small enough to be handled amenably grows to an unmanageable size, resources may be increased to handle the larger problem, or parts of it may be passed on to other organizations, so that the task becomes an interorganizational one (Hirsch, 1975). Alternatively, the task to be handled may shrink to fit the resources available or the amount of information that can be handled adequately in processing it (Meier, 1965). Each of these strategies, and many others, resolve for members of an organization the problem of what to do next by simplifying the manner in which the current situation is interpreted. They offer a way of deciding what to ignore in a more complex formulation to produce a statement of the problem in which uncertainty has been reduced. The success of such strategies, however, turns on the issue of whether the simplified diagnosis of the present and likely future situation is accurate enough to enable the organizational goals to be achieved without encountering unexpected difficulties that lead on to catastrophe.

The central difficulty, therefore, lies in discovering which aspects of the current set of problems facing an organization are prudent to ignore and which should be attended to, and how an acceptable level of safety can be established as a criterion in carrying out this exercise. Wilensky (1967) has suggested that to deal with such situations, one must discover how to recognize high-quality intelligence about the problem in hand, using the term *intelligence* in its military sense. Wilensky's criteria for high-quality intelligence are that it should be 'clear, timely, reliable, valid, adequate and wide-ranging' so that it is understandable by the users, is available when needed, is perceived similarly by different users, 'captures reality,' gives a full account of the context, and poses the major policy alternatives.

This is excellent as a normative statement of what is desirable, but it does little in practical situations to offer tests of clarity, timeliness, or adequacy of intelligence. One means which Wilensky did put forward for tackling these latter issues, however, is by the examination of failures of intelligence, these being more important than failures of control. Taking up this suggestion, this article considers the manner in which such an approach could be used to begin to identify, as Wilensky (1967: 121) puts it, 'the conditions that foster the failure of foresight.' British public inquiries into major public disasters offer sets of information about some aspects of the intelligence failures that led up to them. A number of such inquiries have been scrutinized to find patterns of similarities that make such happenings more understandable and, it is hoped, more avoidable (Turner, 1976). The public inquiries referred to, and others currently being examined, all involve loss of life and damage to property on a large scale. This gives to the reports a tragic clarity arising from a concern to prevent a repetition of such major and unforeseen accidents. The main purpose of the present research, however, is not to produce a general theory of such disasters, although one may emerge incidentally, but to use them as a paradigm for the understanding of organizational failures of foresight, which are also in their way disastrous, although they may lack the public impact produced by a major loss of life.

Foresight and its failure

In accounting for failures of foresight, undesirable events known about in advance but which were unavoidable with the resources available can be disregarded. In addition, little time need be spent on catastrophes that were completely unpredictable. Neither of these categories present problems of explanation. In the former case, because of lack of resources, no action was possible. In the latter, no action could have been taken because of a total lack of information or intelligence. In practice, however, such extremes are rare, and in most cases of undesirable or catastrophic events, some forewarning is available potentially, and some avoiding action is possible notionally.

This situation may be clarified by making use of a definition produced by an early researcher into disaster phenomena. Carr (1932) suggested that 'a catastrophic change is a change in the functional adequacy of certain cultural artefacts' (Killian, 1956: 1–2). A failure of foresight may therefore be regarded as the collapse of precautions that had hitherto been regarded culturally as adequate. Small-scale everyday accidents do not provoke a cultural reevaluation of precautions. There may be a failure of foresight at an individual level when a man drops a plate or falls off a ladder while painting his house, but such events provoke no surprise in the community, and call for no widespread cultural readjustment. By the same token, there is little need for a reevaluation of culturally accepted precautionary devices when accidents, even on a large scale, occur in situations recognized as hazardous. When a trawler is lost in Arctic fishing grounds, or when a wall collapses onto a firefighting team, there is much less comment than when an accident kills passengers on a suburban commuter train.

The concern here, therefore, is to make an examination of some large-scale disasters that are potentially foreseeable and potentially avoidable, and that, at the same time, are sufficiently unexpected and sufficiently disruptive to provoke a cultural reassessment of the artefacts and precautions available to prevent such occurrences. The intention of this examination is to look for a set of organizational patterns that precede such disasters. Having identified such a pattern, one can go on to ask whether it can also be found in the preconditions for other major organizational failures which do not lead necessarily to loss of life, but which, nevertheless, provoke the disruption of cultural assumptions about the efficacy of current precautions, such as the collapse of a major public company.

An extensive literature of disaster studies has grown up since World War II (Fritz, 1961; Wallace, 1956; Rayner, 1957; Barton, 1969; Nosow and Form, 1958), building on the work of such earlier writers as Queen and Mann (1925) and Carr (1932). A number of these studies have set out a variety of developmental models for disasters (Carr, 1932; Powell, Rayner, and Finesinger, 1953; Wallace, 1956; Barton, 1969), but because this literature is oriented to the sequence that begins with a warning of danger and moves through the onset of danger to the problems of alarm, panic, and rescue, none of the sequence patterns presented are of much help in dealing with the organizational events that permit potentially avoidable incidents to occur. Disaster planning literature aimed at management similarly begins with the assumption that a catastrophe will occur, and directs attention to the forming of emergency committees and the organization of rescue and relief plans (Healy, 1969). Accident investigators (Goeller, 1969; Hale and Hale, 1970; Wigglesworth, 1972; Lawrence, 1974) have identified a preaccident period, but have regarded it as an individual rather than an organizational phenomenon.

To make it easier to organize the current data, therefore, a new developmental sequence is set out, taking account of the period when the events leading up to the disaster develop. Since it is assumed that a disaster in the sociological sense involves a basic disruption of the social context and a radical departure from the pattern of normal expectations for a significant portion of the community, the model in Table 1 begins at a notional starting point where matters can be assumed to be reasonably normal – Stage I. The set of culturally held beliefs – Stage Ia – about the world and its hazards are at this point sufficiently accurate to enable individuals and groups to survive successfully in the world. This level of coping with the world is achieved by adhering to a set of normative prescriptions – Stage Ib – that are consonant with accepted beliefs. Such prescriptions about the precautions necessary to avoid recognized hazards are embodied in laws, codes of practice, mores, and folkways. When unfortunate consequences follow on a violation of these sets of norms, there is no need for any cultural readjustment, for such an occurrence serves to strengthen the force of the existing prescriptions.

A disaster or a cultural collapse takes place because of some inaccuracy or inadequacy in the accepted norms and beliefs, but if the disruption is to be of any consequence, the discrepancy between the way the world is thought to operate and the way it really does rarely develops instantaneously. Instead, there is an accumulation of a number of events that are at odds with the picture of the world

Table 1 The sequence of events associated with a failure of foresight

Stage I	**Notionally normal starting point:** (a) Initial culturally accepted beliefs about the world and its hazards (b) Associated precautionary norms set out in laws, codes of practice, mores, and folkways.
Stage II	**Incubation period:** the accumulation of an unnoticed set of events which are at odds with the accepted beliefs about hazards and the norms for their avoidance.
Stage III	**Precipitating event:** forces itself to the attention and transforms general perceptions of Stage II.
Stage IV	**Onset:** the immediate consequences of the collapse of cultural precautions become apparent.
Stage V	**Rescue and salvage – first stage adjustment:** the immediate postcollapse situation is recognized in ad hoc adjustments which permit the work of rescue and salvage to be started.
Stage VI	**Full cultural readjustment:** an inquiry or assessment is carried out, and beliefs and precautionary norms are adjusted to fit the newly gained understanding of the world.

and its hazards represented by existing norms and beliefs. Commonly, in this incubation period – Stage I, a chain of discrepant events develop and accumulate unnoticed. For this to happen, all of these events must fall into one of two categories: either the events are not known to anyone or they are known but not fully understood by all concerned, so that their full range of properties is not appreciated in the same way that they will be after the disaster (Lawrence, 1974). In this incubation stage the failure of foresight develops. It is in the conditions for the development of this stage that the answers to Wilensky's problems about the adequacy of organizational intelligence can be found.

Beyond this stage, a further pattern of development one that begins with the incidence of a precipitating event – Stage III – can be discerned. Such an event arouses attention because of its immediate characteristics. For instance, the train crashes, the building catches fire, or share prices begin to drop. More significantly, the precipitating incident also makes it inevitable that the general perception of all of the events in the incubation period will be transformed, by offering criteria that identify the incubating network of events so that the process of transforming the ill-structured problem into a well-structured problem may begin. The precipitating event is followed immediately by the onset – Stage IV – of the direct and unanticipated consequences of the failure, an onset which occurs with varying rate and intensity, and over an area of varying scope (Carr, 1932). Closely related is the following stage of rescue and salvage – Stage V, in which rapid and adhoc redefinitions of the situation are made by participants to permit a recognition of the most important features of the failure and enable work of rescue and salvage to be carried out. When the immediate effects have subsided, it becomes possible to carry out a more leisurely and less superficial assessment of the incident, and to move toward something like a full cultural adjustment – Stage VI – of beliefs, norms, and precautions, making them compatible with the newly gained understanding of the world.

Reference will be made to this model in the discussion of the data examined, paying particular attention to the incubation period, for there is a special concern to identify the conditions that make it possible for unnoticed, misperceived, and misunderstood events to accumulate in a manner that leads eventually to cultural disruption.

Variable disjunction of information

In an earlier examination of the behavior of managers and others concerned with the scheduling of work through batch-production factories, it was noted (Turner, 1970; Kynaston Reeves and Turner, 1972) that the problem of obtaining an optimal schedule was an ill-structured problem, and that it was a problem with a potentially infinite set of solutions. Groups and individuals tackled this problem, therefore, by the semitacit adoption of a series of rules of thumb which had been found in the past to circumnavigate the central scheduling problem, without the need to specify it precisely.

The various groups in this highly complex situation were trying to manipulate a state of affairs for which they were unable to agree upon a single authoritative description. Because each person had access to a slightly different set of information, each tended to construct slightly differing theories about what was happening, and about what needed to be done. Given sufficient time, money, and energy, it would have been possible to reconcile all the conflicting aspects of these sets to produce one agreed upon set, but in such situations, complexity and uncertainty are high, while time, money, and energy are scarce.

This condition was seen to be an example of a more general state that arises when the amount of information that can be generated or attended to with available resources is considerably less than the amount of information needed to describe fully or take account of the complexity of the situation. Relevant information, or perhaps what Wilensky called high-quality intelligence, under such circumstances, therefore, becomes a scarce resource in itself. The cost of obtaining one piece of information has to be balanced against the cost of obtaining an alternative bit. This state of the variable disjunction of information cannot be dismissed as a lack of communication. Rather, it is a situation in which high complexity and continuous change make it necessary to be extremely selective in the use of communications.

Tonge (1961), in tackling a related issue, drew a distinction between well-structured problems and ill-structured problems that is useful for this discussion. Well-structured problems, Tonge suggested, are numerically described, with specified goals and available routines for their solution. Ill-structured problems, such as batch-production scheduling, often use symbolic or verbal variables, have vague, nonquantifiable goals, and lack available routines for solving them, so that rules of thumb or ad hoc heuristic procedures are commonly used to devise solutions for them.

Data

Since it was likely that the pattern of behavior and the information condition observed in dealing with the batch-production scheduling problem were instances of a more general and significant phenomenon, the examination of disaster reports was consciously selective, in that those disasters likely to display a variable disjunction of information were of particular interest. A number of reports in which it was relatively easy in the official inquiry to attribute the failure to a lack of appreciation of some previously unknown factor or to some clearly recognized lapse from good practice were rejected as being of little interest at the present stage (Micheal Colliery, 1968; Sea Gem, 1967).

The discussion is not intended to apply to all disasters, therefore, but is explicitly an examination of three selected examples of intelligence failure in complex circumstances that promised some similarities with the condition of variable disjunction of information already described.

The three reports of incidents analyzed are the *Report by the Tribunal of Inquiry* (1966–1967) set up to investigate the Aberfan disaster in Wales, the *Report of the Public Inquiry into the Accident at Hixon Level Crossing on January 6th, 1968* (1968), and the *Report of the Summerland Fire Commission* (1974).

In the first incident (Aberfan, 1966–1967), a portion of a colliery tip on a mountainside at Aberfan slid down into the village in 1966, engulfing the school, killing 144 people, including 116 children, 109 of whom were in the school. In the second incident (Hixon, 1968), a large road transporter, 148 feet long, carrying a very heavy transformer was hit by an express train while it was negotiating a new type of automatically controlled half-barrier rail crossing, killing three rail-waymen and eight passengers on the train. The transporter moved at two miles per hour and, therefore, could not clear the crossing in the 24-second warning period. In the third case (Summerland, 1974), a holiday leisure complex at Douglas, Isle of Man, with approximately 3,000 people inside, caught fire, on August 2, 1973. The building, an open structure clad partly in sheet steel and partly in acrylic sheeting, burned rapidly and 50 men, women, and children in the building died.

Detailed notes were taken of the contents of the three reports, and in a second stage, the notes were carefully sifted and analyzed, by labeling and categorizing the phenomena encountered in as accurate a manner as possible. Patterns of relationships between the observed categories were then sought. This procedure is very close to that recommended by Glaser and Strauss (1967), and is intended to develop a basis for handling discussions, not only of the present incidents, but also of future incidents of this kind.

Observed patterns

Major causal features

The common feature which forms the initial starting point for discussion in the Aberfan, Hixon, and Summerland disasters is that in each case the accident occurred when a large complex problem, the limits of which were difficult to specify, was being dealt with by a number of groups and individuals usually operating in separate organizations and separate departments within organizations. Thus, at Aberfan, the ill-structured problem was the running of the pit and its ancillary activities to the satisfaction of H.M. Inspectors of Mines, of the various departments of the National Coal Board, the pit employees, and local residents and their elected representatives. At Hixon, the problem was the introduction and operation of a new type of level crossing to the satisfaction of the various departments within British Rail, the Ministry of Transport, the police, and the wide range of road users, including children, farmers, and those likely to use the crossing with animals, agricultural machinery, or other abnormal loads. Finally, at Summerland, the problem tackled was one of building a new, profitable, and safe form of leisure center, using some new materials. For each case, the dominant factors upon which the inquiry concentrated are sum-marized below, together with a brief indication of the organizational units and subunits involved in each incident.

Aberfan. The Tribunal of Inquiry considered the part played by a number of bodies and organizational units in its lengthy assessment of the events leading up to the tip slide. In addition to evidence taken from technical advisory bodies, the tribunal heard evidence relating to the organization of the colliery where the tip was located and to the role of the area and divisional bodies responsible for this colliery. Evidence concerning involvement of the National Coal Board head-quarters, the activities of a body set up to review organization within the Board, and the part played by the National Union of Mineworkers was reviewed. The tribunal was particularly interested in information about the policies pursued in selecting sites for tips and about the manner in which information about earlier nonfatal tip slides had been disseminated within this very large organization. On this last point, the tribunal discovered that knowledge about the procedures necessary to stabilize tips potentially had been available for many years. An engineer in a local company, which was subsequently incorporated into the National Coal Board, produced a memorandum in 1939 anticipating the causes of the disaster. But subsequent circulation of this document in the National Coal Board was restricted to a small number of the professional engineering groups. This meant that the nature of the problem was not generally appreciated, in spite of the occurrence of other tip slides in postwar years. The London headquarters of the National Coal Board remained unaware that tips constituted a potential source of serious danger until after the Aberfan incident.

Organizations outside the National Coal Board were involved when local residents protested, through the local borough council, about the possible danger from the tips at Aberfan. The local planning committee and borough engineers office were concerned in negotiations with the Board, assisted to some extent by the local Member of Parliament. The tribunal considered at length the unsatisfactory manner in which these representations were handled locally by the Board and its failure to reach a satisfactory conclusion.

Finally the tribunal took much evidence from management and workers at the colliery about the perfunctory manner in which the decision to build a tip over a small stream had been made and about the response of management and workers to the various warning signs that were apparent as this tip grew in size and the slip became imminent.

Although the situation was complex and there were many contributing factors, the Tribunal of Inquiry found that the dominant pattern of thought that contributed to the disaster was one present in the National Coal Board and, more generally, in the coal industry. It can be characterized as a pervasive institutional set of attitudes, beliefs, and perceptions that led to a collective neglect by almost everyone concerned of the problems of tip safety.

This neglect had a number of components. There were historic and institutional precedents in the neglect of tips by the 1938 Commission on Safety in Mines and by H. M. Inspectors of Mines and Quarries. These were reinforced by sets of industrial beliefs in the coal industry that gave little consideration to tips. As a consequence, the perception of potential dangers associated with tips was dimmed, even when slips occurred elsewhere. Few staff were appointed to deal with the problem of tip safety. Organizational practices were concerned more with the problems of mines than with those of tips. Such literature as existed on tip safety was neglected or not given wide circulation. Naturally, this powerful bias in the coal industry affected patterns of decision making so that when, for example, decisions about the siting of new tips were being made, little trouble was taken over the problem.

Hixon. The investigation into this incident drew on evidence from a substantial number of organizations. In British Rail, for example, evidence was taken from the train crew, from those departments responsible for planning and implementing the introduction of new forms of automatic crossing, from those responsible for disseminating publicity to potential users of the crossings, and from those who installed, inspected, and modified the Hixon crossing. Evidence was taken in the Ministry of Transport from the railway inspectorate responsible for approving the new crossings and the procedures associated with them. Those responsible in the police force for circulating information about the new crossings and for briefing police patrols escorting abnormal loads were questioned, as well as policemen who were escorting the load which was in the collision.

The communication links between the Ministry of Transport and the police through the government department responsible for police affairs also came under scrutiny, as did communications between the police and a unit in British Rail responsible for bridge safety. This unit checked routes for abnormal loads that might constitute a danger to weak bridges, but it was not required explicitly to consider such hazards as automatic level crossings. Evidence was also heard from members of two commercial organizations: the company which owned the transformer that was in transit and which had a factory adjacent to the automatic level crossing and the haulage company which owned the transporter. In the latter company, patterns of responsibility and awareness of statutory obligations for the transport of abnormal loads were examined. The inquiry also considered communications between top management, middle management, and the transporter crew, and communications between top management and British Rail over a previous incident concerning a lorry stalled on an automatic level crossing.

Within this complex set of organizational responsibilities and communications, the central and most distinctive contributing feature leading up to the disaster was a failure on the part of a large number of individuals in British Rail departments, in the management of the road hauliers concerned, and in the Ministry of Transport. They failed to bring together creatively the information they all had, or had access to, in a way which would have made clear the danger of the new crossings to a long slow-moving vehicle that was in the middle of an automatic half-barrier crossing when it began to close. Other precautions had been taken, but not this one, and this was the factor which led to the accident. This failure, a failure in creative problem solving, was compounded by a passive administrative stance adopted by other parties involved. Notable among these were the police, who had received the information necessary to avert the disaster, but who failed for a number of reasons to consider it actively. A further contributing factor was the behavior of the drivers and crew of the transporter who could have acted to avert the disaster, had they been alerted to the need for this and to the procedures called for. They became involved in this tragedy as members of the public who were expected to take a responsibility for their own behavior in relation to the hazard of the crossings.

Summerland. The organizational background to the Summerland fire is possibly the most complex and the most diffuse of that of any of the three cases discussed. The leisure center was developed by Douglas Corporation, the local authority of the largest town on the island, with financial assistance from the government of the Isle of Man. The shell of the completed building, owned by the corporation, was leased to a leisure company which had authority to design and build the more decorative part of the interior. There was an important gap in the continuity of the project between the design and construction of the shell under one design team, and the design and furnishing of the building by the lessees, employing a second design team. In addition to its role as developer, the local authority was involved through its planning, engineering, and fire safety committees in scrutinizing successive bylaw, planning, and safety submissions for the building as design and construction progressed.

The design of the shell of the building was placed in the hands of a local architectural practice, which, in turn, obtained agreement for a larger company on the UK mainland to be retained as associate architects. In the second phase, the design and fitting out of the interior, the UK architects were employed as principals by the lessees of the building, the leisure company. Because two of the most important construction materials used were novel, the manufacturers and distributors of these materials were included in the Summerland Fire Commission's inquiries. Additional factors the commission considered to be relevant to its investigation were the extent to which informal contacts between those in the island community were developed at the expense of more formal procedures, and the extent to which the need to have the second phase of the building completed in time for the tourist season led to the cutting of corners through pressure of work.

A final area of investigation concerned staff organization in the completed leisure center, in particular the severely limited nature of the arrangements made for the training of staff in fire procedures.

The commission concluded that the underlying factors were 'many human errors and failures, and it was the accumulation of these, too much reliance on an "old boy" network and some very ill-defined and poor communications which led to the disaster' (Summerland, 1974). These general factors were operating in a situation in which a small architectural firm was undertaking its first large commission, designing a new kind of building, which posed new fire risks, and which was built with new types of construction materials. In addition, the conditions under which it was anticipated that the building would operate were changed significantly during the design process.

The precise patterns of events, and even their dominant components, are different in each case; presumably, this is why parallels have not been drawn more frequently in the past. But looking beyond these immediate differences, a number of similarities can be discerned.

Similarities

The common features of such disasters have been described in detail elsewhere (Turner, 1976), but they may be summarized under the following headings.

Rigidities in perception and belief in organizational settings. The accurate perception of the possibility of disaster was inhibited by cultural and institutional factors. The Aberfan case in particular offers a powerful and tragic instance of the manner in which a failure of perception may be created, structured, and reinforced by a set of institutional, cultural, or subcultural beliefs and their associated practices.

All organizations develop within them elements of continuous culture which are related to their tasks and their environment (Turner, 1971). Part of the effectiveness of organizations stems from their development of such cultures, but this very property also brings with it the danger of a collective blindness to important issues. This is the danger that some vital factors may have been left outside the framework of bounded rationality. When a pervasive and long-established set of beliefs exists within an organization, these beliefs influence the attitudes and perceptions of men and women in the organization. They affect decision-making procedures and mold organizational arrangements and provisions so that there is a possibility of a vicious, self-reinforcing circle growing up, when it is generally believed that an area is not important or problematic (Crozier, 1964; Gouldner, 1954).

The decoy problem. A recurrent feature of the reports analyzed is that in many instances, when some hazard or problem was perceived, action taken to deal with that problem distracted attention from the problems which eventually caused trouble. In other words, a contributory factor to the disasters was the attention paid to some well-defined problem or source of danger which was dealt with, but which distracted attention from another dangerous but ill-structured problem in the background. For example, at Hixon, a number of parties concerned were aware that the process of taking an abnormal load across a level crossing was potentially hazardous. Representatives of both the haulage company and the company owning the transformer assessed the crossing considering the hazard of arcing onto the overhead electric wires; the police escort and the transporter crew stopped to discuss this problem, as well as the problem of negotiating an uneven section of the crossing. But none of these parties considered the particular danger to which a long, slow load might be exposed.

Organizational exclusivity: disregard of nonmembers. In two of the cases, individuals outside the principal organizations concerned had foreseen the danger that led to the disaster, and had complained, only to meet with a high-handed or dismissive response. They were fobbed off with ambiguous or misleading statements, or subjected to public relations exercises, because it was automatically assumed that the organizations knew better than outsiders about the hazards of the situations with which they were dealing. Thus, the local council at Aberfan failed to gain any satisfactory response from the National Coal Board to the expression of its anxiety, and a query from the road hauliers to British Rail about the problems of the new crossings was dismissed by British Rail in a letter 'remarkable for its arrogance and high-handedness,' in the words of the official report.

Information difficulties. Information difficulties are likely to be associated with ill-structured problems, since it is not easy for any of the individuals or parties involved to fully grasp and handle these vague and complex problems. In situations of disjunct information, the simple remedy of better communication will not work unless resources are increased so that the problem is no longer ill-structured, or unless the problem defined is reduced to a size which can be adequately handled by the existing information net (Meier, 1965).

Communication and information handling difficulties are widespread in all organizations, and it would be wrong to suggest that all such cases lead on to disaster. Moreover, the cases examined here are of little value in assessing such a suggestion, since they were originally selected as likely to display a condition of disjunct information.

Nonetheless, the varying types of communication difficulty examined in the three cases are of some interest. In each case, unresolved ambiguities about warning signs, orders and procedures, and responsibilities and controls were noted. For example, at Aberfan, there were a number of disagreements about the state of the tip and about the nature of earlier slips. At Hixon, a requirement by the inspectorate that a warning notice be moved to a position 'facing traffic' on the road was intended to ensure that the notice was at a right angle to the flow of road traffic and visible to approaching traffic. In fact, the notice was moved so that it was parallel to the road and facing stationary traffic at the crossing. At Summerland, considerable ambiguity surrounded the issue of the reaction of the plastic panels when exposed to fire and the conditions under which waivers for their use were issued by the local authority. In both the Hixon and Aberfan cases, some top management groups adopted an idealistic and unrealistic view of the problem area. It is relatively easy for chief executives to assume that their departments have effective safety precautions and that all eventualities have been dealt with when they are remote from those departments. These assumptions are unlikely to be tested by reality except in the case of disaster.

In each case, too, wrong or misleading information was sent from one party to another, sometimes because of interpersonal difficulties between two particular individuals and information was unintentionally distorted. In the Summerland case, an overreliance was placed upon informal networks developed for other purposes. Even when information was available, it was not always made use of, either because the recipients did not perceive or attend to it, or because they failed to see its significance for the actions they were taking. Information about the operation of the new automatic rail crossings was available in every police station, but was buried in a long technical memorandum, which the inquiry characterized as 'mere flotsam in the station,' and which few policemen could be expected to read in detail. At Summerland, some breaches of good practice in, for example, the construction of a void of combustible materials, arose not because information was not available, but because work was being pushed ahead in a state of intense activity.

Involvement of strangers. In both the Hixon and Summerland cases, and particularly in the latter, a contributing factor to the disaster was the presence of numbers of untrained or uninformed people in potentially hazardous situations. When access to a potentially hazardous process or site can be restricted to trained or skilled personnel, the range of incidents likely to activate the hazard is considerably reduced. But when those not directly under the control of or socialized by the organizations concerned can put themselves in a position where they can activate the hazards if they behave improperly from the organization's point of view, the risks are vastly increased. This group, which will often be made up of members of the public, can be referred to as 'strangers.' The basic problem about strangers is that they are difficult to brief. As a group, they are also difficult to define, so that information about the desired procedures must be disseminated to a wide and amorphous group of potential users, many of whom will never actually need it. Because of the difficulty of defining such a group, administrators may also run into error in communicating with them because they adopt oversimplified stereotypes when considering their likely behavior or characteristics. Thus, even when reflecting after the accident on the process of planning the new automatic crossings, a member of the railway inspectorate thought it unreasonable that the inspectorate should have to consider the whole range of road traffic which might potentially use a crossing, rather than the general run of such traffic, an attitude which was not accepted in the final report. Similarly, at Summerland, stereotyped assumptions about the likely behavior of the general public in the event of a fire ignored those parents who were separated from their children who were in the children's cinema on another floor. These parents fought to reach them against the flow of the crowd, increasing congestion on a crowded and dangerous staircase.

The problems created in situations where safe operation relies to some extent upon the safe behavior of strangers are intensified by the fact that the strangers are always located at the moment of danger at a site where they have a number of opportunities to manipulate the situation in ways not foreseen by those designing the abstract safety system. They may thus create complications by manipulating some of the manifold properties which any specific and concrete site possesses.

Failure to comply with existing regulations. Few relevant regulations had been framed in the Aberfan case regarding tip safety, but at Hixon, and particularly at Summerland, regulations that already existed were not satisfactorily complied with. Those concerned either did not realize that the regulations applied to the case in hand or they approached these regulations with a feeling of 'what can we get away with?' At other points, the regulations were not adequately implemented, mainly because they had become out-of-date and difficult to apply to changed technical, social, or cultural conditions. The manner in which theater regulations devised to apply to traditional theaters are to be interpreted when applied to a multiactivity leisure center such as Summerland, with cinemas, bars, and entertainment at several levels within a large enveloping structure, offers a case in point.

Minimizing emergent danger. Another problem which recurs at many points in the three reports is that of a failure to see or to appreciate fully the magnitude of some emergent danger. When possible hazards were recognized, they were commonly underestimated; even when the danger was more clearly visible, many individuals and groups undervalued it. Thus, the warning signs of an impending tip slide at Aberfan were not recognized by some individuals, and those who did see some danger completely failed to anticipate accurately the scale of the possible movement of the coal waste. At Summerland, the danger posed by a small rubbish fire against the side of the building was not appreciated for some time; even when it was, the elaborate fire alarm system built into the complex was not used, and the delay in contacting the fire service was such that one of the first notifications they received was from a ship at sea which could see the blaze on shore. Ambiguity and disagreement among several parties about the status and significance of the evidence pointing to possible danger also served to lead to an undervaluing of such evidence, particularly when the more complacent group was also the more powerful one.

When the full scale of developing danger became impossible to ignore, the apparently straightforward act of strengthening precautions was not always the response; instead, some individuals began to take action to shift the blame, while others sought to take control of the situation by wholly inappropriate and quasi-magical means. Surprisingly, this behavior extended to a tendency for individuals who were exposed to danger themselves to fail to call for help. Such behavior has been noted in more extensive studies, particularly of behavior in fires (Barlay, 1972) and in mining accidents (Lawrence, 1974). This behavior occurs partly because of a fear of sounding an unnecessary alarm, and partly because of psychological pressures to deny danger and to assert one's continued invulnerability (Wolfenstein, 1957).

All of these features of the three reports (summarized in Tables 2 and 3) relate to events leading up to the incidents. Another concern, reflected in the recommendations of the reports, deals with processes of cultural readjustment rather than with the incubation of the disaster.

Nature of recommendations after the disaster: the definition of well-structured problems. An important function of tribunals of inquiry is to make recommendations to prevent a recurrence of the particular kind of disaster being investigated. All three of the reports examined contain such recommendations. Though the recommendations are diverse, they have in common the following feature: each dealt with the problem that caused the disaster as it was later revealed and not as it presented itself to those involved beforehand. The recommendations, therefore, treat the well-structured problem defined and revealed by the disaster, rather than with preexisting, ill-structured problems.

Discussion

An analysis of the features of the organizational and administrative arrangements associated with the three disasters can serve to define the processes by which organizational failures develop. The relation of the common features of the analysis to the model outlined earlier is set out schematically in Table 2. In Stage I, prior to the incubation period, two of the inquiries revealed varying degrees of failure to comply with existing regulations. Where the regulations were still

Table 2 Common features observed in the development of 3 major disasters and their relation to various stages of development

Stage of development	Feature	Comments
Stage I. Initial beliefs and norms	Failure to comply with existing regulations	Violation of existing precautions
Stage II. Incubation period	Rigidities of belief and perception	A. Events unnoticed or misunderstood because of erroneous assumptions
	Decoy phenomena Disregard of complaints from outsiders	
	Information difficulties and noise The involvement of strangers	B. Events unnoticed or misunderstood because of difficulties of handling information in complex situations
	Failure to comply with discredited or out-of-date regulations	C. Effective violation of precautions passing unnoticed because of cultural lag in formal precautions
	Minimizing of emergent danger	D. Events unnoticed or misunderstood because of a reluctance to fear the worst outcome
Stage III. Precipitating event		
Stage IV. Onset		
Stage V. Rescue and salvage		
Stage VI. Full cultural readjustment	Definition of new well-structured problems and appropriate precautions in inquiries following the disaster	The establishment of a new level of precautions and expectations

current and applicable, such behavior represented a violation of existing precautionary norms, and any accident which might have resulted from such behavior would not have made cultural readjustment necessary. There is no problem in accounting for a catastrophe that occurs because a train driver is drunk, a pleasure boat is overloaded, or a company executive fails to observe codes of practice.

Most of the features extracted from the inquiry reports fall, of course, within the second stage of the incubation period, which is precisely the period when failures of foresight are developing. These may be clustered into four groupings within this period.

Table 3 Some examples of the features listed in Table 2

Feature	Example
IIA Rigidities of belief and perception	Major institutional neglect of tips as a potential source of danger (Aberfan)
Decoy phenomena	Local residents mistakenly thought that the danger from tips at Aberfan was associated with the tipping of very fine waste, and they withdrew some of their complaints when it was agreed that this would not be tipped Concern of police and transporter crew at Hixon with the danger of arcing onto overhead wires, and not with collision
Disregard of complaints from outsiders	Complaints from Aberfan residents not adequately dealt with by National Coal Board High-handed response from British Rail to haulage company over stalled lorry on crossing prior to Hixon accident
IIB Information difficulties and noise	Poor communication between individuals because of poor personal relations (Aberfan) Ambiguous orders: does facing traffic mean facing approaching traffic, or stationary traffic at the crossing (Hixon) Information buried in a mass of irrelevant material (Hixon) Information neglected because of pressure of work (Summerland) Police expected government documents to be interpreted for them, but this was not done with the automatic crossings instructions
Involvement of strangers	People using a rail crossing at Hixon were strangers to the rail system Public using the leisure center at Summerland were strangers to the organizations operating the center
IIC Failure to comply with discredited or out-of-date regulations	Uncertainty about how traditional theater regulations should apply to a new concept leisure center such as Summerland
IID Minimizing of emergent danger	Early movements of the tip at Aberfan were not conceived of as leading to major hazard Minor fire at Summerland was dealt with by staff, and there was delay in summoning the fire brigade

Events unnoticed or misunderstood because of erroneous assumptions. Discrepant events begin to accumulate in this period without eliciting comment, either because they are not noticed or because their significance is misunderstood. In each of the cases examined, some events contributing to the disaster were unappreciated because no one expected or was alert for such phenomena, or because they were explained away as alternative, decoy phenomena, so that their full nature was missed. By its very nature, such a condition is a difficult one to observe without the benefit of hindsight, but clues may be sought by an examination of the manner in which those who dissent from accepted organizational views are treated. If the existing orthodoxy automatically dismisses complaints from outsiders as attempts to claim power by nonexpert cranks, the existence of an undue degree of organizational bias and rigidity is suspected. By the same token, when members of the organization adopt over-rigid stereotypes of the problems and the people being dealt with, dangerous misperceptions are again likely to develop.

Events unnoticed or misunderstood because of difficulties in handling information in complex situations. Each of the disaster inquiries revealed a complex and varied pattern of misunderstandings, ambiguities, and failures of communication, some of which contributed to the disaster, and others of which were revealed incidentally and were found to have no bearing on the accident. Perfect communication will never be possible in any but the simplest of systems. And many of the misunderstandings and failures to communicate revealed by public inquiries could be readily duplicated in organizational situations where no disastrous outcome occurs. It is reasonable to expect, however, some kind of relationship between increasing difficulty in information handling and increasing likelihood of failures of communication accumulating in such a way as to lead to the incubation of a disaster.

Tasks that must be handled by large organizations will generate a large number of messages within the organization. Thus, they are more likely to offer an opportunity for failures of communication to develop than are tasks which can be handled in a smaller organization. Similarly, where a task is handled by a number of agencies, there is more likelihood of communication failures occurring than when a task can be contained within a single agency. The likelihood of such failures will be increased further by the fact that each organizational unit or subunit will have developed its own distinctive subculture and its own framework of bounded rationality. This may give rise to erroneous assumptions about the portion of the problem that is being handled by other units. Again, the more prolonged, complex, vague, hasty and large-scale the task, the more likelihood of information handling difficulties arising. Prolonged tasks are likely to be associated with changes in goals, responsibilities, and administrative roles that create difficulties. Large and complex tasks generate more information; vague tasks generate more ambiguities and more noise (Wohlstetter, 1962). Rushed tasks lead to the overlooking of information because of pressure of work. Two factors which were identified as particularly contributing to the complexity and unpredictability of organizational tasks are the design of large complex sites, and the management of groups of strangers who have access to such sites.

Since a state of variable disjunction of information is by definition one in which the resources available to handle information are inadequate, such a condition would be expected to increase the propensity for information difficulties to accumulate in a hazardous manner.

Effective violations of precautions passing unnoticed because of cultural lag in existing precautions. A simple failure to observe existing regulations is one problem, but a more complex situation arises when existing precautionary regulations are discredited, because they are out-of-date or inapplicable to the case in hand, but not yet changed. In such cases, as when existing theater regulations were deemed to be inapplicable to the Summerland leisure center, there may be difficulty in finding an appropriate standard by which to judge the ad hoc solutions arrived at, without the benefit of guidance from well-considered formal precautions.

Events unnoticed or misunderstood because of a reluctance to fear the worst outcome. This tendency was a particularly noticeable one in the evidence submitted to the inquiries studied, and it has been noted also by other observers. Clearly, when existing danger signs are not perceived, given low priority, treated as ambiguous or as sources of disagreement, and considered insignificant because of psychological dispositions or for other reasons, another avenue is provided for the accumulation of events which may combine to lead to disaster.

Stages III to V in Table 2 cover the area of most preexisting disaster studies. No attempt was made in the present study to categorize events falling in these three stages. In Stage VI, however, a role was played by each of the committees or tribunals of inquiry in establishing a new level of precautions and new expectations about their efficacy. In each case, the report weighed and evaluated the behavior revealed by its inquiries, marking it down as responsible or irresponsible, or good or bad practice, even when the behavior may have had no direct bearing upon the particular incident investigated. Each report then concluded by making recommendations which sought to amend existing beliefs and assumptions, and to establish new norms of behavior, to prevent a recurrence of similar incidents.

Conclusion

The present article initiates debate and research into the important question of the conditions under which organizational groupings can make gross errors of perception, judgment, and calculation that lead to unfortunate or disastrous consequences. The above catalog of conditions represents only a first contribution to this debate. Work is currently being pursued to extend the range of disaster reports studied, and to include a consideration of other forms of organizational failures. The overall findings reported here could be restated as the proposition that disaster-provoking events tend to accumulate because they have been overlooked or misinterpreted as a result of false assumptions, poor communications, cultural lag, and misplaced optimism.

At this level of generality, such a proposition may not be particularly unexpected, but it should be considered in the light of two points. First, disasters, other than those arising from natural forces, are not created overnight. It is rare that an individual, by virtue of a single error, can create a disastrous outcome in an area formerly believed to be relatively secure. To achieve such a transformation, he or she needs the unwitting assistance offered by access to the resources and resource flows (Benson, 1975) of large organizations, and time. The three accidents discussed here had been incubating for a number of years. In the case of Aberfan, the accumulation of the basic misconceptions which contributed in a major way to the tragedy began a century or so ago. By contrast with an analysis of 405 accidents in gold mines (Lawrence, 1974), which showed a mean of 1.96 human errors per accident, an approximate count of similar types of error shows that the disasters at Aberfan, Hixon, and Summerland were associated with 36, 61, and 50 errors per disaster, respectively. Small-scale failures can be produced very rapidly, but large-scale failures can only be produced if time and resources are devoted to them.

Second, the listing of general categories fails to convey fully the complexity of the series of events from which the general categories have been drawn. It is not merely that there are 50 or more subtle variations in modes of miscommunication. More than that, the categories of events listed in Tables 2 and 3 represent cultural, institutional, informational, psychological, and task-related phenomena in organizational and interorganizational settings. Each of the disasters arose not because of a single factor, but because of the accumulation of complex branching chains made up of mixes of each kind of these phenomena. A major research task is the production of taxonomies of such interactions if the preconditions of disaster and of other failures of foresight are to be more fully understood.

Barry A. Turner is a lecturer in the Department of Sociology at the University of Exeter, England.

References

Aberfan (1966–1967) *Report by the Tribunal of Inquiry*, House of Commons Paper HC 553, HMSO: London.

Barlay, Stephen (1972) *Fire: An International Report*, Hamish Hamilton: London.

Barton, Allen H. (1969) *Communities in Disaster: A Sociological Analysis of Collective Stress Situations*, Ward Lock Educational: London.

Benson, Kenneth J. (1975) 'The interorganizational net-work as a political economy', *Administrative Science Quarterly*, 20: 229–249.

Carr, Lowell J. (1932) 'Disaster and the sequence-pattern concept of social change', *American Journal of Sociology*, 38: 207–218.

Crozier, Michel (1964) *The Bureaucratic Phenomenon*, Tavistock: London.

Fritz, Charles E. (1961) 'Disaster', in Merton, R. K. and Nisbet, R. A. (eds) *Contemporary Social Problems*, 651–694, Harcourt Brace and World: New York.

Glaser, B. and Strauss, A. (1967) *The Discoveries of Grounded Theory: Strategies for Qualitative Research*, Weidenfeld and Nicolson: London.

Goeller, B. F. (1969) 'Modelling the traffic safety', *Accident Analysis and Prevention*, 1: 167–204.

Gouldner, Alvin (1954) *Patterns of Industrial Bureaucracy*, Free Press: New York.

Hale, A. R. and Hale. M. (1970) 'Accidents in perspective', *Occupational Psychology*, 44: 115–121.

Healy, Richard J. (1969) *Emergency and Disaster Planning*, Wiley: New York.

Hirsch, Paul M. (1975) 'Organizational analysis and industrial sociology: an instance of cultural lag', *The American Sociologist*, 10: 3–12.

Hixon (1968) *Report of the Public Inquiry into the Accident at Hixon Level Crossing on January 6th 1968*, Command paper Cmnd. 3706, HMSO: London.

Killian, Lewis M. (1956) *An Introduction to Methodological Problems of Field Studies in Disasters*, Committee on Disaster Studies Report No. 8, Publication 464, Washington D.C.: National Academy of Sciences, National Research Council.

Kynaston Reeves, Tom and Turner, Barry A. (1972) 'A theory of organization and batch behavior in batch production factories', *Administrative Science Quarterly*, 17: 81–98.

Lawrence, A. C. (1974) 'Human error as a cause of accidents in gold-mining', *Journal of Safety Research*, 6: 78–88.

Lawrence, Paul R. and Lorsch, Jay W. (1967) *Organizations and Environment: Managing Differentiation and Integration*, Harvard University, Division of Research: Boston.

Meier, R. L. (1965) 'Information input overload: features of growth in communications oriented institutions', in Massarik, Fred and Ratoosh, Philburn (eds), *Mathematical Explorations in Behavioral Science*, 233: 273, R. D. Irwin: Homewood, Ill.

Micheal Colliery (1968) *Report of the Inquiry into the Fire at Micheal Colliery*, Fife, Command Paper Cmnd. 3657, HMSO: London.

Nosow, Sigmund and Form, William H. (1958) *Community in Disaster*, Harper: New York.

Powell, John W., Rayner, Jeanette and Finesinger, Jacob E. (1953) 'Responses to disaster in American cultural groups', in US Army Medical Service Graduate School, *Symposium on Stress*, Washington, D.C: Army Medical School Graduate School.

Queen, Stuart A. and Martin Mann, Delbert (1925) *Social Pathology*, Thomas Y. Crowell Co.: New York.

Rayner, Jeanette F. (1957) 'Studies of disaster and other extreme situations – an annotated selected bibliography', *Human Organization*, 16: 30–40.

Sea Gem (1967) *Report of the Inquiry in the Causes of the Accident to the Drilling Rig*, Sea Gem, Command Paper Cmnd. 3409, HMSO: London.

Simon, Herbert (1957) *Administrative Behavior*, Free Press: New York.

Summerland (1974) *Report of the Summerland Fire Commission*, Government Office: Isle of Man.

Thompson, James D. (1967) *Organizations in Action*, McGraw-Hill: New York.

Tonge, Fred M. (1961) *A Heuristic Program for Assembly Line Balancing*, Prentice-Hall: Englewood Cliffs, N. J.

Turner, Barry A. (1970) 'The organisation of production scheduling in complex-batch production situations', in G. Heald (ed.), *Approaches to Organisational Behaviour*, 87–99, Tavistock: London.

Turner, Barry A. (1971) *Exploring the Industrial Sub-culture*, Macmillan: London.

Turner, Barry A. (1976) 'An examination of some of the organisational preconditions associated with some major disasters', presented to Open University Seminar, City University, London, November 1974. Reprinted in G. Peters (ed.) *Human Failures and Systems Failures*, TD432 Unit 4, The Open University Press: Milton Keynes.

Wallace, Anthony F. C. (1956) *Human Behaviour in Extreme Situations: A Survey of the Literature and Suggestions for Further Research*, Committee on Disaster Studies, Report No. 1, Publication 90, National Academy of Sciences, National Research Council: Washington, D.C.

Wigglesworth, E. L. (1972) 'A teaching model of injury causation and a guide for selecting countermeasures', *Occupational Psychology*, 46: 69–78.

Wilensky, H. L. (1967) *Organizational Intelligence*, Basic Books: New York.

Wohlstetter, Roberta (1962) *Pearl Harbor: Warning and Decision*, Stanford University Press: Stanford, Calif.

Wolfenstein, Martha (1957) *Disaster: A Psychological Essay*, Routledge and Kegan Paul: London.

Chapter 9

Thierry (Terry) C. Pauchant and Ian I. Mitroff

CRISIS PRONE VERSUS CRISIS AVOIDING ORGANIZATIONS: IS YOUR COMPANY'S CULTURE ITS OWN WORST ENEMY IN CREATING CRISES?

DEFINING THE 'HEALTH' OF an organization is even more difficult than that of an individual. For one, organizations are more complex. They are composed of innumerable individuals spread out in space and time, literally over the entire globe. For another, an organization is composed of a highly complex interplay between people, technology, products, plants, facilities, marketing, selling, distribution, and financial systems. For still another, all of these various factors are themselves a complex blend of (a) known and unknown, (b) conscious and unconscious, and (c) rational and irrational forces.

In recent years, students of organizations have come to appreciate that one of the most powerful sets of forces acting on organizations is that of organizational culture. Roughly, *culture is to an organization what personality is to an individual*. The parallel is even more striking. Freud and a host of other significant social scientists have shown that some of the most important aspects of personality are unconscious. We should not therefore be surprised to find that the same holds true of organizations: some of their most important aspects are unconscious. As a result, organizations are largely *unaware* of some of the most important forces influencing their actions (Zaleznik and Kets de Vries, 1975; Starbuck *et al.*, 1978; Kets de Vries and Miller, 1985).

One of the more significant ways in which these unconscious forces operate is through *basic, taken-for-granted assumptions* that an organization makes about itself, its customers, employees, and surrounding environment (Mason and Mitroff, 1981; Schein, 1985). Most of the time, the basic assumptions an organization makes about itself and the other factors in its environment don't matter. An organization can 'get by' in 'normal or good times' by not knowing or examining its assumptions very deeply or systematically. But these are not normal times. All organizations everywhere today face enormous pressures from worldwide global competition. In addition, they face a whole new series of threats not experienced on any previous scale before (Mitroff and Kilmann, 1984; Fink, 1986).

These threats are major crises represented by such recent events as (a) the nationwide tampering of a major product, as happened to Johnson and Johnson, (b) major plant and environmental disasters such as Bhopal (Shrivastava, 1987) and Chernobyl, (c) a major tragedy such as the destruction of the space shuttle Challenger which threatened the reputation and existence of the entire space program (Perrow, 1984).

The list of major crises goes on: terrorism, sabotage, product defects, computer breakdowns, hostile takeovers, occupational health diseases, sexual harrassment (Mitroff, Pauchant and Shrivastava, 1988).

In this article, we are primarily concerned with man-made, organizationally induced crises or disasters, *not* natural ones (e.g, earthquakes, floods, hurricanes). Our major questions are: Are some organizations (cultures) crisis prone? Do such cultures create in some way their own crises? What are the differences between 'healthy' versus 'crisis-prone' or 'unhealthy' cultures? We argue that there are indeed strong differences between healthy and unhealthy companies, and in fact, they can be observed in terms of the differences in assumptions that organizations make on five basic categories that have been shown to constitute an organization's culture (see Schein, 1985). The categories are:

1   *Humanity's relationship to nature*. At the corporate level, do the key members view the relationship of the corporation to its environment as one of dominance, submission, harmonizing, finding an appropriate niche, or what?

2   *The nature of reality and truth*. What are the organization's rules, policies, behavior that define what is 'real' and what is not? What is a fact? Truth?

3   *The nature of human nature*. What does it mean to be 'human' and what attributes are considered intrinsic or ultimate? Is human nature good, evil, or neutral?

4   *The nature of human activity*. What is the 'right' thing for human beings to do, on the basis of the above assumptions about reality, the environment, and human nature; to be active, passive, self-developmental, fatalistic, or what?

5   *The nature of human relationship*. What is considered to be the 'right' way for people to relate to each other? Is life cooperative or competitive; individualistic, group collaborative or communal; based on traditional linear authority, law, charisma, or what?

(Adapted from Schein, 1985, p. 86.)

Assumptions made in any one of these categories will have a powerful influence on corporate policies and practice. For example, if the culture of a corporation assumes that the nature of human beings is intrinsically 'bad', then such a corporation will set up a number of controls and a strong system of rewards and punishments to regulate its members' behavior. A culture that sees human nature as 'neutral' or 'good' will use strong controls much less.

Cultural differences between healthy and unhealthy companies

To find whether such differences existed, we interviewed 30 high-ranking executives in 23 organizations. We explored (1) the overall culture of their organizations in relation to crises, and (2) the extent to which their organizations were
involved in crisis management (CM). Our results are based on in-depth interviews averaging two and a half hours. These organizations – which need to
remain anonymous – span ten industries such as food, oil, telecommunications,
defense, etc. They are, for the most part, well known U.S. companies, employing on the average 50,000 employees and generating about $6,500 million of
yearly revenues. Finally, most of the executives interviewed were at the corporate level, with policy making responsibilities in CM and can be considered as
'experts' in CM in their respective companies.

To find such differences, first we established whether the organizations we
studied have a fragmented or integrated effort in CM. To do so we used a total of
nine criteria which have been shown to be important in establishing and maintaining a robust program in CM (Mitroff and Kilmann, 1984; Fink, 1986). For
example, we asked whether their organization had a tracking system to warn of
impending signals of potential crises (Ansoff, 1975; Housel, El Sawy and
Donovan, 1986); whether they simulated and trained for major crises (Basset,
1987; Smart and Vertinsky, 1977); whether they had formally established a
Crisis Management Unit (CMU) (Billings *et al.*, 1980; Milburn, 1972); whether
their CM program was 'championed' by their CEO (Argyris and Schön, 1978;
Collins, 1987); the extent to which their CM efforts cut across different functions and divisions of their organization (Mitroff, Pauchant and Shrivastava,
1987); and so on. An in-depth presentation of these criteria has been presented
elsewhere (Pauchant, 1988a).

Two groups of organizations emerged from this research: 57% of the sample,
or 13 companies, had no or only fragmented efforts in CM; 43% or 10 companies had an integrated effort. *Only 4 companies out of 10 had a relatively integrated
crisis management plan and one third had practically no plans whatsoever.* This finding is
consistent with the results of other researchers (for example, Fink, 1986). This
relative lack of effort in CM is particularly alarming considering that 83% of this
same sample, or 19 companies see themselves as being *more vulnerable to crises
than they were in the past.*

Second, we tried to identify key cultural characteristics between these two
groups to explain the discrepancy between, on the one hand, the relative lack of
CM efforts, and, on the other hand, the general perception of increased
vulnerability to crises.

One fundamental conclusion emerged repeatedly. What differentiates
between corporations with weak and strong efforts in CM was the nature of their
'*organizational identity*'. By this we mean that how executives feel about themselves and their organization is strongly related to their firm's involvement in
CM (Schwartz, 1987).

To differentiate between the two types of companies, we labeled the
unhealthy ones SICs, standing for 'self-inflated corporations', and 'PSRC',
standing for 'positive self-regard corporations'. SICs are essentially narcissistic

(Kohut, 1971, 1977). They care only or mainly about themselves. A crisis is something which happens mainly only to them and not to their customers or their environment. PSRC are exactly the opposite.

We found a strong relation between the conception an organization had of itself and the efforts it mounted in CM in nearly 80% of the companies interviewed. The SIC group exhibited, in the great majority of cases, a fragmented and weak effort in CM, while the PSRC group exhibited a strong and more integrated effort. Let's go through more systematically how these two groups differ on fundamental assumptions.

(1) Humanity's relation to nature

This assumption concerns the definition of nature itself, i.e. how a corporation defines its environment, and its relationship to it. The SIC group tends to define its environment and crises in relation to itself, while the PSRC group tends to view itself in relation to the larger environment. This is particularly evident in the definitions that executives in these organizations give about CM. For example, a typical definition given in the SIC group was: 'An event of a magnitude which threatens the well-being of the entire *corporation* and involves a large portion of top management time and activity', while a typical definition from the PSRC group was: 'An unexpected event that produces great tensions and uncertainty and impact on *the public* as well as on the organization itself'.

When asked to list their primary stakeholders, the SIC group has the tendency to emphasize the importance of its *internal* stakeholders such as partners, managers, top management, CEO, etc., while the PSRC group adds to this list *external* stakeholders such as customers, trade partners, regulators, public at large, etc.

In effect, in the SIC group, which exhibits, as stressed before, the weakest efforts in CM, *corporations confuse their internal structure with the structure of crises.* These corporations are unable to empathize with those crises that could potentially confront their external stakeholders. For example, when asked what could be the worst crisis that customers could face, an executive in a food company from the SIC group seriously answered that the worst crisis would be for his customers to 'not find our product on the shelf'. One could see here the basic incapacity of this executive to put himself in his customers' shoes. When repeatedly questioned, he could acknowledge the fear of food poisoning, death due to tampering, etc.

This lack of empathy, i.e. the fact that these companies do not empathize with others, involves a second aspect of the assumption, i.e. the relationship of the corporation to its environment. Defining the environment in relation to itself, the SIC group views the environment largely from the standpoint of what it can provide or do for the corporation. In other words, the relation of these corporations to their environment is mostly a relation of dominance or subjugation. Customers, regulators, suppliers, etc., are all primarily viewed as *means* for the accomplishment of corporate objectives. For example, in this view, customers are only acknowledged and catered to from the standpoint that they will buy the firm's products. Conversely, PSRC perceive their environment in a broader context. For them, customers need to be catered to, not just because they are potential buyers, but because they are fellow human beings. The relationship between the company and the customer is thus no longer reduced solely to the single act of buying; rather he or she is perceived as a whole person, as an end in themselves.

(2) The nature of reality and truth

We found that the SIC group uses a great number of *defensive mechanisms* when the reality of crises confronts their self-inflated fantasies. These mechanisms are used by individuals to protect their sense and perception of themselves (see for example Klein, 1937; or Kohut, 1971). Some use *denial*, or the *conscious refusal* to acknowledge reality. Others use the mechanism of *disavowal*, i.e. they acknowledge a threatening reality but downplay its importance. For example, an executive in a SIC consulting firm considered its 70% yearly turnover of employees as 'normal' and 'not impacting on the functioning of the firm'. Other firms use the mechanism of *fixation* where the organization expresses a rigid commitment to a particular course of action. For example, an executive in the leisure industry explained that his firm could not involve itself in efforts in CM 'considering our commitment to the bottom line'. Still, another mechanism of defense is developed through the feeling of *grandiosity*, i.e. feeling of omnipotence, perfection and all-powerfulness. For example, an executive in the health industry stressed that his corporation did not develop any efforts in CM considering that his top management believed they were 'bigger than life'. Still, another strategy of defense is *idealization*, i.e. the feeling of omnipotence through the idealization of another. For example, an executive in the oil industry declared that his company could not be threatened by any crises, stating that 'our CEO can handle anything'. Lastly, another strategy of defense is *intellectualization*. For example, an executive in a non-profit organization declared that his firm did not consider terrorism as a major threat, arguing that 'we do "good" to society; who would want to hurt us?'

These different examples show the diverse ways in which the SIC group re-defines reality to suit its fantasies and beliefs about itself. We should stress that we found indications of these defense mechanisms in 100% of the firms constituting the SIC group, whereas we found such examples in only 30% of the PSRC group. We should also note that this misperception of reality is not motivated primarily by *rational* blocks, i.e. executives not being able to rationally apprehend reality, but rather through *emotional* blocks, executives not having the *emotional resources* to face up to critical situations.

(3) The nature of human nature

This basic assumption defines what it means 'to be human'. The SIC group has the tendency to view internal and external stakeholders as 'good' only if they confirm the fantasized sense of perfection of the firm, and as 'bad' or 'evil' if they do not. In this sense, the world is fragmented between 'good' and 'bad' guys, 'us' and 'them'; 'us' being the 'good guys', the 'excellent company', the 'pride of America', and 'them' being all the rest, the 'bad companies', the ones that 'experience crises', the 'ones that disagree with us'. In particular, the media is perceived by most corporations of the SIC group as 'evil' to be controlled or neutralized, considering that this group brings to the world at large news about the lack of perfection of the particular corporations under crisis.

Particularly intriguing in this category is the use of the concept of 'corporate excellence'. In this context, excellence can be seen as a potential additional barrier against dealing with reality, for not allowing a serious effort in CM. For example, an executive in the food industry declared that:

> 'A formal program is not necessary for an excellent company . . .
> Our track record is so good that crisis management is not considered
> as a major risk for us . . . Only bad companies need crisis management
> to cover up their deficiencies.'

In some sense, it seems that the 'search for excellence', popularized by Peters and Waterman (1982) and implemented in many organizations, when pushed to the extreme, goes *against* the establishment of a serious and integrated program of CM. We have found that corporations in the SIC group lack executives in key positions who have the emotional strength to face up to reality and acknowledge that their corporation and the people who manage it are not all-powerful, all-omnipotent, all-perfect and 'all-excellent'.

As can be expected, corporations in the PSRC group do not divide the world up into simplistic 'good-bad' dichotomies. If they acknowledge their strengths and specific competencies, they are also quick to point out their deficiencies and need for improvement. It should be stressed again, that most of these feelings are *unconscious*, i.e. *not available to consciousness*. During the interviews, we met a number of executives who could articulate the nonsensical nature of their wish for perfection, while at the same time demonstrating through their day-to-day behavior the continued need for perfection.

(4) The nature of human activities

This basic assumption dictates what is the 'right' thing to do for human beings. In the SIC group, we found two paramount strategies in relation to CM: 'Doing something for the sake of doing something' and 'fatalism'. Both can be seen as an expression of a weak, damaged or self-inflated sense of corporate identity.

The 'doing something for the sake of doing' strategy, largely practiced by the SIC group, creates an illusion of action and omnipotence (Kohut, 1971). As seen in basic assumption 1, these companies confuse their own organizational structure for the structure of crises. Strategic actions thus *mirror* the company's own culture as opposed to being adapted to the reality presented by crises. Paramount to this strategy is the insistence on engineering and financial actions, i.e. technical and financial quick-fixes. In the 23 companies surveyed, actions on technical issues, such as financial and engineering audits and improvements were *370% more developed* than actions concerning human and social issues, such as the behavioral preparation of executives to cope with the psychological dimensions (e.g. stress, anxiety, breakdowns) of crises (Barnes, 1984; Holsti, 1971; Raphael, 1986). These results are consistent with another study which quantitatively analyzed the CM efforts of 114 *Fortune* 1000 companies. We roughly found the same percentage (Mitroff, Pauchant and Shrivastava, 1988). This is *not* to say that financial and engineering issues are not important in CM. They obviously are. However this indicates that, at the present time, most companies have focused their efforts on what they *are used to doing*. They have not yet come to see that crises require *new* programs of psychological and emotional preparation.

Through adopting an attitude of 'fatalism', the SIC group avoids guilt raised by crises. For example, when we pointed out the paradox that even an 'acknowledged' 'excellent' company such as Johnson and Johnson (J&J) had experienced two major crises from their Tylenol products, the majority of the executives of the SIC group stressed that these accidents were 'random', caused by 'bad luck'; they had to be considered a disaster, i.e. caused from the influence of a 'bad star' from the Latin 'dis' 'bad', and 'astrum' 'star'. Although we personally admire J&J as a company, as well as how they handled their crises, we do not subscribe to the 'disaster' theory, and wish to reintroduce a part of responsibility for J&J in these crises. After all, it is likely that the market success of J&J's products influenced the choice of the psychopath(s) for tampering with them as well as increasing the importance of these crises. The fatalism strategy is a dangerous one; in effect, if it reduces guilt and responsibility for a company's actions. It also justifies the company's doing nothing.

The PSRC group do not, to a great extent, use these same strategies. They believe in strategic action. They accept the guilt and anxiety induced by crises in order to be in a position to act against them. They also have a more balanced and integrated 'crisis portfolio', not focusing only on the technical issues in CM (Mitroff, Pauchant and Shrivastava, 1987). They believe in both technical *and* psychological actions to prepare for and manage crises.

(5) *The nature of human relationship*

Lastly, this basic assumption influences the definition of the 'right' way for people to relate to each other. In the SIC group, this relation is mostly competitive and individualistic. The results of this culture, such as giving a few executives a great amount of power in proportion to their grandiose performances and dramatic results, have perhaps been most exemplified by Wall Street in the last years. The street has a name for its self-inflated heroes; it calls them the 'superstars'. When some firms have realized for awhile huge growths and profits through these individuals, the number of crises experienced by this industry at large such as insider trading cases and dramatic losses, have been well documented. Inversely, we found that the PSRC group uses a paradoxical approach to human relationship, being – at the same time – competitive and cooperative, individualistic and group cooperative. For example, a number of PSRC firms have chosen not one but *several* project managers for their most important projects, acknowledging both the individual and the group, but protecting itself against the loss or the mistakes of one of these managers.

Corporate culture change

The results from our study are frightening. Without exception, the executives who disagreed with their top management on their firm's weak actions in CM stressed that it will take '*a major shift*' in the culture of their company and the views of their top management *before* any serious efforts in CM will be developed. This result is frightening, considering that 2/3 of the companies (14 out of 23) acknowledged that their involvement in CM was in more than 80% of the cases based on a *reaction* to crises as opposed to *pro-action*. For example, one executive in the leisure industry stressed that his company will need a 'serious black-eye' before even considering a CM plan. This means that we will have to wait for major crises, for 'major black-eyes', with *major impact on stakeholders at large and the 'bottom line' before* some companies will develop more integrative and pro-active efforts in CM.

To move the culture of a company from the SIC to the PSRC group requires that a company manage the organizational and individual *anxiety* of its members. We have labeled this process '*management of self*' (Pauchant, 1988a). In essence, such a process attempts to diminish the self-inflated behaviors that go against efforts in CM and increase positive self-regard behaviors that allow an appropriate program of CM. Basic to this process is *to replace anxiety with fear*. It was clear during our interviews that what paralyzed the SIC group from taking appropriate CM actions was the existence of a *diffuse, subjective, vague, non-articulated anxiety* (Kohut, 1971). We should stress that this anxiety was *not consciously acknowledged* by the interviewed executives. What emerged from these interviews was not the anxiety itself, *but the defensive mechanisms executives used to manage it*.

Anxiety and fear are different (May, 1958). Anxiety lacks a specific object while fear is something which is experienced and directed towards a specific object. In other words, one is not anxious of something. To be 'anxious' is to be 'attacked from the rear' or 'from all sides at once' (May, 1950). Not having any specific object to be anxious of, no strategic action is possible to reduce its cause(s), except the defensive mechanisms we have presented in this article, such as denial, feelings of grandiosity, etc. In contrast, fear has a specific object. One is afraid of something. Fear, thus, allows the development of strategic actions, attention being narrowed to a specific object. Different mechanisms can be used to move a corporation from anxiety to fear in relation to CM. Each company, depending on the situation of its organizational identity, will prefer some. We mention here six such strategies.

A first strategy is to bring into the open this phenomenon of anxiety (May, 1950). This article is one way to start a discussion of it. Another strategy is to allow executives and non-executives to have a direct experience with the phenomenon of crises. Organizational crisis simulation workshops, as close as possible to reality, can be used (Basset, 1987). A third strategy is to allow organizational members to conceptualize the dimensions and the complexity of crises. A computerized simulation model would be helpful in this area (Pauchant, 1988a). A fourth strategy could be to sensitize executives to the deeper psychological issues at stake that crises raise. Executive seminars that deal with the psychological aspects are critical (Mitroff and Kilmann, 1984). Similarly the use of psychologists on staff and/or the use of external experts in the area could be useful. A fifth strategy is to attempt to diminish anxiety through different stress management workshops, specifically targeted toward the phenomenon of crises. Lastly, leadership itself is a strong tool for change in the area of CM. However, if the leader, such as the CEO, is perceived as too strong by organizational members, he or she could be idealized, resulting in the defense mechanism of idealization by employees, going against the development of strategic efforts in CM.

A last word: To say that the 'concept of self' or 'organizational identity' is paramount in influencing strategic actions in CM is to view the phenomenon of crises in a different light. It is to acknowledge the *existential nature of crises* (Pauchant, 1988b), i.e. to acknowledge the negative effects of individual and corporate grandiosity and the wish for self-inflated 'excellence'. We are not advocating the development in corporations of workshops on existential philosophy, studying Sartre or Kierkegaard, although it is clear that this branch of philosophy treats the concept of crisis as its central theme (see for example May, 1958). We are however advocating that executives who see the necessity for modifying their corporate culture not only consider the technical issues involved in CM but also the human and social issues. As we have argued, the notion of threats to the basic concept of the self, the fundamental wishes for grandiosity and excellence, are at the crux of the issue. Lastly, we wish to stress that if we have labeled Self-Inflated Corporations as 'sick', we also understand and empathize with their wish to preserve at all cost their organization of experience and sense of identity. However, considering that corporate crises can now involve the large scale death of individuals as in the Bhopal or Chernobyl accidents, we must encourage these organizations to examine their basic sense of identity.

References

Ansoff, H.I. (1975) 'Managing strategic surprise by response to weak signals', *California Management Review*, 18 (2): 21–33.

Argyris, C. and Shön, D.A. (1978) *Organizational learning: A theory of action perspective*, Addison-Wesley: Reading, MA.

Barnes, J., Jr. (1984) 'Cognition biases and their impact on strategic planning', *Strategic Management Journal*, 5: 129–137.

Basset, D.A. (1987) 'Crisis management: Lessons from the FBI' presented at the crisis management seminar, September 14–15, University of Southern California, Center for Crisis Management: Los Angeles, CA.

Billings, R.S., T.W. Milburn and M.L. Schaalman (1980) 'A model of crisis perception: A theoretical and empirical analysis', *Administrative Science Quarterly*, 25: 300–316.

Collins, D.E. (1987) 'Critical lessons learned from the experience in handling product tampering accidents: The case of Johnson and Johnson', Presented at the crisis management seminar, September 14–15, University of Southern California, Center for Crisis Management: Los Angeles, CA.

Fink, S. (1986) *Crisis management: Planning for the inevitable*, AMACOM: New York.

Holsti, O.R. (1971) 'Crisis, stress, and decision making' *International Social Science*, 23: 53–67.

Housel, T.J., El Sawy, O.A. and Donovan, P.F. (1986) 'Information systems for crisis management: Lessons from Southern California Edison' *MIS Quarterly*, Dec.: 389–400.

Kets De Vries, M. and Miller, D. (1985) *The neurotic organization*, Jossey-Bass: San Francisco, CA.

Klein, M. (1937) *The psycho-analysis of children*: 2nd ed., Hogarth: London.

Kohut, H. (1971) *The analysis of the self: A systematic approach to the psychoanalytic treatment of narcissistic disorders*, International University Press: New York.

Kohut, H. (1977) *The restoration of self*, International University: New York.

Mason, R.O. and Mitroff, I.I. (1981) *Challenging strategic planning assumptions*, Wiley: New York.

May, R. (1950) *The meaning of anxiety*, Washington Square: New York.

May, R. (ed.) (1958) *Existence: A new dimension in psychiatry and psychology*, Random House: New York.

Milburn, T.W. (1972) 'The management of crisis', in C.F. Hermann (ed.) *International crises: Insights from behavioral research*, Free Press: New York.

Mitroff, I.I. and Kilmann (1984) *Corporate tragedies: Product tampering, sabotage, and other catastrophes*, Praeger: New York.

Mitroff, I.I., Pauchant, T.C. and Shrivastava, P. (1987) *Forming a crisis portfolio: Putting one's crisis preparations on a firmer footing*, Working paper, Center for Crisis Management, Graduate School of Business Administration, University of Southern California: Los Angeles, CA.

Mitroff, I.I., Pauchant, T.C. and Shrivastava, P. (1988) 'The structure of man-made organizational crises: Conceptual and empirical issues in the development of a general theory of crisis management, '*Technological Forecasting and Social Change*' in press.

Pauchant, T.C. (1988a) *Crisis management and narcissism: A Kohutian perspective*, unpublished doctoral dissertation, Graduate School of Business Administration, University of Southern California: Los Angeles, CA.

Pauchant, T.C. (1988b) *Organizational existentialism. Toward the concept of 'bounded emotionality'*, working paper, Research laboratory, School of Administrative Sciences, Laval University: Quebec City.

Perrow, C. (1984) *Normal accidents: Living with high-risk technologies*, Basic Books: New York.

Peters, T.J. and Waterman, R.H. (1982) *In search of excellence: Lessons from America's best-run companies*, Harper and Row: New York.

Raphael, B. (1986) *When disaster strikes: How individuals and communities cope with catatrophe*, Basic Books: New York.

Schein, E.H. (1985) *Organizational culture and leadership*, Jossey-Bass: San Francisco, CA.

Schwartz, H.S. (1987) 'On the psychodynamics of organizational disaster: The case of the space shuttle Challenger' *The Columbia Journal of World Business*, 22 (1): 59–68.

Shrivastava, P. (1987) *Bhopal: Anatomy of a crisis*, Ballinger: Cambridge, MA.

Smart, C. and Vertinsky, I. (1977) 'Designs for crisis decision units.' *Administrative Science Quarterly*, 22: 640–657.

Starbuck, W.H., Greve, A. and Hedberg, B.L. (1978) 'Responding to crises: Theory and the experience of European businesses', in: C.F. Smart and W.T. Stanbury (eds.), *Studies in crisis management*, Butterworth and Co: Toronto.

Zaleznik, A. and Kets de Vries, M. (1975) *Power and the corporate mind*, Houghton Mifflin: Boston, MA.

Chapter 10

Denis Smith

BEYOND CONTINGENCY PLANNING: TOWARDS A MODEL OF CRISIS MANAGEMENT

Introduction

THE 1980s WILL BE remembered as a consequence of a plethora of major commercial and industrial crises which took place worldwide during the decade. These crises were manifested in a variety of forms. Major industrial accidents involving considerable loss of life took place at Mexico City, Bhopal, Chernobyl and the offshore Piper Alpha oil platform. There were also a series of major transport failures during the decade which undermined public confidence in this sector of the service economy. Notable amongst such accidents were the sinking of the *Herald of Free Enterprise*, the Kings Cross underground station fire, the *Challenger* space shuttle explosion, the failure of the Soviet gas pipeline, the *Exxon Valdez* oil spill and, finally, the Lockerbie/Pan-Am and the Kegworth/M1 aircraft crashes.

Crises were not confined to the industrial sector during this period. The leisure industry was also subject to a series of catastrophic incidents which raised public consciousness of the risks associated with such activities. Football stadiums, for example, provided the locus for a series of major disasters including the fire at the Bradford City ground, the Heysel riot and the Hillsborough stadium disaster (where football supporters were crushed to death following an over-crowding incident). In all three of these events English soccer clubs were involved and each incident contributed to considerable changes being made in the management and organization of the game in the UK.

The opening months of 1990 bode ill for the mitigation of crisis events during the 1990s as a series of major incidents made the headlines in the UK alone. The storms that pounded the coastline of Britain during February and

March, along with the resultant floods, tested emergency plans to the full. The announcement in February that Perrier's bottled water, which was renowned for its purity, was contaminated with traces of benzene sent waves of panic through the market, as did the concern and scientific ambiguity over BSE ('mad cow disease') in British beef. In addition, the news in the British media that French nuclear power stations had an estimated potential failure rate of up to 1 in 20 did little to allay public fears about the potential for disaster realizable in that form of industrial activity.

The implications for management inherent in these various events are obvious. What they require is that organizations should strive to ensure that they have the frameworks and capabilities to cope with high levels of uncertainty and the seemingly increasing magnitude of crisis events. In addition, it is becoming incumbent on organizations to give serious consideration to the vexed and contentious issue of managerial style and culture in promulgating such crises.

The notion that events such as the ones listed above were somehow unforeseen is somewhat spurious, as academics have argued for many years that all systems have a propensity towards failure (see, for example, Perrow, 1984). Consequently, it is no longer enough for managers to consider 'if' a system will fail but rather 'when' that failure will occur. With the emergence in the UK courts of the contentious concept of 'corporate manslaughter' (following the sinking of the *Herald of Free Enterprise*) the climate exists where it will quickly become imperative for organizations to ensure that all necessary steps have been taken to prevent an accident occurring. Claims of 'managerial ignorance' regarding the situation prevailing prior to the disaster will no longer be bliss in providing a defence after the event. If we accept the premise that all organizations will face a crisis at some point in their lifespan, then the major question that needs to be addressed is this: how do we cope with such events when they occur and what steps can be taken to prevent them in the first place?

The former question has been the subject of vigorous debate within the academic and professional literature – perhaps to the detriment of the latter. It would appear that the focus, to date, of such debates has been in terms of developing coping strategies and curing the harm done to the corporate image in the wake of a crisis. The issue of prevention, whilst not ignored completely, has been severely neglected, largely because it raises fundamental questions about the nature of managerial style and organizational culture. These are both enmeshed within the organizational frameworks of power and are therefore difficult to change. In an attempt to shift the balance of analysis, the remainder of this paper will focus its attention on the theoretical aspects of crisis management, thereby attempting to provide a basis for considering the issues raised by pre-crisis managerial style.

The nature of industrial crisis management

As the existence of this journal testifies, crisis management has emerged as an academic specialization which owes its theoretical roots to work undertaken largely in North America. This new sub-field is essentially multidisciplinary in nature, drawing on research in the fields of economics, sociology and political science. As a consequence the term is often defined quite differently depending on the academic context in which it is used.

The problem of definition is an important issue within the study of crisis management and this can be explored by a closer examination of a number of different perspectives on the nature of a crisis. The first is offered by Dyson, who argues that, 'Crisis is clearly a perceptual affair. Industrial crisis has different faces in the sense that a particular crisis is likely to consist of a set of interlocked crises . . .' (Dyson, 1983, p. 28). Accepting the inherent ambiguity that exists within the use of the term it is necessary to assess what a crisis entails for those actors involved within it. Quarantelli (1988), for example, differentiates between those crises which are deemed to be intentional (such as war, civil disturbances, etc.) and those incidents which occur 'accidentally' within the context of a community setting. Such events would include the series of industrial accidents mentioned earlier which resulted in considerable loss of life amongst local residents. Shrivastava *et al.* (1988) develop this point and argue that crises are, '. . . organizationally-based disasters which cause extensive damage and social disruption, involve multiple stakeholders, and unfold through complex technological, organizational and social processes' (p. 285). This raises the issue of crises which are bound by organizational configurations but which nevertheless have the potential to affect a number of other groups which interface with the host organization.

The configuration of individual crisis events can be seen, therefore, as a function of the interactions between a number of smaller events which conspire to generate the main crisis event. The degree of coupling between such events gives rise to the sense of urgency that Wilks and Dyson (1983) see as being important within economically-based crises. They argue that such events can be categorized by virtue of the speed with which they occur. For them, urgency is one of three factors, along with issues of finality and threat, which are essential components of a crisis. They observe that such crises often result in a change in the ownership or management of the organization as the various stakeholders become wary of management's style of operation. In addition, Wilks and Dyson point to an increased likelihood of some form of government intervention in the post-crisis incident phase. This usually takes the form of legislative and policy change although, in certain cases, direct intervention is possible. The systems within which such crises occur often have the interaction between humans and technology as a dominant characteristic and the design of this interface creates the potential for latent failures unless properly managed (Reason, 1987). Perhaps the most celebrated accounts of such failures occur in process engineering and result in catastrophic accidents such as the one at Bhopal. The complex socio-political nature of crisis compounds the technical problem of definition as it is often the case that a technological crisis, due to systems failure, will create a financial crisis at a later point in the organization's lifetime. This situation occurred following the accident at Bhopal as Union Carbide sold off many of its assets in an attempt to avoid a hostile takeover bid (Shrivastava, 1987).

Some authors have gone so far as to suggest that an organization will reach a series of crisis points simply by virtue of its development over time and that the only way in which an organization can develop is to overcome such crises and move on to the next developmental phase (see Greiner, 1972). Indeed, it has been suggested that organizations can have a 'successful' crisis which helps to improve the overall performance of the enterprise. David (1990) states that, '. . . because of the way it focuses attention on how tasks are managed and draws new patterns of cohesion, a successfully handled crisis can benefit an organization' (p. 90). One of the more 'apparently' successful crises to occur in recent years was that experienced by the Perrier corporation. This contamination issue early in 1990 was seen by some French observers as a masterful public relations exercise which served to reinforce Perrier's image of a caring company. However, the reality of the situation was somewhat different as Perrier was forced to divest itself of the soft drinks division in order to fund the repositioning of the bottled water (Coyne, personal communication, 1990). The problem here is that public confidence in a company, or its products, needs to be restored in order to prevent a further crisis occurring as the market translates its concerns into buying behaviour.

In certain cases, governments intervene to restore public confidence in an organization or an entire industrial sector, especially when there is a significant public interest or where the state is the key regulator or operator. In many cases the government itself can be seen as a stakeholder in the crisis event (Zimmerman, 1987), a point borne out in the spate of rail accidents in the UK towards the end of the 1980s. Within this context, Zimmerman argues that the management of human resources is perhaps the greatest contributor to crisis generation and that governments can go some way towards mitigating this problem by changing the status within society of certain key groups, such as maintenance engineers. Such changes do not call for massive investment in new structures, but rather require an extension of existing powers and the development of a culture that sees accidents as routine rather than rare events (Zimmerman, 1987). Such a shift in organizational culture will have to be translated into changes in the nature of decision making.

The scope of the decision making process within crisis situations is often narrowed by the urgent nature of events which require an expeditious resolution of the fundamental problem. In certain cases it is possible to see a crisis affecting the strategic goals of the organization, as witnessed at Bhopal and through such events as the sinking of the *Herald of Free Enterprise*. This strategic theme is developed by Booth (1990), who observes that it is a lack of strategic planning which often lies at the root of an organization's inability to cope with a crisis event. He terms this diffidence towards crisis planning as a 'delayed reaction syndrome' which he defines as, '. . . the reluctance of organisations to invest in crisis management planning until conclusive evidence is available that there is a problem. By this time it is too late to prevent a crisis occurring. The best that can be done is to lessen the impact' (Booth, 1990, p. 1).

It also worth noting the limits of expertise within this complex decision making setting. The conventional wisdom that the appliance of scientific expertise will help to achieve a resolution of contentious issues has been brought into question in recent years. Indeed, some authors have suggested that the application of certain types of technical expertise in risk-based problems may even heighten conflict (see, for example, Smith, 1990). This increase in conflict results from both the trans-scientific nature of risk events and the disparate nature of the scientific body which will inevitably be aligned along partisan lines in contentious areas. Expert judgements of risk are themselves bounded by uncertainty and a belief in the infallibility of such judgements has proved to be a major problem in the generation of crises in the past. In order for management to develop its ability to plan for crisis events it must first recognize the limitations of its own expertise.

It is generally accepted that there are three distinct phases within the process of crisis management, namely, a pre-crisis/disaster phase (which includes warnings of impending crisis), a period of crisis impact/rescue, and finally a period of recovery/demise (see, for example, Cohen and Ahearn, 1980; Raphael, 1986). Following the final phase of a crisis it is necessary for the organization to return to some form of equilibrium, even though this may not be the situation that prevailed before the crisis (Raphael, 1986). In extreme circumstances it is conceivable for the organization to have its existence threatened by the severity of the crisis or by the failure of management to contain the impact of media and governmental intervention. The process of recovery may well extend over a considerable period of time and will be dependent upon a number of factors. These include both the extent of the damage and the ability of rescuers to mitigate the damage.

Within the literature it is possible to identify a series of potential rescuers ranging from the emergency services, through crisis decision teams, to public relations managers. Dealing with the emergency services first, there is a growing awareness that these organizations are themselves subject to a considerable degree of stress as a function of their roles as rescuers (see, for example, Douglas *et al.*, 1988; James, 1988). The effectiveness of rescue teams under conditions of stress is important as they are central to the process of damage limitation and recovery. In many organizations, senior managers are also exposed to high levels of stress as they attempt to cope with crises and consequently much attention has been focused on ways of reducing such stress levels whilst improving the quality of the crisis management process.

Crisis and environmental decision units have been seen by many companies as providing them with opportunities for effectively managing crises away from the normal decision making process. The impact and trauma that is associated with a crisis event is such that it can result in a disjuncture between the various elements of the decision making process. This requires a framework within which the decisions, taken under conditions of crisis, are of a high quality and are also implemented quickly by senior management (Smart and Vertinsky, 1977). Crisis decision units are designed to facilitate such a process and require that the host organization engages in a continual education and training programme to heighten awareness of crisis events amongst its managers. From an examination of the more popular business literature it would certainly appear that the notion of impact mitigation is high on the list of managerial priorities. The issue here becomes one of image management – the interaction between the organization and the media which is essential in order to avoid a protracted trial by the media.

One of the key issues in this regard is managing the 'gap between official and unofficial information' (David, 1990, p. 90). Within this context the aim of a crisis decision unit is to shield senior management from the attention of the media whilst at the same time providing them with the information to manage the situation (David, 1990). In addition, such units allow other sections of the organization to continue to carry out their functional tasks without being distracted by the events of the crisis (David, 1990). However, one possible problem that exists with such a specialized decision unit is that they can engender a 'pass the buck' mentality, as individuals see such problems as belonging to someone else (Hunt and Auster, 1990). In order to overcome this block it is necessary to develop a mutually supportive organizational culture which, at the same time, encourages whistle blowing and bottom-up communication flows as a means of highlighting potential problems.

The most common element in an effective crisis management programme appears therefore to be the presence of a responsive corporate culture which facilitates effective communication and develops intra-organizational support during a crisis. The next section explores this issue in more detail, paying particular attention to the influence of culture on contingency planning.

Rationality and culture – the limits of contingency planning

The culture of an organization is often held as being of critical importance to corporate strategic decision making (see, for example, Freeman and Gilbert, 1988; Johnson and Scholes, 1988), particularly in terms of its perceived ability to respond to a crisis event. Culture presents both an opportunity and a threat for crisis management. On the one hand, the culture of an organization can serve to precipitate a crisis by providing the environment within which such an event can escalate rapidly. Conversely, the prevailing culture can be central to an organization's ability to cope with a threatening situation (see Hunt and Auster, 1990). Mitroff et al. (1989) develop this thesis by arguing that organizations can be considered as being either 'crisis-prone' or 'crisis-prepared.' Their resultant 'onion model' of crisis management has four layers which, moving outwards from the centre, are: core beliefs, organizational beliefs, organizational structure, and, finally, organizational behaviour and plans. These elements of an organization contribute towards its ability to cope with a crisis event. Crisis-prone organizations, they observe, '. . . redefine reality to suit their fantasies and beliefs about themselves . . . the misperception of reality by prone organizations is not, as far as we can determine, motivated primarily by blocks or impairment to rational thinking.' Instead they argue that, 'the misperception of reality was blocked through emotional factors, i.e. by executives not having the emotional resources to face up to critical situations realistically' (Mitroff et al., 1989, p. 275).

Such characteristics of a managerial culture have been highlighted by other writers. Schwartz (1989), for example, has argued that certain organizations may be considered to be 'unhealthy' and that this malaise provides the circumstances within which 'organizational decay' occurs. This decay, he argues, results from an organization's inability to achieve an '. . . illusion of the organization ideal in the face of the failure of the organization to exemplify it.' The difficulty here, '. . . is that such symbolic manipulation places falsehood right at the core of organizational functioning and therefore cannot help but lead to a loss of rationality' (Schwartz, 1989, p. 324). It is this loss of reality that can lead organizations to make decisions which eventually lead to crises.

A tangental perspective on such issues is given by Reason (1987), who likens the potential for systems failure through human error to pathogens within a human body. For most of the time such pathogens are, '. . . either tolerated or kept in check by protective measures. But every now and again a set of circumstances occurs which permits these "resident pathogens" to thwart the defences, thus making the system vulnerable to threats that could otherwise have been withstood' (Reason, 1987, p. 465). Drawing on Rasmussen and Pedersen's (1982) classification of failures as either 'active' or 'passive,' Reason argues that it is the passive failures (resulting from design and construction conditions) which generate the greatest potential for the creation of resident pathogens.

There are a number of issues that can be addressed by management in respect of such failure events. Reason makes the distinction between short- and long-term strategies for action. In the short term, attention needs to be focused on the maintenance cycle and the training programmes for control room staff and this ties in with similar recommendations made by Zimmerman (1987). As a longer-term objective Reason argues that the design of many complex technological systems needs to take account of the human dynamics of their operation and this can only be done by educating the system designers, thereby giving them a fuller appreciation of the strengths and weaknesses of human cognition. In certain cases such a programme would demand a shift in the dominant belief systems in place within bureaucracies. Unfortunately such shifts in corporate culture are difficult to achieve in practice without the support of key managerial staff who are themselves often steeped in the culture that one seeks to change.

It would appear from this brief review of the literature that crises appear to have a number of common characteristics. These include temporal and spatial dimensions; the question of managerial culture and style; finality, threat and urgency; along with a 'threshold level' of harm which determines when a crisis occurs. Each of these factors sets the boundaries of the crisis event, although it is acknowledged that a crisis occurring within a discrete spatial and temporal context may well create the impetus for another event at some later juncture. This raises a question concerning the triggering process which occurs within crisis generation and the speed and degree of interaction (termed 'coupling' by Perrow (1984)) that exists between such events. Mitroff et al. (1989) also point to coupling as being an important attribute of crisis generation. In addition, they list complexity/scientific uncertainty, system/assumption breakdown and anxiety as being important elements within the promulgation of crises. The implications here are that crises arise through a failure of management to fully consider all of the possible disaster scenarios that face the organization. The current managerial thrust is in terms of contingency planning – 'What happens if?' – which is in general woefully inadequate in terms of crisis prevention and it is the latter which should be the aim of crisis management. In order to develop these ideas further the next section will present a model of crises which highlights the preventative elements of the managerial function.

Pulling the pieces together: towards a model of crisis management

If we develop the arguments articulated above a stage further, then it would appear that there are three distinct phases within any given crisis situation. The first is that period leading up to the crisis event in which the organization fails to take account of an impending situation which, '. . . appears to imperil the firm's survival and places the firm under severe time pressures' (Ansoff, 1984, p. 418). This phase can be termed a *crisis of management* in which the actions (or inactions) of management can promulgate the development of an organizational climate and culture within which a relatively minor triggering event can rapidly escalate up through the system and result in a catastrophic failure.

The second phase occurs when the organization is in the throes of an *operational crisis situation*. Because of the threat posed to the organization, its dominant internal environment becomes one of support, rather than departmental bickering or buck passing. This is the phase in which the human face of management is an important element in reducing the organizational impact of the event (David, 1990). Time is of the essence during this phase as the organization, often in collaboration with others, attempts to cope with the implications of the crisis event, especially if it involves loss of life. The aim here is to prevent a worsening of the situation and to generate a climate of support for those involved in the crisis. However, this supportive phase only lasts as long as the tenure of the event itself and quickly turns to a search for culpability.

In the ensuing post-crisis period there is often an attempt to apportion blame and search for scapegoats in an attempt to legitimize organizational operating procedures and managerial styles. This phase can be seen as a *crisis of legitimation* as an organization seeks to restore external confidence in both its managerial structure and operating systems. This phase often attracts government intervention in the crisis process as the state seeks both to secure legitimacy and to take preventative measures. The resultant model is shown in Fig. 1, where it can be seen that there is also a feedback loop which would affect the managerial culture in the post-event phase.

It is possible that the management of a given crisis can be passed on from the host organization either to another organization (or other organizations) or to a specialized crisis decision unit. This will normally occur in the second phase of the model, as witnessed by the role of the emergency services who enter a crisis situation in an attempt to resolve it or limit the resultant damage. In addition, it is possible to see such a transfer taking place in the legitimation phase as attempts are made to apportion blame outside of the organization that played host to the crisis event. This process can be witnessed in the wake of transport accidents, as the regulatory authority is often called upon to legitimate its own policy stance through the actions of the crisis-exposed organization. Finally, other organizations operating in the same sector will also be affected either as a result of close association with the crisis-stricken organization, or through more

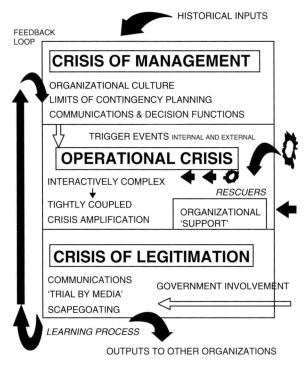

HISTORICAL INPUTS

FEEDBACK
LOOP

CRISIS OF MANAGEMENT

ORGANIZATIONAL CULTURE
LIMITS OF CONTINGENCY PLANNING
COMMUNICATIONS & DECISION FUNCTIONS

TRIGGER EVENTS INTERNAL AND EXTERNAL

OPERATIONAL CRISIS

INTERACTIVELY COMPLEX

TIGHTLY COUPLED
CRISIS AMPLIFICATION

RESCUERS

ORGANIZATIONAL
'SUPPORT'

CRISIS OF LEGITIMATION

COMMUNICATIONS
'TRIAL BY MEDIA'   GOVERNMENT INVOLVEMENT
SCAPEGOATING

LEARNING PROCESS

OUTPUTS TO OTHER ORGANIZATIONS

Figure 1 Model of crisis management

stringent legislation brought into force during the legitimation phase. Here we can see the impact of the crisis being passed on to other organizations which will be forced to modify their own practices in order to meet changes in regulation and public demand.

In the recent past, it is fair to say that most managerial attention has been focused on the operational and legitimation phases of crises. However, in order to reduce the *frequency* of crises (and, arguably, to also limit the consequences) it is necessary for managers to focus attention on the initial formulation period. The implications of this can be illustrated by a brief examination of crisis events.

In the case of the *Challenger* accident, it was apparent that the actions (or inactions) of management in the period prior to the explosion were a major contributory factor in the resultant failure. Had managerial action been taken on the O-ring problem, then two rings would have been used as a fail-safe measure, thereby reducing the risks of a total systems failure (Lambright, 1989). The accident at Bhopal also displays the problems associated with managerial style. Here cutbacks in safety provisions and training programmes eventually led to the generation of an organizational climate in which the degree of coupling between events was so short that the disaster occurred quickly following the initial systems failure. The resultant gas leak led to the death of over 2,500 local residents and created a series of crises for the various organizations involved. For Union Carbide, the crisis almost led to the demise of the company as governments and local publics expressed their vexation over the company's activities throughout the world. The accident also had implications for other chemical companies who came under considerable public scrutiny as local residents became apprehensive about the possibility of a similar accident occurring 'in their backyard' (Jones, 1988).

In February 1990, Perrier, the spring water company, was rocked by the revelation that its supposedly pure water was contaminated by traces of benzene, a known carcinogen, which had entered the water during the bottling process. The initial response of the company illustrates the importance of communications and media relations during the period of a crisis. Crumley (1990) observes that, '. . . Perrier's handling of the disaster was uneven at best, ranging from head-in-sand refusal to talk, to announcements in arch-corporatese, to bursts of pique. One analyst called it "the caveman approach to public relations" ' (p. 52). The result of the discovery in the USA led to a collapse of the company's market share and a recall of some 160 million bottles from world markets at an estimated cost of 29 million ECUS (Crumley, 1990). The end result was that Perrier had to divest its soft drinks division in order to pay for the re-positioning of the bottled water worldwide (Coyne, personal communication, 1990). Whilst the recall restored public confidence in the product, the same effect could have been achieved by effective communications during the early phase of the crisis had the culture of the organization allowed it.

Each of the cases cited above points to a failure of management to control the crisis situation pertaining within the organization. In the case of Union Carbide and Perrier it represents a failure of management to ensure that proper maintenance was being carried out within the plants. As both crises were the result of inadequate maintenance provision they could, arguably, have been prevented. Similarly, the *Challenger* disaster provides evidence of a lack of effective communication within the organization and the apparent willingness of managers to place cost over consequence in the short term – in this case it represents a failure to consider the worst-case scenario. Such cost-benefit scenarios are not uncommon in business and perhaps the best example can be found in the case of the Ford Pinto where the costs of compensation for burn victims were 'outweighed' by the costs of improvements to the vehicle.

The importance of managerial culture is therefore apparent and requires greater attention by those charged with responsibility for risk management. In particular, the issues of communication and control require the foremost cognizance on the part of the senior managers. Within an organizational context the ability of management to communicate effectively is vitally important within a risk management framework. This communications flow must be both bottom-up as well as top-down in order to be effective in preventing disasters, as the processes of communication and risk prediction are intrinsically linked due to the location of expertise within the organization. In addition, the prevention of crisis is also dependent on senior managers being aware of the problems that exist both within the organization and in its immediate environmental setting. The control function of management is also important in this respect, as managers will need to ensure that their decisions are implemented fully and quickly. The issue of communication after the initial crisis impact has undoubtedly attracted the greatest attention within the literature, providing managers with a checklist of procedures to follow in order to avoid 'trial by the media.' In discussing the cases of Perrier and Piper Alpha both Crumley (1990) and Jones (1988) highlight the importance of the companies' initial responses and their handling of the media in mitigating the damage to public relations that the crisis inevitably brings with it. Without effective communications the organization is unable to respond effectively to the rapid change that is associated with a crisis event.

This paper has reviewed some of the key issues relating to crisis management and detailed a model which seeks to explore the various stages through which crises go. Much of the concern expressed in the professional management literature, to date, has focused on the post-crisis phase, as organizations have attempted to manage the negative impact of the event. However, in order to be able to effectively manage crises, we need to look at the culture of the organization and assess its effect on crisis generation. Whilst this might be the most effective way of preventing crises it has been largely neglected by practising managers because of the threat that such changes bring with them. In order to cope with crises, management should be encouraged to acknowledge the limits of their abilities and adapt their contingency planning accordingly. It is only as a result of such a shift in culture that crises will be prevented rather than simply 'managed.'

References

Ansoff, H.I. (1984) *Implanting Strategic Management*, Prentice Hall International: Hemel Hempstead.

Booth, S. (1990) *Crisis management planning: approaches and problems*, paper presented at the Crisis Management Workshop, European Consortium for Political Research: Bochum, 2–7 April 1990.

Cohen, R.E. and Ahearn, F.L. (1980) *Handbook for Mental Health Care of Disaster Victims*, Johns Hopkins University Press: Baltimore, MD.

Crumley, B. (1990) 'Fizzzz went the crisis' *International Management*, April 1990: 52–53.

David, R. (1990) Damage limitation, *Business*, April 1990: 88–91.

Douglas, R.B., Blanks, R., Crowther, A. and Scott, G. (1988) 'A study of stress in West Midlands firemen using ambulatory electrocardiograms', *Work and Stress*, 2: 309–318.

Dyson, K. (1983) 'The cultural, ideological and structural context', in K. Dyson and S. Wilks (eds), *Industrial Crisis: a Comparative Study of the State and Industry*, Martin Robertson: Oxford: 26–66.

Freeman, R.E. and Gilbert, D.R. (1988) *Corporate Strategy and the Search for Ethics*, Prentice Hall: Englewood Cliffs, NJ.

Greiner, L.E. (1972) 'Evolution and revolution as organisations grow' *Harvard Business Review*, July/August, reprinted in D. Asch and C. Bowman (eds), *Readings in Strategic Management*, Macmillan: London: 373–387.

Hunt, C.B. and Auster, E.R. (1990) 'Proactive environemental management: avoiding the toxic trap', *Sloan Management Review*, Winter 1990: 7–18.

James, A. (1988) 'Perceptions of stress in British ambulance personnel' *Work and Stress*, 2: 319–326.

Johnson, G. and Scholes, K. (1988) *Exploring Corporate Strategy*, 2nd ed. Prentice Hall International: Hemel Hempstead.

Jones, T. (1988) *Corporate Killing*. Free Association Books: London.

Lambright, W.H. (1989) *Government-industry relations in the context of disaster: lessons from Apollo and Challenger*, paper presented at the Second International Conference on Industrial and Organizational Crisis Management at the Leonard Stern School of Business: New York University, 3–4 November 1989.

Mitroff, I.I., Pauchant, T., Finney, M. and Pearson, C. (1989) 'Do some organizations cause their own crises? The cultural profiles of crisis-prone vs. crisis-prepared organizations', *Industrial Crisis Quarterly*, 3: 269–283.

Pauchant, T.C., Mitroff, I.M., Weldon, D.N. and Ventolo, G.F. (1990) 'The ever-expanding scope of industrial crises: a systemic study of the Hinsdale telecommunications outage' *Industrial Crisis Quarterly*, 4: 243–261 (this issue).

Perrow, C. (1984) *Normal Accidents: Living with High-Risk Technologies*, Basic Books: New York.

Quarantelli, E.L. (1988) 'Disaster crisis management: a summary of research findings', *Journal of Management Studies*, 25: 373–385.

Raphael, B. (1986) *When disaster strikes: a handbook for the caring professions*, Hyman: London.

Rasmussen, J. and Pedersen, O.M. (1982) *Formalised search strategies for human risk contributions: a framework for further development*, Riso-M-2351, Riso National Laboratory: Roskilde, Denmark.

Reason, J. (1987) 'Cognitive aids in process environments: prostheses or tools?', *International Journal of Man-Machine Studies*, 27: 463–470.

Schwartz, H.S. (1989) 'Organizational disaster and organizational decay: the case of the National Aeronautics and Space Administration' *Industrial Crisis Quarterly*, 3: 319–334.

Shrivastava, P. (1987) *Bhopal: Anatomy of a Crisis*, Ballinger: Cambridge, MA.

Shrivastava, P., Mitroff, I.M., Miller, D. and Miglani, A. (1988) 'Understanding industrial crises', *Journal of Management Studies*, 25: 283–303.

Smart, C. and Vertinsky, I. (1977) 'Designs for crisis decision units', *Administrative Science Quarterly*, 22: 640–657.

Smith, D. (1990) 'Corporate power and the politics of uncertainty: conflicts surrounding major hazard plants at Canvey Island' *Industrial Crisis Quarterly*, 4: 1–26.

Wilks, S. and Dyson, K. (1983) 'The character and economic context of industrial crises', in K. Dyson and S. Wilks (eds), *Industrial Crisis: a Comparative Study of the State and Industry*, Martin Robertson: Oxford: 1–25.

Zimmerman, R. (1987) 'The government's role as stakeholder in industrial crises', *Industrial Crisis Quarterly*, 1 (3): 34–45.

Chapter 11

Karlene H. Roberts

SOME CHARACTERISTICS OF ONE TYPE OF HIGH RELIABILITY ORGANIZATION

A<small>N</small> **INCREASING NUMBER OF** organizations are engaged in production or services that require extraordinary attention to avoiding major errors because errors could lead to destruction of the organization and/or a larger public. These organizations are hazardous (in the engineering sense) and until they experience failure they are generally invisible to the public at large which needs their services but fails to realize the costs required to obtain them. The minute one of these organizations experiences failure a clamoring public demands change. But change in what?

Shrivastava (1986) notes that of the 28 major industrial accidents (those killing at least 50 people) that have occurred in the twentieth century, half have occurred since 1977, and three occurred in 1984. This suggests that the number of organizations capable of killing large numbers of people is growing and that we should devote attention to addressing issues concerned with how to design and operate them safely.

Within the set of hazardous organizations there is a subset which has enjoyed a record of high safety over long periods of time. One can identify this subset by answering the question, 'how many times could this organization have failed resulting in catastrophic consequences that it did not?' If the answer is on the order of tens of thousands of times the organization is 'high reliability' (Roberts and Gargano 1990; Rochlin, La Porte and Roberts 1987). Examples of the hazardous organizations that engage in nearly error free operations are the U.S. air traffic control system, some power distribution grids, aircraft carriers and submarines, and international banking.

The organizational literature and high reliability organizations

Existing research literature assumes that high reliability organizations (HROs) and other kinds of organizations are not different from one another. Approached from a research design perspective the null hypothesis is that 'Organizations do not vary in internal processes as a function of the degree to which their production technologies are perceived as hazardous or the consequences of individual failures vary in severity.'

Is this plausible? Does contemporary organization theory speak to this point? Contemporary organization theories are essentially theories about trial and error (incrementalism), failure tolerant, low reliability organizations. How adequate can such a literature be when addressing phenomena at least partly derived from precisely the opposite conditions?

For a variety of reasons (see Roberts and Rousseau 1989) the organizational literature fails to deal specifically with either hazardous organizations (as exceptions see Perrow 1984; Shrivastava 1986) or with the subset in that category which might be defined as engaging in extremely high levels of performance reliability. In so far as that literature deals with reliability at all, it deals with effectiveness (see for example, Goodman and Pennings 1977; Cameron and Whetton 1983; Lewin and Minton 1986; Zammuto 1983). However, the effectiveness literature covers a whole range of outcomes, and none of them are performance reliability. While the organizations of interest in this research focus on other outcomes, reliability is their number one concern.

Most of the growing literature on risk and crisis management is journalistic. It and more scholarly treatments (for example, Bignell and Fortune 1984; Covello, Menkes and Mumpower 1986; Morone and Woodhouse 1986; Shrivastava 1986; Turner 1976; Rasmussen, Duncan and Leplat 1987; Perrow 1984; Schwartz 1987) generally assume a crisis or major accident has or will happen and addresses damage control. Recently that literature has included some attention to accident prevention. It stems from studies that show ex post facto the flaws in operations or decision structures that contributed to accidents, and seems to suggest that we have reasonable models of how failure free organizations work. Since all of this work focuses on a dependent variable of accident or crisis it is not clear how useful it can be to understanding nearly failure free operations.

Because the risk and crisis management literatures are specialized, one should examine more general organizational literature in search of propositions that can guide observation. When pushed to their logical conclusions in HROs existing propositions from this literature provide paradoxes. Here are two examples.

Generalist organizations will perform more reliably in variable 'crude grained' environments characterized by less rapid fluctuation than will specialist organizations (Freeman and Hannan 1983). Specialist organizations will perform more reliably in stable environments as well as in variable 'fine grained' environments characterized by more rapid changes than will generalist organizations. As we will see, HROs are characterized by both advanced technology (requiring specialist understanding) and high degrees of interdependence (requiring generalist understanding).

If tasks are highly interdependent (as we will see they are in HROs), directly reciprocally influencing one another, then close grouping of performers and tight coordination and control enhances performance reliability (Thompson 1967; Weick 1979). Yet, uncertain environments require sufficient complexity and flexibility within the organization to map the uncertainty (Ashby 1952; Weick 1987). As indicated previously HROs are characterized by extreme interdependence. They also face very uncertain environments as we will see.

Long lists of similar paradoxes can be developed for HROs. They hint that appropriate theory is wanting, and that perhaps a first step in understanding the design and management of such organizations is by examining some of the characteristics of HROs and addressing the issue of how the organizations resolve paradoxes produced by these characteristics.

One type high reliability organization

Nuclear powered aircraft carriers provided the settings in which observations were made to identify characteristics that might describe HROs and that later might prove to differentiate them from organizations in which the primary goal is not performance reliability. The organizations are characterized by interactions among many technologies at different stages of advancement. For example, Command Information Centers rely on vacuum tube computers, while the F/A-18 fighter/attack aircraft, which is also a part of the system, uses extremely advanced computer technology. These and many other ship, aircraft, ordnance, maintenance, and nuclear reactor technologies simultaneously operate interdependently with one another.

These organizations can commit catastrophic errors in a number of ways. Nuclear reactor accidents are possible. The ships and their aircraft (each has nine squadrons representing a variety of complicated technologies) are vulnerable to a myriad of aviation related accidents. Fire, flooding, grounding, collision, and fuel and weapons explosions are also potential results of costly errors. More generally, each ship is a part of a national security system in which error can result in unintended military confrontations that can be catastrophic.

On the flight and hangar decks aircraft that can themselves cause accidents are parked in close proximity with one another, and aircraft, jet fuel, and ordnance are close to one another. This can create unintended interactions. One of the most potentially damaging things that can happen is a deck fire such as the one aboard USS Enterprise on January 9, 1969.

In that accident an auxiliary startup heat exhaust ignited a Zuni rocket-pad missile which struck an aircraft on the other side of the ship during pre-launch deck loading. This set off a chain reaction of aircraft and munitions explosions with 500-pound bombs exploding on the flight deck. Approximately 100 people were killed. Not only were lives lost but because the ship had to be taken to port for repair a seven-billion dollar national asset was unavailable for use.

Each ship is a city with 6,000 men and an airport on the roof. It carries seven different kinds of aircraft configured into nine squadrons. With a flight deck 1092 feet long and 252 feet wide, and a less spacious hangar deck, it is not hard to see that planes must be configured into very small space. It is entirely possible for them to ram into one another doing great harm. Thus, in an attempt to attenuate the possibility of the larger accident the Navy uses as one measure of its effectiveness 'crunch' rate. A crunch occurs when two aircraft touch while being moved on the flight or hangar decks.

The following facts are given simply to illustrate the size and complexity of the organization. Nuclear carriers are 24 stories high and carry enough ship fuel to last 15 years. They have 3,360 compartments and spaces, more than 2,000 telephones, over a billion transistors and diodes; and if stacked, all their technical manuals would be as high as the Washington Monument. One nuclear carrier, USS Enterprise, can supply the power needs for a city the size of Minneapolis, and if taken out of the water and set vertically she would measure 200 feet taller than San Francisco's Transamerica Building or more than 125 feet taller than the Eiffel Tower.

The reliability of this HRO (and that of other aircraft carriers) is defined in terms of peacetime training activities, not her ability to perform in wartime. There is considerable argument both in and outside the military about carrier reliability in the advent of war. Carriers have two major purposes, to project power abroad and to engage in war at sea. The United States has considerable experience projecting power abroad using her carriers and this experience supports the notion that the carriers operate reliably in the kinds of engagements they have experienced.

In the history of the world there have been very few 'wars at sea' (Hughes 1986). This is because neither the strong nor the weak side likes to fight them, each for different reasons. Even in the best planned battles (including battle groups of seven to ten ships) confrontations turn into melees. It is unclear what this says about single ship performance reliability.

Some characteristics of high reliability organizations

While, admittedly it would be best to pull propositions from existing organizational literature to study HROs, the limitations of that literature have been discussed. Only two major organizational studies of hazardous organizations exist and these are of organizations that created catastrophes. Both of these studies focused on components of failure. In one case no direct measures were taken or observations made in organizations (Perrow 1984)[1] and in the other all observations came from one organization (Shrivastava 1986). We can examine the components those authors focus on and ask whether they exist aboard the carriers, and if so whether they are automatically associated with catastrophe. If they have not resulted in catastrophe has the organization taken steps to prevent their doing so?

Perrow (1984) explicates complexity and tight coupling as the key components of 'high risk' technologies. (He assumes *all* hazardous technologies are also high risk and does not differentiate hazard, risk, and reliability.) Since his implicit assumption is that 'high risk' technologies are accidents waiting to happen, it seems complexity and tight coupling contribute to potential accidents.

By complex interactions Perrow means interactions 'of unfamiliar sequences, or unplanned and unexpected sequences, and either not visible or not immediately comprehensible' (Perrow 1984, p. 78). The elements of complexity are baffling interactions, subsystems called upon to serve multiple (and incompatible) functions, proximity, and indirect information sources. This is not how the organization literature typically describes the complexity. (That literature deals with complexity as more of something; more units, more communication lines, etc.) Perrow's example of subsystems serving multiple and incompatible functions is a heater used simultaneously to heat gas in one tank and as a heat exchanger to absorb heat in another. If the heater fails, one tank will be too cool while the other tank overheats.

Proximity and indirect information sources are further indicators of system complexity. When systems are supposed to act independently of one another but are in close proximity there is the possibility they will interact, leading to disaster. Further, when something happens the accident thoroughly upends the organizations such that operators are frequently unable to obtain information first hand, rather their sources are indirect. Operators must rely on the quality of the accident to suggest its underlying dynamic as when fire fighters, unable to get close to a shipboard fire, judge its causes only by knowing the contents of the space on fire.

The second of Perrow's factors, tight coupling, is not the number of connections between two units in an organization. It has to do with the brittleness of those connections. Tightly coupled systems (as opposed to loosely coupled systems) have (1) more time dependent processes (they cannot wait to be attended to), (2) more invariant sequences (B must follow A), (3) overall designs that allow only one way to reach a goal, and (4) little slack. In tightly coupled systems the buffers and redundancies must be designed and thought about in advance. Loosely coupled systems offer more opportunity for immediate, spur of the minute, redundancies and buffers. 'Tight coupling is a mechanical term meaning there is no slack or buffer or give between two items. What happens in one directly affects what happens in the other' (Perrow 1984, pp. 89–90). This is a decidedly engineering perspective, and might be beneficially supplemented with a more sociological or psychological perspective.

Shrivastava (1986) discusses human, organizational, and technical causes of the Bhopal disaster. Low employee morale combined with ongoing labor management conflicts contributed to carelessness. Staff reduction directly contributed to the accident and eroded human back-up systems. Operators had inadequate safety training, and managers and workers had little information about the hazard potential of the plant. Managers had failed to investigate causes of a previous failure, and operators failed to carry out a crucial operation shortly before the accident occurred. While technical failure (nonoperational status) of safety and backup systems were key elements in the catastrophe, they were caused by organizational and managerial carelessness. The potpourri of human factors contributing to the accident might be summarized as factors brought by poor training and motivation, by inadequate staffing, and the lack of core values emphasizing safety and reliability.

The organization factors that Shrivastava identifies as interdependent with the human factors are low importance of the Bhopal plant to its parent, Union Carbide; mistakes made in predicting the economic viability of such a plant before building it; and top management discontinuity in the plant. The techno-logical failures that combined with human and organizational factors to produce the accident were unanticipated interactions among multiple failures in the sys-tem, tight coupling, design flaws in the plant, the use of defective or malfunction-ing equipment, the use of contaminated or sub standard supplies and raw material, and the use of incorrect operating procedures.

In their recognition of the importance of complex interactions, operator manning, training and motivation, Perrow and Shrivastava specifically suggest the importance of interdependence among organizational units (Aiken and Hage 1968; Lincoln 1982; Victor and Blackburn 1987). In his discussion of multiple stakeholders Shrivastava also alludes to the impact of shifting environments (Dill 1958) on the Bhopal accident, but he is not very precise about this. Both Perrow and Shrivastava imply that these are situations with large numbers of constituen-cies and participant groups that result in multiple and conflicting goals. Thus, we add to those factors suggested by Perrow and Shrivastava interdependence, environmental uncertainty and goals.

We agree with these authors that if one observes many of the characteristics they describe operating simultaneously in hazardous technologies these tech-nologies are subject to a high probability of risk. Some of their characteristics do, however, operate in HROs. In some cases they cause no problems in and of themselves. In other cases the organization takes action to mitigate their dys-functional consequences. Particularly because Perrow's analyses are from sec-ondary data sources, it seemed important to not only validate his and Shrivastava's analyses through direct observation but to extend those analyses wherever possible.

Research strategy

To this end, a participant observer 'in depth case study' of the kind Campbell (1977) calls for in effectiveness research was undertaken. Over a three-year period a team of three senior researchers followed two West Coast based car-riers, USS Enterprise and USS Carl Vinson, through their 18-month readiness cycles, beginning when they come out of overhaul and ending after their deployment 'on station' in the Indian Ocean. In addition one team member joined the initial part of the shakedown cruise aboard USS Theodore Roosevelt, off the East Coast of the United States.

Team members went to sea intermittently for periods of five to ten days, making observations and learning jobs done aboard the ships from different vantage points. Field notes were entered into computers every few hours when the pace of the ships' activities permitted. Shipboard activities run on a 24-hour day schedule. Observations were frequently made on 21-hour per day schedules.

Team members represent different social science disciplines and assigned themselves around the ships to insure different perspectives, in order to reduce individual bias. Thus, one team member might 'work the deck' while another observed bridge activities and the third learned how to launch and recover aircraft from the ship's tower. Over the course of the observations all relevant ship and squadron activities were observed by all team members.

Perrow's characteristics

Complexity. We first describe components of complexity, and indicate what the organization does to diminish their negative consequences when it perceives them to be dysfunctional. Aboard carriers all personnel are alerted to the possibility of unexpected organizational sequences and training is constantly engaged in to provide all possible scenarios that trainers can think of. For example, deck fires can happen in many ways and the Navy goes to great pains to provide almost continuous face to face, simulation, and video training about the causes of deck fires and what to do about them. This training is also directed to understanding the complexities of the technologies aboard the ships so that interactions among the hardware and human components can be managed in such a way that baffling interactions do not occur. Exercises are engaged in, however, that have sufficient flexibility to allow people some creativity in problem solving. For example, during her maiden cruise the captain of USS Carl Vinson found himself in such high winds he could not land aircraft safely. He ordered the ship sailed 15 knots astern in order to recover aircraft more safely – a relatively innovative strategy.

Activities that would result in catastrophe if they intermingled (e.g. fueling aircraft while loading munitions) are kept separate. Their intermingling would result in disastrous consequences (the 1969 Enterprise fire provides an example of that). Operator ability to keep such activities separated could be one factor differentiating HROs from less reliable organizations. This ability requires considerable organizational skill because men, munitions, high performance aircraft, and jet fuel, are close to one another. On the flight deck 150–200 men fuel, load ordnance aboard, and maintain aircraft that come and go in 48- to 60-second intervals. The Navy uses many mechanisms to keep things separated that should be separate under these conditions. Again, constant training is observed, deck hands use the buddy system of training in which one man is assigned to closely monitor another. The deck itself is divided into three distinct areas (fly 1, 2, and 3) and men are assigned to work in one area only at the specialized jobs they have been taught. Uniforms are color-coded so that the director of this deck orchestra can keep an eye on the location of people with different job functions. A flight deck handler orchestrates all flight and hangar deck activities noting aircraft states of readiness on a scale model of the two decks in the flight deck control center.

Numerous indirect information sources do exist in this organization, just as in any other technologically complex organization in which one has to rely on lights and dials as signals of the activities of machinery. This is overlayed on carriers with numerous direct information linkages connecting key centers of the entire ship. This reduces the possibility that one will only have indirect information about the state of the ship. For example, the ship's control tower, responsible for all activity on the flight deck and hangar deck, uses more than

20 communication devices to contact critical parts of the ship, ranging from radios to sound powered phones. The landing signal officer (LSO) on the flight deck is connected directly to the airboss (a commander) in the tower in five different ways. There is a regular telephone, a sound powered 'hot' line (akin to two tin cans and a string), a radio, and a public address system. These are supplemented by tower capability to call the deck 'foul' which is the final way to communicate with the LSO. The navigational bridge and tower are connected by three different kinds of communication devices. When the ships are in battle exercises they are also frequently in EMCON, which is electronics emissions control and means that communication is restricted so that potential enemies cannot lock on to ship electronics systems. This means a ship reduces its own direct communications and still operates safely.

Tight Coupling. The hypothesized brittleness of connections in these organizations is evidenced on aircraft carriers in a number of ways. The technologies are tightly coupled in an engineering sense, and the whole is extremely mechanistic, which constitutes brittleness in this case. Most examples of tight coupling we have seen are couplings of information and resources, not of brittleness. During air operations the navigational bridge is tightly coupled to the air tower because most aircraft cannot be recovered unless the minimum wind over the deck is at least sixteen knots.

This is achieved through coordination between navigation and the air boss who cannot begin recovery until the ship has turned into the wind. The boss simply does not have the resource (ready deck) available to do his job until the navigational team acts. In addition, an aircraft pilot is tightly coupled to the tower (airboss) because fuel remaining is a critical factor dictating the need to land or be refueled in the air. The situation is more difficult during night flight operations when everyone is hindered by reduced visual cues.

Tight coupling also occurs for the pilot and the ship from a different standpoint (representing information coupling) during reduced visibility periods or at night. The pilot is guided on final approach to the ship by the carrier's Air Traffic Control Center (CATCC). As the center guides him to the ship the pilot is told to 'call the ball.' When he can see the Fresnel lens or 'meat ball' (the device on the port side of the ship which he uses to adjust his glide slope), the pilot reports this to LSO, CATCC, and tower on a commonly held radio frequency. At this point the LSO takes control of the aircraft, provides advisory information, and ensures the aircraft remains within landing parameters or waves it off the ship if safe landing limits are exceeded. (Many other people can also wave it off.) If the aircraft is low on fuel or has other problems it becomes tightly coupled with other parts of the ship (e.g. the carrier air group commander or CAG).

All the characteristics of tight coupling Perrow mentions (time dependent processes, invariant sequences of operations, overall design that only allows one way to reach a goal, and little slack) are apparent to some degree on the carriers. Flight operations themselves are time dependent processes. One of the jobs done during final approach is done by an enlisted man on the tower (spotter). He stands next to the commander of the tower (boss) and his second in command (miniboss). Using binoculars he calls the type of aircraft arriving on final approach, then the aircraft weight setting for the arresting gear. He then checks the gear position of the aircraft, and calls it to the boss. Finally, he calls repeatedly the status of the deck (foul or clear), and when the deck clears and is ready to take the aircraft aboard he calls what the aircraft in fact did (landed, was waved off, or boltered – tried but failed to trap aboard). He does this sequence of activities in a 48- to 60-second time frame, and then immediately repeats it. Each of his activities is redundant with some activity done elsewhere on the ship. We will return to this later. This is just one example of the many invariant sequences of behavior that occur in these organizations. One cannot call the gear status of the aircraft before reporting the type of aircraft, and it is impossible to call the aircraft weight prior to knowing its type.

In this respect the organization seems designed to allow only one way to reach its goal of getting the aircraft off and back on to the ship. However, the organization itself is built of layers and layers of activities that allow changes in reaching goals. Perhaps one's interpretation of whether there is only one way to reach the goal of bringing the planes on board safely depends on the level of analysis from which the ships are examined.

From the perspective of the spotter it appears there is only one way to get the planes down. But what if a plane is in trouble? As an example, a plane approaching a ship might report that a landing gear light has come on in the cockpit, signaling that the landing gear is not down for landing. The spotter has already begun his sequence of tasks. Now the CAG intervenes with several possible ways to recover the plane safely. With a quick examination of the facts he can order the plane aboard as though nothing happened (and the pilot can bang on his console hoping the light will go out), he can order the deck barrier raised (this is a flexible barrier midship that can catch the aircraft) which is risky for the plane and ship, or he can send the plane to a land-based air field (if he has one available). The one way to reach the goal of a safe landing has turned into several possibilities and the invariant sequences of the spotter are overlaid by many sequential possibilities for the pilot and the CAG. Perhaps Perrow's analysis is restricted to only one level of analysis.

The situation is similar with regard to slack, that is, the perspective one takes determines his estimate of the amount of slack that exists. From the spotter's perspective there is little slack. He has to work in the tight time frame of a few seconds and cannot think about many alternatives. Though even this is a bit deceptive. He knows that if the information about the status of the aircraft that he conveys to the airboss is not consistent with status information coming to the boss from other sources the recovery will be aborted. He might even be a part of the landing termination because he recognizes the inconsistencies and points them out to the airboss who then aborts the recovery. The boss, however, has more flexibility. Because the system has much built in redundancy (discussed later) during the short time frame he can think about alternatives for the aircraft.

The organization does a number of other things to mitigate the harmful consequences of tight coupling. It utilizes extreme hierarchical differentiation. This gives people specific roles within the invariant sequences of behavior and organizes them in the step by step way of reaching goals using one or a limited number of ways. Carriers (in fact all ships) are run by hierarchies. The captain is at the top, his Executive Officer is next, followed by 17 department heads. Junior officers serve as generalist advisors, and limited duty officers, master-chiefs, senior chiefs, and chiefs are specialist operators. This differentiation is necessary for knowing who is ultimately responsible for what. As an officer aboard Enterprise stated, 'Officers send information to enlisted men through intermediaries. These are the senior enlisted (first class petty officers) who aspire to khaki (chiefs, warrant officers, limited duty officers). It's important to reduce bruising of egos that occurs if we try to go around the chain of command to get to the petty officers'. The negative effects of extreme hierarchical differentiation are reduced through the use of bargaining.

For example, at times both supply and maintenance activities must be conducted on the hangar deck. The supply officer or his representative bargains with the maintenance officer or his representative about the specifics of temporary space utilization on the hangar deck.

The negative effects of tight coupling are also lessened by the bargaining required by many to achieve their various priorities. Officers constantly negotiate the social order (Strauss 1978). The focal point of this process is the ship's operations officer who goes around the ship 'collecting' training and readiness requirements from various owners of these issues (airboss, maintenance officer, supply officer, etc.), and designs a number of implementation plans until he reaches one that is acceptable to all parties. His objective is to find a maximizing solution, one which everyone wins something and no one loses big.

As an example, within the broader framework of the admiral's mission requirements, a decision must be made about when to transition from day to night flight operations with the added complication of a change in the flying environment. This decision considers the admiral's readiness exercise needs, the supply officer's requirements to provide flight deck personnel with meals, the captain's requirement to position the ship at a particular spot at a particular time for another day's exercise, the airboss' need to provide adequate rest periods for the deck hands, etc. Various aspects of this decision milieu are given various priorities by each of the officers involved. While the admiral's battle plan priorities are usually highest, ship's company officers often attempt to negotiate change in even these priorities when they feel they will lead to unsafe working conditions. Similar negotiations occur at all levels of the organization.

A number of strategies are used to decrease the negative effects of *both* complexity and tight coupling. One of the first things one is struck with on the carriers is the vast amount of redundancy that occurs. Redundancy takes a variety of forms (Lerner 1986) including back up computers that do the same thing the on line computers do (duplication). It also takes the form of breaking tasks up such that one person may do task 1, 2, and 3, while another does 2, 4, and 5; and yet another does 1, 4, and 6 (overlap). This kind of redundancy is designed to deal with partial system failure, and as we alluded to earlier in our discussion of the spotter's job, is probably an outcome of tight coupling. With regard to air operations on the ships, aircraft status data are kept in two different places on the ship, and the multiple communication systems discussed earlier run throughout the ship and are redundant. Control for the setting of the arresting gear ultimately rests in the hands of at least three different people with oversight by the airboss.

It is not only done to lessen the negative effects of tight coupling and deal with numerous simultaneous outcomes but to decompose the tight time frames that are a part of tight coupling. If things are done quickly, but many pairs of eyes serve as watchdogs, the many pairs of eyes are a substitute for unavailable time. In a short time three pairs of eyes should be able to spot a problem that may take one pair of eyes longer to detect.

High degrees of responsibility and accountability (Tetlock 1985) that we do not see in other kinds of organizations can reduce the problems caused by complexity and tight coupling. Air Department enlisted men aboard Carl Vinson noted that their jobs are constantly cross checked in order to assure reliability and accountability. Enlisted nuclear reactor operators talked about the enormous amount of training required to do their jobs and the enormous amount of tension caused by having to do things right all the time. Flight deck personnel aboard both Carl Vinson and Enterprise called the deck 'organized chaos'. It is organized in the sense that everyone knows his job and chaos in the sense that no one knows what will happen next. In such an environment the buddy system is enormously important for safety. 'A new guy shadows you. If you go to the mess he goes to the mess, if you go to the head he goes to the head. That's the way we train new guys.' 'You can't let people think about what's going on or they wouldn't stay on the flight deck. We're responsible for our own and everyone else's lives.'

Finally, 'cultures of reliability' centering around safety and related issues can be directed against the negative effects of the kinds of factors Perrow discusses. In the embryonic stages of Theodore Roosevelt's development as an organization her captain (CO) briefed newly arriving enlisted men. He stressed the use of the buddy system as a safety device and told his men not to break the rules *unless* safety is at stake. This CO also stressed the fact that he felt he was laying down the culture of the organization, and that subsequent COs would only modify it at the margins. Much discussion ensued aboard Roosevelt about how long it takes to develop a culture and how important continuity of the management team is to that development.

In her early stages of life Carl Vinson had some severe rotation problems and never developed a definitive culture under her first CO. It is very important that the head of a new HRO perceive himself to be constantly in a training mode in terms of developing a culture. It is also important that HROs *are* constantly in training modes. As one officer aboard Enterprise commented, 'Our fundamental responsibility is training. We're like a baseball team that never goes into a season.' (One hopes they never go into a season.)

Weick (1987) notes that training may be dysfunctional to the reliable operations of HROs because training teaches behaviors that may be inappropriate in an emergency. That is entirely possible. As mentioned previously, there is much discussion about whether we can actually fight a war as we train for fighting a war. Weick also notes a system incorporating both centralization and decentralization is difficult to design, and that culture gives order to such a system by providing latitude for interpreting, improvisation, and unique action.

Shrivastava's characteristics

Shrivastava discusses *antecedents* to accidents in 'high risk' organizations, contrasted to Perrow's discussion of components of accidents. First, we consider his human antecedents (training, motivation, and manning). As indicated previously, constant training is an important aspect of carrier operation. In addition to insuring appropriate skill level at any one time, this is done to ameliorate the negative effects of high turnover. Limited duty officers and specialized enlisted personnel turn over less frequently than generalist officers and can help insure adequate training. Motivation is dealt with throughout both training and the 'culture of reliability.' Manning problems are handled with a tremendous amount of redundancy.

Shrivastava's organizational antecedents to accidents are low importance of the plant to its parent, mistakes in determining economic viability, and top management discontinuity. As centers of battle groups aircraft carriers are enormously important to the U.S. maritime strategy. The Navy provides a tremendous land-based support package for them and the other ships in the battle groups. As an example, a significant work force of uniformed and civilian personnel located at Naval installations up and down the West Coast of the United States support the six Pacific carriers and air wings with their combined crews of more than 25,000 men. Our observations are silent with regard to economic viability. The Navy mandates that all top management on its carriers rotate in a planned and systematic succession. As an example, 90-day interval is required between the rotation of a carrier captain and his principal assistant, the executive officer. However, rotation is a constant fact of life in the Navy which generally develops various strategies to lessen its negative organizational consequences, as we have seen with training.

We have already addressed two of the technological factors identified by Shrivastava as contributors to the accident at Bhopal (unanticipated interactions among failures, and tight coupling). Design flaws can and do cause problems for carriers. However, changes in carrier design are incremental allowing management to deal with small changes at any one time. The Navy worries constantly about defective, substandard, and malfunctioning equipment. It fights this battle simultaneously on many fronts, including the constant training of many maintenance people and pressure placed on vendors.

Tables 1 and 2 summarize this discussion. Table 1 lists Perrow's potentially dysfunctional components of 'high risk' technologies and carrier responses to them. Table 2 lists Shrivastava's antecedents to the Bhopal accident and carrier responses to them.

As previously indicated, both Perrow and Shrivastava imply interdependence, environmental uncertainty, and disagreement about goals as characteristics of hazardous technologies. We now turn to these concepts.

Table 1 Perrow's potentially dysfunctional components of 'high risk' technologies and carrier responses to them

Potentially dysfunctional characteristics and processes	Organizational strategies and processes used to lessen each of these dysfunctionalities	Strategies used to reduce the negative effects of both complexity and tight coupling
Complexity		
potential for unexpected sequences	continuous training	redundancy
complex technologies	continuous training	accountability
potential for systems serving incompatible function to interact	job design strategies to keep function separate	responsibility
indirect information sources	main direct information sources	'culture' of reliability
Tight Coupling		
time dependent processes	redundancy	
invariant sequences of operations	hierarchical differentiation	
only one way to reach goal	bargaining	
little slack	redundancy	

Table 2 Shrivastava's antecedents to the Bhopal accident and carrier responses to them

Potentially dysfunctional characteristics and processes	Organizational strategies and processes used to lessen these dysfunctionalities
poor training	continuous training
poor motivation	training/culture
low manning	redundancy
low importance of organization to parent economically inviable	continual support for organization
top management discontinuity	regulations about top management rotation
unanticipated interactions	continuous training
tight coupling	see Table 1
design flaws	
defective, substandard malfunctioning equipment	training, use of many maintenance personnel, pressure on vendors

Interdependence and environmental uncertainty

The ship's activities are highly interdependent with one another: No single unit can do its job without inputs from many others. We find pooled, sequential, and reciprocal interdependence (Thompson 1967). As an illustration of pooled interdependence, units make discrete contributions to the whole and are supported by it. From one perspective the maintenance, weapons, and air departments each contribute discretely to the overall mission of the organization. Each in turn is fed and housed by the whole. As an example of sequential interdependence, flight deck team members are specialists. Planes cannot be hooked to catapults for launch until they have been fueled by one set of people, loaded with ordnance by another set, etc. Each set of men do their jobs in turn. Developing an airplan requires reciprocal interdependence in which officers bargain through the specifics of a flight plan depending on training and mission needs. The nature of the dependencies one sees depends greatly on the level of analysis of the observation. At the individual worker level dependencies are apt to be pooled (though examples of reciprocal interdependence exist), at the level of department decision making they are likely to be reciprocal.

The term interdependence implies that people are mutually dependent on one another. One problem in specification is that the commodities of the dependence are often quite different for any two interdependent people. The tower boss is dependent on the navigation team to position the ship so that the wind over the angle is correct and planes can be recovered. But the boss also depends on the bridge for general direction in doing his job. The bridge team is dependent on the airboss doing his job in a safe manner, while specifically the navigational team on the bridge is dependent on the airboss to provide accurate information about the number of planes in a recovery, etc. Comparing these interdependencies is like comparing apples and oranges and the problem requires future research attention.

In his analysis of organizational and interorganizational developments of disasters Turner (1976) notes that disasters occur when a large, complex problem, the limits of which are difficult to specify, is dealt with by a large number of people. Flight operations is a complex problem, and novel situations arise all the time. The problem of interdependence is born of trying to farm parts of the problem out to various people while trying to maintain some information and resource connectedness among them. As McCann and Galbraith (1981, p. 94) state, 'increasing interdependence, then, results from increasing structural complexity, where complexity arises from horizontal and vertical differentiation, spatial arrangement, or size.'

The existence of environmental uncertainty seems relatively obvious aboard ships. Wars are meant to be uncertain and the ship's job is to constantly train for this event. Other uncertainties include changes in command, orders, and weather. Training exercises are clearly designed to flex the ship with uncertainty.

As indicated previously, hypotheses about close grouping and flexibility derived from the necessity to manage interdependence and cope with environmental uncertainty conflict. Managing interdependence is thought to require extreme hierarchy, while coping with environmental uncertainty requires decentralization. How does a carrier resolve this paradox?

We illustrated the existence of extreme hierarchy. But, in addition to this, decision making is pushed to the lowest levels possible at least in the sense of vetoes. On carriers even the lowest level participant can abort landings. Because ingesting foreign objects can ruin jet engines (and possibly everyone's day on the flight deck) when anyone sees a foreign object on the deck he can call a halt to flight operations. While one would not want to make mistakes about such things very often, mistakes are not punished in this situation. In addition, personnel are trained that when they see a problem they own it either until they solve it or until someone who can solve it takes responsibility for it. Rank is not at issue here. Thus, the organization addresses the paradox derived from hypotheses regarding interdependence and environmental uncertainty with *both* hierarchy and decentralization. In a sense the pyramid is inverted. The organization focuses on training and on letting people use that training. Low level decision making is part of that focus.

Goals

A strong sense of primary mission and operational goals is apparent on carriers which is at odds with what the literature tells us about goals in organizations with numerous constituencies. That this is true is evidenced by a number of things we have been told. The commanding officer of the USS Carl Vinson once said to this author, 'sometimes I think you don't keep your eye on the goal around here. The primary goal is to get the planes off the pointy end of the ship and back down on to the flat end without mishap.' Deck hands aboard Enterprise were consistent in their remarks about the fact that 'when we're flying, we're doing the job of the ship.' A deckhand has never flown an aircraft, yet these people see that mission as pivotal to the success of their organization, and identify with it. They added, 'we don't feel good about the organization when we're in port. That's make work. We do the job of the ship when we're at sea.' One deckhand told it all, 'This is just a bird farm. The birds come in, they get fed, and they go.'

Enormous effort on everyone's part is required to translate these abstract goals into operational goals. Aboard Carl Vinson we were told, 'no one understands the role of the Engineering officer until the lights go out or the steam cats (catapults) go down.' It is impossible to launch aircraft without the catapults. Aircraft handlers aboard Vinson commented, 'if we don't move the aircraft right, we'll get a locked deck [as in any sort of traffic gridlock], there won't be anywhere to move these aircraft short of shoving them off the deck, and planes won't be able to take off and land.' During the shakedown cruise aboard Theodore Roosevelt there was enormous concern about anchoring because if they could not anchor the ship correctly they could not get on with its primary mission (launch and recover aircraft safely).

Bargaining is a successful strategy for operationalizing goals because the superordinate goals are clear to everyone. The organization needs to resolve tensions created by the need for maximal organizational effectiveness today without jeopardizing the ability to do it again tomorrow. Despite multiple constituencies the organization does not fail at specifying and operationalizing goals.

These strategies for obtaining goals may be sharpened in the observer's eyes because they are also strategies for obtaining the basic goal of survival. That goal is sufficiently a part of the ground (as in figure-ground relationship) or fabric of the organization that it is not addressed verbally in an everyday sense as is the goal of getting planes off and back down onto the flight deck. There are at least two reasons for this. One is that lessons of survival are burned in blood over the 68 years of carrier operation, each one becoming a part of the organization's fabric. The second is that it is probably dysfunctional for one consciously to deal with his mortality on a daily basis.

Thus, the survival goal is not always apparent. It is reflected in circumstances such as screaming at deck hands to get behind the foul line (when, in fact, the entire deck is dangerous). It is recognized intermittently when something happens to make it salient. As an example, the day of the Challenger accident all eyes were glued to television sets aboard Vinson. That accident occasioned numerous stories in the ward room about 'the one I walked away from', and this author was shoved against a bulkhead by a senior department head who said 'If you're getting to the point where you think a beam's going to fall and kill you, or that you can't make it across a hangar deck safely during flight operations, then you're a danger to yourself and to us.' The goal is also made salient when senior policy makers try to make the ship engage in practices thought unsafe by its senior officers. As an example, scheduling complexities resulted in Carl Vinson's being delayed in deployment three months after her last graded exercise at sea. Her commanding officer requested two at sea exercises in that interval and his navigator stated, 'if we don't flex, when we do go to sea we'll kill someone.'

These ships, in fact all military ships, cannot only do and suffer great harm, they are intermittently the most total of total institutions (Goffman 1961). That affords considerably more top down control than is possible in other organizations and makes this organization different even within the set of hazardous organizations that operate reliably over long periods of time. It should not be forgotten, however, that the same conditions of totalness provide additional opportunity for lower level control over survivability, as when a deck hand causes a serious fire (or in the 1989 case of the USS Iowa gun turret explosion). The fact that organizational members cannot walk away, and cannot quit, affords the organization greater control through socialization, but also allows small problems to build into epidemic proportions and ramify throughout the organization. Maintaining balance is extremely important in this organization.

The Navy recognizes and has somehow gotten Congress to recognize the virtual impossibility of doing this job without enormous amounts of redundancy (in jobs, communication structures, parts, etc.) and training, both terrifically expensive. When hazardous organizations cut corners on either of these issues disaster is likely to occur (for example, Bhopal, Challenger, Exxon-Valdez, etc.).

Conclusions

Perrow and Shrivastava describe organizational catastrophes resulting from a set of characteristics and processes they define. Sometimes explicitly and sometimes implicitly their message is that if these characteristics exist in hazardous technologies catastrophes will occur no matter how low the probability.

Our observations of three nuclear aircraft carriers show that a number of these characteristics potentially exist or do exist. The organizations have developed strategies for avoiding the negative effects of these characteristics. They also engage in other activities and processes designed to aid in obtaining performance reliability.

Our focus here is on only one kind of HRO, nuclear aircraft carriers. It is possible that all HROs using hazardous technologies do not have all of these strategies and processes. However, one that does not have most, if not all, of them is probably accident prone. And, it is entirely possible for an HRO to engage in cost cutting activities that will render it a 'low reliability' organization. We do not know yet which in the set of strategies and processes are most crucial to organizational success, but suspect that continuous training and redundancy are at the top of the list.

Other organizations have some of the properties observed in HROs. We probably would not observe *all* those characteristics identified here in a nonhigh reliability organization. It does not make sense for organizations to adopt expensive ways to manage themselves if they do not need to. For example, redundancy is tremendously expensive and one cannot see any reason for an organization to have large amounts of it unless it is needed.

It is entirely possible that other hazardous industries, such as nuclear waste disposal, in which activities are less time compressed, have other defining characteristics than those we observe on the carriers. However, we feel that most of the characteristics identified here should operate in most organizations that require advanced technologies and in which the cost of error is so great that it needs to be avoided all together. The development of a complete typology of defining characteristics of HROs poses a major research challenge.

Some of the characteristics identified probably manifest themselves differently across HROs. For example, while we feel certain that the culture of reliability in all HROs includes large doses of safety and accountability, in air squadrons there may be more attention to interpersonal helpfulness than in nuclear power plants. Interdependence may well manifest itself differently, even along different dimensions, across HROs.

Research in HROs and other hazardous organizations is just beginning. As indicated previously, the vast amount of research attention given hazardous organizations focuses on what to do after the accident. This not only seems like 'closing the barn door after the horse has gone', it frequently leaves the researcher in a situation in which the clues to the operation are destroyed and certainly does not focus on the possibility of operational success.

We argue that existing organizational behavior literature is wanting in directing this effort (Roberts and Gargano 1990; Rochlin 1989). A large number of research questions suggest themselves.

As examples of those questions we look here *at only structure and the management of interdependence* (ignoring training, culture, environmental uncertainty, goals, etc.). Across HROs what patterns of structure and rules develop in response to requirements for very reliable performance? While it may appear that HROs lend themselves to bureaucratic, hierarchical structure and formal processes, the tacit assumption of such structures is that errors in the production process are not likely to be large and trial and error learning is acceptable.

In HROs reliability oriented processes compete with production oriented processes. How do divisions of responsibility and distributions of formal authority emerge? To what degree is command responsibility at the 'center' versus distributed on the basis of critical function? Are HRO leaders who are required to maintain reliability in the dominant coalition as predicted by the contingency theorists (Thompson 1967; Galbraith 1973; Pfeffer 1982; Scott 1987)? What are the formal relations between technically skilled, reliability oriented groups and leaders in high status positions responsible for coordination and strategic direction?

Relative to broader structural issues, when is it appropriate for the hierarchy to give way to a pyramid inversion? To the extent that pyramid inversion occurs, to what degree is it driven by time compressed sequences of behaviors, technological imperatives, etc.? How do people come to understand the appropriate time for loosening the structure?

With regard to interdependence, what are the various commodities of exchange and how can they be measured? What are the various patterns of interdependence that emerge in HROs? What processes have emerged to coordinate and manage them in meeting the dual demands of reliability and peak load? How are interdependence and culture related? Is culture more likely to be homogeneous in interdependent networks than in more loosely federated organizations? The list of research questions could go on and on.

While at early research stages reporting properties and processes of HROs is useful, certain comparisons should follow. HROs in different industries should be systematically compared and they should be compared with the other kinds of organizations. Good and poor performing hazardous organizations should be compared. For example, while not a part of an in-depth research effort, a comparison of Boston Edison Company's poor performing (and now not performing) Pilgrim nuclear power plant and Northeast Utilities' high performance Millstone I showed the two plants as similar in design, size, and vintage, but very dissimilar in effectiveness. Their managements were also extremely different (Wessel 1987). Careful comparisons of this sort might elucidate effective management strategies for HROs. Lewin and Minton (1986) suggest this strategy.

Finally, organizations that must use hazardous technologies and wish to achieve high levels of performance reliability should ponder seriously the costs of doing business. A number of human costs not mentioned here are associated with the extremely high financial costs of implementing organizational strategies and processes to maintain high levels of performance reliability.

In this case the human costs include working 20 to 22 hours a day while at sea, living and working in a regimented environment, long periods of time away from family and women, living in close quarters with others, often not being able to get away from the job, etc. These combined costs may be excessive, in which case the organization or its larger constituencies have to compare the value of the service provided against cost. If they choose not to institute all the safeguards discussed here they must contend with the possible outcomes of that action.

Acknowledgements

This research was supported by Office of Naval Research contract #N-00014–86-k-0312 and National Science Foundation grant #F7-08046. The research is part of a multidisciplinary study of high reliability organizations. The ideas in this paper were drawn from the research team, Professors Todd La Porte and Gene Rochlin. The author would like to thank Captains Richard Wolter and Harry Robbins and Commander Charles Zullinger for their contributions; Professor Denise Rousseau for her many reviews of previous versions of this paper; Professors Richard Daft and Arie Lewin for their developmental help; Professor Charles Perrow for his insightful review; and other anonymous reviewers.

Note

1   Other studies of hazardous organizations that failed exist (e.g. Presidential Commission on the Space Shuttle Challenger Accident, 1986). These studies draw on secondary data only.

References

Aiken, M. and J. Hage (1968) 'Organizational Interdependence and Intraorganizational Structure', *Amer. Sociological Rev*, 33: 912–929.

Ashby, W. R. (1952) *A Design for a Brain*, John Wiley: New York.

Bignell, V. and J. Fortune (1984) *Understanding Systems Failures*, Manchester University Press: Dover, NH.

Cameron, K. S. and D. A. Whetton (1983) *Organizational Effectiveness: A Comparison of Multiple Models*, Academic Press: New York.

Campbell, J. P. (1977) 'On the Nature of Organizational Effectiveness', in P. S. Goodman and J. M. Pennings (eds), *New Perspectives on Organizational Effectiveness*, Jossey Bass: San Francisco.

Covello, V., J. Menkes and J. Mumpower (eds) (1986) *Risk Evaluation and Management*, Plenum: New York.

Dill, W. R. (1958) 'Environment as an Influence on Managerial Autonomy', *Admin. Sci. Quart.*, 2: 409–443.

Freeman, J. H. and M. T. Hannan (1983) 'Niche Width and the Dynamics of Organizational Populations', *Amer. J. Sociology*, 88: 1116–1145.

Galbraith, J. (1973) *Designing Complex Organizations*, Addison-Wesley: Reading, MA.

Goffman, E. (1961) *Asylums*. Doubleday: Garden City, NY.

Goodman, P. S. and J. M. Pennings (eds) (1977) *New Perspectives on Organizational Effectiveness*. Jossey-Bass: San Francisco.

Hill, C. A. (RADM) (1989) 'FY 90 Budget . . . The Struggle Ahead', *Wings of Gold*, (Spring), 10.

Hughes, W. P. (Capt) (1986) *Fleet Tactics: Theory and Practice*, Naval Institute Press: Annapolis, MD.

Lerner, A. W. (1986) 'There is More than One Way to Be Redundant: A Comparison of Alternatives for the Design and Use of Redundancy in Organizations', *Admin. and Society*, 18, 334–359.

Lewin, A. Y. and J. W. Minton (1986) 'Determining Organizational Effectiveness: Another Look and an Agenda for Research', *Management Sci.*, 32, 514–538.

Lincoln, J. R. (1982) 'Intra- (and inter-) Organizational Networks', in S. B. Bacharach (ed.), *Research in the Sociology of Organizations*. (vol. 1) 1–38, AI Press: Greenwich, CT.

McCann, J. and J. R. Galbraith (1981) 'Interdepartmental Relations', in P. C. Nystrom and W. H. Starbuck (eds), *Handbook of Organizational Design*, Oxford University Press: Oxford.

Morone, J. G. and E. J. Woodhouse (1986) *Averting Catastrophe: Strategies for Regulating Risky Technologies*, University of California Press: Berkeley.

Perrow, C. (1984) *Normal Accidents: Living with High Risk Technologies*, Basic Books: New York.

Pfeffer, J. (1982) *Organizations and Organization Theory*, Pitman: Boston.

Presidential Commission on the Space Shuttle Challenger Accident (1986) 'United States Presidential Commission on the Space Shuttle Challenger Accident Report to the President'.

Rasmussen, L., K. Duncan and J. Leplat (eds) (1987) *New Technology and Human Error*, John Wiley: New York.

Roberts, K. H. (1989) 'New Challenges in Organizational Research: High Reliability Organizations', *Industrial Crisis Quart.*, 3: 111–125.

Roberts, K. H. and G. Gargano (1990) 'Managing a High Reliability Organization: A Case for Interdependence', in M. A. Von Glinow and S. Morhman (eds), *Managing Complexity in High Tech Organizations*, 146–159, Oxford: New York.

Roberts, K. H. and D. M. Rousseau (1989) 'Research in Nearly Free, High Reliability Organizations: Having the Bubble', *IEEE Trans.*, 36: 132–139.

Rochlin, G. I., (1989) 'Technology, Hierarchy and Organizational Self Design: US Navy Flight Operations as a Case Study', *Industrial Crisis Quart.*, 3: 159–176.

Rochlin, G. I., T. R. La Porte, and K. H. Roberts (1987) 'The Self Designing High Reliability Organization: Aircraft Carrier Flight Operations at Sea', *Naval War College Rev.*, (Autumn), 76–90.

Schwartz, H. S. (1987) 'On the Psychodynamics of Organizational Disaster: The Case of Space Shuttle Challenger', *Columbia J. World Business*, 22.

Scott, W. R. (1987) *Organizations: Rational, Natural, and Open Systems*, (2nd edition), Prentice Hall: Englewood Cliffs, NJ.

Shrivastava, P. (1986) *Bhopal*, New York: Basic Books.

Strauss, A. L. (1978) *Negotiations: Varieties, Contexts, Processes and Social Order*, Jossey Bass: San Francisco.

Tetlock, P. E. (1985) 'Accountability: The Neglected Social Context of Judgement and Choice', in L. L. Cummings and B. M. Staw (eds). *Research in Organizational Behavior*, 297–332, JAI Press: Greenwich, CT.

Thompson, J. D. (1967) *Organizations in Action*, McGraw-Hill: New York.

Turner, B. (1976) 'The Organizational and Interorganizational Development of Disasters', *Admn. Sci. Quart.*, 21: 378–397.

Victor, B. and R. S. Blackburn (1987) 'Interdependence: An Alternative Conceptualization', *Acad. Management Rev.* 12: 486–498.

Weick, K. E. (1979) *The Social Psychology of Organizing*, Addison-Wesley: Reading, MA.

Weick, K. E. (1987) 'Organizational Culture and High Reliability', *California Management Rev.*, 29: 112–127.

Wessel, D. (1987) 'Pilgrim and Millstone, Two Nuclear Plants, Have Disparate Fates', *Wall Street J.*, July 28, p. 1.

Zammuto, R. F. (1983) *Assessing Organizational Effectiveness*, State University of New York Press: Albany.

Chapter 12

Joyce Fortune and Geoff Peters

SYSTEMS ANALYSIS OF FAILURES AS A QUALITY MANAGEMENT TOOL

Systems and systems thinking

SYSTEMS APPROACHES TO DESIGN, engineering and problem analysis are well established (see, for example, Beishon and Peters, 1976 and Rosenhead, 1989). The common feature of these approaches that can be described as systemic (as opposed to just systematic) is that they use the abstract notion of a whole, termed system, as an epistemological device to make sense of real-world complexity.

Checkland and Scholes (1990) define systems thinking in the following way:

> 'There *is* such a notion [as that of system], and systems thinking is simply consciously organised thought which makes use of that concept . . . the most basic core idea of systems thinking [is] that a complex whole may have properties which refer to the whole and are meaningless in terms of the parts which make up the whole. These are the so-called "emergent properties".'

Emergence is one of a group of concepts that lie at the heart of systems thinking. Checkland (1979) places it alongside three others: hierarchy, communication and control; but Ackoff (1971) identifies it as one of a much larger group of 32 concepts and terms. He organizes these 32 items into 'a system of systems concepts' and groups them under headings such as system changes, behavioural classification of systems, and adaptation and learning. Young (1964) also attempts to define and classify the concepts of which systems thinking is comprised, using the simple classification shown in Figure 1.

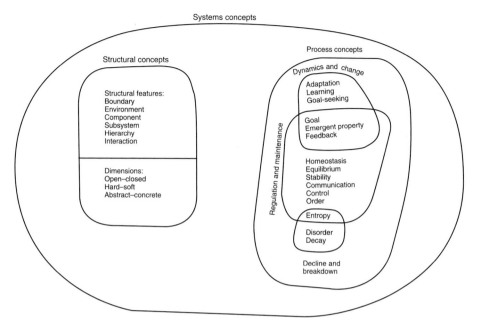

Figure 1 Classifications of systems concepts (Young, 1964)

Systems thinking and failures

Failures do not commonly arise from simple unforeseen causes. They arise out of extremely complicated contexts and are usually the outputs of complex processes. In order to arrive at an understanding of a specific failure with a view to predicting and or preventing future failures it is thus necessary to understand its context. Use of systems thinking to conceptualize this context and to investigate the processes that were taking place allows the investigation to place as much emphasis upon the relationships between subsystems and components as on the subsystems and components themselves. The necessity of this in a quality problem context too should be obvious; for example, the causes of a product proving too expensive to manufacture as a result of specification of extremely tight tolerances and the use of non-standard components can often be traced back to poor relations between design and production.

Quality and failures

Quality and systems analysis of failures are traditionally seen as two distinct subject areas, each with its own body of literature and research. There are, however, significant areas of overlap between them and it can be argued that they have much to learn from each other. They are both primarily concerned with performance and the problems they address are often remarkably similar. It is frequently the question of scale that causes observers to distinguish between a quality problem and a failure. To take an example within the narrow confines of a 'conformance to specification' definition of quality: weld defects in cars coming off a production line may share many common features with the weld problem that led to the collapse of Alexander L. Kielland accommodation rig in the North Sea in 1980, but the former would be treated as a quality problem and the latter as a failure.

When a broader, more modern definition of quality that encompasses the quality of the design and production process as well as the fitness of the final product or service is considered, the overlaps become even more noticeable. In a paper that is much cited in the failures field as an early attempt to use systems thinking in the analysis and prevention of failures, Jenkins (1969) presents a list of 'disasters that could have been avoided with Systems Engineering'.

As can be seen from the following examples taken from his list, the cases he quotes would now be immediately recognized as quality problems:

> 'A large integrated plant complex lost a great deal of money during the first two years of its life because plant reliability and raw material availability had not been assessed properly.
>
> A fibre manufacturer responded quickly to an increase in demand by installing additional spinning capacity without ensuring that its raw material supply was adequate and so lost money by tying up valuable capital resources.'

Given this common ground between quality and systems analysis of failures it seems appropriate to examine whether any of the body of knowledge and expertise that is currently identified with systems analysis of failures, and seen as distinct from quality, can contribute to the management of quality.

This paper concentrates on one particular area where significant scope for transfer appears to exist: the use of a meta-method for problem analysis at the system level.

Problem analysis in quality and in failures

In recent years, there has been a marked shift towards the use of integrated approaches to quality within organizations. Broadly speaking, these approaches are based on either the teachings of so-called quality gurus (Crosby's zero defects, Deming's 14 points, etc.), or the need to be seen to conform to certain national, international, or customers' standards (e.g. BS5750, ISO 9000, Q-101), or, sometimes, a combination of the two. Recognition of the need to set in place mechanisms for tackling quality problems is to be found within most of the approaches that are commonly used, though at the more detailed level of description, the mechanisms suggested vary. Crosby (1982) for example, recommends the use of quality circles, or similar teams, whilst Juran (1964) puts forward a more complex arrangement whereby a group of people manage an improvement programme and 'employ' problem-solving specialists to undertake it.

When a problem-solving mechanism is in place, it usually provides an umbrella under which many problems can be tackled at the same time, and in similar ways, by different groups of people. In some companies, an explicit problem-solving method such as the PDCA (plan/do/check/act) cycle is used, but it is more common for problems to be tackled on an *ad hoc* basis, with techniques such as brainstorming, pareto analysis and cause and effect diagrams being brought into play as and when they are judged necessary.

One of the basic principles behind many of the problem-solving mechanisms that are used is that participants are free to operate upon problems that they select themselves as being of greatest concern to them and their closest colleagues. This principle is adopted so as to secure commitment to the problem-solving process. One problem that is inherent in this approach, though, is that it leads to solutions being found to easily definable, lower-level problems whilst higher-level, higher consequence, over-arching problems are neglected. For example, once a Statistical Process Control (SPC) scheme has been introduced and been seen to work well, investigations into future problems are likely to be confined to individual processes, even in cases where the roots of the problems lie within the control system itself. Because individuals experience different smaller aspects of the same larger problem a huge amount of evidence may have to pile up before the scheme itself is suspected, and even then the problem solvers may lack the means or motivation to tackle complex, poorly defined problems. Systems analysis of failures offers a way of clarifying, investigating and dealing with such higher-level problems or problem messes.

Systems failures

Most significant failures arise from highly complex human activities where many transformations are taking place and so they are particularly appropriate subjects for the application of systems approaches. One particular systems approach, the failures method (Fortune, 1993), has been specifically designed for the study of failure. It takes on board the importance of context by viewing a failure in terms of the system or number of systems from which it can be perceived to have emerged and examining the system's relationships with its wider systems and its environment. The method also provides a means of examining the relationships between the subsystems and components within the system's boundary. By modelling failures in systems terms it allows them to be understood.

The failures method

The failures method has two key features: perception and representation of the failure situation as a system(s); and comparison of that system(s) with a model of a robust system that is capable of purposeful activity without failure, and with other models based on typical failures. A recent version of the method is shown in outline in Figure 2.

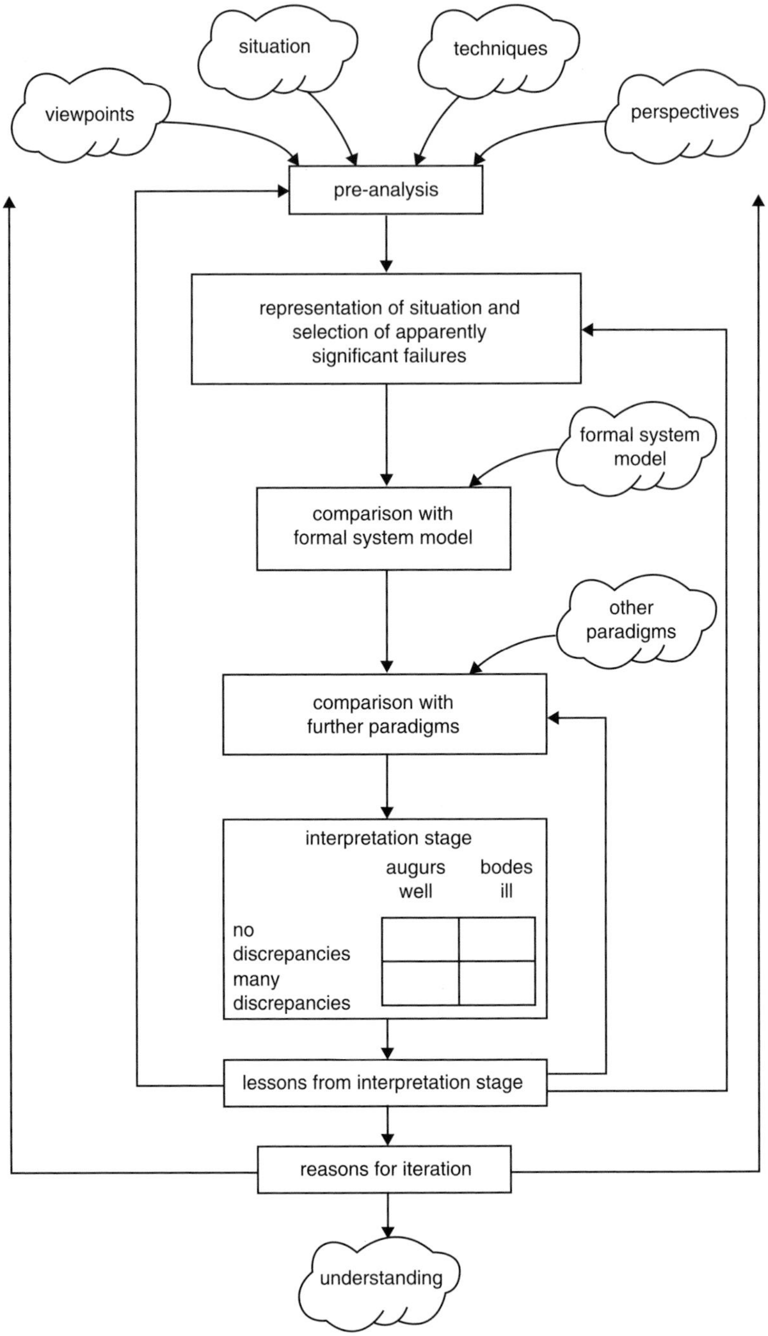

Figure 2 The failures method

Use of the method begins with the analyst being faced with a mass of information about a situation that someone has identified as a failure or potential failure. The initial appraisal stage requires sufficient knowledge of the situation in systems terms to be amassed to enable the analyst to represent the situation, or aspects of it, in forms where it can be compared with various paradigms. This can be achieved by means of a five-step process:

1 Preanalysis
  Define the role of the analyst and the purpose of the analysis. Gather together source material. Examine the situation from different viewpoints and organize the information into a form(s) that will render it usable. This may involve the use of rich pictures, spray diagrams, multiple cause diagrams, databases and so on. Exact methods for the pre-analysis are not prescribed, but systems analyses are proscribed.
2 Select apparently significant failure(s)
  The situation itself will have already been labelled a failure or potential failure in general terms (otherwise the study would not have been undertaken), but now the precise aspects of the situation that are to form the subject of the analysis must be specified in accordance with the role, purpose and viewpoints identified in step 1.
3 Perception of systems
  Structure relevant aspects of the situation into a range of systems forms. Put trial boundaries around the various systems and give each option a name.
4 Selection
  Select the system that will form the first basis for comparison (against the formal system paradigm). This may be one of the systems that was perceived in step 3 or a combination of a number of them.
5 Clarification and description
  This begins with clarification of the nature of the system selected in step 4 and ends with representation of the system in an appropriate format. It will be necessary to describe in systems terms the components, subsystems, environment, goals, flows, outputs, inputs, levels, states, connections and so on of the selected system in order to reach an adequate understanding of its processes, structure, climate and behaviour.

The bases for comparison against which representations of the situation are examined are termed paradigms. The authors have allowed for the possibility that the paradigms which are deployed can be expanded according to the experiences of the practitioners using the method. At present, the standard list of paradigms comprises:

- Formal system
- Control
- Communications
- Human factors
- Various engineering reliability models such as Failure Mode and Effect Analysis (FMEA), fault trees, cascade failure and common mode failure.

A full description of these paradigms is given in Watson and Fortune (1993). Of the paradigms included, the most valuable by far has proved to be formal system, a successful application of which is described in Fortune and Peters (1990).

Formal system paradigm

This model, which unites most core systems concepts, is shown diagrammatically in Figure 3. It is adapted from Checkland (1981) and is essentially a compilation of the features which should be present if a set of activities is to comprise a system capable of purposeful activity without failure. The paradigm is termed formal system, where the word formal is being used in the sense of providing a form or a structural framework into which something can be fitted. Its features are:

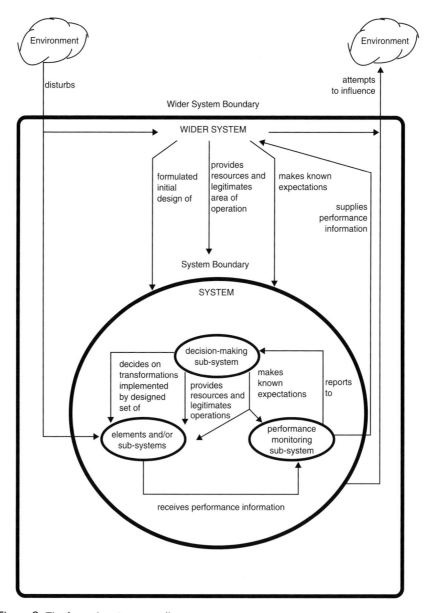

Figure 3 The formal system paradigm

- a continuous purpose or mission
- a measure of performance
- a decision-taking process
- a degree of connectivity between the components
- an environment with which the system interacts
- boundaries separating the system from its wider system and the wider system from the environment
- resources
- some guarantee of continuity.

In addition to the formal system being made up of elements and subsystems as shown in Figure 3, the subsystems themselves can be considered as formal systems in their own right with their own decision-making and performance-monitoring components. The hierarchical nature of such systems is further highlighted by a similar relationship existing between the subsystems and the system as between the system and the wider system. Although a system is said to have expectations of its subsystems, the subsystems are assumed to have a certain amount of autonomy in deciding how those expectations are met.

The formal system paradigm has graduated to a central place in the method so that it is always applied first. At each comparison stage, it is necessary to decide whether the results indicate a need to go back and learn more about the situation, to deploy more comparisons or to bring together the results of the comparisons to give a new understanding of the failure. Up until now, these decisions about whether iteration was necessary have been matters of judgement, but the authors are in the process of producing guidelines which will be incorporated in a revised version of the method.

In general terms, studies of a wide range of failures have shown groups of commonly recurring features such as:

- Deficiencies in the apparent organizational structure such as a lack of a performance-measuring subsystem or a control decision system.
- No clear statements or purpose supplied in comprehensible form from the wider system.
- Deficiency in the performance of one or more subsystems.
- Subsystems with ineffective means of communication inadequately designed subsystems.
- Inadequately designed subsystems.

Application

The failures method described here has now been widely applied. One example that provides a good illustration of its use in the context of a quality problem concerns science education in primary schools over the decade 1975–1985. A study of this problem area began by representing relevant aspects of the situation in system form. A map of the resulting 'science education in primary schools system' is shown in Figure 4.

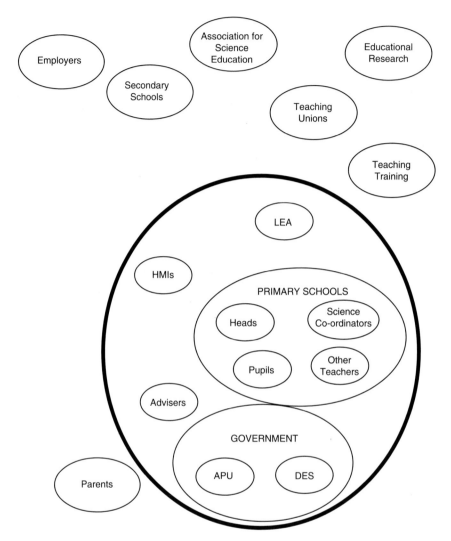

Figure 4 Systems map of the science education in primary schools system, LEA, local education authority; HMIs, Her Majesty's Inspectors; DES, Department of Education and Science; APU, Assessment of Performance Unit

A comparison was then made between this system and the formal system paradigm. This comparison, which is represented diagrammatically in Figure 5, revealed a number of interesting insights, some of which were explored further using other paradigms. It showed, for example, that the decision-making subsystem did not make its expectations known to the performance-monitoring subsystem. The wider system had not made its expectations known either, nor had it formulated the initial design of the system. The system as a whole was not cohesive and had little influence over its environment; indeed, the performance-monitoring subsystem was the only part of the system to have significant links with the environment.

An extended version of this study can be found in Fortune *et al.* (1993).

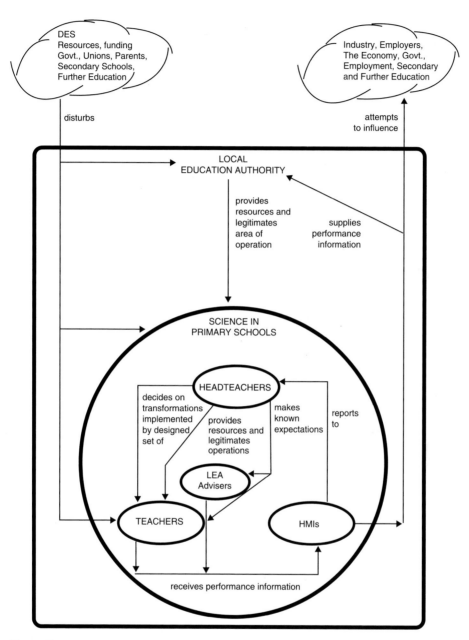

Figure 5 Comparison between science education in primary schools system and the formal system paradigm. LEA, Local Education Authority, HMIs, Her Majesty's Inspectors; DES, Department of Education and Science

Conclusion

The authors would like to suggest that, given the close links that can be demonstrated between systems analysis of failures and quality, and the importance of having tools available to tackle high-level or systemic quality problems, the potential usefulness of the failures method in the quality management context should be taken on board. Mechanisms must be found for addressing those problems rather than concentrating on their lower-level symptoms; not only is the potential payback much greater, it should, in the longer term, be possible to reduce the total amount of resources invested in problem solving.

References

Ackoff, R. L. (1971) 'Towards a System of Systems Concepts', *Management Science*, 17, p. 11.

Beishon, J. and G. Peters (1976) *Systems Behaviour*. Harper & Row: New York.

Checkland, P. B. (1979) 'The Shape of the Systems Movement', *Journal of Applied Systems Analysis*, 6.

Checkland, P. B. (1981) *Systems Thinking, Systems Practise*, Wiley: Chichester.

Checkland, P. B. and J. Scholes (1990) *Soft Systems Methodology in Action*. Wiley: Chichester.

Crosby, P. B. (1982) *Quality is Free*, The New American Library Inc.

Fortune, J. (1993) *Studying Systems Failures*, Open University Press: Milton Keynes.

Fortune, J. and G. Peters (1990) 'The Formal System Paradigm for Studying Failures', *Technology Analysis and Strategic Management*, 2, p. 4.

Fortune, J., G. Peters and L. Rawlinson-Winder (1993) 'Science Teaching in Primary Schools – A Systems Study', *Journal of Curriculum Studies*, 25, p. 4.

Jenkins, G. M. (1969) 'The Systems Approach', *Journal of Systems Engineering*, 1, p. 1.

Juran, J. M. (1964) *Managerial Breakthrough*. McGraw Hill.

Rosenhead, J. (ed.) (1989) *Rational Analysis for a Problematic World*, Wiley: Chichester.

Watson, L. and J. Fortune (1993) *Systems Paradigms*, Open University Press: Milton Keynes.

Young, O. R. (1964) *General Systems: Yearbook Vol. 9*, Society for General Systems Research.

Chapter 13

Barry A. Turner and Brian Toft

ORGANIZATIONAL LEARNING
FROM DISASTERS

Introduction

WE CAN LEARN FROM the past only if we are able to recognize similarities between our past experience and our present situation. All forms of learning based upon feedback require that we link patterns from the past with those cues which might alert us to related patterns in the foreseeable future. In many fields of industrial engineering we have become skilled at making such links, with the result that thousands of routine industrial operations can now be carried out much more safely than they were 50, 20 or even 10 years ago. Where we are less skilled is in learning fully the lessons offered to us by major failures in large-scale complex systems.

To extend such learning it is necessary to start with the assumption that major failures in large-scale systems are not wholly unique, so they can be analysed to provide information which will reduce the chances of similar events recurring. It is gradually becoming clear that many disasters and large-scale accidents display similar features and characteristics, so the possibility of gaining a greater understanding of these disturbing events is presented to us [1].

Although major large-scale failures are high-intensity events, they also occur with low frequency within any one industrial sector, so to learn from them we must make use of a wide range of comparisons from different industrial sectors. To facilitate such comparisons a framework must be developed which aids recognition of similar types of causal patterns, disregarding the differing contexts in which they may occur. Much recent research has been moving towards the development of such a framework, suggesting that the majority of large-scale accidents arise from combinations of individual, group, social and organizational factors, and that these combinations display recurring configurations when detached from their specific technical contexts [1–5].

Public accident inquiries have an important role to play in these learning processes, but they are normally under pressure to give all of their attention to the matter in hand, and they have little opportunity to develop more wide-ranging analyses or to contribute directly to the emerging debate about system patterns which might aid learning.

Public inquiries after major accidents already have to serve a number of purposes: they respond to public concern by trying to ascertain exactly how the events in question came about; they provide an authoritative investigatory basis for any subsequent legal action related to liability; and they attempt to provide information which will ensure that accidents will not arise from similar causes in the future. To make any progress at all towards this latter goal an inquiry must, of course, be efficiently carried out, any resulting conclusions must be disseminated effectively and their implications must be translated by individuals and by organizations into appropriate preventive action. These cycles of events are, however, rarely considered in a unified fashion, and in this paper we wish to correct this omission and to address some issues which bear upon the problems of the effective generations, dissemination and use of information relevant to large-scale accident prevention.

After a major accident, some kind of corrective action is likely to be initiated spontaneously by operators of similar plant, or operators in related industries, merely upon the basis of reports of an accident occurring, or upon the basis of reports of an inquiry in the national or the technical press. A widely publicised component failure, for example, might prompt checks upon similar components elsewhere. But the primary focus for action based upon the lessons of the inquiry lies in the recommendations of that inquiry, and if we are concerned to minimize and contain the adverse outcomes associated with major hazards it is important to look at the nature of inquiry recommendations and at the response to them.

In a current study we have been examining the recommendations made in reports from 19 public inquiries into major accidents, and in order to determine in detail the nature of the response to the inquiries we have followed this up by interviewing representatives of the array of organizations involved with five of these incidents. We chose to look at public inquiries into major accidents which took place in Britain between 1965 and 1975, these inquiries having already had their findings subjected to some detailed analysis [1]. The incidents studied more intensively were all accidents which triggered fires or explosions. The study is not yet complete and the analysis reported here is an interim one.

When we examined recommendations from these major accident inquiries, we found that it was possible to discern recurrent types of recommendations [6]. An accident is always a physical event, and all inquiries made recommendations demanding technical improvements and requiring that certain physical changes be made to plant and equipment. But these large-scale inquiries also normally recognized that the accidents were not solely technical events. They clearly acknowledged them to be *socio*-technical in nature, and over 80% of their recommendations were accordingly concerned with organizational and pro-cedural matters. Recommendations were thus concerned to clarify administrative procedures and arrangements, to draw attention to personnel issues such as the need for staff training, or to call retrospectively for improved safety precautions to be installed by, for example, the revision or work procedures or by the modification of existing rules or regulations. Organizational recommendations also typically exhibited concern about information flows, calling for improved communication about hazards within and outside organizations, demanding the formulation and dissemination of new rules or procedures, and recommending increased supervision, monitoring or inspection of organizational activities by in-house staff, by external agencies or both. Finally, most of these major public inquiries attempted to develop foresight by making recommendations which offered the possibility of forestalling future problems, doing this by calling for the initiation of programmes of experimental investigations, for example, or by directing calls for action to organizations not immediately implicated in the particular incident under scrutiny.

Such an analysis of recommendations displays to us both the areas which were of concern to those conducting these inquiries and the model of diagnosis and prevention which the inquiry body tacitly adopted. These particular public inquiries sought to control hazards and to prevent the recurrence of major incidents by advocating action at a physical, an administrative and at a communications level, as well as sometimes proposing actions which ranged more widely where future plans to deal with a particular hazard were concerned. The model behind these arrays of practical recommendations stresses the importance of: selecting appropriate physical safety precautions; identifying and eliminating ambiguous situations; keeping working practices, rules and procedures up-to-date; training staff appropriately; improving communication about hazardous matters; and attending to the supervision and monitoring of processes and individuals within the organizations concerned.

This kind of approach is broadly in keeping with the direction of the recent research referred to above, but it is presented in specific rather than general terms in each case. Organizations in any sector could doubtless learn much about emergency planning for industrial hazards merely by considering their own operations alongside this very general checklist. But we should ask here whether there are also other ways of making maximum use of the considerable volume of investigation which goes into such accident inquiries, in order to ensure that any wider applicability of their findings is brought to notice and that the response to their recommendations is effective.

One of the problems which such inquiries face in attempting to learn from their investigations is that of marshalling the evidence so that appropriate relationships can be observed and the appropriate deductions made. Since the evidence taken by an inquiry will run to many hundreds of thousands of words, it is, on occasion, difficult for the interrelationships between events to be fully appreciated.

It may then, in turn, prove difficult to extract all the lessons to be learnt from an incident; if members of the investigating team are not able to comprehend fully all the implications of the evidence which they have at their disposal, they may unwittingly end up with a limited set of recommendations. The complexity of events associated with large-scale incidents may thus generate 'blind spots' in the lessons drawn from them, and it would be a contribution to organizational learning if such blind spots could be reduced or eliminated.

A technique known as Schematic Report Analysis has been developed in the course of examining public inquiry reports, in order to explore the combinations of unnoticed events which develop in the 'incubation period' prior to a major disaster. This technique has been used not only to summarize a number of public inquiry reports but also to analyse other types of incidents, for example, the build-up to the Yom Kippur War [7] and the causation of instances of structural failure [8].

In recent developments of this technique, Schematic Report Analysis has been used first to translate the written synthesis of evidence gathered about a particular incident into a graphic form, and then to locate recommendations within this format in a way which links them to the relevant aspects of the accident investigation. Thus, by summarizing large amounts of information into a readily comprehensible form, such diagrams could assist those investigating accidents to clarify their own diagnoses and to identify more clearly the connections being proposed between diagnosis and recommendation.

A fuller account of this technique is available elsewhere [9], but the accompanying figures give some indication of the approach which has been used. Figure 1 illustrates how the events of the incubation period of one particular unwanted incident, in this case a methane explosion at Cambrian Colliery, Wales, can be displayed in a single schematic presentation. In Fig. 2, the various branches of the causal analysis have been isolated and each recommendation of the inquiry has been related to the train of events which it is intended to prevent recurring. It can readily be seen that the schematic diagram subdivides into six separate yet interrelated clusters of events, but the recommendations made as a result of the inquiry seek only to intervene in three of those clusters. Whether this omission was due to an oversight on the part of the investigators, or whether, as seems more likely, they were unable to formulate appropriate corrective courses of action, the diagram set out in Fig. 2 points up the relationship between the inquiry and the recommendations more clearly and more immediately than does the original report. The development and wider use of this and related techniques clearly have a part to play in improving organizational learning after major accidents. As well as assisting the analysis of the evidence, they can help to spread the findings of the inquiry in a more readily accessible form. Very full versions of Schematic Report Diagrams can be stored as nested sets using proprietary programs such as Macintosh Filevision, and diagrams generated from such stores can readily be used as training aids.

As indicated above, work currently in hand at Exeter (with the support of the Economic and Social Research Council) is investigating the long-term feedback cycle instituted by accident inquiries. Following the examination of inquiry recommendations, this project is making a detailed exploratory investigation of the response to recommendations made by five major inquiries concerned with large fires and explosions 10 years or more ago. The recommendations of the five inquiries called for action by a total of 23 organizations. Of these, only one refused to cooperate with the research, although four other organizations declined indirectly, on the grounds that no one with knowledge of the incident

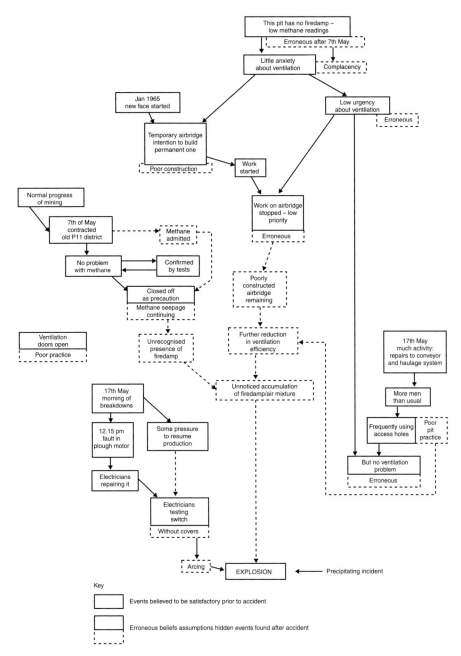

Figure 1 Outlining of individual event SRAD Cambrian Colliery Accident.
Source: Ref. 1.

and its aftermath was now available, staff having died, retired or moved on. A further four organizations had gone out of business since the incident, but interviews were conducted satisfactorily with representatives of the remaining 14 organizations involved.

Although the analysis of these interviews is still in an early stage, some

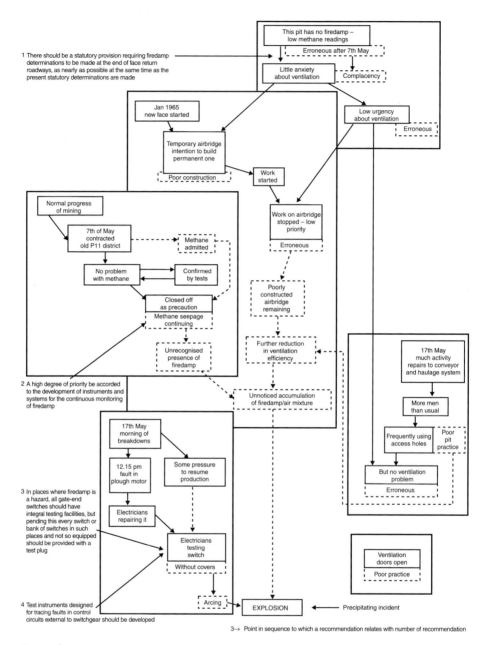

Figure 2 SRAD showing main clusters of events for Cambrian Colliery Accident

preliminary observations arising from them seem to be of sufficient interest to set out here. A point which is immediately striking is the emotional impact which involvement in a major accident has upon those concerned. Even after an interval of 10 years or more, these effects appear to be massive and enduring. One senior manager still did not wish to talk about the incident which his organization was involved with, because it still upset him to think about it, even though his organization bore no responsibility for the accident. As a result of the effects of the accident, some of those interviewed reported that their connection with the accident had triggered a major shift in preoccupations and activities. One architectural practice, for example, had shifted emphasis of its work so that the bulk of its work was concerned with safety matters, whilst an individual in another practice responded to the shock of discovering the fire potential of furniture used in his building by spending several years designing safer alternative fittings.

A second observation relates to the clarity of recall about the incidents in question by individuals, even after an interval of 10 years or more. We have no independent means of confirming the *accuracy* of recall, and all studies of memory and recollection would lead us to expect systematic distortion in such retrospective accounts, but informants' discussions of what had taken place had a very vivid and immediate quality. They had no difficulty in presenting their clear account of what had taken place, of the lessons which had been learned, and of how the implementation process had been carried out. They had all clearly carried away and retained, in a very accessible form, their own personal lessons from the incident.

If such an incident recurred, of course, these personal learning experiences would not be the only issue which it would be important to ask about. It would be equally relevant to ask whether the lessons absorbed by these individuals with direct responsibility for response to the earlier accident had been satisfactorily transferred to the 'memory' of the organization; for this to occur, they would need not just to have made an impact upon this particular band of individuals, but to have been translated into a form where they had become a pervasive and accepted part of the organization's mode of operation [10]. Our inquiries are centrally concerned with the extent to which this institutionalization occurred, but as yet we have no conclusions to offer on this point.

As far as organizational responses are concerned, the accounts collected did suggest that action was taken to implement relevant recommendations from the inquiry, and that it was taken very quickly, delays in implementation occuring only when large outlays of capital expenditure were needed. In such cases, the shortfall in safety during the interim period was typically made up by the devising of new rules and regulations, and by safety campaigns to make staff particularly aware of the problem. A clear preference was expressed within these organizations for forms of safety training which actively involved employees in safety practices and procedures, rather than merely making them the passive recipients of additional sets of regulations or directives.

As one would expect following incidents which had excited considerable public concern, the recommendations for action were considered at the highest level in all 14 organizations, followed subsequently by a meeting or a series of meetings with lower levels of management, and supplemented in some organizations by information programmes aimed at the general workforce. Such a pattern of endorsement of action from the top of the organization clearly contributed to the speed and scope of the reaction to the recommendations within the organizations.

Whilst the diffusion of information about the response to hazard within organizations could readily follow the normal hierarchical pattern used for other types of in-house communications, clear differences could be discerned when issues of broader diffusion were discussed. In very large national organizations which constituted industries in their own right, difficulties of communication arising from sheer size were compensated for by the possibility of using standard communication channels to ensure widespread and rapid dissemination of a particular warning or instruction to all parts of the industry with a reasonable degree of certainty about its delivery. By contrast, in a fragmented or decentralized sphere of operations, the differential response of small organizations to information about hazard seemed to be associated with a lack of cross-communication between small competitors about such matters, few enquiries being made of others about their level of hazard awareness.

A systems model for the reduction of socio-technical failures

These preliminary observations from our study may serve to raise some questions about the manner in which recommendations contribute to feedback and learning, about the assumptions which underlie them, and about mechanisms for ensuring that they are more widely known after an investigation. They raise the question also of whether it would be desirable and feasible to establish some kind of unitary hazard reporting system which would overcome the problems of hazard communication within fragmented and decentralized sectors of activity to which we have just referred. To help to clarify discussion about organizational learning and adequate feedback after major incidents, it might be helpful to try to formulate such a system in model form.

The elements of such a hypothetical model are set out in Fig. 3, which is based upon earlier work in which one of the authors was concerned to apply systems thinking to the problem of reducing the incidence of socio-technical failures [6, 11]. It is sketched out here not as an immediate policy proposal, but in order to illuminate the issues which proposals that moved any way towards such a system would need to confront.

The schematic model in Fig. 3 is best understood by considering a proposal to initiate a project which would bring about some change in the environment, a proposal to build a bridge, say, or to construct a power station. The left-hand side of the diagram sets out in a schematic form the kinds of events which might then be expected to follow, as the design is specified and transmuted into more detailed proposals which can be reviewed for their acceptability. The implementation of the accepted design and the development of operational instructions for the project enable the accepted cycle to be completed by the generation of the changes initially envisaged – the bridge is built and carries traffic, or the power station is finished and generates electricity.

What this cycle does not include are the activities suggested on the right-hand side of the diagram, activities concerned with learning about design. Typically we do have some kinds of activities which provide us with opportunities for design learning but these are rarely seen either as complete elements in themselves or as key contributors to an overall learning system, particularly when the information from failures is being considered. Here we are pointing to the need

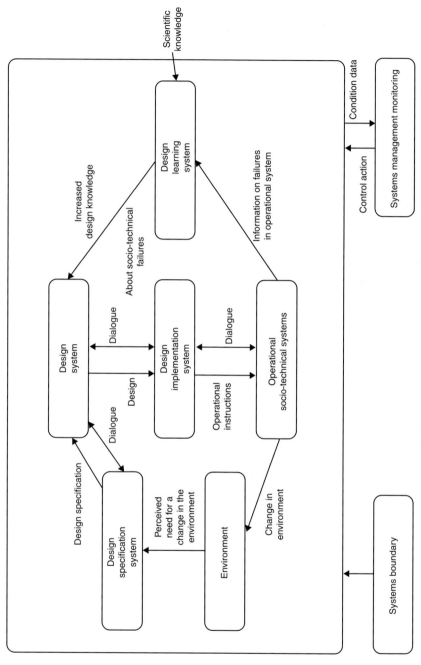

Figure 3 A socio-technical failure reducing system

for a set of procedures which could help to ensure that the lessons which can be drawn from socio-technical failures are incorporated into training and working practices in the future. This could be achieved by making wider provision for the collection, collation and analysis of data from known socio-technical failures, as well as from other sources, and by making arrangements to incorporate this information into design and implementation, and into the management of these processes.

We have expanded the model further in Fig. 4 to move a little way away from the wholly schematic, by trying to specify some of the sub-systems which a unitary arrangement for reducing socio-technical systems failure might contain. We hope that this model, initially formulated earlier this year [6] by the application of a 'Systems Approach' [12, 13], might provide an organizing framework within which discussions of the improvement of the management of industrial hazards might take place.

In the expanded model, operations have also been separated out into three levels of functioning. At the first level the Design Implementation and the Operational Socio-technical Systems are to be found. The second level contains the first level plus the Design and the Design Specification Systems, whilst the third level of the model adds the Design Learning System to the first two levels. Within each system, the sub-systems shown are intended to be illustrative of the activities likely to be taking place, rather than being an exhaustive specification.

The core sequence assumed in the model is the same as that already discussed for Fig. 3: a desire for change in the environment prompts the specification of a possible project design, which will, we hope, be devised with the benefit of opinions sought from concerned actors in the system. The completed specifications will then be translated into firm proposals, through the activities of sub-systems concerned, among other things, with problem-solving and the collation of designs from separate sections of the project in order to avoid difficulties of mismatching.

A Simulated Systems sub-unit is included in the model to emphasize the importance of the possibility of non-destructive testing of proposals in as many failure modes as possible before the design to be implemented is finalized. Here, as in other parts of the system, good communications and a two-way dialogue are important in reducing the possibility of failure.

As in the simplified model, the Design Implementation System translates the proposals of the Design System into operational instructions which would include information about cost, the provision of labour, the ordering of materials and so on. A token sample of sub-units is included here for illustrative purposes.

The Operational System can then be brought into action to start to engineer the proposed project, setting up the required socio-technical system in order to do so. This should generate both the changes initially specified for the project, and also 'condition data' which may be used to monitor the project, and to initiate corrective control action where this is possible.

As with the earlier diagram, the principal focus of interest for present purposes is to be found at the highest level of the model, in the interaction of the processes already outlined with the Design Learning System, which is here sketched out in a little more detail. Should the project fail catastrophically, or

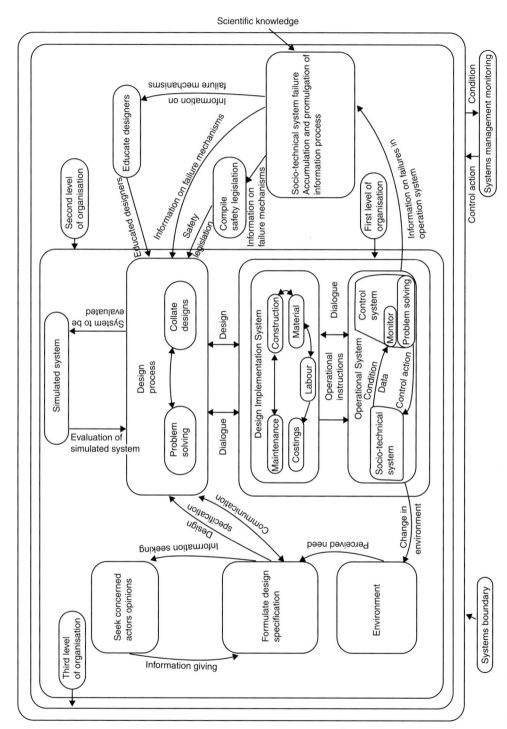

Figure 4 Expanded socio-technical failure reducing systems model

should it malfunction to a level which produces a 'near-miss' catastrophe, the procedures indicated here would be brought into play. The three processes specifically identified here set out some of the important general modes of reaction which are involved.

As discussed earlier, this part of the system is expected to receive information from a variety of sources about socio-technical failures, together with relevant academic research findings. As these are accumulated, the system would be expected to:

a   transmit information directly to the Designer Education Systems, so that information about failures and the responses to them could be made available to designers, engineers, managers and others in training, making them much more aware of the problems and mechanisms of failure;
b   pass information on to sub-systems concerned with the production of Codes of Practice and Safety Legislation in order to influence procedures and work practices; and
c   communicate the knowledge gained directly to industry via trade journals and other publications, special notices (as at present in civil aviation), and training courses, to ensure that current experience influences practice as soon as possible.

To many there will be little that is novel in this model, except perhaps in its clear diagrammatic formulation; it merely proposes that in designing and operating large-scale socio-technical systems we should make maximum use of available information by setting up and maintaining negative feedback loops to improve our control of such systems. But when we look at practice, the logic of the model looks less self-evident. Engineering institutions are resistant to suggestions that they might install procedures for reporting on and learning from failures. Research into such matters can only be carried out with extreme circumspection if at all, and specialists in the insurance industry who possess information which is vital to the operation of a Design Learning System are reluctant in the extreme to consider making use of this information in the way outlined by the model, either because they fail to see any connection between such discussions as the present one and their own commercial concerns, or because of the contraints and anxieties imposed upon them by the need for confidentiality and by associated legal limitations upon the dissemination of failure-related information.

We suggested above that this model might provide a framework for the discussion of some of the issues connected with learning from disasters. The difficulties in moving current practitioners a very small step along the way towards the constructive use of failure-derived information indicates clearly that a sociological analysis of current practices in any industry operating large-scale hazardous systems would reveal a pattern much different from the model outlined, with the partial exception, perhaps, of the nuclear industry [14, 15].

We should note too that the model itself has its drawbacks. An all-embracing information-gathering and reporting system would be difficult to devise and to operate, and it might generate undesirable side-effects by accelerating current trends towards the over-centralization of information in our society. It could also be accused of placing an undue faith in a purely cognitive approach to issues of hazard management and failure prevention, neglecting many of the social, emotional and aesthetic aspects of the processes discussed, and making no overt provision for assessing the way in which issues of commercial, political and military power might impinge upon our understanding of, and our response to, large-scale systems failures. With all of these provisos, however, serious discussion of the issues raised by the model is needed if we are successfully to confront the potential for catastrophic losses which results from the continued development in our societies of large-scale systems with high energy concentrations.

Conclusions

At every large-scale accident inquiry the hope is expressed that the investigations will ensure that 'this shall not happen again'. But, in practice, adequate learning is often constrained. Several factors contribute to this: frequently there is an assumption that the particular large-scale incident is unique and unlikely to recur – even, perhaps, that it is pointless to look for regularities in such 'Acts of God'. Often there is also no readily available perspective making it easy to interpret findings at an appropriately general level, and no set of techniques for discerning all relevant patterns in the events surrounding the accident. Learning about such failures is further inhibited if too limited a range of possible comparisons is scanned. Large-scale failures do not recur with great frequency in any single field of activity, and we need to look outside our own industrial sector, examining incidents in other industries and in non-industrial settings if we are to maximize our chances of spotting repeated patterns and of learning from them. The final stage in developing adequate organizational learning after a disaster requires the lessons identified to be passed on effectively to those who need to know about them, and that they be passed on in such a way that appropriate action indicated by them is encouraged.

In general, then, as the model discussed in this paper indicates, learning from disasters requires: first, a wide-ranging investigation; second, an outlook and techniques which enable appropriate lessons to be drawn from events which are often similar only at some general systemic level; and finally, an efficient capability to transmit information from these lessons to those most in need of it. Much remains to be done in identifying patterns of contemporary institutional reactions to failure, and in devising ways of minimizing such failures in the future.

References

1. Turner, B. A. (1978) *Man-made Disasters*, Wykeham Press: London.
2. Bignell, B. and Fortune; J. (1984) *Understanding Systems Failures*, Manchester University Press: Manchester.
3. Perrow, C. (1984) *Normal Accidents: Living with High-Risk Technologies*, Basic Books: New York.
4. Pidgeon, N. F. and Turner, B. A. (1986) ' "Human error" and socio-technical

systems failure in structural engineering', in *Modelling Human Error in Structural Design and Construction*, (ed. A. Nowak), ASCE: New York.

5. Pidgeon, N. F., Turner, B. A. and Blockley, D. I. (1986) *The sociological management of safety*, paper presented to the British Sociological Association Conference on Science, Technology and Society: Leeds, 6–9 April.

6. Toft, B. (1987) *Schematic Report Analysis Diagramming: an aid to organisational learning*, unpublished research paper, Department of Sociology, University of Exeter: UK.

7. Stech, F. J. (1979) *Political and Military Intention Estimation*, Mathtech, Bethesda: Maryland.

8. Pidgeon, N. F., Blockley, D. I and Turner, B. A. (1986) 'Design practice and snow loading: lessons from a roof collapse', *The Structural Engineer*, 64A:(3) 67–71.

9. Toft, B. and Turner, B. A. (1987) 'The Schematic Report Analysis Diagram: a simple aid to learning from large-scale failures', *International CIS Journal*, 1 (2), May, 12–23.

10. Kletz, T. A. (1980) 'Organisations have no memory', *Loss Prevention Manual*, 13.

11. Toft, B. (1984) *Human Factor Failure in Complex Systems*, unpublished undergraduate dissertation, Department of Independent Studies, University of Lancaster: UK.

12. Lockett, M. and Spear, R. (1980) *Organisation as Systems*, Open University Press, Milton Keynes: UK.

13. Checkland, P. (1981) *Systems Thinking, Systems Practice*, Wiley: New York.

14. Kalfsbeer, H. W. (1987) *The Organisation and Use of Abnormal Occurrence Data*, Technical Note No. 1.87.72, PER 1320/87, Ispra Joint Research Centre: Varese.

15. Amesz, J., Francocci, G., Primavera, R. and ven der Pas, A. (1982) *The European Abnormal Occurrences Reporting System*, PER 672/82, Ispra Joint Research Centre: Varese.

Chapter 14

Karl E. Weick

ENACTED SENSEMAKING IN CRISIS SITUATIONS[1]

Introduction

CRISES ARE CHARACTERIZED BY low probablility/high con-sequence events that threaten the most fundamental goals of an organization. Because of their low probability, these events defy interpretations and impose severe demands on sensemaking. The less adequate the sensemaking process directed at a crisis, the more likely it is that the crisis will get out of control. That straightforward proposition conceals a difficult dilemma because people think by acting. To sort out a crisis as it unfolds often requires action which simultaneously generates the raw material that is used for sensemaking and affects the unfolding crisis itself. There is a delicate tradeoff between dangerous action which produces understanding and safe inaction which produces confusion. The purpose of this article is to explore the complications of that tension.

Two exhibits highlight the central issue. The first involves explorers, the second involves the last paragraph of Union Carbide's procedure for dealing with gas leaks.

(1)   'An explorer can never know what he is exploring until it has been explored' (Bateson, 1972, p. xvi).

(2)   'The [Bhopal] plant's operating manual for methyl isocyanate offered little guidance in the event of a large leak. After telling the operators to dump the gas into a spare tank if a leak in a storage tank cannot be stopped or isolated, the manual says: "There may be other situations not covered above. The situation will determine the appropriate action. We will learn more and more as we gain actual experience"' (Diamond, 28 January 1985, p. 7).

Bateson's description of exploring illustrates the key point about sensemaking The explorer cannot know what he is facing until he faces it, and then looks back over the episode to sort out what happened, a sequence that involves retrospective sensemaking. But the act of exploring itself has an impact on what is being explored, which means that parts of what the explorer discovers retrospectively are consequences of his own making. Furthermore, the exploring itself is guided by preconceptions of some kind, even though they may be generic preconceptions such as 'this will have made sense once I explore it although right now it seems senseless' (Weick, Gilfillan and Keith, 1973).

The explorer who enacts a sensible environment is no different from the operator of a console in a chemical plant control room who confronts a puzzling assortment of dials, lights and sounds and discovers, through action, what the problem is, but in doing so, shapes the problem itself (see McHugh, 1968, for an analogue). Both the explorer and the control room operator understand the problem they face only after they have faced it and only after their actions have become inextricably wound into it.

Imagine that the control room operator faces a gas leak and the admonition from the Union Carbide procedure cited above. Carbide is right when it says experience is the source of learning, but it is wrong when it says, 'The situation will determine the appropriate action'. People often don't know what the 'appropriate action' is until they take some action and see what happens. Thus, actions determine the situation. Furthermore, it is less often true that 'situations' determine appropriate action than that 'preconceptions' determine appropriate action. Finally, the judgement of 'appropriateness' is likely to be a motivated assessment constructed partially to validate earlier reasoning. These corrections show not so much that Carbide's statement is in error, as that Carbide's assessment is incomplete because it misrepresents the contribution of action to human understanding.

Understanding is facilitated by action, but action affects events and can make things worse. Action during crisis is not just an issue of control, it is an epistemological issue. If action is a means to get feedback, learn, and build an understanding of unknown environments, then a reluctance to act could be associated with less understanding and more errors.

In the remainder of this article I will enlarge these introductory ideas in three ways. First, I will describe the concept of enactment that drives this analysis. Second, I will discuss how cognition and understanding are affected by commitment, capacity, and expectations during crises. I conclude with a brief survey of implications for crisis management.

The enactment perspective

Assumptions of the enactment perspective

The concept of enactment is a synthesis, tailored for organizational settings, of four lines of scholarship: self-fulfilling prophecies (E. E. Jones, 1986; R. A. Jones, 1977; Snyder, 1984), retrospective sensemaking (Staw, 1980; Weick,

1979), commitment (Salancik, 1977; Staw, 1982), and social information processing (Salancik and Pfeffer, 1978). The term 'enactment' is used to preserve the central point that when people act, they bring events and structures into existence and set them in motion. People who act in organizations often produce structures, constraints, and opportunities that were not there before they took action.

Enactment involves both a process, enactment, and a product, an enacted environment.

Enactment is the social process by which a 'material and symbolic record of action' (Smircich and Stubbart, 1985, p. 726) is laid down. The process occurs in two steps. First, portions of the field of experience are bracketed and singled out for closer attention on the basis of preconceptions. Second, people act within the context of these bracketed elements, under the guidance of preconceptions, and often shape these elements in the direction of preconceptions (Powers, 1973). Thus, action tends to confirm preconceptions.

An enacted environment is the residuum of changes produced by enactment. The word 'residuum' is preferred to the word 'residue' because residuum emphasizes that what is left after a process cannot be ignored or left out of account because it has potential significance (Webster's Dictionary of Synonyms, 1951, p. 694). The product of enactment is not an accident, an afterthought, or a byproduct. Instead, it is an orderly, material, social construction that is subject to multiple interpretations. Enacted environments contain real objects such as reactors, pipes and valves. The existence of these objects is not questioned, but their significance, meaning, and content is. These objects are inconsequential until they are acted upon and then incorporated retrospectively into events, situations, and explanations.

The external residuum of enacted changes is summarized internally by people in the form of a plausible map by which observed actions produced observed consequences. Since the summary map contains if–then assertions, it is called a cause map (Weick and Bougon, 1986) and is the source of expectations for future action. When we assert that the organization and the environment are in the mind of the actor, this means two things. It means that cause maps affect the construction of new experience through the mechanism of expectations and it means that cause maps affect the interpretation of old experience through the mechanism of labelling.

Thus, an enacted environment has both a public and a private face. Publicly, it is a construction that is usually visible to observers other than the actor. Privately, it is a map of if–then assertions in which actions are related to outcomes. These assertions serve as expectations about what will happen in the future.

At the heart of enactment is the idea that cognition lies in the path of the action. Action precedes cognition and focuses cognition. The sensemaking sequence implied in the phrase, 'How can I know what I think until I see what I say?' involves the action of talking, which lays down traces that are examined, so that cognitions can be inferred. These inferred cognitions then become preconceptions which partially affect the next episode of talk, which means the next set of traces deposited by talk are affected partially by previous labels and partially by current context. These earlier inferences also affect how the next episode of talk is examined and what is seen. This sensemaking sequence has the potential to become closed and detached from the context in which it occurs. However, that potential is seldom realized because preconceptions are usually weak, actions are usually novel, and memories are usually flawed.

Relationship of enactment perspective to crisis literature

The enactment perspective is applied to crisis situations in this article in an attempt to address Shrivastava's (1987, p. 118) observation that we do not yet understand much about how individual actions can cause an industrial crisis. The analysis of enactment suggests that individual actions involved in sensemaking can cause a crisis, but also manage it to lower levels of danger. Actions often construct the reasons for their occurrence as they unfold, which means their consequences are difficult to forecast in advance. Our actions are always a little further along than is our understanding of those actions, which means we can intensify crises literally before we know what we are doing. Unwitting escalation of crises is especially likely when technologies are complex, highly interactive, non-routine, and poorly understood. The very action which enables people to gain some understanding of these complex technologies can also cause those technologies to escalate and kill.

To learn more about how sensemaking can be decoupled from escalation, we focus on triggered events: 'a specific event that is identifiable in time and place and traceable to specific man-made causes' (Shrivastava, 1987, p. 8). Triggered events are places where interventions can have an effect, these events involve judgement which can deteriorate when pressure increases (Staw, Sandelands and Dutton, 1981), and these events can escalate into a crisis.

The enactment perspective is about both crisis prevention and crisis management. We share with Ayres and Rohatgi (1987, p. 41) the assumption that 'while the probability of operator error can often be reduced, there is no evidence whatever that it can be eliminated altogether. . . . Human errors are fundamentally "caused" by human variability, which cannot be designed away'. This assumption suggests to us that errors are inevitable, so the key issue is how to keep errors from enlarging. Errors are less likely to enlarge if they are understood more fully, more quickly. If we can understand the process of sensemaking during a crisis, then we can help people to prevent larger crises by smarter management of small crises. It is this sense in which enactment blurs the line between crisis prevention and crisis management. By understanding triggering events and the ways in which small sensemaking actions can grow into large senseless disasters, we hope to develop a better understanding of how crises can be isolated and contained.

The enactment approach shares an interest with Billings, Milburn, and Schaalman (1980) in triggering events, and complements their analysis by emphasizing that action is instrumental to crisis perception. The enactment perspective focuses on 'proactive crisis management' in Mitroff, Shrivastava, and Udwadia (1987) and develops specifically the activities of pre-assessment, prevention, preparation, and coping. The threat–rigidity cycle (Staw, Sandelands and Dutton, 1981) is in the background throughout our analysis since we assume that action often manages threat toward lower levels of intensity thereby reducing the tendency toward rigid problem solving.

Crises obviously are overdetermined and human sensemaking may play only a small part in their development. Nevertheless, crises engage human action, human action can amplify small deviations into major crises, and in any search for causes, we invariably can find some human act which may have set the crisis in motion. It is our contention that actions devoted to sensemaking play a central role in the genesis of crises and therefore need to be understood if we are to manage and prevent crises.

The enacted quality of crises

Shrivastava's (1987) analysis of Bhopal can be read for themes of enactment, as when he observes that 'the initial response to the crisis sets the tone for the rest of the effort' (p. 134). From the standpoint of enactment, initial responses do more than set the tone; they determine the trajectory of the crisis. Since people know what they have done only after they do it, people and their actions rapidly become part of the crisis. That is unavoidable. To become part of the problem means that people enact some of the environment they face. Had they not acted or had they acted differently, they would face a different set of problems, opportunities and constraints.

All crises have an enacted quality once a person takes the first action. Suppose that a gauge shows an unexpected increase in temperature. That is not enactment. Suppose further that in response to the unexpected temperature increase people tap the gauge or call the supervisor or proceed with a tea break or walk out to look at the tank whose temperature is being measured. That still is not enactment, because all that exists so far is a simple stimulus and response. But the response of tapping, calling, drinking, or walking produces a new stimulus that would not have been there had the first been ignored. The 'second stimulus' is now a partial human construction. The assumptions that underlie the choice of that first response contribute to enactment and the second stimulus. As action continues through more cycles, the human responses which stimulate further action become increasingly important components of the crisis. 'When a triggering event occurs, spontaneous reactions by different stakeholders solve some of the immediate problems, but they also create new problems – thus prolonging the crisis and making it worse' (Shrivastava, 1987), p. 24).

Thus, from the perspective of enactment, what is striking is that crises can have small, volitional beginnings in human action. Small events are carried forward, cumulate with other events, and over time systematically construct an environment that is a rare combination of unexpected simultaneous failures.

Shrivastava (1987, p. 42) identified 'the leakage of toxic gas' as the triggering event at Bhopal, but my choice would be the failure to insert a slip blind into a pipe being cleaned, which allowed water to back up and enter the MIC tank and catalyse a complex chemical interaction (Ayres and Rohatgi, 1987, p. 32;

Shrivastava, 1987, p. 46). The slip blind oversight occurred in close proximity to the 'leakage of toxic gas'; it was a small deviation that amplified because MIC was stored in 60 ton tanks rather than 55 gallon drums, and it resulted from a proximate combination of preconceptions about a job and its safety, inadequate supervision, and inadequate training.

It is not sufficient to deal with the enacted quality of crises by striving to make the technology operator-proof. All that does is move the dynamics of enactment to an earlier point in time where incomplete designs are enacted into unreliable technology by fallible designers who believe they can bypass the very human variability that has already been exhibited by their design process.

The enacted quality of crises is especially visible when we apply the concepts of commitment, capacity, and expectations to crisis conditions.

Enactment and commitment

The importance of commitment (Salancik, 1977) for enactment is straight-forward. Normally, when people act, their reasons for doing things are either self-evident or uninteresting, especially when the actions themselves can be undone, minimized, or disowned. Actions that are neither visible nor permanent can be explained with casual, transient explanations. As those actions become more public and irrevocable, however, they become harder to undo; and when those same actions are also volitional, they become harder to disown. When action is irrevocable, public and volitional, the search for explanations becomes less casual because more is at stake. Explanations that are developed retrospectively to justify committed actions are often stronger than beliefs developed under other, less involving, conditions. A tenacious justification can produce selective attention, confident action, and self-confirmation. Tenacious justifications prefigure both perception and action, which means they are often self-confirming.

Tenacious justifications can be forces for good or evil in crises. They are forces for good because they generate meaning in times of ambiguity, surprise, and confusion (Staw, 1980). Justifications provide sufficient structure for people to get their bearings and then create fuller, more accurate views of what is happening and what their options are.

The dark side of commitment is that it produces blind spots. Once a person becomes committed to an action, and then builds an explanation that justifies that action, the explanation tends to persist and become transformed into an assumption, that is taken for granted. Once this transformation has occurred it is unlikely that the assumption will be readily viewed as a potential contributor to a crisis.

For example, the public, irrevocable choice at Bhopal to keep the dangerous process of MIC production secret, was justified in terms of competitive advantage and the prevention of 'unnecessary' alarm. As a result, the commitment to secrecy was one of the last assumptions workers considered as a contributor to the crisis. To minimize alarm, the warning siren at Bhopal was not turned on until gas actually started to leak into the atmosphere, the siren was turned off after 5 minutes, and it was not restarted until gas had been escaping for 90 minutes. The commitment to secrecy induced a blind spot toward a partial solution, necessary alarm.

As another example, the public, irrevocable decision by Bhopal management to announce that all safety violations reported to them in a September 1982 report, had been corrected (Ayres and Rohatgi, 1987, p. 36), was justified by actions which took safety for granted and inadvertently allowed it to deteriorate steadily in several different places. Thus, the eventual public, irrevocable choice to disconnect the refrigeration equipment that kept MIC temperature under control, was justified as a relatively safe means to save electricity, reduce costs, and recover freon which could be used elsewhere in the plant. It was the uncontrolled heating of MIT in Tank 610 that led to rupture of the safety valves and venting of the gas.

When people make a public commitment that an operating gauge is inoperative, the last thing they will consider during a crisis is that the gauge is operating. Had they not made the commitment, the blind spot would not be so persistent. When a person becomes committed to the view that fluctuations in electricity cause 90 per cent of the variances that are seen in gauges, the possibility that a much different percentage is more accurate will not be entertained until the crisis is at an advanced stage.

Given the effects of commitments on attention, practitioners and researchers alike might learn more about crisis potential (Mitroff, Shrivastava and Udwadia, 1987, p. 290) if they see which people are 'on record' as making irreversible assertions about technology, operators, and capabilities. Those assertions, and their associated justifications, will have been shielded from scrutiny more than other assertions in which less is at stake. The practices and assumptions that those justifications shield may be significant contributors to crisis.

Enactment and capacity

Action in the form of capacity can affect crisis management through perception, distribution of competence and control within a hierarchy, and number and diversity of actors.

Capacity and response repertoire affect crisis perception, because people see those events they feel they have the capacity to do something about. As capacities change, so too do perceptions and actions. This relationship is one of the crucial leverage points to improve crisis management.

The rationale for these relationships has been described by Jervis (1976, pp. 374–5). '(T)he predisposition to perceive a threat varies with the person's beliefs about his ability to take effective counteraction if he perceives the danger. . . . Whether they are vigilant or defensive depends in large part on whether they think they can act effectively on the undesired information'.

If people think they can do lots of things, then they can afford to pay attention to a wider variety of inputs because, whatever they see, they will have some way to cope with it. The more a person sees of any situation, the higher the probability that the person will see the specific change that needs to be made to dampen the crisis. Accuracy in perception comes from an expanded response capacity. Perrow (1984) argues that operators who have specialized expertise do not see the 'big picture' as crises develop and therefore miss key events. That scenario is consistent with the proposition that capacity affects perception. Specialists can do a few things well, which means that they search the world to see if it needs what they can do. If it doesn't, they do nothing else because they see nothing else.

If people are aware that volitional action may enact conditions that intensify or de-escalate crises, and if they are also aware of their actions and capacities, this heightened awareness could allow them to see more of a developing crisis. Seeing more of the developing crisis, people should then be able to see more places where they could intervene and make an actual difference in what is developing. The joint beliefs, 'I have capacity' and 'capacity makes a difference', should reduce defensive perception and allow people to see more. As they see more, there is a greater probability that they will see some place where their intervention can make a difference.

Capacity can also affect crisis management by the way in which it is distributed in a hierarchy. Perrow (1984, p. 10) notes that 'operators need to be able to take independent and creative action because they are closest to the system, yet centralization, tight coupling, and prescribed steps prevent decentralized action'.

Action of any kind may be prevented or slowed in a centralized system. Hermann (1963) has noted when crises occur, authority becomes contracted in one of three ways: it moves to higher levels of the hierarchy, fewer people exercise authority, or there is an increase in the number of occasions when authority is exercised even though the number of units exercising it remain constant (p. 70).

The danger in centralization and contraction of authority is that there may be a reduction in the level of competence directed at the problem as well as an overall reduction in the use of action to develop meaning. For example, Bhopal had relatively unsophisticated sensing devices and had to rely on workers to sense problems by means of the 'tear gas effect of the vapor' (Diamond, 28 January, 1985, p. 6). But the presence of that vivid indicator was still not enough because the tearing was given little attention by authorities. Furthermore, if people had moved around at Bhopal, they would have heard gurgling and rumbling in the MIC tank, seen drops of water near the tank, and felt tearing in their eyes.

The person in authority is not necessarily the most competent person to deal with a crisis, so a contraction of authority leads either to less action or more confusion. Career ladders in crisis-prone organizations are crucial antecedents for coping. People who come up through the technical ranks have hands-on experience and the requisite knowledge to sense variations in the technological environment they face. Those who administer without a technical background have less requisite expertise and miss more.

Diamond (30 January, 1985, p. 6), in his account of Bhopal, noted that during the crisis, 'K. V. Shetty, the plant superintendent for the shift, had come racing over from the main gate on a bicycle, workers said. "He came in pretty much in a panic", Mr Day said. "He said, 'what should we do?' " Mr Shetty, who declined to be interviewed, was on the administrative and not the technical side of the factory, the workers said'.

Capacity can also affect crisis potential through staffing decisions that affect the diversity of acts that are available. Enactment is labour-intensive, which means understaffing has serious effects. Even though the Bhopal plant had few automated controls, high manual control over processes, and a potentially large amount of action data from which understanding could be built, these potential assets were neutralized because operating staffs had been cut from 12 to 6 people per shift. Thus, knowledge was reduced, not because of automation, but because of understaffing. If action is the means to understanding, then the number and quality of actors available to do that acting and interpretation become crucial variables.

Turnover is as much a threat to capacity as is understaffing, but for a different reason. Institutional memory is an important component of crisis management. People can see only those categories and assumptions that they store in cause maps built up from previous experience. If those cause maps are varied and rich, people should see more, and good institutional memory would be an asset. However, if cause maps are filled with only a handful of overworked justifications, then perception should be limited and inaccurate, and a good memory would be a liability.

Shrivastava (1987, p. 52) reported that there was no institutional memory at Bhopal because turnover in top management was high and Smith (1984, p. 908) made the same observation about crisis management in the US government. In both cases, there are few beliefs that control seeing. It might seem desirable for a few preconceptions to be carried in institutional memory because then people will perceive more of what is 'really there'. Perception, however, is never free of preconceptions, and when people perceive without institutional memories, they are likely to be influenced by salient distractions (e.g. Kirwan, 1987) or by experience gained in settings that are irrelevant to present problems.

If more people are in constant touch with the system, this will make it easier to detect and correct anomalies and also to implant more reliable environments. These outcomes should be especially likely when the people doing the enactment have diverse experience, novel categories and justifications, and diverse activities at which they are skilled and in terms of which they perceive the world. We are not talking about specialists isolated from one another. Instead, we are talking about heterogeneous teams of diverse people with sufficient mutual respect that they maintain dense interaction with one another. Teams able to meet these demands are scarce, do not come cheap, and may be most likely to form if high levels of professionalism are associated with them.

Enactment and expectations

The assumptions that top management make about components within the firm often influence enactment in a manner similar to the mechanism of self-fulfilling prophecy. Many of these assumptions can increase or decrease the likelihood that small errors will escalate into major crises. Thus, assumptions are an important source of crisis prevention.

This mechanism is clearly visible in Bhopal where top management assumed that the Bhopal plant was unimportant and therefore allocated limited resources to maintain it. That assumption of unimportance set in motion a self-confirming vicious circle in which worker indifference and management cost-cutting became mutually reinforcing and resulted in deteriorating conditions that became more dangerous. ' "The whole industrial culture of Union Carbide at Bhopal went down the drain", said Mr Pareek, the former project engineer. "The plant was losing money, and top management decided that saving money was more important than safety. Maintenance practices became poor, and things generally got sloppy. The plant didn't seem to have a future, and a lot of skilled people became depressed and left as a result" ' (Diamond, 28 January, 1985, p. 6).

A plant perceived as unimportant proceeds to act out, through turnover, sloppy procedures, inattention to details, and lower standards, the prophecy implied in top management's expectations. A vicious circle is created and conditions become increasingly dangerous. Notice that the most crucial assumption does not involve safety directly. Instead, the crucial assumptions focus on themes of competence, importance, and value. Susceptibility to crisis varies as a function of top management assumptions about which units are important.

When cost cutting is focused on less important units, it is not just decreased maintenance which raises susceptibility to crisis. Instead, it is all of the indirect effects on workers of the perception that their unit doesn't matter. This perception results in increased inattention, indifference, turnover, low cost improvisation, and working-to-rule, all of which remove slack, lower the threshold at which a crisis will escalate, and increase the number of separate places at which a crisis could start. As slack decreases, the technology becomes more interactively complex (Perrow, 1984), which means there are more places where a minor lapse can escalate just when there are more minor lapses occurring.

The point is, this scenario starts with top management perceptions that set in motion enactments that confirm the perceptions. Furthermore, the initial perceptions were concerned with strategy, not safety. Strategy became an inadvertent source of crisis through its effects on realities constructed by disheartened workers. The realities they enacted removed buffers, dampers, and controls between steps in the technology, made it harder for errors to be contained, and easier for errors to get started.

Implications for crisis management

Crisis management is often portrayed as reactive activity directed at problems that are already escalating. That portrait is too narrow and I have tried to show why.

Perrow (1984) captured the core issue in crisis management, but did so in a way that exhibited rather than remedied the blind spot that concerns us. He observed that 'our ability to organize does not match the inherent hazards of some of our organized activities' (p. 10). The potential blindspot in that otherwise tight description is the reference to 'inherent hazard'.

Hazards are not given nor do they necessarily inhere in organized activity. Instead, they are often constructed and put into place by human actors. Their development is indeterminant rather than fixed, and crisis management can mean quick action that deflects a triggering event as it unfolds rather than delayed action that mops up after the triggering event has run its course. These possibilities are more likely to be seen if we think of large crises as the outcome of smaller scale enactments.

When the enactment perspective is applied to crisis situations, several aspects stand out that are normally overlooked.

To look for enactment themes in crises, for example, is to listen for verbs of enactment, words like manual control, intervene, cope, probe, alter, design, solve, decouple, try, peek and poke (Perrow, 1984, p. 333), talk, disregard, and improvise. These verbs may signify actions that have the potential to construct or limit later stages in an unfolding crisis.

To look for enactment themes in crises is also to assess the forcefulness of actions and the ambiguity of the situation (Perrow, 1984, p. 83) in which those actions occur. As forcefulness and ambiguity increase, enactment is more consequential, and more of the unfolding crisis is under the direct control of human action. Conversely, as action becomes more tentative and situations become more clearly structured, enactment processes will play a smaller role in crisis development and management. Enactment, therefore, will have most effect on those portions of a crisis which are loosely coupled. If pipe cleaning procedures are not standardized, if supervision is intermittent, if job specifications are vague, or if warning devices are activated capriciously, then these loosely coupled activities will be susceptible to alteration through enactment. Human action will produce environments involving pipes, supervision, specifications, and alarms, either in dangerous or safe combinations, because these are the most influencible elements. Loose coupling does not guarantee safety. Instead, it guarantees susceptibility to human action, and those actions can either reduce or increase hazards.

Enactment affects crisis management through several means such as the psychology of control, effects of action on stress levels, speed of interactions, and ideology.

An enactment perspective suggests that crisis events are more controllable than was first thought. That suggestion, by itself, can be self-affirming because as perceptions of control increase, stress decreases, and as stress decreases, perceptual narrowing also decreases which means people see more when they inspect any display (George, 1986). As people see more, they are more likely to notice things they can do something about, which confirms the perception of control and also reduces crisis intensity to lower levels by virtue of early intervention in its development.

Enactment can also reduce the perceptual narrowing produced by stress in another way. When people take some action, they often transform a more complex task into a simpler task. This occurs because action clarifies what the problem may be, specific action renders many cues and options irrelevant, and action consolidates an otherwise unorganized set of environmental elements. All of these simplifications gain significance in the context of stress because there is good evidence that stress has less adverse effects on performance of simple tasks than on performance of complex tasks (Eysenck, 1982). Since stress is an accompaniment of all crises, and since many crises escalate because of the secondary effects of crisis-induced stress, the beneficial effect of action in the form of task simplification is important.

Not only does action simplify tasks, it also often slows down the effects of one variable on another. Perrow (1984) has shown tight coupling, in the presence of interactive complexity, leads to rapid escalation of crisis events. Action such as rearrangements of traffic patterns by air traffic controllers (Weick, 1987) often dampens the tight coupling between variables and reduces both the speed and magnitude with which connected variables affect one another. Especially if a controller becomes a step in a process (Perrow, 1984, p. 331), the actions of that controller can slow the speed with which the process unfolds and can also slow the speed with which unanticipated interactions occur.

Perhaps the most important implication of enactment is that it might serve as the basis for an ideology of crisis prevention and management. By ideology, we mean a 'relatively coherent set of beliefs that bind people together and explain their worlds in terms of cause-and-effect relations' (Beyer, 1981, p. 166). Enactment leverages human involvement in systems and, as a coherent set of beliefs about the form and outcomes of such involvement, could elicit self-control and voluntary co-operation similar to that elicited by more formal structures designed to do the same thing (Meyer, 1982, p. 55).

An ideology built around the preceding ideas would mean that people have a fuller idea of how individuals generate their own environments including crisis environments, have an appreciation that the strength of commitments is a manipulable variable that has tangible environment effects, see the importance of expertise in action and the value of multiple small actions, understand how structures can accelerate or decelerate responsive action, and see more potential cause of crises and more places where interventions are possible, while maintaining an awareness of the necessity to balance dangerous action with safe inaction in the interest of diagnosis.

If these beliefs were adopted as a component of crisis management, people could think about crises in ways that highlight their own actions and decisions as determinants of the conditions they want to prevent.

The activity of crisis management, viewed through the lens of enactment, involves such things as managing crises to lower levels of intensity, increasing skill levels and heightening the awareness of existing skill levels in the interest of expanded perception, appreciation of the ways in which small interventions can amplify, and being exquisitely aware of commitments that may bias diagnoses.

Perrow (1984) has, I think, correctly identified a new cause of human-made catastrophes, 'interactive complexity in the presence of tight coupling, producing a system accident' (p. 11). Recent benchmark catastrophes such as Chernobyl, Bhopal, and Challenger all fit this recipe. The way to counteract catastrophes, therefore, is to reduce tight coupling and interactive complexity. To do this, it seems important not to blame technology, but rather to look for and exaggerate all possible human contributions to crises in the hope that we can spot some previously unnoticed contributions where we can exert leverage. Therefore, even if the relative importance of enactment is exaggerated and borders on hyperbole, the important outcome of such exaggeration could be discovery of unexpected places to gain control over crises. The enactment perspective urges people to include their own actions more prominently in the mental experiments they run to discover potential crises of which they may be the chief agents.

Note

1   I acknowledge with appreciation the comments of Barbara Kelly, Reuben McDaniel, and Douglas Orton on an early version of this manuscript.

References

Ayres, R. U. and Rohatgi, P. K. (1987) 'Bhopal: lessons for technological decision-makers', *Technology in Society*, 9: 19–45.

Bateson, G. (1972) *Steps to an Ecology of Mind*, New York: Ballantine.

Beyer, J. M. (1981) 'Ideologies, values, and decision-making in organizations', in Nystrom, P. C. and Starbuck, W. H. (eds), *Handbook of Organizational Design*, Vol 2, 166–202, New York: Oxford University Press.

Billings, R. S., Milburn, T. W. and Schaalman, M. L. (1980) 'A model of crisis perception: a theoretical analysis', *Administrative Science Quarterly*, 25: 300–16.

Diamond, S. (1985) 'The Bhopal disaster: how it happened', *New York Times*, 28 January, 1, 6, 7.

Diamond, S. (1985) 'The disaster in Bhopal: workers recall horror', *New York Times*, 30 January, 1, 6.

Eysenck, M. S. (1982) *Attention and Arousal*, New York: Springer-Verlag.

George, A. L. (1986) 'The impact of crisis-induced stress on decision-making', in Solomon, F. and Marston, R. Q. (eds), *The Medical Implications of Nuclear War*. Washington DC: National Academy of Sciences Press.

Hermann, C. F. (1963) 'Some consequences of crisis which limit the viability of organizations', *Administrative Science Quarterly*, 8: 61–82.

Jervis, R. (1976) *Perception and Misperception in International Politics*, Princeton, NJ: Princeton University Press.

Jones, E. E. (1986) 'Interpreting interpersonal behavior: The effects of expectancies', *Science*, 234: 41–6.

Jones, R. A. (1977) *Self-Fulfilling Prophecies*, Hillside, NJ: Erlbaum.

Kirwan, B. (1987) 'Human reliability analysis of an offshore emergency blowdown system', *Applied Ergonomics*, 18: 23–33.

McHugh, P. (1968) *Defining the Situation*, Indianapolis: Bobbs-Merrill.

Meyer, A. D. (1982) 'How ideologies supplant formal structures and shape responses to environment', *Journal of Management Studies*, 19: 45–61.

Mitroff, I. I., Shrivastava, P. and Udwadia, F. (1987) 'Effective crisis management', *Executive*, 1, 283–92.

Perrow, C. (1984) *Normal Accidents*, New York: Basic Books.

Powers, W. T. (1973) *Behavior: The Control of Perception*, Chicago: Aldine.

Salancik, G. R. (1977) 'Commitment and the control of organizational behavior and belief, in Staw, B. M. and Salancik, G. R. (eds), *New Directions in Organizational Behavior*, 1–54, Chicago: St. Clair.

Salancik, G. R. and Pfeffer, J. (1978) 'A social information processing approach to job attitude and task design', *Administrative Science Quarterly*, 23, 224–53.

Shrivastava, P. (1987) *Bhopal: Anatomy of a Crisis*, Cambridge, MA: Ballinger.

Smircich, L. and Stubbart, C. (1985) 'Strategic management in an enacted world', *Academy of Management Review*, 10: 724–36.

Smith, R. J. (1984) 'Crisis management under strain', *Science*, 225: 907–9.

Snyder, M. (1984) 'When belief creates reality', in Berkowitz, L. (ed.), *Advances in Experimental Social Psychology*, Vol. 18, 247–305, New York: Academic Press.

Staw, B. M. (1980) 'Rationality and justification in organizational life', in Cummings, L. and Staw, B. (eds), *Research in Organizational Behavior*, Vol. 2, 45–80, Greenwich, CT: JAI Press.

Staw, B. M. (1982) 'Counterforces to change', in Goodman, P. S. and Associates (eds), *Change in Organizations: New Perspectives on Theory, Research, and Practice*, 87–121, San Fransisco: Jossey-Bass.

Staw, B. M., Sandelands, L. E. and Dutton, J. E. (1981) 'Threat-rigidity effects in organizational behavior: a multi-level analysis', *Administrative Science Quarterly*, 26: 501–24.

Webster's Dictionary of Synonyms, First Ed. (1951) Springfield, MA: Merriam.

Weick, K. E. (1979) *The Social Psychology of Organizing*, 2nd ed., Reading, MA: Addison-Wesley.

Weick, K. E. (1987) 'Organizational culture as a source of high reliability', *California Management Review*, 29 (2): 112–27.

Weick, K. E. and Bougon, M. G. (1986) 'Organizations as cause maps', in Sims, H. P. Jr. and Gioia, D. A. (eds), *Social Cognition in Organizations*, 102–35, San Francisco: Jossey-Bass.

Weick, K. E., Gilfillan, D. P. and Keith, T. (1973) 'The effect of composer credibility on orchestra performance', *Sociometry*, 36: 435–62.

Chapter 15

Larry Barton

MODELING THE CRISIS
MANAGEMENT PROCESS

ALTHOUGH CRISIS MANAGEMENT IS a relatively new managerial science, the process by which organizations attempt to anticipate and create models for responding to a serious incident is hardly new. Military units constitute the most historically formidable groups that have routinely tested various scenarios for centuries, a tradition now adopted by financial and transportation entities, manufacturers and a host of other enterprises.

What is a model

The systems and procedures used by these organizations inevitably are a reflection of the management culture and system to which that group is accustomed. For example, British Petroleum, arguably one of the world's best prepared multinationals, has literally weathered rough seas on almost every continent in the drilling and exploration – and all of the resulting human and technological hazards associated with such – and regularly trains teams of engineers as well as executives on dozens of 'what if?' scenarios.

As Denis Smith and Dominic Elliott note, modeling a crisis is only as good as the data that is injected into underlying assumptions about the basic strengths and weaknesses of the organization and the quality of the talent that will be tasked with managing the incident and the subsequent business resumption. While some risk managers infuse a rigor into their methodology, such as benchmarking comparable companies and charting the kinds of crises that have injured workers and their employers, modeling cannot be based on newspaper clippings and historical anecdote alone.

Modeling for a crisis must be systemized in order to be effective; in essence, sound historical research must be blended with current benchmarking practices of competing organizations; it must be tested against high standards on the inherent reliability of data, preferably by using actuaries, risk managers, seismologists – any credentialed individual who can validate or challenge assumptions in the draft plan.

The limitations to modeling are painfully obvious to anyone who has ever witnessed a management team grappling with the headaches, financial costs and human costs associated with a catastrophe, often prompted by the volatile question: 'why didn't anyone here ever tell me this could happen?' While modeling may not document each and every possible scenario that could cripple an organization, sound modeling has clear benefits: it elevates management thinking to a new level of probability versus possibility, and it stimulates management to address whether it has sufficient resources to bring the organization to normalcy after such an incident occurs.

The culture gap

Thus, we see that this chapter provides a sound introduction to the role that culture plays in anticipating organizational disaster. Barry A. Turner notes that when a model is weak, assumptive or poorly constructed, one can anticipate a 'degree of cultural collapse.' Of course, possibly the organizational culture was weak in the first place. Regardless of where cultural dysfunctions are headquartered – the CEO, risk manager, operations chief or investors – failing to assess the role of culture could make a bad situation far worse because culture is, indeed, the private and public reflection of organizational values.

Turner notes that 'members of organizations can never be sure that their present actions will be adequate for the attainment of their desired goals,' and this observation is hardly defeatist: it captures, very precisely, the fact that humans can make mistakes but it is far better that we err on the side of anticipating more, not fewer problems...ones that injure more people, communities and enterprises, not fewer.

If appreciating organizational culture is essence for a sound crisis response, it is also true that having access to quality intelligence is a prerequisite for success. When we turn our back on this research – as well as obvious risks – we can encounter 'failures of foresight' that can lead a management team to believe it has low exposure to risk. Thus, we find a colossal paradox in modeling crisis: there is not a major corporation in the world that does not insure its building, intellectual property and human assets (smartly transferring risk to a third party), but these same organizations that acknowledge risk by purchasing insurance often will not invest in the intelligence gathering and risk management process needed to reduce their exposure accordingly.

Mirroring the work of a sound social scientist, Turner believes that norms and beliefs – that underpinning of culture discussed earlier – must be candidly assessed by management as part of the crisis modeling process; this 'preaccident period' offers an unusual opportunity for executives to think through those 'what if?' scenarios and prepare their teams accordingly. Alas, many fail to acknowledge risk or the need for preparation. We see this when the United Nations acknowledges that tsunami warning and communication systems were woefully inadequate for the devastation that shook Sri Lanka and much of Asia in January 2005 despite pleas by seismologists, public health experts and meteorologists for decades. These same post-accident appraisals of dysfunctional culture are typical after almost every high profile natural or corporate disaster, prompting investigators to commonly focus on three questions: what did you know? When did you know it? What did you do about it?

Joining Smith and Elliott, Turner observes that 'major causal features' often dot the human and organization radar screen early but are undetected by senior managers – sometimes because they choose not to hear bad news or because they are hesitant to spend the capital necessary to correct a deficiency. This leads one to question who actually owns and manages the 'radar screen' at the organization; for example, in many pharmaceutical companies we find that the screen is owned by regulatory and customer managers who often hear about complaints on medicines early; in banks, it is often an auditing team that may detect the kind of massive fraud that encircled the Singapore investment community largely due to one zealot whose massive success masked a web of deceit. Turner calls this 'tip safety,' and others may call it a radar screen, but in reality, we are really talking about a simple equation: great intelligence and common sense can save lies and spare an organization.

Crisis avoidance

In their assessment of how executives perceive and react to threats and signals on their respective radar screens, Pauchant and Mitroff found that although many executives recognized the potential of crisis, most had taken only modest efforts to create a formal crisis management plan. Once again we find that culture – a sense of 'that can't happen here' – permeates many organizations because, they assert, admitting risk may actually be an acknowledgment that the company is somehow weak or ill-prepared.

Loss is often stated in financial or reputational terms, but inevitably there is a human toll that is impossible to quantify. Pauchant and Mitroff note that when crisis struck following the loss of the Space Shuttle Challenger or mass illness associated with technical and construction errors at the Chernobyl nuclear power plant – social and political scientists often look to the culture behind these entities as much as technological factors that caused harm.

The notion of healthy and unhealthy companies is simplistic but it is a starting point in which we can ascertain whether those who prepare for and anticipate risk have a more proven track record to sustain and overcome major catastrophes. In this regard, the authors note that 'corporations confuse their internal structure with the structure of crises' and assert that many ill-prepared companies have an inherent deficiency: they think of themselves first and not of the consequences of their actions (or lack of actions) upon their customers and other stakeholders.

In analyzing different groups of companies, the authors attempt to argue that there is an intellectualization among some managers; these individuals, they assert, may have egos that are beyond reason, may be managing in denial that anyone would want to harm their company or that they are simply not conscious of the hazards inherent in their specific enterprise. They assert, correctly, that companies tend to focus on what they are doing rather than exploring the hypothetical arena of 'what's the worst that could happen to us?' That journey of due diligence is not only meaningful, it is, indeed, a fiduciary bond between manager and stakeholder. It is also one that most managers tend to find to be a costly detour away from 'mission critical' – producing product, creating revenue and meeting obligations. Athough the authors come perilously close to trying to suggest that only 'good' companies are crisis prepared, they suggest that decision making and culture must have an equal seat at the crisis preparation table.

Crisis management models

If the platform suggested in this section thus far is sound – namely that a healthy organization must acknowledge its cultural strengths and weaknesses before it can be mature enough to properly assess organizational risk – then logic leads us to embrace Denis Smith's analysis that decision making is the centerpiece of sound crisis prevention and management. Indeed, he notes that 'it is a lack of strategic planning which often lies at the root of an organization's inability to cope with a crisis event,' and this is indeed substantiated by literally hundreds of studies into where problems – ignored or mismanaged during their initial hours – escalated into full-scale crises.

Smith observes that three phases exist in the process of crisis management: pre-disaster, impact/rescue, and recovery. During all three phases, and the many sub-phases inherent in each, the role of information is paramount; indeed, next to responding to human injury and loss, it is arguably the single most important ingredient of the entire process because without accurate and updated information, any strategic decision could be suspect. He notes that the gap between official and unofficial information (e.g. hearsay, rumor) is often wide and pronounced, opening the doors for managers to miss key points on their radar screen and thus underestimate the impact of a disaster. If this same failure to process and respond to information existed at airports around the world, transportation would come to an immediate halt in the aftermath of mid-air collisions. For reasons noted by authors earlier in the chapter, the role of culture and deniability simply makes it easier for good people to ignore signals of impending danger.

The presence of an 'effective crisis management programme' is a sound investment of time and energy, Smith asserts, because educating professionals about the risks of their organization is a powerful way for the organization to acknowledge the possibility that a single event, or chain of events, could throw the entity into chaos. The model of crisis management that he advances: crisis of management, operational crisis and crisis of legitimization supports the earlier assessment as to the power, and relevance, of assuring that management has quality information at its disposal when it makes milestone decisions during and after a crisis. In the prominent case of Perrier, in which abnormally high levels of benzene were detected in bottled water, it is noted that company officials under-estimated public reaction, and of health ministers, to what at first appeared to be a problem. This 'problem' rapidly escalated into a crisis of management because managers did not have sound information – from their own field sales managers, from epidemiologists and from the news media – in which to make sound decisions.

Reliability organizations and environments

Do organizations vary in terms of the various qualitative and quantitative issues that are inherent in their management structure? Karlene Roberts believes that a study of high reliability organizations (HRO) offers some glimpse into how various technologies play a role in anticipating, calculating and responding to errors and accidents, notably in aircraft environments. Considering the magnitude of humans, weaponry and aircraft confined in a small space, and the interreliability of these three factors, one can assume that complexity is as important as reliability when it comes to proper governance of such a national asset.

Of all factors, 'tight coupling' may be one of the most important, because whether we are examining the Union Carbide Bhopal debacle – a complex facility that was plagued by poor infrastructure planning at the outset let alone human failures once launched – we see that regardless of any reliability technologies an organization may embed in its systems, ultimately a human judgment – hopefully one informed by credible data, experience and substantive knowledge – guides any decision, whether it be to launch a missile or close a plant. It is obvious that no single unit of an organization can be effective if it is not considering the ramifications of its decisions and the reliability of its technologies.

Summary

Systems – any system – is complex. Clearly the field of crisis management has matured over the past decade, not only because the quality of scholarly research and industry focus has become sharper (often at the expense of companies who suffered a major public debacle) but also because our collective sense of loss – human, financial and reputation – is more astute. In reality, although psychologists like to often remind us that people can rebound after a critical incident, many organizations do not – plants close, human service agencies cut their staff, entire nations can be crippled after a tsunami. We continue to grow and learn from catastrophe on scales both modest and monumental.

The crisis of management: cultural and psychological dynamics of risk and crisis management

Chapter 16

Jens Rasmussen

HUMAN ERRORS: A TAXONOMY FOR DESCRIBING HUMAN MALFUNCTION IN INDUSTRIAL INSTALLATIONS

Introduction

AT PRESENT WE WITNESS a large interest in the involvement of human operators in the reliability and safety of industrial installations as well as in methods for incorporation of the effects of human errors in quantitative risk assessment. Two features of the present situation are particularly important when considering the development of quantitative methods: One is the need to consider the human role in rare events due to the risk involved in large scale industrial installations. Another one is the introduction of interface equipment based on the rapidly developing information technology. Together these features lead to a pronounced need for replacement of empirical design guides by tools and methods for analytical human performance prediction and error probability estimation.

Analytical techniques are based on a causal model of the role of parts and components of a system in the accidental chains of events leading from the initial fault or disturbance to the unacceptable consequences. Until recently, most analytical effort for including human errors has been spent on verification of the safety of existing, operating process plants of traditional design with respect to the man-machine interface, as for instance, the use of Therp (Swain, 1976) on nuclear power plants (WASH 1400). This situation has led to a definition of errors and quantification of error rates in terms referring to the structure and elements of the external human task, and *not* in terms of human functions and capabilities and their limitations. Generally, current methods are based on a taxonomy of human errors in terms of erroneous sequencing or performance of task elements or steps; i.e. the analytical approach is based on a model of the task rather than a model of the man performing the task. Human functions and features are then taken into consideration by means of 'performance shaping factors' (Swain, 1976, 1980).

Unfortunately this means that only little guidance for predicting human performance with new designs of man-machine interfaces can be derived. To be able to collect empirical data for human performance for transfer to another task context than the one supplying the data, a generic psychological classification of human errors must be applied which has well specified relations to generic task properties and environmental features.

Only little is published on such generic psychological error mechanisms, probably because human errors have been considered to be a weakness of operators which could be cured by improved training and better instructions and because the pace of change of work situations has been slow enough to allow for purely empirical methods. Typically, some of the early attempts to find generic psychological error mechanisms from analysis of professional task performance are from aviation research to improve cockpit designs – see for instance Fitts and Jones (1947). Theoretical studies of psychological error mechanisms have only started quite recently. James Reason (1975, 1976, 1977) has published analysis of human errors based on explicit models of human performance and has made attempts to sketch a taxonomy of error mechanisms from the analysis of 'every day slips and lapses'.

Based on analysis of event reports from nuclear power plants an attempt has been made to characterize human error mechanisms in generic terms (Rasmussen, 1980) and the results of this analysis have been adopted in a proposal for a taxonomy for practical data collection by an OECD/CSNI group of experts (Rasmussen et al., 1981). Recently, also Norman (1979, 1980) has published analysis of every day 'slips of mind' including initial attempts to develop more generic classification schemes for description of human errors. However, before discussing a taxonomy of human errors, it will be necessary to consider a definition of human errors in more detail.

Definition and characteristics of human errors

Basically it is very difficult to give a satisfactory definition of human errors. Frequently they are identified after the fact: If a system performs less satisfactorily than it normally does – due to a human act or to a disturbance which could have been counteracted by a reasonable human act – the cause will very likely be identified as a human error. This is probably because the analyst will not have the information – or psychological background – which is necessary to trace through the human performance in the explanatory causal backtracking process to find a possible causal input (see Rasmussen, 1980).

A more fruitful point of view is to consider human errors as instances of man-machine or man-task misfits. In case of systematic or frequent misfits, the cause will typically be considered to be a design error. Occasional misfits are typically caused by variability on part of the system or the man and are considered to be system failures or human errors, respectively.

However, human variability is an important ingredient in adaptation and learning and the ability to adapt to peculiarities in system performance and optimize interaction is the very reason for having people in a system. To optimize performance, to develop smooth and efficient skills, it is very important to have opportunities to perform trial and error experiments, and human errors can in a way be considered as unsuccessful experiments with unacceptable consequences. Typically they are only classified as human errors because they are performed in an 'unkind' work environment. An unkind work environment is then defined by the fact that it is not possible for a man to observe and reverse the effects of inappropriate variations in performance before they lead to unacceptable consequences.

When the effect of human variability is observable and reversible, the definition of error is related to a reference or norm in terms of the successful outcome of the activity. However, if observability and/or reversibility of inappropriate performance are not present; if, for instance, the effect of errors is delayed in time, is depending on further steps in a sequence, or is dependent upon possible latent conditions, as is often the case in industrial installations, then an established successful procedure becomes the man's only immediate reference for a judgement of errors, which therefore are related to the activity per se, rather than to a fulfilment of the related goal.

In practice it will be very difficult to arrange data collection related to those human errors which are immediately observable and reversible by the acting person and, therefore, may be corrected without further notice. In particular, it will be very difficult to determine the frequency of opportunities for such errors which will be needed to derive error rates or probabilities of error in a specific situation.

The features of observability and reversibility vary with error types and with task context and depend on very specific and detailed characteristics of the interface. Consequently, different task settings will be potential sources of data for the various error types. In order to transfer error data to predict performance in a new task design, it is necessary to have a match between observability and reversibility features of the new task and those used as data sources for each of the various relevant error mechanisms. It is, therefore, necessary to identify and characterize the features of a task which prevent error reversal during the analysed events and which, during data collection, will act as a selective filter upon the initial repertoire of errors committed. This should probably not be part of the event analysis itself but be performed as a background task analysis for the work situations included in the data collection.

The analytical problems involved depend very much on the nature of the work situation. In process plant control, for instance, the work situation is highly structured and the effects of human errors can be analysed. However, due to the processes which are not immediately visible, the recovery problem is rather complex. In general work safety, the work situation is very unstructured, which causes analytical problems; on the other hand, the 'processes' are typically rather concrete and visible, and recovery features can be more readily defined.

By analytical systems assessment, the consequences and probabilities of accidental chains of events are predicted from a causal model based on knowledge of failure modes of the components of the system and the related failure rates. To facilitate systematic analysis, a library of 'mini-fault-trees' for standard components is generally used. Probabilities for the failure modes related to different branches of the tree are typically conditioned by operating and environmental parameters. The basic idea is that the components can be represented by an input-output model with known transfer functions for the various failure modes. Similarly, human system 'components' have been represented by input-output models with transfer characteristics which can be modified by error mechanisms (see Fig. 1).

Already from the above discussion of the definition of human errors, it appears that this model is unrealistic since it does not take into consideration the selective filtering of error mechanisms depending upon reversibility features of the task context. Furthermore, the model lacks the aspect of human intention and expectance; in reality, there is no one-to-one relationship between the external task performance and the internal human functions which are used. This relationship depends on human value perception and upon subjective goals and performance criteria derived from such values. From the subjective goals and the expectations about the state of the system, information is sought and collected actively. Trained people ask questions to the system, biased by their experience and immediate expectations; they do not passively receive and filter an information input (see Fig. 2).

It follows that error mechanisms and failure modes depend on mental functions and knowledge which are activated by subjective factors. They cannot be directly observed but must be inferred from characteristics of the task and the work situation together with the external manifestation of the error. For this to be possible, a model of human information processing must be available. Such a model must relate elements of human decision making and action to internal information processes for which generic psychological mechanisms and limitations can be identified. An attempt to develop such a model from analysis

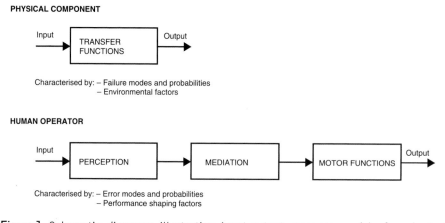

Figure 1 Schematic diagrams illustrating input-output response model of a physical component used for failure analysis and the analogical model frequently adopted for human operators

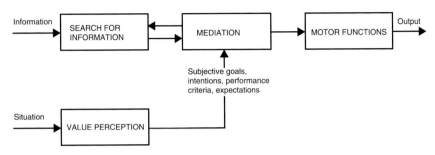

Figure 2 Model of a human operator must include active intentions, expectations and subjective goals

of verbal protocols and cases of human malfunction has been described elsewhere (Rasmussen, 1976, 1980).

In this model, a distinction is drawn between three levels of behaviour: skill-, rule-, and knowledge-based performance, see Fig. 3. This distinction is tightly related to the norm or reference used for error judgement, since different concepts are used to control behaviour: In the skill-based domain, including automated, more or less subconscious routines, performance is controlled by stored patterns of behaviour in a time-space domain. Errors are related to variability of force, space or time coordination. The rule-based domain includes performance in familiar situations controlled by stored rules for coordination of subroutines, and errors are typically related to mechanisms like wrong classification or recognition of situations, erroneous associations to tasks, or to memory slips in recall of procedures. Since rule-based behaviour is used to control skill-based subroutines, the error mechanisms related to skill-based routines are always active. Rule-based behaviour is not directly goal-controlled, but goal oriented, and the immediate criteria for errors deal with whether the relevant rules are recalled and followed correctly or not. This is the case, unless the total task is considered explicitly as one integrated whole and ultimate error correction is included in the error definition. However, in that case, transfer of data to and from a different task context is not possible.

The third behavioural domain is called upon in case of unique, unfamiliar situations for which actions must be planned from an analysis and decision based on knowledge of the functional, physical properties of the system and the priority of the various goals. In this domain, the internal data processing functions used for the task are very person and situation dependent and vary with details in the task context, with the extent and type of knowledge immediately available to the person, and with his subjective preferences. In general, errors in this domain can only be defined in relation to the goal of the task and generic error mechanisms can only be defined from very detailed studies based on verbal protocols which can supply data on the actual data process.

Data collection and prediction based on a breakdown of task performance in the knowledge-based domain is only possible for very tightly controlled experimental situations, not for real-life task settings (Rasmussen, 1980). Consequently, the present taxonomy only includes inappropriate reading of input information together with errors of inference leading to unsuccessful

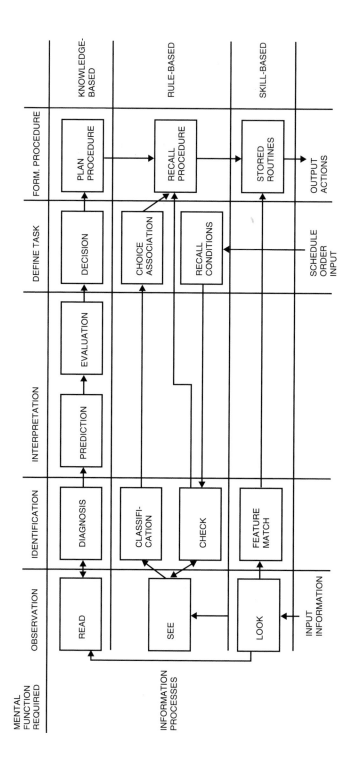

Figure 3 The diagram illustrates how the same required mental function can be served by different information processes – each with particular error mechanisms

performance due to latent, not considered, conditions or to unacceptable side effects. Both are failures in functional reasoning about a causal network.

An important set of error mechanisms is related to failure in selecting the proper level of behaviour in an abnormal situation, here called errors of discrimination. These error mechanisms are consequences of the fact that data in the environment cannot be considered input information to a passive data processor. In the three levels of behaviour, a man uses basically different information which is derived from the data, viz. information in the form of signals, signs, or symbols (Rasmussen, 1980). Which interpretation he uses depends on an active choice and error mechanisms are related to his bias or fixation for this choice.

Fig. 3 illustrates the characteristic data processes of the three levels. Clearly, the mental processes and the related error mechanisms are different for the various levels. The level applied in a given situation depends strongly upon the degree of training of the operator, and it is seen that error data collected from routine task situations are not applicable in unfamiliar, infrequent situations (such as emergencies) irrespective of the effects of stress and similar factors. In passing it can be mentioned that 'tunnel vision' during emergency situations can be the effect not only of stress, but can be caused by the fundamental nature of the diagnostic task (cognitive tunnelling, Moray, 1981) and of the capacity requirements of higher level mental tasks (Rasmussen, 1981).

The generic mental functions at the three levels of behaviour as illustrated in the schematic diagram of Fig. 3 must be related to a more general description of that internal mental function which was not performed as required by the external task. In order to be able to identify the internal function which failed on the basis of the external effects of errors alone, this description must be independent on the level of human behaviour and based alone on a rational breakdown of the decision sequence into the phases of detection, identification, decision, etc., as indicated on top of Fig. 3.

So far we have considered only *what* went wrong (the internal mental function that failed) and *how* it went wrong (the internal failure mechanism) together with the effect upon the external task, the external mode of malfunction. It is necessary also to consider explicitly the cause of the malfunction, *why* it happened, especially whether the change in the work situation, which is ascribed the role of cause, is related to spontaneous human variability or is a change in the external work condition, in the form of a change in task content or an irrelevant, distracting event. In conclusion, these factors add up to a description of a human error in the form of a causal chain of events as shown in Fig. 4.

How far back in this chain one needs to go to identify the category to be selected as the nominal cause for which data is collected depends upon the actual use. To judge reliability of an existing task, it is only necessary to consider the external mode of failure; to judge training and interface design for improvement, the mechanism of failure must be considered; and to evaluate the work situation, the external causes must also be identified.

Fig. 4 includes five aspects of human errors which are useful as five dimensions in a multi-facet classification system. These dimensions are not completely

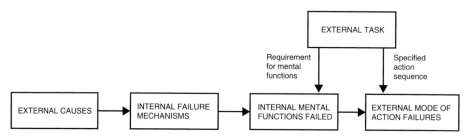

Figure 4 Typical characteristics of an accidental chain of events including human malfunction

independent, significant correlations are found for subsets of tasks and work situations. Furthermore, the members of the different categories are not mutually exclusive and, therefore, generic fault trees or prototypical decision-error-trees are not feasible to characterize human performance. We prefer the use of a multi-facet description from which error-trees can be derived for specific applications, as described later. This solution also seems to be preferable for computer administration and analysis of data since a good resolution can be obtained with a limited number of classes in each dimension.

Performance shaping factors

The causal chain of events of Fig. 4 only considers the information processing aspects of the man-machine interaction; i.e. the chain of events related to changes in the conditions for human decisions or to the process of decision making itself. However, the work environment influences man in a much more complex way than through the information domain alone, as illustrated by Fig. 5. It appears to be necessary to include conditioning factors related to affective, motivating aspects of the work situation as well as physiological factors. Such factors will not directly appear in the causal chain of events but may influence it by changing human limits of capability, subjective preferences in choice of mental strategies and goals etc. Some of these factors can only be identified by careful analysis of the actual work 'climate' and are frequently not considered in normal event report. Together with the categories of Fig. 5. such conditioning factors result in the taxonomy of human errors illustrated by Fig. 6.

The taxonomy for event analysis including human malfunction

The categories of the taxonomy directly related to the inappropriate human performance are shown on Fig. 6. When used for data collection in process plant environments, a number of categories are added for description of the circumstances for the event, including characteristics of the process plant and its immediate operational state; the manner of detection of the event; the ultim-ate consequences upon plant operation; the systems and components affected;

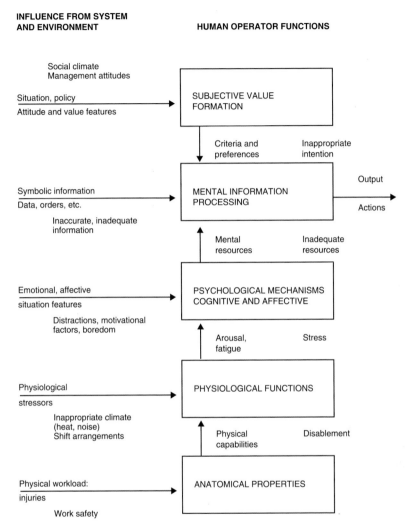

**INFLUENCE FROM SYSTEM
AND ENVIRONMENT**

HUMAN OPERATOR FUNCTIONS

Social climate
Management attitudes

Situation, policy

Attitude and value features

SUBJECTIVE VALUE
FORMATION

Criteria and   Inappropriate
preferences   intention

Symbolic information

Data, orders, etc.

Inaccurate, inadequate
information

MENTAL INFORMATION
PROCESSING

Output

Actions

Mental   Inadequate
resources   resources

Emotional, affective

situation features

Distractions, motivational
factors, boredom

PSYCHOLOGICAL MECHANISMS
COGNITIVE AND AFFECTIVE

Arousal,   Stress
fatigue

Physiological

stressors

Inappropriate climate
(heat, noise)
Shift arrangements

PHYSIOLOGICAL FUNCTIONS

Physical   Disablement
capabilities

Physical workload:

injuries

Work safety

ANATOMICAL PROPERTIES

Figure 5 The diagram illustrates the complex interaction in a man-machine system which controls the mismatch features in an error situation

the personnel category involved; the work location; etc. These categories are discussed in more detail in Rasmussen *et al.*, 1981.

When used for data collection, a number of conventions are needed to avoid too much ambiguity and guidelines for event analysis should be used for consistent classification. Guidelines are proposed elsewhere (Hollnagel *et al.*, 1981) and examples are given in the following discussion of the categories, which is ordered according to the logical sequence of analysis. It will be clear from the discussion that the important feature of the taxonomy proposed will be the structure and its dimensions, not the detailed numbers of categories, which may vary with the specific application.

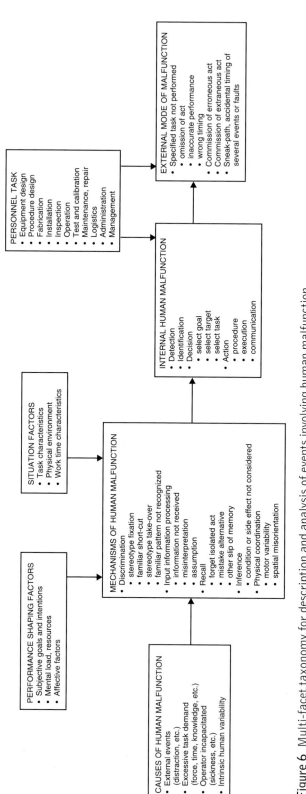

Figure 6 Multi-facet taxonomy for description and analysis of events involving human malfunction

Personnel task

Identification of the task performed is important to characterize the circumstances during which the malfunction occurred. The categories included in Fig. 7 are rather general and only useful for routine event reporting. In proper data collection campaigns, the tasks involved must be analysed and the location of the failure in the task more precisely identified. Furthermore, task analysis must be performed to determine the bias resulting from the potential for immediate error correction together with the frequency of error opportunities.

External mode of malfunction

This category describes the immediate, observable effect of human malfunction upon the task performance and the way in which it initiates the consequent chain of accidental events. The category serves to characterize the sensitivity of the system to the malfunction in a few classes which are useful for monitoring a plant system by routine reports and which relates to the information needed in reliability analysis (whether the specified task is performed) and for risk analysis (effects of erroneous acts). For predictive analysis, the classes are not very useful and more specific external modes should be determined from a correlation of error mechanisms, internal functions and the result of a task analysis as described below.

Internal human malfunction

This category identified the internal mental function of the man's decision making which was not performed as required by the task. It is based upon a model of human decision making as a rational sequence of elements as indicated in Fig. 3, which may be performed as stated or bypassed by habitual leaps. Event analysis should serve to identify the decision process that has been erroneously performed or has been inappropriately bypassed by a habitual leap.

The use of these decision categories is ambiguous in several ways and some conventions are necessary to give consistent classifications. First of all, human performance has basically a hierarchical structure and it may consequently be a matter of choice as to which level the decision categories are used and how they are brought into use. This choice will depend on the circumstances during which inappropriate human performance is found and on the amount and quality of the information available from the event. One typical example will be a skilled operator making a single erroneous decision during normal or near-normal work situations. In this case, the decision categories will be used on a high level of task planning, partly because highly professional people are only making 'decisions' at a high level to control their skilled and more subconscious routines as illustrated in Fig. 3, and partly because routine event reports do not include information which enables an identification of decision errors at a lower level, even though they may appear; e.g. if a skilled routine must be modified. A repair

**INTERNAL HUMAN MALFUNCTION
WHAT FAILED?**

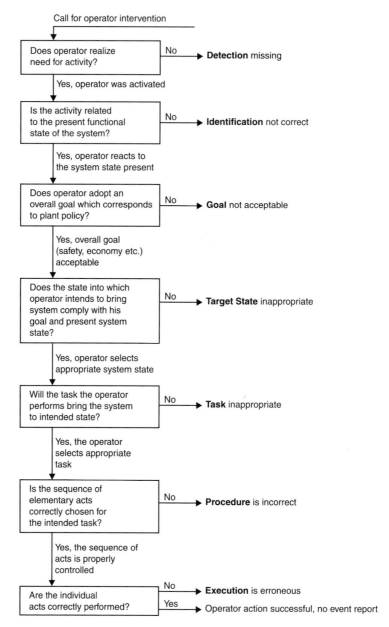

Figure 7 Guide to identify the internal human malfunction from event analysis

task can be taken as an example: If the equipment fault is incorrectly diagnosed, the inappropriate mental function is classified as 'identification'. However, if the fault is correctly identified and the task of replacement properly mentioned but inappropriately planned because the internal state of the equipment is not properly identified at a lower level, then the mental malfunction will be classified as 'inappropriate procedure'.

For cases including several inappropriate human decisions which are related in the chain of events, we normally only classify the first malfunction when the source of information is routine reports. This is due to the consideration that the situation following an erroneous decision is too complex to allow the analyst to judge the basis of the subsequent decisions and the normal classification categories may not apply. The variability, e.g. for human decision making, in a situation created by acts based on misidentification of the state of the system, is only accessible through very detailed in situ analyses based on interviews.

A systematic guide to the analysis of simple routine event reports, to identify 'what was wrong', is proposed in Fig. 7.

Mechanisms of human malfunction

The categories of mechanisms of human malfunction are closely related to the categories of human behaviour which are represented in the model of Fig. 3. The categories of 'internal human malfunction' and those of 'mechanisms of human malfunctions', which are related to categories of internal human information processes and of internal human mechanisms, respectively, are basically different concepts and should therefore be considered separately during event analysis. During normal work situations, there is a rather close correlation between information process types and of mechanisms used for the activity. Since, however, event analysis will include situations of all degrees of familiarity for operators, we maintain that the categories of information processes and psychological mechanisms should be kept separate during analysis.

As discussed above, the mechanisms of malfunction must be deduced from the observable evidence by means of a model of human performance, and the analysis must therefore follow guidelines derived from such a model as, for instance, proposed in Fig. 8 derived from the three level model of Fig. 3. The categories proposed should not be taken as a final set; it includes the categories which have been found typical from a preliminary analysis of 200 U.S. Licencee Event Reports (Rasmussen, 1980). Since they have been found to cover the larger part of the cases, an immediate classification as proposed during event recording will save the effort for detailed data collection in the more complex situations.

An important situation for which detailed data collection and analysis are needed is when operators respond to abnormal situations and have realized that knowledge-based reasoning is needed. In this knowledge-based domain there is very little correlation between the activity types of identification, decision and planning, and the underlying types of psychological mechanisms related to functional, causal deduction and search which will be applied in all the activities. In the present taxonomy, all mechanisms related to this level of behaviour are lumped in the category of malfunction during inference such as inadequate consideration of causal conditions or side effects. Future studies, e.g. in training simulator sessions, will hopefully serve to make this category more detailed, as

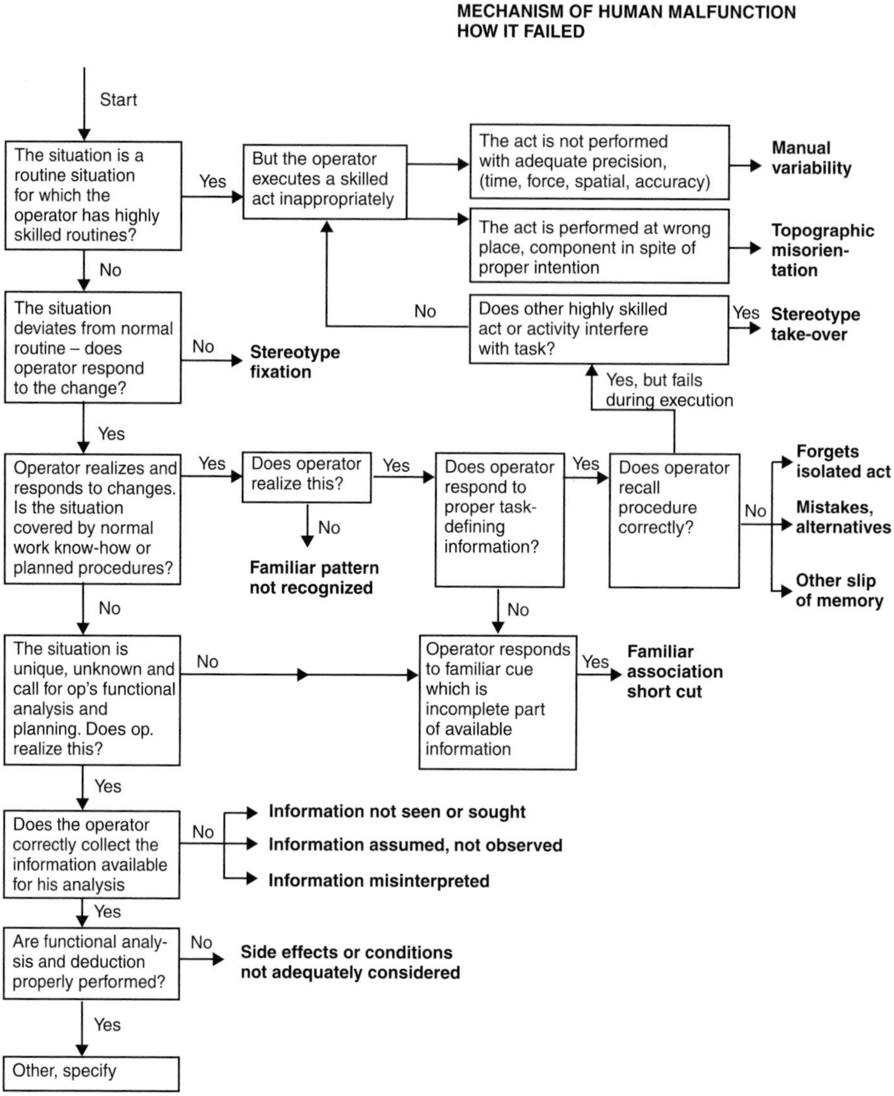

**MECHANISM OF HUMAN MALFUNCTION
HOW IT FAILED**

Start

The situation is a routine situation for which the operator has highly skilled routines?	Yes →	But the operator executes a skilled act inappropriately	→ The act is not performed with adequate precision, (time, force, spatial, accuracy) → **Manual variability**

→ The act is performed at wrong place, component in spite of proper intention → **Topographic misorientation**

No

| The situation deviates from normal routine – does operator respond to the change? | No → **Stereotype fixation** |

No → Does other highly skilled act or activity interfere with task? → Yes **Stereotype take-over**

Yes, but fails during execution

Yes

| Operator realizes and responds to changes. Is the situation covered by normal work know-how or planned procedures? | Yes → | Does operator realize this? | Yes → | Does operator respond to proper task-defining information? | Yes → | Does operator recall procedure correctly? | → **Forgets isolated act** |

No ↓
Familiar pattern not recognized

No → **Mistakes, alternatives**

→ **Other slip of memory**

No

No ↓

| The situation is unique, unknown and call for op's functional analysis and planning. Does op. realize this? | No → | Operator responds to familiar cue which is incomplete part of available information | Yes → **Familiar association short cut** |

Yes

| Does the operator correctly collect the information available for his analysis | No → **Information not seen or sought**
→ **Information assumed, not observed**
→ **Information misinterpreted** |

Yes

| Are functional analysis and deduction properly performed? | No → **Side effects or conditions not adequately considered** |

Yes

Other, specify

Figure 8 Guide for event analysis to identify the mechanism of human malfunction

well as more infrequent categories now lumped in the category 'other'. It is therefore important to have good, free text descriptions of cases relating to these two categories.

Causes of human malfunction

This category should identify the possible external causes of the inappropriate human action. As discussed in a previous section, a malfunction implies a *change* from normal or expected function and this change can be due to a spontaneous internal human variability or a change in the external task condition. Identification of possible external causes is important for several reasons. First of all, there is a natural tendency, when analysing the chain of events implied in maloperation of a system, to accept a human error as the explanation if an inappropriate human act is met by the causal backtracking – 'it is human to err'. Special care is therefore needed to identify external causes. Secondly, such external causes may be important since they influence frequency and also may indicate causal coupling to other chains of event.

The category of causes within the present taxonomy should only be taken as illustrative. Specific sets should be identified in the different specific applications since they will be very context dependent. A decision tree to guide data collection can therefore only be a framework ensuring consideration of the major classes, such as the one illustrated in Fig. 9.

Performance shaping and situation factors

These categories include general conditions which may influence error probability, but – according to our definition – do not cause errors. The distinction between the two categories is only caused by the fact that the set here called performance shaping factors can only be identified by careful human factors analysis, whereas the situation factors are readily recognizable. The class 'task characteristics' is important in relation to error mechanisms, since it should identify whether the task is familiar to the person or not, and whether it is performed according to schedule or not. This information gives clue to identification of the level of behaviour called upon (compare Fig. 3).

Human error prediction

In the sections above, references have been made to the use of the taxonomy for event analysis and some of the problems involved have been discussed. Event analysis implies a breakdown of the event into the features given by the taxonomy, and the quality of the taxonomy is related to the extent to which the causal flow and the mechanisms controlling the event propagation are maintained and can be regenerated from the data. When used for error prediction, the taxonomy must serve a synthesis of the relevant, possible chains of events during human performance from the elements contained in the categories together with an estimate of the probability – or at least a ranking of the significance of the possible events. A discussion of the problems involved in prediction of human errors in general is presented elsewhere (Rasmussen, 1979) and is outside the scope of the present paper and, accordingly, only an illustrative indication of the use of the taxonomy is considered.

Prediction of human malfunction in a task considered in isolation is not very meaningful. The basis for any human error prediction in the present context will be the result of a functional analysis of the technical system or the task environment including a failure analysis. This analysis will serve to identify the requirements for human actions. It will specify the required human task in

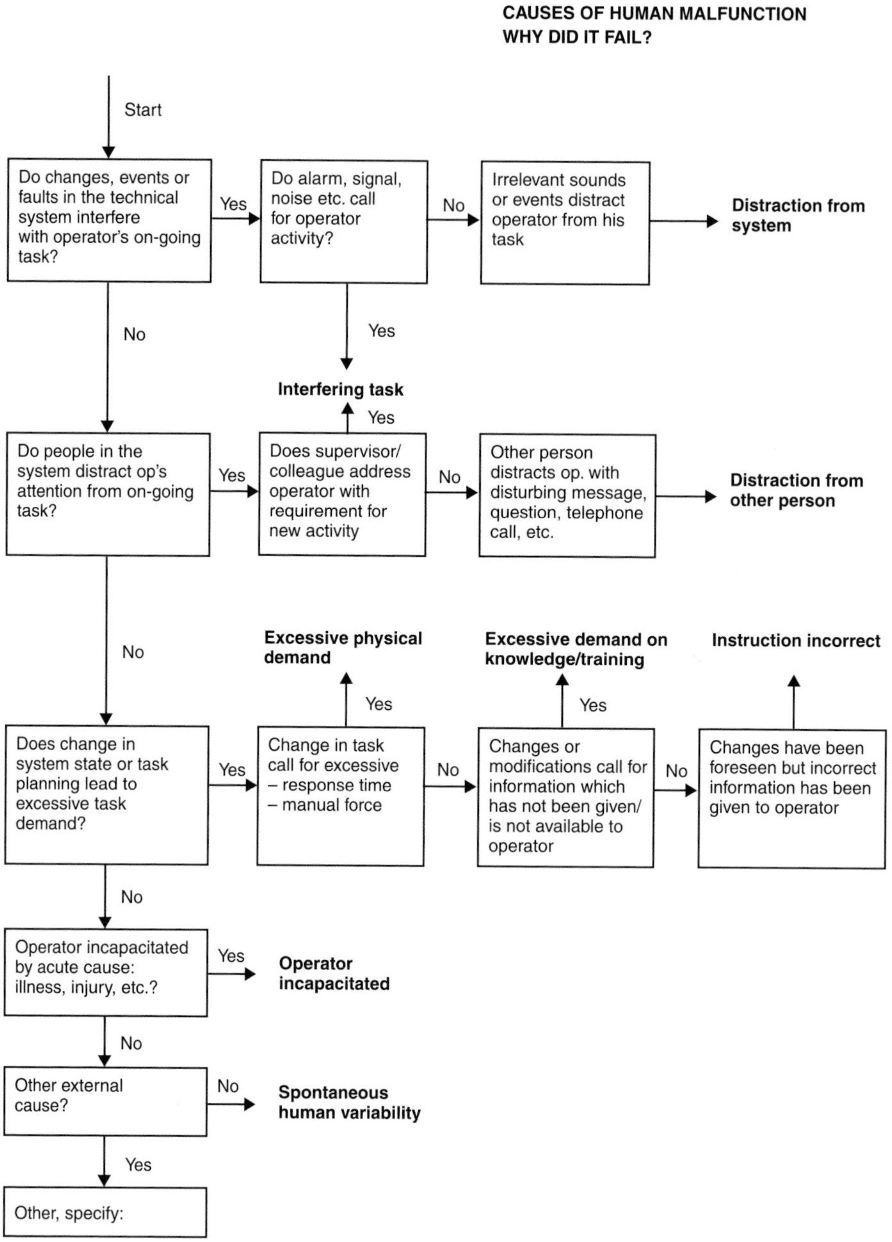

**CAUSES OF HUMAN MALFUNCTION
WHY DID IT FAIL?**

Start

| Do changes, events or faults in the technical system interfere with operator's on-going task? | →Yes→ | Do alarm, signal, noise etc. call for operator activity? | →No→ | Irrelevant sounds or events distract operator from his task | → | **Distraction from system** |

No↓ (from first box)

Yes↓ (from alarm box)

Interfering task
↑Yes

| Do people in the system distract op's attention from on-going task? | →Yes→ | Does supervisor/ colleague address operator with requirement for new activity | →No→ | Other person distracts op. with disturbing message, question, telephone call, etc. | → | **Distraction from other person** |

No↓

Excessive physical demand   **Excessive demand on knowledge/training**   **Instruction incorrect**
↑Yes   ↑Yes

| Does change in system state or task planning lead to excessive task demand? | →Yes→ | Change in task call for excessive – response time – manual force | →No→ | Changes or modifications call for information which has not been given/ is not available to operator | →No→ | Changes have been foreseen but incorrect information has been given to operator |

No↓

| Operator incapacitated by acute cause: illness, injury, etc.? | →Yes→ | **Operator incapacitated** |

No↓

| Other external cause? | →No→ | **Spontaneous human variability** |

Yes↓

| Other, specify: |

Figure 9 Guide for event analysis to identify external causes of human malfunction

terms of an action sequence required to bring the system from one – normal or disturbed – state to another. At the same time, probability estimates for the relevant equipment failures and other non-human caused events will be very useful to serve as stop rules to prevent search for irrelevant human error mechanisms.

When the task requirements related to different plant states are formulated, the problem of prediction is to determine whether the person will detect the need for action, identify the actual state of the system, choose the proper target state and so forth – in short, the internal mental functions which are required by the task and could be wrong should be determined. Next, the internal mechanisms of malfunction are correlated to the required mental functions and their effect upon the actual task performance can be determined in detail. This means that the relevant external modes of failure for the actual task are identified and the related specific fault trees can be constructed.

If we consider as a simple example the act of closing a valve, this can be unsuccessful due to different causal mechanisms. It may be opened fully instead of closed due to a 'mistake of alternatives' or due to 'stereotype fixation' (if it operates in reverse to usual). Closing may be omitted due to simple 'slip of memory' – with high probability, if the act is 'functionally isolated' from the main course of the task. Or a wrong valve may be closed, in which case we have two coupled errors and it is important to predict the mistaken valve. Depending upon the error mechanism involved, this valve will be topographically close ('topographic misorientation'), have a name or label which can be mistaken ('mistake of alternatives', A for B for instance) or be part of a very familiar routine which is similar to the present task (psychologically close, 'stereotype take-over').

The message of this simple example is that the causal relationships among mechanisms, mental function and task elements must be maintained during the analysis in order to identify the external mode of error and to relate frequencies or probabilities to the ultimate effects – and to predict couplings between multiple errors. When the ultimate effect of the errors and potential for error correction are identified from the systems analysis, the probable causes of errors are estimated to judge error probability and potential for coupling to other events. Based on the proposed multi-facet taxonomy, general formats to guide identification of relevant chains of events including human error in systems analysis can be formed.

An illustrative example for action errors is shown in Fig. 10, based on a combination of the categories of internal malfunction, mechanisms of malfunction, together with causes and external effects. A practical implementation of such preformatted analysis guides have been developed by Taylor (1979). Since errors of intention are very complex and situation specific, such general guides for this kind of error are not feasible at present. However, error prediction for familiar tasks for which the procedure is known is an important part of systems reliability analysis and risk analysis and tools like the action analysis format of Fig. 10 have proved useful.

Conclusion

In the present paper, it has been stressed several times that the important aspect of the proposed taxonomy is the structure, not the elements used within the various categories. There is, at present, a widespread interest in quantification of human performance which appears to be somewhat premature, since the qualitative structures and categories which are necessary to define the items to be measured or counted are not properly sorted out. This cannot be done without

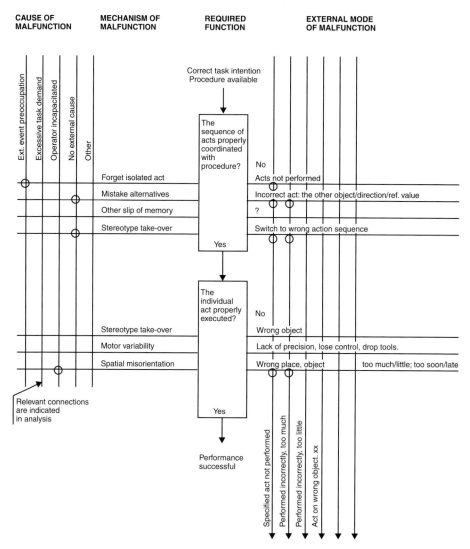

Figure 10 Schematic format for prediction of error in action sequence. Will serve to generate fault trees in a failure mode and effect analysis. For illustrative purpose, only a limited number of items in the different categories are included

careful studies of human performance and errors in actual work situations in order to reach a better understanding of the complexity of human error situations and the data needed to characterize them. The purpose of the present taxonomy has been to contribute to the basis for such studies by means of more systematic experiments in data collection schemes for real-life work situations.

References

Fitts, P.M. and Jones, R.E. (1947) 'Analysis of factors contributing, to 460 "pilot-error" experiences in operating aircraft controls, Report TSEAA-694–12, Aeromedical

Laboratory, Wright-Patterson Air Force Base: Dayton, Ohio, reprinted in W.H. Sinaiko (Ed.), *Selected papers on human factors in the design and use of control systems*, New York: Dover, 1961.

Hollnagel, E., Pedersen, O.M. and Rasmussen, J. (1981) *Notes on human performance analysis*, Risø-M-2285.

Moray, N. (1981) 'The role of attention in the detection of errors and the diagnosis of failures in man-machine systems', to be published, in J. Rasmussen and W.B. Rouse (Eds), *Human detection and diagnosis of system failures*, Plenum Press: New York.

Norman, D.A. (1979) *Slips of the mind and an outline for a theory of action*, Report CHIP 88, Center for Human Information Processing, University of California: San Diego.

Norman, D.A. (1980) *Errors in human performance*, Report No. 8004, Center for Human Information Processing, University of California: San Diego.

Rasmussen, J. (1976) 'Outlines of a hybrid model of the process operator', in Sheridan and Johannsen (Eds), *Monitoring behaviour and supervisory control*, Plenum Press: New York.

Rasmussen, J. (1979) 'Notes on human error analysis and prediction', in G. Apostolakis and G. Volta (Eds), *Synthesis and analysis methods for safety and reliability studies*, Plenum Press: London.

Rasmussen, J. (1980) 'What can be learned from human error reports?', in K.D. Duncan, M.M. Gruneberg and D. Wallis (Eds), *Changes in working life*, John Wiley & Sons.

Rasmussen, J. (1980) *Some trends in man-machine interface design for industrial process plants*, Risø-M-2228, also in proceedings of ASSOPO 80 – an IFIP/IFAC symposium, Norway.

Rasmussen, J. (1981) 'Models of mental strategies in process plant diagnosis' to be published, in: J. Rasmussen and W.B. Rouse (Eds), *Human detection and diagnosis of system failures*, Plenum Press: New York.

Rasmussen, J., Pedersen, O.M.P., Carnino, A., Griffon, M., Mancini, G. and Gagnolet, A. (1981) *Classification system for reporting events involving human malfunction*, Risø-M-2240.

Reason, J.T. (1975) 'How did I come to do that?', *New Behaviour*, April 24, 1975.

Reason, J.T. (1976) 'Absent minds', *New Society*, November 4, 1976.

Reason, J.T. (1977) 'Skill and error in everyday life', in: M. Howe (Ed.), *Adult learning*, Wiley: London.

Swain, A. (1976) *Sandia human factors program for weapon development*, SAND 76–0326 Sandia Laboratories.

Swain, A. (1980) *Handbook of human reliability analysis with emphasis on NPP applications*, draft report NUREG/CR-1278.

Taylor, J.R. (1979) *A background to risk analysis*, Vol. 1 to 4, Electronics Department, Risø National Laboratory.

Chapter 17

James Reason

THE CONTRIBUTION OF LATENT HUMAN FAILURES TO THE BREAKDOWN OF COMPLEX SYSTEMS

Introduction

THE PAST FEW YEARS have seen a succession of major disasters afflicting a wide range of complex technologies: nuclear power plants, chemical installations, spacecraft, 'roll-on-roll-off' ferries, commercial and military aircraft, off-shore oil platforms and railway networks. If we were to focus only upon the surface details, each of these accidents could be regarded as a singular event, unique in its aetiology and consequences. At a more general level, however, these catastrophes are seen to share a number of important features.

(i) They occurred within complex socio-technical systems, most of which possessed elaborate safety devices. That is, these systems required the precise coordination of a large number of human and mechanical elements, and were defended against the uncontrolled release of mass and energy by the deliberate redundancy and diversity of equipment, by automatic shut-down mechanisms and by physical barriers.

(ii) These accidents arose from the adverse conjunction of several diverse causal sequences, each necessary but none sufficient to breach the system's defences by itself. Moreover, a large number of the root causes were present within the system long before the accident sequence was apparent.

(iii) Human rather than technical failures played the dominant roles in all of these accidents.

Even when they involved faulty components, it was subsequently judged that appropriate human action could have avoided or mitigated the tragic outcome.

Thanks to the abundance and sophistication of engineered safety measures, many high-risk technologies are now largely proof against single failures, either of humans or components. This represents an enormous engineering achievement. But it carries a penalty. The existence of elaborate 'defences in depth' renders the system opaque to those who control it. The availability of cheap computing power (which provided many of these defences) means that, in several modern technologies, human operators are increasingly remote from the processes that they nominally govern. For much of the time, their task entails little more than monitoring the system to ensure that it functions within acceptable limits.

A point has been reached in the development of technology where the greatest dangers stem not so much from the breakdown of a major component or from isolated operator errors, as from the insidious accumulation of delayed-action human failures occurring primarily within the organizational and managerial sectors. These residual problems do not belong exclusively to either the machine or the human domains. They emerge from a complex and as yet little understood interaction between the technical and social aspects of the system.

Such problems can no longer be solved by the application of still more 'engineering fixes' nor are they amenable to the conventional remedies of human factors specialists. Further improvements in reliability will require more effective methods of risk management. These, in turn, depend upon acquiring a better understanding of the breakdown of complex socio-technical systems, and the development of new techniques of risk assessment. This paper sketches out some of the issues that must be confronted if this ambitious programme is to succeed.

Active and latent human failures

Close examination of several recent disasters (especially Bhopal, Challenger, Chernobyl, Zeebrugge and King's Cross) shows the need to distinguish two ways in which human beings contribute to the breakdown of complex systems (see also Rasmussen and Pedersen (1983)).

(i)   Active failures: those errors and violations having an immediate adverse effect. These are generally associated with the activities of 'front-line' operators: control room personnel, ships' crews, train drivers, signalmen, pilots, air traffic controllers, etc.

(ii) Latent failures: these are decisions or actions, the damaging consequences of which may lie dormant for a long time, only becoming evident when they combine with local triggering factors (that is, active failures, technical faults, atypical system conditions, etc.) to breach the system's defences. Their defining feature is that they were present within the system well before the onset of a recognizable accident sequence. They are most likely to be spawned by those whose activities are removed in both time and space from the direct human–machine interface: designers, high-level decision makers, regulators, managers and maintenance staff.

Two recent accident investigations, in particular, have dramatically reversed the usual practice of focusing upon the actions of the 'front-line' operators (Sheen, 1987; Fennell 1988). Both the Zeebrugge and King's Cross inquiries concluded that rather than being the main instigators of these disasters, those at the human –machine interface were the inheritors of system defects created by poor design, conflicting goals, defective organization and bad management decisions. Their part, in effect, was simply that of creating the conditions under which these latent failures could reveal themselves.

There is a growing awareness within the human reliability community that attempts to discover and remedy these latent failures will achieve greater safety benefits than will localized efforts to minimize active failures. So far, much of the work of human factors specialists has focused upon improving the immediate human–system interface. Whereas this is undeniably an important enterprise, it only addresses a relatively small part of the total safety problem, being aimed at reducing the active failure tip of the causal iceberg. The remainder of this paper will focus upon latent rather than active failures, beginning with some quantitative evidence from the nuclear power industry.

Some data in support of the latent failure argument

The Institute of Nuclear Power Operations (INPO) manages the Significant Event and Information Network for its member utilities both within and outside the United States. In 1985 they issued an analysis of 180 significant event reports received in 1983–84 (INPO 1985). A total of 387 root causes were identified. These were assigned to five main categories: human performance problems, 52%; design deficiencies, 33%; manufacturing deficiences, 7%; external causes, 3%; and an 'other unknown' category, 5%.

The human performance problems were further broken down into the following subcategories: deficient procedures or documentation, 43%; lack of knowledge or training, 18%; failure to follow procedures, 16%; deficient planning or scheduling, 10%; miscommunication, 6%; deficient supervision, 3%; policy problems, 2%; and 'other', 2%.

There are two important conclusions to be drawn from these data. First, at least 92% of all root causes were man-made. Secondly, only a relatively small proportion of the root causes (approximately 8% of the total) were initiated by the operators. The majority had their origins in either maintenance-related activities, or in fallible decisions taken within the organizational and managerial domains.

The major role played by maintenance-related errors in causing nuclear power plant events has also been established by two independent studies (Rasmussen 1980; NUMARC 1985). Of these, simple omissions (the failure to carry out necessary actions) formed the largest single category of identified human problems in nuclear power plant operations.

A resident pathogen metaphor

It is suggested that latent failures are analogous to the 'resident pathogens' within the human body, which combine with external factors (stress, toxic agencies, etc.) to bring about disease. Like cancers and cardiovascular disorders, accidents in complex, defended systems do not arise from single causes. They occur through the unforeseen (and often unforeseeable) concatenation of several distinct factors, each one necessary but singly insufficient to cause the catastrophic breakdown. This view leads to a number of general assumptions about accident causation.

(i)   The likelihood of an accident is a function of the total number of pathogens (or latent failures) resident within the system. All systems have a certain number. But the more abundant they are, the greater is the probability that a given set of pathogens will meet just those local triggers necessary to complete an accident sequence.

(ii)   The more complex, interactive, tightly coupled and opaque the system (Perrow 1984), the greater will be the number of resident pathogens. However, it is likely that simpler systems will require fewer pathogens to bring about an accident as they have fewer defences.

(iii) The higher an individual's position within an organization, the greater is his or her opportunity for generating pathogens.

(iv)   It is virtually impossible to foresee all the local triggers, though some could and should be anticipated. Resident pathogens, on the other hand, can be assessed, given adequate access and system knowledge.

(v)   It therefore follows that the efforts of safety specialists could be directed more profitably towards the proactive identification and neutralization of latent failures, rather than at the prevention of active failures, as they have largely been in the past.

These assumptions raise some further questions: how can we best gauge the 'morbidity' of high-risk systems? Do systems have general indicators, comparable to a white cell count or a blood pressure reading, from which it is possible to gain some snapshot impression of their overall state of health?

A general framework for accident causation

The resident pathogen metaphor is far from being a workable theory. Its terms are still unacceptably vague. Moreover, it shares a number of features with the now largely discredited accident proneness theory, although the pathogen view operates at a systemic rather than at an individual level.

Accident proneness theory floundered when it was established that unequal accident liability was, in reality, a 'club' with a rapidly changing membership (see Reason 1974). In addition, attempts to find a clearly defined accident-prone personality proved largely fruitless.

The pathogen metaphor would suffer a similar fate if it turned out that latent failures could only be identified retrospectively in relation to a specific set of accident circumstances in a particular system. For the analogy to have any value, it is necessary to establish a generic set of indicators relating to system 'morbidity', and then to demonstrate clear connections between these indicators and accident liability across a wide range of complex systems and in a variety of accident conditions.

In what follows, an attempt will be made to develop the pathogen metaphor into a theoretical framework for considering the aetiology of accidents in complex technological systems. The challenge is not just to provide an account of how active and latent failures combine to produce accidents, but also to show where and how more effective remedial measures might be applied.

Before considering the pathology of complex systems, we must first identify their essential, 'healthy' components. These are the basic elements of production. All complex technologies are involved in some form of production, whether it be energy, a chemical substance, or the mass transportation of people by land, sea or air. There are five basic elements to any productive system: decision makers, line management, preconditions, productive activities and defences.

(i) Decision makers. These include both the architects and the senior executives of the system. Once in operation, the latter set the production and safety goals for the system as a whole. They also direct, at a strategic level, the means by which these goals should be met. A large part of their function is concerned with the allocation of finite resources. These comprise money, equipment, people and time.

(ii) Line management. These are the departmental specialists who implement the strategies of the decision makers within their particular spheres of operation: operations, training, sales, maintenance, finance, safety, engineering support, personnel, and so on.

(iii) Preconditions. Effective production requires more than just machines and people. The equipment must be reliable and of the right kind. The workforce must be skilled, alert, knowledgeable and motivated.

(iv) Productive activities. These are the actual performances of machines and people: the temporal and spatial coordination of mechanical and human activities needed to deliver the right product at the right time.

(v) Defences. Where the productive activities involve exposure to hazards, both the human and mechanical components of the system need to be provided with safeguards sufficient to prevent forseeable injury, damage or costly outages.

The human contributions to accidents are summarized in figure 1. They are linked there to each of the basic elements of production, portrayed as 'planes' lying one behind the other in an ordered sequence. The question at issue is: how do fallible decisions translate into unsafe acts capable of breaching the system's defences?

It is assumed that latent failures (resident pathogens) have their primary systemic origin in the errors of high-level decision makers. But they are also introduced

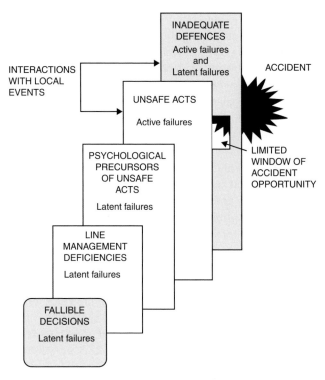

Figure 1 Showing the relationship between various human contributions to accidents and the basic elements of production. Latent failures have their primary systematic origins in the fallible decisions made by senior executives. They are subsequently translated into different forms as the effects of these decisions pass through the system during the production process

into all levels of the system by the human condition. Error proneness and the capacities for being stressed, failing to perceive hazards, being ignorant of the system, and having less than ideal motivation are brought by each individual into the workplace.

Even in the best run organizations, a significant number of influential decisions will subsequently prove to be mistaken. Fallible decisions are an inevitable part of the design and management process. The issue is not so much how to prevent them, but how to ensure that their adverse consequences are detected and recovered.

All organizations must allocate limited resources to two distinct goals: production and safety. In the long term, these are clearly compatible. But short-term conflicts of interest will arise in which the resources given to production could diminish safety, and conversely. There are a number of reasons why these dilemmas will tend to be resolved in favour of production rather than safety goals.

First, resources directed at improving productivity have relatively certain outcomes; those aimed at enhancing safety do not, at least in the short term (Brehmer, 1988). This is due to the large part played by stochastic factors in accident causation.

Secondly, the feedback generated by the pursuit of production goals is generally unambiguous, rapid, compelling and (when the news is good) highly reinforcing. In sharp contrast, that derived from the pursuit of safety goals is largely negative, intermittent, often deceptive and perhaps only compelling after a major accident or a string of incidents.

Even when decision makers attend to this feedback, they do not always interpret it correctly. Defensive 'filters' may be interposed, which protect them from bad news and encourage extrapunitive reactions. Thus a bad safety record can be attributed to operator carelessness or incompetence. This position is frequently consolidated by cataloguing the various engineering safety devices and safe operating practices that have been put in place. These are understandable reactions, but they none the less block the discovery of effective counter-measures and contribute to further fallible decisions.

At the line management level, the consequences of fallible decisions manifest themselves differently in the various specialist departments. Within the operations department, they can take the form of undermanning, inadequate procedures, poor scheduling and unsafe assignments. In the training department, they can result in the transmission of inadequate skills, rules and knowledge to the workforce. Maintenance deficiencies can reveal themselves in poor planning and shoddy workmanship. Failures of procurement show up as dangerous and defective equipment. The list goes on, but all the factors mentioned above played a significant part in the aetiology of the Bhopal, Challenger, Chernobyl and King's Cross disasters.

Psychological precursors are latent states. They create the potential for a wide variety of unsafe acts. The precise nature of these acts will be a complex function of the task, the environmental influences and the presence of hazards. Each precursor can give rise to many unsafe acts, depending on the prevailing conditions.

There is a many-to-many mapping between line management deficiencies and these psychological precursors. Failures in the training department, for example, can translate into a variety of precursors: high workload, undue time pressure, inappropriate preception of hazards, ignorance of the system and motivational difficulties. Likewise, any one precondition (for example, undue time pressure) could be the product of many line management deficiencies: poor sheduling, inadequate procedures, inappropriate training and maintenance failures.

A useful way of thinking about these transformations is as types converting into tokens. Deficient training is a general failure type that can reveal itself, at the precursor level, as a variety of pathogenic tokens. Such a view has important remedial implications. Rectifying a failure type could, in principle, eliminate a large class of tokens. The type–token distinction is a hierarchical one. Precondition tokens at the precursor level become types for the creation of tokens at unsafe act level.

A psychological precursor, either alone or in combination with others, can play a major role in provoking and shaping an almost infinitely large set of unsafe acts. The stochastic character of this onward mapping reveals the futility of 'tokenism': the concentration of remedial efforts upon preventing the recurrence of specific unsafe acts. Although certain of these acts may fall into a recognizable category (for example, failing to wear personal safety equipment) and so be amenable to targeted safety programmes, the vast majority of them are unforeseeable and occasionally quite bizarre.

This view of accident causation suggests that unsafe acts are best reduced by eliminating their psychological precursors rather than the acts themselves. However, it must be accepted that whatever measures are taken, some unsafe acts will still occur. It is therefore necessary to provide a variety of defences to intervene between the act and its adverse consequences. Such defences can be both physical and psychological. The latter are as yet relatively unexploited, and involve procedures designed to improve error detection and recovery.

Very few unsafe acts will result in damage or injury. In a highly protected system, the probability that the consequences of an isolated action will penetrate the various layers of defence is vanishingly small. Several causal factors are required to create a 'trajectory of opportunity' through these multiple defences. Many of the causal contributions will come from latent failures in the organizational structure, or in the defences themselves. Others will be local triggering factors. These could be a set of unsafe acts committed during some atypical (but not necessarily abnormal) system state. Examples of the latter are the unusually low temperature on the night preceding the Challenger launch, the voltage–generator tests carried out just before the annual maintenance shut-down in the Chernobyl-4 reactor, and the nose-down trim of the Herald of Free Enterprise because of a combination of unusually high tide and unsuitable docking facilities.

A significant number of accidents in complex systems arise from the deliberate or unwitting disabling of defences by operators in pursuit of what, at the time, seem to be sensible or necessary goals. The test plan at Chernobyl required that the emergency core cooling system should be switched off, and the need to improvise in an unfamiliar and increasingly unstable power regime later led the operators to strip the reactor of its remaining defences. At Zeebrugge, the overworked and undermanned crew of the Herald of Free Enterprise left harbour with the bow doors open. This was an oversight caused by a bizarre combination of active failures (Sheen 1987), but it was also compounded by strong management pressures to meet the stringent schedule for the Dover docking.

Managing safer operations

An effective safety information system has been found to rank second only to top management concern with safety in discriminating between safe and unsafe companies, matched on other variables (Kjellen 1983). The feedback loops and indicators that could go to make up such a system are shown in figure 2.

Loop 1 (reporting accidents, lost time injuries, etc.) represents the minimum requirement. In most cases, however, the information supplied is too little and too late for effective proactive control. The events that safety management seeks to prevent have already occurred.

Loop 2 is potentially available through unsafe act auditing procedures. In

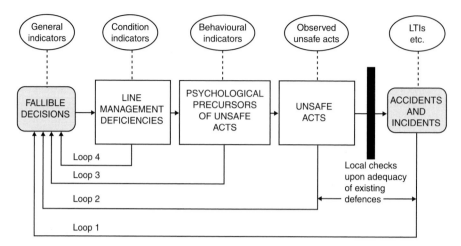

Figure 2 The actual and potential feedback loops and indicators associated with each of the basic elements of production. Loop 1 already exists in most systems, and communicates information about accidents, lost time, injuries, etc. Loop 2 is potentially available through Unsafe Act Auditing. Loops 3 and 4 could provide information regarding latent failures; though in practice they are rarely seen in place

practice, however, this information is usually only disseminated to the lower, supervisory levels of the organization.

The main thrust of the present view of accident causation is towards the establishment of loops 3 and 4. It argues that the most effective way of managing safety is by acting upon types rather than tokens; that is, by influencing system and individual states occurring early on in the history of a possible accident. To identify these indicators, and to find ways of neutralizing the general failure types so revealed constitute the major challenges facing contemporary accident researchers. For the moment, however, we will consider only the most global of these diagnostic signs: the general indicators associated with top-level decision making.

The general indicators shown in figure 2 cover two broad aspects of a system's safety management. The first relates to the variety and sensitivity of its feedback loops. The second deals with the senior executives' responses to safety-related data. No amount of feedback will enhance system safety if the information supplied is not acted upon in a timely and effective manner.

Westrum (1988) has provided a useful classification of the ways in which organizations differ in their responses to safety-related information. These reactions fall into three groups: denial, repair and reform actions.

(i)   Denial actions. These may take one or both of the following forms: suppression, 'whistleblowers' are punished or dismissed and their observations removed from the record; and encapsulation, the observers are retained, but the validity of their observation is disputed or denied.

(ii) Repair actions. Externally, these can take the form of a public relations exercise in which the observations are allowed to emerge, but in a reassuring and sugar-coated manner. Internally, the problem is admitted, but it is only addressed at a local level. 'Offending' operators are disciplined or relocated. Dangerous items of equipment are modified to prevent the recurrence of a specific kind of observed failure. The wider implications of the problem are denied.

(iii) Reform actions. These take two forms: dissemination, the problem is admitted to be global, and global action is taken upon it; reorganization, action on the problem leads to a fundamental reappraisal and reform of the system as a whole.

The more effective the organization, the more likely it is to respond to safety data with reform actions. Less adequate organizations will confine themselves to either denial or repair actions. This leads to a tripartite classification of organizations.

(i) Pathological organizations possess inadequate safety measures, even under normal circumstances. They habitually sacrifice safety for greater productivity, often under severe economic pressure, and they actively circumvent safety regulations.

(ii) Calculative organizations try to do the best job they can by using 'by-the-book' methods. These are usually adequate under normal operating circumstances, but often fail to thwart the development of the multiple-cause accidents, discussed earlier.

(iii) Generative organizations set safety targets for themselves beyond ordinary expectations, and fulfill them because they are willing to do unusual things in unconventional ways. They emphasise results more than methods, and value substance more than form. Notable exemplars of this last category have been investigated by La Porte and his colleagues at the University of California, Berkeley.

High-reliability organizations

The La Porte group (see La Porte and Consolini 1988) has made an intensive study of three high-reliability organizations: the Federal Aviation Authority's air traffic control system, Pacific Gas and Electric's power generating system and two U.S. Navy nuclear aircraft carriers. These organizations share at least two goals: to avoid altogether major failures that could cripple or even destroy, the system; and to cope safely with periods of very high peak demand and production whenever they arise. All of these organizations perform complex and hazardous tasks under considerable time pressure, and they do so with a very low error rate and an almost total absence of catastrophic failure. What are the ingredients? Can we 'bottle' them?

Perhaps the most significant feature of these organizations is their complex yet highly adaptive structural reactions to changing levels of hazard. Each organization has three distinct authority structures: routine, high-tempo and emergency. Each structure has its own characteristic practices, communication pathways and leadership patterns.

The routine mode reveals the familiar hierarchical pattern of rank-dependent authority. This is the face of the organization most evident to the casual observer. It functions with the use of extensive 'standard operating procedures'.

Just beneath the surface of this bureaucratic structure is the high-tempo mode, practised by the same individuals, but in quite a different manner. Authority is no longer based upon rank, but upon functional skills. Formal status defers to expertise. Communications switch from largely vertical channels to being richly horizontal among task-related groups.

Within these high-tempo groups, the La Porte team noted an extraordinary sensitivity to the incipient overloading of any one of its members. For example, when an air traffic controller has an unusually large number of aircraft on his screen, supervisors and other controllers will gather around silently and watch for danger points. When found, they are shown by pointing at the screen. Few words are spoken. When the load has eased, the impromptu support group fades away as quietly as it arrived.

The emergency mode is triggered by unequivocal signs that a well-defined danger is imminent. Authority patterns in this mode are based upon a preprogrammed and well-rehearsed allocation of duties. Individuals regroup themselves into different functional units on the basis of a predetermined plan, tailored to the particular nature of the emergency. La Porte and Consolini (1988) comment upon these co-existing structures as follows: 'Contemporary organization theory literature does little to alert one to the likelihood of these multi-layered, nested authority systems. We are familiar with different types of organization that parallel each of these modes. There are bureaucratic organizations, professional ones, and disaster response ones. We have not thought that all three might be usable by the same organizational membership.'

Can we build these adaptive structural ingredients into high-risk organizations at their outset, or must they evolve painfully and serendipitously over many years of hazardous operating experience? It is probably too early to tell. But it is clear that a close study of high-reliability organizations should feature prominently on the research agendas of those concerned with understanding and preventing the kinds of disaster discussed in this paper. Just as in medicine, it is probably easier to characterize sick systems rather than healthy ones. Yet we need to pursue both of these goals concurrently if we are to understand and then create the organizational bases of system reliability.

Many people contributed to the ideas expressed in this paper. Two, in particular, deserve special mention. Patrick Hudson of the University of Leiden was the first to apply the type–token distinction in the context of accident causation. The production-based framework for accident causation emerged from discussions with John Wreathall of Science Applications International Corporation (Columbus, Ohio).

References

Brehmer, B. (1988) *Changing decisions about safety in organizations*, World Bank Workshop on Safety Control and Risk Management, 18–20 October, Washington D.C.

Fennell, D. (1988) *Investigation into the King's Cross underground fire*, Department of Transport, London: HMSO.

INPO (1985) *An analysis of root causes in 1983 and 1984 significant event reports*, Institute of Nuclear, Power Operations: Atlanta, Georgia.

Kjellen, U. (1983) *The Deviation Concept in Occupational Accident Control*, TRITA/AOG-0019, Arbetsolycksfalls Gruppen, Royal Institute of Technology: Stockholm.

La Porte, T. R. and Consolini, P. M. (1988) *Working in practice but not in theory: theoretical challenges of high reliability organizations*, Annual Meeting of the American Political Science Association, 1–4 September, Washington D.C.

NUMARC (1985) *A maintenance analysis of safety significant events*, Nuclear Utility Management and Human Resources Committee, Institute of Nuclear Power Operations: Atlanta, GA.

Perrow, C. (1984) *Normal accidents: living with high risk technologies*, Basic Books: New York.

Rasmussen, J. (1980) 'What can be learned from human error reports' in *Changes in working life* (ed. K. Duncan, M. Gruneberg and D. Wallis), Wiley: London.

Rasmussen, J. and Pedersen, O. M. (1983) 'Human factors in probabilistic risk analysis and risk management', in *Operational safety of nuclear power plants*, vol. 1, Vienna: International Atomic Energy Agency.

Reason, J. T. (1974) *Man in motion*, Weidenfeld: London.

Sheen, Mr Justice (1987) *Herald of Free Enterprise* Report of Court no. 8074, Department of Transport, HMSO: London.

Westrum, R. (1988) *Organizational and inter-organizational thought*, World Bank Workshop on Safety Control and Risk Management, 18–20 October, Washington D.C.

Chapter 18

Karl E. Weick

THE COLLAPSE OF SENSEMAKING IN ORGANIZATIONS: THE MANN GULCH DISASTER

THE DEATH OF 13 men in the Mann Gulch fire disaster, made famous in Norman Maclean's *Young Men and Fire*, is analyzed as the interactive disintegration of role structure and sensemaking in a minimal organization. Four potential sources of resilience that make groups less vulnerable to disruptions of sensemaking are proposed to forestall disintegration, including improvisation, virtual role systems, the attitude of wisdom, and norms of respectful interaction. The analysis is then embedded in the organizational literature to show that we need to reexamine our thinking about temporary systems, structuration, nondisclosive intimacy, intergroup dynamics, and team building.

The purpose of this article is to reanalyze the Mann Gulch fire disaster in Montana described in Norman Maclean's (1992) award-winning book *Young Men and Fire* to illustrate a gap in our current understanding of organizations. I want to focus on two questions: Why do organizations unravel? And how can organizations be made more resilient? Before doing so, however, I want to strip Maclean's elegant prose away from the events in Mann Gulch and simply review them to provide a context for the analysis.

The incident

As Maclean puts it, at its heart, the Mann Gulch disaster is a story of a race (p. 224). The smokejumpers in the race (excluding foreman 'Wag' Wagner Dodge and ranger Jim Harrison) were ages 17–28, unmarried, seven of them were forestry students (p. 27), and 12 of them had seen military service (p. 220).

They were a highly select group (p. 27) and often described themselves as professional adventurers (p. 26).

A lightning storm passed over the Mann Gulch area at 4PM on August 4, 1949 and is believed to have set a small fire in a dead tree. The next day, August 5, 1949, the temperature was 97 degrees and the fire danger rating was 74 out of a possible 100 (p. 42), which means 'explosive potential' (p. 79). When the fire was spotted by a forest ranger, the smokejumpers were dispatched to fight it. Sixteen of them flew out of Missoula, Montana at 2:30PM in a C-47 transport. Wind conditions that day were turbulent, and one smokejumper got sick on the airplane, didn't jump, returned to the base with the plane, and resigned from the smokejumpers as soon as he landed ('his repressions had caught up with him,' p. 51). The smokejumpers and their cargo were dropped on the south side of Mann Gulch at 4:10PM from 2000 feet rather than the normal 1200 feet, due to the turbulence (p. 48). The parachute that was connected to their radio failed to open, and the radio was pulverized when it hit the ground. The crew met ranger Jim Harrison who had been fighting the fire alone for four hours (p. 62), collected their supplies, and ate supper. About 5:10 (p. 57) they started to move along the south side of the gulch to surround the fire (p. 62). Dodge and Harrison, however, having scouted ahead, were worried that the thick forest near which they had landed might be a 'death trap' (p. 64). They told the second in command, William Hellman, to take the crew across to the north side of the gulch and march them toward the river along the side of the hill. While Hellman did this, Dodge and Harrison ate a quick meal. Dodge rejoined the crew at 5:40PM and took his position at the head of the line moving toward the river. He could see flames flapping back and forth on the south slope as he looked to his left (p. 69).

At this point the reader hits the most chilling sentence in the entire book: 'Then Dodge saw it?' (p. 70). What he saw was that the fire had crossed the gulch just 200 yards ahead and was moving toward them (p. 70). Dodge turned the crew around and had them angle up the 76-percent hill toward the ridge at the top (p. 175). They were soon moving through bunch grass that was two and a half feet tall and were quickly losing ground to the 30-foot-high flames that were soon moving toward them at 610 feet per minute (p. 274). Dodge yelled at the crew to drop their tools, and then, to everyone's astonishment, he lit a fire in front of them and ordered them to lie down in the area it had burned. No one did, and they all ran for the ridge. Two people, Sallee and Rumsey, made it through a crevice in the ridge unburned, Hellman made it over the ridge burned horribly and died at noon the next day, Dodge lived by lying down in the ashes of his escape fire, and one other person, Joseph Sylvia, lived for a short while and then died. The hands on Harrison's watch melted at 5:56 (p. 90), which has been treated officially as the time the 13 people died.

After the fire passed, Dodge found Sallee and Rumsey, and Rumsey stayed to care for Hellman while Sallee and Dodge hiked out for help. They walked into the Meriwether ranger station at 8:50PM (p. 113), and rescue parties immediately set out to recover the dead and dying. All the dead were found in an area of 100 yards by 300 yards (p. 111). It took 450 men five more days to get the 4,500-acre Mann Gulch fire under control (pp. 24, 33). At the time the crew jumped on the fire, it was classified as a Class C fire, meaning its scope was between 10 and 99 acres.

The Forest Service inquiry held after the fire, judged by many to be inadequate, concluded that 'there is no evidence of disregard by those responsible for the jumper crew of the elements of risk which they are expected to take into account in placing jumper crews on fires.' The board also felt that the men would have been saved had they 'heeded Dodge's efforts to get them to go into the escape fire area with him' (quoted in Maclean, p. 151). Several parents brought suit against the Forest Service, claiming that people should not have been jumped in the first place (p. 149), but these claims were dismissed by the Ninth Circuit U.S. Court of Appeals, where Warren E. Burger argued the Forest Service's case (p. 151).

Since Mann Gulch, there have been no deaths by burning among Forest Service firefighters, and people are now equipped with backup radios (p. 219), better physical conditioning, the tactic of building an escape fire, knowledge that fires in timber west of the Continental Divide burn differently than do fires in grass east of the Divide, and the insistence that crew safety take precedence over fire suppression.

The methodology

Among the sources of evidence Maclean used to construct this case study were interviews, trace records, archival records, direct observation, personal experience, and mathematical models.

Since Maclean did not begin to gather documents on Mann Gulch until 1976 (p. 156) and did not start to work in earnest on this project until his seventy-fourth birthday in 1977, the lapse of almost 28 years since the disaster made interviewing difficult, especially since Dodge had died of Hodgkin's disease five years after the fire (p. 106). Maclean located and interviewed both living witnesses of the blaze, Sallee and Rumsey, and persuaded both to accompany him and Laird Robinson, a guide at the Smokejumper base, on a visit back to the site on July 1, 1978. Maclean also knew Dodge's wife and had talked to her informally (p. 40). He attempted to interview relatives of some who lost their lives but found them too distraught 27 years later to be of much help (p. 154). He also attempted to interview (p. 239) a member of the Forest Service inquiry team, A. J. Cramer who, in 1951, had persuaded Sallee, Rumsey, and ranger Robert Jansson to alter their testimony about the timing of key incidents. Cramer was the custodian of seven or eight watches that had been removed from victims (p. 233), only one of which (Harrison's) was released and used as the official time of the disaster (5:56PM). To this day it remains unclear why the Forest Service made such a strong effort to locate the disaster closer to 6:00PM than to 5:30, which was suggested by testimony from Jansson, who was near the river when the fire blew up, and from a recovered watch that read 5:42. Maclean had continuing access to two Forest Service insiders, Bud Moore and Laird Robinson (p. 162). He also interviewed experts on precedents for the escape fire (p. 104) and on the nature of death by fire (p. 213).

The use of trace records, or physical evidence of past behaviors, is illustrated by the location during a 1979 trip to the gulch, of the wooden cross that had been placed in 1949 to mark the spot where Dodge lit his escape fire (p. 206). The year before, 1978, during the trip into the gulch with Sallee and Rumsey, Maclean located the rusty can of potatoes that had been discarded after Hellman drank its salty water through two knife slits Rumsey had made in the can (p. 173). He also located the flat rocks on which Hellman and Sylvia had rested while awaiting rescue, the juniper tree that was just beyond the crevice Sallee and Rumsey squeezed through on the ridge (p. 207), and Henry Thol, Jr.'s flashlight (p. 183). Considering the lapse of time, the destructive forces of nature over 28 years, and the power of a blowup fire to melt and displace everything in its path, discovery of these traces is surprising as well as helpful in reconstructing events.

Archival records are crucial to the development of the case, although the Forest Service made a considerable effort after its inquiry to scatter the documents (p. 153) and to classify most of them 'Confidential' (p. 158), perhaps fearing it would be charged with negligence. Records used by Maclean included statistical reports of fire suppression by smokejumpers in Forest Service Region 1 (e.g. p. 24); the report of the Forest Service Board of Review issued shortly after the incident (dated September 29, 1949, which many felt was too soon for the board to do an adequate job); statements made to the board by people such as the C-47 pilot, parents of the dead crew (p. 150), and the spotter on the aircraft (p. 42); court reports of litigation brought by parents of smokejumpers against the Forest Service; photographs, virtually all of which were retrieved for him by women in the Forest Service who were eager to help him tell the story (p. 160); early records of the smokejumpers organization, which was nine years old at the time of the disaster; reports of the 1957 task force on crew safety (p. 221); and contemporary reports of the disaster in the media, such as the report in the August 22, 1949 issue of *Life* magazine.

Direct observation occurred during Maclean's three visits to Mann Gulch in 1976, 1977, and 1978 (p. 183, trips made much more difficult because of the inaccessibility of the area (pp. 191–192). The most important of these three visits is the trip to the gulch with Sallee and Rumsey, during which the latter pair reenacted what they did and what they saw intermittently through the dense smoke. When their accounts were matched against subsequent hard data (e.g. their estimation of where Dodge lit his escape fire compared against discovery of the actual cross planted in 1949 to mark the spot), it was found that their reconstruction of events prior to the time they made it to safety through the crevice is less accurate than their memory for events and locations after they made it to safety. This suggests to Maclean that 'we don't remember as exactly the desperate moments when our lives are in the balance as we remember the moments after, when the balance has tipped in our favor' (p. 212). Direct observation also occurred when Maclean and Robinson themselves hiked the steep slopes of Mann Gulch under summer conditions of heat and slippery, tall grass that resembled the conditions present in the disaster of 1949. The two men repeatedly compared photos and maps from 1949 with physical outcroppings in front of them to see more clearly what they were looking at (e.g. photos misrepresent the steepness of the slope, p. 175). There were also informal experiments, as when Rod Norum, an athlete and specialist on fire behavior, retraced Dodge's route from the point at which he rejoined the crew, moved as fast as possible over the route Dodge covered, and was unable to reach the grave markers as fast as the crew did (p. 67). During these trips, Maclean took special note of prevailing winds by observing their effect on the direction in which rotted timber fell. These observations were used to build a theory of how wind currents in the gulch could have produced the blowup (p. 133).

Personal experience was part of the case because, in 1949, Maclean had visited the Mann Gulch fire while it was still burning (p. 1). Maclean also was a Forest Service firefighter (not a smokejumper) at age 15 and nearly lost his life in the Fish Creek fire, a fire much like the one in Mann Gulch (p. 4). Maclean also reports using his practical experience as a woodsman to suggest initial hypotheses regarding what happened at Mann Gulch (e.g. he infers wind patterns in the gulch from observations of unusual wave action in the adjacent Missouri River, p. 131).

Having collected data using the above sources, but still feeling gaps in his understanding of precisely how the race between fire and men unfolded, Maclean taught himself mathematics and turned to mathematical modeling. He worked with two mathematicians, Frank Albini and Richard Rothermel, who had built mathematical models of how fires spread. The group ran the predictive models in reverse to see what the fire in Mann Gulch must have been like to generate the reports on its progress that were found in interviews, reports, and actual measurements. It is the combination of output from the model and subjective reports that provide the revealing time line of the final 16 minutes (pp. 267–277).

If these several sources of evidence are combined and assessed for the adequacy with which they address 'sources of invalidity,' it will be found that they combat 12 of the 15 sources listed by Runkel and McGrath (1972: 191) and are only 'moderately vulnerable' to the other three. Of course, an experienced woodsman and storyteller who has 'always tried to be accurate with facts' (p. 259) would expect that. The rest of us in organizational studies may be pardoned, however, if we find those numbers a good reason to take these data seriously.

Cosmology episodes in Mann Gulch

Early in the book (p. 65), Maclean asks the question on which I want to focus: 'what the structure of a small outfit should be when its business is to meet sudden danger and prevent disaster.' This question is timely because the work of organizations is increasingly done in small temporary outfits in which the stakes are high and where foul-ups can have serious consequences (Heydebrand, 1989; Ancona and Caldwell, 1992). Thus, if we understand what happened at Mann Gulch, we may be able to learn some valuable lessons in how to conceptualize and cope with contemporary organizations.

Let me first be clear about why I think the crew of smokejumpers at Mann Gulch was an organization. First, they have a series of interlocking routines, which is crucial in Westley's (1990: 339) definition of an organization as 'a series of interlocking routines, habituated action patterns that bring the same people together around the same activities in the same time and places.' The crew at Mann Gulch have routine, habituated action patterns, they come together from a common pool of people, and while this set of individual smokejumpers had not come together at the same places or times, they did come together around the same episodes of fire. Westley's definition suggests it doesn't take much to qualify as an organization. The other side is, it also may not take much to stop being one.

Second, the Mann Gulch crew fits the five criteria for a simple organizational structure proposed by Mintzberg (1983: 158). These five include coordination by direct supervision, strategy planned at the top, little formalized behavior, organic structure, and the person in charge tending to formulate plans intuitively, meaning that the plans are generally a direct 'extension of his own personality.' Structures like this are found most often in entrepreneurial firms.

And third, the Mann Gulch crew has 'generic subjectivity' (Wiley, 1988), meaning that roles and rules exist that enable individuals to be interchanged with little disruption to the ongoing pattern of interaction. In the crew at Mann Gulch there were at least three roles: leader, second in command, and crewmember. The person in the lead sizes up the situation, makes decisions, yells orders, picks trails, sets the pace, and identifies escape routes (pp. 65–66). The second in command brings up the rear of the crew as it hikes, repeats orders, sees that the orders are understood, helps the individuals coordinate their actions, and tends to be closer to the crew and more of a buddy with them than does the leader. And finally, the crew clears a fire line around the fire, cleans up after the fire, and maintains trails. Thus, the crew at Mann Gulch is an organization by virtue of a role structure of interlocking routines.

I want to argue that the tragedy at Mann Gulch alerts us to an unsuspected source of vulnerability in organizations. Minimal organizations, such as we find in the crew at Mann Gulch, are susceptible to sudden losses of meaning, which have been variously described as fundamental surprises (Reason, 1990) or events that are inconceivable (Lanir, 1989), hidden (Westrum, 1982), or incomprehensible (Perrow, 1984). Each of these labels points to the low probability that the event could occur, which is why it is meaningless. But these explanations say less about the astonishment of the perceiver, and even less about the perceiver's inability to rebuild some sense of what is happening.

To shift the analytic focus in implausible events from probabilities to feelings and social construction, I have borrowed the term 'cosmology' from philosophy and stretched it. Cosmology refers to a branch of philosophy often subsumed under metaphysics that combines rational speculation and scientific evidence to understand the universe as a totality of phenomena. Cosmology is the ultimate macro perspective, directed at issues of time, space, change, and contingency as they relate to the origin and structure of the universe. Integrations of these issues, however, are not just the handiwork of philosophers. Others also make their peace with these issues, as reflected in what they take for granted. People, including those who are smokejumpers, act as if events cohere in time and space and that change unfolds in an orderly manner. These everyday cosmologies are subject to disruption. And when they are severely disrupted, I call this a cosmology episode (Weick, 1985: 51–52). A cosmology episode occurs when people suddenly and deeply feel that the universe is no longer a rational, orderly system. What makes such an episode so shattering is that both the sense of what is occurring and the means to rebuild that sense collapse together.

Stated more informally, a cosmology episode feels like vu jade – the opposite of deja vu: I've never been here before, I have no idea where I am, and I have no idea who can help me. This is what the smokejumpers may have felt increasingly as the afternoon wore on and they lost what little organization structure they had to start with. As they lost structure they became more anxious and found it harder to make sense of what was happening, until they finally were unable to make any sense whatsoever of the one thing that would have saved their lives, an escape fire. The disaster at Mann Gulch was produced by the inter-related collapse of sensemaking and structure. If we can understand this collapse, we may be able to forestall similar disasters in other organizations.

Sensemaking in Mann Gulch

Although most organizational analyses begin and end with decision making, there is growing dissatisfaction with this orthodoxy. Reed (1991) showed how far the concept of decision making has been stretched, singling out the patching that James G. March has done in recent discussions of decision making. March (1989: 14) wrote that 'decision making is a highly contextual, sacred activity, surrounded by myth and ritual, and as much concerned with the interpretive order as with the specifics of particular choices.' Reed (1991: 561) summarized March this way:

> 'decision making preferences are often inconsistent, unstable, and externally driven; the linkages between decisions and actions are loosely-coupled and interactive rather than linear; the past is notoriously unreliable as a guide to the present or the future; and . . . political and symbolic considerations play a central, perhaps overriding, role in decision making.'

Reed wondered aloud whether, if March is right in these descriptions, decision making should continue to set the agenda for organizational studies. At some point a retreat from classic principles becomes a rout.

There have been at least three distinct responses to these problems. First, there has been a shift, reminiscent of Neisser and Winograd's (1988) work on memory, toward examining naturalistic decision making (Orasanu and Connolly, 1993), with more attention to situational assessment and sensemaking (Klein, 1993). Second, people have replaced an interest in decision making with an interest in power, noting, for example, that 'power is most strategically deployed in the design and implementation of paradigmatic frameworks within which the very meaning of such actions as "making decisions" is defined' (Brown, 1978: 376). And third, people are replacing the less appropriate normative models of rationality (e.g. Hirsch, Michaels, and Friedman, 1987) based on asocial 'economic man' (Beach and Lipshitz, 1993) with more appropriate models of rationality that are more sophisticated about social relations, such as the model of contextual rationality (White, 1988).

Reed (1991) described contextual rationality as action motivated to create and maintain institutions and traditions that express some conception of right behavior and a good life with others. Contextual rationality is sensitive to the fact that social actors need to create and maintain intersubjectively binding normative structures that sustain and enrich their relationships. Thus, organizations become important because they can provide meaning and order in the face of environments that impose ill-defined, contradictory demands.

One way to shift the focus from decision making to meaning is to look more closely at sensemaking in organizations. The basic idea of sensemaking is that reality is an ongoing accomplishment that emerges from efforts to create order and make retrospective sense of what occurs.

Recognition primed decision making, a model based in part on command decisions made by firefighters, has features of sensemaking in its reliance on past experience, although it remains grounded in decision making (Klein, 1993). Sensemaking emphasizes that people try to make things rationally accountable to themselves and others. Thus, in the words of Morgan, Frost, and Pondy (1983: 24),

> 'individuals are not seen as living in, and acting out their lives in relation to, a wider reality, so much as creating and sustaining images of a wider reality, in part to rationalize what they are doing. They realize their reality, by reading into their situation patterns of significant meaning.'

When the smokejumpers landed at Mann Gulch, they expected to find what they had come to call a 10:00 fire. A 10:00 fire is one that can be surrounded completely and isolated by 10:00 the next morning. The spotters on the aircraft that carried the smokejumpers 'figured the crew would have it under control by 10:00 the next morning' (Maclean, p. 43). People rationalized this image until it was too late. And because they did, less and less of what they saw made sense:

1.   The crew expects a 10:00 fire but grows uneasy when this fire does not act like one.
2.   Crewmembers wonder how this fire can be all that serious if Dodge and Harrison eat supper while they hike toward the river.
3.   People are often unclear who is in charge of the crew (p. 65).
4.   The flames on the south side of the gulch look intense, yet one of the smokejumpers, David Navon is taking pictures, so people conclude the fire can't be that serious, even though their senses tell them otherwise.
5.   Crewmembers know they are moving toward the river where they will be safe from the fire, only to see Dodge inexplicably turn them around, away from the river, and start angling upslope, but not running straight for the top. Why? (Dodge is the only one who sees the fire jump the gulch ahead of them.)

6.   As the fire gains on them, Dodge says, 'Drop your tools,' but if the people in the crew do that, then who are they? Firefighters? With no tools?

7.   The foreman lights a fire that seems to be right in the middle of the only escape route people can see.

8.   The foreman points to the fire he has started and yells, 'Join me,' whatever that means. But his second in command sounds like he's saying, 'To hell with that, I'm getting out of here' (p. 95).

9.   Each individual faces the dilemma, I must be my own boss yet follow orders unhesitatingly, but I can't comprehend what the orders mean, and I'm losing my race with the advancing fire (pp. 219–220).

As Mann Gulch loses its resemblance to a 10:00 fire, it does so in ways that make it increasingly hard to socially construct reality. When the noise created by wind, flames, and exploding trees is deafening; when people are strung out in a line and relative strangers to begin with; when they are people who, in Maclean's words, 'love the universe but are not intimidated by it' (p. 28); and when the temperature is approaching a lethal 140 degrees (p. 220), people can neither validate their impressions with a trusted neighbor nor pay close attention to a boss who is also unknown and whose commands make no sense whatsoever. As if these were not obstacles enough, it is hard to make common sense when each person sees something different or nothing at all because of the smoke.

The crew's stubborn belief that it faced a 10:00 fire is a powerful reminder that positive illusions (Taylor, 1989) can kill people. But the more general point is that organizations can be good at decision making and still falter. They falter because of deficient sensemaking. The world of decision making is about strategic rationality. It is built from clear questions and clear answers that attempt to remove ignorance (Daft and MacIntosh, 1981). The world of sensemaking is different. Sensemaking is about contextual rationality. It is built out of vague questions, muddy answers, and negotiated agreements that attempt to reduce confusion. People in Mann Gulch did not face questions like where should we go, when do we take a stand, or what should our strategy be? Instead, they faced the more basic, the more frightening feeling that their old labels were no longer working. They were outstripping their past experience and were not sure either what was up or who they were. Until they develop some sense of issues like this, there is nothing to decide.

Role structure in Mann Gulch

Sensemaking was not the only problem in Mann Gulch. There were also problems of structure. It seems plausible to argue that a major contributor to this disaster was the loss of the only structure that kept these people organized, their role system. There were two key events that destroyed the organization that tied these people together. First, when Dodge told Hellman to take the crew to the north side of the gulch and have it follow a contour down toward the river, the crew got confused, the spaces between members widened appreciably, and Navon – the person taking pictures (p. 71) – made a bid to take over the leadership of the group (p. 651). Notice what this does to the role system. There is now no one at the end of the line repeating orders as a check on the accuracy with which they are understood. Furthermore, the person who is leading them, Hellman, is more familiar with implementing orders than with constructing them or plotting possible escape routes. So the crew is left for a crucial period of time with ill-structured, unacknowledged orders shouted by someone who is unaccustomed to being firm or noticing escape routes. Both routines and interlocking are beginning to come apart.

The second, and in some way more unsettling threat to the role system occurred when Dodge told the retreating crew 'throw away your tools!' (p. 226). A fire crew that retreats from a fire should find its identity and morale strained. If the retreating people are then also told to discard the very things that are their reason for being there in the first place, then the moment quickly turns existential. If I am no longer a firefighter, then who am I? With the fire bearing down, the only possible answer becomes, an endangered person in a world where it is every man for himself. Thus, people who, in Maclean's words, had perpetually been almost their own boss (p. 218) suddenly became completely their own boss at the worst possible moment. As the entity of a crew dissolved, it is not surprising that the final command from the 'crew' leader to jump into an escape fire was heard not as a legitimate order but as the ravings of someone who had 'gone nuts' (p. 75). Dodge's command lost its basis of legitimacy when the smokejumpers threw away their organization along with their tools.

Panic in Mann Gulch

With these observations as background, we can now look more closely at the process of a cosmology episode, an interlude in which the orderliness of the universe is called into question because both understanding and procedures for sensemaking collapse together. People stop thinking and panic. What is interesting about this collapse is that it was discussed by Freud (1959: 28) in the context of panic in military groups:

> 'A panic arises if a group of that kind [military group] becomes disintegrated. Its characteristics are that none of the orders given by superiors are any longer listened to, and that each individual is only solicitous on his own account, and without any consideration for the rest. The mutual ties have ceased to exist, and a gigantic and senseless fear is set free.'

Unlike earlier formulations, such as McDougall's (1920), which had argued that panic leads to group disintegration, Freud, reversing this causality, argued that group disintegration precipitates panic. By group disintegration, Freud meant 'the cessation of all the feelings of consideration which the members of the group otherwise show one another' (p. 29). He described the mechanism involved this way:

'If an individual in panic fear begins to be solicitous only on his own account, he bears witness in so doing to the fact that the emotional ties, which have hitherto made the danger seem small to him, have ceased to exist. Now that he is by himself in facing the danger, he may surely think it greater.'

It is certainly true in Mann Gulch that there is a real, palpable danger that can be seen, felt, heard, and smelled by the smokejumpers. But this is not the first time they have confronted danger. It may, however, be the first time they have confronted danger as a member of a disintegrating organization. As the crew moved toward the river and became more spread out, individuals were isolated and left without explanations or emotional support for their reactions. As the ties weakened, the sense of danger increased, and the means to cope became more primitive. The world rapidly shifted from a cosmos to chaos as it became emptied of order and rationality.

It is intriguing that the three people who survived the disaster did so in ways that seem to forestall group disintegration. Sallee and Rumsey stuck together, their small group of two people did not disintegrate, which helped them keep their fear under control. As a result, they escaped through a crack in the ridge that the others either didn't see or thought was too small to squeeze through. Wag Dodge, as the formal leader of a group he presumed still existed, ordered his followers to join him in the escape fire. Dodge continued to see a group and to think about its well-being, which helped keep his own fear under control. The rest of the people, however, took less notice of one another. Consequently, the group, as they knew it, disintegrated. As their group disintegrated, the smokejumpers became more frightened, stopped thinking sooner, pulled apart even more, and in doing so, lost a leader-follower relationship as well as access to the novel ideas of other people who are a lot like them. As these relationships disappeared, individuals reverted to primitive tendencies of flight. Unfortunately, this response was too simple to match the complexity of the Mann Gulch fire.

What holds organization in place may be more tenuous than we realize. The recipe for disorganization in Mann Gulch is not all that rare in everyday life. The recipe reads, Thrust people into unfamiliar roles, leave some key roles unfilled, make the task more ambiguous, discredit the role system, and make all of these changes in a context in which small events can combine into something monstrous. Faced with similar conditions, organizations that seem much sturdier may also come crashing down (Miller, 1990; Miles and Snow, 1992), much like Icarus who overreached his competence as he flew toward the sun and also perished because of fire.

From vulnerability to resilience

The steady erosion of sense and structure reached its climax in the refusal of the crew to escape one fire by walking into another one that was intentionally set. A closer look at that escape fire allows us to move from a discussion of what went wrong at Mann Gulch, to a discussion of what makes organizations more resilient. I want to discuss four sources of resilience: (1) improvisation and bricolage, (2) virtual role systems, (3) the attitude of wisdom, and (4) respectful interaction.

Improvisation and bricolage

The escape fire is a good place to start in the search for sources of resilience simply because it is clear evidence that, minimal though the organization of the crew might have been, there still was a solution to the crisis inside the group. The problem was, no one but Dodge recognized this. The question then becomes: How could more people either see this escape fire as a solution or develop their own solution? This is not an easy question to answer because, from everything we know, Dodge's invention of burning a hole in a fire should not have happened. It should not have happened because there is good evidence that when people are put under pressure, they regress to their most habituated ways of responding (e.g. Barthol and Ku, 1959). This is what we see in the 15 people who reject Dodge's order to join him and who resort instead to flight, a more overlearned tendency. What we do not expect under life-threatening pressure is creativity.

The tactic of lighting a fire to create an area where people can escape a major prairie fire is mentioned in James Fenimore Cooper's 1827 novel *The Prairie*, but there is no evidence Dodge knew this source (Maclean, p. 104). Furthermore, most of Dodge's experience had been in timbered country where such a tactic wouldn't work. In timber, an escape fire is too slow and consumes too much oxygen (p. 105). And the fire that Dodge built did not burn long enough to clear an area in which people could move around and dodge the fire as they did in the prairie fire. There was just room enough to lie down in the ashes where the heat was less intense (p. 104).

While no one can say how or why the escape fire was created, there is a line of argument that is consistent with what we know. Bruner (1983: 183) described creativity as 'figuring out how to use what you already know in order to go beyond what you currently think.' With this as background, it now becomes relevant that Dodge was an experienced woodsman, with lots of hands-on experience. He was what we now would call a bricoleur, someone able to create order out of whatever materials were at hand (e.g. Levi-Strauss, 1966; Harper, 1987). Dodge would have known at least two things about fires. He would have known the famous fire triangle – you must have oxygen, flammable material, and temperature above the point of ignition to create a fire (Maclean. p. 35). A shortage of any one of these would prevent a fire. In his case, the escape fire removed flammable material. And since Dodge had been with the Forest Service longer than anyone else on the crew, he would also have known more fully their four guidelines at that time for dealing with fire emergencies (p. 100). These included (1) start a backfire if you can, (2) get to the top of a ridge where the fuel is thinner, (3) turn into the fire and try to work through it, and (4) don't allow the fire to pick the spot where it hits you. Dodge's invention, if we stretch a bit, fits all four. It is a backfire, though not in the conventional sense of a fire built to stop a fire. The escape fire is lit near the top of a ridge, Dodge turns into the main fire and works through it by burning a hole in it, and he chooses where the fire hits him. The 15 who tried to outrun the fire moved toward the ridge but by not facing the fire, they allowed it to pick the spot where it hit them.

The collapse of role systems need not result in disaster if people develop skills in improvisation and bricolage (see Janowitz, 1959: 481). Bricoleurs remain creative under pressure, precisely because they routinely act in chaotic conditions and pull order out of them. Thus, when situations unravel, this is simply normal natural trouble for bricoleurs, and they proceed with whatever materials are at hand. Knowing these materials intimately, they then are able, usually in the company of other similarly skilled people, to form the materials or insights into novel combinations.

While improvised fire fighting may sound improbable, in fact, Park Service firefighters like those stationed at the Grand Canyon approximate just such a style. Stephen Pyne (1989), a Park Service firefighter, observed that people like him typically have discretion to dispatch themselves, which is unfathomable to the Forest Service crews that rely on dispatchers, specialization, regimentation, rules, and a conscious preference for the strength of the whole rather than the versatility and resourcefulness of the parts. Forest Service people marvel at the freedom of movement among the Park people. Park Service people marvel at how much power the Forest Service is able to mobilize on a fire. Pyne (1989: 122) described the Park Service fire operations as a nonstandard 'eclectic assembly of compromises' built of discretion and mobility. In contrast to the Forest Service, where people do everything by the book, 'The Park Service has no books; it puts a premium on the individual. Its collective behavior is tribal, and it protects its permanent ranks.' If improvisation were given more attention in the job description of a crew person, that person's receptiveness to and generation of role improvisations might be enhanced. As a result, when one organizational order collapses, a substitute might be invented immediately. Swift replacement of a traditional order with an improvised order would forestall the paralysis that can follow a command to 'drop your tools.'

Virtual role systems

Social construction of reality is next to impossible amidst the chaos of a fire, unless social construction takes place inside one person's head, where the role system is reconstituted and run. Even though the role system at Mann Gulch collapsed, this kind of collapse need not result in disaster if the system remains intact in the individual's mind. If each individual in the crew mentally takes all roles and therefore can then register escape routes and acknowledge commands and facilitate coordination, then each person literally becomes a group (Schutz, 1961). And, in the manner of a holograph, each person can reconstitute the group and assume whatever role is vacated, pick up the activities, and run a credible version of the role. Furthermore, people can run the group in their head and use it for continued guidance of their own individual action. It makes just as much sense to talk about a virtual role system as it does to talk about a virtual anything else (e.g. Bruner, 1986: 337). An organization can continue to function in the imagination long after it has ceased to function in tangible distributed activities. For the Mann Gulch fire, this issue has bearing on the question of escape routes. In our research on accidents in flight operations off nuclear carriers (Weick and Roberts, 1993), Karlene Roberts and I found that people who avoid accidents live by the credo, 'never get into anything without making sure you have a way out.' At the very last moment in the Mann Gulch tragedy, Dodge discovered a way out. The point is that if other people had been able to simulate Dodge and/or his role in their imagination, they too might have been less puzzled by his solution or better able to invent a different sensible solution for themselves.

The attitude of wisdom

To understand the role of wisdom (Bigelow, 1992) as a source of resilience, we need to return to the crew's belief that all fires are 10:00 fires. This belief was consistent with members' experience. As Maclean put it, if the major purpose of your group is to 'put out fires so fast they don't have time to become big ones' (p. 31), then you won't learn much about fighting big fires. Nor will you learn what Maclean calls the first principle of reality: 'little things suddenly and literally can become big as hell, the ordinary can suddenly become monstrous, ad the upgulch breezes can suddenly turn to murder' (p. 217). To state the point more generally, what most organizations miss, and what explains why most organizations fail to learn (Scott, 1987: 282), is that 'Reality backs up while it is approached by the subject who tries to understand it. Ignorance and knowledge grow together' (Meacham, 1983: 130). To put it a different way,

> 'Each new domain of knowledge appears simple from the distance of ignorance. The more we learn about a particular domain, the greater the number of uncertainties, doubts. questions and complexities. Each bit of knowledge serves as the thesis from which additional questions or antithesis arise.'
>
> (Meacham, 1983: 120)

The role system best able to accept the reality that ignorance and knowledge grow together may be one in which the organizational culture values wisdom. Meacham (1983: 187) argued that wisdom is an attitude rather than a skill or a body of information.

To be wise is not to know particular facts but to know without excessive confidence or excessive cautiousness. Wisdom is thus not a belief, a value, a set of facts, a corpus of knowledge or information in some specialized area, or a set of special abilities or skills. Wisdom is an attitude taken by persons toward the beliefs, values, knowledge, information, abilities, and skills that are held, a tendency to doubt that these are necessarily true or valid and to doubt that they are an exhaustive set of those things that could be known.

In a fluid world, wise people know that they don't fully understand what is happening right now, because they have never seen precisely this event before. Extreme confidence and extreme caution both can destroy what organizations most need in changing times, namely, curiosity, openness, and complex sensing. The overconfident shun curiosity because they feel they know most of what there is to know. The overcautious shun curiosity for fear it will only deepen their uncertainties. Both the cautious and the confident are closed-minded, which means neither makes good judgments. It is this sense in which wisdom, which avoids extremes, improves adaptability.

A good example of wisdom in groups is the Naskapi Indians' use of caribou shoulder bones to locate game (Weick, 1979). They hold bones over a fire until they crack and then hunt in the directions to which the cracks point. This ritual is effective because the decision is not influenced by the outcomes of past hunts, which means the stock of animals is not depleted. More important, the final decision is not influenced by the inevitable patterning in human choice, which enables hunted animals to become sensitized to humans and take evasive action. The wisdom inherent in this practice derives from its ambivalence toward the past. Any attempt to hunt for caribou is both a new experience and an old experience. It is new in the sense that time has elapsed, the composition of the hunter band has changed, the caribou have learned new things, and so forth. But the hunt is also old in the sense that if you've seen one hunt, you've seen them all. There are always hunters, weapons, stealth, decoys, tracks, odors, and winds. The practice of divination incorporates the attitude of wisdom because past experience is discounted when a new set of cracks forms a crude map for the hunt. But past experience is also given some weight, because a seasoned hunter 'reads' the cracks and injects some of his own past experience into an interpretation of what the cracks mean. The reader is crucial. If the reader's hunches dominate, randomization is lost. If the cracks dominate, then the experience base is discarded. The cracks are a lot like the four guidelines for fire emergencies that Dodge may have relied on when he invented the escape fire. They embody experience, but they invite doubt, reassembly, and shaping to fit novelties in the present.

Respectful interaction

The final suggestion about how to counteract vulnerability makes explicit the preceding focus on the individual and social interaction. Respectful interaction depends on intersubjectivity (Wiley, 1988: 258), which has two defining characteristics: (1) Intersubjectivity emerges from the interchange and synthesis of meanings among two or more communicating selves, and (2) the self or subject gets transformed during interaction such that a joint or merged subjectivity develops. It is possible that many role systems do not change fast enough to keep up with a rapidly changing environment. The only form that can keep up is one based on face-to-face interaction. And it is here, rather than in routines, that we are best able to see the core of organizing. This may be why interaction in airline cockpit crews, such as discussed by Foushee (1984), strikes us so often as a plausible microcosm of what happens in much larger systems. In a cockpit under crisis, the only unit that makes sense (pun intended) is face-to-face synthesis of meaning.

Intersubjectivity was lost on everyone at Mann Gulch, everyone, that is, but Sallee and Rumsey. They stuck together and lived. Dodge went his own individual way with a burst of improvisation, and he too lived. Perhaps it's more important that you have a partner than an organization when you fight fires. A partner makes social construction easier. A partner is a second source of ideas. A partner strengthens independent judgment in the face of a majority. And a partner enlarges the pool of data that are considered. Partnerships that endure are likely to be those that adhere to Campbell's three imperatives for social life, based on a reanalysis of Asch's (1952) conformity experiment:

(1)   Respect the reports of others and be willing to base beliefs and actions on them (trust);
(2)   Report honestly so that others may use your observations in coming to valid beliefs (honesty); and,
(3)   Respect your own perceptions and beliefs and seek to integrate them with the reports of others without depreciating them or yourselves (self-respect) (adapted from Campbell, 1990: 45–46).

Earlier I noted a growing interest in contextual rationality, understood as actions that create and maintain institutions and traditions that express some conception of right behavior and a good life with others (Reed, 1991). Campbell's maxims operationalize this good life with others as trust, honesty, and self-respect in moment-to-moment interaction. This triangle of trust, honesty, and self-respect is conspicuously missing (e.g. King, 1989: 448) in several well-documented disasters in which faulty interaction processes led to increased fear, diminished communication, and death. For example, in the Tenerife air disaster (Weick, 1990), the copilot of the KLM aircraft had a strong hunch that another 747 airplane was on the takeoff runway directly in front of them when his own captain began takeoff without clearance. But the copilot said nothing about either the suspicions or the illegal departure. Transient cockpit crews, tied together by narrow definitions of formal responsibilities, and headed by captains who mis-takenly assume that their decision-making ability is unaffected by increases in stress (Helmreich et al., 1985), have few protections against a sudden loss of meaning such as the preposterous possibility that a captain is taking off without clearance, directly into the path of another 747.

Even when people try to act with honesty, trust, and self-respect, if they do so with little social support, their efforts are compromised. For example, lin-guists who analyzed the conversations at Tenerife and in the crash of Air Florida flight 90 in Washington concluded that the copilots in both cases used 'devices of mitigation' to soften the effects of their requests and suggestions.

A mitigated instruction might be phrased as a question or hedged with qualifications such as 'would' or 'could.' . . . (I)t was found that the speech of subordinate crew members was much more likely to be mitigated than the speech of captains. It was also found that topics introduced in mitigated speech were less likely to be followed-up by other crew members and less likely to be ratified by the captain. Both of these effects relate directly to the situation in which a subordinate crew member makes a correct solution that is ignored. . . . The value of training in unmitigated speech is strongly suggested by these results (O'Hare and Roscoe, 1940: 219).

If a role system collapses among people for whom trust, honesty, and self-respect are underdeveloped, then they are on their own. And fear often swamps their resourcefulness. If, however, a role system collapses among people where trust, honesty, and self-respect are more fully developed, then new options, such as mutual adaptation, blind imitation of creative solutions, and trusting compliance, are created. When a formal structure collapses, there is no leader, no roles, no routines, no sense. That is what we may be seeing in Mann Gulch. Dodge can't lead because the role system in which he is a leader disappears. But what is worse, Dodge can't rely on his crewmembers to trust him, question him, or pay attention to him, because they don't know him and there is no time to change this. The key question is: When formal structure collapses, what, if anything, is left? The answer to that question may well be one of life or death.

Structures for resilience

While the answer to that question is not a matter of life or death for organizational theorists, they do have an interest in how it comes out. A theorist who hears Maclean's question, 'what the structure of a small outfit should be when its business is to meet sudden danger and prevent disaster,' might come back with a series of follow-up questions based on thinking in organizational studies. I look briefly at four such questions to link Mann Gulch with other concepts and to suggest how these linkages might guide further research.

First, there is the follow-up question. Is 'small' necessarily a key dimension, since this group is also young and transient? Maclean calls the 16-person smoke-jumper crew 'small,' except that it is conventional in the group literature to treat any group of more than 10 people as large (Bass, 1990: 604). Because there is so little communication within the crew and because it operates largely through obtrusive controls like rules and supervision (Perrow, 1986), it acts more like a large formal group with mediated communication than a small informal group with direct communication.

It is striking how little communication occurred during the three and a half hours of this episode. There was little discussion during the noisy, bumpy plane ride, and even less as individuals retrieved equipment scattered on the north slope. After a quick meal together, people began hiking toward the river but quickly got separated from one another. Then they were suddenly turned around, told to run for the ridge, and quickly ran out of breath as they scaled the steep south slope. The minimal communication is potentially important because of the growing evidence (e.g. Eisenhardt, 1993: 132) that nonstop talk, both vocal and nonverbal, is a crucial source of coordination in complex systems that are susceptible to catastrophic disasters.

The lack of communication, coupled with the fact that this is a temporary group in the early stages of its history, should heighten the group's vulnerability to disruption. As Bass (1990: 637) put it, 'Groups that are unable to interact easily or that do not have the formal or informal structure that enables quick reactions are likely to experience stress (Bass, 1960). Panic ensues when members of a group lack superordinate goals – goals that transcend the self-interests of each participant.' While the smokejumpers have the obvious superordinate goal of containing fires, their group ties may not be sufficiently developed for this to be a group goal that overrides self-interest. Or Bass's proposition itself may be incomplete, failing to acknowledge that unless superordinate goals are overlearned, they will be discarded in situations of danger.

Second, there is the follow-up question, Is 'structure' what we need to understand in Mann Gulch, or might structuring also be important? By structure, I mean 'a complex medium of control which is continually produced and recreated in interaction and yet shapes that interaction: structures are constituted and constitutive . . . of interpersonal cognitive processes, power dependencies, and contextual constraints' (Ranson, Hinings, and Greenwood, 1980: 1, 3). Structuring, then, consists of two patterns and the relationships between them. The first pattern, which Ranson *et al.* variously described as informal structure, agency, or social construction, consists of interaction patterns that stabilize meaning by creating shared interpretive schemes. I refer to this pattern as shared provinces of meaning, or meaning. The second pattern, variously described as configuration, contextual constraints, or a vehicle that embodies dominant meanings, refers to a framework of roles, rules, procedures, configured activities, and authority relations that reflect and facilitate meanings. I refer to this second pattern as structural frameworks of constraint, or frameworks.

Meanings affect frameworks, which affect meaning. This is the basic point of the growing body of work on structuration (e.g. Riley, 1983; Poole, Seibold, and McPhee, 1985), understood as the mutual constitution of frameworks and meanings (Ranson, Hinings, and Greenwood, 1980) or relations and typifications (DiMaggio, 1991) or structures and structuring (Barley, 1986). Missing in this work is attention to reversals of structuration (Giddens, 1984). The use of descriptive words in structuration theory such as 'continually produced,' 'recreated in interaction,' 'constituted,' and 'constitutive' directs attention away from losses of frameworks and losses of meaning. For example, Ranson, Hinings, and Greenwood (1980: 5) asserted that the 'deep structure of schema which are taken for granted by members enables them to recognize, interpret, and negotiate even strange and unanticipated situations, and thus continuously to create and reenact the sense and meaning of structural forms during the course of interaction.' The Mann Gulch disaster is a case in which people were unable to negotiate strangeness. Frameworks and meanings destroyed rather than constructed one another.

This fugitive quality of meaning and frameworks in Mann Gulch suggests that the process of structuring itself may be more unstable than we realized. Structuring, understood as constitutive relations between meaning and frameworks, may be a deviation-amplifying cause loop (Maruyama, 1963; Weick, 1979) capable of intensifying either an increase or decrease in either of the two connected elements. Typically, we see instances of increase in which more shared meanings lead to more elaborate frameworks of roles, which lead to further developments of shared meaning, etc. What we fail to realize is that, when elements are tied together in this direct manner, once one of them declines, this decline can also spread and become amplified as it does so. Fewer shared meanings lead to less elaborate frameworks, less meaning, less elaborate frameworks, and so on. Processes that mutually constitute also have the capability to mutually destroy one another.

If structuration is treated as a deviation-amplifying process, then this suggests the kind of structure that could have prevented the Mann Gulch disaster. What people needed was a structure in which there was both an inverse and a direct relationship between role systems and meaning. This is the only pattern that can maintain resilience in the face of crisis. The resilience can take one of two forms. Assume that we start with an amplifying system like the one in Mann Gulch. The role system lost its structure, which led to a loss of meaning, which led to a further loss of structure, and so on. This is the pattern associated with a deviation-amplifying feedback loop in which an initial change unfolds unchecked in the same direction. One way to prevent this amplification is to retain the direct relation between structure and meaning (less role structure leads to less meaning, more structure leads to more meaning) but create an inverse relation between meaning and structure (less meaning, more structure, and vice versa). This inverse relationship can be understood as follows: When meaning becomes problematic and decreases, this is a signal for people to pay more attention to their formal and informal social ties and to reaffirm and/or reconstruct them. These actions produce more structure, which then increases meaning, which then decreases the attention directed at structure. Puzzlement intensifies attentiveness to the social, which reduces puzzlement.

The other form of control arises when a change in structure, rather than a change in meaning, is responsible for counteracting the fluctuations in sensibleness. In this variation, less structure leads to more meaning, and more meaning then produces more structure. The inverse relationship between structure and meaning can be understood this way: When social ties deteriorate, people try harder to make their own individual sense of what is happening, both socially and in the world. These operations increase meaning, and they increase the tendency to reshape structure consistent with heightened meaning. Alienation intensifies attentiveness to meaning, which reduces alienation.

What is common to both of these controlled forms is an alternation between attention to frameworks and attention to meanings. More attention to one leads to more ignorance of the other, followed by efforts to correct this imbalance, which then creates a new imbalance. In the first scenario, when meaning declines, people pay more attention to frameworks, they ignore meaning temporarily, and as social relations become clearer, their attention shifts back to meanings. In the second scenario, when social relations decline, people pay more attention to meaning, they ignore frameworks temporarily, and as meanings become clearer, attention shifts back to frameworks. Both scenarios illustrate operations of wisdom: In Meacham's words, ignorance and knowledge grow together. Either of these two controlled patterns should reduce the likelihood of disaster in Mann Gulch. As the smokejumpers begin to lose structure they either also lose meaning, which alerts them to be more attentive to the structure they are losing or they gain individual meaning, which leads them to realign structure. The second alternative may be visible in the actions taken by Dodge and Rumsey and Sallee.

This may seem like a great deal of fretting about one single word in Maclean's question, 'structure.' What I have tried to show is that when we transform this word from a static image into a process, we spot what looks like a potential for collapse in any process of social sensemaking that is tied together by constitutive relations. And we find that social sensemaking may be most stable when it is simultaneously constitutive and destructive, when it is capable of increasing both ignorance and knowledge at the same time. That seems like a fair return for reflecting on a single word.

Third, there is the follow-up question, Is 'outfit' the best way to describe the smokejumpers? An outfit is normally defined as 'a group associated in an undertaking requiring close cooperation, as a military unit' (Random House, 1987: 1374). The smokejumpers are tied together largely by pooled interdependence, since the job of each one is to clear adjacent portions of a perimeter area around a blaze so that the fire stops for lack of fuel. Individual efforts to clear away debris are pooled and form a fire line. What is significant about pooled interdependence is that it can function without much cohesion (Bass, 1990: 622). And this is what may have trapped the crew. Given the constantly changing composition of the smokejumping crews, the task largely structured their relations. Simply acting in concert was enough, and there was no need to know each other well in addition. This social form resembles what Eisenberg (1990: 160) called nondisclosive intimacy, by which he meant relationships rooted in collective action that stress 'coordination of action over the alignment of cognitions, mutual respect over agreement, trust over empathy, diversity over homogeneity, loose over tight coupling, and strategic communication over unrestricted candor.' Nondisclosive intimacy is a sufficient ground for relating as long as the task stays constant and the environment remains stable.

What the Mann Gulch disaster suggests is that nondisclosive intimacy may limit the development of emotional ties that keep panic under control in the face of obstacles. Closer ties permit clearer thinking, which enables people to find paths around obstacles. For example, when Rumsey squeezed through a crevice in the ridge just ahead of the fire, he collapsed 'half hysterically' into a juniper bush, where he would have soon burned to death. His partner Sallee stopped next to him, looked at him coldly, never said a word, and just stood there until Rumsey roused himself, and the two then ran together over the ridge and down to a rock slide where they were better able to move around and duck the worst flames (Maclean, p. 107). Sallee's surprisingly nuanced prodding of his partner suggests the power of close ties to moderate panic.

One might expect that the less threatening the environment, the less important are relational issues in transient groups, but as Perrow (1984) emphasized in his normal accident theory, there are few safe environments. If events are increasingly interdependent, then small unrelated flaws can interact to produce something monstrous. Maclean saw this clearly at Mann Gulch: The colossal fire blowup in Mann Gulch was 'shaped by little screwups that fitted together tighter and tighter until all became one and the same thing – the fateful blowup. Such is much of tragedy in modern times and probably always has been except that past tragedy refrained from speaking of its association with screwups and blowups' (Maclean, 1992: 92).

Nondisclosive intimacy is not the only alternative to 'outfit' as a way to describe the smokejumpers. Smith (1983) argued that individual behaviors, perceptions of reality, identities, and acts of leadership are influenced by intergroup processes. Of special relevance to Mann Gulch is Smith's reanalysis of the many groups that formed among the 16 members of the Uruguayan soccer team who survived for 10 weeks in an inaccessible region of the Chilean Andes mountains after their aircraft, carrying 43 people, crashed (see Read, 1974 for the original account of this event). Aside from the eerie coincidence that both disasters involved 16 young males, Smith's analysis makes the important point that 16 people are not just an outfit, they are a social system within which multiple groups emerge and relate to one another. It is these intergroup relationships that determine what will be seen as acts of leadership and which people may be capable of supplying those acts. In the Andes crash, demands shifted from caring for the wounded, in which two medical students took the lead, to acquiring food and water, where the team captain became leader, to articulating that the group would not be rescued and could sustain life only if people consumed the flesh of the dead, to executing and resymbolizing this survival tactic, to selecting and equipping an expeditionary group to hike out and look for help, and finally to finding someone able to explain and rationalize their decisions to the world once they had been rescued.

What Smith shows is that this group of 16 forms and reforms in many different directions during its history, each time with a different coherent structure of people at the top, middle, and bottom, each with different roles. What also becomes clear is that any attempt to pinpoint the leader or to explain survival by looking at a single set of actions is doomed to failure because it does not reflect how needs change as a crisis unfolds, nor does it reflect how different coherent groupings form to meet the new needs.

The team in the Andes had 10 weeks and changing threats of bleeding, hygiene, starvation, avalanche, expedition, rescue, and accounting, whereas the team in Mann Gulch had more like 10 minutes and the increasingly singular threat of being engulfed in fire. Part of the problem in Mann Gulch is the very inability for intergroup structures to form. The inability to form subgroups within the system may be due to such things as time pressure, the relative unfamiliarity of the smokejumpers with one another compared with the interdependent members of a visible sports team, the inability to communicate, the articulation of a common threat very late in the smokejumpers' exposure to Mann Gulch, and ambiguity about means that would clearly remove the threat, compared with the relative clarity of the means needed by the soccer players to deal with each of their threats.

The point is, whatever chance the smokejumpers might have had to survive Mann Gulch is not seen as clearly if we view them as a single group rather than as a social system capable of differentiating into many different sets of subgroups.

The earlier discussion of virtual role systems suggested that an intergroup perspective could be simulated in the head and that this should heighten resilience. Smith makes it clear that, virtual or not, intergroup dynamics affect survival, even if we overlook them in our efforts to understand the group or the 'outfit.'

As a fourth and final follow-up question. If there is a structure that enables people to meet sudden danger, who builds and maintains it? A partial answer is Ken Smith's intergroup analysis, suggesting that the needed structure consists of many structures, built and maintained by a shifting configuration of the same people. As I said, this perspective makes sense when time is extended, demands change, and there is no formal leader at the beginning of the episode. But there is a leader in Mann Gulch, the foreman. There is also a second in command and the remaining crew, which means there is a top (foreman), middle (second in command), and bottom (remaining crew). If we take this a priori structure seriously, then the Mann Gulch disaster can be understood as a dramatic failure of leadership, reminiscent of those lapses in leadership increasingly well documented by people who study cockpit/crew resource management in aircraft accidents (e.g. Wiener, Kanki, and Helmreich, 1993).

The captain of an aircrew, who is analogous to a player-coach on a basketball team (Hackman, 1993: 55), can often have his or her greatest impact on team functioning before people get into a tight, time-critical situation. Ginnett (1993) has shown that aircraft captains identified by check airmen as excellent team leaders spent more time team building when the team first formed than did leaders judged as less expert. Leaders of highly effective teams briefed their crewmembers on four issues: the task, crew boundaries, standards and expected behaviors (norms), and authority dynamics. Captains spent most time on those of the four that were not predefined by the organizational context within which the crew worked. Typically, this meant that excellent captains did not spend much time on routinized tasks, but less-excellent captains did. Crew boundaries were enlarged and made more permeable by excellent captains when, for example, they regarded the flight attendants, gate personnel, and air traffic controllers as members of the total flight crew. This contrasts with less-excellent captains, who drew a boundary around the people in the cockpit and separated them from everyone else.

Excellent captains modeled norms that made it clear that safety, effective communication, and cooperation were expected from everyone. Of special interest, because so little communication occurred at Mann Gulch, is how the norm, 'communication is important,' was expressed. Excellent crews expect one another to enact any of these four exchanges: '(1) I need to talk to you; (2) I listen to you; (3) I need you to talk to me; or even (4) I expect you to talk to me' (Ginnett, 1993: 88). These four complement and operationalize the spirit of Campbell's social imperatives of trust, honesty, and self-respect. But they also show the importance of inquiry, advocacy, and assertion when people do not understand the reasons why other people are doing something or ignoring something (Helmreich and Foushee, 1993: 21).

Issues of authority are handled differently by excellent captains. They shift their behaviors between complete democracy and complete autocracy during the briefing and thereafter, which makes it clear that they are capable of a range of styles. They establish competence and their capability to assume legitimate authority by doing the briefing in a rational manner, comfortably, with appropriate technical language, all of which suggests that they have given some thought to the upcoming flight and have constructed a framework within which the crew will work.

Less autocratic than this enactment of their legitimate authority is their willingness to disavow perfection. A good example of a statement that tells crewmembers they too must take responsibility for one another is this: 'I just want you guys to understand that they assign the seats in this airplane based on seniority, not on the basis of competence. So anything you can see or do that will help out, I'd sure appreciate hearing about it' (Ginnett, 1993: 90). Notice that the captain is not saying, I am not competent to be the captain. Instead, the captain is saying, we're all fallible. We all make mistakes. Let's keep an eye on one another and speak up when we think a mistake is being made.

Most democratic and participative is the captain's behavior to engage the crew. Briefings held by excellent captains last no longer than do those of the less-excellent captains, but excellent captains talk less, listen more, and resort less to 'canned presentations.'

Taken together, all of these team-building activities increase the probability that constructive, informed interactions can still occur among relative strangers even when they get in a jam. If we compare the leadership of aircraft captains to leadership in Mann Gulch, it is clear that Wag Dodge did not build his team of smokejumpers in advance. Furthermore, members of the smokejumper crew did not keep each other informed of what they were doing or the reasons for their actions or the situational model they were using to generate these reasons. These multiple failures of leadership may be the result of inadequate training, inadequate understanding of leadership processes in the late '40s, or may be attributable to a culture emphasizing individual work rather than group work. Or these failures of leadership may reflect the fact that even the best leaders and the most team-conscious members can still suffer when structures begin to pull apart, leaving in their wake senselessness, panic, and cosmological questions. If people are lucky, and interpersonally adept, their exposure to questions of cosmology is confined to an episode. If they are not, that exposure stretches much further. Which is just about where Maclean would want us to end.

References

Ancona, Deborah G. and Caldwell, David F. (1992) "Bridging the boundary: External activity and performance in organizational teams", *Administrative Science Quarterly*, 37: 634–665.

Asch, Solomon (1952) *Social Psychology*, Prentice-Hall: Englewood Cliffs, NJ.

Barley, Stephen R. (1986) "Technology as an occasion for structuring: Evidence from observations of CT scanners and the social order of radiology departments", *Administrative Science Quarterly*, 31: 78–108.

Barthol, R. P. and Ku, N. D. (1959) "Regression under stress to first learned behavior", *Journal of Abnormal and Social Psychology*, 59: 134–136.

Bass, Bernard M. (1960) *Leadership, Psychology, and Organizational Behavior*, Harper: New York.

— (1990) Bass and Stogdill, *Handbook of Leadership*, Free Press: New York.

Beach, Lee R. and Raanan Lipshitz (1993) "Why classical decision theory is an inappropriate standard for evaluation and aiding most human decision making", in Klein, Gary A., Orasnu, Judith, Calderwood, Roberta and Zsambok, Caroline E. (eds), *Decision Making in Action: Models and Methods*, 2135, Ablex: Norwood, NJ.

Bigelow, John (1992) "Developing managerial wisdom", *Journal of Management Inquiry*, 1: 143–153.

Brown, Richard Harvey (1978) "Bureaucracy as praxis: Toward a political phenomenology of formal organizations", *Administrative Science Quarterly*, 23: 365–382.

Bruner, Jerome (1983) *In Search of Mind*, Harper: New York.

Bruner, Jerome (1986) *Actual Minds, Possible Worlds*, Harvard University Press: Cambridge, MA.

Campbell, Donald T. (1990) "Asch's moral epistemology for socially shared knowledge." in Irwin Rock (ed.), *The Legacy of Solomon Asch: Essays in Cognition and Social Psychology*, 39–52, Erlbaum: Hillsdale, NJ.

Daft, Richard L. and MacIntosh, Norman B. (1981) "A tentative exploration into the amount and equivocality of information processing in organizational work units", *Administrative Science Quarterly*, 26: 207–224.

DiMaggio, Paul (1991) "The micro-macro dilemma in organizational research: Implications of role-system theory", in Joan Huber (ed.), *Micro-macro Changes in Sociology*, 7–98, Sage: Newbury Park, CA.

Eisenberg, Eric M. (1990) "Jamming: Transcendence through organizing", *Communication Research*, 17: 139–164.

Eisenhardt, Kathleen M. (1993) "High reliability organizations meet high velocity environments: Common dilemmas in nuclear power plants, aircraft carriers, and microcomputer firms", in Karlene H. Roberts (ed.), *New Challenges to Understanding Organizations*, 117–135, Macmillan: New York.

Foushee, H. Clayton (1984) "Dyads and triads at 35,000 feet", *American Psychologist*, 39: 885–898.

Freud, Sigmund (1959) *Group Psychology and the Analysis of the Ego*, first published in 1922, Norton: New York.

Giddens, Anthony (1984) *The Constitution of Society*, University of California Press: Berkeley.

Ginnett, Robert C. (1993) "Crews as groups: Their formation and their leadership", in Weiner, Earl L., Kanki, Barbara G. and Helmreich, Robert L. (eds), *Cockpit Resource Management*, 71–98, Academic Press: San Diego.

Hackman, J. Richard (1993) "Teams, leaders, and organizations: New directions for crew-oriented flight training", in Wiener, Earl L., Kanki, Barbara G. and Helmreich, Robert L. (eds), *Cockpit Resource Management*, 47–69, Academic Press: San Diego.

Harper, Douglas (1987) *Working Knowledge: Skill and Community in a Small Shop*, University of Chicago Press: Chicago.

Helmreich, Robert L. and Foushee, Clayton (1993) "Why crew resource management? Empirical and theoretical bases of human factors training in aviation", in Weiner, Earl L., Kanki, Barbara G. and Helmreich, Robert L. (eds), *Cockpit Resource Management*, 35, Academic Press: San Diego.

Helmreich, Robert L., Foushee, Clayton H., Benson, R. and Russini, W. (1985) "Cockpit resource management: Exploring the attitude-performance linkage", paper presented at Third Aviation Psychology Symposium, Ohio State University.

Heydebrand, Wolf V. (1989) "New organizational forms" *Work and Occupations*, 16: 323–357.

Hirsch, Paul, Michaels, Stuart and Friedman, Ray (1987) " "Dirty hands" vs. "clean models": Is sociology in danger of being seduced by economics?", *Theory and Society*, 16: 317–336.

Janowitz, Morris (1959) "Changing patterns of organizational authority: The military establishment", *Administrative Science Quarterly*, 3: 473–493.

King, Jonathan B. (1989) "Confronting chaos", *Journal of Business Ethics*, 8: 39–50.

Klein, Gary A. (1993) "A recognition-primed decision (RPD) model of rapid decision making", in Klein, Gary A., Orasanu, Judith, Calderwood, Roberta and Zsambok, Caroline E. (eds) *Decision Making in Action: Models and Methods*, 138–147, Ablex: Norwood, N.J.

Lanir, Zvi (1989) "The reasonable choice of disaster: The shooting down of the Libyan airliner on 21 February 1973", *Journal of Strategic Studies*, 12: 479–493.

Levi-Strauss, Claude (1966) *The Savage Mind*, University of Chicago Press: Chicago.

McDougall, William (1920) *The Group Mind*, Putnam: New York.

Maclean, Norman (1992) *Young Men and Fire*, University of Chicago Press: Chicago.

March, James G. (1989) *Decisions and Organizations*, Blackwell: Oxford.

Maruyama, Magorah (1963) "The second cybernetics: Deviation-amplifying mutual causal process", *American Scientist*, 51: 164–179.

Meacham, John A. (1983) "Wisdom and the context of knowledge", in Kuhn, D. and Meacham, J.A. (eds), *Contributions in Human Development*, 8: 111–134, Karger: Basel.

Miles, Ray E. and Snow, Charles C. (1992) "Causes of failure in network organizations" *California Management Review*, 84 (4): 53–72.

Miller, Danny (1990) *The Icarus Paradox*, Harper: New York.

Mintzberg, Henry (1983) *Structure in Fives: Designing Effective Organizations*, Prentice-Hall: Englewood Cliffs, NJ.

Morgan, Gareth, Frost, Peter J. and Pondy, Louis R. (1983) "Organizational symbolism", in Pondy, L. R., Frost, P. J., Morgan, G. and Dandridge, T. C. (eds), *Organizational Symbolism*, 935, JAI Press: Greenwich, CT.

Neisser, Ulric and Winograd, Eugene (1988) *Remembering Reconsidered: Ecological and Traditional Approaches to the Study of Memory*, Cambridge University Press: New York.

O'Hare, David, and Roscoe, Stanley (1940) *1990 Flightdeck Performance: The Human Factor*, Iowa State University Press: Ames, IA.

Orasanu, Judith and Connolly, Terry (1993) "The reinvention of decision making", in Gary A. Klein, Orasanu, Judith, Calderwood, Roberta and Zsambok, Caroline E. (eds), *Decision Making in Action: Models and Methods*, 3–20, Ablex: Norwood, NJ.

Perrow, Charles (1984) *Normal Accidents*, Basic Books: New York.

— (1986) *Complex Organizations*, 3rd ed., Random House: New York.

Poole, M. Scott, Seibold, David R. and McPhee, Robert D. (1985) "Group decision-making as a structurational process", *Quarterly Journal of Speech*, 71: 74–102

Pyne, Stephen (1989) *Fire on the Rim*, Weidenfeld & Nicolson: New York.

Random House (1987) *Dictionary of the English Language*, 2nd ed.: Unabridged, Random House: New York.

Ranson, Stewart, Hinings, Bob and Greenwood, Royston T. (1980) "The structuring of organizational structures", *Administrative Science Quarterly*, 25: 7–17.

Read, P. P. (1974) *Alive*, Pan Books: London.

Reason, James (1990) *Human Error*, Cambridge University Press: New York.

Reed, M. (1991) "Organizations and rationality: The odd couple" *Journal of Management Studies*, 28: 559–567.

Riley, Patricia (1983) "A structurationalist account of political culture" *Administrative Science Quarterly*, 28: 414–437.

Runkel, Phillip J. and McGrath, Joseph E. (1972) *Research on Human Behavior*, Holt, Rinehart, and Winston: New York.

Schutz, William C. (1961) "The ego, FIRO theory and the leader as completer", in Louis Petrullo and Bernard M. Bass (eds), *Leadership and Interpersonal Behavior*: 48–65, Holt, Rinehart, and Winston: New York.

Scott, W. Richard (1987) *Organizations: Rational, Natural, and Open Systems*, Prentice-Hall: Englewood Cliffs, NJ.

Smith, Ken K. (1983) "An intergroup perspective on individual behavior" in Hackman, Richard J., Lawler, Edward E. and Porter, Lyman M. (eds), *Perspectives on Behavior in Organizations*, 397–408, McGraw-Hill: New York.

Taylor, Shelby E. (1989) *Positive Illusions*, Basic Books: New York.

Weick, Karl E. (1979) *The Social Psychology of Organizing*, 2nd ed, Addison-Wesley: Reading. MA.

— (1985) "Cosmos vs. chaos: Sense and nonsense in electronic contexts", *Organizational Dynamics*, 14 (Autumn): 50–64.

— (1990) "The vulnerable system: Analysis of the Tenerife air disaster", *Journal of Management*, 16: 571–593.

Weick, Karl E., and Roberts, Karlene H. (1993) "Collective mind in organizations: Heedful interrelating on flight decks", *Administrative Science Quarterly*, 38: 357–381.

Westley, Frances R. (1990) "Middle managers and strategy: Microdynamics of inclusion", *Strategic Management Journal*, 11: 337–351.

Westrum, Ron (1982) "Social intelligence about hidden events", *Knowledge*, 3: 381–400.

White, S. K. (1988) *The Recent Work of Jurgen Habermas: Reason, Justice, and Modernity*, Cambridge University Press: Cambridge.

Wiener, Earl L., Kanki, Barbara G. and Helmreich, Robert L. (1993) *Cockpit Resource Management*, Academic Press: San Diego.

Wiley, Norbert (1988) "The micro-macro problem in social theory", *Sociological Theory*, 6: 254–261.

Chapter 19

Willard W. Radell

STORMING AND CATASTROPHIC SYSTEM FAILURES

Introduction

> The experiences of civilization teach many lessons that go unheeded
> until some great disaster comes as an object-lesson to recall to men's
> minds things known but half-forgotten.
>
> (Powell, 1989, p. 150)

PRESENT AT MANY INDUSTRIAL disasters is a phenomenon that plays a role in setting up the conditions for system failures but is seldom blamed by post-mortem investigative boards of inquiry. It is a phenomenon that transcends type of enterprise or economic system. Both capitalism and socialism can foster its development, and it can occur within private business as well as in bureaucratized government agencies. The tragic catalyst for so many otherwise disparate catastrophes and 'accidents' is the phenomenon of storming (Radell, 1990).

Storming is an acceleration in the pace of activity at the end of a planning period that occurs as a response to an arbitrary, time-dependent incentive system. Storming phenomena are best known by Soviet studies specialists who observed many cases of storming in the now defunct centrally planned economies (Linz, 1988, pp. 186–187). So common was it in traditional pre-Gorbachev Soviet factories that citizens and specialists called it *shturmovshchina* (Nove, 1986, pp. 227–228). While the English equivalent, 'storming,' is not commonly used in the West, the phenomenon occurs with sufficient frequency, and with severe enough potential consequences, that the term should probably find its way into the lexicon of educated people.

Storming is distinct from its well-known cousin, the speed-up, in that with storming the intention is not to ratchet production to higher production levels in small increments. When storming is practiced an attempt is being made to effect a level of activity that significantly exceeds past practice for the purpose of satisfying a schedule or plan that rewards completion by an arbitrary dead-line. Most of the participants in a storming situation know that the accelerated pace cannot be sustained indefinitely.

When storming works well and without catastrophe, managers are thought to have performed well and the system that produced the storming is typically pronounced fit for the next episode of rush. After a period of accelerated production in which planning goals have been met and rewards distributed, the risks taken to achieve the results within arbitrary time spans are largely invisible. After repeated periods of successful storming, the true long-run costs are masked by the highly visible short-run successes. Having a track record of successful storming, managers are lulled into believing that the risk of failure is decreasing with each success. Starbuck and Milliken call this 'fine-tuning the odds until something breaks' (1988).

Because risks and costs are hidden in successful storming events, we learn most from cases in which storming fails. Storming spring-loads a system with stress so that sometimes a simple, low probability triggering event can set off a chain of cascading failures in an already overwrought system (Shrivastava et al., 1988). Although the specific triggering events are different in each catastrophic failure and failures certainly can occur without storming, a surprisingly large number of industrial and transportation disasters have occurred during storming episodes. Of the vast pool of storming events, those that will be analyzed here are the cases in which storming played a critical role in a disaster. It is from these cases that it is possible to trace out the pattern of storming behaviors and to begin to explore ways to determine when storming has gone too far.

Context

Storming phenomena can be understood best in the context of established theories of industrial crises and accidents. While storming, managers create a synthetic crisis in an attempt to tap pools of hidden organizational slack and to make the enterprise more 'χ-efficient' (Liebenstein, 1966). Managers reason that if a goal is set that exceeds past practice, greater organizational efficiency will be the result. Active and passive stakeholders in storming decisions, including insurance companies that are underwriting the risk of catastrophic failure, often do not suspect that the accelerated level of activity will lead to disaster.

Rushing to meet a goal tied to an arbitrary, time-dependent incentive system is a sub-set of what Perrow (1984) calls 'production pressures.' Storming is a type of production pressure during which achievement of a quantitative output goal is tied to a specific incentive system. In the context of Perrow's 'normal accidents,' storming makes an organization more 'tightly coupled,' leading to more complex interaction among system components. The exponentially increasing complexity that is characteristic of the formative stages of a normal accident creates a 'significant degree of incomprehensibility' that makes timely recovery from an accident difficult or impossible. Unable to adequately understand the new complex interactions induced by linking the incentive sub-system to the production system, managers are unable to 'decouple' the sub-systems quickly enough to mitigate or prevent disaster (Perrow, 1984, p. 106). With organizational slack squeezed out of the production system in the storming attempts, 'the safety ends of safety devices' (Perrow, 1984, p. 207) are undermined in favor of using the devices to facilitate achieving the production goal without reducing the level of risk. With the effect of safety devices neutralized, storming processes tend to induce error and to magnify the consequent cost of error. Although Perrow concludes that 'private gain . . . does not seem to be the overriding problem' (p. 339), production pressure tied to an arbitrary, time-dependent incentive system makes the assumption of higher risk levels by line managers and production workers almost inevitable.

Storming can also be viewed as imposing an extra-optimal level of stress on a complex system. Such stress is especially dangerous when it is imposed on a group that is trapped in 'organizational decay' (Schwartz, 1989, pp. 319–334). If managers view the factory mechanistically instead of as '. . . a complex socio-economic system that requires frequent human intervention' (Shrivastava, 1987, p. 48), then transition to the 'crisis prone organization' is made more likely. Once the management culture is decaying in the service of mechanistic pressure to produce, important events go '. . . unnoticed or misunderstood because of a reluctance to fear the worst outcome' (Turner, 1978, p. 102).

Staw and Ross (1987) provide other psychological forces that can lead to disaster in storming situations.

(1) 'Reinforcement traps' cause persistence when withdrawal is called for because until the ultimate disaster, rushing in pursuit of a short-term goal is positively rewarded (p. 48).
(2) 'Self-justification' causes managers to '. . . justify an ineffective course of action by increasing their commitment to it' (p. 51).
(3) 'Self-inference' describes the tendency of managers to attach significance to decisions that have been publicly and freely affirmed.
(4) 'Information processing' filters information to put a positive spin on the chosen course of action.
(5) Group 'face-saving' occurs when a number of managers endorse the goal, making individual withdrawal more difficult.
(6) 'Norms' convey 'attributions of heroism' when exceeded. Against all odds the goal is pursued. The larger the egos of the managers, the more likely is persistence in the direction of escalating risk.

Ironically, those who are in the best position to detect the adverse consequences of extra-optimal storming are often the least likely to change direction before a catastrophic system failure. Knowing when to say when on storming requires careful study of those cases in which storming has led to disaster. The Soviet case is used both because it provides the origin of the concept and because it is a polar case of storming in a centrally planned economy. The Wilberg mine fire, Three

Mile Island, Chernobyl, and the failure of the space shuttle *Challenger* are used for detailed exploration of the storming phenomenon because all were subjects of detailed post-mortem investigation.

Pre-*Perestroika* Soviet storming

When plotted on a graph, traditional Soviet factory production looked like an electrocardiogram with the sharp peaks at the ends of months and years. The incentive to rush stemmed from managerial bonuses that were tied to output target fulfillment to the exclusion of other enterprise objectives such as quality, safety, and preservation of plant and equipment. When all planning goals could not be met simultaneously there were great rewards for meeting the output objective alone. On the other hand, if the old Soviet enterprise met other objectives but failed to satisfy the planned output norm, the result was a significant reduction in pay and benefits. Half of a manager's annual income hinged on the difference between meeting 99.9% and 100.1% of planned output. Consequently, it was not uncommon for Soviet factories to produce over 40% of monthly output in the last ten days of the month, and less than 20% in the first ten days (Birman, 1988, p. 215). Gorbachev disparaged this phenomenon as:

> . . . jerky production [that] also does tangible damage. It is no secret that at the beginning of the month many plants stand idle longer than they function. But at the end of the month they begin a headlong rush, as a result of which output quality is low. This chronic disease must be eradicated.   (1987, p. 390)

It is clear that a significant result of Soviet storming was an accounting business cycle which peaked at the end and troughed at the beginning of planning periods.

If the only results of storming were increased production and more complete utilization of hidden reserves, then storming would not be undesirable. But the rush to meet the planned objective also creates significant allocation distortions. Neglected machine maintenance during the storming period leads to an abnormal rate of machine breakdowns in the post-storming period. This aspect of storming was detected by Roca in his interviews with Cuban emigre managers who reported that:

> There was psychological pressure to maintain production at all costs in the sugar mill. The mill must not be stopped, and if that happens it must be restarted immediately. Our maintenance department was pressured by the production chief to restart the machinery without concern for any possible permanent damage to the equipment . . .
> (1986, p. 163)

If employees are worked past the point of fatigue, higher than average absenteeism is common immediately after the end of the planning period. As mentioned by Gorbachev, quality control declines as plant managers attempt to coax from their factories more output than they were designed to yield. Waste rates increase, since workers have less time to plan optimal mixes of raw materials. In addition, managers who anticipate the rush at the end of planning periods tend to hoard capital, labor, and raw materials to accommodate the expected waste. This hoarding creates a general rise in the capital/output, labor/output, and materials/output ratios, reflecting the chronically depressed levels of productivity that were associated with Soviet storming. Once storming becomes common practice, even managers not wishing to storm are locked into the system as suppliers delay deliveries of inputs until the end of the accounting period.

When institutional incentives encourage storming, a rising cost of production is expected to follow. In engineering-economic studies the daily rated capacity of a plant is that output which yields minimum unit costs. On a storming day the attempt to produce more than a plant's rated capacity will cause an increase in daily average cost. Exceeding the minimum daily unit cost increases the average cost for the entire planning period. If, after the storming period, fatigued workers choose to be absent in greater numbers and neglected machines begin to fail, daily output falls below that which minimizes daily unit costs, increasing the annual average cost of production. Such post-storming behavior will at the same time require future storming to make up for the deficiency of output. Thus, the practice of storming meant that there was seldom a day when a Soviet factory produced at its most efficient level.

Nuclear storming

In the United States before 1979, storming commonly occurred in nuclear power plant construction. On the eve of the accident at the Three Mile Island unit 2 nuclear power plant (TMI-2), 19 of the 66 power reactors brought into service at that time had been started in Decembers. One of the plants started in the last days of 1978 was TMI-2, which was owned by General Public Utilities (GPU). Because of the bad operating experience of TMI in the brief time that it operated, there was a strong suspicion that TMI-2 was stormed into operation in the last days of 1978 to reap pecuniary advantage. Was the operator of TMI the only utility likely to have practiced storming? The answer may be seen in Table 1.

The 19 December starts seen in Table 1 greatly exceed the 5–6 December starts that would be expected if the decision to generate power commercially were randomly distributed among the months of the year. The Poisson probability that the 19 or more December starts would randomly occur around the expected 5.5 per month is less than .0000006. Because TMI-2 was brought on-line late in December of 1978, and did not behave well in the few short months it operated commercially, it was widely believed that it was one of the 19 that may have been stormed on-line.

Pecuniary considerations may have driven managers to attempt to bring TMI-2 on line, ready or not, before the end of 1978. Among the special

Table 1 Month of initial commercial power production: nuclear power plants commissioned, 1960–1978

Initial operating month	Frequency
January	2
February	2
March	9
April	2
May	3
June	4
July	8
August	5
September	5
October	2
November	5
December	19

Source: US NRC, 1979, pp. 1–2.

financial advantages tied to timing of commercial operation before the end of a year were investment tax credits of which GPU had $27 million (GPU, 1979, p. 26). Another financial advantage to a late December 1978 start-up was '. . . a $5 million decrease in income tax expense due to the flow-through of a portion of the excess of tax over book depreciation, resulting from Three Mile Island Unit 2's being placed in service in December 1978 . . .' (GPU, 1979, p. 30). Finally, the owner of TMI-2 had hoped that an early start for the reactor would allow rate relief since the company had '. . . requested that action be timed to the commercial operation of TMI Unit 2, which was delayed until late December 1978 because of technical start-up problems' (GPU, 1979, p. 2). Since the technical problems continued to the catastrophic end of its short three-month commercial life, it is likely that the lure of pecuniary advantages tempted managers to storm TMI-2 on line before it was ready.

Chernobyl presents a somewhat different example both in scale and type of storming. Apparently the plant operators at Chernobyl felt several types of pressure simultaneously. On the one hand, their enterprise plan called for the safety test that would trigger the catastrophe, and that had to be completed in a narrow time frame. The narrow time frame was dictated by the overall enterprise plan which required that quotas of power production be maintained. Finally, the operators were necessarily pressured into load-management demands from the grid. The pressure to complete the safety test on an intrinsically unsafe graphite reactor on schedule illustrates how meaningless apparent objectives become when a system is primed for failure through excessive stress and insufficient buffers. Even after the accident, dangerous practices persisted as Chernobyl's management continued '. . . to resolve questions of the station's operation at any cost and was its top priority, to the detriment of the quality of repair work and the maintenance of especially complex equipment' (Gubarev and Odinets, 1988, p. 3).

Unfortunately, utility managers who are able to storm a reactor on line before the end of a tax year, or who are able to squeeze in a safety test while avoiding accidents, are considered good managers. The nature of risk in storming is that only a few reactors will behave very badly and impose enormous costs, while the most likely outcome is that the stormed reactor will behave acceptably well. The problem is that we do not know which reactors will operate in a dangerous manner after being stormed into service or during a squeezed safety test.

However uncertain are the risks of storming, US utility managers have learned from the accident at TMI-2 how not to storm. Since 1979 there have been no more December starts-up of nuclear power plants than would be expected on a random basis.

The Wilberg mine disaster

> Just prior to the beginning of the 4:00 p.m. shift, there had been a lot of discussion among the afternoon-shift miners. Some had been apprehensive about working that day. Management was in the process of trying to break a production record on the 5th Right section, and some employees were concerned for their safety due to escape routes off the tailgate and bleeders being blocked from falls.
>
> (UMWA (1987), p. 6)

> The air compressor was inadvertently turned on and operated continuously for about 69 hours before the fire started . . . The primary cause of the fire was failure of mine management to remove the air compressor from service or properly repair the air compressor when it was known to be in an unsafe condition . . . The following factors contributed to the severity of the accident: . . . the increased number of miners present on the section because of an attempt to set a production record.
>
> (MSHA (1987), p. 92)

> Except for the acknowledged attempt to set a production record, normal mining was in progress in the No. 5 Right longwall section.
>
> (Nagy (1987), p. 2)

The Mine Safety and Health Administration (MSHA) and United Mine Workers of America (UMWA) reports are in stark disagreement as to the proximate event that triggered the Wilberg mine disaster. One cites flash ignition of the lubricating oil in a badly neglected compressor as the source while the other report implies that a bearing fire on an overloaded and undermaintained conveyor belt initiated the tragedy. Whichever version is accepted, it is clear that storming figured prominently in either scenario.

On 19 December 1984, the management of Emery Mining Corporation, operator of Utah Power's Wilberg Mine in Orangeville, Utah, attempted to set a 24-hour coal production record. By mid-afternoon the record pace of the previous shifts meant that achievement of the goal would be determined by the ability of the 4 PM to midnight shift to maintain the record breaking pace. To personally supervise the push for the record, an unusual number of managers were in the mine. Equipment usually shut down between shifts was left running while the second and third shifts changed in the mine to continue the record pace. An inexperienced belt operator was assigned to the conveyor belt on the third shift and ordered '. . . to keep it running and not to shut it off for any reason' (UMWA, p. 6). At about 9 PM a fire started near the belt mouth of the 5th Right longwall section that would kill 27 Emery employees. While the fire was the proximate cause of the deaths, storming on 19 December, and in the months leading to the fire, created the climate of rush that made the mortality rate in the 5th Right section so high.

Storming began at Wilberg Mine in 1979 when 'two-entry' mining began in conjunction with longwall mining. Wilberg was originally designed as a 'multiple-entry' mine with several ventilation paths. In the 'two-entry' Wilberg mine, the single ventilation path almost guaranteed that fire near the mouth would yield a high mortality rate. Taking the long view, the set-up for the disaster began when the Wilberg mine was allowed to 'revert to a system that the 1969 Mine Act sought to eliminate (two-entry ventilation plans)' (UMWA, p. 53). As a result, a single fire could both block exit and poison the single stream of ventilation air.

Short-run storming decisions were also instrumental in the disaster. All alternative paths of escape were blocked by administrative decision. Bleeder tunnels used to purge toxic gasses were clogged with rock falls that were left uncorrected by Mine Safety and Health Administration (MSHA) waivers granted to Emery management. As late as 19 November, 1984, a MSHA inspector was told '. . . not to get shook up about the cave-in in the 5th Right return . . .' (UMWA, p. 56). Why were the waivers sought by the mining company? According to the UMWA report on the disaster, the company wished to avoid '. . . the inconvenience and downtime of shooting another overcast over the belt' (UMWA, p. 61).

Despite strong will and heroism on the part of would-be rescuers, the rescue efforts were more chaotic and riskier than would ordinarily be the case in a crisis as a result of pre-crisis storming decisions. Significantly, 'the number of persons present in the longwall mining area was more than twice the normal work complement as an acknowledged effort was being made that particular day to set [a] production record' (Nagy, p. 1). The decision to storm meant that there was an unusually large number of people in the mine, meaning that any disaster would lead to a greater probability of greater loss of life. Some of the extra people were managers who would ordinarily be above ground where they could manage coherent rescue efforts. The loss of so many managers in the first minutes of the disaster, including the Mine Manager, the Vice President of Operations, the General Mine Foreman, the Longwall Mine Foreman, the Maintenance Foreman, the Service Foreman, and the Longwall Coordinator, created confusion. Chains of command and information had so thoroughly broken that when the MSHA teams arrived there was no way to tell how many rescuers were in the mine, where they had gone, and whether they also needed to be rescued. As stated in the UMWA report, 'there were no controls placed over those entering the mine, or where they were in the mine. As the fire spread, so did the personnel fighting the fire' (UMWA, p. 23). In the moments after the fire was detected, a warehouseman and a bath-houseman, whose duties and training had not included managing mine rescues, had '. . . to dig through papers in the office to find numbers to call. Approximately 35 minutes after the fire was detected, the first call was made . . .' (UMWA, p. 21). In the absence of experienced above ground management, the MSHA team arrived to find that '. . . no one had taken the air off the fire' and 'the rescuers, mostly inexperienced, continued to travel past the fire' to 'fight it from the back side' (UMWA, p. 22). The lack of on-site management in the early hours of the disaster can be ascribed to the attempt to set a production record.

The MSHA report listed the source of the fire as a compressor which caught fire after extreme under-maintenance and abuse. As the official report noted, 'there was no record of air compressor examinations . . .' nor was there evidence '. . . that the required weekly examinations and tests . . .' were being performed (MSHA, 1987, p. 57). Since the compressor's 'over-temperature safety switch was intentionally by-passed . . ., the only protective device installed . . . to protect . . . against overheating . . . [was] defeated' (MSHA, p. 88). During the investigation of the disaster, MSHA discovered that the compressor had run '. . . unused and unattended for about 69 hours prior to the fire' (MSHA, p. 61). Ingersoll-Rand's service manual for the compressor specifies that for 'every eight hours of operation this (air intake) service indicator should be checked to determine if servicing is required' (Ingersoll-Rand, 1977, p. 35). When a production system is being strained to its maximum capacity in preparation to break a record, maintenance tends to be driven lower on the list of priorities. Although the compressor was charged with starting the fire, the storming process taking place on 19 December had the potential for other disastrous failures.

Fires had occurred before at Wilberg, usually on the conveyor belt. When conveyor belt bearings got red-hot, workers were directed to spray the bearings with water and keep the belt moving until a shift change or until the bearing started flaming. On the night of 19 December the Continuous Belt Fire Detection system (CBFD) was apparently not functioning properly and the person whose duties included monitoring the system could not see the alarm light panels from all of his workstations. Despite the high volume of coal on the conveyor because '. . . the company was pushing for a production record . . . there is no evidence that the area was cleaned at any time during the shift' (UMWA, p. 47). Plant wiring carried with it potential for disaster as some cables had less rated current carrying capacity than the machines they were serving. Added risk came from circuits that by-passed circuit breakers, a condition miners referred to as being 'jumpered out.' Further adding to the risk of disaster was the lack of independent circuits on the mine's emergency water pumps, which meant that when the mine power was shut off in the emergency, would-be rescuers were left without water to fight the fire. Another wiring problem endangered rescuers when combustible gasses from the fire built up. The power was shut off while the mine was evacuated. But the plant's diesel fired back-up power supply automatically started an electrical ventilation fan which increased the probability of ignition of the gasses while at the same time providing fresh air for the fire. By 24 December 1984 it was decided that the only way to override the renegade back-up system was to literally kill it. '. . . A helicopter carrying a sharpshooter with a high-powered rifle, shot holes into the radiator of the diesel motor' (UMWA, p. 19).

What happened at Wilberg Mine on 19 December 1984 went beyond a sacrifice of safety for production. Safety is often compromised for some accept- able purpose (Why not set the speed limit on interstate highways at 45 mph?). At Wilberg, storming caused too many corners to be cut, caused too many channels of information to be ignored, eliminated too many pools of organizational slack, and set up a situation in which any one of a number of triggering events could have led to catastrophic system failure. The attempt to set a production record with the organizational and technical resources available on 19 December carried a greater degree of risk than would have been accepted freely by Emery employees if a more realistic estimate of the level of risk had been known. Single-minded pursuit of an arbitrary production record within a fixed period of time was not allowed to be hindered by fears of the risk of catastrophic failure.

Shuttle mission 51-L

> In nearly all accidents we need to distinguish two different levels of causation. The first is the immediate technical or mechanical reason for the accident: the second is the underlying human reason.
>
> (Gordon (1978), p. 251)

For many years the National Aeronautics and Space Administration (NASA) successfully stormed its way to achievements like the Apollo missions to the moon. NASA's ability to respond successfully to President Kennedy's arbitrary, end of the decade lunar landing objective created a 'can-do' attitude that excluded few possibilities. The *Challenger* disaster of 26 January, 1986 appears as a single failure in an otherwise successful venture. Yet investigation into the events leading up to the tragedy raises the suspicion that more was involved than the failure of the O-rings on one of the two rocket boosters. Storming at NASA, always in the background, took on a critical negative role in the *Challenger* disaster.

With the *Challenger* disaster there is no doubt that storming was being conducted deliberately and with large effect. The launch rate had been increased slowly between 1981 and 1984 with 2 shuttles orbited in 1981, 3 in 1982, 4 in 1983, and 5 in 1984. Beginning in 1985 the launch rate was increased signifi- cantly to 9, with 15 shuttle launches planned for 1986. Astronout John Young, in a 4 March 1986 memo, assigned a central role to storming.

> From watching the presidential commission open-session interviews on television, it is clear that none of the direct participants have the

faintest doubt that they did anything but absolutely the correct thing
in launching 51-L at every step of the way. While it is difficult to
believe that any humans can have such complete and total confidence,
it is even more difficult to understand a management system that
allows us to fly a solid rocket booster single-seal design that explo-
sively and dynamically verifies its Criticality 1 performance [Critical-
ity 1 designates components whose failure yields catastrophe] . . .
There is only one driving reason that such a potentially dangerous
system would ever be allowed to fly — launch schedule pressure.

(Young, 1986)

Careful reading of the final report of the Presidential Commission on the Space
Shuttle *Challenger* Accident (hereafter: Rogers Commission) leaves no doubt
that storming contributed significantly to the disaster. The 'heavy emphasis . . .
on the schedule . . . to build up to 24 missions a year brought a number of
difficulties . . .' (Rogers Commission, 1986, p. 164).

One motive to increase the launch rate was economic. The early feasibility
studies from the Nixon years trumpeted the shuttle as a space truck that would
economically orbit freight. At some point policy-makers outside NASA got the
idea that the shuttle venture would eventually break-even or make a small profit.
By the 1980s it was believed that a hand-crafted shuttle, with an on-board crew,
could economically compete with simpler, mass-produced European launch
vehicles. President Reagan declared in 1982 that the shuttle '. . . is the primary
space launch system for both national security and civil government missions . . .
The first priority of the STS program is to make the system fully operational and
cost-effective in providing routine access to space . . .' (Rogers Commission,
p. 164). To be cost-effective, NASA had lined up a number of cash-paying
customers for launches. From a need to satisfy those customers came '. . . a
requirement to launch a certain number of flights per year and to launch them
on time,' a practice that '. . . may occasionally have obscured engineering concerns' (Rogers Commission, p. 165). Concern with burgeoning budget deficits
in the early 1980s also contributed to the pressure to bring in cash as NASA was
faced with the same stringency in appropations as other federal agencies. Since
fixed costs are a big percentage of shuttle expenses, any attempt to make the
shuttle 'pay' in the economic sense requires a more rapid launch rate.

Another motive for speeding up shuttle launches was political. Influential
members of Congress and the White House were routinely wined and dined at
shuttle launches to protect the source of government support for NASA operations. Playing on the human desire to be associated with the 'right stuff,'
NASA had become adept at the public relations end of operating a very large
government agency. When President Reagan, echoing President Nixon's desire
that non-technical civilians have the opportunity to ride into orbit, requested
politician, teacher, and journalist missions, NASA complied willingly. It would
have been bad PR not to have done so. Every time a civilian was added to a
mission, a payload specialist originally scheduled for the mission had to be
bumped. Some payloads were not compatible with the remaining array of
payload specialists and the already complex launch preparations were further

complicated by the need to juggle payload manifests among various missions. Software engineers had to struggle to finish avionic programs, while lead-time dropped, shortening the hours that shuttle crews logged on the mission simulators. Thus, with no additional resources, NASA was forced into a situation in which '. . . the political advantages of implementing those late changes [in mission manifests] outweighed our general objections' (Rogers Commission, p. 173).

Political and economic motives combined to produce an excessive multiplicity of objectives in the shuttle program. At first, the shuttle was to be a next step toward the development of a large space station, and to function as the kind of large scale project that could maintain the scientific and technical skills necessary to maintain US leadership in aerospace technology. At some point the idea of the shuttle being a 'good investment in our future' was transformed into 'it should be cost-effective.' Later Strategic Defense Initiative (SDI or 'Star Wars'), Politician-in-Space, Teacher-in-Space, and Journalist-in-Space missions were abruptly ordered by the White House and supported by Congress with no significant increase in financial resources to deal with the increasing demands being placed on the system. As stated in the Rogers Commission Report, 'NASA cannot both accept the relatively spur-of-the-moment missions that its can-do attitude tends to generate and also maintain the planning and scheduling discipline required to operate as a space truck on a routine and cost-effective basis' (Rogers Commission, pp. 171–172). When objectives multiply with time constraints on each, and without an increase in the resources necessary to meet those objectives, storming becomes inevitable, and at some point, dangerous.

When storming is becoming dangerous it almost always qualifies as folly by Tuchman's definition in that there are usually people close to the situation who recognize the higher risk level and sound a warning (Tuchman, 1984, p. 5). Rockwell International, primary contract for the shuttle orbiters, was against launch with cold temperatures. Also adamant against the shuttle launch on a morning as cold as 26 January were the Morton-Thiokol engineers whose primary concern was the behavior of the solid rocket booster O-rings when exposed to cold. The response of the NASA bureaucracy to the engineers' concern was 'my God Thiokol, when do you want me to launch, next April?' (Rogers Commission, p. 96). Under pressure from NASA to keep moving toward a launch, Morton-Thiokol engineers were told '. . . we have to make a management decision.' One manager/engineer was told 'to take off his engineering hat and put on his management hat' (Rogers Commission, p. 93). The storming mentality was allowed to win out over the technical judgement of those closest to the component that would fail catastrophically. The burden of proof was shifted from the past practise of engineers proving that their components were safe, to proving beyond a shadow of doubt that the components they engineered were not safe. Such a shift makes it almost impossible for those who see that storming has gone too far to stop the system before catastrophe.

As was true at Wilberg, the attempt to accelerate the launch rate created stresses that could have led to alternative catastrophe scenarios. Storming-induced bottlenecks added risk with each launch of the shuttle. Aside from the excessive overtime and spare parts shortages, the higher launch rate caused shortages of basic shuttle components. Cannibalization on landing at Edwards

Air Force Base with the parts shipped back to Kennedy Space Center to be installed immediately before the next launch increased the risk that the cannibalized part or an adjacent part in either the donor or host shuttle would be damaged. Software engineering was another critical area whose reserves had been squeezed out by the accelerated launch rate. At the time of Mission 51-L, flight crews had only a bare minimum of time on shuttle simulators. NASA's software engineers had not been provided with the necessary resources to accomodate both the large number of manifest changes caused by floating objectives and at the same time to deal safely with the accelerated launch rate. As is true with other storming-induced catastrophes, participants are not expected to ask the question, how much can we safely do with what we have?

Lessons

Although storming is a rational tendency in organizations, many stakeholders have a legitimate interest in keeping it from becoming excessive. Consumers, employees, nearby residents, stock-holders, insurers and responsible government officials all have an interest in keeping storming within the boundaries of acceptable risk. There are no simple ways to effect better regulation of storming, but by watching for tell-tale signs, the organizational equivalent of a governor on a steam engine could be built into production systems.

Study of storming phenomena yields a number of characteristics that can signal the need for organizational adjustment.

(1) Storming makes production into a sporting event, with beginning and end, with victory and the threat of defeat, and with winners and losers. In contrast, successful production is a continuous process.

(2) Information must flow freely from those closest to the adverse consequences of the storming to the highest level of management at which the pressure originated. Moreover, the information must be acted upon when there is the potential for disaster. Richard Feynman of the Rogers Commission wondered why it was that the engineers at Morton-Thiokol, who knew the most about how the shuttle boosters worked, could not get the message through to the managers at the top that cold temperatures would adversely affect the safety of a launch decision.

(3) Storming is more than cutting corners. Negative information is screened out. To counteract this tendency the formal organizational structure needs to facilitate the flow of negative information just as positive information is already facilitated.

(4) Bury the myth that overly ambitious goals will yield more performance than will less ambitious goals that reflect current constraints and resources. The lesson of the 'theory of second best' developed by economists is that a strategy that seeks to achieve goals that are based on realistic assessments of available resources will outperform a strategy that aims to exceed a system's ability to produce.

(5) It is dangerous to '. . . reward "performance" when it is measured

poorly . . .' (Weisbrod, p. 54). 'Poorly measured' can refer to quantitative goals that while easy to measure, oversimplify the complex goals of an organization. A bonus system that rewards a 10% increase in 'output' when avoidance of disaster and maintenance of quality control are excluded from the calculation of output is dangerous.

(6) Insurers could take a more active role in evaluating the tightness of the coupling of the systems they are underwriting. If changes in the degree of system tautness were responded to with assessment of higher premiums, extra-optimal storming would be less likely to occur.

(7) There need to be persons present in a potential storming situation who are not part of the storming process itself. Ideally, these watchers would be safety professionals who have no stake in the pursuit of short-term goals and who have no direct responsibility to maintain production rates. The watchers will be best at preventing extra-optimal storming if they are paid from the corporate level, or by the insurer rather than by the local production facility they are watching.

(8) Watchers should periodically ask managers what it is they are trying to accomplish. People engaged in storming do not think in terms of optima. Rather they seek to maximize this or minimize that. If a watcher hears too many maximizing words in the answers, when asking about objectives, it may be time to suggest a cool down.

(9) Watchers should listen for monistic goals. When storming is excessive, policy is framed around the attainment of a single objective. Phrases like 'the wagon is loaded, let's get moving now,' are clues that a primary objective is being pursued without regard for secondary or tertiary adverse consequences (Smith, p. 1497).

(10) Watchers should monitor the role of 'net costs vs. net benefits' in managers' decision making. While excessive storming is under way, considerations of economic rationality become secondary. Up until the moment of catastrophic system failure, short-term gains appear to exceed both short-term and long-term costs. There are often attempts to shift costs into subsequent time periods to make storming decisions look better in the short run. Since discrepancies between apparent costs and benefits and actual costs and benefits of storming almost always show up as deterioration in either quality or sub-system reliability, watchers should be keen to detect changes in quality of output and subsystem failure rates.

Scope and implications of storming behavior

Not all catastrophes are caused by storming, and most storming does not cause catastrophe. But storming is so often the essential catalyst that allows an event to trigger a disaster that much may be gained by learning to recognize excessive storming. Management theorists and industrial psychologists speak of an optimal level of stress. If stress levels are too low, performance levels drop. If they are too high, performance levels also drop. Storming exemplifies a situation in which maximum stress levels continue until an arbitrary time deadline is met. It should not be surprising that disastrous performance levels occasionally result. What makes storming so potentially dangerous is that it often fails at peak levels of short-term performance. Immediately before the catastrophic failure the system seems to be working better than ever before. A euphoria sets in that puts a positive spin on almost all information. As problems appear, they are disposed of with more than usual satisfaction as the expeditor knows that continued pursuit of the short-term goal has been assured.

The lure of higher productivity is almost irresistible. Even reasonable people can get caught up in the pursuit of the grand objective without regard for how much it will cost to achieve. Immediately after the *Challenger* disaster, politician-in-space Jake Garn affirmed his belief that NASA could maintain the accelerated flight schedule of 1986, as well as continuing the civilian in space programs, by stating that '. . . the program was mature enough. I think they are capable of that schedule' (Large and McGinley, 1986, p. 1). Again in March of 1991 Senator Garn expressed concern that NASA had been too conservative after *Challenger* in not sticking to a more aggressive launch schedule. Garn disparaged NASA's lack of willingness to 'take the smallest chance' (Associated Press, 1991). It is often at the point that the natural, human, 'hurry-up, let's get on with it' attitude is most widely held that we assume the greatest risk of catastrophic failure. It is then that we are most likely to ignore negative information paths and exaggerate positive information about system performance.

As more is learned about storming as a phenomenon, it should be possible for managers and safety professionals to detect excessive storming before it becomes a problem. Deliberately slowing down a system or de-linking incentives from short-term (time dependent) results are not likely to be popular with managers trained in the old 'management by objective' (MBO) school. 'Setting a schedule and working toward it' to 'produce a tension that releases more and more energy as we drive toward a due date' (Mali, 1972, pp. 279–280) can be a dangerous prescription when tied directly to the incentive system. Hopefully, we can find better ways to value different types of information in a storming episode. We need better ways to assign priorities in a management information system so that, as Hopper suggested, from millions of pieces of information we can distinguish between two simultaneous messages received by chemical plant managers that (1) 'a valve is malfunctioning that will destroy the plant if not fixed, and (2) Joe Blow worked 2 hours overtime last week' (Hopper, 1986, pp. 1095–1096).

In essence, excessive storming is 'folly,' possessing the three necessary criteria outlined by Tuchman (1984, pp. 4–7, 19, 25, 41, 234).

(1) In each of the case studies presented in this paper there were people who felt the activity was counter-productive as it was taking place and not merely in retrospect.
(2) In each case, alternatives were available that would have favorably altered the outcomes.
(3) Each case was a group policy and not the action of one person.

It is not an easy matter to detect when normal storming has become crusading and folly, but one symptom, Tuchman warns, is the 'refusal to benefit from experience.' When Rockwell International decided to stretch the production schedule on the shuttle *Endeavour* to four years to reflect budget constraints and 'safety considerations,' they were taking a step toward reducing storming in their part of the shuttle program (Wood, 1991, p. 12:2). Heroic portrayals of storming run so deep in human culture that it is difficult to assert that the deliberate slowing down of production systems may be responsible, courageous behavior. As is learned about storming it is hoped that other organizations will do as Rockwell did with *Endeavour*'s production scheduling. Managers who are sensitive to the potential dangers of storming are more likely to be able to pull back before a stressed system enters the realm of unanticipated high risks and unexpectedly expensive consequences.

References

Associated Press (1991) 'Senator accuses NASA of timidity', *Johnstown Tribune-Democrat*, 11 March: A-11.

Birman, I. (1988) 'The imbalance of the Soviet economy,' *Soviet Studies*, 40: 215. *Industrial Crisis Quarterly, Vol. 6, No. 4.*

GPU (General Public Utilities) (1979) *GPU Annual Report*, 1978.

Gorbachev, M. (1987) *Selected Speeches and Articles*, Progress: Moscow.

Gordon, J.E. (1978) *Structures, or Why Things Don't Fall Down*, Plenum: New York.

Gubarev, V. and Odinets, M. (1988) 'Chernobyl, two years later: echo of the "zone" ', Pravda, 24 April: 3; translated excepts in *Current Digest of the Soviet Press*, 40, 25 May 1988: 13.

Hopper, G. (1986) (quoted) 'Admiral Hopper talks to AAAS staff', *Science*, 233: 1095–1096.

Ingersoll-Rand (1977) Operation and Maintenance Manual, Models 5M, 7M, and 9M. Appendix J, MSHA, *Report of Investigation: Underground Coal Mine Fire*, Wilberg Mine.

Large, A.J. and McGinley, L. (1986) 'Tragedy in space'. *Wall Street Journal*, 29 January: 1.

Liebenstein, H. (1966) 'Allocative efficiency vs. X-efficiency' *American Economic Review*, June: 392–415.

Linz, S.J. (1988) 'Managerial autonomy in Soviet firms', *Soviet Studies*, 40: 175–195.

Mali, P. (1972) *Managing by Objectives*, Wiley Interscience: New York.

Mine Safety and Health Administration (MSHA), US Department of Labor, 1987, *Report of Investigation: Underground Coal Mine Fire*, Wilberg Mine.

Nagy, J. (1987) Wilberg Mine fire: cause, location, and initial development. Appendix H, MSHA, *Report of Investigation: Underground Coal Mine Fire*, Wilberg Mine.

Nove, A. (1986) *The Soviet Economic System*, Allen & Unwin: Boston, MA.

Perrow, C. (1984) *Normal Accidents*, Basic: New York.

Powell, J.W. (1989) 'The lesson of Conemaugh', *North American Review*, 149: 150–156.

Radell, W.W. (1990) 'Storming: the losing edge', *Scholars*, 2: 24–31.

Roca, S. (1986) 'State enterprises in Cuba under the new system of planning and management (SDPE)', *Cuban Studies*, 16: 153–179.

Rogers Commission (W.P. Rogers, Chair) (1986) *Report of the Presidential Commission on the Space Shuttle Challenger Accident.*

Schwartz, H.S. (1989) 'Organizational disaster and organizational decay: the case of the National Aeronautics and Space Administration', *Industrial Crisis Quarterly*, 3: 319–334.

Shrivastava, P. (1987) *Bhopal: Anatomy of a Crisis*, Ballinger: Cambridge, MA.

Shrivastava, P., Mitroff, I.I., Miller, D. and Miglani, A. (1988) 'Understanding industrial crises', *Journal of Management Studies*, 25: 285–303.

Smith, R.J. (1986) 'Experts ponder effect of pressures on shuttle blowup' *Science*, 231: 1495–1498.

Starbuck, W.H. and Milliken, F.J. (1988) 'Challenger: fine-tuning the odds until something breaks', *Journal of Management Studies*, 25: 319–340.

Staw, B.M. and Ross, J. (1987) 'Behavior in escalation situations: antecedents, prototypes, and solutions' *Research in Organizational Behavior*, 9: 39–78.

Tuchman, B.W. (1984) *The March of Folly*, Knopf: New York.

Turner, B.A. (1978) *Man-made Disasters*, Crane, Russak & Co: New York.

UMWA (United Mine Workers of America) (1987) *The Wilberg Mine Disaster*.

US NRC (Nuclear Regulatory Commission) (1979) *Nuclear Power Plant Operating Experience*, 1978.

Weisbrod, B.A. (1989) 'Rewarding performance that is hard to measure: the private nonprofit sector' *Science*, 244: 541.

Wood, D.B. (1991) ' "Endeavour" aims at a safe flight' *Christian Science Monitor*, 9 January: 12.

Young, J.W. (1986) (quoted) 'Astronauts express opinions on shuttle launch safety'. *Aviation Week and Space Technology*, 17 March: 28–29.

Chapter 20

Denis Smith

THE CRISIS OF MANAGEMENT: MANAGING AHEAD OF THE CURVE

Introduction

ONE MIGHT ARGUE THAT the prevention of crisis is the ultimate goal of the crisis management process. Crisis prevention remains, however, an elusive process for many organizations, as a cursory review of the business and popular press will testify. In the same week that the UK's MG Rover group finally collapsed, there were also a range of other problems including: riots in China (which were targeted at Japan and Japanese organizations); the conviction of a senior Manager following a major fraud in an Australian company; problems within the Italian government; and a multiple-fatality fire in a Paris hotel (Clement, 2005; Harrison, 2005; Lichfield and Harries, 2005; Marks, 2005; McNeill, 2005; Popham, 2005). The nature and range of these events serves to illustrate the dynamic and diverse nature of 'crises' and raises questions about the capability of organizations to prevent such 'problems' from incubating.

In virtually every case of a 'crisis', the causal processes involved are both 'complex' and multi-faceted. Put another way, crises invariably do not originate from simple root causes, but from the interaction between multiple issues and processes. This, in turn, generates emergent properties that arise out of these interactions. The ability of 'management' to identify and intervene to prevent crises from occurring could, therefore, be seen as an important attribute for an organization. However, as events would seem to corroborate, the processes through which such crises are incubated and develop remain, perhaps, the most difficult point for intervention on the part of 'management' (represented as both a functional area within the organization and as a professional process). There are several reasons for this.

In the first instance, it is difficult to anticipate the likely outcomes of those 'events' where the causal factors are not perceived by managers as being linked 'logically', in terms of a cause and effect relationship, with the eventual outcome. Problems around emergent properties serve as a good example of these difficulties, and managers will invariably make a series of assumptions about the way that the organization functions, that might well cause difficulties when dealing with emergent issues in the build up to a crisis. Such emergent properties are the unforeseen products of the interaction between the various elements of the organization as a 'system' and they challenge the 'linear-process' mindset that underpins much management theory and practice.

Second most managers would generally believe that they are doing a good job and many are convinced that their actions could not lead to a crisis or catastrophic failure within the organization. When combined with a tendency to reject critical views about the ways that we perform, this minimization of the hazards present within the organization can generate problems for the identification of potential crisis events and their precursors (Turner, 1976, 1978). Again, the identification of such precursors represents a significant challenge for 'management'.

Third, the scale and extent of the interconnections that take place between the various elements of the organizations in which we work often make it difficult to see problems in a holistic manner. In our increasingly globalized world, in which our supply chains and networks extend over large areas (expressed in both space and time), these interactions are of major importance. The compression of the various decision horizons and the impact that this can have upon the performance of the organization is also an important factor in the generation of crisis potential, as is the speed of interactions that can occur within elements of the system (Perrow, 1984; Radell, 1990, 1992).

Fourth, the skills required to work in the 'steady-state' environment of an organization will invariably be different to the task demands that are generated in the period that is designated as a crisis. Managers are normally recruited because of their abilities to manage the 'normal' activities and processes of the organization and not for their abilities to deal with crisis. There are a set of problems around the skills and knowledge that managers have, and the ways that this set of capabilities can interact with the rules that exist in the organization, to create a range of performance problems. The skills and knowledge held by managers interacts with the 'regulatory' setting in which they operate to create potential problems, especially around error generation (Rasmussen, 1982, 1983; Reason, 1990a, 1997, 2001). There are also some critical decision points within a crisis time-line that can have a significance beyond the recognition of those people involved in the process. Handy has termed such decisions as 'points of inflection' (Handy, 1994, 1995) and we will come back to a discussion around the ways in which multiple points of inflection might interact to allow a crisis to escalate. Also of importance here is the capability of managers to 'make sense' (Weick, 1993, 1995, 2001) of the processes that are occurring around these various points of inflection. A failure both to make sense of the situation, and to take action on the basis of an inaccurate view of the problems that are faced at that point in time, will help to generate subsequent points of inflection further down the time-line.

Finally, there are a series of difficulties that surround our abilities to deal with the various 'routine' decisions within organizations. In some cases, these decisions may generate conditions that may help shape the generation of errors lower down the organizational hierarchy. Also of importance within an increasingly interconnected setting, is the recognition of the significance associated with certain choices across both space and time and the impact that they can have on failure generation.

Taken together, these factors can interact to allow for the generation of a set of conditions that may inhibit management's capabilities to identify and manage the precursors to crisis. In this respect, the works by Radell, Rasmussen, Reason and Weick, offer some interesting perspectives on our understanding of the manner in which organizations generate the potential for failure.

Errors, skills, capabilities and the incubation of crisis

There has been a long history of research into the processes by which error within organizations can generate problems relating to failure potential. In his seminal work, Turner conceptualized the processes by which organizations can 'incubate' the potential for disaster and he identified a number of key underlying factors that shaped this process (Turner, 1976, 1978). In some respects, Turner was the first to fully identify the complex interaction that took place between both strategic and operational level factors in the creation of disaster potential. His work suggested that, for some organizations, the very processes that are used to structure decision-making and the 'transformations' that typify the organizations core processes and products may well create the conditions that can generate a crisis. For Radell, the manner in which organizations compress their various decision-making horizons and transformation process can generate problems through the 'storming' effect this can have. He argued that the compression of the design-testing-production timeline can often serve to generate conditions that can ultimately swamp management's abilities to deal with those problems that occur. In some cases, this storming process prevents product-related problems from being recognized early and this has the effect of magnifying the impact of any problems by damaging the organization's reputation. Such problems become compounded in those organizations where there are complex supply and distribution chains. In addition, the challenges that are generated by new, emergent forms of crisis have also been widely discussed in terms of their potential abilities to overwhelm management's capabilities to deal with the problems that are generated (Erikson, 1994; Gladwell, 2000; Perrow, 1984; Sagan, 1993; Tenner, 1996).

Both Rasmussen and Reason have made significant contributions to our understanding of the nature of error within organizations and the processes that can help to generate it. Rasmussen argues that it is possible to see skills-, rules-and knowledge-based factors shaping the generation of error (Rasmussen, 1982, 1983). This raises important questions concerning the ways in which organizations recruit and train their staff and the processes that they employ for knowledge capture, codification and dissemination. Reason builds upon this initial framework around skills-rules-knowledge and also points to the role of latent factors in shaping the conditions in which 'operational' level errors can occur.

Despite the significance of this body of research, some questions remain, however, as to whether it has had the required impact on management theory and practice that it deserves. Taken together, this research points to the ways in which organizations can seek to focus attention around generating resilience as well as dealing with vulnerability within 'systems' of work. This is especially important as a consequence, in the ways that managerial decisions can erode and bypass organizational defences.

Eroding organizational defences

Turner made the point that organizational defences are based upon the precautionary norms that managers and systems designers put into place to control the portfolio of hazardous events that are deemed to be 'credible'. It is the gap between these precautionary norms and the hazards that are generated that creates a problem regarding organizational failures. Whilst put this way it does not sound too profound, it should be noted that this was an extremely important advance in thinking at the time of Turner's early work, and the concept of incubation has laid a robust platform for subsequent work to explore the issues that underpinned these gaps in defences. Turner's contribution to the literature is very significant as he also outlined a number of factors that contributed to the creation of these gaps in defences and provided us with a means of exploring the processes of incubation in practice. Table 1 takes these issues and raises some potential implications for management. It should be noted that the issues identified here are not meant to be inclusive, but are simply indicative of the wider implications. Each organization will generate specific issues around the core elements of incubation and the issues raised here represent a starting point for a wider audit of crisis potential. It should also be noted that there are also important interactions taking place between these core elements and that these will also generate problems. As a consequence, it is possible to generate second order and possibly third order issues on the basis of the various interactions that can take place between the managerial implications identified in Table 1.

A key element within the incubation process is the manner in which people make errors (slips, lapses and mistakes) and also violate (Reason, 1990b). The psychology of this process was not dealt with in detail by Turner but has been developed by both Rasmussen and Reason. Reason, in particular, has shown how the interactions between latent and active errors, along with the erosion of organizational defences and the generation of a flawed culture, can create a basis from which failures can escalate rapidly. Reason uses the metaphor of Swiss cheese to explain the manner in which holes in multiple layers of defences can allow those defences to become breached under certain conditions. It is at the level of creating holes in the multiple layers of defences within the organization that the work of Turner and Reason overlap. Figure 1 illustrates a hypothetical situation in which layers of defences are breached. It is possible to see the broader

Table 1 Elements of incubation

Issues raised by Turner around the processes of incubation	Implications for 'management'
Rigid core beliefs and managerial perceptions	− strong core beliefs will prevent any acceptance of counter views to those expressed within the dominant organizational 'paradigm'. − expert views are also important in shaping an (un)willingness to accept challenges to assumptions around safety − perceptions around control will be important in shaping the willingness of managers to consider the limitations of existing control strategies relative to the perceived portfolio of hazards facing the organization − Core beliefs (and values) have implications for the ways in which an organisation's stance on corporate responsibility will impact upon crisis creation and management − evidence-based decision-making may prove to be an important issue around complex, non-linear, socio-technical problems − precautionary approaches to risk provide a way of challenging core beliefs and assumptions (for example, an absence of any evidence of harm should not be seen as a proof of safety)
The presence of decoy phenomena	− development of capabilities around hazard identification and prioritizing aimed at in − move away from restricted 'worst case' scenario approaches to a more inclusive consideration of the hazard portfolio − expert views on the risks involved may result in a greater focus on less important issues which then serve as decoys from the main problems
Disregard of complaints from outsiders	− impacts upon managerial sense making and generates a siege mentality amongst managers that becomes more apparent under conditions of crisis − may strengthen resistance around challenges to core beliefs, values and assumptions − the involvement of external 'critics' as part of the organisation's strategic approach to crisis will help to ensure that all potential crises are considered and reduce the risk of perceptual minimisation
Difficulties around information flows	− problems of communication across disciplinary boundaries − need for real time communication and information transfer across networks within tightly coupled systems − more effective information flows will allow for the identification of latent error potential

Continued

Table 1 *continued*

Issues raised by Turner around the processes of incubation	Implications for 'management'
	– raises issues around the management of knowledge within networks and supply chains
The involvement of outsiders within the 'system'	– role and significance of 'critical, non-expert' commentators within decision making (termed 'critical evaluators' by Janus)
	– role of external 'agents' in exposing vulnerability within the system (either as a contributor to any potential trigger or by increasing the consequences of an incident)
	– the creation of vulnerability within 'outsiders' through poor and ineffective communication around safety procedures and protocols
Perceptually minimising the hazard(s)	– need for more effective use of evidence within decision-making and a more explicit presentation of the uncertainty surrounding risk calculations
	– programmes for awareness raising on the potential for crisis (cross-sector comparisons etc.)
	– greater recognition of the impacts of 'storming' on the vulnerability of the organization and its associated networks and supply chains
Presence of a confused regulatory position	– shift in approach away from a compliance-based approach to dealing with potential hazard issues
	– greater use of a precautionary approach to hazards
	– move towards a more 'ethically-based' approach (moving beyond regulatory requirements) (strategic corporate social responsibility)

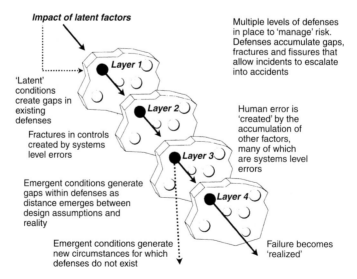

Figure 1 Elements of the Swiss Cheese model in practice

contextual issues raised by Turner as also providing us with greater insight into the broader context in which such errors are generated.

If we consider the range of incubation processes as a means of generating and developing holes in various defence levels within the organization then the combined effects of such latent and active errors will be to allow failure to cascade quickly through the system. This, combined with the difficulties of sensemaking around the 'gaps' in defences, will generate a sense of confusion amongst decision-makers and system operators that will allow an event to escalate. If the system in use is tightly coupled, or if the decision horizons have been compressed to the point at which 'storming' takes place, then the conditions will be in place for a crisis to develop. The storming process represents a further example of how management can respond to one set of task demands (within a short term time horizon) but, at the same time, create problems further down the time-line. Again, the processes of sensemaking are clearly of importance here.

Our aim for the remainder of this discussion is to outline a framework for conceptualizing this process within the initial phase of a crisis and to assess the importance of error, sensemaking and decision processes in the creation of an environment in which both incubation and escalation can take place. However, we may choose to describe this complex process, the problems that sit at the heart of failure generation are generally common and they centre on a number of factors.

Firstly, there are issues around the behaviour of non-linear systems and the processes through which emergence takes place within organizations. Much of the body of management theory is based upon a set of assumptions around cause-and-effect relationships (that is, they are set within a linear system of operating). This represents a significant problem in terms of crisis generation, as it serves to generate assumptions about controls and human behaviours on the part of managers. Recent work has pointed to the importance of non-linear processes within organizations (Axelrod and Cohen, 1999; Taylor, 2001; Urry, 2003) as well as to a range of, what have been described as, organizational *mis*behaviours (Ackroyd and Thompson, 1999). These misbehaviours would include a range of work around violations, human error (Reason, 1990a, 1990b, 1997, 2001) and the limitations associated with expert knowledge claims (Angell, 1996; Beck, 1986, 1992; Epstein, 1996; Giddens, 1990; Michael, 1992; Smith, 1990). These issues are of importance in generating some of the emergent conditions that create difficulties for managers as a consequence of the linear approaches to control that are taken by organizations.

Secondly, there is often little actual 'evidence' available to decision-makers in support of their attempts to address a range of those potential hazards that could escalate into crises. For many crises, whilst there were warnings and concerns about potential problems, there was often insufficient evidence available to force decision-makers to deal with the problem. The beliefs and assumptions held by decision-makers and, to an extent, their values, would need to be changed by such 'evidence' and so it would invariably have to be unequivocal. One 'solution' to this problem associated with a lack of clear evidence has been to try and adopt a more precautionary approach to dealing with hazards, especially around public policy and health issues (Calman and Smith, 2001). However, such an approach has also been criticized for stifling innovation and change, as well as requiring a significant change in the mindset of many decision-makers in order to be effective. Further work is needed in the area of the precautionary approach to assess its importance as an element of crisis management policy and practice. Whilst the core precepts of the precautionary principle are robust[1], the ways in which these elements of the principle can be put into place needs more careful consideration.

These issues of prevention, precaution and evidence-based decision-making sit in the initial 'crisis of management' phase and relate to the processes by which crisis potential becomes incubated. Invariably, there are also a series of issues concerning the cost of prevention, especially when considered on the basis of no 'evidence of harm'. This is an issue that has caused many organizations to make assumptions around safety as they trade-off risk and profitability/performance (Angell, 1996; Chiles, 2002; Collee and Bradley, 1997; Flynn and Marsden, 1992; Moorhead, Ference, and Neck, 1991; Puchan, 2001; Stephens and Brynner, 2001). The problems associated with a priori evidence, a precautionary approach, informed consent and the role of predictive validity around decision making remain significant barriers to crisis identification.

Thirdly, in an increasingly interconnected world, it is likely that the conditions for failure in one part of the organization may well have been generated elsewhere within the organization or, in certain cases, in other organizations. The structure and tightly coupled nature of our supply chains (especially in terms of the length and levels of interaction within them), the role of 'transport' (in its various physical and electronic forms) in our globalized economies, and the speed at which problems can emerge relative to our abilities to intervene around mitigation, all conspire to generate significant problems for management (Taylor, 2001). If we add to this the vulnerabilities of those various 'supply' and 'value' chains to malicious attack, then the problems take on a further degree of complexity. The terrorist attacks in Tokyo, New York, Madrid, and London all illustrated the vulnerability of transport systems to malicious actions (Baxter and Downing, 2001; Murakami, 1997; Posner, 2003; Walker, 2002). Even in those cases where there is no direct action to cause harm, the 'coupling' and 'complexity' (Perrow, 1984) within the system can generate significant problems around delays and disruption.

An example that illustrates this problem can be found in the outbreak of SARS that took place in 2003 (Bloom, 2003; Chan-Yeung and Yu, 2003; Wenzel and Edmond, 2003). Here, a disease outbreak in China was quickly transferred to a number of countries in a matter of days. The outbreak generated considerable concern and significantly increased the task demands placed upon health-care providers in a number of countries that were geographically removed from the source of the outbreak. Whilst disease outbreaks might be considered an extreme example of such connectivity, examples also exist around the food industry (Anon, 2003; Brown, 2003; Collee and Bradley, 1997; Narden, 2003; Pennington, 2003; Yoo, 2003) and product recalls and bans (Angell, 1996; Puchan, 2001; Siomkos, 1999; Stephens and Brynner, 2001) that also point to the nature and extent of the role of the coupling and complexity within supply chains.

The importance of the crisis of management phase comes from the fact that it represents the processes through which managers become the 'authors of their own misfortune', and create a set of conditions, protocols and practices that will ultimately allow an incident to escalate into an accident and beyond. In order to begin to address this process, we need to explore the processes of incubation, escalation and the role of human agency (especially management) in the generation of crisis. In order to set these issues into context, we need to establish a framework that allows us to manage problems 'ahead of the curve'. In this case, the curve can be seen as representing the escalating nature of a crisis, the increasing task demands associated with such escalation, and the points of intervention that will be required to bring the event back within acceptable limits and control parameters.

Managing ahead of the curve: dealing with the points of inflection

It is possible to conceptualize an emerging crisis, as an escalating set of task demands that impact upon the organization in ways that challenge the capabilities of managers and 'operators' to bring the 'event' back to within their 'sphere of control'. At the point that they lose control, we can argue that the event has become a crisis. Figure 2 attempts to conceptualize this process and assumes that a crisis is reached when the organization moves beyond its abilities to contain the task demands of the 'event' and it escalates still further beyond the limits of existing contingency plans. At this point, external resource will be required (or even imposed upon the organization) in order to recover from the damage caused and to prevent further escalation of the 'event'. The problem space referred to here is that area around the point of inflection. It is here that the event can either be brought back under control or can escalate still further. The problem space can be seen to include that period just before and after the inflection points, as this period will have a significant bearing on the nature of

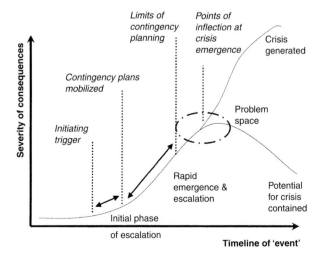

Figure 2 Crisis emergence and the point of inflection

the subsequent decisions. Figure 2 invariably simplifies the process and several qualifying comments need to be made at this juncture. Of particular importance here will be the point at which the organization's contingency plans are brought into effect. It can be argued that they should be mobilized (along with the crisis teams) at the time where it becomes clear that that event has the potential to escalate into a crisis. The aim of any contingency process is to stop an event from escalating to the point where the organization 'loses' control and there will be several important decision processes in this process (which can also be expressed as points of inflection).

The period leading up to the critical point of inflection is clearly important and it is here that the processes of incubation and the creation of latent conditions will allow for the rapid escalation of the event, as will the various processes around emergence, coupling/complexity and storming. It is necessary to expand our assessment of the period leading up to the rapid emergence of the event and the eventual process of bringing the event back under control. Figure 3 attempts to elaborate on the processes that take place within this period and it is possible to identify three main phases that need to be explored in more detail.

The initial phase of the incident, that period leading up to the initiating event, serves to generate the potential for subsequent failure by the interaction of the incubation factors, latent and active error processes that take place over time within the organization. In essence, this process is 'the crisis of management', because it is here that the problems around performance within the management structures will generate the bedrock for crisis. The vulnerability that is created will then be exposed by the triggering event and this will allow the crisis to generate. The next phase is between the initiating event and the point at which the organization's contingency, or crisis management, plans are brought into operation. In the early phases of the crisis, the organization responds to the initiating event within the framework of its contingency planning processes. The decisions and actions taken at this point will ultimately shape the event. The performance of the organization here will also be a function of its previous

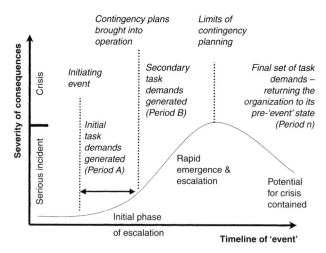

Figure 3 Initial escalation of an incident up to the limits of the existing contingency plans

testing of its contingency plans, the training of teams, and the integration of learning from previous crisis events (both internal and external to the organization). It is clear that learning also plays a major role in this initial phase of a crisis, a point that has been made elsewhere (Smith, 1995; Toft and Reynolds, 1994; Turner, 1976, 1978). Clearly, if the organization does not have any contingency plans or processes in place then there will be a rapid 'escalation' of the conditions associated with the event. These will invariably generate task demands that will swamp the abilities of 'management' to cope and this may allow for further escalation to take place. If there are gaps in existing controls, or if the event generates emergent conditions for which there are no controls, then the event will quickly move beyond the limitations of existing contingency plans. The time taken to do this is important, as any undue delays may result in the incident escalating to a point where it becomes a crisis by its own volition. Although this would normally be considered as part of the operational crisis phase, there is a period of overlap between the two phases, in which the actions of management can continue to have an important influence on the generation of a crisis. A failure to mobilize the necessary resource or actions that are based on false assumptions will serve to shape the subsequent phases of the event narrative. The processes of sensemaking are therefore important in this phase as, without the benefits of the formal crisis management procedures, managers will have to deal with the initial demands of this event as well as manage the demands of the core business activities. Clearly, there are important issues here around the ways that managers are trained and developed as part of the organization's human resources strategy.

Similarly, the compression of the various time horizons for core business processes will also have an important bearing on the generation of task demands at this point. Radell's observations around the processes of 'storming' serve as an example of how core business processes may both generate the potential for a crisis, but also inhibit the response of the organization in dealing with the early phases of the event as it emerges. By compressing the decision horizons for key projects, the organization will increase the 'coupling' and 'complexity' that is inherent in the system and increase the potential for emergent properties in the process. Taken together this will generate additional task demands for management that may serve to overwhelm its capabilities, with the result that incidents escalate into more serious, and potentially catastrophic, events.

The second phase of this process occurs once the organization's crisis management procedures have been activated. It is assumed here that this will involve formal structures for crisis management teams (working at several cross-functional levels) as well as a framework of existing contingency processes around media handling, problem solving and information management. The actions of 'management' in this phase will also have an impact on the containment of the crisis event and the eventual return of the organization to a 'normal' (or near normal) state. There will be a series of secondary, or second-order, task demands generated at this point that will be a function of the ways in which the event has escalated to this point. This phase is critical, in that it represents a point at which the organization can finally control the escalation of the event. Once it moves beyond the existing contingency capabilities of the organization, then the event will be deemed to be a crisis, as it will be visible to outside observers as a function of its scale, will have generated damage, and will also require significant external resources in order to bring it back under control. It is possible that this period in the evolution of a crisis can be long standing and the organization may be put into a position where it effectively moves from one pre-crisis stage to another, but without ever fully recovering.

The final stage (shown in Figure 3 as period *n*) will represent the processes by which the organization is returned to a state close to the 'pre-crisis' position (although it could be argued that, depending on the nature of the event, this can never be fully achieved). Problems occur once the organization moves beyond the limits of its contingency plans as this may mean that the event has developed in such a way that it has generated conditions that were not considered as initially plausible by those managers responsible for assessing the risks. Managers will, therefore, need to make a number of decisions that could make the event escalate even further. It is at this stage that the notion of a point of inflection takes on an important new dynamic within this process.

Moving towards crisis: points of inflection as failures in management

The issue of anticipating and managing potential elements of organizational failure was addressed by Handy (Handy, 1994, 1995) who argued that there was a need to consider the potential for problem escalation at what he termed the 'point of inflection'. In many respects, this concept serves as a useful metaphor for our considerations here around the various 'crisis of management' processes. Handy points to the trajectory that organizations have and the manner in which this trajectory can quickly escalate into a 'crisis' event. He argues that we often only consider taking action to address a problem when we have passed the optimal point for intervention. This can be seen as a result of a number of factors including, our abilities to make sense of what is happening, the processes of denial, and the paralysis that can often be created by high-impact, high-pressure incidents.

In many respects, these arguments have been advanced by several authors working in the area of crisis management. Perrow, for example, pointed to the importance of 'tight coupling' and 'interactive complexity' in which the inter-action between elements of the organization and its activities will quickly lead to the cascade of an initiating event to generate a catastrophic failure (Perrow, 1984). Gladwell also identifies a similar notion of an 'inflection' point, which he terms a 'tipping point' (Gladwell, 2000). Conceptually, therefore, this notion of a critical decision and action point has a broad base within the academic litera-ture. For our present purposes the area around the point of inflection can be considered as a problem space, in that it will involve a considerable amount of sensemaking and problem solving. It can also generate further problems as a function of the decision making process that takes place within this period. In some cases, it is possible to see organizations embedding the pre-conditions for subsequent crises as part of their attempt to manage earlier crisis events (Sipika and Smith, 1993) and this leads to the development of a continued erosion of

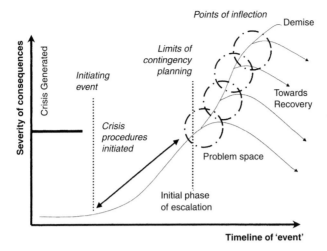

Figure 4 The point of inflection and the emergence of crisis conditions

organizational resilience. We can argue here that there are multiple points of infection within the context of a crisis (see Figure 4), as there will be a considerable amount of emergence within that period beyond the limits of the organization's contingency planning processes.

The challenge for management is to be able to work within this problem space around the various points of inflection in such a way as to prevent further escalation. However, this is a dynamic and extremely challenging process and one for which most managers have not been trained. We can consider these various points of inflection as generating a 'vulnerable pathway' within the organization and this needs to be developed in more detail at this point.

Pathways of vulnerability

The final point to make in this paper relates to the processes by which vulnerability is created and embedded within the organization. The concept of vulnerable pathways has been set out in more detail elsewhere (Smith, 2000, 2005) and only some of the main issues will be outlined here as a means of drawing this discussion together. The intention at this point is to link together the notions of vulnerable pathways with the points of inflection in an attempt to identify an area that requires further theoretical development and empirical research.

In essence, a vulnerable pathway links together the various points of inflection along with the products of incubation and the development of latent conditions. The outcome of this process is that the activities of management within the 'crisis of management' phase will create the pre-conditions for these pathways. The decisions taken at the various points of inflection will shape the route that the crisis follows. In addition, the crisis process will inevitably display a range of emergent properties that are of importance in allowing defences to be eroded or bypassed. This has been an issue that has attracted a considerable amount of attention within the broad social science literature, but has not had the attention that it deserves within mainstream management theory. In many cases, such failures combine with the assumptions of systems designers and managers to generate a set of beliefs regarding the manner in which failure can occur. Of particular importance in this regard is the manner in which these design assumptions can combine with the assumptions held by managers to create the conditions in which the point of inflection can be created.

Another perspective on this process sees the point of inflection as existing at the interface between stabile and chaotic conditions facing an organization. Figure 4 highlighted the manner in which an escalating failure exceeds the limits of the contingency plans in place to deal with the perceived portfolio of failure. At the various points of inflection, the decisions and actions taken in response to the prevailing systems' conditions may allow the problem to escalate further and move the organization into what could be considered as a chaotic state. The emerging curve of an escalating crisis can be seen to mark the shift from a stable to a chaotic state. This relationship between the crisis literature and the developing research in the fields of complexity and chaos is an area that may prove to be particularly fruitful for our understanding of the various processes at work in this initial period of a crisis. Again, more empirical and theoretical work is needed in this area.

Conclusions

This chapter has sought to draw upon some of the main findings of other papers in this book and to extend the discussion of the processes that are in operation around the initial stages of a crisis. The chapter has argued that the creation of the various products of incubation will ensure that the decisions taken, especially at the various points of inflection within the crisis timeline, will allow the crisis to escalate beyond the capabilities of the organization to contain it unless the process is carefully managed. This represents a major challenge for organizations and may even cast doubt upon the validity of many current approaches to dealing with business continuity management.

There is, however, a need for much more research in this area if we are to elaborate upon our understanding of these processes and, perhaps more to the point, to translate them into a format that will prove accessible and useful to practicing managers. It is that translation of research into practice that is the biggest challenge to the academic community.

Note

1   This is especially the case around the view that the absence of any evidence of harm is not a proof of safety, and that where the potential consequences are great, then a more cautious approach should be taken.

References

Ackroyd, S. and Thompson, P. (1999) *Organizational Misbehaviour*, SAGE: London.

Angell, M. (1996) *Science on trial. The clash of medical evidence and the law in the breast implant case*, W.W. Norton and Company: New York, NY.

Anon. (2003) 'Meat from U.S. mad cow traced to 8 states', Guam, CNN.com, accessed 31/12/2003, on-line ed. http://edition.cnn.com/2003/US/12/28/mad.cow/index.html

Axelrod, R. and Cohen, M. D. (1999) *Harnessing complexity. Organizational implications of a scientific frontier*, The Free Press: New York.

Baxter, J. and Downing, M. (eds.) (2001) *The day that shook the world. Understanding September 11th*, BBC Worldwide Ltd: London.

Beck, U. (1986) *Risikogesellschaft: Auf dem Weg in eine andere Moderne*, Suhrkamp Verlag: Frankfurt.

Beck, U. (1992) *Risk society. Towards a new modernity*, M. Ritter, trans., SAGE: London.

Bloom, B. R. (2003) 'Lessons from SARS', *Science*, 300: 701.

Brown, D. L. (2003) 'Canada awaits test results on cow: Government plays down relevance of infected animal's origin', *Washington Post*, accessed 14:20 on 31/12/2003 ed.: A12. (http://www.washingtonpost.com/ac2/wp-dyn/A39764–2003Dec29?language=printer).

Calman, K. and Smith, D. (2001) 'Works in theory but not in practice? Some notes on the precautionary principle', *Public Administration*, 79 (1): 185–204.

Chan-Yeung, M. and Yu, W. C. (2003) 'Outbreak of severe acute respiratory syndrome in Hong Kong Special Administrative Region: case report', *British Medical Journal*, 326: 350–352.

Chiles, J. R. (2002) *Inviting disaster. Lessons from the edge of technology*, Harper Business: New York.

Clement, B. (2005) 'We've worked so hard, and they do this to us', *The Independent*, Saturday 16th April 2005, p. 5.

Collee, J. G. and Bradley, R. (1997) 'BSE: a decade on – part 2', *The Lancet*, 349: 715–721.

Epstein, S. (1996) *Impure science. AIDS, activism, and the politics of knowledge*, University of California Press: Berkeley, CA.

Erikson, K. (1994) *A new species of trouble. Explorations in disaster, trauma, and community*, W.W. Norton and Company: New York.

Flynn, A. and Marsden, T. (1992) 'Food regulation in a period of agricultural retreat: the British experience', *Geoforum*, 23 (1): 85–93.

Giddens, A. (1990) *The consequences of modernity*, Polity Press: Cambridge.

Gladwell, M. (2000) *The Tipping Point. How little things can make a big difference*. Abacus: London.

Handy, C. (1994) *The empty raincoat: making sense of the future*, Hutchinson: London.

Handy, C. (1995) *The age of unreason. New thinking for a new world*, Random House: London.

Harrison, M. (2005) 'Blair pledges £150m to aid Rover as Chinese pull out of rescue deal', *The Independent*, Saturday 16th April 2005, p. 4.

Lichfield, J. and Harries, R. (2005) 'Twenty die in blaze at Paris hotel used to house migrants', *The Independent*, Saturday 16th April, p. 20.

McNeill, D. (2005) 'Panicked China reins in rioters as anti-Japanese protests spread', *The Independent*, Saturday, 16th April, p. 24.

Marks, K. (2005) 'Jail for man behind "Australia's Enron" after £2bn collapse', *The Independent*, Saturday 16th April, p. 22.

Michael, M. (1992) 'Lay discourses of science: science-in-general, science-in-particular, and self', *Science, Technology and Human Values*, 17 (3): 313–333.

Moorhead, G., Ference, R. and Neck, C. P. (1991) 'Group decision fiascoes continue: Space Shuttle Challenger and a revised groupthink framework', *Human Relations*, 44 (6): 539–550.

Murakami, H. (1997) *Underground. The Tokyo gas attack and the Japanese psyche*, A. Birnbaum and P. Gabriel, trans., The Harvill Press: London.

Narden, B. (2003) 'Cow's meat reached retailers in eight states', *Washington Post*, Section A, accessed 14:21 on 31/12/2003, on-line ed.: A01. (http://www.washingtonpost.com/ac2/wp-dyn/A37014–2003Dec28?language=printer).

Pennington, H. (2003) *When food kills. BSE, E.coli and disaster science*, Oxford University Press: Oxford.

Perrow, C. (1984) *Normal Accidents*, Basic Books: New York.

Popham, P. (2005) 'Berlusconi's coalition in crisis after partner quits', *The Independent*, Saturday 16th April, p. 20.

Posner, G. (2003) *Why America slept. The failure to prevent 9/11*, Random House: New York, NY.

Puchan, H. (2001) 'The Mercedes-Benz A-class crisis', *Corporate Communications: An International Journal*, 6 (1): 42–46.

Radell, W. W. (1990) 'Storming: the losing edge', *Scholars*, 2: 24–31.

Radell, W. W. (1992) 'Storming and catastrophic system failures', *Industrial Crisis Quarterly*, 6: 295–312.

Rasmussen, J. (1982) 'Human errors: A taxonomy for describing human malfunction in industrial installations', *Journal of Occupational Accidents*, 4: 311–333.

Rasmussen, J. (1983) 'Skills, rules, knowledge: signals, signs and symbols and other distinctions in human performance models', *IEEE Transactions on Systems, Man and Cybernetics*, 13: 257–267.

Reason, J. T. (1990a). 'The contribution of latent human failures to the breakdown of complex systems', *Philosophical Transactions of the Royal Society of London B*, 37: 475–484.

Reason, J. T. (1990b) *Human error*, Oxford University Press: Oxford.

Reason, J. T. (1997) *Managing the risks of organizational accidents*, Ashgate: Aldershot.

Reason, J. T. (2001) 'Understanding adverse events: the human factor', in C. Vincent (ed.), *Clinical risk management. Enhancing patient safety*, 2nd ed.: 9–30, BMJ Books: London.

Sagan, S. D. (1993) *The limits of safety. Organizations, accidents, and nuclear weapons*, Princeton University Press: Princeton, NJ.

Siomkos, G. J. (1999) 'On achieving exoneration after a product safety industrial crisis', *Journal of Business & Industrial Marketing*, 14 (1): 17–29.

Sipika, C. and Smith, D. (1993) 'From disaster to crisis: the failed turnaround of Pan American Airlines', *Journal of Contingencies and Crisis Management*, 1 (3): 138–151.

Smith, D. (1990) 'Corporate power and the politics of uncertainty: Risk management at the Canvey Island complex', *Industrial Crisis Quarterly*, 4 (1): 1–26.

Smith, D. (1995) 'The Dark Side of Excellence: Managing Strategic Failures', in J. Thompson (ed.), *Handbook of Strategic Management*, 161–191. Butterworth-Heinemann: London.

Smith, D. (2000) 'On a wing and a prayer? Exploring the human components of technological failure', *Systems Research and Behavioral Science*, 17: 543–559.

Smith, D. (2005) 'Business (not) as usual – crisis management, service interruption and the vulnerability of organisations', *Journal of Services Marketing*, 19 (5): 309–320.

Stephens, T. and Brynner, R. (2001) *Dark remedy. The impact of Thalidomide and its revival as a vital medicine*, Perseus Publishing: Cambridge, Mass.

Taylor, M. C. (2001) *The moment of complexity – emerging network culture*, Chicago University Press: Chicago.

Tenner, E. (1996) *Why things bite back. Technology and the revenge effect*, Fourth Estate: London.

Toft, B. and Reynolds, S. (1994) *Learning from disasters*, Butterworth: London.

Turner, B. A. (1976) 'The organizational and interorganizational development of disasters', *Administrative Science Quarterly*, 21: 378–397.

Turner, B. A. (1978) *Man-made disasters*, Wykeham: London.

Urry, J. (2003) *Global complexity*, Polity: Cambridge.

Walker, D. M. (2002) '9/11: the implications for public-sector management', *Public Administration Review*, 62 (Special Issue): 94–97.

Weick, K. E. (1993) 'The collapse of sensemaking in organizations: The Mann Gulch Disaster', *Administrative Science Quarterly*, 38: 628–652.

Weick, K. E. (1995) *Sensemaking in organizations*, SAGE: Thousand Oaks.

Weick, K. E. (2001) *Making sense of the organization*, Blackwell: Oxford.

Wenzel, R. P. and Edmond, M. B. (2003) 'Managing SARS amidst uncertainty', *New England Journal of Medicine*, 348 (20): 1947–1948.

Yoo, J.-S. (2003) USDA envoys discuss mad cow in S. Korea, *Chicago Tribune*, accessed at 17:24 on 1/1/2004, on-line ed. http://www.chicagotribune.com/news/nationworld/sns-ap-mad-cow-skorea,1,6036653.story.

Crisis management in practice

Chapter 21

Carolyne Smart and Ilan Vertinsky

DESIGNS FOR CRISIS DECISION UNITS

T HE PAPERS OF HEDBERG, Nystrom, and Starbuck (1976) and Turner (1976) are excellent examples of a growing literature that deals with causes of organizational crises and designs for their prevention. Yet in a world of sharp discontinuities, crises are inevitable. Reducing their frequency may unfortunately result in a reduction of the organization's coping resources. Designs for preventing crises should be complemented by development of capabilities for coping with crises. This paper deals with the design of the specialized decision process that emerges once a crisis has begun.

The microcosm of crisis decision making is presented through a conceptual model describing the major variables affecting the quality of decision making and the implementation of decisions during a crisis. In particular, attention is focused on those links in the model that define areas of a decision unit's vulnerability to malfunctions. The model is presented by means of a flow graph where pluses imply positive impacts and minuses imply inverse interrelationships. The paper then investigates some of the major areas of organizational susceptibility to pathologies and explores design features aimed at preventing these pathologies.

Quality of decisions and implementation during a crisis: a conceptual model

The Figure displays some of the major links that contribute to the lowering of decision quality within a group and that lead to dysfunctions within the implementation process during a crisis.

Decision quality (Box 0) is inversely related to the rates of the four types of

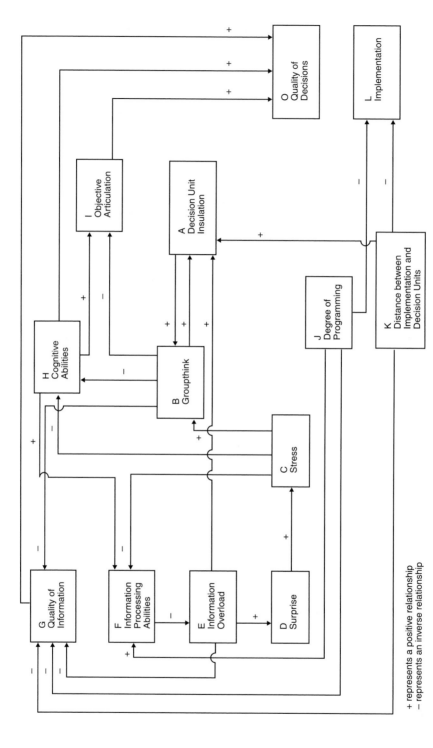

+ represents a positive relationship
– represents an inverse relationship

Figure 1 A conceptual model of crisis decision and implementation processes

decision errors: rejecting a correct course of action, accepting a wrong solution to a problem, solving the wrong problem, and solving the right problem correctly but too late (Raiffa, 1968).

Decision quality depends upon three factors: the quality of information inputs into the decision process (Box G), the fidelity of objective articulation and tradeoff evaluation (Box I), and cognitive abilities of the decision group (Box H).

The quality of information inputs into the decision process depends on the ability of the system to effectively absorb information flows, thus preventing overloads (Box E) and to reduce noise in communication channels. Noise depends upon the distance between units in the organization (Box K) (distance in the psychological sense not necessarily geographical). Information overload results in dysfunctional selective attention, retention of information, and delays and subversion of communication flows. The special dynamics of group decision making under stress – 'groupthink' – also introduce pathological filters into information processing.

Articulation of objectives and fidelity in assessing tradeoffs are essential to the choice process. Especially relevant to the study of crisis is the ability to preserve the appropriate posture of risk taking and insulate such posture from the impact of short-term circumstances. In the model, the major impacts are groupthink, which introduces a risk bias, and general cognitive abilities, which affect the scope of objectives attended.

Cognitive abilities are the abilities of the decision unit to interpret information, generate options creatively, calculate and make choices between alternative courses of action. Changes in cognitive abilities during a crisis are attributed mainly to the groupthink phenomenon (Box B) and stress (Box C).

Implementation (Box L) depends on the distance between decision and implementation units (Box K) and the ability of organizational units to realign their procedures with new states of the system, an ability which is inversely related to the degree of programming in the organization (Box J). One should note that the two evaluative variables, quality of decision and implementation, are not additive. When decision quality is high, lack of implementation voids its value to the organization. When decision quality is low, however, lack of implementation may have a positive buffering impact on the organization. In a crisis one must secure a high-quality decision-making process, the outputs of which are duly and precisely implemented. High-quality decisions increase the implementation units' trust in the decision unit and increase degree of compliance with directives. High-quality decisions tend also, in the long run, to reduce the demands imposed on the management information system by improving the process of problem definition and making economical use of information.

Crisis decision-making pathologies

Analysis for design may proceed in two ways, by adopting a developmental point of view or by adopting a preventive perspective. The latter provides a more economical closure for the analysis, while sacrificing many relevant design aspects. The preventive focus is more appropriate here since, from a cost-benefit point of view, the general development of the organization should not be attuned to rare circumstances – and by definition crises are rare events. Therefore, the focus is on specific components and links of the model that are potential sources of pathologies in the decision and implementation processes during a crisis.

A decision process consists of articulation of objectives, generation of alternate courses of action, appraisal of their feasibility, evaluation of the consequences of given alternatives, and a choice of that alternative which contributes most to the attainment of organizational objectives.

The following classes of crises-specific pathologies affect one or more of these components of decision making:

1. Narrowing of cognitive processes – affecting primarily alternative generation and calculation of consequences
2. Information distortion – affecting the appraisal of feasibility of alternatives and identification of their consequences
3. Group pathologies – affecting the range of alternatives considered, the appraisal of the alternatives' feasibility, identification of true objectives, and evaluation of consequences
4. Rigidities in programming – affecting primarily the scope of alternatives generated and the choice process
5. Lack of decision readiness – affecting indirectly all the above pathologies by intensifying the stress rooted in the crisis situation.

Rigidities in programming and information distortion are the key constraints upon the implementation process. Rigidities of programming increase the friction associated with a substantial organizational change while information distortion inhibits the effectiveness of any control system.

Narrowing of cognitive processes

During crises when individuals are under great stress and important decisions must be made within a short time, certain pathologies may arise in the decision process that reduce its quality, for example, more errors of calculation and fewer options considered. Although a moderate level of stress may promote learning in a decision situation (Cangelosi and Dill, 1965), during a crisis stress is usually of such a magnitude that it promotes dysfunctional behavior. Holsti (1971: 62) suggested that an 'increasingly severe crisis tends to make creative policy making both more important and less likely.'

Creative decision making in part depends on an input of ideas from a wide variety of individuals reflecting different experiences and expertise. During a crisis, there is a tendency, however, for a contraction of authority to occur in an organization (Hermann, 1963). Authority for decision making shifts to higher levels and there is a reduction in the number of persons participating in the decision process (Mulder, van Eck, and de Jong, 1971: 21).

As the decision/authority unit contracts, the amount of stress on decision makers increases since each member feels a greater responsibility for potential failure. The greater the level of felt stress, the greater the perceived pressure for decisiveness. Stress leads to the narrowing of cognitive processes. An individual under stress screens out some essential environmental cues thereby adopting a restricted perspective of the decision situation (Easterbrook, 1959; Holsti, 1971). With decreasing levels of cognitive efficiency, behavior becomes less adaptive and the resulting decision is often of poor quality (Levine, 1971; Robinson, 1972).

Stress-related maladaptive behavior is manifested in numerous ways. Milburn (1972) suggested that stress has a curvilinear effect on individual performance. While a moderate level of stress may be conducive to good decision making, high levels of stress lead to a breakdown in perceptual accuracy and reduced ability to focus on relevant information from the environment. Paige (1968) and Albers (1966) have suggested that, under great stress, decision makers become increasingly concerned with short-range issues at the expense of long-range outcomes. Stress also promotes a rigidity in problem solving, a functional fixedness that reduces the individual's capacity for abstract reasoning and tolerance for ambiguity (Beier, 1951; Smock, 1955; Loomis, 1960). The impaired cognitive abilities of the individual may result in an inability to predict the consequences of various alternate courses of action (Holsti, 1972).

> 'The consensus of most behavioral research is that men operating under . . . acute stress are scarcely capable of considered judgement. Strain and fatigue commonly produce actions which are caricatures of day-to-day behavior.'
>
> (Nathan (1975) 259)

Information distortion

During crises changes in information-processing abilities throughout the organization also contribute to reduced efficiency in making decisions. Under crisis-induced stress, the number of communication channels used for collection and distribution of information between the decision unit and the rest of the organization is reduced (Hermann, 1963). This is in part a result of the tendency toward centralization noted previously and the debilitating impact of a high volume of information competing for the attention of fewer decision makers.

Overload of information and the need to respond quickly force decision makers to use fewer channels, hence further reducing their alternate information sources and shortening their horizons.[1] Under conditions of information overload, an organization may use mechanisms such as omission, delay of response, filtering and processing incorrect information in order to cope with emerging threats (Miller, 1960). These mechanisms if employed in an ad hoc fashion may cause great distortion of information. Clearly with appropriate planning the dysfunctions of these mechanisms can be minimized. Planned omissions, managed delays, and functional filtering are important parts of any management information system coping with capacity overruns.

Lanzetta and Roby (1957) found that the error rate on task performance was correlated positively with the increased volume of information received by decision makers. Information overload and the perceived need to respond quickly tend to force decision makers to shorten their decision horizons. This tendency increases the probability of decision error.

Information distortion also occurs as a result of the position of a decision unit in the organizational network and the impact a position has upon the timing and information content that reaches decision makers. In hierarchical organizations information must travel through a lengthy filtering process before it reaches the decision unit. The information content reflects the accumulation of information processing selectivities in intermediate stages. Downs (1967) calculated that in a six-level hierarchy, there may be a 98 percent loss of informational content between the lowest and highest level of the organization. Citing Tullock (1965), Downs noted that information is subject to hierarchical distortion in both quantity and quality. The quantity of information received by senior decision makers is reduced as a result of the high cost of communication and their own limited cognitive capacities. Quality of information is distorted due to perceptual differences resulting, in part, from specialization of individuals at each organizational level.

Individuals at lower levels of the organization have a parochial range of interests in contrast to the holistic organizational perspectives of senior decision makers. The filtering process in upward communications therefore reflects information needs and perspectives of lower echelons rather than the needs of recipients. Ackoff (1967) noted that decision makers often suffer from an overabundance of irrelevant information, while Crozier (1963: 51) stated, 'Those who have the necessary information do not have the power to decide, and those who have the power to decide cannot get the necessary information.'

As noted previously, both an overload and an underload of information can exist in different stages of a crisis. Taylor (1975: 410) argued that the information-processing capacity of a decision maker should be viewed as having both upper and lower bounds. Taylor's argument for a band of efficient information processing capacity is made on the basis of optimal levels of stress-related arousal. In the case of a crisis, however, overload and underload of information are both causes of high levels of stress. It has been demonstrated that information deprivation leads individuals to seek out stimuli (Jones, Wilkinson, and Braden, 1961; Suedfeld, 1971). This psychological state may lead a decision maker to seize upon irrelevant or incorrect information without appropriate discrimination.

Group pathologies

Under conditions of crisis-induced stress there is a tendency for participation in decision making to be limited to a small number of individuals. Specifically, the individuals included in the decision unit tend to be from the highest levels of the organization and have the personal confidence of the head of the organization (Hermann, 1972: 288). Consequently, the central decision unit is likely to consist of a tightly knit, homogeneous group, led by a strong leader. The group is usually insulated from the rest of the organization by a sense of shared responsibility, trust, and mutual support.

Special dynamics of the group structure itself can contribute to error under such conditions. Janis (1972) suggested that during crises, under a particular combination of circumstances, in-group pressures in the decision unit bring about a deterioration of mental efficiency, reality testing, and moral judgment. This promotes a condition called groupthink. Janis noted (1972: 13):

> The concept of groupthink pinpoints an entirely different source of trouble, residing neither in the individual nor in the organizational setting. Over and beyond all the familiar sources of human error is a powerful source of defective judgment that arises in cohesive groups – the concurrence seeking tendency, which fosters overoptimism, lack of vigilance, and sloganistic thinking about the weakness and immorality of out groups.

Individuals become committed to group decisions, and, as a result, their own personal attitudes and models of reality shift to reflect that of the group in an attempt to maintain inner consistency. De Rivera (1968: 27) has also noted the effects of group pressures on the individual's sense of reality, suggesting that for a decision maker, 'changing his view of reality means losing emotional contact with the group.'

Groupthink is most likely to occur under the following conditions: when the decision unit displays high cohesion, when the decision unit is insulated from the advice of qualified experts, and when a strong leader actively promotes a solution to a problem. Cohesive groups are not all prone to groupthink. Groupthink results only when the above attributes are present. For example, virtually the same group of individuals in the U.S. government was involved in the decision processes that led to the Bay of Pigs Invasion and to the blockade at the time of the Cuban missile crisis. The effects of groupthink in the first situation resulted in a course of action that was an unmitigated disaster, while the second action is usually considered a model of rational crisis-decision making.

There are eight major symptoms of groupthink.

1. Most or all group members develop an illusion of invulnerability, which promotes excessive optimism and encourages decisions of very high risk.
2. Group members ignore warnings and negative feedback that might force a reassessment of a decision. Attempts are made to rationalize the status quo.
3. Group members display an inviolate belief in their own morality. The ethical and moral consequences of a decision may be ignored entirely.
4. Group members hold sterotyped views of the enemy in adversarial situations. The adversary is regarded as immoral and too evil to attempt genuine negotiations to resolve conflicts, or too stupid and too weak to take any effective counteractions.

5. The group applies direct pressure to any member who expresses doubts about a course of action or questions arguments supporting policies that are favored by the majority. The potentially negative ramifications of a decision are never discussed. In this manner the concurrence-seeking norm is reinforced.

6. Individual members practice self-censorship. They avoid deviating from group consensus by keeping silent about their own doubts and misgivings. This occurs not because of a lack of faith in one's own ideas, but through a fear of losing approval of fellow group members. The assumption that silence means consent reinforces self-censorship.

7. Group members share an illusion that unanimity means truth.

8. Groups develop mindguards – self-appointed members who try to shield the decision unit from information that may go against shared beliefs.

When a decision unit displays most of these symptoms in a crisis situation, it will generally produce poor quality decisions that are likely to bring on a disaster for the organization. The dynamics of groupthink may reinforce some dysfunctional individual behavior patterns. Staw (1976) found that decision makers in some instances may increase their commitment to poor decisions, even at the risk of further negative consequences, to avoid cognitive dissonance.

Rigidities in programming

To ensure coordination, economical information processing, and reliable and efficient routine responses in non-crisis situations, organizations develop standard operating procedures (SOPs). SOPs ensure alignment of interpretation between senders and recipients of messages, and increase predictability of responses to alternative stimuli. To achieve alignment and predictability SOPs demand a restricted repertoire of messages and meanings. Economy of communications is achieved at the price of poverty of expression. Novel situations requiring communications that do not fit into established molds are either ignored or forced into the mold. The new situation triggers the responses the old situation merits or no response at all.

Crisis situations often involve sharp discontinuities requiring realignments of resources, roles, and functions, thus interrupting regular communication networks. The economies obtained by institutionalized SOPs and detailed programming become liabilities, as unlearning may be sometimes a more difficult short-term task than learning.

The process of organizational socialization is geared to penalize deviations from SOPs. In the short run overcoming the existing structure of rewards and penalties may be difficult especially if the reward system is also rigidly programmed. Allison (1971) suggested that most SOPs are highly resistant to change since they are usually grounded in the norms or basic attitudes of the organization and the operating style of its members.

There are, however, some situations in which a network of SOPs may be harnessed for effective coping with a novel situation. This will be the case if (1) a communication strategy exists that uses the predictable, reliable responses in new patterns to yield the correct path of action or (2) the need for change was anticipated and capacity for it built in existing procedures.

Lack of decision readiness

Degree of preparedness, both in psychological terms and in terms of decision capabilities, is an important determinant of the degree of stress resulting from surprise, and in the ability of an organization to cope with the event. Rarity of events contributes to the degree of surprise they generate. Lack of experience induces higher stress since it means that an organization has no repertoire of responses to help it cope with unknown events and the effects of the potential impact are uncertain. Fink, Beak, and Taddeo (1971) have suggested that the intensity of a crisis depends upon the degree of change required in the organization to adapt successfully. The more unfamiliar the event, the greater will be the requirement for adaptation and change to cope with the event, and thus, the greater the level of stress generated.

Surprise occurrence of familiar situations may also induce stress but such stress has a shorter life span than the stress produced by the uncertainty of unfamiliar situations (Cyert and March, 1963). Under conditions of uncertainty, there is a need to develop a model of the situation with an appropriate repertoire of responses. Such a concept-formation process typically is slow. It requires simultaneous discrimination among alternate possible models of the situation and estimation of their parameters. In a familiar situation, the availability of a model for the situation permits quick convergence in reconciling new data from the surprise with existing concepts in the organization.

Implementation failures

Crisis situations require precise and quick implementation of decisions. In large organizations, most problems require the support of others for implementation of solutions. Rarely does the decision unit itself have the ability to implement directly. Thus, an actual decision may be timely, well thought out, and represent the best action in a crisis, but the organization may still end up in a disaster through faulty implementation techniques. MacCrimmon (1973) suggested that in organizations with multiple implementation units, there is considerable room for discretionary action resulting in accidental or purposeful misimplementation. Difficulties in implementation seem rooted in three areas: action units are not motivated to carry out the decision selected; noisy channels of communication and inflexible procedures affecting coordination may delay receipt of messages and timing of actions; and the action units may not understand their orders.

As noted before, mobilization for coping with crises may disrupt existing organizational patterns. The uncertainty produced by organizational reshuffling may strengthen the tendency of units to engage in defensive moves for preserving their territories. Uncertainty may heighten the commitment to parochial goals, which represent to individuals the familiar. Different degrees of exposure to crises and therefore different degrees of felt threat may increase the existing differences in perceived organizational priorities between units. While an external threat may be the best motivator for long-term organizational cohesiveness, in the short run differentiated exposure to this threat may intensify internal organizational conflicts. Even when alignment between units' motives and organizational needs is achieved, implementation may fail because units do not understand or are incapable of executing the required course of action.

In the discussion of standard operating procedures and interunit communications, it was suggested that needs generated by novel situations will be ignored or interpreted to fit existing molds. Such resistance to change unintentionally subverts directives. Control systems which may provide quick feedback to central decision units for corrective actions also often suffer from rigidity of programming and therefore fail to signal implementation failures.

Prescriptions for crisis

The Table presents design features for preventing the crisis pathologies just discussed. While generally the prescriptions will contribute positively to alleviating a specific pathology, they may also have undesirable side effects. Improvements typically come at a cost. The balance of costs and benefits depends upon the contingency, the organization, and the particular role players in the decision situation. The following discussion attempts to illustrate some of these tradeoffs by examining the suggested prescriptions for improving decision quality and for increasing decision implementation during a crisis.

Preventing premature consensus

Dominant leadership has been recognized as an element of group dynamics that can lead to error in the decision process, particularly as such leadership promotes a quick convergence on a single alternative (Maier, 1967; Janis, 1972). This tendency can be alleviated by the decision leader encouraging critical evaluation of policies, perhaps assigning a specific role to each group member, and encouraging the expression of a variety of different points of view and expressions of doubts. Varying opinions from members are more likely to be considered if, as Thibaut and Kelley (1959) suggested, the leader refrains from critical evaluation and acts merely to guide the discussion. Although this procedure can work if the leader is committed to ensuring critical appraisal, it is difficult for most organizational members to overcome traditional hierarchical norms of deference to the leader. If one group or individual is intent on pleasing the leader, the process can be subverted. Open criticism in debates can lead to damaged feelings if members are carried away in their roles as critical evaluators. 'Feelings of rejection, depression, and anger might be evoked so often when this role assignment is put into practice that it could have a corrosive effect on morale and working relations within the group' (Janis, 1972: 210).

Table 1 Designs for crisis: preventive measures

Major problems	Characteristics and symptoms	Prescriptions
Narrowing of cognitive processes, premature consensus resulting from limited alternative generation	Preferred solution promoted by strong central leadership	Encourage critical evaluation and various points of view, remain nonevaluative at outset of policy session
	Reduced cognitive abilities as a result of increased stress	Rotate decision members or have separate crisis- and noncrisis-decision units
		Develop stress profiles on leaders and use stress reduction techniques (TM, relaxation)
		Use behavioral modification techniques to increase individual thresholds of stress tolerance
	Limited information from fewer sources as a result of pressure and stress	Vary membership of decision unit to ensure leaders are exposed to new points of view
		Generate alternatives to current solution for a specific time period
	Reduction in decision-unit size, fewer alternate points of view from all parts organization (insulation)	Members of a decision unit should discuss alternatives with associates in their own units to obtain fresh opinions and reactions
		Invite outside experts to give their opinions to the decision group
	Functional fixedness in problem solving	Use creative problem-solving techniques for generating alternatives such as brainstorming, synectics, morphology
	Attention to short-range issues at the expense of long-range issues	Shift focus deliberately to evaluate long-range issues
		Develop specialized responsibility to advocate the long-range perspective
		Encourage entire decision group to generate additional alternatives with a long-range focus

Continued

Table 1 *continued*

Major problems	Characteristics and symptoms	Prescriptions
Information distortion	Information overload as a result of reduced size of the decision unit and increased information inputs	Develop better scanning techniques and efficient monitoring devices to flag trends above threshold levels; use special formats for presenting information
	Time delays in intelligence reports	Use special information systems for crises based on data compression and effective sampling techniques
		Use special communications channels (hotlines)
		Establish special crisis units for data assembly and coordination
		Set up outside channels of information to cut through hierarchy
		Develop new flexible SOPs
	Preference for agreeable information mindguards*	Diversify jobs
		Use role playing and psychodrama Protect minority points of view
		Communicate directly with outside groups not part of the decision unit
	Stereotypes of the adversary, cultural blocks*	Construct scenarios of adversary's alternatives
		Carefully reconsider and reinterpret signals from adversary
		Use expert advice on foreign cultures, cross-cultural training
Group pathologies	Illusions of invulnerability of decision group and high risk propensity*	Set up independent resource and capability appraisals
		Shift risk propensity from group level to lower individual levels: record acceptable risk levels before an alternative is selected

Major problems	Characteristics and symptoms	Prescriptions
		Construct worst-outcome scenarios for realistic appraisal of seriousness of proposed alternative
	Rationalization of warnings which may force a reassessment of current policies*	Assign at least one member of decision group the role of devil's advocate
		Structure evaluation of each proposal, emphasizing negative aspects (dialectical approach)
	Belief in the inherent morality of the decision group*	Form subgroups to reduce the possibility of the group developing a concurrence-seeking norm
	Pressures on members to conform to accepted group policies*	Protect minority opinions
		Use dialectic approach or independent groups to work on the same problems but with different leaders
	Suppression of personal doubts*	Encourage expression of objections and doubts
		Set up anonymous channels for expressing opinions and providing information to the group (Delphi technique)
	Cognitive biases and faulty conceptualization	Formal bias-correcting programs (computer routines) for assessment of subjective probabilities
Rigidities in programming	Responses made in fixed patterns which may be unsuited to the situation	Expand repertoire to SOPs to take into account a greater number of contingencies
	Resistance to changing established procedure	Introduce more individual discretion into SOPs
		Incorporate dialectical approach into procedures
Lack of decision readiness	Surprise leading to increased levels of stress	Use environmental scanning procedures and trigger mechanisms
		Create scenarios
		Establish contingency plans
		Create a crisis-planning group

Continued

Table 1 *continued*

Major problems	Characteristics and symptoms	Prescriptions
Implementation pathologies	Lack of motivation or sense of urgency	Expand organizational structure to include more groups in decision making
		Establish independent policy planning and evaluation groups composed of members from implementation units
		Set up indoctrination programs (goal training)
	Unit alienation and lack of understanding	Manipulate organizational rituals to focus on primary goals
		Place trusted people in the field to coordinate
		Use drills to simulate crises
		Plan triggering cues for automatic implementation
	Role conflicts and political games	Clarify communications, shorten channels
		Use dual SOPs for routine and crisis situations with established trigger rules for movement between regimes
		Set up fishscale structures

*Characteristics of groupthink

Impartiality by the leader in a discussion may also be a drawback. The group may be deprived of the services of one of the best decision makers in the organization. The result may be a lower quality decision than would have resulted if the leader had participated. There is also the danger that nondirection by the leader may result in a decision that is completely unacceptable to the leader. The proper role of the leader lies somewhere between the two extremes.

Critical evaluation and the exploration of a wide range of policy alternatives is a time-consuming process. The organization may not have the time to adopt such procedures. Especially in a crisis, a decision on a response must be reached very quickly to head off disaster. In crisis periods the high level of stress felt by the decision unit contributes to reduced cognitive abilities. Increased generation and evaluation of alternatives may contribute to information overload, which in turn increases the probability of information distortion – another source of error. Premature consensus can be prevented by inviting the opinions of outside experts, seeking opinions from associates in the organization, and generating alternatives through brainstorming, through synectics, and other creative problem-solving techniques (Arnold, 1962; Stein, 1974). These techniques may prevent premature consensus, but they also substantially increase the probability of information overload. Janis (1972) noted that while the use of outside experts and trusted associates provides the decision unit with fresh perspectives, there is always the danger of a breach of security or an information leak in an expanded group. In highly competitive situations this is most undesirable and potentially damaging to the organization. If expert assistance is to be used effectively, assistants must be consulted early in the decision process before convergence on a particular alternative starts.

Special effort should be made by the leader to ensure that a long-range perspective is introduced early into the deliberations by assigning special responsibility to certain members for developing such a focus. Incremental decisions made for short-term expediency may have severe consequences on future policies and negotiating positions.

A program for crisis prevention must also consider the individual decision makers and their ability either to avoid stress or to manage it. Selecting organizational members for stressful positions should be done not merely on the basis of technical competence and know-how but also in terms of capabilities to handle stress. A variety of stress-reducing techniques, can be incorporated into the daily routine of appropriate role players. Individuals may undergo behavioral modification treatment to raise their tolerance to stress (Budzynski, 1973). Rotating decision makers or replacing them with new individuals selected and trained for these high-stress situations is another possibility.

Preventing information distortion

Information overload is a serious problem for decision units given the requirements of increased information flows and the debilitating effects of heightened stress and shortened time horizons during a crisis. More information does not necessarily mean better information. Improved scanning techniques and monitoring devices of the information environment and presentation in special formats can help ensure that information received by the decision unit is of the proper quality as well as a manageable quantity. Special information systems for crisis situations may be developed based on data compression through effective sampling techniques or coding and flagging only those critical trends above a given threshold. Such special systems could include extraordinary channels of communication to cut through the organizational hierarchy and, in some instances, to utilize direct links with the environment or more than one source of the same information (Downs, 1967). These techniques will also help reduce the effects of time delays, decision unit insulation, and the screening process at various levels of the hierarchy as information is filtered upward. In terms of resources, however, such systems can be costly for the organization. In many instances, personnel are diverted from their regular pursuits to participate, sometimes at the expense of the day-to-day functioning of other parts of the organization. Most certainly there are costs of system development that must be incurred. Expansion of organizational systems may also have the drawback of making the organization more unwieldy, especially in the ability to effect coordination. Through the proliferation of sub-groups there is an increased danger of empire building, which can lead to intraorganizational conflict and bargaining. This in turn will affect the ability to implement decisions.

Personal biases and stereotypes of the adversary are major factors contributing to information distortion. Role playing and psychodrama may help to overcome the influence of stereotypes and increase understanding of the adversary. Scenario building is another technique that promotes understanding of a rival's actions and warnings and enables the decision group to predict responses to an action with greater accuracy (Janis, 1972). Such role playing can be expanded to include general crisis training or drills, which has the secondary effect of reducing stress on individuals when a real crisis develops. The cost of techniques like role playing and cross-cultural training may be prohibitive because they are so time consuming; ideally these techniques should be developed as part of precrisis training.

Prevention of errors in judgment resulting from group pathologies

Some errors of judgment are the result of group dynamics and are manifested in symptoms of groupthink. Solutions to problems such as the propensity to take increased risks and illusions of invulnerability may be found through role playing and scenario building. In addition, attempts should be made to reduce risk propensity by focusing on individual responsibilities thereby avoiding a group-induced shift toward greater risk taking (Wallach, Kogan, and Bem, 1964). Techniques such as building scenarios of the worst possible outcome will aid in evaluating the seriousness of proposed actions realistically and reduce the propensity toward high-risk alternatives.

Since units subject to groupthink try to rationalize away warnings and other disturbing data that may require a reevaluation of policy, to ensure full evaluation of all alternatives, at least one member should be assigned the role of devil's advocate. This technique is based on the premise that conflict is the best means of exposing hidden assumptions. In this manner, both good and bad aspects of a proposal are examined. There is a danger, however, that devil's advocates may become tokens or 'domesticated.' An institutionalized devil's advocate can paradoxically lead to a false sense of security in the decision unit. Group members may develop the 'comforting feeling that they have considered all sides of the issue and that the policy chosen has weathered challenges from within the decision-making circle' (Janis, 1972: 215). One way to avoid tokenism is to rotate the responsibility to play devil's advocate among the group members. The dialectical approach is a more formal vehicle, which uses structured debate to bring forth alternative views of the world. Mason (1969: B408) noted that use of dialectics forces 'exposing hidden assumptions and developing a new conceptualization of the planning problem the organization faces.'

Pressures on group members to conform to majority opinions can be avoided through the use of subgroups that meet separately under different leaders and report back to the decision unit. Techniques such as Delphi allow anonymous expression of opinion and questioning, and thus could also serve to protect minority viewpoints. Mitroff and Pondy (1974) have suggested that Kantian Delphi is superior to traditional Delphi techniques, which result in positions based on minimum compromise not the best decisions. The goal in Kantian Delphi is not consensus but the elicitation of diverse points of view from many disciplines. In this manner the information base is enlarged beyond that which any one individual possesses. The technique is particularly good for poorly structured problems.

Preventing rigidities in programming

Organizations attempt to minimize the probability of decision pathologies either by expanding the repertoire of programmed solutions to include more contingencies, or by introducing higher levels of individual discretion into SOPs. The strategy of expanding SOPs involves high development and maintenance costs to the organization. This strategy is effective only in coping with anticipated events. The vulnerability of the organization is increased when novel situations occur. Complex but inappropriate decision programs may delay organizational realignment necessary to cope with the novel decision situation. While an expanded repertoire of SOPs will reduce the number of errors which occur when information is forced into rigid formats, the complexity involved will increase random noise in the information system and make the tracing of errors more difficult. The strategy of allowing more individual discretion in SOPs gives greater flexibility but organizational economies obtained by standardization and programming are lost.

Every organization must develop SOPs to obtain an appropriate balance between flexibility and standardization to fit its specific environment. To guard against the introduction of biases, however, a dialectic component can be built into every information processing and decision program. The dialectic will ensure that counterplans are developed for all major decisions and contradictory points of view are examined. In this manner any latent biases can be identified. This procedure is similar to the dialectical approach suggested as a measure to prevent group pathologies – episodic dialectics are supplemented by routine programmed dialectics.

Improving decision readiness

An organization that is engaged in constant drills in anticipation of rare events may avoid the strategic damage inherent in surprise. Constant scanning of the organizational environment for possible threats, coupled with imaginative scenario building of yet unrealized contingencies, may reduce the chance of surprise. It may be possible to form special intelligence groups whose major responsibility would be the identification of possible rare events with threat potential and whose members would be freed from daily organizational decision making. The formation of special groups may offer an advantage to the organization in the anticipation of the future. The problem associated with such independent centers, however, is that of credibility. Often the hyperinnovative tendencies of such groups cause a loss of credibility and isolation from power, with resulting inability to influence decision processes. Involving organizational members through rotation in activities of such institutions may partially eliminate this problem of credibility.

Enrichment of the organizational repertoire of responses – contingency plans – with appropriate, sensitive trigger mechanisms may reduce the chance of crisis, either by mitigating the seriousness of an event by a timely appropriate response, or by reducing the surprise associated with the event.

Preventing implementation failures

There are two components to the prevention of implementation pathologies. The first consists of general organizational development of abilities for coping with crises: the second component involves structural changes and enrichment of the repertoire of SOPs.

Motivation of implementation units to carry out decisions can be improved by involving at least one representative from each unit in the actual decision process. When a group solves a problem, each member of the group participating feels responsible for making the solution work. If a solution has been imposed without consultation, however, there is not the same commitment to implementation. Action groups involved with the decision will also be more aware of critical timing factors. Maier noted (1967: 249), 'a low-quality solution that has good acceptance can be more effective than a higher-quality solution that lacks acceptance.' Motivation of implementation units can also be improved by thorough indoctrination programs for all members of the organization to develop a heightened commitment to goals. While this procedure will not entirely remove the problems of political games and bargaining between units, there will be some reduction in the incompatibility of goal structures between the diverse units of the organization. Problems of comprehension are also reduced by participation in the decision process. Implementation units frequently do not understand the reasons for choosing a course of action that they regard as arbitrary or threatening. Hence, a tendency to subvert the implementation process either consciously or unconsciously often emerges. Participation in the decision process increases understanding of the decision through exposure to all the alternatives considered and the reasons for their rejection. Participation leads to a widened perspective of the total crisis, including overall organization goals, not just a narrow perspective dominated by self-interest. Commitment to and understanding of the decision facilitate diffusion of information throughout the organization.

Noisy channels of communication between decision and implementation units can result in misinterpretation and lack of coordination. This in part can be alleviated by the decision unit placing trusted people in the field to effect coordination. Usually such people will be in direct communication with the decision unit to reduce the probability of error. SOPs increase inertia and lead to subversion of new directives but the commitment to SOPs can be made to work to the advantage of the organization. Special cues for triggering new automatic programs for crisis situations can be developed and incorporated in SOPs. These cues can be reinforced by the use of precrisis drills and simulations. Thus, during an actual crisis much of the required behavior is pre-programmed, reducing the latitude for error.

For major improvements to be made in implementation, the organization must make a strong commitment to precrisis training. Most of these solutions, with the exception of greater participation in the decision process, cannot be carried out during a crisis. The organization must also be prepared to allocate resources for development of these programs since they are not without cost, both in time and in money.

The second component of a strategy for preventing implementation failures consists of some basic modifications in the organization's structure. Dual structures, one for routine and the other for crisis situations, can be developed with appropriate transition rules between crisis and non-crisis regimes. The crisis-triggered regime will be characterized by a flexible repertoire of operating procedures capable of accommodating unanticipated changes required by novel situations. Its structure is aimed at reducing the distances between implementation units and the central unit by increasing overlaps of group memberships to form a fishscale structure. Key positions in staff and line units will be filled by crisis specialists – executives selected on the basis of creative adaptive abilities in high-stress situations. Special emergency communication networks and other organizational resource reserves should be developed emphasizing rapid mobilization.

The dual structure is similar to the adaptive management or project management form proposed by Ansoff and Brandenburg (1971). Personnel are assigned on a temporary basis to projects; when needs change the personnel are reassigned. Ansoff and Brandenburg suggested that this type of structure is particularly suited for situations requiring flexible strategic and operational responses. Membership in the crisis management team, however, should remain relatively stable since permanent decision-making groups tend to perform better than ad hoc groups (Hall and Williams, 1966).

Conclusion

Designs for crisis decision making attempt to (1) prevent certain biases that are specific to stressful situations, (2) increase flexibility and sensitivity of line units, and (3) develop computational and processing capabilities in the organization to meet sudden increasing demands imposed upon decision units.

The prescriptions proposed in the paper can be classified into three categories:

1. Minor structural and procedural modifications of the crisis-decision process – for example, scenario building, dialectics, use of devil's advocates.

2. Major general development of capabilities – for example, build up of information processing capabilities, selective recruitment of executives, improvement in line units' sensitivities to commands through drills.
3. Creation of dual specialized structures, one for routine decision making and one for crisis decision making.

The first class of prescriptions is limited in scope but general in application. The main choice is one of design – selecting between a general organizational development strategy and the creation of dual structures. Through specialization, better coping abilities can be attained but at a cost of maintaining idle structures and the need to develop the capability of transition between these structures.

Clearly the size, the general resource capabilities, and the objectives of an organization must be considered in deciding between these two strategies. A large organization with a stable environment but vulnerable to the impacts of discontinuities – for example, a centralized, undiversified, low-slack organization – should maintain a dual specialized structure. The costs of general development and maintenance of crisis-coping capabilities will far exceed the costs of developing a contingency skeleton organization ready to move in and manage the crisis. In contrast, a small organization coping with a fluctuating environment may benefit from a general development of crisis-coping capabilities.

Note

1   Miller (1956) studied the capacity of individuals to process and retain information. He found that short-term capacity of individuals is limited to seven chunks of information.

References

Ackoff, Russell L. (1967) 'Management misinformation systems', *Management Science*, 14: B147–B156.

Albers, Robert J. (1966) 'Anxiety and time perspectives', *Dissertation Abstracts*, 21: 4848.

Allison, Graham T. (1971) *Essence of Decision*, Boston: Little, Brown.

Ansoff, H. Igor, and Brandenburg, R. G. (1971) 'A language for organizational design: parts I and II', *Management Science*, 17: B705–B731.

Arnold, John E. (1962) 'Useful creative techniques' in Parnes, S. J. and Harding, H. F. (eds), *A Sourcebook for Creative Thinking*, 251–268, New York: Scribner's.

Beier, Ernst G. (1951) 'The effects of induced anxiety on flexibility of intellectual functioning, *Psychological Monographs*, 65: no. 326

Budzynski, T. H. (1973) 'Biofeedback procedures in the clinic', *Seminars in Psychiatry*, 5: 537–547.

Cangelosi, Vincent E., and Dill, William R. (1965) 'Organizational learning: observations towards a theory', *Administrative Science Quarterly*, 10: 173–203.

Crozier, Michel (1963) *The Bureaucratic Phenomenon*, Chicago: University of Chicago Press.

Cyert, Richard M., and March, James G. (1963) *A Behavioral Theory of the Firm*, Englewood Cliffs, NJ: Prentice-Hall.

de Rivera, Joseph H. (1968) *The Psychological Dimension of Foreign Policy*, Columbus, OH: Merrill.

Downs, Anthony (1967) *Inside Bureaucracy*, Boston: Little, Brown.

Easterbrook, J. A. (1959) 'The effect of emotion on cue utilization and the organization of behavior', *Psychological Review*, 66: 183–201.

Fink, S. L., Beak, J. and Taddeo, K. (1971) 'Organizational crises and change', *Journal of Applied Behavioral Science*, 7: 15–37.

Hall, Jay and Williams, Martha S. (1966) 'A comparison of decision-making performances in established and ad hoc groups', *Journal of Personality and Social Psychology*, 3: 214–222.

Hedberg, Bo L. T., Nystrom, Paul C., and Starbuck, William H. (1976) 'Camping on seesaws: prescriptions for a self-designing organization', *Administrative Science Quarterly*, 21: 41–65.

Hermann, Charles F. (1963) 'Some consequences of crisis which limit the viability of organizations', *Administrative Science Quarterly*, 8: 61–82.

Hermann, Charles F. (1972) *International Crises: Insights from Behavioral Research*, New York: Free Press.

Holsti, Kalevei J. (1966) 'Resolving international conflicts: a taxonomy of behavior and some figures on procedures', *Journal of Conflict Resolution*, 10: 272–296.

Holsti, Ole R. (1971) 'Crises, stress, and decision-making', *International Social Science Journal*, 23: 53–67.

Holsti, Ole R. (1972) *Crisis, Escalation, War,* Montreal: McGill-Queens University Press.

Janis, Irving L. (1972) *Victims of Groupthink*, Boston: Houghton Mifflin.

Jones, A., Wilkinson, H. J. and Braden, I. (1961) 'Information deprivation as a motivational variable', *Journal of Experimental Psychology*, 66: 126–137.

Lanzetta, John T., and Roby, Thornton B. (1957) 'Effects of work-group structure and certain task variables on group performance', *Journal of Abnormal and Social Psychology*, 53: 307–314.

Levine, Seymour (1971) 'Stress and behavior' *Scientific American*, 224: 26–31.

Loomis, C. P. (1960) *Social Systems: Essays on Their Persistence and Change*, New York: D. Van Nostrand.

MacCrimmon, Kenneth R. (1973) *Theories of Collective Decision*, Review paper, 4th International Research Conference on Subjective Probability, Utility and Decision Making, Rome.

Maier, Norman R. F. (1967) 'Assets and liabilities in group problem solving: the need for an integrative function', *Psychological Review*, 74: 239–249.

Mason, Richard O. (1969) 'A dialectical approach to strategic planning', *Management Science*, 15: B403–B414.

Milburn, Thomas W. (1972) 'The management of crisis' in Charles F. Hermann (ed), *International Crises: Insights from Behavioral Research*, 249–277', New York: Free Press.

Miller, G. A. (1956) 'The magical number seven, plus or minus two: some limits on our capacity for processing information', *Psychological Review*, 63: 81–97.

Miller, J. G. (1960) 'Information input overload and psychopathology', *American Journal of Psychiatry*, 16: 695–704.

Mitroff, Ian I., and Pondy, Louis R. (1974) 'On the organization of inquiry: a comparison of some radically different approaches to policy analysis', *Public Administration Review*, 34: 471–479.

Mulder, Mauk, Ritsema van Eck and de Jong, Rendel D. (1971) 'An organization in crisis and non-crisis situations', *Human Relations*, 24: 19–41.

Nathan, James A. (1975) 'The missile crisis' *World Politics*, 27: 256–281.

Paige, Glenn D. (1968) *The Korean Decision*, New York: Free Press.

Raiffa, Howard (1968) *Decision Analysis*, Reading, MA: Addison-Wesley.

Robinson, James A. (1972) 'Crisis: an appraisal of concepts and theories' in Charles F. Hermann (ed.), *International Crises: Insights from Behavioral Research*, 20–35, New York: Free Press.

Smock, Charles D. (1955) 'The influence of psychological stress on the "intolerance of ambiguity"', *Journal of Abnormal Psychology*, 50: 177–182.

Staw, Barry M. (1976) 'Knee-deep in the big muddy: a study of escalating commitment to a chosen course of action', *Organizational Behavior and Human Performance*, 16: 27–44.

Stein, Morris I. (1974) *Stimulating Creativity*, New York: Academic Press.

Suedfeld, Peter (1971) 'Information processing as a personality model', in Schroder, M. Harold and Suedfeld, Peter (eds), *Personality Theory and Information Processing*, 3–14. New York: Ronald Press.

Taylor, Ronald N. (1975) 'Psychological determinants of bounded rationality: implications for decision-making strategies', *Decision Sciences*, 6: 409–429.

Thibaut, J. W., and Kelley, H. H. (1959) *The Social Psychology of Groups*, New York: Wiley.

Tullock, Gordon (1965) *The Politics of Bureaucracy*, Washington DC: Public Affairs Press.

Turner, Barry A. (1976) 'The organizational and interorganizational development of disasters', *Adminstrative Science Quarterly*, 21: 378–397.

Wallach, Michael A., Kogan, Nathan and Bem, Daryl J. (1964) 'Diffusion of responsibility and level of risk taking in groups', *Journal of Abnormal and Social Psychology*, 68: 263–274.

Chapter 22

Karl E. Weick and Karlene H. Roberts

COLLECTIVE MINDS IN ORGANIZATIONS: HEEDFUL INTERRELATING ON FLIGHT DECKS

THE CONCEPT OF COLLECTIVE mind is developed to explain organizational performance in situations requiring nearly continuous operational reliability. Collective mind is conceptualized as a pattern of heedful interrelations of actions in a social system. Actors in the system construct their actions (contributions), understanding that the system consists of connected actions by themselves and others (representation), and interrelate their actions within the system (subordination). Ongoing variation in the heed with which individual contributions, representations, and subordinations are interrelated influences comprehension of unfolding events and the incidence of errors. As heedful interrelating and mindful comprehension increase, organizational errors decrease. Flight operations on aircraft carriers exemplify the constructs presented. Implications for organization theory and practice are drawn.*

Some organizations require nearly error-free operations all the time because otherwise they are capable of experiencing catastrophes. One such organization is an aircraft carrier, which an informant in Rochlin, LaPorte, and Roberts' (1987: 78) study described as follows:

> . . . imagine that it's a busy day, and you shrink San Francisco Airport to only one short runway and one ramp and one gate. Make planes take off and land at the same time, at half the present time interval, rock the runway from side to side, and require that everyone who leaves in the morning returns that same day. Make sure the equipment is so close to the edge of the envelope that it's fragile. Then turn off the radar to avoid detection, impose strict controls on radios, fuel the aircraft in place with their engines running, put an enemy

in the air, and scatter live bombs and rockets around. Now wet the whole thing down with sea water and oil, and man it with 20-year-olds, half of whom have never seen an airplane close-up. Oh and by the way, try not to kill anyone.

Even though carriers represent 'a million accidents waiting to happen' (Wilson, 1986: 21), almost none of them do. Here, we examine why not. The explanation we wish to explore is that organizations concerned with reliability enact aggregate mental processes that are more fully developed than those found in organizations concerned with efficiency. By fully developed mental processes, we mean that organizations preoccupied with reliability may spend more time and effort organizing for controlled information processing (Schneider and Schiffrin, 1977), mindful attention (Langer, 1989), and heedful action (Ryle, 1949). These intensified efforts enable people to understand more of the complexity they face, which then enables them to respond with fewer errors. Reliable systems are smart systems.

Before we can test this line of reasoning we need to develop a language of organizational mind that enables us to describe collective mental processes in organizations. In developing it, we move back and forth between concepts of mind and details of reliable performance in flight operations on a modern super carrier.[1] We use flight operations to illustrate organizational mind for a number of reasons: The technology is relatively simple, the coordination among activities is explicit and visible, the socialization is continuous, agents working alone have less grasp of the entire system than they do when working together, the system is constructed of interdependent know-how, teams of people think on their feet and do the 'right thing' in novel situations, and the consequences of any lapse in attention are swift and disabling. Because our efforts to understand deck operations got us thinking about the possibility that performance is mediated by collective mental processes, we use these operations to illustrate that thinking, but the processes of mind we discuss are presumed to be inherent in all organizations. What may vary across organizations is the felt need to develop these processes to more advanced levels.

The idea of group mind

Discussions of collective mental processes have been rare, despite the fact that people claim to be studying 'social' cognition (e.g. Schneider, 1991). The preoccupation with individual cognition has left organizational theorists ill-equipped to do much more with the so-called cognitive revolution than apply it to organizational concerns, one brain at a time. There are a few exceptions, however, and we introduce our own discussion of collective mind with a brief review of three recent attempts to engage the topic of group mind.

Wegner and his associates (Wegner, Giuliano, and Hertel, 1985; Wegner, 1987; Wegner, Erber, and Raymond, 1991) suggested that group mind may take the form of cognitive interdependence focused around memory processes. They argued that people in close relationships enact a single transactive memory system, complete with differentiated responsibility for remembering different portions of common experience. People know the locations rather than the details of common events and rely on one another to contribute missing details that cue their own retrieval. Transactive memory systems are integrated and differentiated structures in the sense that connected individuals often hold related information in different locations. When people trade lower-order, detailed, disparate information, they often discover higher-order themes, generalizations, and ideas that subsume these details. It is these integrations of disparate inputs that seem to embody the 'magical transformation' that group mind theorists sought to understand (Wegner, Giuliano, and Hertel, 1985: 268). The important point Wegner contributes to our understanding of collective mental processes is that group mind is not indexed by within-group similarity of attitudes, understanding, or language, nor can it be understood without close attention to communications processes among group members (Wegner, Giuliano, and Hertel, 1985: 254–255). Both of these lessons will be evident in our reformulation.

Work in artificial intelligence provides the backdrop for two additional attempts to conceptualize group mind: Sandelands and Stablein's (1987) description of organizations as mental entities capable of thought and Hutchins' (1990, 1991) description of organizations as distributed information-processing systems. The relevant ideas are associated with theories of 'connectionism,' embodied in so-called 'neural networks.' Despite claims that their work is grounded in the brain's microanatomy, connectionists repeatedly refer to 'neurological plausibility' (Quinlan, 1991: 41), 'neuron-like units' (Churchland, 1992: 32), 'brain-style processing' (Rumelhart, 1992: 69), or 'neural inspiration' (Boden, 1990: 18). This qualification is warranted because the 'neural' networks examined by connectionists are simply computational models that involve synchronous parallel processing among many interrelated unreliable and/or simple processing units (Quinlan, 1991: 40). The basic idea is that knowledge in very large networks of very simple processing units resides in patterns of connections, not in individuated local symbols. As Boden (1990: 14) explained, any 'unit's activity is regulated by the activity of neighboring units, connected to it by inhibitory or excitatory links whose strength can very according to design and/or learning.' Thus, any one unit can represent several different concepts, and the same concept in a different context may activate a slightly different network of units.

Connectionism by itself, however, is a shaky basis on which to erect a theory of organizational mind. The framework remains grounded in a device that models a single, relatively tightly coupled actor as opposed to a loosely coupled system of multiple actors, such as an organization. Connectionists have difficulty simulating emotion and motivation (Dreyfus and Dreyfus, 1990), as well as everyday thought and reasoning (Rumelhart, 1992). In computational models there is no turnover of units akin to that found in organizations, where units are replaced or moved to other locations. And the inputs connectionists investigate are relatively simple items such as numerals, words, or phrases, with the outputs being more or less accurate renderings of these inputs (e.g. Elman, 1992). This contrasts with organizational researchers who pay more attention to complex inputs, such as traditional competitors who make overtures to cooperate, and to outputs that consist of action as well as thought.

What connectionism contributes to organizational theory is the insight that complex patterns can be encoded by patterns of activation and inhibition among simple units, if those units are richly connected. This means that relatively simple actors may be able to apprehend complex inputs if they are organized in ways that resemble neural networks. Connectionists also raise the possibility that mind is 'located' in connections and the weights put on them rather than in entities. Thus, to understand mind is to be attentive to process, relating, and method, as well as to structures and content.

Sandelands and Stablein (1987: 139–141) found parallels between the organization of neurons in the brain and the organization of activities in organizations. They used this parallel to argue that connected activities encode concepts and ideas in organizations much like connected neurons encode concepts and ideas in brains. Ideas encoded in behaviors appear to interact in ways that suggest operations of intelligent processing. These parallels are consistent with the idea that organizations are minds. The important lessons from Sandelands and Stablein's analysis are that connections between behaviors, rather than people, may be the crucial 'locus' for mind and that intelligence is to be found in patterns of behavior rather than in individual knowledge.

Hutchins (1990, 1991: 289) has used connectionist networks, such as the 'constraint satisfaction network,' to model how interpretations based on distributed cognitions are formed. These simulations are part of a larger inquiry into how teams coordinate action (Hutchins, 1990) and the extent to which distributed processing amplifies or counteracts errors that form in individual units. Hutchins' analysis suggests that systems maintain the flexible, robust action associated with mindful performance if individuals have overlapping rather than mutually exclusive task knowledge. Overlapping knowledge allows for redundant representation that enables people to take responsibility for all parts of the process to which they can make a contribution (Hutchins, 1990: 210).

The potential fit between connectionist imagery and organizational concepts can be inferred from Hutchins' (1990: 209) description of coordination by mutual constraint in naval navigation teams:

> [The] sequence of action to be taken [in group performance] need not be explicitly represented anywhere in the system. If participants know how to coordinate their activities with the technologies and people with which they interact, the global structure of the task performance will emerge from the local interactions of the members. The structure of the activities of the group is determined by a set of local computations rather than by the implementation of the sort of global plan that appears in the solo performer's procedure. In the team situation, a set of behavioral dependencies are set up. These dependencies shape the behavior pattern of the group.

The lessons we use from Hutchins' work include the importance of redundant representation, the emergence of global structure from local interactions, and behavioral dependencies as the substrate of distributed processing.

Our own attempt to describe group mind has been informed by these three sources but is based on a different set of assumptions. We pay more attention to the form of connections than to the strength of connections and more attention to mind as activity than to mind as entity. To make this shift in emphasis clear, we avoid the phrases 'group mind' and 'organizational mind' in favor of the phrase 'collective mind.' The word 'collective' unlike the words 'group' or 'organization' refers to individuals who act as if they are a group. People who act as if they are a group interrelate their actions with more or less care, and focusing on the way this interrelating is done reveals collective mental processes that differ in their degree of development. Our focus is at once on individuals and the collective, since only individuals can contribute to a collective mind, but a collective mind is distinct from an individual mind because it inheres in the pattern of interrelated activities among many people.

We begin the discussion of collective mind by following the lead of Ryle (1949) and developing the concept of mind as a disposition to act with heed. We then follow the lead of Asch (1952) and develop the concept of collective interrelating as contributing, representing, and subordinating, and illustrate these activities with examples from carrier operations. We next combine the notions of heed and interrelating into the concept of collective mind as heedful interrelating and suggest social processes that may account for variations in heedful interrelating. Finally, we describe three examples of heedful interrelating, two from carrier operations and one from the laboratory, and present an extended example of heedless interrelating that resulted in a $38-million accident.

Mind as disposition to heed

'Mind' is a noun similar to nouns like faith, hope, charity, role, and culture. 'Mind' is not the name of a person, place, or thing but, rather, is a dispositional term that denotes a propensity to act in a certain manner or style. As Ryle (1949: 51) said,

> The statement 'the mind is its own place' as theorists might construe it, is not true, for the mind is not even a metaphorical 'place.' On the contrary, the chessboard, the platform, the scholar's desk, the judge's bench, the lorry-driver's seat, the studio and the football field are among its places. These are where people work and play stupidly or intelligently.

That mind is actualized in patterns of behavior that can range from stupid to intelligent can be seen in the example Ryle (1949: 33) used of a clown who trips and stumbles just as clumsy people do. What's different is that 'he trips and stumbles on purpose and after much rehearsal and at the golden moment and where the children can see him and so as not to hurt himself.' When a clown trips artfully, people applaud the style of the action, the fact that tripping is done with care, judgment, wit, and appreciation of the mood of the spectators. In short, the tripping is done with heed. Heed is not itself a behavior but it refers to the way behaviors such as tripping, falling, and recovering are assembled. Artful tripping is called heedful, not so much because the tripping involves action preceded by thought but because the behaviors patterned into the action of tripping suggest to the observer qualities such as 'noticing, taking care, attending, applying one's mind, concentrating, putting one's heart into something, thinking what one is doing, alertness, interest, intentness, studying and trying' (Ryle, 1949: 136). These inferences, based on the style of the action, are called 'heed concepts' and support the conclusion that the behaviors were combined intelligently rather than stupidly.

The word 'heed' captures an important set of qualities of mind that elude the more stark vocabulary of cognition. These nuances of heed are especially appropriate to our interest in systems preoccupied with failure-free performance. People act heedfully when they act more or less carefully, critically, consistently, purposefully, attentively, studiously, vigilantly, conscientiously, pertinaciously (Ryle, 1949: 151). Heed adverbs attach qualities of mind directly to performances, as in the description, 'the airboss monitored the pilot's growing load of tasks attentively.' Notice that the statement does not say that the airboss was doing two things, monitoring and also checking to be sure that the monitoring was done carefully. Instead, the statement asserts that, having been coached to monitor carefully, his present monitoring reflects this style. Mind is in the monitoring itself, not in some separate episode of theorizing about monitoring.

Heedful performance is not the same thing as habitual performance. In habitual action, each performance is a replica of its predecessor, whereas in heedful performance, each action is modified by its predecessor (Ryle, 1949: 42). In heedful performance, the agent is still learning. Furthermore, heedful performance is the outcome of training and experience that weave together thinking, feeling, and willing. Habitual performance is the outcome of drill and repetition.

When heed declines, performance is said to be heedless, careless, unmindful, thoughtless, unconcerned, indifferent. Heedless performance suggests a failure of intelligence rather than a failure of knowledge. It is a failure to see, to take note of, to be attentive to. Heedless performance is not about ignorance, cognition (Lyons, 1980: 57), and facts. It is about stupidity, competence, and know-how. Thus, mind refers to stretches of human behavior that exhibit qualities of intellect and character (Ryle, 1949: 126).

Group as interrelated activity

Ryle's ideas focus on individual mind. To extend his ideas to groups, we first have to specify the crucial performances in groups that could reflect a disposition to heed. To pinpoint these crucial performances, we derive four defining properties of group performance from Asch's (1952: 251–255) discussion of 'mutually shared fields' and illustrate these properties with carrier examples.[2]

The first defining property of group performance is that individuals create the social forces of group life when they act as if there were such forces. As Asch (1952: 251) explained it,

> We must see group phenomena as both the product and condition of actions of individuals. . . . There are no forces between individuals as organisms; yet to all intents and purposes they act as if there were, and they actually create social forces. Group action achieves the kind of result that would be understandable if all participants were acting under the direction of a single organizing center. No such center exists: between individuals is a hiatus, which nevertheless, they succeed in overcoming with surprising effectiveness.

An example from carriers occurs during flight operations. The men in the tower (Air Department) monitor and give instructions to incoming and departing aircraft. Simultaneously, the men on the landing signal officers' platform do the same thing. They are backed up by the men in Air Operations who monitor and instruct aircraft at some distance from the ship. From the aviator's viewpoint, he receives integrated information about his current status and future behavior from an integrated source when, in reality, the several sources are relatively independent of one another and located in different parts of the ship.

The second defining property of group performance is that when people act as if there are social forces, they construct their actions (contribute) while envisaging a social system of joint actions (represent), and interrelate that constructed action with the system that is envisaged (subordinate). Asch (1952: 251–252) explained this as follows:

> There are group actions that are possible only when each participant has a representation that includes the actions of others and their relations. The respective actions converge relevantly, assist and supplement each other only when the joint situation is represented in each and when the representations are structurally similar. Only when these conditions are given can individuals subordinate themselves to the requirements of joint action. These representations and the actions that they initiate/bring group facts into existence and produce the phenomenal solidity of group process.

The simultaneous envisaging and interrelating that create a system occur when a pilot taxies onto the catapult for launching, is attached to it, and advances his engines to full power. Even though pilots have to rely on the catapult crew, they remain vigilant to see if representations are similar. Pilots keep asking themselves questions like, 'Does it feel right?' or 'Is the rhythm wrong?' The referent for the question, 'Does it feel right' however, is not the aircraft but the joint situation to which he has subordinated himself. If a person on the deck signals the pilot to reduce his engines from full power, he won't do so until someone stands in front of the plane, directly over the catapult, and signals for a reduction in power. Only then is the pilot reasonably certain that the joint situation has changed. He now trusts that the catapult won't be triggered suddenly and fling his underpowered aircraft into a person and then into the ocean.

The third defining property of group performance is that contributing, representing, and subordinating create a joint situation of interrelations among activities, which Asch (1952: 252) referred to as a system.

When these conditions are given we have a social system or a process of a definite form that embraces the actions of a number of individuals. Such a system does not reside in the individuals taken separately, though each individual contributes to it; nor does it reside outside them; it is present in the interrelations between the activities of individuals.

An example from carriers is a pilot landing an aircraft on a deck. This is not a solitary act. A pilot doesn't really land; he is 'recovered.' And recovery is a set of interrelated activities among air traffic controllers, landing signal officers, the control tower, navigators, deck hands, the helmsman driving the ship, etc. As the recovery of a single aircraft nears completion in the form of a successful trap, nine to ten people on the landing signal officer's platform, up to 15 more people in the tower, and two to three more people on the bridge observe the recovery and can wave the aircraft off if there is a problem. While this can be understood as an example of redundancy, it can also be interpreted as activities that can be interrelated more or less adequately, depending on the care with which contributing, representing, and subordinating are done.

The fourth and final defining property of group performance suggested by Asch is that the effects produced by a pattern of interrelated activities vary as a function of the style (e.g. heedful-heedless) as well as the strength (e.g. loose-tight) with which the activities are tied together. This is suggested by the statement that, in a system of interrelated activities, individuals can work with, for, or against each other.

The form the interrelated actions take-on a team or in an office-is a datum of precisely the same kind as any other fact. One could say that all the facts of the system can be expressed as the sum of the actions of individuals. The statement is misleading, however, if one fails to add that the individuals would not be capable of these particular actions unless they were responding to (or envisaging the possibility of) the system. Once the process described is in motion it is no longer the individual 'as such' who determines its direction, nor the group acting upon the individual as an external force, but individuals working with, for, or against each other (Asch, 1952: 252).

It is these varying forms of interrelation that embody collective mind. An example of interrelating on carriers can be seen when ordnance is loaded onto an aircraft and its safety mechanisms are removed. If there is a sudden change of mission, the live ordnance must be disarmed, removed, and replaced by other ordnance that is now activated, all of this under enormous time pressure. These interrelated activities, even though tightly coupled, can become more or less dangerous depending on how the interrelating is done.

In one incident observed, senior officers kept changing the schedule of the next day's flight events through the night, which necessitated a repeated change in ordnance up to the moment the day launches began. A petty officer changing bombs underneath an aircraft, where the pilot couldn't see him, lost a leg when the pilot moved the 36,000-pound aircraft over him. The petty officer should have tied the plane down before going underneath to change the load but failed to do so because there was insufficient time, a situation created by continual indecision at the top. Thus, the senior officers share the blame for this accident because they should have resolved their indecision in ways that were more mindful of the demands it placed on the system.

Although Asch argued that interrelated activities are the essence of groups, he said little about how these interrelations occur or how they vary over time. Instead, he treated interrelations as a variable and interrelating as a constant. If we treat interrelations as a variable and interrelating as a process, this suggests a way to conceptualize collective mind.

Heedful interrelating as collective mind

The insights of Ryle and Asch can be combined into a concept of collective mind if we argue that dispositions toward heed are expressed in actions that construct interrelating. Contributing, representing, and subordinating, actions that form a distinct pattern external to any given individual, become the medium through which collective mind is manifest. Variations in heedful interrelating correspond to variations in collective mind and comprehension.

We assume, as Follett (1924: 146–153) did, that mind begins with actions, which we refer to here as contributions. The contributions of any one individual begin to actualize collective mind to the degree that heedful representation and heedful subordination define those contributions. A heedful contribution enacts collective mind as it begins to converge with, supplement, assist, and become defined in relation to the imagined requirements of joint action presumed to flow from some social activity system.

Similar conduct flows from other contributing individuals in the activity system toward others imagined to be in that system. These separate efforts vary in the heedfulness with which they interrelate, and these variations form a pattern. Since the object of these activities ('the envisaged system' to use Asch's phrase) is itself being constituted as these activities become more or less inter-related, the emergent properties of this object are not contained fully in the representation of any one person nor are they finalized at any moment in time. A single emergent property may appear in more than one representation, but seldom in all. And different properties are shared in common by different subsets of people. Asch seems to have had this distributed representation of the envisaged system in mind when he referred to 'structurally similar representa-tions.' This pattern of distributed representation explains the transindividual quality of collective mind. Portions of the envisaged system are known to all, but all of it is known to none.

The collective mind is 'located' in the process of interrelating just as the individual mind for Ryle was 'located' in the activities of lorry driving, chess playing, or article writing. Collective mind exists potentially as a kind of capacity in an ongoing activity stream and emerges in the style with which activities are interrelated. These patterns of interrelating are as close to a physical substrate for collective mind as we are likely to find. There is nothing mystical about all this. Collective mind is manifest when individuals construct mutually shared fields. The collective mind that emerges during the interrelating of an activity system is more developed and more capable of intelligent action the more heedfully that interrelating is done.

A crude way to represent the development of a collective mind is by means of a matrix in which the rows are people and the columns are either the larger activities of contributing, representing, and subordinating, or their component behaviors (e.g. converging with, assisting, or supplementing). Initially, the cell entries can be a simple 'yes' or 'no.' 'Yes' means a person performs that action heedfully; 'no' means the action is done heedlessly. The more 'yeses' in the matrix, the more developed the collective mind.

We portray collective mind in terms of method rather than content, structuring rather than structure, connecting rather than connections. Interrelations are not given but are constructed and reconstructed continually by individuals (Blumer, 1969: 110) through the ongoing activities of contributing, representing, and subordinating. Although these activities are done by individuals, their referent is a socially structured field. Individual activities are shaped by this envisioned field and are meaningless apart from it. When people make efforts to interrelate, these efforts can range from heedful to heedless. The more heed reflected in a pattern of interrelations, the more developed the collective mind and the greater the capability to comprehend unexpected events that evolve rapidly in unexpected ways. When we say that a collective mind 'comprehends' unexpected events, we mean that heedful interrelating connects sufficient individual know-how to meet situational demands. For organizations concerned with reliability, those demands often consist of unexpected, nonsequential interactions among small failures that are hard to see and hard to believe. These incomprehensible failures often build quickly into catastrophes (Perrow, 1984: 7–12, 22, 78, 88).

An increase in heedful interrelating can prevent or correct these failures of comprehension in at least three ways. First, longer stretches of time can be connected, as when more know-how is brought forward from the past and is elaborated into new contributions and representations that extrapolate farther into the future. Second, comprehension can be improved if more activities are connected, such as when interrelations span earlier and later stages of task sequences. And third, comprehension can be increased if more levels of experience are connected, as when newcomers who take nothing for granted interrelate more often with old-timers who think they have seen it all. Each of these three changes makes the pattern of interrelations more complex and better able to sense and regulate the complexity created by unexpected events. A system that is tied together more densely across time, activities, and experience comprehends more of what is occurring because the scope of heedful action reaches into more places. When heed is spread across more activities and more connections, there should be more understanding and fewer errors. A collective mind that becomes more comprehensive, comprehends more.

Variations in heed

If collective mind is embodied in the interrelating of social activities, and if collective mind is developed more or less fully depending on the amount of heedfulness with which that interrelating is done, we must address the issue of what accounts for variations in heed. We suspect the answer lies in Mead's (1934: 186) insight that mind is 'the individual importation of social process.' We understand the phrase 'social process' to mean a set of ongoing interactions in a social activity system from which participants continually extract a changing sense of self-interrelation and then reenact that sense back into the system. This ongoing interaction process is recapitulated in individual lives and continues despite the replacement of people.

Mead stressed the reality of recapitulation, as did others. Ryle (1949: 27), for example, observed that 'this trick of talking to oneself in silence is acquired neither quickly nor without effort; and it is a necessary condition to our acquiring it that we should have previously learned to talk intelligently aloud and have heard and understood other people doing so. Keeping our thoughts to ourselves is a sophisticated accomplishment.' Asch (1952: 257) described the relationship between the individual and the group as the only part-whole relation in nature 'that depends on recapitulation of the structure of the whole in the part.' The same point is made by Morgan (1986) and Hutchins (1990: 211), using the more recent imagery of holograms. System capacities that are relevant for the functioning of the whole are built into its parts. In each of these renderings, social processes are the prior resources from which individual mind, self, and action are fashioned (Mead, 1934: 191–192). This means that collective mind precedes the individual mind and that heedful interrelating foreshadows heedful contributing.

Patterns of heedful interrelating in ongoing social processes may be internalized and recapitulated by individuals more or less adequately as they move in and out of the system. If heedful interrelating is visible, rewarded, modeled, discussed, and preserved in vivid stories, there is a good chance that newcomers will learn this style of responding, will incorporate it into their definition of who they are in the system, and will reaffirm and perhaps even augment this style as they act. To illustrate, Walsh and Ungson (1991: 60) defined organization as a 'network of intersubjectively shared meanings that are sustained through the development and use of a common language and everyday social interactions.' Among the shared meanings and language on carriers we heard these four assertions:

(1)   If it's not written down you can do it;
(2)   Look for clouds in every silver lining;
(3)   Most positions on this deck were brought in blood; and
(4)   Never get into something you can't get out of.

Each of these guidelines, if practiced openly, represents an image of heedful interrelating that can be internalized and acted back into the system. If such guidelines are neglected, ignored, or mocked, however, interrelating still goes on, but it is done with indifference and carelessness.

Whether heedful images survive or die depends importantly on interactions among those who differ in their experience with the system. While these interactions have been the focus of preliminary discussions of communities of practice (e.g. Lave and Wenger, 1991: 98–100) involving apprentices and experts, we highlight a neglected portion of the process, namely, the effects of socialization on the insiders doing the socializing (Sutton and Louis, 1987).

When experienced insiders answer the questions of inexperienced newcomers, the insiders themselves are often resocialized. This is significant because it may remind insiders how to act heedfully and how to talk about heedful action. Newcomers are often a pretext for insiders to reconstruct what they knew but forgot. Heedful know-how becomes more salient and more differentiated when insiders see what they say to newcomers and discover that they thought more thoughts than they thought they did.

Whether collective mind gets renewed during resocialization may be determined largely by the candor and narrative skills of insiders and the attentiveness of newcomers. Candid insiders who use memorable stories to describe failures as well as successes, their doubts as well as their certainties, and what works as well as what fails, help newcomers infer dispositions of heed and carelessness. Insiders who narrate richly also often remind themselves of forgotten details when they reconstruct a previous event. And these reminders increase the substance of mind because they increase the number of examples of heed in work.

Narrative skills (Bruner, 1986; Weick and Browning, 1986; Orr, 1990) are important for collective mind because stories organize know-how, tacit knowledge, nuance, sequence, multiple causation, means-end relations, and consequences into a memorable plot. The ease with which a single story integrates diverse themes of heed in action foreshadows the capability of individuals to do the same. A coherent story of heed is mind writ small. And a repertoire of war stories, which grows larger through the memorable exercise of heed in novel settings, is mind writ large.

The quality of collective mind is heavily dependent on the way insiders interact with newcomers (e.g. Van Maanen, 1976). If insiders are taciturn, indifferent, preoccupied, available only in stylized performances, less than candid, or simply not available at all, newcomers are in danger of acting without heed because they have only banal conversations to internalize. They have learned little about heedful interdependence. When these newcomers act and try to anticipate the contributions of others, their actions will be stupid, and mistakes will happen. These mistakes may represent small failures that produce learning (Sitkin, 1992). More ominous is the possibility that these mistakes may also represent a weakening of system capacity for heedful responding. When there is a loss of particulars about how heed can be expressed in representation and subordination, reliable performance suffers. As seasoned people become more peripheral to socialization, there should be a higher incidence of serious accidents.

We have dwelt on insider participation simply because this participation is a conspicuous phenomenon that allows us to describe collective mind, but anything that changes the ongoing interaction (e.g. preoccupation with personalities rather than with the task) can also change the capability of that interaction to preserve and convey dispositions of heed. Those changes in turn should affect the quality of mind, the likelihood of comprehension, and the incidence of error.

Illustrations of heed in interrelating

The concepts of heed, interrelating, contributing, representing, subordinating, intelligent action, comprehension, recapitulation, and resocialization come together in the concept of collective mind as heedful interrelating. Applying the language of collective mind to four examples of complex systems, we illustrate the adequate comprehension produced by heedful interrelating and the problematic comprehension produced by heedless interrelating.

Heedful interrelating

The first example of interrelating that is heedful involves a laboratory analogue of collective mind (Weick and Gilfillan, 1971). Three people who can neither see nor talk with one another are given target numbers between 1 and 30. Whenever a target number is announced, each person is to contribute some number between 0 and 10 such that, when all three contributions are added together, they sum to the target number.

There are many ways to solve this problem (e.g. a target number of 13 can be achieved with a 3s strategy, $4-4-5$, or a 10s strategy, $10-3-0$). Once a group evolves a strategy, people are removed one at a time, and strangers, who know nothing of the strategy in use, enter. The questions are, how do old-timers interrelate with newcomers, what strategy emerges, how soon does it emerge, and how stable is it!

Austere as these operations are, they have the rudiments of a collective mind. A newcomer knows a number of things:

(1) There are others in the activity system but they must be envisioned, since it is impossible to communicate with them (representation);
(2) The two other people have had some experience with the system and with the game (there are imagined requirements to which one must subordinate);
(3) Each contribution is important and must interrelate with the others (contributions must converge, supplement, assist, and be defined in relation to one another);
(4) To learn the existing system or to create a new one requires attention, careful calculations, and clear signals of intent (heedful contribution, representation, and subordination); and,
(5) Casual, indifferent interrelating will not be punished severely, because people are anonymous, and the rewards for participation are trivial (heedless responding is an option).

Just as the newcomers know these things, so do the old-timers. When these three people try to work out and maintain a system that hits each target on the first try, they are attempting to interrelate. They contribute, represent, and subordinate with varying amounts of heed. Their interrelating is better able to distinguish a mistake from an intentional effort to change strategy the more heedfully it was assembled. Likewise, heedful interrelating can 'read' a newcomer's intentions quickly, whereas heedless interrelating cannot. These discriminations are not accomplished by single individuals but are accomplished by interrelated activities and the heedfulness with which those activities are defined in relation to one another. Heedful action at any one of these three positions can be undermined if it is not reciprocated at the other two. What is undermined, however, is a pattern of interrelations, not a person. A pattern of nonreciprocated heedfulness represents a loss of intelligence that is reflected in missed targets and slow change.

Heedful interrelating on carriers looks a lot like the pattern of interrelating seen in the common-target game. A vivid example of this similarity is Gillcrist's (1990: 287–288) account of what it feels like to land and taxi on a carrier deck at night. Having successfully trapped onto the deck, Gillcrist watched the flight director's two amber wands:

> I raised the hook handle with my right hand and simultaneously added a lot of power to get the Crusader moving forward. There was an urgency in the taxi signal movement of the wands, telling me that there must be another plane close behind me in the groove. They wanted to get my airplane completely across the foul line as quickly as possible. Taxiing at night was more carefully done than in the light of day, however. We'd had enough airplanes taxi over the side at night to learn that lesson. . . . The wands pointed to another set of wands further up the flight deck and I began to follow their direction as my F-8 was taxied all the way to the first spot on the bow. 'God, how I hate this.' I muttered to myself. 'Do they really have to do this or are they just trying to scare me?' In spotting me in the first taxi spot on the bow, the taxi director was turning the F-8 so close to the edge of the flight deck that the cockpit actually swung in an arc over the deck's edge. All I could see was black rushing water eighty feet below. 'Jesus' I said to myself, 'I hope that guy knows what he is doing.'

The taxi director does know what he is doing, as does the pilot, but that alone does not keep the plane from dropping off the deck. The interrelating of their know-how keeps the plane on the deck. A command from the director that is not executed by the pilot or a pilot deviation that is not corrected by the director are equally dangerous and not controllable by either party alone. The activities of taxiing and directing remain failure-free to the extent that they are interrelated heedfully.

A third example of heedful interrelating is of special interest because so much of it appears to involve the mind of one individual, in this case, the person responsible for deck operations (the bos'n). One of the people in this position who was interviewed had 23 years of experience on 16 carriers. At the time he joined this carrier's crew, it took six hours to spot 45 aircraft on the deck. He reduced that time to two hours and 45 minutes, which gave his crew more time to relax and maintain their alertness.

This person tries constantly to prevent the four worst things that can happen on a deck: It catches fire, becomes fouled, locked (nothing can move), or a plane is immobilized in the landing area. The more times a plane is moved to prevent any of these conditions, the higher the probability that it will brush against another plane ('crunch'), be damaged, and be out of service until repaired.

This bos'n, who is responsible for the smooth functioning of deck operations, gets up an hour early each day just to think about the kind of environment he will create on the deck that day, given the schedule of operations. This thinking is individual mind at work, but it also illustrates how collective mind is represented in the head of one person. The bos'n is dealing with collective mind when he represents the capabilities and weaknesses of imagined crewmembers' responses in his thinking, when he tailors sequences of activities so that improvisation and flexible response are activated as an expected part of the day's adaptive response, and when he counts on the interrelations among crewmembers themselves to 'mind' the day's activities.

The bos'n does not plan specific step-by-step operations but, rather, plans which crews will do the planning and deciding, when, and with what resources at hand. The system will decide the operations, and the bos'n sets up the system that will do this. The bos'n does this by attempting to recognize the strengths and weaknesses of the various crews working for him. The pieces of the system he sets up may interrelate stupidly or intelligently, in large part because they will either duplicate or undermine the heedful contributing, representing, and subordinating he anticipates.

Heedless interrelating

When interrelating breaks down, individuals represent others in the system in less detail, contributions are shaped less by anticipated responses, and the boundaries of the envisaged system are drawn more narrowly, with the result that subordination becomes meaningless. Attention is focused on the local situation rather than the joint situation. People still may act heedfully, but not with respect to others. Interrelating becomes careless. Key people and activities are overlooked. As interrelating deteriorates and becomes more primitive, there is less comprehension of the implications of unfolding events, slower correction of errors, and more opportunities for small errors to combine and amplify. When these events are set in motion and sustained through heedless interrelating, there is a greater chance that small lapses can enlarge into disasters.

An incident that happened during a nighttime launch and recovery, which was described to us in interviews and correspondence, illustrates the steady loss of collective mind as interrelating became less heedful. This incident began to unfold during a night launch in which one-third of the planes in the mission were still on deck waiting to be launched, even though other planes were already beginning to be recovered.

Aircraft A, which was in the air and the fourth plane in line to land, had an apparent hydraulic failure, although the pilot was able to get his gear and tail hook down. This failure meant that if the plane were landed, its wings could not be folded, and it would take up twice the space normally allotted to it. This complicates the landing of all planes behind it.

While the pilot of plane A was trying to get help for his problem on a radio channel, plane B, an F-14, which was number three in order of landing, had a compound hydraulic failure, and none of his back-up hydraulic systems appeared to work, something that was unheard of. Plane C, which was fifth in line to land, then developed a control problem. Thus, the airboss was faced, first, with several A-7 aircraft that still had to be launched. This is not a trivial complication, because the only catapult available for these aircraft was the one whose blast-deflector panel extends part way into the area where planes land. Second, the airboss had a string of planes about to land that included (1) a normally operating A-7, (2) a normally operating A-7, (3) plane B with a compound hydraulic failure, (4) plane A with a hydraulic failure but gear and tail hook down, and (5) plane C with an apparent control problem.

The first plane was taken out of the landing pattern and the second was landed. Plane B, the one with the most severe problems, was told to land and then had to be waved off because the person operating the deflector panel for launches lowered the panel one second too late to allow B to land. The deflector operator had not been informed that an emergency existed. Plane B and its increasingly frightened pilot were reinserted into the landing pattern behind plane C for a second pass at the deck. Plane B then experienced an additional hydraulic failure. Plane A landed without incident, as did plane C. Plane C had corrected its control problem, but no one was informed. Thus, plane B's second pass was delayed longer than necessary because he had to wait for C to land in the mistaken belief that C still had a problem. The pilot of plane B became increasingly agitated and less and less able to help diagnose what might be wrong with his aircraft. The decision was made to send plane B to a land base, but it ran out of fuel on the way and the pilot and his RIO (radar intercept officer) had to eject. Both were rescued, but a $38-million aircraft was lost. If aircraft B had not been waved off the first time it tried to land, it would have been safely recovered. If we analyze this incident as a loss of collective mind produced by heedless interrelating, we look for two things: events that became incomprehensible, signifying a loss of mind, and increasingly heedless interrelating.

There were several events that became harder to comprehend. The failure of the hydraulic system in aircraft B was puzzling. The triggering of additional hydraulic failures was even more so. To have three of five aircraft on final approach declare emergencies was itself something that was hard to comprehend, as was the problem of how to recover three disabled planes while launching three more immediately.

Incomprehensible events made interrelating more difficult, which then made the events even harder to comprehend. The loss of heed in interrelating was spread among contributions, representations, and subordinations. The squadron representative who tried to deal with the stressed pilot in plane B was not himself a pilot (he was an RIO), and he did not scan systematically for possible sources of the problem. Instead, he simply told the pilot assorted things to try, not realizing that, in the pilot's doing so, additional systems on the plane began to fail. He didn't realize these growing complications because the pilot was both imprecise in his reports of trouble and slow to describe what happened when he tested some hypothesis proposed by the representative. And the representative did nothing to change the pilot's style of contributing.

But heedless interrelating was not confined to exchanges between pilot and representative. The RIO in plane B made no effort to calm the pilot or help him diagnose. The deflector operator was not treated as a person in the recovery system. Three different problems were discussed on two radio frequencies, which made it difficult to sort out which plane had which problem. No one seemed to register that the squadron representative was himself getting farther behind and making increasingly heedless contributions. The airboss in command of the tower was an F-14 pilot, but he was preoccupied with the five incoming and the three outgoing aircraft and could not be pulled completely into the activity system that was dealing with the F-14 problem. As heed began to be withdrawn from the system, activities and people became isolated, the system began to pull apart, the problems became more incomprehensible, and it became harder for individuals to interrelate with a system of activities that was rapidly losing its form. The pattern of interrelated activities lost intelligence and mind as contributions became more thoughtless and less interdependent.

Had the pattern of interrelations been more heedful, it might have detected what was subsequently said to be the most likely cause of the failures in plane B. Although the aircraft was never recovered, the navy's investigation of the incident concluded that too many demands were placed on the emergency back-up systems, and the plane became less and less flyable. Sustained heedful interrelating might well have registered that the growing number of attempted solutions had in fact created a new problem that was worse than any problem that was present to begin with.[3]

It is important to realize that our analysis, using the concepts of collective mind and heedful interrelating, implies something more than the simple advice, 'be careful.' People can't be careful unless they take account of others and unless others do the same. Being careful is a social rather than a solitary act. To act with care, people have to envision their contributions in the context of requirements for joint action. Furthermore, to act with care does not mean that one plans how to do this and then applies the plan to the action. Care is not cultivated apart from action. It is expressed in action and through action. Thus people can't be careful, they are careful (or careless). The care is in the action.

The preceding analysis also suggests that it is crucial to pay attention to mind, because accidents are not just issues of ignorance and cognition, they are issues of inattention and conduct as well. The examples of incomprehension mentioned above are not simply issues of fact and thinking. Facts by themselves are of no help if they cannot be communicated or heard or applied or interpreted or incorporated into activities or placed in contexts, in short, if they are not addressed mindfully. One 'fact' of this incident is that plane B could have landed had it not been waved off because of the extended deflector. Furthermore, individuals within the system were not ignorant of crucial details (e.g. the pilot of plane C knew he no longer had a problem).

One interpretation of this incident is that individuals were smarter than the system, but the problem was more complex than any one individual could understand. Heedful interrelating of activities constructs a substrate that is more complex and, therefore, better able to comprehend complex events than is true for smart but isolated individuals. The F-14 may have been lost because heedful interrelating was lost. Heightened attentiveness to social process might have prevented both losses.

Discussion

We conclude from our analysis that carrier operations are a struggle for alertness and that the concept of heedful interrelating helps capture this struggle. We began with the question, How can we analyze a complex social activity system in which fluctuations in comprehension seem to be consequential? We focused on heed (understood as dispositions to act with attentiveness, alertness, and care), conduct (understood as behavior that takes into account the expectations of others), and mind (understood as integration of feeling, thinking, and willing).

We were able to talk about group mind without reification, because we grounded our ideas in individual actions and then treated those actions as the means by which a distinct higher-order pattern of interrelated activities emerged. This pattern shaped the actions that produced it, persisted despite changes in personnel, and changed despite unchanging personnel. Thus, we did not reify social entities, because we argued that they emerge from individual actions that construct interrelations. But neither did we reify individual entities, because we argued that they emerge through selective importation, interpretation, and re-enactment of the social order that they constitute.

In broadening our focus, we conceptualized mind as action that constructs mental processes rather than as mental processes that construct action. We proposed that variations in contributing, representing, and subordinating produce collective mind. Common hallmarks of mind such as alertness, attentiveness, understanding, and relating to the world were treated as coincident with and immanent in the connecting activities. To connect is to mind.

For the collective mind, the connections that matter are those that link distributed activities, and the ways those connections are accomplished embody much of what we have come to mean by the word 'mind.' The ways people connect their activities make conduct mindful. Mindless actions ignore interrelating or accomplish it haphazardly and with indifference (Bellah et al., 1991).

As a result of our analysis, we now see the importance of disentangling the development of mind from the development of a group. In Asch's description of the essence of group life, as well as in other discussions of group cognition, the development of mind is confounded with the development of the group. As a group matures and moves from inclusion through control to affection (Schutz,

1958), or as it moves from forming through storming, norming, and performing (Tuckman, 1965), both interrelating and intimacy develop jointly. If a mature group has few accidents or an immature group has many, it is difficult to see what role, if any, mind may play in this. An immature group of relative strangers with few shared norms, minimal disclosure, and formal relationships might well find it hard to cope with nonroutine events. But this has nothing to do with mind.

In our analysis we have assumed that there is something like a two-by-two matrix in which a group can be developed or undeveloped and a collective mind can be developed or undeveloped. And we assume that the combinations of developed-group-undeveloped mind and undeveloped-group-developed mind are possible. These two combinations are crucial to any proposal that collective mind is a distinct process in social life.

The combination of developed-group-undeveloped mind is found in the phenomenon of groupthink (Janis, 1982), as well as in cults (Galanter, 1989), interactions at NASA prior to the Challenger disaster (Starbuck and Milliken, 1988), and ethnocentric research groups (Weick, 1983). Common among these examples is subordination to a system that is envisaged carelessly, or, as Janis (1982: 174) put it, there is an overestimation of the group's power, morality, and invulnerability. Furthermore, contributions are made thoughtlessly; as Janis (1982: 175) put it, there is self-censorship of deviations, doubts, and counter-arguments. And, finally, representations are careless; members maintain the false assumption that silence means consent (Janis, 1982: 175). In the presence of heedless interrelating, comprehension declines, regardless of how long the group has been together, and disasters result.

The combination of undeveloped-group-developed mind is found in ad hoc project teams, such as those that produce television specials (e.g. Peters, 1992: 189–200) or motion pictures (Faulkner and Anderson, 1987), and in temporary systems such as those that form in aircraft cockpits (Ginnett, 1990), around jazz improvisation (Eisenberg, 1990), in response to crises (Rochlin, 1989), or in high-velocity environments (Eisenhardt, 1993). The common feature shared among these diverse settings is best captured by Eisenberg (1990: 160), who characterized them as built from nondisclosive intimacy that 'stresses coordin-ation of action over alignment of cognitions, mutual respect over agreement, trust over empathy, diversity over homogeneity, loose over tight coupling, and strategic communication over unrestricted candor.'

Translated into the language of heedful interrelating, what Eisenberg depicted were relationships in which shared values, openness, and disclosure, all hallmarks of a developed group, were not fully developed, but in which collect-ive mind was developed. Nondisclosive intimacy is characterized by heedful contributing (e.g. loose coupling, diversity, strategic communication), heedful representing (e.g. mutual respect, coordination of action), and heedful subordin-ating (e.g. trust).

If heedful interrelating can occur in an undeveloped group, this changes the way we think about the well-known stages of group development. If people are observed to contribute, represent, and subordinate with heed, these actions can be interpreted as operations that construct a well-developed collective mind;

however, those same actions can also be seen as the orienting, clarifying, and testing associated with the early stages of a new group just beginning to form (McGrath, 1984: 152–162). By one set of criteria, that associated with group formation, people engaged in forming are immature. By another set of criteria, that associated with collective mind, these acts of forming represent well-developed mental processes.

These opposed criteria suggest that groups may be smartest in their early stages. As they grow older, they lose mind when interrelating becomes more routine, more casual, more automatic. This line of reasoning is consistent with Gersick's (1988) demonstration that groups tend to re-form halfway through their history. In our language, this midcourse reshuffling can be understood as redoing the pattern of interrelations that constitute mind, thereby renewing mind itself. If groups steadily lose mind and comprehension as they age, their capability for comprehension may show a dramatic increase halfway through their history. If that is plausible, the sudden surge in comprehension should be accompanied by a sudden decrease in the number of accidents they produce.

The conceptualization of topics in organizational theory

Our analysis of collective mind and heedful interrelating throws new light on several topics in organizational theory, including organizational types, the measurement of performance, and normal accidents.

The concept of mind may be an important tool in comparative analysis. LaPorte and Consolini (1991) argued that high-reliability organizations such as aircraft carriers differ in many ways from organizations usually portrayed in organizational theory as (for convenience) high-efficiency organizations. Typical efficiency organizations practice incremental decision making, their errors do not have a lethal edge, they use simple low-hazard technologies, they are governed by single rather than multilayered authority systems, they are more often in the private than the public sector, they are not preoccupied with perfection, their operations are carried on at one level of intensity, they experience few nasty surprises, and they can rely on computation or judgment as decision strategies (Thompson and Tuden, 1959) but seldom need to employ both at the same time. LaPorte and Consolini (1991: 19) concluded that existing organizational theory is inadequate to understand systems in which the 'consequences and costs associated with major failures in some technical operations are greater than the value of the lessons learned from them.'

Our analysis suggests that most of these differences can be subsumed under the generalization that high-efficiency organizations have simpler minds than do high-reliability organizations. If dispositions toward individual and collective heed were increased in most organizations in conjunction with increases in task-related interdependence and flexibility in the sequencing of tasks, then we would expect these organizations to act more like high-reliability systems. Changes of precisely this kind seem to be inherent in recent interventions to improve total quality management (e.g. U.S. General Accounting Office, 1991).

Our point is simply that confounded in many comparisons among organizations that differ on conspicuous grounds, such as structure and technology, are less conspicuous but potentially more powerful differences in the capability for collective mind. A smart system does the right thing regardless of its structure and regardless of whether the environment is stable or turbulent. We suspect that organic systems, because of their capacity to reconfigure themselves temporarily into more mechanistic structures, have more fully developed minds than do mechanistic systems.

We also suspect that newer organizational forms, such as networks (Powell, 1990), self-designing systems (Hedberg, Nystrom, and Starbuck, 1976), cognitive oligopolies (Porac, Thomas, and Baden-Fuller, 1989: 413), and interpretation systems (Daft and Weick, 1984) have more capacity for mind than do M forms, U forms, and matrix forms. But all of these conjectures, which flow from the idea of collective mind, require that we pay as much attention to social processes and microdynamics as we now pay to the statics of structure, strategy, and demographics.

The concept of mind also suggests a view of performance that complements concepts such as activities (Homans, 1950), the active task (Dornbusch and Scott, 1975), task structure (Hackman, 1990: 10), group task design (Hackman, 1987), and production functions (McGrath, 1990). It adds to all of these a concern with the style or manner of performance. Not only can performance be high or low, productive or unproductive, or adequate or inadequate, it can also be heedful or heedless. Heedful performance might or might not be judged productive, depending on how productivity is defined.

Most important, the concept of mind allows us to talk about careful versus careless performance, not just performance that is productive or unproductive. This shift makes it easier to talk about performance in systems in which the next careless error may be the last trial. The language of care is more suited to systems concerned with reliability than is the language of efficiency.

Much of the interest in organizations that are vulnerable to catastrophic accidents can be traced to Perrow's (1981) initial analysis of Three Mile Island, followed by his expansion of this analysis into other industries (Perrow, 1984). In the expanded analysis, Perrow suggested that technologies that are both tightly coupled and interactively complex are the most dangerous, because small events can escalate rapidly into a catastrophe. Nuclear aircraft carriers such as those we have studied are especially prone to normal accidents (see Perrow, 1984: 97) because they comprise not one but several tightly coupled, interactively complex technologies. These include jet aircraft, nuclear weapons carried on aircraft, nuclear weapons stored on board the ship, and nuclear reactors used to power the ship. Furthermore, the marine navigation system and the air traffic control system on a ship are tightly coupled technologies, although they are slightly less complex than the nuclear technologies.

Despite their high potential for normal accidents, carriers are relatively safe. Our analysis suggests that one of the reasons carriers are safe is because of, not in spite of, tight coupling.

Our analysis raises the possibility that technological tight coupling is dangerous in the presence of interactive complexity, unless it is mediated by a mutually shared field that is well developed. This mutually shared field, built from heedful interrelating, is itself tightly coupled, but this tight coupling is social rather than technical. We suspect that normal accidents represent a breakdown of social processes and comprehension rather than a failure of technology. Inadequate comprehension can be traced to flawed mind rather than flawed equipment.

The conceptualization of practice

The mindset for practice implicit in the preceding analysis has little room for heroic, autonomous individuals. A well-developed organization mind, capable of reliable performance is thoroughly social. It is built of ongoing interrelating and dense interrelations. Thus, interpersonal skills are not a luxury in high-reliability systems. They are a necessity. These skills enable people to represent and sub-ordinate themselves to communities of practice. As people move toward indi-vidualism and fewer interconnections, organization mind is simplified and soon becomes indistinguishable from individual mind. With this change comes height-ened vulnerability to accidents. Cockpit crews that function as individuals rather than teams show this rapid breakdown in ability to understand what is happening (Orlady and Foushee, 1987). Sustained success in coping with emergency condi-tions seems to occur when the activities of the crew are more fully interrelated and when members' contributions, representations, and subordination create a pattern of joint action. The chronic fear in high-reliability systems that events will prove to be incomprehensible (Perrow, 1984) may be a realistic fear only when social skills are underdeveloped. With more development of social skills goes more development of organization mind and heightened understanding of environments.

A different way to state the point that mind is dependent on social skills is to argue that it is easier for systems to lose mind than to gain it. A culture that encourages individualism, survival of the fittest, macho heroics, and can-do reactions will often neglect heedful practice of representation and subordination. Without representation and subordination, comprehension reverts to one brain at a time. No matter how visionary or smart or forward-looking or aggressive that one brain may be, it is no match for conditions of interactive complexity. Cooperation is imperative for the development of mind.

Reliable performance may require a well-developed collective mind in the form of a complex, attentive system tied together by trust. That prescription sounds simple enough. Nevertheless, conventional understanding seems to favor a different configuration: a simple, automatic system tied together by suspicion and redundancy. The latter scenario makes sense in a world in which individuals can comprehend what is going on. But when individual comprehension proves inadequate, one of the few remaining sources of comprehension is social entities. Variation in the development of these entities may spell the difference between prosperity and disaster.

Notes

*   We acknowledge with deep gratitude, generous and extensive help with previous versions of this manuscript from Sue Ashford, Michael Cohen, Dan Denison, Jane Dutton, Les Gasser, Joel Kahn, Rod Kramer, Peter Manning, Dave Meader, Debra Meyerson, Walter Nord, Linda Pike, Joe Porac, Bob Quinn, Lance Sandelands, Paul Schaffner, Howard Schwartz, Kathie Sutcliffe, Bob Sutton, Diane Vaughan, Jim Walsh, Rod White, Mayer Zald, and the anonymous reviewers for *Administrative Science Quarterly*.

1   Unless otherwise cited, aircraft carrier examples are drawn from field observation notes of air operations and interviews aboard Nimitz class carriers made by the second author and others over a five-year period. Researchers spent from four days to three weeks aboard the carriers at any one time. They usually made observations from different vantage points during the evolutions of various events. Observations were entered into computer systems and later organizational members for clarity of meaning. Examples are also drawn from quarterly workshop discussions with senior officers from those carriers over the two years. The primary observational research methodology was to triangulate observations made by three faculty researchers, as suggested by Glaser and Strauss (1967) and Eisenhardt (1989). The methodology is more fully discussed in Roberts, Stout, and Halpern (1993). Paper-and-pencil data were also collected and are discussed elsewhere (Roberts, Rousseau, and LaPorte, 1993). That research was supported by Office of Naval Research contract #N–00014–86-k–0312 and National Science Foundation grant #F7–08046.

2   We could just as easily have used Blumer's (1969: 78–79 discussion of 'the mutual alignment of action.'

3   There is a limit to heedfulness, given the number and skill of participants, and on this night this ship was at that limit. The system was overloaded, and the situation was one that managers of high-technology weapons systems worry about all the time. They call it OBE (overcome by events). Given perhaps only minor differences in the situation, the outcomes might have been different. In this situation, for example, had the carrier air group commander come to the tower (which he often does), he would have added yet another set of eyes and ears, with their attendant skills. Perhaps he could have monitored one aspect of the situation while the boss and mini boss took charge of others, and the situation would have been a more heedful one. Had the squadron representative in the tower been a pilot, he might have searched through his own repertoire of things that can go wrong and helped the F–14's pilot calm down and solve his problem, increasing the heedfulness of the situation.

References

Asch, Solomon E. (1952) *Social Psychology*, Englewood Cliffs, NJ: Prentice-Hall.

Bellah, Robert N., Madsen, Richard, Sullivan, William M., Swidler, Ann and Steven M. Tipton (1991) *The Good Society*, Knopf: New York.

Blumer, Herbert (1969) *Symbolic Interaction*, University of California Press: Berkeley.

Boden, Margaret A. (1990) "Introduction", in Margaret A. Boden (ed.), *The Philosophy of Artificial Intelligence*, 1–21, Oxford University Press: New York.

Bruner, Jerome (1986) *Actual Minds. Possible Worlds*, Harvard University Press: Cambridge, MA.

Churchland, Paul M. (1992) "A deeper unity: Some Feyerabendian themes in neuro-computational form", in Steven Davis (ed.), *Connectionism: Theory and Practice*, 30–50, Oxford University Press: New York.

Daft, Richard, and Weick, Karl E. (1984) "Toward a model of organizations as interpretation systems", *Academy of Management Review* 9: 284–295.

Dornbusch, Sandford M. and Scott, W. Richard (1975) *Evaluation and the Exercise of Authority*, Jossey-Bass: San Francisco.

Dreyfus, Hubert L., and Dreyfus, Stuart E. (1990) "Making a mind versus modeling the brain: Artificial intelligence back at a branch point", in Margaret A. Boden (ed.), *The Philosophy of Artificial Intelligence*, 300–333, Oxford University Press: New York.

Eisenberg, Eric (1990) "Jamming: Transcendence through organizing", *Communication Research*, 17: 139–164.

Eisenhardt, Kathleen M. (1989) "Building theories from case study research", *Academy of Management Review*, 14: 532–550.

Eisenhardt, Kathleen M. (1993) "High reliability organizations meet high velocity environments: Common dilemmas in nuclear power plants, aircraft carriers, and microcomputer firms", in Karlene Roberts (ed.), *New Challenges to Understanding Organizations*, 117–135, Macmillan: New York.

Elman, Jeffrey L. (1992) "Grammatical structure and distributed representations", in Steven Davis (ed.), *Connectionism: Theory and Practice*, 138–178, Oxford University Press: New York.

Faulkner, Robert R., and Anderson, A. B. (1987) "Short-term projects and emergent careers: Evidence from Hollywood", *American Journal of Sociology*, 92: 879–909.

Follett, Mary Parker (1924) *Creative Experience*, New York: Longmans, Green.

Galanter, Marc (1989) *Cults*, Oxford University Press: New York.

Gersick, Connie G. (1988) "Time and transition in work teams: Toward a new model of group development", *Academy of Management Journal*, 31: 9–41.

Gillcrist, P. T. (1990) *Feet Wet: Reflections of a Carrier*, Presidio Press: Novato, CA.

Ginnett, Robert C. (1990) "Airline cockpit crew", in J. Richard Hackman (ed.), *Groups That Work (and Those That Don't)*, 427–448, Jossey-Bass: San Francisco.

Glaser, Barney, and Strauss, Anselm L. (1967) *The Discovery of Grounded Theory: Strategies for Qualitative Research*, Aldine: Chicago.

Hackman, J. Richard (1987) "The design of work teams", in Jay Lorsch (ed.), *Handbook of Organizational Behavior*, 315–342, Prentice-Hall: Englewood Cliffs, NJ.

Hackman, J. Richard (ed.) (1990) *Groups That Work (and Those That Don't)*, Jossey-Bass: San Francisco.

Hedberg, Bo L. T., Nystrom, Paul C. and Starbuck, William H. (1976) "Camping on seesaws: Prescriptions for a self-designing organization", *Administrative Science Quarterly*, 21: 41–65.

Homans, George C. (1950) *The Human Group*, Harcourt: New York.

Hutchins, Edwin (1990) "The technology of team navigation", in Galegher, Jolene, Kraut, Robert E., and Egido, Carmen (eds), *Intellectual Teamwork*, 191–220, Erlbaum: Hillsdale, NJ.

Hutchins, Edwin (1991) "The social organization of distributed cognition", in Resnick, Lauren, B., Levine, John M. and Teasley, Stephanie D. (eds) *Perspectives on Socially Shared Cognition*, 283–307, American Psychological Association: Washington DC.

Janis, Irving (1982) *Groupthink*, 2nd ed, Houghton-Mifflin: Boston.

Langer, Eleanor J. (1989) "Minding matters: The consequences of mindlessness-mindfulness", in Leonard Berkowitz (ed.), *Advances in Experimental Social Psychology*, 22: 137–17, Academic Press: New York.

LaPorte, Todd R. and Consolini, Paula M. (1991) "Working in practice but not in theory: Theoretical challenges of high-reliability organizations", *Journal of Public Administration Research and Theory*, 1: 19–47.

Lave, Jean, and Wenger, Etienne (1991) Situated Learning: Legitimate Peripheral Participation, Cambridge University Press: New York.

Lyons, William (1980) *Gilbert Ryle: An Introduction to His Philosophy*, Humanities Press: Atlantic Highlands, NJ.

McGrath, Joseph E. (1984) *Groups: Interaction and Performance*, Prentice-Hall: Englewood Cliffs, NJ.

McGrath, Joseph E. (1990) "Time matters in groups", in Galegher, Jolene, Kraut, Robert, E. and Egido, Carmen (eds), *Intellectual Teamwork*, 23–61, Erlbaum: Hillsdale, NJ.

Mead, George Herbert (1934) *Mind, Self, and Society*, University of Chicago Press: Chicago.

Morgan, Gareth (1986) *Images of Organization*, Sage: Beverly Hills, CA.

Orlady, Harry W. and Foushee, H. Clayton (1987) *Cockpit Resource Management Training*, Springfield, VA: National Technical Information Service (N87–22634).

Orr, Julian E. (1990) "Sharing knowledge, celebrating identity: Community memory in a service culture", in Middleton, David and Edwards, Derek (eds), *Collective Remembering*, 169–189, Sage: Newbury Park, CA.

Perrow, Charles (1981) "The President's Commission and the normal accident", in Sills, D., Wolf, C. and Shelanski, V. (eds), *The Accident at Three Mile Island: The Human Dimensions*, 173–184, Westview Press: Boulder, CO.

Perrow, Charles (1984) *Normal Accidents*. Basic Books: New York.

Peters, Tom (1992) *Liberation Management*, Knopf: New York.

Porac, Joseph F., Thomas, Howard and Baden-Fuller, Charles (1989) "Competitive groups as cognitive communities: The case of Scottish knitwear manufacturers" *Journal of Management Studies*, 26: 397–416.

Powell, Walter W. (1990) "Neither market nor hierarchy: Network forms of organization", in Staw, Barry M. and Cummings, Larry L. (eds), *Research in Organizational Behavior*, 12: 295–336, JAI Press: Greenwich, CT.

Quinlan, Phillip (1991) *Connectionism and Psychology*, University of Chicago Press: Chicago.

Roberts, Karlene H., Rousseau, Denise M. and LaPorte, Todd R. (1993) "The culture of high reliability: Quantitative and qualitative assessment aboard nuclear powered aircraft carriers", *Journal of High Technology Management Research* (in press).

Roberts, Karlene H., Stout, Susan and Halpern, Jennifer J. (1993) "Decision dynamics in two high reliability military organizations", *Management Science* (in press).

Rochlin, Gene I. (1989) "Organizational self-design is a crisis-avoidance strategy: U.S. naval flight operations as a case study", *Industrial Crisis Quarterly*, 3: 159–176.

Rochlin, Gene I., LaPorte, Todd R. and Roberts, Karlene H. (1987) "The self-designing high-reliability organization: Aircraft carrier flight operations at sea", *Naval War College Review*, 40 (4): 76–90.

Rumelhart, David E. (1992) "Towards a microstructural account of human reasoning", in Davis, Steven (ed.), *Connectionism: Theory and Practice*, 69–83, Oxford University Press: New York.

Ryle, Gilbert (1949) *The Concept of Mind*, University of Chicago Press: Chicago.

Sandelands, Lloyd E., and Stablein, Ralph E. (1987) "The concept of organization mind", in Bacharach, Samuel and DiTomaso, Nancy (eds), *Research in the Sociology of Organizations*, 5: 135–161, JAI Press: Greenwich, CT.

Schneider, David J. (1991) "Social cognition", in Porter, Lyman W. and Rosenzweig, Mark R. (eds), *Annual Review of Psychology*, 42: 527–561, Annual Reviews: Palo Alto, CA.

Schneider, W., and Shiffrin, R. M. (1977) "Controlled and automatic human information processing: I. Detection, search and attention", *Psychological Review*, 84: 1–66.

Schutz, William C. (1958) *FIRO A Three-Dimensional Theory of Interpersonal Behavior*, Holt, Rinehart, and Winston: New York.

Sitkin, Sim (1992) "Learning through failure: The strategy of small losses", in Barry Staw and Cummings, Larly (eds), *Research in Organizational Behavior*, 14: 231–266, JAI Press: Greenwich, CT.

Starbuck, William H., and Milliken, Francis J. (1988) "Challenger: Finetuning the odds until something breaks", *Journal of Management Studies*, 25: 319–340.

Sutton, Robert I. and Louis, Meryl R. (1987) "How selecting and socializing newcomers influences insiders", *Human Resource is Management*, 26: 347–361.

Thompson, James D., and Tuden, Arthur (1959) "Strategies, structures, and processes of organizational decision", in James D. Thompson (ed.), Comparative Studies in Organization: 195–216, University of Pittsburgh Press: Pittsburgh.

Tuckman, Bruce W. (1965) "Developmental sequence in small groups", *Psychological Bulletin*, 63: 384–399.

U.S. General Accounting Office (1991) *Management Practices*, U.S. Companies Improve Performance through Ouality Efforts. Document GAO/NSIAD–91–19O, U.S. Government Printing Office: Washington DC.

Van Maanen, John (1976) "Breaking in: Socialization to work" in Robert Duhin (ed.), *Handbook of Work, Organization and Society*: 67–130, Rand McNally: Chicago.

Walsh, James P. and Ungson, Gerardo R. (1991) "Organizational memory" Academy of Management Review, 16: 57–91.

Wegner, Daniel M. (1987) "Transactive memory: A contemporary analysis of the group mind", in Brian Mullen and George R. Goethals (eds), Theories of Group Behavior 185–208, Springer-Verlag: New York.

Wegner, Daniel M., Erber, Ralph and Raymond, Paula (1991) "Transactive memory in close relationships" *Journal of Personality and Social Psychology*, 61: 923–929.

Wegner, Daniel M., Giuliano, Toni and Hertel, Paula T. (1985) "Cognitive interdependence in close relationships", in William J. Ickes (ed.), Compatible and Incompatible Relationships, 253–276, Springer-Verlag: New York.

Weick, Karl E. (1983) "Contradictions in a community of scholars: The cohesion-accuracy tradeoff", *Review of Higher Education*, 6 (4): 253–267.

Weick, Karl E., and Browning, Larry (1986) "Arguments and narration in organizational communication" *Journal of Management*, 12: 243–259.

Weick, Karl E., and Gilfillan, David P. (1971) "Fate of arbitrary traditions in a laboratory microculture", *Journal of Personality and Social Psychology*, 17: 179–191.

Wilson, G. C. (1986) *Supercarrier*, Macmillan: New York.

Chapter 23

Dominic Elliott and Denis Smith

FOOTBALL STADIA DISASTERS IN THE UNITED KINGDOM: LEARNING FROM TRAGEDY?[1]

Introduction

SPORTING EVENTS HAVE ATTRACTED large crowds for many centuries and have long created managerial problems for those charged with their control. The Colosseum, for example, which was built during the first century AD to accommodate 50,000 spectators, had some 80 entrance/exits; showing that even the Romans were aware of some basic crowd safety ideas associated with, what has become known as, 'complex space'. As stadia and crowd sizes have increased, so too have the problems of managing such events. Recent events have illustrated how great the potential for accidents are within stadia, and concern over crowd safety in such circumstances has been growing. However, the roots of the current problems associated with crowd safety and control in the United Kingdom can be traced back to the nineteenth century when many of today's stadia were built. This paper represents an attempt to explore the implications of managing large crowds in complex space and offers some insights into the nature of such problems within the United Kingdom by reference to a series of disasters involving British football fans.

Until recently, the issue of managing crowds, as opposed to managing hooligans, had taken a back seat in the minds of many. Indeed, Inglis (1987) comments that,

'A century ago clubs did virtually nothing to protect spectators. Thousands were packed onto badly constructed slopes with hardly a wooden barrier in sight. About the best that can be said of the early grounds is that with only ropes around the pitches there was little to stop a build up of pressure sending hundreds pouring onto the pitch.' (p. 28)

Given the scale of crowds at some matches it was only a matter of time before disaster struck. In April, 1902, at a Scotland–England match, held at Ibrox Park, Glasgow, a 'temporary' wooden and iron structure collapsed killing 26 and injuring another 500 spectators. This was to be the first of many horrific incidents at sports stadia, although it would appear that the regulators were slow to learn the lessons that they taught. Indeed, in his report on the Hillsborough disaster, Lord Justice Taylor (1989) was forced to comment that:

'It is a depressing and chastening fact that this is the ninth official report covering crowd safety and control at football grounds. After eight previous reports and three editions of the Green Guide, it seems astounding that 95 people could die from overcrowding before the very eyes of those controlling the event.' (p. 4)

At the time of Taylor's inquiry in 1989/90, it seemed that both the scale and frequency of stadia disasters was increasing and that firm managerial action was required to ensure that further events did not occur.

Stadia disasters in the United Kingdom show a remarkable degree of similarity in terms of the response of the regulators involved. In the initial 'legitimation' phase that exists after crises (Smith, 1990b), specific legislative controls were developed to deal with the demands of that particular incident. Consequently, there has been a piecemeal framework of control developed and the fundamental problems associated with managing complex space have not been broadly addressed. Much of the attention of regulators has been focused on the technical solutions to complex space problems. The Moelwyn-Hughes report (1946), for example, legally specified the maximum capacities for grounds. Following the Ibrox Park accident in Scotland, 'The Guide to Safety at Sports Grounds' (or Green Guide) was published in an attempt to provide guidelines to clubs on ground safety. The eventual response to the Ibrox event and its subsequent inquiry was the passing of The Safety at Sports Ground Act (1975) which sought to deal with the problems of egress from grounds and other issues of crowd control. The Popplewell Report (1986) finally sought to control the sale and consumption of alcohol in and around football grounds. In the wake of the Bradford fire, specific recommendations concerning the maintenance and construction of stands were postulated. Finally, the Taylor Report (1989) made specific recommendations about the control of crowds and the use of wire cages to prevent pitch invasions.

Obviously, such a fragmented approach brings with it its own inherent problems. Canter (1989), for example, is critical of any piecemeal approach to developing safety, arguing that:

'As a consequence there is never any possibility of examining the system of legislation as a whole, of seeing the directions in which it is accumulating or of developing radical solutions that will deal with fundamental problems. A further problem is that rules and principles get built into the legislation in the early years and, provided it cannot be demonstrated that somebody has been injured because of these rules, there is a powerful inertia in the system of controls operating against the changing the rules.' (p. 92)

An excellent example of this 'inertia' concerns the role of Scicon consultants, who provided technical information to the Wheatley Report (1971). Their findings, regarding rules for crowd movement, speeds and passageway widths, were considered preliminary and, therefore, requiring further research. However, these figures have been used extensively, despite the fact that more recent work has shed doubt on their accuracy. In essence, we see the creation of a technical paradigm which then becomes virtually impossible to shift (see Fischer, 1991). Finally, Canter (1989) puts forward the idea that once the problem of crowd safety and control is seen as a technical question – determined by barrier strengths, the width of passageways and other technical considerations – then the mind set becomes one that seeks only technical solutions. This culture of technocracy (see Fischer, 1990; 1991) is held to be important in luring organizations into a false sense of security and is virtually impossible to challenge by potential victims (Smith, 1990a). What is quite obvious from this brief introduction is that the football industry in the United Kingdom has something to learn from the academic research that has been carried out in the area of crisis management. This paper seeks to begin that process by examining a number of football disasters within the context of established crisis management frameworks.

While research on organizational and environmental crises is increasing in scope and developing in intellectual rigor (Pauchant and Douville, 1993), there is still much work that needs to be undertaken in analyzing specific cases of crisis. There are few events that capture public and regulatory attention more than those that involve multiple fatalities. The modes by which such disasters unfurl can be seen to include transport failures (Schwartz, 1988; Smith, 1992a; Weick, 1990), industrial processes (Kunreuther, 1987; Shrivastava, 1992), product failures (Siomkos, 1989; Siomkos and Kurzbard, 1992), geophysical, engineering and structural failures (Blockley, 1980; Turner, 1978) and crowd-related accidents (Jacobs and 't Hart, 1992; 't Hart and Pijnenburg, 1989). This paper considers the latter events – multiple fatalities in public spaces – in more detail and focuses on a specific sub-group of such disasters, namely those involving accidents at sports stadia in the United Kingdom.

The literature on crisis management is not homogenous and certain paradigmatic conflicts exist within this emergent field. Given that the process of crisis management is closely related to strategic management (see Mitroff, Pauchant and Pearson, 1992; Smith, 1992b), it could be argued that the crisis management literature also suffers from some of the same paradigmatic conflicts that beset the older discipline.[2] In particular, it is important to recognize the distinction between those who are concerned with a largely reactive mode of crisis management and those who advocate a more strategic approach to the problem. The 'body bag' approach of the former group is epitomized in the contingency-based approaches to disaster management and recovery. Examples of such work concern issues of evacuation (Zelinsky and Kosinski, 1991), media response (Regester, 1989) and the medical response to disasters (Noji, 1991; Costanzo, 1992). In terms of the latter group, the work of Kets de Vries and Miller (1984; 1987) and Pauchant and Mitroff (1992) serve to illustrate the more organic approaches to the process of crisis management that exist within the literature. Here authors are concerned with issues of prevention and change rather than simply with response. The issues center around the process of organizational learning and cultural change, or put another way, this perspective provides a challenge to the technocratic circle of crisis. We have argued elsewhere (Smith, 1992b; 1993; Smith and Sipika, 1993) that there are a number of critical elements within crisis causation and that these can be considered as the 7Cs of crisis management (see Figure 1). The 7Cs can be considered to fall into two groups. The cold square represents the more technocratic aspects of crisis management, whereas the warm triangle elements represent the more organic aspects of the process[3] (Smith, 1993). These 7Cs are held to interact with the cultural web of the organization and can produce a sense of 'managerial omnipotence' which prevents an effective recognition of the malaise present within organizations (Smith, 1992b). In addition, the 7Cs can be seen to operate in each of the three phases of crisis management that are shown in Figure 2. They are of particular importance in providing the climate within which crises can be incubated and determine the effectiveness of organizational responses to the demands of the event.

How then do we break into this cycle of crisis? The issue for managers of sports stadia is how to maximize their profits while ensuring that they have a credible team or event to bring in the crowds. This then has to be reconciled with the need to ensure that those who visit the venue are assured of their safety. Such a juggling act ensures that crisis management continues to be a hydra-headed beast (Smith, 1992a). In order to deal with the problem in an effective manner we have to look closely at the 'cultural web' (Johnson and Scholes, 1989) of the various organizations concerned and assess how this interacts with the crisis recipe that is in place (Smith, 1992b). This recipe can be considered as a set of assumptions and beliefs which are present among, and taken for granted by, all organizational members (Johnson and Scholes, 1989). The importance of the recipe lies in the fact that it serves as an anchor for the various situations

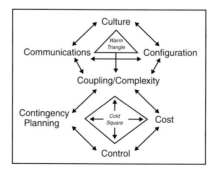

Figure 1 The 7Cs of crisis management
Source: Smith 1992a, 1992b and 1993

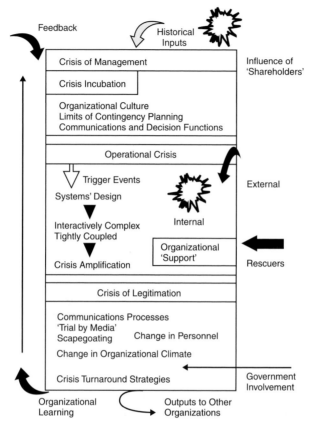

Figure 2 Three phases of crisis management
Source: Smith

faced by managers and provides a foundation for strategic decision making and the role of beliefs and assumptions therein (Johnson and Scholes, 1989). In this context, the recipe of the organization has much in common with the inner layers of Pauchant and Mitroff's (1992) 'Onion Model' of crisis management. By using these frameworks, this paper will explore the fatal accident events within United Kingdom football stadia and will move on to suggest policy recommendations to ensure that the organizations concerned can take remedial action to prevent their recurrence.

Match of the day: The development of the United Kingdom soccer industry

The Football League in the United Kingdom is organized as a cartel. While each club is a separate legal entity and is owned and managed by different persons each is also very much part of a league. Without membership of a league there is very little point to existence. The Football Association and Football League exert a tremendous influence over clubs. Expulsion from either would lead to the demise of any club. The background to most crises lies in the nature of the organizations that play host to them and the environment within which they operate. Stadia disasters also fall within this rubric and it is important to briefly set out the broader context of the industry prior to detailing the specifics of the events under consideration in this paper.

The United Kingdom football industry is a multi-million pound operation. Its popularity is indicated by the estimated 23.7 million people who watched the 1986 World Cup game between England and Argentina on the United Kingdom television network (Canter, 1989). The Football League was formed in 1888 by the twelve clubs in England thought to have the highest potential gates (Inglis, 1987), emphasizing from the start the importance of commercial considerations within the professional game. However, Sloane (1971) has argued that football clubs do not seek to maximize profits but are utility maximizers subject to basic financial constraints. The *Economist* (22/4/89), in reporting on the financial state of football league clubs after the Hillsborough tragedy, claimed that almost all league clubs would be considered as bankrupt if they were to be judged by criteria in the Insolvency Act (see also, Arnold, 1991; Bird, 1982; Gratton and Lisewiski, Jennett, 1984). This contrasts with the American National Football League who are thought to have a more conventional profit-maximizing approach to the organization of their game. Given the financial state of many United Kingdom league clubs one would have expected more closures or mergers than the handful that have occurred since 1980. That this has not happened is no doubt due to the presence of a significant number of rich benefactors who are willing to put their own money into clubs for largely sentimental reasons. It is truly ironic that many so called hard nosed business men are willing to throw cash into a virtual bottomless pit that is a modern football club. This approach to the financial aspects of the game's management is reinforced by a survey of objectives of football league clubs carried out by Arnold and Benveniste (1988). They found that playing success scored higher than either financial success or financial stability in the minds of most managers and chairmen. This tends to support the earlier contention that league football clubs are utility maximizers. However, what is of more interest within the context of this paper was the finding that ground improvements were mentioned in only three percent of responses as being of importance.

Given the recent history of disasters within football, the findings of Arnold and Benveniste are of great concern, especially when set against the broad economic environment within which clubs operate. The Chester Report (1983), into the structure and financing of football, found that, despite falling attendances, gate receipts as a whole had increased due to the much higher entry costs for spectators. However, the report states that, despite increased revenue, 'clubs in the Football League are going through their most difficult period ever' (p. vi) and that part of this burden arises as a result of the costs inherent in the Safety at Sports Grounds Act (Chester, 1983). The report quotes a figure of $11 million as representing the costs of conforming with the Act, with an additional $50 million being spent on new stands and other improvements over the period 1970–1983. These problems have been made worse by the general state of the United Kingdom economy since the late 1970s combined with the spiraling transfer and wages bills facing clubs. The report also points to the creation of a binary divide between the most successful clubs and those who languish in the lower divisions. The report is also highly critical of clubs' apparent unwillingness to put customer comfort and satisfaction higher on their agendas, observing that it is the latter that will serve to increase market share (see also, Arnold and Benveniste, 1988). Given the close connections between football clubs in the United Kingdom, one might have expected a great deal of inter-organizational learning to have occurred in the wake of the various tragedies. Prior to addressing the reasons why such learning has palpably failed in the United Kingdom, it is first necessary to outline each of the chosen events in turn.

Ibrox – 1971

The Ibrox Stadium in Glasgow is the home ground of Rangers FC which is among the richest clubs in Europe. It is ironic perhaps that such a club should play host to such an incident, given the resources that it had at its disposal. The 1971 Ibrox disaster took place on the Stadium's Stairway 13. This particular stairway had already been the scene of three major incidents in 1961, 1967 and 1969 which had led to the deaths of two and injuries to eight and twenty four respectively (Inglis, 1987). Stairway 13 was long and steep and similar to some of the entrances to the London Underground system. In 1971, at the end of the derby match against Celtic, spectators leaving by the stairway fell. Two explanations for the catastrophe were suggested. Canter (1989) reports the cause of the incidents as being,

> 'when spectators who had started to leave early . . . turned back at the sound of cheering from the stands. In the crush which resulted between those leaving and those returning, 66 people died and 140 were injured. Steel barriers were bent in the crush, which suggests that a force of at least 4,450 newtons was exerted at that point.' (p. 89)

An alternative explanation for the event states simply that the tragedy occurred as spectators left the stadium. The additional factor of the crowd changing direction is thus omitted (Inglis, 1987) and the implication is that the design of the exit was insufficient to cope with the crowd. In the first instance the cause is closely related to a 'chance' late goal causing the confusion which led to the crush, in the latter instance it is a case of poor stadium design. The subsequent enquiry, while not apportioning blame, found the Rangers' management complacent in their attitude to previous problems. *The Times* newspaper in its report on the accident (4/1/71) commented on the delay in people seeking to leave the stand being aware of the crush below them on the stair. Clearly the relentless, uninformed mass of leaving spectators played a major cause in the deaths of the other spectators. A local military policeman, talking to *The Times* (5/1/71) said,

> 'This is the sort of thing that could happen with a smaller number of people. The clubs should make civilized accommodation available for

their supporters – give them seats under cover – instead of herding them into areas where they are pushed and jammed like animals.'

Despite the large number of deaths, the limited coverage of the disaster by the national press indicates a low degree of public interest at the time. A leading article in the *Economist* (9/1/71) referred to the bleak year for football with much of the emphasis being on the financial performance of clubs. Regarding safety, the *Economist* stated that,

'It is sure that after half a century of neglect by successive govern-ments, the safety of crowds at football matches will be taken seriously at last.'

The Government's response to Ibrox was to commission a report into the safety of crowds at football grounds. The findings of the report led ultimately to the Safety at Sports Grounds Act which was passed with the proviso that it should only cover clubs in the upper divisions in Scotland and England. Arising from the earlier reports of Harrington and Lang, and stimulated by Ibrox, a voluntary code, commonly known as the Green Guide was published in 1973. The club itself made a few amendments to stairway 13 in the aftermath of the disaster and, in 1977, a complete redesign of the ground was undertaken and stairway 13 was completely removed.

Bradford – 1985

Bradford City FC was founded in 1903 and by 1908 the club had successfully achieved promotion into the first division and constructed the main stand, which was eventually to burn down. Despite its successes in the earlier half of this century, Bradford had slipped into the lower divisions by the 1950s and this lack of success was reflected in a worsening financial situation. The club was under threat of closure in both 1965 and again in 1983 (Shaw, 1985). The financial situation facing the club was combined with worries over the state of the ground itself which had been built at the turn of the century. During the 1950s, two stands at Valley Parade were demolished because of concerns about their safety (Inglis, 1987) and during the early 1980's similar concerns were expressed about the main stand. A visit from the Health and Safety Executive (HSE) in 1980 produced a statement observing that,

'There was very little compliance with the Guide to Safety at Sports Grounds, and Mr. Newman (club secretary) said that although he knew of the existence of the Guide it was not really his responsibility to see whether or not particular recommendations of the Guide were met.'

While only designated grounds were obliged to meet the guidelines expressed in the guide, other clubs were supposed to use it for guidance. The mounting financial pressures faced by clubs in the lower divisions, conspire to ensure that only lip service was paid to the Green Guide given its financial implications. The dilemma is set out by Inglis (1985) who observes that,

'No club wants to have an unsafe ground, but the third and fourth division clubs have always resisted moves to include them in the Act because they argue that the costs involved would bankrupt them or be inappropriate in view of their rapidly declining attendance figures.' (p. 2)

The HSE was to continue to express its concerns to the club's management. In a letter to the club in September 1981, the HSE Inspector indicated his concerns over further hazards that required attention. These included worries over, 'the void area between the concrete supporting structure and the wood floor should, after the removal of rubbish, be completely blanked off.'

Further inspections by the HSE in 1981 prompted questions being raised regarding evacuation from the main stand:

'I would also ask you to consider the evacuation procedure for the main stand, this is largely constructed of wood and from paragraph 8 of the code you will see that it should be capable of evacuation in 2.5 minutes. Please consider the above points and write to me detailing your proposals.' (p. 23)

Significantly, there was no response from the club to the HSE's letter.

The HSE was not the only statutory authority aware of the potential risks at the stadium. The poor state of the ground had led the club to seek financial support from the Football Trust. A letter (18/7/84) from West Yorkshire County Council was written, at the request of the club, in support of its application. Here the Council, as the licensing authority for the ground, drew attention to aspects of the ground which required attention. In particular, the Council observed that the main stand created particular problems as, 'The timber construction is a fire hazard, and in particular, there is a build up of combustible materials in the voids beneath the seats. A carelessly discarded cigarette could give rise to a fire risk' (Quoted in Popplewell, 1985, p. 20).

The letter was despatched in July, 1984 and a copy was also sent to the fire service. Popplewell (1985) reports that the latter, 'took the view that it was a matter of good housekeeping for the occupiers of the football ground to deal with and saw no reason to take the matter any further' (p. 19).

It is clear from the evidence of these communications that not only were the club aware of the potential for disaster but that a variety of statutory bodies also shared this knowledge. The major problem was with the main stand. This structure, which was built in 1908, was about 90 meters long and set on the side of a hill with a void between the weathered floor of the stand and the ground below. Over a period of time, papers, sweet wrappers and litter had collected in this void, creating a fire hazard. The stand was divided into two longitudinal sections separated by a fence of about 4–5 feet high. Two gaps in this fence allowed access between the front and rear parts of the stand and these were located approximately one third of the way in from either end. To the front of the stand there was a small terrace. Access to the stand was from the rear, through a dark passageway which ran across its full length. The exit gates and entry turnstiles were located off this passageway. To prevent the admission of non-paying customers many of these gates and turnstiles were locked shut during the game, thereby preventing exit during any match. Toilets and refreshment bars were also located at the back of the stand, resulting in crowding at halftime. Finally, the stand was covered by a wooden roof covered with roofing felt. The scene was set, therefore, for a major incident involving significant numbers of people exposed to fire risks, with only a limited means of egress available to them.

A crowd of some 11,000 attended the ground on May 11, 1985 for the final match of the season to celebrate the teams success. Shortly before half time a fire broke out in the main stand. The fire caused little concern, at first, as is evident by photographic evidence. Popplewell (1985) reports that, 'Those in the immediate area of the fire seemed to think that it was simply some paper which had caught fire, that it was of no particular significance, and that within a short period of time steps would be taken to deal with it' (p. 7).

One spectator left his nephew to get a fire extinguisher from the rear of the stand although this had been removed due to fears of its misuse by unruly spectators. A Police Constable, called to investigate the fire, called to colleagues on the touchline to get a fire extinguisher: 'Owing to the background noise they thought he had asked for the fire brigade and they therefore radioed to the fire brigade' (Popplewell, 1985, p. 7).

This request was made at about 15:42, by 15:44 flames were clearly visible and within two further minutes the whole stand was on fire. Spectators proved reluctant to move as PC Lyles reported:

> 'We did not get much reaction from people in the stand, obviously they were watching the match and in fairness the fire did not look serious from where they were sitting. A few of them moved out into the aisles towards the top of the steps.' (p. 7)

An absence of loud hailers and an inability for the police to cut into the public address system hindered police attempts to direct spectators. The police personal radio sets, which were designed for only one officer to speak at a time, also caused communication problems as they were unable to cope with the demands of the event. The amount of 'traffic' resulted in poor sound quality, a problem exacerbated by background noise and more importantly by the sheer weight of pressure on the system. Eventually, when the seriousness of the fire became clear, spectators began to move; some escaped onto the pitch, although many sought to leave by the usual exits at the rear of the stand, many of which were locked shut. While some exits were forced open and other non-signposted exits were used as escape routes many spectators were caught in a trap, caught between the fire and the barred exits which resulted in a high loss of life.

Heysel – 1985

Pictures of Bradford stunned the nation and emphasized that peaceful, law abiding spectators could be victim to tragedy in a football stadium. The Heysel disaster, just over two weeks later, returned the focus of public attention back to the link between safety and hooliganism. The Heysel Stadium in Brussels, was chosen as the venue for the final of the European Cup between Juventus of Italy and Liverpool of England. The stadium was opened in 1930 and was a regular venue for football matches and other sporting events. However, the condition of the ground was questioned at the investigation into the tragedy. Popplewell (1986), reported that,

> 'Having regard to the state of the crush barriers and fences, and the general condition of the terraces it seems unlikely, had it been located in this country, that a certificate would have been issued under the Safety of Sports Ground Act 1975 for this part of the ground.' (p. 4)

While the state of the terraces as a contributory factor in the event may be debatable, the suitability of the stadium as a venue for such an important match must be questioned. This is especially so given the reputation of the English fans' behavior. Miller (1985) states that,

> 'Nobody of whatever nationality could attempt to defend England's wretched record of crowd behavior, but it must be said that the Heysel Stadium . . . was ill equipped both in its structure and in its segregation of rival supporters to cope with a match in which there were bound to be such tensions.' (pp. 1–2)

Given these concerns about English fans, it is surprising that Inglis (1990) reports allegations that the UEFA inspectors spent less than 30 minutes checking the suitability of the ground for the Cup Final. Again, one sees evidence of the lack of managerial foresight in preparing for the event.

The Belgian authorities determined that Juventus and Liverpool fans would be segregated in separate parts of the ground. In addition, areas for 'neutral' spectators would be located in block 'M', beside Juventus supporters in blocks 'N' and 'O', and in block 'Z' beside Liverpool supporters in blocks 'X' and 'Y'. Additional barriers around the neutral areas were also erected although these were not considered to be adequate. To the flank of block 'Z', the site of the disaster, was a wall rising from two meters high at one end to three meters at the other. It was a brick wall which was not fixed in anyway to the concrete wall it sat upon.

Responsibility for policing inside the ground was split between the Brussels Police (Juventus end) and the National Gendarmerie (Liverpool end). Problems of communication were evident as were the inherent difficulties of coordinating the activities of two separate organizations. The Gendarmerie officer in charge at the stadium had failed to attend any of a number of meetings to discuss arrangements for the match with his counterpart in the Brussels police and other official bodies (Popplewell, 1986). The lack of apparent planning by the police was commented upon by a number of observers (see coverage of the event in *The Times*, *Guardian* and *Financial Times* of May 30 & 31, 1985) and Peter Robinson of Liverpool claimed in an interview that,

> 'When we arrived at the stadium on Wednesday, I immediately said that police were needed in the empty security zone, because it was clear that the neutral zone was predominantly filled by Italians with predominantly black and white colors and that the barriers, which they say the police had approved the day before would not be adequate.'
>
> (The Times, 5/31/85, p. 3)

The attempts to segregate the opposing fans had obviously broken down. Many Italian fans were able, one way or another, to acquire tickets for block 'Z' which should have been neutral. The security arrangements had assumed that opposing fans would not be located in such close proximity to one another and the systems in place were deemed to be inadequate to cope with the conflict that followed.

Police reports indicated a series of incidents throughout the afternoon before the game. At 17:15 a police report indicated a mass invasion of block 'M' (neutral) from blocks (Juventus) 'O' and 'N' which were overcrowded (Popplewell 1986, p. 6). At the other end of the ground:

> 'somewhere between 18:15 and 18:30, the English fans fired flares and rockets and threw stones into Block "Z", which was beginning to be occupied by what were clearly Italian supporters. There was also a number of English supporters in Block "Z" who sought to escape into Block "Y" . . . It appears there were about 15,000 spectators in Blocks "X" & "Y" and about 5,000 in Block "Z"'.
>
> (Popplewell, 1986, p. 7)

Precise figures for the numbers of spectators, were unavailable because of the lack of specific turnstiles for each block and gaps in the boundary wall sufficiently wide to enable admission without a ticket or payment.

Between 19:15 and 19:30 three charges by English spectators from Blocks 'X' and 'Y' on block 'Z' took place (Popplewell, 1986). The first two were repulsed although the third successfully broke through the security barriers. A report in *The Times* newspaper suggests that the Belgian police had withdrawn at this stage to await reinforcements although the Popplewell report appears vague on this point. As the Juventus supporters sought to escape from the onslaught of English supporters they were forced along the boundary walls furthest from block Y. As the crush built up more pressure was exerted on the perimeter wall and a section of about six meters in length collapsed. People tumbled down among the rubble, others followed close behind, unable to stop themselves because of the pressure of people behind them, seeking to escape from the English supporters. Most of the 38 victims died from suffocation or crushing and some four hundred were injured.

Hillsborough

Hillsborough, the home ground of Sheffield Wednesday, was widely considered to be one of the better quality grounds in the United Kingdom. The West Stand, built in 1965 in readiness for use as a venue for the 1966 World Cup, had a capacity of,

> '4465 seats in an upper tier, and open terraces in front. Next to the other two stands it looks rather ordinary, but the view it provides is excellent, as are its facilities, and it does close off the ground effectively without cramping the style of either of its neighbors.'
>
> (Inglis, 1987, p. 97)

The terraces to the front of the stand had a capacity of about 10,100 and was split into a number of separate pens, each surrounded by fencing on three sides. This division into pens was the result of an overcrowding incident during the 1981 FA Cup semi-final held at the ground. Capacity for each pen was determined by a process of fans finding their own level, despite the fact that approximate capacities for each pen had been calculated. Access between the pens was possible by gates located to the very rear of each pen. When these gates were open the back row of terracing had access between pens. 'In practice, when substantial numbers are present, these gateways are not readily visible or accessible. The present layout of the pens, fences, crush barriers and gates has resulted from a series of piecemeal changes' (Taylor, 1989, p. 5).

Crush barriers were also located in parallel with the goal line. To the front of the terraces lay a 2.5 meter high fence, turned inwards at the top, preventing access to the pitch. Gates were located at intervals, along this fence, none were wider than one meter.

Entry to the West Stand and terraces was from the Leppings Lane end. Because of the close proximity of housing and the River Don there was not as much room for turnstiles as there was for access to other parts of the ground. Lack of room also meant that the area immediately outside the ground could become quickly congested. Thus access for 29,800 spectators in the south and east sides of the ground was through 60 turnstiles (500:1) compared to 23 turnstiles serving the 23,250 capacity (1,000:1) in the north and west sides. From Leppings Lane, spectators made their way through a set of perimeter gates[4] to the turnstiles. Seven turnstiles were available for the potential 10,100 standing spectators (1450:1). A rate of 600 admissions per hour was considered quick, given good conditions. The layout of the turnstiles was confusing; the use of letters and numbers, out of sequence, to denote groups of turnstiles as well as individual ones required time for the individual spectator, who was unfamiliar with the ground, to make sense of. This confusion was exacerbated by the presence of a dividing fence running from the perimeter fence to the ground itself. Any spectator who found themselves on the wrong side of the fence would be forced to fight against the tide of people to the other side. Entrances A and C were located on one side of this fence, Entrance B on the other. Turnstiles for the former two entrances were denoted by numbers and the latter by letters.

Having successfully made sense of the external layout spectators, on entering the ground, were drawn by a combination of signposting and layout towards a tunnel which led to terracing in pens 3 and 4, directly behind the goal. Where the tunnel emerged onto the terraces, the way ahead was bisected by the radial fence separating pens 3 and 4. A short spur of wall projected forward on either side of the tunnel opening which had the effect of guiding those emerging from the tunnel forward into pens 3 and 4 rather than into other adjacent pens. Overcrowding of pens 3 and 4 had been so severe in 1988 that this tunnel had been blocked off by police officers. However, no record of this was made in the post match de-brief and it was not included in the operational order for 1989. It should be noted that there was virtually no control of the numbers of spectators going into each of the pens. In summary, the layout of the Leppings Lane end had developed both internally and externally, in a piecemeal manner and yet despite these changes the safety certificate was not amended.[5] This layout was to have a key impact on the disaster of 15 April.

Liverpool FC and Nottingham Forest FC were to meet one another in the semi-finals of the FA cup in an exact duplication of the previous year's match. Despite having the larger average attendance, Liverpool supporters were given the smaller side of the ground, accessed from Leppings Lane, to assist in ensuring strict segregation. By 2 p.m., although pens 3 and 4 were filling quickly a surprisingly small number of Liverpool fans had taken their places upon the terraces. By 2.15 p.m. the numbers in pens 3 and 4 were large enough to warrant a request, via the public address system, for fans to move forward to make room. Outside the Leppings Lane entrance large crowds of fans were beginning to collect. By 2.50 p.m. pens 3 and 4 were reportedly:

> 'already full to a degree which caused serious discomfort to many well used to enduring pressure on the terraces. The numbers at that time were clearly in excess of the maximum density stated by the Home Office Guide to Safety at Sports Grounds'.
>
> (Taylor, 1989, p. 11)

Outside the ground, as kickoff approached, the crowd became more anxious to ensure quick access. Given the numbers of turnstiles progress was likely to be slow. Progress was further slowed by the rising pressure, pushing and shoving. It was clear that the crowd would be unable to enter the ground by 3:00 p.m. A request, from a Police Constable, for the kickoff to be postponed was rejected. Technical problems affecting communication between officers outside the ground and the control room were also reported at this time. Superintendent Marshall, the officer in charge outside the Leppings Lane, fearful of fatalities occurring outside the ground, requested permission (at 2:47 p.m.) to open the exit gates, adjacent to the turnstiles, to relieve the pressure. At 2:52 p.m. authorization to open exit gates was given. The largest entry was through Gate C which opened into the area directly behind the terraces. The most obvious route to the terraces, as described, was through the tunnel to pens 3 and 4 which were already overcrowded.

Intense pressure built up in the tunnel, pressure which took advantage of any movement forward in the pens ahead, thereby increasing the pressure on the fans trapped inside the pens. Against a background of noise within the stadium the police officers in front of the pens did not immediately notice what was wrong. The narrow exit gates to the front of pens 3 and 4 sprang open due to the pressure. Police officers sought to close them and to either push back fans spilling out of them or to redirect them to the wing pens. As awareness of the problem grew further problems of communication were evident: 'At Gate 3, a constable, now aware of the crisis, followed strictly his written orders and radioed for permission to open that gate. Receiving no reply, he took it upon himself to open it' (Taylor, 1989, p. 13).

While some fans sought to escape through the gates, others tried to climb the perimeter fence. These were pushed back at first by police who suspected a pitch invasion. The overcrowding remained unnoticed by the control room[6], they too assumed that the fans spilling onto the pitch were involved in an attempted pitch invasion. Photographic evidence also shows that before 3:00 p.m. spectators were being pulled out of the terrace by spectators sitting in the stand above. At some stage one of the crush barriers in pen 3 broke, providing an unbroken thrust of pressure from the rear of the tunnel to the front of the terrace.

> 'The crushing force was transmitted and dispersed so that all along the front of pen 3 fans were pressed hard up against the low wall and the wire of the fence above it. . . . The pressure stayed and for those crushed breathless by it, standing or prone, life was ebbing away. If no relief came in four minutes there would be irreversible brain damage; if longer death'.
>
> (Taylor, 1989, p. 13)

The most noticeable thing about video evidence of the incident is the slowness with which the police appear to comprehend what is going on. Even after those officers closest to pens 3 and 4 'came alive to the situation' many other officers clearly believed it to be a case of crowd trouble. By 3:06 p.m. the police control room were aware of the seriousness of the problem and requested that the match be stopped. It was not until 3:12 p.m. however, that any attempt to seal off the entrance to the tunnel was made. Chief Superintendent Nesbit of the traffic police arrived on the pitch at about this time and set about organizing the extraction of casualties from pen 3. At 3:13 p.m. a request from the police to the fire brigade for cutting equipment was made. By this time, many of the fans were either already dead or were dying from the crushing.

Discussion

> 'With the growing accumulation of research data and the increased sophistication of conceptual models, the recognition is slowly dawning that CM (crisis management) encompasses a diverse and complex set of activities, phases and factors'.
>
> (Mitroff et al., 1989, p. 270)

Each of the tragedies outlined earlier illustrate, in their different ways, the development of crisis events and the need for effective crisis management. In all cases there is evidence of crisis incubation and a failure to consider the possibility of crisis amplification by those responsible for managing the stadia. Having outlined the chronology of the four events, this final section seeks to examine them within the theoretical frameworks outlined earlier.

Crisis of management

Pauchant and Mitroff (1988) and Mitroff *et al.* (1989) have emphasized the importance of culture in determining the proneness of organizations to crisis. This is illustrated by their Onion Model of Crisis Management which shows the relationships between organizational culture, managerial beliefs, and structure and strategy. At the innermost, core level, are the fundamental beliefs that influence the way in which an organization, or individuals therein, process information collected for the decision making process. This 'mindset', which is akin to the cultural web of the organization, will determine the range of policy options which are considered to be acceptable to the host organizations. For example, Taylor (1990) reports that,

> 'Amazingly, complacency was still to be found after Hillsborough. It was chilling to hear the same refrain from directors at several clubs I visited. "Hillsborough was horrible – but, of course, it couldn't have happened here." Couldn't it? The Hillsborough ground was regarded by many as one of the best in the country.' (p. 4)

This complacent assumption indicates a mindset that will not place importance on financing improvements to the layout of their stadia. Given this assumption and the finding by Arnold and Benveniste (1988) that playing success is the most important objective for clubs, it is likely that available monies are more likely to be spent on team improvements rather than ground safety. The continued use of stairway 13 at Ibrox (despite three serious incidents there) and the poor housekeeping at Bradford (despite warnings over a period of at least five years) are both indicators of the low priority given to ground improvements, and accordingly to crowd safety, by clubs. That ground safety is viewed by many as simply a question of fulfilling legislative requirements is demonstrated by Popplewell (1985):

> 'There seems to be a general view that the Green Guide has no application unless the ground is designated. Nothing could be more misconceived. I recommend that the next edition of the Green Guide should make it clear that it applies to all sports grounds, not simply those designate.' (p. 30)

The priority given to team improvements, to the detriment of ground safety, by clubs may suggest that a separation of ownership from use is required to ensure that grounds receive the attention they require.

Culture is however, only one of a number of factors which serve to precipitate crises (Smith, 1992a; 1992b). Cost is another important facet of the process. For example, Bradford City AFC was twice faced with bankruptcy in the twenty years prior to the tragedy which indicates the funding climate within which decisions were made. The cost of improvements, given the limited financial resources and priorities of the club, meant limited maintenance of, and improvement to, the ground. At Ibrox, the replacement of stairway 13 required significant investment by the club and was hastened after the deaths of sixty six spectators which helped to increase the priority of such investment. Piecemeal improvements to the Leppings Lane end of the Hillsborough stadium must also be in part attributable to the shortage of financial resources. The cost of redesigning the entrances to allow turnstiles to service specific pens was no doubt considered to be prohibitive before the tragedy, in the absence of any evidence of significant immediate risk. Finances for new stands and layout improvements may suddenly be available as their priority becomes only too evident in the wake of a disaster.

Much of the focus so far has been on the stadia and clubs that hosted these disasters. The involvement of other parties, however, must not be overlooked. The failure of the various inspection bodies to follow up expressed concern prior to the Bradford fire or the allegedly lax inspection of Heysel by UEFA officials are examples of a crisis of management that goes beyond stadia managers themselves. Problems surrounding the effectiveness of communication are also relevant here. For example, the failure of the HSE to pass on their concerns about the Bradford Stadium to the fire brigade serves to illustrate the importance of effective inter-organizational communication. The different configurations or structures of these organizations may also impede communication between them and their ability to act. Thus because the Green Guide stated that a fire hazard was a matter for the fire brigade, officials from the HSE did not feel it necessary for them to take responsibility for a problem which they had identified but which was deemed the responsibility of another agency. This might be viewed as the actions of a bureaucracy which does not encourage its officers to use their initiative but rather encourages them to follow the prescribed procedures. Poor communication also played a part in the build up to the Heysel tragedy. The officer in charge of the Gendarmerie failed to turn up to pre-match meetings arranged to determine coordination between the Brussels City Police and the Gendarmes. Given the importance of policing in conforming to plan and a need to follow a contingency plan in case of emergencies this failure can be seen as an important factor in enabling the tragedy to occur as it did.

The culture of stadia managers and other parties can be seen as critical in creating an environment in which warning signs, in some instances extreme warnings, are ignored. The importance of cost in compressing developmental pressures, discounting what are perceived as long term risks is closely linked to this cultural environment. Communication failures and organizational structures and rules influencing the degree of autonomy for individual employees have also been shown to have a critical influence in this build up to the 'operational crisis.'

Operational crisis

The operational crisis is child to the preceding crisis of management. Just as children are shaped by their parent, the crisis of management will influence the ability of the organizations involved to cope with the demands of the crisis event. The absence of the Officer in Charge of the Gendarmerie at Heysel from pre-match briefings limited the effectiveness of his response during the crisis. Greater concern for security at the expense of safety, led to the locking of exits and removal of fire fighting equipment from the Bradford Stadium. The assumptions of management and a denial of risk underpin these decisions. While examples of the various 7C's may be found having an effect during the crisis, certain of them are regularly more critical than others. The coupling and complexity of events is often visible in the operational phase of crises. At Hillsborough, the poor layout at the Leppings Lane entrance, the internal signs which served to focus the entering fans on the tunnel to pens 3 and 4, the acute overcrowding which was aggravated by a further influx of fans through the open gate and a failure, at the time, to appreciate the links between these facets were in one sense the root cause of the tragedy. The interaction between the components of the system ensured that once the build-up began, then it was inevitable that disaster would ensue.

Problems of communication also tend to come to the forefront during disasters. The configuration or structure of the organization, which is important in determining how work is coordinated, is also critical here. Where organizations coordinate by contingency plan, communication needs are determined by two key factors. First, the relevance of the original plan to the crisis circumstances and secondly the familiarity of individual operatives with the plan. Contingency plans may be seen as the product of organizations used to a fairly simple and stable environment trying to make sense of the unknown. Individuals are expected to carry out duties in accordance with the plan. As the lives of others may depend on each person undertaking their assignment in a prescribed way, as is the case with the fire service, little scope for the use of initiative is allowed. Organizational structure and culture will reinforce this by creating environments which do not reward such behavior. Clearly such organizations are likely to face serious difficulties in times of crisis which do not correlate closely to the contingency plan. This contrasts sharply with a training scheme organized by the Scottish police service which has created a simulation scheme that enables officers to develop a wide range of skills and may be applied in a range of situations rather than confine them to strict contingency plans.

At Hillsborough, permission to open the gates to the pitch was required from the central control. It is difficult to determine how long the officer waited for authorization before opening the gate to pen 3 on his own initiative. A reliance on control and coordination through a central point of authority, requires excellent communications which are often not available for the duration of a crisis incident:

> 'Mr. Greenwood's request for the match to be stopped and various
> messages from Constables reporting the distress in the pens did not

register. Likewise, communication from Leppings Lane to control was unreliable. Undoubtedly these breakdowns made it more difficult for those in command to make proper assessments and exercise effective command.

(Taylor, 1989, p. 54)

The failure of the controlling officer to assume responsibility for the coordination of the rescue from the pens, leaving it for the senior traffic officer to do some six minutes later, suggests that serious problems existed within the control room. The limitations of police radios, the level of background noise and finally an attempt to use hand signals indicates the difficulties of communicating in circumstances such as these. All four of these stadia disasters occurred with crowds in what might be described as complex spaces. Canter (1989) argues that it is not simply the weight and site of such crowds that causes crushes but:

> 'the communicative and behavioral inertia, which means that once a crowd starts on one course of action it is slow to react to circumstances, partly because of difficulty in passing information all the way from the site of the danger to the fringes. Typically, those at the back of such a crowd never realize how dangerous conditions have become at the front'. (p. 88)

The need for excellent monitoring of such crowds and the need to ensure effective communication to them from the controlling agencies is clear. The requirement for good quality public address systems which can be accessed by those coordinating either the control or the rescue function is imperative. At Ibrox and Hillsborough the predicament of those caught up in the middle of the crush is clearly not comprehended by those on the edge of it. Quick communication might have played a part in reducing the number of casualties. At Bradford, the effective use of a PA system might have marshaled people more quickly and encouraged them to find proper exits.

Crisis of legitimation

We have discussed culture and its importance in the development of an environment in which crisis can occur. It is also of key importance at the point where the post crisis phase feeds into the incubation of another crisis (Smith and Sipika, (1993)). Consideration needs to be given to the structure and culture of the organization in order to help ensure that learning occurs within the organization. The contribution of non-compliance to the spirit of the Safety at Sports Grounds Act (1975) to the Bradford and Hillsborough disasters indicates a failure to learn within the football industry. There is an apparent willingness for government, football authorities and clubs to seek technical solutions and formulas to help ensure that such tragedies never happen again. Sadly, purely technical solutions rarely take full account of the complexity of crowd-related disaster, as Canter (1989) illustrates in his discussion of human behavior:

'There is one other very simple flaw in the engineering considerations. The calculation of the use of a set of exits is made by identifying all the exit widths available to people in particular spectating
positions and dividing the total number of unit widths by the total
number of people. This is an elementary averaging exercise. But
anybody who has looked around in a theatre, or at any other public
place of entertainment at the end of the performance, will have
noticed that, unlike engineers' numbers, people do not divide themselves evenly between the exits available. People will tend to go to
the exits they know or to the ones that lead in directions they wish
to take'. (p. 96)

A technocratic approach is still advocated by those in respected advisory positions to the FA and Football League, as was evident at a recent Home Office
conference on crowd safety and control. Stadia, it was proposed, would be
designed on the assumption of an average person. No allowances for the differences between adults and children was made, let alone the range of differences
between adults. Such technical 'solutions' only serve to create a climate of
incubation unless the core behavioral aspects of organizations is also addressed.
This contrasts sharply with the police response to the Hillsborough disaster:

'It is a matter of regret that at the hearing, and in their submissions,
the South Yorkshire Police were not prepared to concede they were in
any respect at fault in what occurred. Mr. Duckenfield, under pressure of cross-examination, apologized for blaming the Liverpool fans
for causing the deaths. But, that aside, the police case was to blame
the fans for being late and drunk, and to blame the Club for failing to
monitor the pens. It was argued that the fatal crush was not caused by
the influx through Gate C but was due to barrier 124a being defective. Such an unrealistic approach gives cause for anxiety as to whether
lessons have been learned. It would have been more encouraging for
the future if responsibility had been faced'.

(Taylor, 1989, p. 50)

Culture at a general level may also influence decisions. References to football
fans as animals were frequently reproduced in the media, helping to create an
environment in which it becomes permissible to treat football fans like animals.
It does not take a genius to make the link between animals and the 'wire cages'
which housed the majority of standing supporters in the late 1980's. Peter
Jenkins (1989), of Liverpool Football Club, expresses concerns about the poor
management of many clubs: 'As businesses, many clubs are poorly managed by
people who are sometimes incompetent to run large organizations and who
often treat supporters as an embarrassing mob rather than as customers to be
wooed' (p. 18).

It is perhaps this attitude, among those who are charged with the development
of the game, more than any other that needs to be changed.

A failure to search for the underlying causes of tragedy combined with a search for simple technical solutions as a panacea for ground safety problems and a complacent attitude among senior managers, inevitably leads to a certainty that football disasters are not things of the past. The technocratic solutions, while convincing in the wake of a disaster, are inadequate in themselves unless attempts are made to ensure that the 'softer' elements of the organization – culture, communication and configuration – are also addressed. While a great deal has been achieved in the United Kingdom since Hillsborough and Bradford, it took the combined effects of two major loss-of-life events and the subsequent changes in legislation to highlight the real risks that football fans faced as they spent an afternoon on the terraces. The process of organizational learning for crises requires that managers address the full range of organizational characteristics that combine to generate such events (Smith, 1993). The quick fix technical solutions that fail to change the core values and assumptions of the organization will result in a further period of incubation before the problem reemerges at a later date and in another form. The football industry owes it to those who lost their lives in the United Kingdom tragedies, that further loss-of-life events are prevented by making changes at the core rather than at the periphery.

Acknowledgments

The authors are grateful to a number individuals who have assisted them in the course of their research. These include, Police Inspectors Bernie Swift, John Jeffrey, Ray Johnston (Merseyside Police) and Deputy Chief Constable Peter Hayes, Assistant Chief Constable Walter Jackson, Superintendent Tom Cooper (South Yorkshire Police). In addition, the authors would like to express their thanks to Thierry Pauchant and two anonymous referees for their comments on an earlier version of this paper. As usual all errors of interpretation remain ours.

Notes

1   This paper is dedicated to the memory of those football supporters who lost their lives in the various disasters covered by this paper. It is hoped that their deaths will not be in vain.

2   There is a considerable literature which deals with the differing perspectives on the strategy process and the various 'schools' that exist within the discipline. Notable among the more recent exchanges in this area are the papers by Mintzberg (1990a; 1990b; 1991) and Ansoff (1991).

3   This distinction draws upon the work of Pascale and Athos (1981), Peters and Waterman (1982) and Hampden-Turner (1990).

4   These gates have now been removed and there is a large area in which queuing can take place.

5   In the wake of a disaster, a number of changes were made to the design of the ground which were aimed at removing the problems caused by the funneling of fans into the pens at the Leppings Lane end.

6   It should be noted that the Police control box provided at the ground was very small and located at the Leppings Lane end of the stadium. This box is now used to house the entertainments officer who plays music at half time and a new Police control room has been built.

References

Ansoff, I. (1991) "Critique of Henry Mintzberg's 'The Design School: reconsidering the basic premises of strategic management' ", *Strategic Management Journal*, 12 (6) pp. 449–461.

Arnold, A. J. (1991) "An Industry in Decline? The Trend in Football League Gate Receipts," *The Service Industries Journal*, Vol. 11, April, pp. 179–188.

Arnold, A. J. and Benveniste, I. (1988) "Wealth and Poverty in the English Football League", *Accounting and Business Research*, Vol. 17 No. 67, pp. 195–203.

Bird, P. J. (1982) "The Demand for League Football", *Applied Economics*, 14, pp. 637–649.

Blockley, D. I. (1980) *The Nature of Structural Design and Safety*, Ellis-Horwood: Chichester.

Canter, D. (1989) *Football In Its Place: An Environmental Psychology of Football Grounds*. Routledge: London.

Chester, N. (1983) *Report of the Committee of Enquiry into Structure and Finance: The Football League*, The Football League: Lytham St. Annes.

Costanzo, S. (1992) "The role of public health services in disaster prevention", *Disaster Prevention and Management*, 1 (1): 72–76.

Economist (8–14) Jan. 1971), p. 13.

Economist (1989).

Fischer, F. (1990) *Technocracy and the Politics of Expertise*, Sage: Newbury Park, California.

Fischer, F. (1991) "Risk assessment and environmental crisis: toward an integration of science and participation", *Industrial Crisis Quarterly*, 5 (2): 113–132.

Gratton, C. and Lisewiski, B. (1981) "The Economics of Sport in Britain: a case of market failure", *British Review of Economic Issues*, Vol. 3, No. 8, pp. 63–75.

Hampden-Turner, C. (1990) *Creating Corporate Culture: from Discord to Harmony*, Economist Books/Addison-Wesley Publishing: Reading, Massachusetts.

Inglis, S. (1985) "Design faults hampered escape but outdated wood structures common to many other clubs", *Guardian*, 5/13/85, p. 2.

Inglis, S. (1987) *The Football Grounds of Great Britain*, Collins-Willow: London.

Inglis, S. (1990) *The Football Grounds of Europe*, Harper-Collins: London.

Jacobs, B. and 't Hart, P. (1992) "Disaster at Hillsborough Stadium: a comparative analysis" in Parker, D. and Handmer, J. (eds) (1992) *Hazard management and emergency planning*. James and James: London, pp. 127–151.

Jennett, N. (1984) "Attendances, Uncertainty of Outcome and Policy in Scottish League Football", *Scottish Journal of Political Economy*, Vol. 31, No. 2, June 1984, pp. 176–198.

Johnson, G. and Scholes, K. (1989) *Exploring Corporate Strategy*, 2nd ed., Prentice Hall International: Hemel Hempstead.

Kets de Vries, M. and Miller, D. (1984) *The Neurotic Organization*, Jossey Bass: San Francisco, California.

Kets de Vries, M. and Miller, D. (1987) *Unstable at the Top: Inside the Troubled Organization*, Mentor Books: New York.

Kunreuther, H. (ed) (1987) *Insuring and Managing Hazardous Risks: From Seveso to Bhopal and Beyond*, Springer Verlag: New York.

Miller, D. (1985) "41 soccer fans die in stampede at Euro Cup final", *The Times*, 5/30/1985.

Mintzberg, H. (1990a) "The Design School: reconsidering the basic premises of strategic management", *Strategic Management Journal*, 11 (3): 171–195.

Mintzberg, H. (1990b) "Strategy formation: schools of thought", in Frederickson, J. (ed.) (1990) *Perspectives on Strategic Management*, Harper Row: New York, pp. 105–135.

Mintzberg, H. (1991) "Learning 1, Planning O: Reply to Igor Ansoff" *Strategic Management Journal*, 12 (6): 463–466.

Mintzberg, H. and Waters, J. H. (1985) "Of strategies deliberate and emergent", *Strategic Management Journal*, Vol. 6, pp. 257–72.

Mitroff, I. I., Pauchant, T., Finney, M. and Pearson, C. (1989) "Do some organizations cause their own crises? The cultural profiles of crisis-prone vs. crisis-prepared organizations", *Industrial Crisis Quarterly*, 3 (4): 269–283.

Noji, E. K. (1991) "The medical consequences of earthquakes: coordinating the medical and rescue response", *Disaster Management*, 4 (1): 32–40.

Pascale, R. T. and Athos, A. G. (1981) *The Art of Japanese Management*, Simon and Schuster: New York.

Pauchant, T. and Douville, R. (1993) "Recent research in crisis management: a study of 24 authors' publications from 1986 to 1991", *Industrial & Environmental Crisis Quarterly*, 7 (1): 43–66.

Pauchant, T. C. and Mitroff, I. I. (1988) "Crisis-prone versus crisis-avoiding organizations: is your company's culture its own worst enemy in creating crises?", *Industrial Crisis Quarterly*, 2, pp. 53–63.

Pauchant, T. and Mitroff, I. I. (1992) *The crisis-prone organization*, Jossey-Bass Publishers: San Francisco, California.

Peters, T. and Waterman, J. (1982) *In Search of Excellence*, Warner Books: New York.

Pithers, M., "Safety inspectors failed to tell fire brigade about Bradford risk", *The Times*, 6/13/85.

Popplewell, O. "Committee of Inquiry into Crowd Safety and Control at Sports Grounds: Interim Report", HMSO, 1985.

Popplewell, O. "Committee of Inquiry into Crowd Safety and Control at Sports Grounds: Final Report", HMSO, 1986.

Regester, M. (1989) *Crisis Management: What to do When the Unthinkable Happens*, Hutchinson: London.

Schwartz, H. (1988) "The symbol of the space shuttle and the degeneration of the American dream" *Journal of Organizational Change Management*, 1 (2): 5–20.

Shaw, P. (1985) "The tragic last lap", *Guardian*, 5/13/85, p. 22.

Shrivastava, P. (1992) *Bhopal: Anatomy of a Crisis*, 2nd Edition, Paul Chapman Publishing: London.

Siomkos, G. (1989) "Managing product-harm crises", *Industrial Crisis Quarterly*, 3 (1): 41–60.

Siomkos, G. and Kurzbard, G. (1992) "Product harm crisis at the crossroads: monitoring recovery of replacement products", *Industrial Crisis Quarterly*, 6 (4): 279–294.

Sloane, P. J. (1971) "The Economics of Professional Football: the football club as a utility maximizer", *Scottish Journal of Political Economy*, Vol. 17 no. 2.

Smith, D. (1990a) "Corporate power and the politics of uncertainty: risk management at the Canvey Island complex", *Industrial Crisis Quarterly*, 4 (1): pp. 1–26.

Smith, D. (1990b) "Beyond contingency planning: towards a model of crisis management", *Industrial Crisis Quarterly*, 4 (4): 263–275.

Smith, D. (1992a) "The Kegworth aircrash – a crisis in three phases?", *Disaster Management*, 4 (2): 63–72.

Smith, D. (1992b) "The strategic implications of crisis management: a commentary on

Mitroff *et al.*", in Shrivastava, P., Huff, A. and Dutton, J. (eds) *Advances in Strategic Management*, Vol. 8, JAI Press: Greenwich, Connecticut.

Smith, D. (1993) "Crisis Management in the Public Sector: Lessons from the Prison Service", in Wilson, J. and Hinton, P. (eds) (1993) *The Public Services and the 1990s: issues in public service, finance and management*, Tudor Press: London. (Forthcoming).

Smith, D. and Sipika, C. (1993) "A model of post-crisis turnaround strategies", Long Range Planning, 26 (1): 28–38.

Taylor, P. "The Hillsborough Stadium Disaster: Interim Report", HMSO, 1989.

Taylor, P. "The Hillsborough Stadium Disaster: Final Report", HMSO, 1990.

t'Hart, P. and Pijnenburg, B. (1989) "The Heizel Stadium Tragedy" in Rosenthal, U., Charles, M., and t'Hart, P. (eds) *Coping with Crises*, pp. 197–224, Charles C. Thomas: Illinois.

The Times, (4/1/71) p.2.

Turner, B. A. (1978) *Man-made Disasters*, Wykeham: London.

Weick, K. (1990) "The vulnerable system: an analysis of the Tenerife air disaster", *Journal of Management*, 16 (3): 571–593.

Zelinsky, W. and Kosinski, L. A. (1991) *The Emergency Evacuation of Cities: A Cross-National Historical and Geographical Study*, Savage: Rowman and Littlefield Publishers.

Chapter 24

Dominic Elliott

CRISIS MANAGEMENT INTO PRACTICE

Introduction

LEAVING ASIDE STRICT DEFINITIONS of crisis, which, as Boin's earlier chapter argues, may be problematic, there is a growing interest around issues of hazard and crisis within social, political and economic debates (see for example, Turner, 1976; Shrivastava, 1987; Giddens, 1990; Beck, 1992). This interest reflects the far reaching impacts of events including toxic releases at Seveso and Bhopal, the nuclear accidents at Three Mile Island and Chernobyl and, more recently, terrorist attacks in Istanbul, Madrid, Beslan and New York's World Trade Center. Natural disasters may also trigger organizational and societal crises as the devastating impact of the Indian Ocean Tsunami and countless earthquakes demonstrate. All of these events reflect the large costs to organizations, society and individuals, both economically and psychologically, of crises. Less dramatically, although causing much disruption, power failures in 2002/3 affected millions of people and businesses in London, New York, New Zealand and Rome indicating the vulnerability of the 'developed world's' utility infrastructure. The range and diversity of such crises, and their impacts, raises significant questions concerning crisis causality, prevention, response and turnaround (see, for example, Turner, 1976; Perrow, 1984; Shrivastava, 1987; Pauchant and Mitroff, 1988; Smith, 1990). More fundamentally, perhaps, this range of incidents raises questions about how effectively organizational crises are managed. As Smith identified in our opening chapter, crisis management has emerged as both an academic discipline and a community of practice. It is largely with practice that this chapter is concerned.

The aim of this chapter is to provide a brief comment on the three papers included within this section before proceeding to examine some areas of practice. We use as our starting point Pearson and Clair's (1998) model of the crisis management process as a pointer towards identifying those areas that provide opportunities for managerial intervention. We identify a growing but largely immature literature which seeks to develop insights in the areas identified. Close parallels between the fields of organizational crisis and strategic management are identified.

As identified earlier, a key contribution of Turner (1976, 1978) to the development of theory was his notion of man-made crises. The concern of much of the preceding work dealing with disasters (see, for example, Quarantelli, 1988; Dynes and Aguirre, 1979) focused upon the practicalities of responding to disastrous events. Understandably, since then much academic work has focused upon developing an understanding of the underlying causes of crisis (see, for example, Perrow, 1984; Shrivastava, 1987; Pauchant and Mitroff, 1988, 1992; Hynes and Prasad, 1997; Wicks, 2001). Also a small literature has dealt with how organizations may learn from crisis.

A key debate within the field of strategic management, with direct relevance to the field of crisis, concerns capturing the essence of strategy, be it in formulation, implementation or both (see, for example, Mintzberg, 1990, 1993; Ansoff, 1991). Mintzberg and Waters (1985) identified the discrepancy between how organizations intended to act and how they actually behaved. Mintzberg and Waters distinguished between deliberate and emergent strategies. This simple observation lies at the heart of the debate between those who espouse a classical approach to strategy and those who take a more processual view (see, for example, Whittington, 2002). Put more simply it is the pull between identifying what we should do and managing what we can. Strong parallels can be drawn between strategic and crisis management. In Elliott, Swartz and Herbane (2002) the detailed identification of a prescriptive approach to business continuity management is balanced by a lengthy consideration of business continuity into practice. This balancing theme recognises the limitations of the many prescriptive approaches to crisis management, whilst acknowledging the benefits of exploiting a systematic process for identifying potential hazards, points of failure, triggers and possible remedies. The central aim of the business continuity planning is to develop a rich picture of an organizations environment and of its competencies. Business continuity management concerns the ways in which organizational change is effected. The knowledge emerging from the planning process, if managed effectively, may provide the basis for successful crisis management. This tension between prescriptive and non-prescriptive approaches is perhaps why this section is the shortest. Crisis management into practice is very difficult to achieve.

Overview of papers

Smart and Vertinsky's (1977) analysis of crisis decision units is one of the few papers which might be regarded as seminal. It draws upon a large literature and owes much to Allison's (1971) analysis of the Cuban missile crisis. Smart and

Vertinsky's model of 'crisis decision and implementation processes' raises many questions that have been picked up since. Much of this work has concerned organizational design and control within high reliability organizations and the interaction between individual human error and the organization management of complex systems (see, for example, Perrow, 1984; Rasmussen, 1982; Reason, 1990; Weick, 1993; La Porte, 1996). It is the research agenda shaped by this paper that makes it stand out. From a practical perspective the paper not only brings together a considerable literature, it develops theory and provides practical advice to managers.

Weick (1993) paper is included because it represents an example of the work dealing with High Reliable Organizations (HROs). Its particular concern is with collective mental processes within organizations. Weick and Roberts see the paper as a significant contribution to the study of collective cognition, an area largely ignored due to greater interest in the process of individual cognition. As Smart and Vertinsky's work indicated an understanding of collective cognitive processes is vital to understanding organization performance at times of crisis. The work emanates from a longer project of work which sought to better understand organizations operating in potentially highly risky activities, yet appeared to have done so reliably. The broad research project sought to identify how these organizations were 'similar to and different from "garden variety" organizations' (Roberts, 1993: 2). It is the emphasis upon the group within organizations that is vital and the group bound together by trust. They conclude with the view that

> 'A culture that encourages individualism, survival of the fittest, macho heroics, and can-do reactions will often neglect heedful practice of representation and subordination. Without representation and subordination, comprehension reverts to one brain at a time. No matter how visionary or smart or forward-looking or aggressive that one brain may be, it is no match for conditions of interactive complexity. Cooperation is imperative for the development of mind.'

The third paper, Elliott and Smith's (1993a) analysis of a series of soccer stadia disasters in the UK highlights both their underlying causes and operational difficulties. It is included because it reflects the status of our work at a point in time. It is four case studies in one. The UK football industry experienced a series of crisis events that have shared a common set of causal factors (Elliott and Smith, 1993a, 1997). It addresses one limitation of the current crisis management literature, namely that most previous studies of crisis have focused upon individual incidents (see, for example, Turner, 1976, 1978; Perrow, 1984; Shrivastava, 1987; Pauchant and Douville, 1993; Weick, 1993; Vaughan, 1996; Hynes and Prasad, 1997). Further, four of these crises, Bolton (1946), Ibrox (1971), Bradford (1985) and Hillsborough (1989) were investigated via high profile public inquiries, each of which made recommendations concerning regulation and safety management within stadia. This provided the opportunity to map out changing patterns of regulation in response to a series of crisis incidents, a primary concern of this paper. Finally, an industry level of analysis allows us to consider the interplay between different stakeholders, most notably between regulators and regulated. It provides the basis for determining the degree to which cultural readjustment, at an organizational level, results from the interaction of a range of institutional level factors (Scott, 1995; Wicks, 2001).

The paper illustrates the incubation of many crises within an industry, resulting from a mindset of vulnerability (Wicks, 2001) and describes in detail how those responsible for managing an event failed to do so during each stage of the crisis, from incubation, through the focal incident into a period of potential cultural readjustment. It offers an example of theory applied to practice and is an ideal finishing point for this collection.

This section is shockingly small given the importance of crisis management practice. This reflects the priorities of much research dealing with complex constructs at a more theoretical level. There is recent work that may achieve seminal status related to better understanding crisis management practice. Flin's (1996) work on leadership is one study which springs to mind. However, much that is written on practice is based upon flimsy, possibly anecdotal evidence and whilst relevant for a specific context has not achieved a level at which findings can be generalized. The richness of earlier sections of this book highlight where much research attention has been directed.

As Boin identifies earlier, two questions have clearly inspired the work he reviews. First, they seek to find out the causes and dynamics of organizational crisis. Second, they explore what organizations can do to cope with these crises. The authors give us different answers, as we have seen above. It appears that we have developed a better understanding of the causes and dynamics of crises than an identification of how organizations can better cope with crises. The result of much management research reminds me of the old joke about the visitor to New York asking a local for directions to a particular hotel. The response 'I wouldn't start from here'. It is clearly worthy to better understand the causes of crises that they may be prevented but has sufficient attention been placed upon the management process?

In a recent review of crisis management Pearson and Clair (1998) identified a process for crisis management that identifies the following components.

- Executive concerns about risk (see, for example, Elliott, Swartz and Herbane, 2002)
- Environmental context
  - Institutionalized practices (see, for example, Vaughan, 1996; Brown and Jones, 2000; Wicks, 2001)
  - Industry regulations (see, for example, Elliott and Smith, 1993a, 1997; Hynes and Prasad, 1997; Hood, Rothstein and Baldwin, 2001; Wells, 2001)
- Organizational crisis management preparedness (see, for example, Pauchant and Mitroff, 1988, 1992)
- Individual and collective reactions
  - Shattered assumptions (see, for example, Pauchant and Mitroff, 1988, 1992)

    o Impaired cognitive, emotional and behavioural responses (see, for example, Smith, 2002a)
- Planned and ad hoc responses
  o Team versus individual (see for example, Flin 1996, Smith, 2002b)
  o Coordination of stakeholders (see for example, Mitchell, Agle and Wood, 1997)
  o Information dissemination (see, for example, Heath, 2001)
  o Organizational/industry visibility (Elliott and Smith, 2005).

Again, despite this breadth of potential application it seems surprising, given the wealth of publications concerning crisis management practice, that there are few papers regarded as seminal. This may be because much published work is in book form (see, for example, Flin, 1996) or is written for the popular market (see, for example, Hiles and Barnes, 1999). Although the literature developed by practitioners is extremely rich and full of insight, there is a tendency for it to make sweeping generalizations. For example, Hiles and Barnes title their book *The Definitive Handbook of Business Continuity Management* (1999) ambitious for a profession still establishing itself. This chapter now briefly reviews some of the ongoing work which fits with each of these headings.

Executive concerns about risk

Tombs (2001: 29) has described the system of health and safety regulation within the UK as one of 'piecemeal prescriptive measures, which were complex and sometimes incomprehensible to the people affected by them'. Tombs (2001) suggests that patterns of self regulation are unlikely, on their own, to raise executive concerns about risk. Within the UK there have been attempts to place matters of risk higher on the corporate agenda, most notably by the Turnbull Report (1999) and Jones and Sutherland (1999). These efforts represent an effort to encourage directors to consider the risks that may face them within the sectors in which their organizations operate. Although it suggests that near misses should provide one source of information there is much evidence to indicate that such knowledge is often ignored or explained away (see, for example, Turner, 1976; Elliott and Smith, 1993b). The Turnbull report calls upon all listed companies, incorporated within the UK to disclose whether their risk management systems accord with it, but leaves it to the market to decide how to respond to cases of departure from it. A thorough critique of self regulation is beyond the scope of this chapter but a number of criticisms of it may be found (see, for example, Smith and Tombs, 1995; Wells, 2001; Elliott and McGuinness, 2002).

As Knight and Pretty (2001) have suggested, ultimately responsibility for risk lies with the chief executive who should steer a clear corporate approach towards its management, balancing 'healthy risk taking' with the dangerous dimension of it. It is the CEO who must oversee the process of managing market, operational, hazard and strategic risks, although day to day control may be delegated to individual managers. However, Knight and Pretty (2001), despite making an articulate case for the CEO's leading role, fail to suggest how that officer might be persuaded to give it the priority it requires. There have been growing calls for making company directors individually responsible for risk management. At the time of writing, directors of Balfour Beatty (a railway maintenance company) are being tried for their company's role in the Hatfield railway disaster. There is talk of individual directors being sued by shareholders and policy holders in the Equitable Life insurance company. Slapper and Tombs (1999) reported that some five company directors were imprisoned 1996–9 for manslaughter, yet without any impact upon the rate of injuries and deaths at work during that period, suggesting that such prosecutions have little impact. Slapper and Tombs (1999) identify a range of measures which they hold might be more compelling to organizations, including punitive fines, enforced adverse publicity, corporate probation, but they conclude that without effective enforcement there is little likelihood of risk and crisis management measures rising up the management agenda.

Environmental context

Stakeholders

Crises impact upon a wide range of stakeholders. For example, when Firestone tyres, fitted to Ford vehicles, were implicated in a large number of fatal accidents both Firestone Tyres and Ford sought to deflect blame for the event away from themselves (see Elliott, 2005). On 6 August 2000 a US Government agency raised concerns about the safety of Firestone Tyres. Sears Roebuck, a distributor, immediately stopped sales of suspect tyres. Ford announced a voluntary recall on 11 August some two days after the official concerns on 9 August. Ford identified a range of possible causes including, an earlier strike in the plant where Firestone tyres were produced and design flaws in the rubber coating on the tyres; firmly placing responsibility for the failure upon Firestone. The United Steel Workers Union threatened Firestone with strike action, selecting a moment of peak vulnerability for the employer. Lawyers were quick to offer their services on a no win, no fee basis. Goodyear was quick to exploit their vulnerability with a number of tactical movements of stock and prices. The media was quick to highlight the conflict between Ford and Firestone and to provide coverage of consumer and consumer group concerns. In this example there was no single event as is often assumed of crises; this escalation resulted from the accumulation of many incidents which combined to create crises for the organizations concerned. The crisis unfolded through many interactions between diverse stakeholders. Crises involve many different stakeholders and it may not always be clear which are the key ones, at first sight. In this case the distributors were amongst the first to act; the labour unions attempts to exploit Firestone's weakness is indicative of poor labour relations preceding the crisis. Stakeholder relations before, during and after a crisis combine to form a key component of the environmental context.

As Barton (2001) has suggested, organizations held in high regard will, generally, be allowed greater room for manoeuvre in managing their response to a crisis than organizations held in low regard. Elliott, Sipika and Smith (1993 and Elliott (2005) use the contrasting examples of Perrier's product contamination with Johnson and Johnsons' Tylenol Tampering to illustrate how the positive reputation of the latter aided its crisis management and subsequent recovery. The media may therefore be seen as another key stakeholder. It is evident that any crisis response must also take into consideration the diversity of stakeholder involvement and need if management efforts are to be effective. Recent developments in stakeholder theory include Mitchell, Agle and Wood's (1997) framework for determining stakeholder saliency using a 'metric' of power, urgency and legitimacy. The application of such a framework to a crisis scenario represents a significant opportunity for research.

Political, social and economic context

Where stakeholders represent one area of interest it is obvious that the traditional business environment provides other areas of interest. In some ways study of these has been neglected, although not ignored as Shrivastava's (1987) analysis of Bhopal indicates. Elliott, Swartz and Herbane (2002) include such 'environmental' analysis as a key element of planning for crisis. In this context organizations make decisions about the product/service markets in which they operate. IBM's decision to divest its PC business to Lenovo represents a deliberate decision to ditch an almost 'sacred' business because it no longer fitted with the corporate behemoth's strategy and image (Teather and Watts, 2004).

The social and political context may also play a key role as demonstrated by the coincidence of a contamination of Coca Cola products during 1999 with one of Belgian poultry. Any understanding of the crisis must be viewed against the peculiar circumstances of that period. The crisis prompted the largest product recall in Coca Cola's history. Affecting much of Western Europe, the events were centred on Belgium which was in the midst of a major health scare. Criticisms of the Belgian Government's handling of the dioxin contamination of chicken and eggs had led to the resignations of its Ministers for Agriculture and Public Health, respectively. Little more than a week later, news of Coca Cola's difficulties emerged (see Elliott, Smith and Sipika, 2003).

Organizational crisis management preparedness

Investment in preparing for organizational crisis takes at least two forms. At one level organizations will make decisions about the degree of time and resource to be put into business continuity plans and processes (see below). At a second level, organizations may consider the role played by core beliefs and assumptions in creating either a crisis prone or a crisis resistant culture (see, for example, Pauchant and Mitroff 1988, 1992). Pauchant and Mitroff's (1988) influential work is included within Section Two. Their later work (Pauchant and Mitroff, 1992) develops more fully the tool they employ to determine the degree to which an organization may tend towards crisis proneness at each of the four levels of their Onion Model. Although there is some interplay between the different layers of the 'onion' deeply held beliefs and assumptions play a key role in shaping structures and, ultimately, organizational behaviour. Other authors have also identified barriers to change in the form of defective information processing. For example, Argyris and Schön (1978) describe 'defensive routines' through which organizations may inhibit an effective response to disturbing stimuli. Argyris (1994) defined defensive reasoning as consisting of

> 'all policies, practices and actions that prevent human beings from having to experience embarrassment or threat and, at the same time, prevent them from examining the nature and causes of that embarrassment or threat.' (p. 78)

People and groups within organizations employ a range of strategies to resist change, even when events highlight inadequacies in systems, procedures and beliefs.

From a practical perspective, there is some agreement that crisis preparedness in the forms of business continuity plans are simply an outward manifestation of inward beliefs. Effective preparations for crisis require investments at both a practical and at a deeper level of culture, assumptions and beliefs.

Individual and collective reactions: teams, leadership and decision making

The successful management of individuals and groups of people is key to effective crisis management, at all stages of the process, from preparing through response to learning and prevention. It is perhaps in this area that there is much from which organizational researchers may draw from other disciplines. For example, Elliott *et al.* (2002) make some use of Mintzberg's (1983) configurations to better understand the contribution of structure to effective crisis management. Smith (2000) draws upon the work of Belbin (1981) to explore individual roles and crisis management teams. As Smith (2000) observes decision making under stress will be influenced by a range of factors including information availability, feedback flows, and the impacts of personality and stress upon an individual's decision making abilities. Many studies of decision making also exploit Janis and Mann's (1977) groupthink.

There is a growing expectation that organizations should possess the competences to handle crisis events. Within the UK, the loss of the Piper Alpha Oil Rig was a catalyst for the development of crisis management capabilities. This was reflected in a number of official publications (see, for example, Home Office 1997a, 1997b). In the wake of 9/11, the Report, commissioned by the President and Congress, identified in its recommendations the need for adopting a standard 'Incident Command System' for the coordination of emergency response. Structures, protocols, mutual understanding and effective communications underpin effective crisis management. In the UK a three tier, strategic, coordinating and tactical, structure is employed by the emergency services when dealing with a major incident (see Flin, 1996). Such structures have increasingly been used in sectors such as Finance (see Elliott et al. 2002). The purpose of such structures is to ensure the effective coordination of an organization's response to an incident.

A key contribution to the organizational crisis literature concerns the so called 'High Reliable Organizations'. Resulting from a study of organizations operating complex, potentially hazardous technologies, they posses the potential for catastrophic failure. The focus of one study (Roberts, 1993) were organizations that had continued to operate safely despite their catastrophic potential. Emerging from this research is the view that complex technologies require complex social systems to manage them. Such social systems requires not only good communications, but an organizational climate in which individuals may question and challenge when things do not make sense. Additionally, individuals should be selected for such teams on the basis of their interpersonal skills as well as their technical skills. As technologies have become more complex than any individual can fully understand the group becomes the unit of control. The descriptions of HRO's put forward by Roberts (1993) and Weick (1993) resemble, to some extent the learning organisation.

Planned and ad hoc responses

Business continuity management

In an organizational context, business continuity management (BCM) has evolved into a process that identifies an organization's exposure to internal and external threats by synthesising hard and soft assets to provide effective prevention and recovery (Elliott, Swartz and Herbane, 2002). Essential to its success is a thorough understanding of the wide range of threats (internal and external) facing an organization. Figure 1 identifies one possible process for BCM; it provides a starting point for considering crisis management in practice.

The scope of risk and crisis management can be focused or broad, reflecting the managerial mindset of an organization. Shrivastava and Mitroff's (1987) typology of crisis may be used as a focus for identifying the range of potential failures facing an organization before proceeding to a consideration of the impact upon business objectives of each of these. This is undertaken through the Business Impact Analysis (BIA), the 'backbone of the entire business continuity exercise' Meredith (1999: 139). It determines priorities and, therefore, many of the financial commitments to business continuity. The BIA involves assessing the likely financial and operational consequences of a crisis. It may be defined as a group of business activities undertaken within an organization. Such activities may occur within or between departments. For a fuller discussion of how a BIA might be undertaken see Elliott et al. (2002). In brief it should identify the range of potential crises, organizational objectives, an outline of key processes and the identification of (flowcharts etc.) linkages and dependencies with other business units, suppliers, customers and other agencies etc. (Elliott et al., 2002). The aim

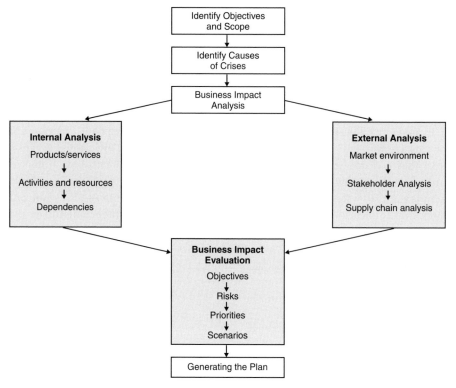

Figure 1 A process for business continuity management
Source: Elliott, Swartz and Herbane (2002)

of the process is to stimulate a consideration of threats and their likely impact upon business processes. Overall, the BIA offers a preliminary analysis of some of the idiosyncrasies of an organization's resource, systems and operations.

Business Impact Evaluation

The Business Impact Evaluation (BIE) constitutes the final step in the planning process. It seeks to pull together the preceding analyses into a cohesive whole as a prelude to drafting the business continuity plan. The BIE re-evaluates the initial objectives, set at the outset of the BCP process and assesses the risk against those objectives. It determines the priorities for business resumption and appropriate investments. Key considerations are an assessment of the resources that each business unit and function requires to resume at an appropriate time. This may result from a reflection upon a range of alternative 'resumption scenarios.' According to Elliott *et al.* (2002) the BIE comprises of four analyses. First, a refining of the business continuity objectives. Second, an evaluation of the risks. Third, the establishment of priorities for business recovery, and fourth the development of business interruption scenarios.

Objectives

In order to have practical and 'testable' objectives, those which have been identified prior to the BIA should be refined in order to elucidate the minimum required level at which each function or business process can operate. These amended objectives may include reference to temporal issues. For example:

- Customer contact must be re-established within two hours
- Invoicing must be resumed within one week for major customers and return to normal within two weeks
- Deliveries from suppliers must recommence within 4 hours
- Level 1 ICT systems must be operational within 45 minutes.

Through the incorporation of greater detail into these objectives, a further sequence of events and timings can be devised and incorporated into the draft business continuity plan.

Risk assessment

The term Risk Assessment describes the process of gauging the most likely outcomes of a set of events and the consequences of those outcomes. At a personal level, informal assessments of risk are a more or less continual mental process from when to pull out from a junction in a car, judging when to complement a colleague on their appearance through to purchasing decisions and so forth. The risk management discipline has sought to formalize risk assessment in an attempt to reduce the effects of personal bias. However, a limitation where complex systems are concerned is that identifying all possible outcomes and consequences is problematic. It has been argued that any attempt to quantify risk will fail because no matter the degree of sophistication of the mathematics all risk assessment is inherently value laden (Toft and Reynolds, 1992). Nevertheless, a structured approach to risk assessment may be better than none. But, a good understanding of the aims and objectives of such a process is more important than a detailed statistical knowledge. A simple matrix, with axes depicting the degree of threat against the likelihood (probability) of occurrence, is commonly used to categorize risks and hence to prioritize remedial actions (Figure 2).

Although providing a useful rule of thumb it does not take into account the extent to which an organization has the potential to control an incident, nor for any asessment of the extent to which certain 'risks' might be deemed acceptable to an organization or to other stakeholders. For example, Johnson & Johnson might have deemed that the public would treat them sympathetically if they suffered from a repeat malicious product tampering episode. In many instances the trade offs will not be as extreme as in the case of the Tylenol poisonings and organizations must themselves balance investment in preparations against what the public or other groups may consider that they should do. The outcome of this process should be to provide a rich understanding of the threats and hazards facing an organization. The next stage, once priorities have been determined, is

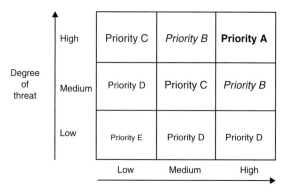

Figure 2 Risk assessment matrix
Source: Elliott, Swartz and Herbane (2002)

to translate the knowledge into a series of plans. A fuller discussion of this process may be seen in Elliott *et al.* (2002). For the purpose of this chapter we proceed to a necessarily brief consideration of how incidents might be managed.

Communications

Communications management may be the most written about subject in the field of organizational crisis yet remain the least well executed. How might corporate image and reputation help or hinder an organization's crisis response? The wealth of material dealing with crisis from a communications perspective indicates that its importance is well understood (see, for example, Stone, 1995; Regester, 1987). Communications may concern cultural norms which help or hinder the flow of information within organizations. Individuals may possess expert or hierarchical power which makes others reluctant to challenge either their decisions or their view of events. The use of humour may also prove a powerful discouragement to free communications (see, for example, Elliott and Smith, 1993b). The flow of communication may also be impeded by malfunctioning or inadequate systems. The 9/11 Commission recommended the increased assignment of radio spectrum for public safety purposes (The 9/11 Commission Report, 2003 p. 397). Popplewell (1985) identified limited police radio systems as a problem during the Bradford Stadium Fire. Technology may also play a role in allowing a crisis to escalate more quickly as the internet and mobile phones add to more traditional means of communication. In the case of the Aurora, outlined in detail below, passenger mobile phones allowed media contact with many on board the vessel which was, effectively, in quarantine.

Traditionally, however, crisis communications has largely been concerned with managing the perceptions and expectations of a variety of stakeholder groups outside and inside the organization. Barton (2001) highlights the importance of communicating internally, an area possibly seen as secondary in importance if column inches is the metric. For Barton (2001) employees may be seen as a key resource as ambassadors and as a potential source of useful information. For Barton (2001) preparing the ground with effective pre-crisis communications is vital. Firestone's employees threatened strike action when their employer experienced a major crisis, suggesting longer term difficulties. Internal goodwill, it is evident, is as vital as that outside an organization. As Shrivastava (1987: 5) observed

> 'Crisis communications is not a short term, one shot public relations effort, or a one way transfer of pertinent information from organisations to the public. Instead it should be viewed as establishment of permanent long term communicative relationships with multiple internal and external stakeholders. Communication implies not only the transfer of information, but an exchange of information and underlying assumptions, and discourse aimed at reaching a common understanding of issues'

An organization's reputational context will be determined by the fit of crisis communications with a number of factors including:

- ongoing marketing communications,
- relationships with the media
- history of previous incidents, (expressed in terms of the affected organization and its broader industrial sector)
- previous experience of successfully dealing with events
- stakeholder relationships
- organizational culture and structure.

Effective communications requires getting the right message to the right stakeholder group. During the pre-crisis stage, this requires that organizations identify:

- Who their stakeholders are
- What problems the crisis causes for them
- What their initial perceptions of the organization are
- The best means of communicating with them
- The message or information that they require.

Elliott *et al.* (1999) report that utility companies maintain detailed databases of customers in order that they can quickly identify the likely consequences of an interruption. Such databases may include at risk groups; be they elderly residents, young families or major industries requiring significant resources. Some databases record when groups may have been affected by previous interruptions or where influential environmental groups or politicians are located. From a self-interested point of view, this provides a useful warning of public embarrassment. Such monitoring requires significant investment and commitment. A growing dimension of marketing concerns the development of relationships within industrial and consumer markets (Egan, 1995). Relationships are increasingly seen as the key to success and it may be a truism to say that most relationships founder when truly tested. An increasing amount of evidence suggests that strong loyalties can be developed where there is a long record of assistance during crises.

Service recovery

A final section of this chapter is concerned with examining the links between the related field of service recovery and organizational crisis. It offers some new perspectives on crisis, grounded in a related business discipline. Services recovery (Elliott, Harris and Baron, 2005) recognizes the cumulative impact of many service failures which, together, may constitute a crisis (Elliott, Harris and Baron, 2005). For example, in late 2003 the Novo virus broke out on P&O cruise ship Aurora triggering an international problem (see, for example, Vasagar and Tremlett, 2003; Searle, Charter, and Bird 2003). A non-exhaustive list of stakeholders includes the almost 600 passengers and crew who were confined to cabins; the passengers and crew unaffected by the virus; P&O (the owners of the cruise ship); the Greek and Spanish Government agencies; potential cruise customers; the lawyers who sought to contact Aurora passengers with a view to encouraging litigation; and the world's media. Time pressures were evident in that the cruise was intended to last for 17 days with specified stops at ports located around the Mediterranean Ocean. The scale of the virus outbreak required the speedy allocation of further medical personnel and resources (Dolan, 2003). The scale of the virus outbreak and the extended scope triggered by the negative reactions of the Greek and Spanish authorities took P&O by surprise. This extended scope created high levels of ambiguity and uncertainty as P&O sought to control the tangible health problems, but found the scope of the political and media induced crises more difficult to manage. Greek port authorities refused permission for docking at Athens and the Spanish Government closed its border with Gibraltar to Aurora passengers. The media crisis was further exacerbated by the ease with which passengers could use modern technology to communicate with family, friends, lawyers and the media, creating another layer of uncertainty. P&O's credibility came into question as some passengers criticized the company for its slow and tardy response. The media reexamined past virus outbreaks on P&O cruise ships, thereby questioning the company's ability to manage. Although ostensibly a crisis triggered by the cumulative impact of many passengers and staff catching a virus, the scale and scope of the crisis were greatly exacerbated by other stakeholders and by the extensive media scrutiny, fuelled in part, by the desire of some customers for compensation (Hamilton, 2003).

Under the umbrella of 'service recovery', research has concentrated upon identifying and classifying types of service failures in different settings (Johnston, 1994; Kelley, Hoffman and Davis, 1993). Research has also considered the appropriateness of specific recovery strategies from the customer perspective (Hoffman and Kelley, 2000; Webster and Sundaram, 1998). Mattila (2001), for example, argues for consideration of the customer's assessment of the *magnitude* of the failure when designing an appropriate response. Finally, research has focused on the recovery evaluation process from the individual customer's perspective (Tax and Brown, 2000). Swanson and Kelley (2001), for example, investigated how customer attributions for service recovery (locus of causality, stability and control), affected verbal behaviour related to recovery. Although there is a recognition within this literature that an organization requires a coordinated effort to deal with service recovery the unit of analysis remains at the level of the individual encounter (see, for example, Lewis and Spyrakopoulos, 2001).

However, from a crisis management perspective, Elliott *et al.* (2005) identify at least four limitations of this approach. First, there is little consideration of the *cumulative impact and significance of individual failure incidents*. A crisis occurs, it may be argued, when many customers experience a negative moment of truth, resulting in either the removal of their custom or in significant adverse publicity resulting in potential customers spending elsewhere. It is thus the cumulative impact of many negative experiences that combine to cause a crisis. It may also be argued that, given the myriad of negative encounters, service organizations receive many warning signals and that crisis avoidance may be facilitated by more effective reading of such signals. For example, in the case of the Ford-Firestone crisis, concerns about the safety of Firestone tyres and Ford vehicles were raised as early as 1992, some eight years before the public crisis and product recall.

Second, a service recovery 'approach' *fails to anticipate the role other stakeholders* may play in escalating dissatisfaction into a crisis. For example, the actions of the Greek and Spanish authorities further exacerbated the potential for dissatisfaction of customers by denying them access to parts of their itinerary.

Third, what do current service recovery measures, implemented within the context of the individual customer encounter, reveal about *core cultural assumptions* that influence crisis incubation? For example, are recovery procedures simply a 'tick the box' exercise to satisfy internal quality audits, or are they aimed at resolving both customer problems as perceived by customers and the underlying systems, processes, practices and cultural assumptions which underpin an organization's service recovery approach.

Fourth, the negative publicity associated with organizational crises is often the result of back-stage service failures by an organization being brought to the attention of a wider audience on the front-stage in the focal crisis incident. For example, once evidence was made public of passenger illnesses, and other passenger inconveniences, on earlier Aurora cruises; people began to question P&O's capabilities. It was no longer considered 'bad luck' on P&O's part. For example, one passenger reported

> 'My wife and I took a cruise on the Aurora 18 months ago when it was new. It had constant problems with the waste plumbing. Our toilet frequently blocked, the whole corridor had no flush for 2 days. The staff mopped up the overspill with bath towels – I have no idea if these were re-circulated. A number of areas smelt of sewerage.'
>
> (Paul Evans, England)

It is highly unlikely that all their employees were unaware of back-stage service failures, and yet something prevented action being taken, thus leading to the incubation of a crisis. A services marketing emphasis on service *failure and recovery processes with external customers* would be unlikely to uncover the reasons for back-stage failures, nor why they were not acted upon.

A central issue in services recovery is customer involvement and participation, particularly during the operational phase of a crisis. Due to the influence of on-site customer participation, the social component of the socio-technical system plays a different, arguably more significant, role in a crisis within a service context than in one within a manufacturing context. Despite this there has been little research within the crisis management literature regarding customers, highlighting a possible weakness of that literature that Elliott *et al.* (2005) have labelled 'orgo-centrism,' that is the degree to which it focuses upon the organizational response to crisis, arguably to the detriment of other stakeholders, most significantly customers. This reflects the roots of crisis management as a sub-field that lie firmly within the area of organization studies. P&O's response to the Aurora crisis, seen through the accounts of passengers, demonstrates characteristics of orgo-centricism, with little regard for the customers' reactions/perceptions of the crisis response actions. Ms Seaborn, aged 35, from Heywood in Greater Manchester, said she came down with the bug on Monday after staff took her passport to stop her leaving the ship and flying home from Gibraltar.

> 'It was an absolute nightmare. We were held hostage. We got a clean bill of health from the doctor, but they wouldn't let us off or give us our passports. A P&O executive said they would only give them to us after we set sail from Gibraltar. I am suing them for kidnap – they didn't need to keep us on the ship did they?'

Customers are clearly vital stakeholders in the all stages of crisis. There is often a financial incentive, in terms of compensation payouts in many crisis situations, which encourages customers to exacerbate any failure. In a service setting, where customers participate in service production, they may act as a rogue element, contributing in ways that are both difficult to predict and to control. While there is evidence that customer-to-customer interactions can act as a de-fuser of dissatisfaction with a service organization, the stabilizing effect can become a de-stabilizing effect if customers begin to regularly attribute blame to other customers and/or communicate their perceptions of the organization's crisis response actions by word of mouth to the detriment of the company's image. It is argued, therefore, that service business continuity processes would benefit from the inclusion of an effective process for monitoring complaining behaviour between customers.

Conclusions

This chapter has digressed from the format followed in the majority of this collection. This is deliberate and represents an effort to encourage greater consideration of how crisis management thinking may penetrate organizations. The practice of crisis management emanates from deeply held beliefs, the influence of defence mechanisms, deficient decision making processes, how individuals make sense of the world, the preparation organizations make to management crises and all the other issues identified throughout this collection. However, ultimately, the purpose of this reflection should be upon making organizations and individuals better able to develop crisis resilient properties or, if crises occur, to manage them effectively. Pearson and Clair's (1998) contribution sought to bring crisis management back into management research mainstream. With the many examples of organizational crises it seems obvious that such an objective remains as important today as ever.

References

Allison, G. T. (1971) *Essence of Decision*, Little Brown: London.

Ansoff, I. (1991) 'Critique Of Henry Mintzberg's "The Design School": Reconsidering The Basic Premises Of Strategic Management', *Strategic Management Journal*, Vol. 12, pp 449–461.

Argyris, C. (1994) 'Good Communications that Blocks Learning', *Harvard Business Review*, pp. 77–85.

Argyris, C. and Schön, D. A. (1978) *Organizational Learning: A Theory of Action Perspective*, Addison-Wesley: Reading, MA.

Barton, L. (2001) *Crisis in Organizations*, South-Western Thomson Learning: Cincinatti.

Beck, U. (1992) *Risk Society: Towards a new modernity*. SAGE: London.

Belbin, R. M. (1981) *Management teams, why they succeed or fail*, Butterworth Heinemann: Oxford.

Brown, A. and Jones, M. (2000) 'Honourable members and dishonourable deeds: sensemaking, impression management and legitimation in the "Arms to Iraq" affair', *Human Relations*, 53: 655–689.

Dolan, A. (2003) 'New Bug Ship Storm', *The Daily Mail*, p. 4.

Dynes R. and Aguirre, B. (1979) 'Organisational Adaptations to Crises: Mechanisms of Co-Ordination and Structural Change', *Disasters*, Vol. 3, No. 1, pp. 71–74.

Egan, C. (1995) *Creating competitive advantage*, Butterworth Heinemann: London.

Elliott, D. (2005) 'Risk and Crisis Management', in Gill, M. (ed.) *International Security Handbook*, Perpetuity Press: Leicester.

Elliott, D. and McGuinness, M. (2002) 'Public Inquiries, Panacea or Placebo', *Journal of Contingencies and Crisis Management*, Vol. 10, Issue 1.

Elliott, D. and Smith, D. (1993a) 'Learning from Tragedy: Sports Stadia Disasters in the UK', *Industrial and Environmental Crisis Quarterly*, Vol. 7, No. 3, pp. 205–230.

Elliott, D. and Smith D. (1993b) 'Knights in Shining Armour', *Disaster Management*, Vol. 5, No. 1, pp. 35–41, ISSN 09534962.

Elliott, D. and Smith, D. (1997) 'Waiting for the next one', in Frosdick, S. and Walley, L. (eds) (1997) *Sport and Safety Management*, Oxford: Butterworth-Heinmann, pp. 85–107.

Elliott, D. and Smith, D. (2006) 'Patterns of Regulatory Behaviour in the UK Football Industry', submitted, *Journal of Management Studies*, in press.

Elliott, D., Harris, K. and Baron, S. (2005) 'Crisis Management and Services Marketing', *Journal of Services Marketing* (in press).

Elliott, D., Sipika, C. and Smith, D. (1993) 'Message in a Bottle: Perrier,' *Proceedings of the World Academy of Marketing*, University of Istanbul, pp. 559–563.

Elliot, D., Swartz, E. and Herbane, B. (1999) *Business Continuity Management*, London: Income Data Services (IDS).

Elliott, D., Swartz, E. and Herbane, B. (2002) *Business Continuity Management: A Crisis Management approach*, Routledge: London.

Flin, R. (1996) *Sitting in the hot seat*, John Wiley: London.

Giddens, A. (1990) *The Consequences of Modernity,* Stanford University Press: Stanford.

Hamilton, A. (2003), 'Full Steam Ahead', *The Times*, Tuesday November 4th, p. 1.

Heath, R. L. (2001) *The Handbook of public relations*, SAGE: Thousand Oaks, CA.

Hiles, A. and Barnes, P. (1999) *The Definitive Handbook of Business Continuity Management*, John Wiley: Chichester.

Hoffman, K.D and Kelley, S.W. (2000) 'Perceived Justice Needs and Recovery Evaluation: a Contingency Approach', *European Journal of Marketing*, Vol. 34, No. 3–4, pp. 418–432.

Home Office (1997a) *Business as Usual: Maximising business resilience to terrorist bombings*, Home Office: London.

Home Office (1997b) *Bombs, Protecting People and Property*, 3rd Edition, Home Office: London.

Hood, C., Rothstein, H. and Baldwin, R. (2001) *The Government of Risk*, Oxford University Press: Oxford.

Hynes, T. and Prasad, P. (1997) Mock bureaucracy in Mining Disasters, *Journal of Management Studies*, Vol. 34, No. 4, pp. 601–623.

Janis, I. and Mann, L. (1977) *Decision Making*, Free Press: New York.

Johnston, R. (1994) *Service Recovery: An Empirical Study*, Warwick University Business School: Coventry, UK.

Jones, M. and Sutherland, G. (1999) *Implementing Turnbull: A Boardroom briefing*, ICEAW: London.

Kelley, S.W., Hoffman, K.D. and Davis, M.A. (1993) 'A Typology of Retail Failures and Recoveries', *Journal of Retailing*, Vol. 69 (Winter), pp. 429–452.

Knight, R. and Pretty, D. (2001) 'Philosophies of risk, shareholder value and the CEO', in Pickford, J. (ed) *Mastering Risk Volume 1*, Financial Times: London.

La Porte, T. (1996) 'A Strawman Speaks Up: Comments on the Limits of Safety', *Journal of Contingencies and Crisis Management*, Vol. 2, No. 4 pp. 207–212.

Lewis, B.R. and Spyrakopoulos, S. (2001) 'Services Failures and Recovery in Retail Banking: The Customers' Perspective', *International Journal of Bank Marketing*, Vol. 19, No. 1, pp. 37–47.

Mattila, A.S. (2001) 'The Effectiveness of Service Recovery in a Multi-industry Setting', *Journal of Services Marketing*, Vol. 15, No. 7, pp. 583–96.

Meredith, W. (1999) 'Business Impact Analysis', in Hiles, A. and Barnes, P. (1999) *The Definitive Handbook of Business Continuity Management*, John Wiley: Chichester.

Mintzberg, H. (1983) *The Structuring of Organisations*, Prentice Hall: Englewood Cliffs, New Jersey.

Mintzberg, H. (1990) 'The Design School: Reconsidering The Basic Premises Of Strategic Management', *Strategic Management Journal*, Vol. 11, pp. 171–195.

Mintzberg, H. (1993) 'The Pitfalls Of Strategic Planning', *California Management Review*, Vol. 36, No. 1, pp. 32–47.

Mintzberg, H. and Waters, J. (1985) 'Of Strategies, Deliberate and Emergent', *Stategic Management Journal*, Vol. 6, pp. 257–272.

Mitchell, R.K, Agle, B.R. and Wood, D.J. (1997) 'Toward a Theory of Stakeholder Identification and Salience: Defining the Principle of Who and What Really Counts', *Academy of Management Review*, 22 (4) pp. 853–886.

Pauchant, T.C. and Douville, R. (1993) 'Recent Research in Crisis Management: a Study of 24 Authors' publications from 1986 to 1991', *Industrial and Environmental Crisis Quarterly*, 7 (1) pp. 43–66.

Pauchant, T.C. and Mitroff, I. (1988) 'Crisis Prone Versus Crisis Avoiding Organizations: Is your Company's Culture its own worst Enemy in Creating Crisis?', *Industrial Crisis Quarterly*, 2 pp. 53–63.

Pauchant, T.C. and Mitroff, I. (1992) *Transforming the Crisis-Prone Organization. Preventing Individual Organizational and Environmental Tragedies*, Jossey-Bass Publishers: San Francisco.

Pearson, C. and Clair, J. (1998) 'Reframing Crisis Management', *Academy of Management Review*, Vol. 22, No. 1, pp. 59–76.

Perrow, C. (1984) *Normal Accidents*, Basic Books: New York.

Popplewell, O. (1985) *Committee Of Inquiry Into Crowd Safety And Control At Sports Grounds: Interim Report*, HMSO: London.

Quarantelli, E. (1988) 'Disaster Crisis Management: A Summary Of Research Findings', *Journal Of Management Studies*, Vol. 25, 4, July.

Rasmussen, J. (1982) 'Human errors: A taxonomy for describing human malfunction in industrial installations', *Journal of Occupational Accidents*, 4: 311–335.

Reason, J. (1990) 'The contribution of latent human failures to the breakdown of complex systems', *Philosophical Transactions of the Royal Society of London, B*, 37: 475–484.

Regester, M. (1987) *Crisis Management*, Hutchinson Business.

Regester, M. and Larkin, J. (1997) *Risk Issues and Crisis Management*, Kogan Page: London.

Roberts, K. (1993) Introduction in *New Challenges to Understanding Organizations* Macmillan: New York.

Scott, W. R. (1995) *Institutions and Organizations*, SAGE: Thousand Oaks.

Searle, D., Charter, D. and Bird, S. (2003) 'Straw Protests at Spanish Closure of Rock Border', *The Times*, Tuesday November 4th, p. 11.

Shrivastava, P. (1987) *Bhopal*, Ballinger: Cambridge, Mass.

Shrivastava, P. (1992) *Bhopal*, (2nd edition) Paul Chapman Books: London.

Shrivastava, P. and Mitroff, I. (1987) Strategic Management of Corporate Crises, Columbia Journal of World Business 22 (1): 5–11.

Slapper, G. and Tombs, S. (1999) *Corporate Crime*, Longman: London.

Smart C. and Vertinsky, I. (1977) 'Designs For Crisis Decision Units', *Administrative Science Quarterly*, Vol. 22, pp. 640–657.

Smith, D. (1990) 'Beyond contingency planning – Towards a model of crisis management', *Industrial Crisis Quarterly*, 4 (4): 263–275.

Smith, D. (2000) 'Crisis Management Teams: Issues in the Management of Operational Crises', *Risk Management: An International Journal*, Vol. 2, No. 3, pp 61–78.

Smith, D. and Tombs, S. (1995) 'Beyond Self Regulation: Towards A Critique Of Self Regulation As A Control Strategy For Hazardous Activities', *Journal Of Management Studies*, Vol 32, Pt 5 (September), pp. 619–637.

Smith, D. (2002a) 'Not by error, but by design – the murderous reign of Harold Shipman', *Public Policy and Administration*, 17 (4), pp. 55–74.

Smith, D. (2002b) 'Management and Medicine – Issues in quality, risk and culture', *Clinician Management*, 11 (1), pp.1–6.

Stone, N. (1995) *The Management and Practice of Public Relations*, Macmillan: London.

Swanson, S.R. and Kelley, S.W. (2001) 'Service Recovery Attributions and Word-of-Mouth Intentions', *European Journal of Marketing*, Vol. 35, No. 1/2, pp. 194–211.

Tax, S. and Brown, S. (2000) 'Service Recovery: research Insights and Practices', in Swartz, T. and Iacobucci, D. (eds), *Handbook of Services Marketing and Management*, SAGE: Thousand Oaks, CA, pp. 271–86.

Teather, D. and Watts, J. (2004) 'End of an era as firm that brought us the pc sells out to Chinese pretender for $1.75bn', *The Guardian*, p. 3.

The 9/11 Commission Report (2003) W. H. Norton & Company Ltd: New York.

Toft, B. and Reynolds, S. (1992) *Learning from Disasters*, Butterworth: London.

Tombs, S. (2001) 'Enforcing safety law in Britain: Beyond Robens', *Risk Management: An International Journal*, Vol. 3 (2): 29–41.

Turnbull, N. (1999) *Internal Control: Guidance for directors on the Combined Code,* ICAEW: London.

Turner, B. (1976) The Organisational and Interorganisational Development of Disasters, *Administrative Science Quarterly*, Vol. 21, pp. 378–397.

Turner, B. (1978) *Man-Made Disasters*, Wykeham: London.

Vasagar, J. and Tremlett, G. (2003) 'Anglo-Spanish Relations on the Sick List as Cruise Liner Sails Out, *The Guardian*, Tuesday November 4th, p. 3.

Vaughan, D. (1996) *The Challenger Launch Decision Risky technology culture, and deviance at NASA*, University of Chicago Press: Chicago.

Webster, C. and Sundaram, D. (1998) 'Service Consumption and Criticality in Failure Recovery', *Journal of Business Research,* Vol. 41, pp. 153–59.

Weick, K. (1993) 'The Vulnerable System' in Roberts, K. (ed.), *New Challenges to Understanding Organizations*, Macmillan: New York.

Wells, C. (2001) *Corporations and Criminal Responsibility*, Oxford University Press: Oxford.

Whittington, R. (2002) *What is strategy and does it matter?* Routledge: London.

Wicks, D. (2001) 'Institutionalized Mindsets of invulnerability: Differentiated Institutional Fields and the Antecedents of Organizational crisis', *Organizational Studies*, 22 (4): 659–692.

Conclusions

Chapter 25

Denis Smith and Dominic Elliott

RESPONDING TO THE DEMANDS OF CRISES: ISSUES AROUND FUTURE DEVELOPMENTS IN THEORY AND PRACTICE

Introduction

THE PAPERS IN THIS book have been brought together to provide a point of entry into the literature on crisis management and to stimulate further debate around some of the core issues within it. Inevitably in a collection of this nature, there are gaps and omissions in the coverage of the issues. However, it is our contention here that these contributions offer an opportunity to explore multiple perspectives on the issues that are both important as anchors for subsequent research and also provide insights into a range of current problems surrounding crisis management in practice. The papers offer a range of perspectives on the processes by which crises are created, escalate and are managed. They also represent a historical perspective on the ways in which research has developed over time and raise some questions concerning the future directions for research into both theory and practice. Both of these elements are important here and need to be elaborated upon in more detail.

First, the historical context surrounding the development of the crisis management research is important because it provides us with some insights into the importance of key issues as they were developed at various points of time. They also provide us with markers for the development of theoretical perspectives on the key issues. Second, the impact of research upon practice is an important factor in terms of our understanding of the complex and evolving processes that underpin how we make sense of crisis generation and management. The issues of theory and practice are inextricably interwoven within the context of crisis management and also represent further problems in terms of our understanding of the processes that are in operation.

Crisis research in context

Any study of the historical development of the crisis and disaster literatures will note a number of developmental stages, each with its own particular foci of attention. Each of these stages of research marks an important aspect of the evolution of the research literature and serves to explain the current configuration of research within the various sub-communities of scholars. The initial body of research was concerned with societal responses to a range of natural hazards. Whilst there was some early work that focused on human-induced hazards (notably Bird, 1962), the majority of the research was concerned with catastrophic events that were triggered by 'natural' phenomenon. It is our contention here that the year 1976 was an important landmark within the literature as it coincided with publication of Turner's seminal work (Turner, 1976, 1978) that has, without doubt, shaped much of the later thinking amongst subsequent generations of researchers around 'man-made disasters'.

The initial stage of research (prior to Turner's seminal paper) was concerned with two broad themes. The first was primarily focused upon organizational and societal responses to disaster. Much of this work had the nature of community response at its core and the work on organizations was largely concerned with their role as 'rescuers' in order to mitigate the effects of disasters. There was, with some notable exceptions (Bird, 1962), little systematic and widespread research or attention focused on the role of organizations, and those who worked within them, upon the generation of such events. Much of this early work came out of either a sociological or a geographical tradition and this reflects an initial interest, either in the community response to natural hazards or the importance of place and the interaction with the natural environment, within those disciplines (Haggett, 2000; Hewitt, 1997; Kennedy, 1979; Quarantelli, 1978a, 1978b, 1998a, 1998b; Stallings, 1978, 1998; Whyte and Burton, 1980). There is still a strong contribution to natural hazard research from these communities, although there are some subtle distinctions that can be made between the two main bodies of work.

For sociologists, there is a tendency to see 'disasters' as having a geo-physical trigger, rather than a technological one (Stallings, 2005). To an extent, geographers have continued with this approach, although the distinction between the possible triggers remains an area of some debate (Haggett, 2000; Hewitt, 1997, 1998; Kennedy, 1979; Smith, 2005b, 2005c; Steinberg, 2000, 2001, 2002). Essentially, however, the major thrust of this work in Sociology has been concerned with the impact of geo-physical processes in causing harm to human communities (Smith, K., 2001). The work that has focused its attention on more human-induced forms of 'event' has been considered by some as sitting outside of this core 'disaster' research perspective, although there are some interesting lessons that can be learnt irrespective of the 'triggers' for these 'events' (Hewitt, 1998; Smith, 2005b). For example, the work on the impacts caused by war and genocide, AIDS and other forms of communicable disease and the impact of a range of technological hazards have all served to enrich our understanding of the nature of 'crisis'. Similarly, that work undertaken into a range of environmental crises and problems has also provided the research community with considerable insights into the processes that underpin the emergence and development of crisis events (Bird, 1962; Davis, 2002; Davis, 2001; Irwin, Dale and Smith, 1996). In many cases, much of this research also has the notion of 'community' at its core rather than providing a focus on the organization as a generator of crises.

The second major theme of this early period of research focused its attention upon decision-making around international relations and the hazards associated with the Cold War period. The backdrop of tensions between the superpowers during this period and the policy notion of 'mutually assured destruction' meant that the potential consequences of poor policy decisions were high. The existence of many intercontinental ballistic missiles, and their continued proliferation and distribution, continued to generate 'flash points' in international relations that ensured that 'risk' and 'crisis' became firmly embedded within the public consciousness. Political science (and, to an extent, sociology) thus had an early interest in the issues of crises, largely from the perspective of international crises and conflicts (Carnesale and Glaser, 1982; Holsti, 1980; Janis, 1982, 1989; Kennedy, 1971; Kramer et al., 1990; Medland, 1990; Wilkenfeld, 1991). Such celebrated events as the Bay of Pigs, the Cuban Missile Crisis, the Vietnam and Korean wars, and a succession of conflicts in the Middle East, all offered the prospect for an escalation of localized conflicts into a global war. Early work on risk management also emerged in this period due to a broad concern with the reliability of the delivery systems for weapons of mass destruction – the holders of such weapons wanted to be reassured that the risks of 'friendly fire' were minimized and so sought to develop techniques around systems reliability. The generation of techniques such as 'fault and event trees' and a range of processes around 'loss prevention' which became associated with this area of work, were to make their way into mainstream industrial activities and generated the discipline of risk analysis (see, for example, Irwin, Smith and Griffiths, 1982).

Following on from Turner's early paper in human-induced 'disasters', the increasing concern with the causes of, and successful management of, organizationally-based 'crises' marked the recognition of the 'man-made' nature of industrial crises. This can be seen to have triggered the beginnings of a second stage in research that marked the beginning of a more multi-disciplinary approach to dealing with problems that drew upon the work of the early period, but also sought a better understanding of the underlying causes of crisis events (Perrow, 1984; Shrivastava, 1987; Tansel, 1995; Tenner, 1996). Work within a number of social science disciplines continued to develop, although there was an increased dissemination of the findings of that research across disciplinary boundaries. Geographers continued to argue for a wider consideration of the role of space, place and time in shaping the configuration of crisis events (Smith, 2005a, 2005b) and psychologists have sought to enhance our understanding of the role of human error in generating failures (Reason, 1990a, 1990b). A key development in this research was the transfer of the military applications of human performance models and frameworks into the ergonomics and human factors disciplines and the dissemination of those concepts into wider industrial settings. The techniques developed within this area also became applied across a range of civilian applications from aviation to nuclear power, and provided considerable insights into our understanding of both 'active' and 'latent' errors in accident generation. As this stage of research matured it became more concerned with understanding of both the causes and the successful management of organizational crises. More importantly perhaps, this research has provided a significant critique of the processes and practices of management. Management theory, however, has been a relatively late convert to a consideration of the problems around crises

Putting management into crisis

Early work within the management literature around crisis had a focus on the development of contingency-based responses to crisis events. The influence of this work can still be seen in the current focus on business continuity management, the performance of crisis management teams and the range of issues around reputation management. Until relatively recently, the critical views on the role of management as a causal agent in crisis generation have come from outside of the discipline. This changed in the mid-1980s as management schools realized that corporate excesses, poor management practices and an over-reliance upon 'technocratic' forms of decision-making, presented significant challenges to management theory and practice. Since that period, there have been several advances made in our understanding of the role of management in both generating the *conditions* for, and dealing with the *demands* of, crises in ways that can allow such events to escalate. It is only relatively recently however, that management's role in the prevention of crises has taken on the importance that it deserves within the discipline. Despite an increasing recognition of the value of crisis prevention, there is still some resistance from organizations towards adopting a proactive approach. The problems of 'preventative' crisis management are that the benefits are invariably intangible – put simply, there is often no evidence of any direct benefit because a crisis has not occurred! On the other hand, the costs of such a preventative process invariably appear on the bottom line, whereas the recognition of the benefits may become clouded in the minds of managers (Smith, 2004). Crisis management has, however, become a means of reflecting upon the limitations of management education and the didactics of processes surrounding management schools – an issue that has caused some to question the validity of the main approaches to management education in the new millennium.

Against this background, crisis management has emerged as what can be considered as a 'composite' discipline, in which the varying perspectives on the issues require a multi-disciplinary approach to the problems. The papers presented in this book have covered a range of issues that are relevant to management activities around the creation of core conditions and demands from crisis. In addition, the interconnections between the various strands of research offer us a range of additional perspectives into the issues around crisis. There are several issues that can be brought together at this point that offer considerable potential for the future direction of crisis management.

First, there is the issue of developing the practice of crisis management as a functional process within organizations. Second, there is the potential for new research areas that emerge out of the testing of current theoretical perspectives as a means of shaping management in practice. Boin (2005, this volume) highlights the problem in his observation that

> '. . . the theories forwarded in these articles must be tested in empirical research that compares both failed and failure-free organizations (in both the public and private sector). The combination between multidisciplinary and empirical research holds the biggest promise for a paradigm of organizational crisis studies.'

As a concluding section to this book, we would like to take up these comments and suggest some key areas for future work and changes in practice.

Developing practice?

There are several themes that emerge out of a cursory examination of the literature on crisis and risk that would seem to offer important lessons for practice. These could be seen to centre on (but not be limited to) the processes by which early warnings of vulnerability can be generated and acted upon, the processes by which we can communicate around the complex, ill-defined dynamics of 'crisis', and the processes by which organizations learn from near miss events and problems in other organizations, as well as from major crisis events across a range of organizations and activities.

The terrorist attacks of 9/11 (in the USA), 3/11 (in Spain) and 7/7 (in London) highlighted the vulnerability that exists in much of our day-to-day activities from any concerted attempt to cause harm. In addition, the loss of the space shuttle Columbia, the continuing problems around BSE ('mad cow' disease), AIDS, and more recently bird flu all point to the difficulties in managing complex socio-technical problems. A key challenge for organizations is their ability to develop robust systems for the analysis of crisis potential and the identification of those 'points of inflection' that can allow a crisis to escalate.

The various phases of a crisis will also challenge the abilities of management to respond to the task demands of an 'event' as it escalates (both BSE and AIDS illustrate the difficulties that exist in trying to respond to a problem once it has passed a critical point). The demands here for managers can be seen to centre around: creating abilities for obtaining early warnings of problems, the leveraging of information from networks, developing an understanding of the processes by which escalation can occur within the 'specific' context of the organization, and a greater understanding of the particular task demands that could be generated by emergence within the 'system' and their impact upon management's abilities to perform effectively.

However, even where vulnerabilities are well known, there may be difficulties in implementing solutions. For example, the severe earthquake in March

2005, off the coast of Sumatra, Indonesia, illustrated the importance of effective early warning systems as well as possessing the means to communicate to potentially vulnerable populations. The fact that warnings were available, but that there was not the means to communicate those warnings, has triggered considerable policy-related activity around communication strategies in the countries and regions that were devastated. It remains to be seen how long the will to maintain such an impetus for more effective communications will last. All too often, a number of barriers to learning from crises are seen to impact upon the effectiveness of such initiatives.

Barriers may exist, for example, to prevent learning in the first instance or to prevent the translation of acquired knowledge into new operating norms and practices. Our section dealing with crisis in practice is largely concerned with the mechanics of crisis management. It provides a pointer to a wider literature, yet as we noted, there is still much scope for development and future insights may arise from ongoing work in the field of organizational learning from crisis (see, for example, Elliott and Smith, 1993, 1997, 2006). There are also important issues around the creation of a learning organization in practice, as opposed to in theory, as there are a number of barriers that appear to prevent organizations from learning effective lessons from crises (Elliott, Smith and McGuinness, 2000; Smith, D., 2001).

Developing research?

There are several areas for future research that can be seen to emerge out of the papers presented here. Of course, the point could be made that the material here is not representative of some of the more recent research and, as such, this is inevitably a skewed perspective. However, it is our view that there are several areas of research that need to be highlighted as they represent important areas for future work.

Firstly, the notion of place within crises is an issue that has been neglected in the literature. Whilst there has been work that has focused on particular crises, which have been physically located within place, there has not been research that has sought to explore the impact of place upon the generation of crises. Place, impacts upon the symbolic nature of crisis and can serve to increase the psychological trauma associated with a catastrophic event. The attacks of 9-11 serve to illustrate the importance of the symbolic nature of crises that are often associated with a sense of place.

A second issue concerns the impact of time upon crises. In a globalized environment, time is an important variable for multi-national, multi-locational organizations. Given the issues around emergence, and the interconnected nature of organizations and their supply chains, the spatial context of crises will become increasingly important. Scale also becomes an important element of this process. As organizations seek to gain economies of scale and move towards just in time management, then there is an increased risk of a hazardous event generating more significant consequences. Scale and time interact together to generate the particular characteristics of a crisis. A high impact event that takes place within a constrained timeframe will generate different issues for organizations than more 'chronic' problems.

Thirdly, the processes by which escalation and emergence impact upon organizational abilities to both predict and prevent crises is an important area for future work. The controversy around high reliability organizations represents an important opportunity to examine the potential that might exist for organizations to deal with these issues. It might also help to suggest potential organizational structures and strategies that would allow for increased mitigation and control around crisis response.

Fourthly, the relationships between organizational learning and crisis need to be more fully explored. There is a contribution to be made at individual, group, organization and industry levels and it is clear that our understanding of organizational learning processes, per se, remains under-developed.

Fifthly, the role of communications at each of the stages of crisis is one that increases in importance as the speed at which crises escalate increases. Communication is made all the more problematic around issues of space and time and it is also a key component of the processes of organizational learning and crisis escalation. Finally, greater attention needs to be placed upon translating theoretical developments into better practice. It is our view, ultimately, that the purpose of research in this field is to enable managers, policy makers and communities to be better prepared for preventing and dealing with crises.

Conclusions

The authors in this collection of papers have identified a wide range of examples of organizational and societal crises at various points throughout this book. Many of these reflect failures of hindsight and foresight (see Turner, 1976, 1978) and the inabilities of managers and other stakeholder groups to successfully deal with the challenges facing them. As Starbuck *et al.* (1978) and Miller (1988) noted, a powerful source of organizational disintegration may be linked to an inappropriate reliance of managers upon 'proven' success formulas or programmes. Organizational learning, of the double loop variety may provide one means of mitigating against such a reliance on formulaic solutions by seeking to address core issues around the development of crises.

There is a further weakness within the literature regarding the origins of much of the current 'seminal' work, which can be seen as emanating from a limited part of the world. One of the most influential frameworks of crisis management, itself borrowed from social psychology highlights the importance of individual and collective beliefs. We wonder whether the emerging crisis management paradigm should be scrutinized for fallacious assumptions and beliefs. As the discipline matures there will be a greater need for the rigorous empirical research called for by Boin (2006) in order to test the nature of those theories in practice.

Research into crisis management has begun to generate some significant challenges to mainstream management theory and practice. The core of the challenge centres on the control-based approaches that are taken to management and the manner in which the assumptions that this generates can create problems for control. The inherent paradox here is that management assumptions create gaps in controls which management fails to recognize because of the assumptions that it holds about the ways that organizations work.

A possible weakness of this collection is its focus upon failing organizations, with the limited inclusion of literature drawn from studies of so called high reliability organizations. The field of crisis is not alone in its focus upon the negative. Fox (2004) identified the focus of social scientists in general, and anthropologists in particular, upon the dysfunctional rather than the desirable. Another deficiency concerns the background of much of this research, which is grounded in a North American and Western European context. Ideally, any future collection should be in a position to draw upon a wider community of scholarship and, ideally, incorporate Asian, South American and African perspectives on the process. A future collection might also do well to devote greater space to better understanding the crisis resistant organization or to considering analyses of crises that originate in other cultures. In this collection we have sought to be thought provoking, rather than comprehensive. We have also avoided seeking to identify a range of issues for the future. We have no crystal ball. We reiterate our view that crisis management is maturing as an academic field of inquiry and in the emergence of communities of practice across the disciplines of risk, crisis, disaster, business continuity and management as a whole. We do not pretend that there is any panacea to the problems caused by complexity, emergence or the panoply of factors surrounding crisis causality and management. There are many placebos to be found across the popular literature, but we do believe that good research can feed through into better crisis management practice.

Finally, we have sought to provide an overview of some of the key debates that have taken place within the crisis management literature. These include the various ways of conceptualizing the crisis process, the ways in which failure potential becomes embedded within organizational systems and processes, the manner in which we make sense of crisis events and issues around problems associated with managing the 'acute' phase of a crisis as well as dealing with its aftermath. We are well aware that any such collection will be eclectic. We hope that we have provided sufficient references to the key works not included. However, we do not claim this to be a definitive work, more a progress report which also serves as an entry point into the diverse bodies of research that characterize the emerging field of crisis management.

References

Bird, M. J. (1962) *The town that died. The story of the world's greatest man-made explosion before Hiroshima*, G.P. Putnam's Sons: New York.

Boin, A. (2006) 'Organizations and Crisis: The emergence of a research paradigm' in Smith, D. and Elliott, D. (eds) '*Key Readings in Crisis Management: Systems and structures for prevention and recovery*', Routledge: London.

Carnesale, A. and Glaser, C. (1982) 'ICBM Vulnerability: The Cures are Worse Than the Disease', *International Security*, 7 (1): 70–85.

Davis, D. (2002) *When smoke ran like water: Tales of environmental deception and the battle against pollution*, Perseus Press: Oxford.

Davis, M. (2001) *Late Victorian holocausts: El Nino famines and the making of the Third World*, Verso: London.

Elliot, D. and Smith, D. (1993) 'Football stadia disasters in the United Kingdom: Learning from tragedy', *Industrial and Environmental Crisis Quarterly*, 7(3), pp. 205–229.

Elliot, D. and Smith, D. (1997) 'Waiting for the next one', in Frosdick, S. and Walley, L. (eds) (1997) *Sport and Safety Management*, Oxford: Butterworth-Heinmann, pp. 85–107.

Elliot, D. and Smith, D. (2006) Active learning from Crisis: Regulation, precaution and the UK football industry's response to disaster', *Journal of Management Studies*, 43 (2), pp. 289–317.

Elliott, D., Smith, D. and McGuinness, M. (2000) 'Exploring the failure to learn: Crises and the barriers to learning', *Review of Business*, 21 (3): 17–24.

Fox, K. (2004) *Watching the English,* Hodder and Stoughton: London.

Haggett, P. (2000) *The geographical structure of epidemics*, Oxford University Press: Oxford.

Hewitt, K. (1997) *Regions of risk: A geographical introduction to disasters*, Addison Wesley Longman Ltd.: Harlow.

Hewitt, K. (1998) 'Excluded perspectives in the social construction of disaster', in E. L. Quarantelli (ed.), *What is a disaster? Perspectives on the question*, 75–91. Routledge: London.

Holsti, O. R. (1980) 'Historians, Social Scientists, and Crisis Management: An Alternative View' *Journal of Conflict Resolution*, 24 (4): 665–682.

Irwin, A., Dale, A. and Smith, D. (1996) 'Science and Hell's Kitchen – The local understanding of hazard issues', in A. Irwin and B. Wynne (eds), *Misunderstanding Science? The public reconstruction of science and technology*, 47–64, Cambridge University Press: Cambridge.

Irwin, A., Smith, D. and Griffiths, R. F. (1982) 'Risk analysis and public policy for major hazards', *Physics in Technology*, 13 (6): 258–265.

Janis, I. L. (1982) *Groupthink: Psychological studies of policy decisions and fiascos* (2nd ed.), Houghton Mifflin: Boston.

Janis, I. L. (1989) *Crucial decisions: Leadership in policymaking and crisis management*, Free Press: New York.

Kennedy, B. A. (1979) 'A naughty world' *Transactions of the Institute of British Geographers*, New Series 4: 550–558.

Kennedy, R. F. (1971) *Thirteen days. A memoir of the Cuban missile crisis*, NY: W.W. Norton & Company: New York.

Kramer, M., Allyn, B. J., Blight, J. G., and Welch, D. A. (1990) 'Remembering the Cuban Missile Crisis: Should We Swallow Oral History?' *International Security*, 15 (1): 212–218.

Medland, W. J. (1990) 'The Cuban Missile Crisis: Evolving Historical Perspectives', *History Teacher*, 23 (4): 433–447.

Miller, D. (1988) 'Organizational Pathology and Industrial Crisis,' *Industrial Crisis Quarterly*, pp. 65–74.

Perrow, C. (1984) *Normal Accidents*, Basic Books: New York.

Quarantelli, E. L. (ed.) (1978a) *Disasters – theory and research*, SAGE: Beverly Hills, CA.

Quarantelli, E. L. (1978b) 'Some basic themes in Sociological studies of disaster' in E. L. Quarantelli (ed.), *Disasters – theory and research*, 1–14, SAGE: Beverly Hills, CA.

Quarantelli, E. L. (1998a) 'Introduction: The basic question, its importance, and how it is addressed in this volume', in E. L. Quarantelli (ed.), *What is a disaster? Perspectives on the question*, 1–7. Routledge: London.

Quarantelli, E. L. (ed.) (1998b) *What is a disaster? Perspectives on the question*, Routledge: London.

Reason, J. T. (1990a) 'The contribution of latent human failures to the breakdown of complex systems', *Philosophical Transactions of the Royal Society of London B*, 37: 475–484.

Reason, J. T. (1990b) *Human error*, Oxford: Oxford University Press.

Shrivastava, P. (1987) *Bhopal: Anatomy of a crisis*, Ballinger Publishing Company: Cambridge, Mass.

Smith, D. (2001) 'Crisis as a catalyst for change: Issues in the management of uncertainty and organizational vulnerability', *E-risk: Business as usual?*, 81–88, British Bankers Association/Deliotte and Touche: London.

Smith, D. (2004) 'For whom the bell tolls: Imagining accidents and the development of crisis simulation in organisations', *Simulation and Gaming*, 35 (3): 347–362.

Smith, D. (2005a) 'Business (not) as usual – crisis management, service interruption and the vulnerability of organisations', *Journal of Services Marketing*, 19 (5): forthcoming.

Smith, D. (2005b) 'In the eyes of the beholder? Making sense of the system(s) of disaster(s)' in R. W. Perry and E. L. Quarantelli (eds.), *What is a disaster? New answers to old questions*, Xlbris: Philadelphia.

Smith, D. (2005c) 'Through a glass darkly – a response to Stallings' "Disaster, Crisis, Collective Stress, and Mass Deprivation"', In R. W. Perry and E. L. Quarantelli (eds), *What is a disaster? New answers to old questions*, Xlibris: Philadelphia.

Smith, K. (2001) *Environmental hazards. Assessing risk and reducing disaster.* (3rd. ed.) Routledge: London.

Stallings, R. (1978) 'The structural patterns of four types of organizations in disaster', in E. L. Quarantelli (ed.), *Disasters – theory and research*, 87–103, SAGE: Beverly Hills, CA.

Stallings, R. (1998) 'Disaster and the theory of social order', in E. L. Quarantelli (ed.), *What is a Disaster? Perspectives on the question*, 127–145, Routledge: London.

Stallings, R. (2005) 'Disaster, crisis, collective stress, and mass deprivation', in R. W. Perry and E. L. Quarantelli (eds), *What is a disaster? New perspectives on old questions*, Xlbris: Philadelphia.

Starbuck, W., Greve, A. and Hedberg, B (1978) 'Responding to Crisis', *Journal of Business Administration*, Spring (Reprinted in Quinn, J. and Mintzberg, H. (eds) (1992) *The Strategy Process*, second edition, pp. 785–793).

Steinberg, T. (2000) *Acts of God. The unnatural history of natural disasters in America*, Oxford University Press: New York.

Steinberg, T. (2001) 'The secret history of natural disaster', *Environmental Hazards*, 3: 31–35.

Steinberg, T. (2002) 'Down to earth: Nature, agency, and power in history', *The American Historical Review*, Vol. 107: 58 paragraphs. accessed 2nd January 2004 online: http://www.historycooperative.org/journals/ahr/107.3/ah0302000798.html

Tansel, B. (1995) 'Natural and manmade disasters: accepting and managing risks' *Safety Science*, 20: 91–99.

Tenner, E. (1996) *Why things bite back. Technology and the revenge effect*, Fourth Estate: London.

Turner, B. A. (1976) 'The organizational and interorganizational development of disasters', *Administrative Science Quarterly*, 21: 378–397.

Turner, B. A. (1978) *Man-made disasters*, Wykeham: London.

Whyte, A. V. and Burton, I. (eds) (1980) *Environmental risk assessment*, Vol. SCOPE 15, Wiley: Chichester.

Wilkenfeld, J. (1991) 'Trigger-Response Transitions in Foreign Policy Crises', 1929–1985, *Journal of Conflict Resolution*, 35 (1): 143–169.

Index

Note: page numbers in **bold** denote references to figures/illustrations/tables.